# About the Author

**DOROTHY SEYLER** is Professor Emerita of English at Northern Virginia Community College. A Phi Beta Kappa graduate of the College of William and Mary, Dr. Seyler holds advanced degrees from Columbia University and the State University of New York at Albany. She taught at Ohio State University, the University of Kentucky, and Nassau Community College before moving with her family to Northern Virginia.

She is the author of *Understanding Argument, Doing Research* (second edition), *The Reading Context* and *Steps to College Reading* (both in their third editions), and *Patterns of Reflection* (now in its seventh edition). In 2007 Dr. Seyler was elected to membership in the Cosmos Club in Washington, DC.

Professor Seyler has published articles in professional journals and popular magazines. She is currently working on a narrative nonfiction book on early-nineteenth-century traveler William John Bankes. She enjoys tennis and golf, traveling, and writing about both sports and travel.

# Contents

# Preface

I have written in previous prefaces to *Read, Reason, Write* that being asked to prepare a new edition is much like being asked back to a friend's home. Although you count on it, you are still delighted when the invitation comes. I am happy that the ninth edition kept old friends and made new ones as well and that once again I am writing a preface, this time to the tenth edition. With the ninth edition, *Read, Reason, Write* became 25 years old! Over all of these years, the text has grown in size—most books have—but also in stature within the teaching community and in its value to students. Of course, even though I have retired from full-time teaching, neither this text nor I am getting older—only better.

Although some important new material strengthens the tenth edition, the essential character of *Read, Reason, Write* remains the same. This text still unites instruction in critical reading and analysis, argument, and research strategies with a rich collection of readings that provide both practice for these skills and new ideas and insights for readers. A key purpose of *Read, Reason, Write* remains the same: to help students develop into better writers of the kinds of papers they are most often required to write, both in college and in the work-place, that is, summaries, analyses, reports, arguments, and documented essays. To fulfill this key purpose, the text must do more than offer instruction and opportunities for practice; it must also show students how these skills connect in important ways. Through all of its years, this text has been committed to showing students how reading, analytic, argumentative, and research skills are interrelated and how these skills combine to develop each student's critical thinking ability.

## FEATURES OF *READ, REASON, WRITE*

- An emphasis on good reading skills for effective arguing and writing.
- Instruction, models, and practice in understanding reading context and analyzing elements of style.
- Instruction, models, and practice in writing summaries and book reviews.
- Focus on argument as contextual: written (or spoken) to a specific audience with the expectation of counterarguments.
- Explanations and models of various types of arguments that bridge the gap between an understanding of logical structures and the ways we actually write arguments.

- Presentation of Aristotelian, Toulmin, and Rogerian models of argument as useful guides to analyzing the arguments of others and organizing one's own arguments.
- In-depth coverage of induction, deduction, analogy, and logical fallacies.
- Guidelines and revision boxes throughout the text that provide an easy reference for students.
- Instruction, models, and practice in finding and evaluating sources and in composing and documenting researched papers.
- A rich collection of readings, both timely and classic, that provides examples of the varied uses of language and strategies for argument.
- A brief but comprehensive introduction to reading and analyzing literature, found in the Appendix.

## NEW FEATURES IN THE TENTH EDITION

This new edition continues the key features of previous editions while adding new material that will make it even more helpful to both students and instructors. Significant changes include:

- A shift to the use of four-color in the text, providing a more pleasing look throughout while also enhancing the coverage of visual argument.
- More visuals throughout the text, consistent with the increased use of visuals in all print media as well as online.
- A big book is a pain in the back—pack! For the last two editions, we have put this text on a diet, and we've continued this trend a bit more in the tenth edition for a slimmer look, without any loss of teaching materials and still with a wealth of readings from which to select. Students should be comfortable studying from *Read, Reason, Write* and working with it in class.
- An updating of APA documentation style, consistent with the sixth edition of the *Publication Manual of the American Psychological Association.*
- With 31 readings in the instructional chapters and 58 readings in the anthology chapters, the tenth edition has a total of 89 readings in addition to 8 student essays and the literature in the Appendix. Forty-nine of the readings are new, and some readings from the ninth edition are in new places, paired with new readings, providing a fresh perspective.
- Of the nine chapters in the anthology section, two are entirely new. The others have many new readings, updating the issues examined in each chapter. For example, the chapter on the environment now focuses on the economic and political problems of climate change and the variety of proposed solutions, including the hotly debated geo-engineering solutions.
- One of the new chapters is all about the Internet and social media, providing a revealing look at the changes to our society brought about by Facebook and Twitter, and by the availability of information worldwide through the Internet.

- The other new chapter, the final one, is still about America, but now its future is debated and examined in less optimistic terms, as writers look at the culture divide and the extremes in both political parties. Both new chapters offer much that demands our attention as we seek to understand and shape the course of this new century.

## ACKNOWLEDGMENTS

No book of value is written alone. I am pleased to acknowledge the contributions of others in shaping this text. My thanks are due—as always—to the library staff at the Annandale Campus of Northern Virginia Community College who over the years helped me find needed information. I would also like to thank all of the students whose essays grace this text. They should be proud of the skill and effort they put into their writing.

I appreciate as well the many good suggestions of the following reviewers of the tenth edition:

Anita August
*Sacred Heart University*

Diane Badur
*Black Hawk College*

Jody Briones
*Texas A & M University-Kingsville*

Marie Eckstrom
*Rio Hondo College*

Laura Gabrion
*Macomb Community College*

Vernon Gravely
*Southeast Missouri State University*

Beth Hafner
*Clinton Community College*

Dee Huntinger
*Western Illinois University*

Richard Magee
*Sacred Heart University*

Kevin McCarthy
*Dartmouth University*

Dianne Smith
*Southeast Missouri State University*

Stephen Thomas
*Northern Kentucky University*

Mary Waguespack
*Loyola U. of New Orleans*

My former editor Steve Pensinger needs to be remembered for steering me through four editions. I am also grateful to Tim Julet and Alexis Walker for guidance through the fifth edition and to Chris Narozny, developmental editor of the sixth edition. My hat's off to Lisa Moore, executive editor for the sixth and seventh editions; to Christopher Bennem, sponsoring editor for the eighth, ninth, and now tenth editions. Last, but not least, my thanks go to past developmental editors Joshua Feldman and Phil Butcher and current developmental editor Janice Wiggins-Clarke. I have been blessed with a chorus of voices enriching this text through my wonderful journey with this book: May you all live long and prosper!

I'll close by once again dedicating *Read, Reason, Write* to my daughter Ruth who, in spite of her own career and interests, continues to give generously of her time, reading possible essays for each new edition and listening patiently to my endless debates about changes. And for all students who use my text: May you understand that it is the liberal education that makes continued growth of the human spirit both possible and pleasurable.

**Dorothy U. Seyler**

**Professor Emerita**

**Northern Virginia Community College**

# Critical Reading and Analysis

# Writers and Their Sources

READ: What is the situation in the photo—who are the two figures, where are they, how do they differ?

REASON: What ideas are suggested by the photo?

REFLECT/WRITE: Why might this visual have been chosen for Chapter 1?

" **A** re you happy with your new car?" Oscar asks.

"Oh, yes, I love my new car," Rachel responds.

"Why?" queries Oscar.

"Oh, it's just great—and dad paid for most of it," Rachel exclaims.

"So you like it because it was cheap," Oscar says. "But, wasn't your father going to pay for whatever car you chose?"

"Well, yes—within reason."

"Then why did you choose the Corolla? Why is it so great?"

Rachel ponders a moment and then replies: "It's small enough for me to feel comfortable driving it, but not so small that I would be frightened by trucks. It gets good mileage, and Toyota cars have a good reputation."

"Hmm. Maybe I should think about a Corolla. Then again, I wouldn't part with my Miata!" Oscar proclaims.

A simple conversation, right? In fact, this dialogue represents an **argument.** You may not recognize it as a "typical" argument. After all, there is no real dispute between Oscar and Rachel—no yelling, no hurt feelings. But in its most basic form, an argument is a *claim* (Rachel's car is great) supported by *reasons* (the car's size, mileage, and brand). Similar arguments could be made in favor of this car in other contexts. For instance, Rachel might have seen (and been persuaded by) a television or online Toyota advertisement, or she might have read an article making similar claims in a magazine such as *Consumer Reports*. In turn, she might decide to develop her argument into an essay or speech for one of her courses.

## READING, WRITING, AND THE CONTEXTS OF ARGUMENT

Arguments, it seems, are everywhere. Well, what about this textbook, you counter. Its purpose is to inform, not to present an argument. True—to a degree. But textbook authors also make choices about what is important to include and how students should learn the material. Even writing primarily designed to inform says to readers: Do it my way! Well, what about novels, you "argue." Surely they are not arguments. A good point—to a degree. The ideas about human life and experience we find in novels are more subtle, more indirect, than the points we meet head-on in many arguments. Still, expressive writing presents ideas, ways of seeing the world. It seems that arguments can be simple or profound, clearly stated or implied. And we can find them in much—if not most—of our uses of language.

You can accept this larger scope of argument and still expect that in your course on argument and critical thinking you probably will not be asked to write a textbook or a novel. You might, though, be asked to write a summary or a style analysis, so you should think about how those tasks might connect to the world of argument. Count on this: You will be asked to write! Why work on your writing skills? Here are good answers to this question:

- Communication skills are the single most important skill sought by employers.
- The better writer you become, the better reader you will be.

- The more confident a writer you become, the more efficiently you will handle written assignments in all your courses.
- The more you write, the more you learn about who you are and what really matters to you.

You are about to face a variety of writing assignments. Always think about what role each assignment asks of you. Are you a student demonstrating knowledge? A citizen arguing for tougher drunk-driving laws? A scholar presenting the results of research? A friend having a conversation about a new car? Any writer—including you—will take on different roles, writing for different audiences, using different strategies to reach each audience. There are many kinds of argument and many ways to be successful—or unsuccessful—in preparing them. Your argument course will be challenging. This text will help you meet that challenge.

## RESPONDING TO SOURCES

If this is a text about *writing* arguments, why does it contain so many readings? (You noticed!) There are good reasons for the readings you find here:

- College and the workplace demand that you learn complex information through reading. This text will give you lots of practice.
- You need to read to develop your critical thinking skills.
- Your reading will often serve as a basis for writing. In a course on argument, the focus of attention shifts from you to your subject, a subject others have debated before you. You will need to understand the issue, think carefully about the views of others, and only then join in the conversation.

To understand how critical thinkers may respond to sources, let's examine "The Gettysburg Address," Abraham Lincoln's famous speech dedicating the Gettysburg Civil War battlefield. We can use this document to see the various ways writers respond—in writing—to the writing of others.

### THE GETTYSBURG ADDRESS | ABRAHAM LINCOLN

Fourscore and seven years ago our fathers brought forth on this continent a new nation, conceived in liberty and dedicated to the proposition that all men are created equal. Now we are engaged in a great civil war, testing whether that nation, or any nation so conceived and so dedicated, can long endure. We are met on a great battlefield of that war. We have come to dedicate a portion of that field as a final resting place for those who here gave their lives that that nation might live. It is altogether fitting and proper that we should do this. But, in a larger sense, we cannot dedicate—we cannot consecrate—we cannot hallow—this ground. The brave men, living and dead, who struggled here have consecrated it far above our poor power to add or to detract.

The world will little note nor long remember what we say here, but it can never forget what they did here. It is for us, the living, rather to be dedicated here to the unfinished work which they who fought here have thus far so nobly advanced. It is rather for us to be here dedicated to the great task remaining before us—that from these honored dead we take increased devotion to that cause for which they gave the last full measure of devotion; that we here highly resolve that these dead shall not have died in vain; that this nation, under God, shall have a new birth of freedom; and that government of the people, by the people, for the people shall not perish from the earth.

## What Does It Say?                                  THE RESPONSE TO CONTENT

Instructors often ask students to *summarize* their reading of a complex chapter, a supplementary text, or a series of journal articles on library reserve. Frequently, book report assignments specify that summary and evaluation be combined. Your purpose in writing a summary is to show your understanding of the work's main ideas and of the relationships among those ideas. If you can put what you have read into your own words and focus on the text's chief points, then you have command of that material. Here is a sample restatement of Lincoln's "Address":

> Our nation was initially built on a belief in liberty and equality, but its future is now being tested by civil war. It is appropriate for us to dedicate this battle-field, but those who fought here have dedicated it better than we. We should dedicate ourselves to continue the fight to maintain this nation and its principles of government.

Sometimes it is easier to recite or quote famous or difficult works than to state, more simply and in your own words, what has been written. The ability to summarize reflects strong writing skills. For more coverage of writing summaries, see pages 13–16. (For coverage of paraphrasing, a task similar to summary, see also p. 16.)

## How Is It Written?
## How Does It Compare
## with Another Work?                                  THE ANALYTIC RESPONSE

Summary requirements are often combined with analysis or evaluation, as in a book report. Most of the time you will be expected to *do something* with what you have read, and to summarize will be insufficient. Frequently you will be asked to analyze a work—that is, to explain the writer's choice of style (or the work's larger rhetorical context). You will want to examine sentence patterns, organization, metaphors, and other techniques selected by the writer to convey attitude and give force to ideas. Developing your skills in analysis will make you both a better reader and a better writer.

Many writers have examined Lincoln's word choice, sentence structure, and choice of metaphors to make clear the sources of power in this speech.* Analyzing Lincoln's style, you might examine, among other elements, his effective use of *tricolon:* the threefold repetition of a grammatical structure, with the three points placed in ascending order of significance.

> Lincoln uses two effective tricolons in his brief address. The first focuses on the occasion for his speech, the dedication of the battlefield: "we cannot dedicate—we cannot consecrate—we cannot hallow. . . ." The best that the living can do is formally dedicate; only those who died there for the principle of liberty are capable of making the battlefield "hallow." The second tricolon presents Lincoln's concept of democratic government, a government "of the people, by the people, for the people." The purpose of government—"for the people"—resides in the position of greatest significance.

A second type of analysis, a comparison of styles of two writers, is a frequent variation of the analytic assignment. By focusing on similarities and differences in writing styles, you can see more clearly the role of choice in writing and may also examine the issue of the degree to which differences in purpose affect style. One student, for example, produced a thoughtful and interesting study of Lincoln's style in contrast to that of Martin Luther King Jr., as revealed in his "I Have a Dream" speech (see pp. 222–26):

> Although Lincoln's sentence structure is tighter than King's and King likes the rhythms created by repetition, both men reflect their familiarity with the King James Bible in their use of its cadences and expressions. Instead of saying eighty-seven years ago, Lincoln, seeking solemnity, selects the biblical expression "Fourscore and seven years ago." Similarly, King borrows from the Bible and echoes Lincoln when he writes "Five score years ago."

## Is It Logical?
## Is It Adequately Developed?
## Does It Achieve Its Purpose?              THE EVALUATION RESPONSE

Even when the stated purpose of an essay is "pure" analysis, the analysis implies a judgment. We analyze Lincoln's style because we recognize that "The Gettysburg Address" is a great piece of writing and we want to see how it achieves its power. On other occasions, evaluation is the stated purpose for close reading and analysis. The columnist who challenges a previously published editorial has analyzed the editorial and found it flawed. The columnist may fault the editor's logic or lack of adequate or relevant support for the editorial's main idea. In each case the columnist makes a negative evaluation of the editorial, but that judgment is an informed one based on the columnist's knowledge of language and the principles of good argument.

Part of the ability to judge wisely lies in recognizing each writer's (or speaker's) purpose, audience, and occasion. It would be inappropriate to assert

---

*See, for example, Gilbert Highet's essay, "The Gettysburg Address," in *The Clerk of Oxenford: Essays on Literature and Life* (New York: Oxford UP, 1954), to which I am indebted in the following analysis.

that Lincoln's address is weakened by its lack of facts about the battle. The historian's purpose is to record the number killed or to analyze the generals' military tactics. Lincoln's purpose was different.

> As Lincoln reflected upon this young country's being torn apart by civil strife, he saw the dedication of the Gettysburg battlefield as an opportunity to challenge the country to fight for its survival and the principles upon which it was founded. The result was a brief but moving speech that appropriately examines the connection between the life and death of soldiers and the birth and survival of a nation.

These sentences establish a basis for an analysis of Lincoln's train of thought and use of metaphors, an analysis grounded in an understanding of Lincoln's purpose and the context in which he spoke.

## How Does It Help Me to Understand Other Works, Ideas, Events?          THE RESEARCH RESPONSE

Frequently you will read not to analyze or evaluate but rather to use the source as part of learning about a particular subject. Lincoln's address is significant for the Civil War historian both as an event of that war and as an influence on our thinking about that war. "The Gettysburg Address" is also vital to the biographer's study of Lincoln's life or to the literary critic's study either of famous speeches or of the Bible's influence on English writing styles. Thus Lincoln's brief speech is a valuable source for students in a variety of disciplines. It becomes part of their research process. Able researchers study it carefully, analyze it thoroughly, place it in its proper historical, literary, and personal contexts, and use it to develop their own arguments.

To practice reading and responding to sources, study the following article by Deborah Tannen. The exercises that follow will check your reading skills and your understanding of the various responses to reading just discussed. Use the prereading questions to become engaged with Tannen's essay.

## WHO DOES THE TALKING HERE?   |   DEBORAH TANNEN

Professor of linguistics at Georgetown University, Deborah Tannen writes popular books on the uses of language by "ordinary" people. Among her many books are *Talking from 9 to 5* (1994) and *I Only Say This Because I Love You* (2004). Her response to the debate over who talks more, men or women, was published in the *Washington Post* on July 15, 2007.

PREREADING QUESTIONS  What is the occasion for Tannen's article—what is she responding to? Who does most of the talking in your family—and are you okay with the answer?

It's no surprise that a one-page article published this month in the journal    1
*Science* inspired innumerable newspaper columns and articles. The study, by Matthias Mehl and four colleagues, claims to lay to rest, once and for all, the

stereotype that women talk more than men, by proving—scientifically—that women and men talk equally.

2    The notion that women talk more was reinforced last year when Louann Brizendine's "The Female Brain" cited the finding that women utter, on average, 20,000 words a day, men 7,000. (Brizendine later disavowed the statistic, as there was no study to back it up.) Mehl and his colleagues outfitted 396 college students with devices that recorded their speech. The female subjects spoke an average of 16,215 words a day, the men 15,669. The difference is insignificant. Case closed.

3    Or is it? Can we learn who talks more by counting words? No, according to a forthcoming article surveying 70 studies of gender differences in talkativeness. (Imagine—70 studies published in scientific journals, and we're still asking the question.) In their survey, Campbell Leaper and Melanie Ayres found that counting words yielded no consistent differences, though number of words per speaking turn did. (Men, on average, used more.)

4    This doesn't surprise me. In my own research on gender and language, I quickly surmised that to understand who talks more, you have to ask: What's the situation? What are the speakers using words for?

5    The following experience conveys the importance of situation. I was addressing a small group in a suburban Virginia living room. One man stood out because he talked a lot, while his wife, who was sitting beside him, said nothing at all. I described to the group a complaint common among women about men they live with: At the end of a day she tells him what happened, what she thought and how she felt about it. Then she asks, "How was your day?"—and is disappointed when he replies, "Fine," "Nothing much" or "Same old rat race."

6    The loquacious man spoke up. "You're right," he said. Pointing to his wife, he added, "She's the talker in our family." Everyone laughed. But he explained, "It's true. When we come home, she does all the talking. If she didn't, we'd spend the evening in silence."

7    The "how was your day?" conversation typifies the kind of talk women tend to do more

Who is the most passive figure in this group?

of: spoken to intimates and focusing on personal experience, your own or others'. I call this "rapport-talk." It contrasts with "report-talk"—giving or exchanging information about impersonal topics, which men tend to do more.

Studies that find men talking more are usually carried out in formal experi-   8 ments or public contexts such as meetings. For example, Marjorie Swacker observed an academic conference where women presented 40 percent of the papers and were 42 percent of the audience but asked only 27 percent of the questions; their questions were, on average, also shorter by half than the men's questions. And David and Myra Sadker showed that boys talk more in mixed-sex classrooms—a context common among college students, a factor skewing the results of Mehl's new study.

Many men's comfort with "public talking" explains why a man who tells his   9 wife he has nothing to report about his day might later find a funny story to tell at dinner with two other couples (leaving his wife wondering, "Why didn't he tell me first?").

In addition to situation, you have to consider what speakers are doing with   10 words. Campbell and Ayres note that many studies find women doing more "affiliative speech" such as showing support, agreeing or acknowledging others' comments. Drawing on studies of children at play as well as my own research of adults talking, I often put it this way: For women and girls, talk is the glue that holds a relationship together. Their best friend is the one they tell everything to. Spending an evening at home with a spouse is when this kind of talk comes into its own. Since this situation is uncommon among college students, it's another factor skewing the new study's results.

Women's rapport-talk probably explains why many people think women   11 talk more. A man wants to read the paper, his wife wants to talk; his girlfriend or sister spends hours on the phone with her friend or her mother. He concludes: Women talk more.

Yet Leaper and Ayres observed an overall pattern of men speaking more.   12 That's a conclusion women often come to when men hold forth at meetings, in social groups or when delivering one-on-one lectures. All of us—women and men—tend to notice others talking more in situations where we talk less.

Counting may be a start—or a stop along the way—to understanding gen-   13 der differences. But it's understanding when we tend to talk and what we're doing with words that yields insights we can count on.

Source: From *The Washington Post*, July 15, 2007, copyright Deborah Tannen. Reprinted by permission.

## QUESTIONS FOR READING AND REASONING

1. What was the conclusion of the researchers who presented their study in *Science*?

2. Why are their results not telling the whole story, according to Tannen? Instead of counting words, what should we study?

3.  What two kinds of talk does Tannen label? Which gender does the most of each type of talking?

4.  What is Tannen's main idea or thesis?

**QUESTIONS FOR REFLECTION AND WRITING**

5.  How do the details—and the style—in the opening and concluding paragraphs contribute to the author's point? Write a paragraph answer to this question. Then consider: Which one of the different responses to reading does your paragraph illustrate?

6.  Do you agree with Tannen that understanding how words are used must be part of any study of men and women talking? If so, why? If not, how would you respond to her argument?

7.  "The Gettysburg Address" is a valuable document for several kinds of research projects. For what kinds of research would Tannen's essay be useful? List several possibilities and be prepared to discuss your list with classmates.

## ACTIVE READING: USE YOUR MIND!

Reading is not about looking at black marks on a page—or turning the pages as quickly as we can. Reading means constructing meaning, getting a message. We read with our brains, not our eyes and hands! This concept is often underscored by the term *active reading*. To help you always achieve active reading, not passive page turning, follow these guidelines.

## GUIDELINES for Active Reading

- **Understand your purpose in reading.** Do not just start turning pages to complete an assignment. Think first about your purpose. Are you reading for knowledge on which you will be tested? Focus on your purpose as you read, asking yourself, "What do I need to learn from this work?"

- **Reflect on the title before reading further.** Titles are the first words writers give us. Take time to look for clues in a title that may reveal the work's subject and perhaps the writer's approach or attitude as well. Henry Fairlie's title "The Idiocy of Urban Life," for example, tells you both Fairlie's subject (urban or city living) and his position (urban living is idiotic).

- **Become part of the writer's audience.** Not all writers have you and me in mind when they write. As an active reader, you need to "join" a writer's audience by learning about the writer, about the time in which the piece was written, and about the writer's expected audience. For readings in this text you are aided by introductory notes; be sure to study them.

- **Predict what is coming.** Look for a writer's main idea or purpose statement. Study the work's organization. Then use this information to anticipate what is coming. When you read "There are three good reasons for requiring a dress code in schools," you know the writer will list *three* reasons.
- **Concentrate.** Slow down and give your full attention to reading. Watch for transition and connecting words that show you how the parts of a text connect. Read an entire article or chapter at one time—or you will need to start over to make sense of the piece.
- **Annotate as you read.** The more senses you use, the more active your involvement. That means marking the text as you read (or taking notes if the material is not yours). Underline key sentences, such as the writer's thesis. Then, in the margin, indicate that it is the thesis. With a series of examples (or reasons), label them and number them. When you look up a word's definition, write the definition in the margin next to the word. Draw diagrams to illustrate concepts; draw arrows to connect example to idea. Studies have shown that students who annotate their texts get higher grades. Do what successful students do.
- **Keep a reading journal.** In addition to annotating what you read, you may want to develop the habit of writing regularly in a journal. A reading journal gives you a place to note impressions and reflections on your reading, your initial reactions to assignments, and ideas you may use in your next writing.

## EXERCISE: Active Reading

Read the following selection, noting the annotations that have been started for you. As you read, add your own annotations. Then write a journal entry—four to five sentences at least—to capture your reactions to the following column.

## POLITICAL ADS AND THE VOTERS THEY ATTRACT   | RICHARD MORIN

A former journalist with the *Washington Post,* Richard Morin wrote a regular Sunday column titled "Unconventional Wisdom" that presented interesting new information from the social sciences. The following column appeared November 23, 2003.

Even though it pains me to report it, those negative political advertisements designed to scare the pants off us appear to work quite well. But here's a surprise—so do those positive ads filled with happy children and cascading violins.  1

Topic.

What's the connection? Both depend on manipulating the emotions of viewers.  2

Note: Both types of ads work—why?

What's more, emotion-drenched political ads are most effective among sophisticated voters, who probably would be the most chagrined to learn that they're suckers for political mudslinging and cheerleading, claims Ted Brader, a political science professor and researcher at the Institute for Social Research at the University of Michigan.  3

4    "Emotions are so central to what makes us tick," Brader said. "Political scientists for years have basically ignored them. But if you think about what causes us to do anything in life, political or otherwise, there are always strong emotions involved."

5    His study, which he is expanding into a book, began as research for his PhD at Harvard University. Brader recruited 286 voting-age men and women in 11 Massachusetts communities during the weeks leading up to the 1998 Democratic gubernatorial primary. The race pitted incumbent Attorney General Scott Harshbarger against former state senator Patricia McGovern.

6    Test subjects were randomly assigned to one of four groups. Each group watched a half-hour local news broadcast that featured one of four seemingly genuine 30-second campaign ads that Brader had prepared. Two ads were positive in tone and two were negative. The names of the candidates were alternated so that each one was featured an equal number of times in the ads.

7    The scripts for the two positive ads were identical. What was different were the accompanying sounds and images. One ad featured uplifting "cues"—symphonic music and warm, colorful images of children intended to inspire an even more enthusiastic reaction to the upbeat message—while the other used bland visual and audio enhancements.

8    The scripts for the two negative ads also were the same. But one featured tense, discordant music and grainy pictures of crime scenes to create a sense of fear. The other ad lacked the scary special effects.

9    The test subjects answered a survey before and after the experiment that measured, among other things, interest in the campaign and candidate preference. And yes, after the study the participants were let in on the secret. "They were 'debriefed' after their participation and given a written explanation that the political ads they saw were completely fictitious, made by me for the study and not by the candidates, and there was not necessarily any connection between what is said in the ads and the candidates' actual positions," Brader said.

10    It's good that he did eventually 'fess up, because the enhanced ads worked better than Brader or his faculty advisers suspected they would. When enthusiasm cues were added to a positive script, the test subjects' self-reported likelihood to vote on Election Day was a whopping 29 percentage points higher than those of subjects who saw the positive ad without the emotion-enhancing cues.

11    The negative ad with fear-inducing cues was particularly effective in persuading viewers to vote for the candidate promoted in the ad. Nearly 10 percent of those who saw the "fear" ad switched allegiance, and 20 to 25 percent were less certain of their choice after seeing their favored candidate dragged through the mud.

12    Those exposed to fear cues also could remember more details of related news stories shown in the broadcast. It also made them more likely to want to obtain more information about the candidates, suggesting one benefit to negative ads: "They may scare people into thinking" about political campaigns, Brader said.

Brader also found that better-informed, better-educated voters were 13 more susceptible to fear-inducing and enthusiasm-enhancing ads than less-knowledgeable voters. "That really contradicts the traditional claim that emotional appeals work primarily on the ignorant masses," or those who are otherwise easily led, he said.

Why are smarties so susceptible to emotional ads? Brader doesn't know. It 14 could be, he said, that such ads "resonate with people who are already emotional about politics to begin with because they have a vested interest."

For political consultants, this is news they can use. "Candidates should aim 15 positive ads at their base of support and fear ads at undecided and opposing voters," Brader advised. "Front-runners, incumbents in times of peace and prosperity, and members of the majority party in a district should rely principally on enthusiasm. Their opponents—trailing candidates, challengers, members of the minority party—should be drawn to the use of fear."

Source: From *The Washington Post*, November 23, 2003. Reprinted by permission of the author.

## WRITING SUMMARIES

Preparing a good summary is not as easy as it may seem. *A summary briefly restates, in your own words, the main points of a work in a way that does not misrepresent or distort the original.* A good summary shows your grasp of main ideas and your ability to express them clearly. You need to condense the original while giving all key ideas appropriate attention. As a student you may be assigned a summary to

- show that you have read and understood assigned works;
- complete a test question;
- have a record of what you have read for future study or to prepare for class discussion; or
- explain the main ideas in a work that you will also examine in some other way, such as in a book review.

When assigned a summary, pay careful attention to word choice. Avoid judgment words, such as "Brown then proceeds to develop the *silly* idea that. . . ." Follow these guidelines for writing good summaries.

## GUIDELINES for Writing Summaries

1. **Write in a direct, objective style, using your own words.** Use few, if any, direct quotations, probably none in a one-paragraph summary.
2. **Begin with a reference to the writer (full name) and the title of the work, and then state the writer's thesis.** (You may also want to include where and when the work was published.)

3. **Complete the summary by providing other key ideas.** Show the reader how the main ideas connect and relate to one another.

4. **Do not include specific examples, illustrations, or background sections.**

5. **Combine main ideas into fewer sentences than were used in the original.**

6. **Keep the parts of your summary in the same balance as you find in the original.** If the author devotes about 30 percent of the essay to one idea, that idea should get about 30 percent of the space in your summary.

7. **Select precise, accurate verbs to show the author's relationship to ideas.** Write Jones *argues*, Jones *asserts*, Jones *believes*. Do not use vague verbs that provide only a list of disconnected ideas. Do *not* write Jones *talks about*, Jones *goes on to say*.

8. **Do not make any judgments about the writer's style or ideas.** Do *not* include your personal reaction to the work.

## EXERCISE: Summary

With these guidelines in mind, read the following two summaries of Deborah Tannen's "Who Does the Talking Here?" (see pp. 7–9). Then answer the question: What is flawed or weak about each summary? To aid your analysis, (1) underline or highlight all words or phrases that are inappropriate in each summary, and (2) put the number of the guideline next to any passage that does not adhere to that guideline.

### SUMMARY 1

I really thought that Deborah Tannen's essay contained some interesting ideas about how men and women talk. Tannen mentioned a study in which men and women used almost the same number of words. She goes on to talk about a man who talked a lot at a meeting in Virginia. Tannen also says that women talk more to make others feel good. I'm a man, and I don't like to make small talk.

### SUMMARY 2

In Deborah Tannen's "Who Does the Talking Here?" (published July 15, 2007), she talks about studies to test who talks more—men or women. Some people think the case is closed—they both talk about the same number of words. Tannen goes on to say that she thinks people use words differently. Men talk a lot at events; they use "report-talk." Women use "rapport-talk" to strengthen relationships; their language is a glue to maintain relationships. So just counting words does not work. You have to know why someone is speaking.

Although we can agree that the writers of these summaries have read Tannen's essay, we can also find weaknesses in each summary. Certainly the second summary is more helpful than the first, but it can be strengthened by eliminating some details, combining some ideas, and putting more focus on Tannen's main idea. Here is a much-improved version:

### REVISED SUMMARY

In Deborah Tannen's essay "Who Does the Talking Here?" (published July 15, 2007), Tannen asserts that recent studies to determine if men or women do the most talking are not helpful in answering that question. These studies focus on just counting the words that men and women use. Tannen argues that the only useful study of this issue is one that examines how each gender uses words and in which situations each gender does the most talking. She explains that men tend to use "report-talk" whereas women tend to use "rapport-talk." That is, men will do much of the talking in meetings when they have something to report. Women, on the other hand, will do more of the talking when they are seeking to connect in a relationship, to make people feel good. So, if we want to really understand the differences, we need to stop counting words and listen to what each gender is actually doing with the words that are spoken.

At times you may need to write a summary of a page or two rather than one paragraph. Frequently, long reports are preceded by a one-page summary. A longer summary may become part of an article-length review of an important book. Or instructors may want a longer summary of a lengthy or complicated article or text chapter. The following is an example of a summary of a lengthy article on cardiovascular health.

### SAMPLE LONGER SUMMARY

In her article "The Good Heart," Anne Underwood (*Newsweek,* October 3, 2005) explores recent studies regarding heart disease that, in various ways, reveal the important role that one's attitudes have on physical health, especially the health of the heart. She begins with the results of a study published in the *New England Journal of Medicine* that examined the dramatic increase in cardiovascular deaths after an earthquake in Los Angeles in 1994. People who were not hurt by the quake died as a result of the fear and stress brought on by the event. As Underwood explains in detail, however, studies continue to show that psychological and social factors affect coronaries even more than sudden shocks such as earthquakes. For example, according to Dr. Michael Frenneaux, depression "at least doubles an otherwise healthy person's heart-attack risk." A Duke University study showed that high levels of hostility also raised the risk of death by heart disease. Another study showed that childhood traumas can increase heart disease risks by 30 to 70 percent. Adults currently living under work and family stress also increase their risks significantly.

How do attitudes make a difference? A number of studies demonstrate that negative attitudes, anger, and hostile feelings directly affect the chemistry of the body in ways that damage blood vessels. They also can raise blood pressure. Less directly, people with these attitudes and under stress often eat more, exercise less, and are more likely to smoke. These behaviors add to one's risk. Some physicians are seeking to use this information to increase the longevity of heart patients. They are advising weight loss and exercise, yoga and therapy, recognizing, as Underwood concludes, that "the heart does not beat in isolation, nor does the mind brood alone."

Observe the differences between the longer summary of Anne Underwood's article and the paragraph summary of Deborah Tannen's essay:

- Some key ideas or terms may be presented in direct quotation.
- Results of studies may be given in some detail.
- Appropriate transitional and connecting words are used to show how the parts of the summary connect.
- The author's name is often repeated to keep the reader's attention on the article summarized, not on the author of the summary.

## USING PARAPHRASE

Paraphrasing is similar to summary in that the goal is an accurate presentation of the information and ideas of someone else. Unlike summary, an entire short work is paraphrased, often a poem (see p. 572 for a paraphrase of a poem) or a complex prose section that needs a simpler, usually longer, restatement so that you are clear about its meaning. We paraphrase short but complex statements, whereas we summarize an entire essay or chapter of a book.

Another use of paraphrasing is to restate some of the information or ideas from a source as a part of developing our own writing. Writers do this extensively in a researched essay, but they may also paraphrase just parts of a source to add value to their own discussion or, perhaps, to be clear about a writer's ideas that they will then evaluate or challenge in some way. In the readings in this text, you will find writers time and again drawing on just one or two sources as a basis for disagreement or to support and develop their own ideas. To illustrate, instead of preparing a summary of Lincoln's entire speech, suppose you want to use his opening point as a lead-in to commenting on our own times; you might write:

> Lincoln's famous brief speech at the dedication of the Gettysburg battlefield begins with the observation that our nation was initially built on a belief in liberty and equality, but the country's future is now being tested by civil war. We are not facing an actual civil war today, but some would argue that we are facing a culture war, a war of opposing values and beliefs, that seems to be tearing our country apart.

Paraphrasing—putting the idea into your own words—is a much more effective use of Lincoln's speech than quoting his first two sentences. It's his idea that you want to use, not his actual language. But note that you give credit to Lincoln for the idea. Summary, paraphrasing, and direct quoting all share this one same characteristic: You must let your readers or listeners know that you are drawing on the information or ideas of someone else.

# ACKNOWLEDGING SOURCES INFORMALLY

As you have seen in the summaries and paraphrases above, even when you are not writing a formally documented paper, you must identify each source by author. What follows are some of the conventions of writing to use when writing about sources.

## Referring to People and Sources

Readers in academic, professional, and business contexts expect writers to follow specific conventions of style when referring to authors and to various kinds of sources. Study the following guidelines and examples and then mark the next few pages for easy reference—perhaps by turning down a corner of the first and last pages.

### References to People

- In a first reference, give the person's full name (both the given name and the surname): *Ellen Goodman, Robert J. Samuelson.* In second and subsequent references, use only the last name (surname): *Goodman, Samuelson.*
- Do not use Mr., Mrs., or Ms. Special titles such as President, Chief Justice, or Doctor may be used in the first reference with the person's full name.
- Never refer to an author by her or his first name. Write *Tannen,* not *Deborah; Lincoln,* not *Abraham.*

### References to Titles of Works

Titles of works must *always* be written as titles. Titles are indicated by capitalization and by either quotation marks or italics.

### Guidelines for Capitalizing Titles

- The first and last words are capitalized.
- The first word of a subtitle is capitalized.
- All other words in titles are capitalized except
  — Articles (*a, an, the*).
  — Coordinating conjunctions (*and, or, but, for, nor, yet, so*).
  — Prepositions (*in, for, about*).

### Titles Requiring Quotation Marks

Titles of works published within other works—within a book, magazine, or newspaper—are indicated by quotation marks.

| | |
|---|---|
| ESSAYS | "The Real Pregnancy Problem" |
| SHORT STORIES | "The Story of an Hour" |
| POEMS | "To Daffodils" |

| ARTICLES | "Choose Your Utopia" |
| CHAPTERS | "Writers and Their Sources" |
| LECTURES | "Crazy Mixed-Up Families" |
| TV EPISODES | "Pride and Prejudice" (one drama on the television show *Masterpiece Theatre*) |

### *Titles Requiring Italics*

Titles of works that are separate publications and, by extension, titles of items such as works of art and websites are in italics.

| PLAYS | *A Raisin in the Sun* |
| NOVELS | *War and Peace* |
| NONFICTION BOOKS | *Read, Reason, Write* |
| BOOK-LENGTH POEMS | *The Odyssey* |
| MAGAZINES AND JOURNALS | *Wired* |
| NEWSPAPERS | *Wall Street Journal* |
| FILMS | *The Wizard of Oz* |
| PAINTINGS | *The Birth of Venus* |
| TELEVISION PROGRAMS | *Star Trek* |
| WEBSITES | *worldwildlife.org* |
| DATABASES | *ProQuest* |

Read the following article (published April 13, 2008, in the *Washington Post*) and respond by answering the questions that follow. Observe, as you read, how the author refers to the various sources he uses to develop his article and how he presents material from those sources. We will use this article as a guide to handling quotations.

## THE FUTURE IS NOW: IT'S HEADING RIGHT AT US, BUT WE NEVER SEE IT COMING
JOEL ACHENBACH

A former humor columnist and currently a staff writer for the *Washington Post*, Joel Achenbach also has a regular blog on *washingtonpost.com*. His books include anthologies of his columns and *Captured by Aliens: The Search for Life and Truth in a Very Large Universe* (2003). The following article was published April 13, 2008.

PREREADING QUESTIONS  What is nanotechnology? What do you think will be the next big change—and what field will it come from?

1      The most important things happening in the world today won't make tomorrow's front page. They won't get mentioned by presidential candidates or Chris Matthews[1] or Bill O'Reilly[2] or any of the other folks yammering and snorting on cable television.

---
[1] Political talk-show host on MSNBC.—Ed.
[2] Radio and television talk-show host on the FOX News Channel.—Ed.

They'll be happening in laboratories—out of sight, inscrutable and   2
unhyped until the very moment when they change life as we know it.

Science and technology form a two-headed, unstoppable change agent.   3
Problem is, most of us are mystified and intimidated by such things as biotech-nology, or nanotechnology, or the various other -ologies that seem to be threatening to merge into a single unspeakable and incomprehensible thing called biotechnonanogenomicology. We vaguely understand that this stuff is changing our lives, but we feel as though it's all out of our control. We're just hanging on tight, like Kirk and Spock when the Enterprise starts vibrating at Warp 8.

What's unnerving is the velocity at which the future sometimes arrives.   4
Consider the Internet. This powerful but highly disruptive technology crept out of the lab (a Pentagon think tank, actually) and all but devoured modern civilization—with almost no advance warning. The first use of the word "inter-net" to refer to a computer network seems to have appeared in this newspa-per on Sept. 26, 1988, in the Financial section, on page F30—about as deep into the paper as you can go without hitting the bedrock of the classified ads.

The entire reference: "SMS Data Products Group Inc. in McLean won a   5
$1,005,048 contract from the Air Force to supply a defense data network internet protocol router." Perhaps the unmellifluous compound noun "data network internet protocol router" is one reason more of us didn't pay atten-tion. A couple of months later, "Internet"—still lacking the "the" before its name—finally elbowed its way to the front page when a virus shut down thou-sands of computers. The story referred to "a research network called Internet," which "links as many as 50,000 computers, allowing users to send a variety of information to each other." The scientists knew that computer networks could be powerful. But how many knew that this Internet thing would change the way we communicate, publish, sell, shop, conduct research, find old friends, do homework, plan trips and on and on?

Joe Lykken, a theoretical physicist at the Fermilab research center in   6
Illinois, tells a story about something that happened in 1990. A Fermilab visi-tor, an English fellow by the name of Tim Berners-Lee, had a new trick he wanted to demonstrate to the physicists. He typed some code into a little blank box on the computer screen. Up popped a page of data.

Lykken's reaction: *Eh.*                                                7

He could already see someone else's data on a computer. He could have   8
the colleague e-mail it to him and open it as a document. Why view it on a separate page on some computer network?

But of course, this unimpressive piece of software was the precursor to   9
what is known today as the World Wide Web. "We had no idea that we were seeing not only a revolution, but a trillion-dollar idea," Lykken says.

Now let us pause to reflect upon the fact that Joe Lykken is a very smart  10
guy—you don't get to be a theoretical physicist unless you have the kind of brain that can practically bend silverware at a distance—and even he, with that giant cerebral cortex and the billions of neurons flashing and winking, saw the proto-Web and harrumphed. It's not just us mortals, even scientists don't always grasp the significance of innovations. Tomorrow's revolutionary technology

may be in plain sight, but everyone's eyes, clouded by conventional thinking, just can't detect it. "Even smart people are really pretty incapable of envisioning a situation that's substantially different from what they're in," says Christine Peterson, vice president of Foresight Nanotech Institute in Menlo Park, Calif.

11      So where does that leave the rest of us?

12      In technological Palookaville.

13      Science is becoming ever more specialized; technology is increasingly a series of black boxes, impenetrable to but a few. Americans' poor science literacy means that science and technology exist in a walled garden, a geek ghetto. We are a technocracy in which most of us don't really understand what's happening around us. We stagger through a world of technological and medical miracles. We're zombified by progress.

14      Peterson has one recommendation: Read science fiction, especially "hard science fiction" that sticks rigorously to the scientifically possible. "If you look out into the long-term future and what you see looks like science fiction, it might be wrong," she says. "But if it doesn't look like science fiction, it's definitely wrong."

15      That's exciting—and a little scary. We want the blessings of science (say, cheaper energy sources) but not the terrors (monsters spawned by atomic radiation that destroy entire cities with their fiery breath).

16      Eric Horvitz, one of the sharpest minds at Microsoft, spends a lot of time thinking about the Next Big Thing. Among his other duties, he's president of the Association for the Advancement of Artificial Intelligence. He thinks that, sometime in the decades ahead, artificial systems will be modeled on living things. In the Horvitz view, life is marked by robustness, flexibility, adaptability. That's where computers need to go. Life, he says, shows scientists "what we can do as engineers—better, potentially."

17      Our ability to monkey around with life itself is a reminder that ethics, religion and old-fashioned common sense will be needed in abundance in decades to come. . . . How smart and flexible and rambunctious do we want our computers to be? Let's not mess around with that Matrix business.

18      Every forward-thinking person almost ritually brings up the mortality issue. What'll happen to society if one day people can stop the aging process? Or if only rich people can stop getting old?

19      It's interesting that politicians rarely address such matters. The future in general is something of a suspect topic . . . a little goofy. Right now we're all focused on the next primary, the summer conventions, the Olympics and their political implications, the fall election. The political cycle enforces an emphasis on the immediate rather than the important.

20      And in fact, any prediction of what the world will be like more than, say, a year from now is a matter of hubris. The professional visionaries don't even talk about predictions or forecasts but prefer the word "scenarios." When Sen. John McCain, for example, declares that radical Islam is the transcendent challenge of the 21st century, he's being sincere, but he's also being a bit of a soothsayer. Environmental problems and resource scarcity could easily be the

dominant global dilemma. Or a virus with which we've yet to make our acquaintance. Or some other "wild card."

Says Lykken, "Our ability to predict is incredibly poor. What we all thought 21 when I was a kid was that by now we'd all be flying around in anti-gravity cars on Mars."

Futurists didn't completely miss on space travel—it's just that the things 22 flying around Mars are robotic and take neat pictures and sometimes land and sniff the soil.

Some predictions are bang-on, such as sci-fi writer Arthur C. Clarke's dec- 23 laration in 1945 that there would someday be communications satellites orbiting the Earth. But Clarke's satellites had to be occupied by repairmen who would maintain the huge computers required for space communications. Even in the late 1960s, when Clarke collaborated with Stanley Kubrick on the screenplay to *2001: A Space Odyssey,* he assumed that computers would, over time, get bigger. "The HAL 9000 computer fills half the spaceship," Lykken notes.

Says science-fiction writer Ben Bova, "We have built into us an idea that 24 tomorrow is going to be pretty much like today, which is very wrong."

The future is often viewed as an endless resource of innovation that will 25 make problems go away—even though, if the past is any judge, innovations create their own set of new problems. Climate change is at least in part a consequence of the invention of the steam engine in the early 1700s and all the industrial advances that followed.

Look again at the Internet. It's a fantastic tool, but it also threatens to dis- 26 perse information we'd rather keep under wraps, such as our personal medical data, or even the instructions for making a fission bomb.

We need to keep our eyes open. The future is going to be here sooner 27 than we think. It'll surprise us. We'll try to figure out why we missed so many clues. And we'll go back and search the archives, and see that thing we should have noticed on page F30.

QUESTIONS FOR READING AND REASONING

1. What is Achenbach's subject? What is his thesis? Where does he state it?
2. What two agents together are likely to produce the next big change?
3. Summarize the evidence Achenbach provides to support the idea that we don't recognize the next big change until it is here.
4. If we want to try to anticipate the next big change, what should we do?

5. What prediction did Arthur C. Clarke get right? In what way was his imagination incorrect? What can readers infer from this example?

6. Are big changes always good? Explain.

7. How does Achenbach identify most of his sources? He does not identify Chris Matthews or Bill O'Reilly in paragraph 1. What does this tell you about his expected audience?

# PRESENTING DIRECT QUOTATIONS: A GUIDE TO FORM AND STYLE

Although most of your papers will be written in your own words and style, you will sometimes use direct quotations. Just as there is a correct form for references to people and to works, there is a correct form for presenting borrowed material in direct quotations. Study the guidelines and examples and then mark these pages, as you did the others, for easy reference.

## Reasons for Using Quotation Marks

We use quotation marks in four ways:

- To indicate dialogue in works of fiction and drama
- To indicate the titles of some kinds of works
- To indicate the words that others have spoken or written
- To separate ourselves from or call into question particular uses of words

The following guidelines apply to all four uses of quotation marks, but the focus will be on the third use.

## A Brief Guide to Quoting

1. *Quote accurately.* Do not misrepresent what someone else has written. Take time to compare what you have written with the original.

2. *Put all words taken from a source within quotation marks.* (To take words from a source without using quotation marks is to plagiarize, a form of stealing punished in academic and professional communities.)

3. *Never change any of the words within your quotation marks.* Indicate any deleted words with ellipses [spaced periods (. . .)]. If you need to add words to make the meaning clear, place the added words in [square brackets], not (parentheses).

4. *Always make the source of the quoted words clear.* If you do not provide the author of the quoted material, readers will have to assume that you are calling those words into question—the fourth reason for quoting. Observe that Achenbach introduces Joe Lykken in paragraph 6 and then uses his last name or "he" through the next three paragraphs so that readers always know to whom he is referring and quoting.

5.  *When quoting an author who is quoted by the author of the source you are using, you must make clear that you are getting that author's words from your source, not directly from that author.*
    For example:

    | ORIGINAL: | "We had no idea that we were seeing not only a revolution, but a trillion-dollar idea." |
    |---|---|
    | INCORRECT: | Referring to his first experience with the World Wide Web, Lykken observed: "We had no idea that we were seeing . . . a revolution." |
    | CORRECT: | To make his point about our failure to recognize big changes when they first appear, Achenbach quotes theoretical physicist Joe Lykken's response to first seeing the World Wide Web: "We had no idea that we were seeing . . . a revolution." |

6.  *Place commas and periods inside the closing quotation mark—even when only one word is quoted:* Unable to anticipate big changes coming from modern science, we are, Achenbach observes, in "technological Palookaville."

7.  *Place colons and semicolons outside the closing quotation mark:* Achenbach jokingly explains our reaction to the complexities of modern technologies in his essay "The Future Is Now": "We're zombified by progress."

8.  *Do not quote unnecessary punctuation.* When you place quoted material at the end of a sentence you have written, use only the punctuation needed to complete your sentence.

    | ORIGINAL: | The next big change will be "happening in laboratories—out of sight, inscrutable, and unhyped." |
    |---|---|
    | INCORRECT: | Achenbach explains that we will be surprised by the next big change because it will, initially, be hidden, "happening in laboratories—." |
    | CORRECT: | Achenbach explains that we will be surprised by the next big change because it will, initially, be hidden, "happening in laboratories." |

9.  *When the words you quote are only a part of your sentence, do not capitalize the first quoted word, even if it was capitalized in the source.* **Exception:** You introduce the quoted material with a colon.

    | INCORRECT: | Achenbach observes that "The future is often viewed as an endless resource of innovation." |
    |---|---|
    | CORRECT: | Achenbach observes that "the future is often viewed as an endless resource of innovation." |
    | ALSO CORRECT: | Achenbach argues that we count too much on modern science to solve problems: "The future is often viewed as an endless resource of innovation." |

10. *Use single quotation marks (the apostrophe key on your keyboard) to identify quoted material within quoted material:*

Achenbach explains that futurists "prefer the word 'scenarios.'"

11. *Depending on the structure of your sentence, use a colon, a comma, or no punctuation before a quoted passage.* A colon provides a formal introduction to a quoted passage. (See the example in item 9.) Use a comma only when your sentence requires it. Quoted words presented in a "that" clause are not preceded by a comma.

| | |
|---|---|
| **ORIGINAL:** | "What's unnerving is the velocity at which the future sometimes arrives." |
| **CORRECT:** | "What's unnerving," Achenbach notes, "is the velocity at which the future sometimes arrives." |
| **ALSO CORRECT:** | Achenbach observes that we are often unnerved by "the velocity at which the future sometimes arrives." |

12. *To keep quotations brief, omit irrelevant portions. Indicate missing words with ellipses.* For example: Achenbach explains that "we want the blessings of science . . . but not the terrors." Some instructors want the ellipses placed in square brackets—[. . .]—to show that you have added them to the original. Modern Language Association (MLA) style does not require the square brackets unless you are quoting a passage that already has ellipses as part of that passage. The better choice would be not to quote that passage.

13. *Consider the poor reader.*

- Always give enough context to make the quoted material clear.
- Do not put so many bits and pieces of quoted passages into one sentence that your reader struggles to follow the ideas.
- Make sure that your sentences are complete and correctly constructed. Quoting is never an excuse for a sentence fragment or distorted construction.

**NOTE:** All examples of quoting given above are in the present tense. We write that "Achenbach notes," "Achenbach believes," "Achenbach asserts." Even though his article was written in the past, we use the present tense to describe his ongoing ideas.

## FOR READING AND ANALYSIS

As you read the following article, practice active reading, including annotating each essay. Concentrate first on what the author has to say, but also observe the organization of the essay and the author's use of quotations and references to other authors and works.

## TURNING THE PAGE   | ANNA QUINDLEN

A columnist for *Newsweek,* Anna Quindlen is also the author of several nonfiction books, including *Loud and Clear* (2005), and several novels, including *Black and Blue* (1998) and *Every Last One* (2010). The following essay appeared in *Newsweek* on March 26, 2010.

PREREADING QUESTIONS  Given the essay's title and what you know about the author, what do you expect the essay to be about? Do you prefer to turn the page or scroll a Kindle? Why?

The stages of a writer's professional life are marked not by a name on an  1
office door, but by a name in ink. There was the morning when my father came home carrying a stack of Sunday papers because my byline was on page one, and the evening that I persuaded a security guard to hand over an early edition, still warm from the presses, with my first column. But there's nothing to compare to the day when someone—in my case, the FedEx guy—hands over a hardcover book with your name on the cover. And with apologies to all the techies out there, I'm just not sure the moment would have had the same grandeur had my work been downloaded instead into an e-reader.

The book is dead, I keep hearing, as I sit writing yet another in a room  2
lined with them. Technology has killed it. The libraries of the world are doomed to become museums, storage facilities for a form as antediluvian as cave paintings. Americans, however, tend to bring an either-or mentality to most things, from politics to prose. The invention of television led to predictions about the demise of radio. The making of movies was to be the death knell of live theater; recorded music, the end of concerts. All these forms still exist—sometimes overshadowed by their siblings, but not smothered by them. And despite the direst predictions, reading continues to be part of the life of the mind, even as computers replace pencils, and books fly into handhelds as well as onto store shelves. Anton Chekhov, meet Steve Jobs.

3    There's no question that reading off-paper, as I think of it, will increase in the years to come. The nurse-midwives of literacy, public librarians, are already loaning e-readers; a library that got 10 as gifts reported that within a half hour they had all been checked out. And there's no question that once again we will be treated to lamentations suggesting that true literacy has become a lost art. The difference this time is that we will confront elitism from both sides. Not only do literary purists now complain of the evanescent nature of letters onscreen, the tech aficionados have become equally disdainful of the old form. "This book stinks," read an online review of the bestseller *Game Change* before the release of the digital version. "The thing reeks of paper and ink."

4    Perhaps those of us who merely want to hunker down and be transported should look past both sides to concern ourselves with function instead of form. I am cheered by the Gallup poll that asks a simple question: do you happen to be reading any books or novels at present? In 1952 a mere 18 percent of respondents said yes. The last time the survey was done, in 2005, that number was 47 percent. So much for the good old days.

5    But not so fast: the National Endowment for the Arts released a report in 2007 that said reading fiction was declining sharply, especially among younger people. Market research done for booksellers has found that the number of so-called avid readers, those who buy more than 10 books a year, skews older and overwhelmingly female. One of the most surprising studies indicates that the biggest users of e-readers are not the YouTube young but affluent middle-aged men. (Some analysts suggest that this may be about adaptable font size; oh, our failing eyes!) The baby boomers are saving publishing; after them, the deluge?

6    The most provocative account of the effect of technology on literacy is now 16 years old, and while it remains a good read—in ink on paper but not, alas, digitally—the passage of time shows that its dark view of the future is overstated. Sven Birkerts's *The Gutenberg Elegies* notes, correctly, that "our entire collective subjective history—the soul of our societal body—is encoded

in print." But the author rejects the notion that words can appear on a computer screen in a satisfactory fashion: "The assumptions that underlie their significance are entirely different depending on whether we are staring at a book or a circuit—generated text," he says.

Is that true? Is Jane Austen somehow less perceptive or entertaining when 7 the words "It is a truth universally acknowledged" appear onscreen? It's disconcerting to read that many of the bestselling novels in Japan in recent years have been cell-phone books. But it's also cheering to hear from e-book owners who say they find themselves reading more because the books come to them rather than the other way around. I remember an impassioned eulogy for the typewriter delivered years ago by one of my newspaper colleagues: how, he asked, could we write on a keyboard that *made no sound*? Just fine, it turned out.

There is and has always been more than a whiff of snobbery about lamen- 8 tations that reading is doomed to extinction. That's because they're really judgments on human nature. If you've convinced yourself that America is a deeply anti-intellectual country, it must follow that we don't read, or we read the wrong things, or we read them in the wrong fashion. And now we have gleeful e-elitism as well, the notion that the conventional product, printed and bound, is a hopeless dinosaur. Tech snobbery is every bit as silly as the literary variety. Both ignore the tremendous power of book love. As Kafka once said, "A book must be the ax for the frozen sea within us."

Reading is not simply an intellectual pursuit but an emotional and spiritual 9 one. It lights the candle in the hurricane lamp of self; that's why it survives. There are book clubs and book Web sites and books on tape and books online. There are still millions of people who like the paper version, at least for now. And if that changes—well, what is a book, really? Is it its body, or its soul? Would Dickens have recognized a paperback of *A Christmas Carol*, or, for that matter, a Braille version? Even on a cell-phone screen, Tiny Tim can God-bless us, every one.

Source: From *Newsweek*, March 26, 2010. Reprinted by permission of International Creative Management, Inc. Copyright © 2010 by Anna Quindlen.

## QUESTIONS FOR READING

1.  What marks stages in a writer's life? In what form are these stages most enjoyed by Quindlen?
2.  What has been the prediction for the future of books?
3.  Are more or fewer people reading today (2005) than in 1952? Who, today, are doing most of the reading?
4.  What two forms of snobbery can be found in the discussion about the future of books and reading?

QUESTIONS FOR REASONING AND ANALYSIS

5.  In paragraph 9, Quindlen offers a definition of reading that includes a metaphor. Explain her concepts of reading in your own words.

6.  Quindlen begins by expressing her pleasure in seeing her name on the cover of a print book. What position does she accept by the end of the essay?

7.  The author refers to several writers throughout her essay. What does this tell you about the audience she expects? Can you identify Chekhov, Birkerts, Austen, Kafka, and Dickens? (Do a quick online search to identify any who are unfamiliar to you.)

QUESTIONS FOR REFLECTION AND WRITING

8.  What characteristic of e-books may help to keep reading alive and well in the future? Do you agree that e-books may be the salvation of future "book" reading? Why or why not?

9.  Would you describe yourself as a reader? (How many books do you read in a year?) Do you prefer print or digital books? How would you explain your preference in a discussion with friends?

1.  A number of years ago, Bill Gates argued that e-books will replace paper books. What are the advantages of e-books? What are the advantages of paper books? Are there any disadvantages to either type of book? Which do you prefer? How would you argue for your preference?

2.  Write a one-paragraph summary of Anna Quindlen's essay. Be sure that your summary clearly states the author's main idea, the claim of her argument. Take your time and polish your word choice.

3.  Read actively and then prepare a one-and-a-half-page summary of Linda J. Waite's "Social Science Finds: 'Marriage Matters'" (pp. 454–62). Your readers want an accurate and balanced but much shorter version of the original because they will not be reading the original article. Explain not only what the writer's main ideas are but also how the writer develops her essay. That is, what kind of research supports the article's thesis? Pay close attention to your word choice.

## GOING ONLINE

Anna Quindlen refers to several writers in her essay. Select one unfamiliar to you and see what you can learn online. Prepare a page of information to share with your class.

# Responding Critically to Sources

READ: What is the situation? Who is hiding under the bed?

REASON: Whom do we expect to be under the bed? What strategy has been used?

REFLECT/WRITE: What makes this cartoon clever?

In some contexts, the word *critical* carries the idea of harsh judgment: "The manager was critical of her secretary's long phone conversations." In other contexts, though, the term means to evaluate carefully. When we speak of the critical reader or critical thinker, we have in mind someone who reads actively, who thinks about issues, and who makes informed judgments. Here is a profile of the critical reader or thinker:

## TRAITS OF THE CRITICAL READER/THINKER

- **Focused on the facts.**
  Give me the facts and show me that they are relevant to the issue.
- **Analytic.**
  What strategies has the writer/speaker used to develop the argument?
- **Open-minded.**
  Prepared to listen to different points of view, to learn from others.
- **Questioning/skeptical.**
  What other conclusions could be supported by the evidence presented?
  How thorough has the writer/speaker been?
  What persuasive strategies are used?
- **Creative.**
  What are some entirely different ways of looking at the issue or problem?
- **Intellectually active, not passive.**
  Willing to analyze logic and evidence.
  Willing to consider many possibilities.
  Willing, after careful evaluation, to reach a judgment, to take a stand on issues.

## EXAMINING THE RHETORICAL CONTEXT OF A SOURCE

Reading critically requires preparation. Instead of "jumping into reading," begin by asking questions about the work's rhetorical context. Rhetoric is about the *art of writing* (or *speaking*). Someone has chosen to shape a text in a particular way at this time for an imagined audience to accomplish a specific goal. The better you understand all of the decisions shaping a particular text, the better you will understand that work. And, then, the better you will be able to judge the significance of that work. So, you need, as much as possible, to answer the following five questions before reading. Then complete your answers while you read—or by doing research and thinking critically after you finish reading.

## Who Is the Author?

Key questions to answer include:

- *Does the author have a reputation for honesty, thoroughness, and fairness?* Read the biographical note, if there is one. Ask your instructor about the author or learn about the author in a biographical dictionary or online. Try *Book Review Digest* (in your library or online) for reviews of the author's books.
- *Is the author writing within his or her area of expertise?* People can voice opinions on any subject, but they cannot transfer expertise from one subject area to another. A football player endorsing a political candidate is a citizen with an opinion, not an expert on politics.
- *Is the author identified with a particular group or set of beliefs? Does the biography place the writer or speaker in a particular institution or organization?* For example, a member of a Republican administration may be expected to favor a Republican president's policies. A Roman Catholic priest may be expected to take a stand against abortion. These kinds of details provide hints, but you should not decide, absolutely, what a writer's position is until you have read the work with care. Be alert to reasonable expectations but avoid stereotyping.

## What Type—or Genre—of Source Is It?

Are you reading a researched and documented essay by a specialist—or the text of a speech delivered the previous week to a specific audience? Is the work an editorial—or a letter to the editor? Does the syndicated columnist (such as Dave Barry, who appears later in this chapter) write humorous columns? Is the cartoon a comic strip or a political cartoon from the editorial page of a newspaper? (You will see both kinds of cartoons in this text.) Know what kind of text you are reading before you start. That's the only way to give yourself the context you need to be a good critical reader.

## What Kind of Audience Does the Author Anticipate?

Understanding the intended audience helps you answer questions about the depth and sophistication of the work and a possible bias or slant.

- *Does the author expect a popular audience, a general but educated audience, or a specialist audience of shared expertise? Does the author anticipate an audience that shares cultural, political, or religious values?* Often you can judge the expected audience by noting the kind of publication in which the article appears, the publisher of the book, or the venue for the speech. For example, *Reader's Digest* is written for a mass audience, and *Psychology Today* for a general but more knowledgeable reader. By contrast, articles in the *Journal of the American Medical Association* are written by physicians and research scientists for a specialized reader. (It would be inappropriate, then, for a general reader to complain that an article in *JAMA* is not well written because it is too difficult.)

- *Does the author expect an audience favorable to his or her views? Or with a "wait and see" attitude? Or even hostile?* Some newspapers and television news organizations are consistently liberal whereas others are noticeably conservative. (Do you know the political leanings of your local paper? Of the TV news that you watch? Of the blogs you choose?) Remember: All arguments are "slanted" or "biased"—that is, they take a stand. That's as it should be. Just be sure to read or listen with an awareness of the author's particular background, interests, and possible stands on issues.

## What Is the Author's Primary Purpose?

Is the work primarily informative or persuasive in intent? Designed to entertain or be inspiring? Think about the title. Read a book's preface to learn of the author's goals. Pay attention to tone as you read.

## What Are the Author's Sources of Information?

Much of our judgment of an author and a work is based on the quality of the author's choice of sources. So always ask yourself: Where was the information obtained? Are sources clearly identified? Be suspicious of those who want us to believe that their unnamed "sources" are "reliable." Pay close attention to dates. A biography of King George III published in 1940 may still be the best source. An article urging more development based on county population statistics from the 1990s is no longer reliable.

**NOTE:** None of the readings in this textbook were written for publication in this textbook. They have all come from some other context. To read them with understanding you must identify the original context and think about how that should guide your reading.

## EXERCISES: Examining the Context

1. For each of the following works, comment on what you might expect to find. Consider author, occasion, audience, and reliability.
   a. An article on the Republican administration, written by a former campaign worker for a Democratic presidential candidate.
   b. A discussion, published in the Boston *Globe,* of the New England Patriots' hope for the next Super Bowl.
   c. A letter to the editor about conservation, written by a member of the Sierra Club. (What is the Sierra Club? Check out its website.)
   d. A column in *Newsweek* on economics. (Look at the business section of this magazine. Your library has it.)
   e. A 1988 article in *Nutrition Today* on the best diets.

    f.  A biography of Benjamin Franklin published by Oxford University Press.

    g.  A *Family Circle* article about a special vegetarian diet written by a physician. (Who is the audience for this magazine? Where is it sold?)

    h.  A *New York Times* editorial written after the Supreme Court's striking down of Washington, DC's handgun restrictions.

    i.  A speech on new handgun technology delivered at a convention of the National Rifle Association.

    j.  An editorial in your local newspaper titled "Stop the Highway Killing."

2.  Analyze an issue of your favorite magazine. Look first at the editorial pages and the articles written by staff, then at articles contributed by other writers. Answer these questions for both staff writers and contributors:

    a.  Who is the audience?

    b.  What is the purpose of the articles and of the entire magazine?

    c.  What type of article dominates the issue?

3.  Select one environmental website and study what is offered. The EnviroLink Network (www.envirolink.org) will lead you to many sites. Write down the name of the site you chose and its address (URL). Then answer these questions:

    a.  Who is the intended audience?

    b.  What seems to be the primary purpose or goal of the site?

    c.  What type of material dominates the site?

    d.  For what kinds of writing assignments might you use material from the site?

## ANALYZING THE STYLE OF A SOURCE

Critical readers read for implication and are alert to tone or nuance. When you read, think not only about *what* is said but also about *how* it is said. Consider the following passage:

> Bush's stupid "war"—so much for the Congress declaring war—drags on, costing unhappy taxpayers billions, while the "greatest army in the world" cannot find the real villain hiding somewhere in a cave.

This passage observes that the Iraq War continues, costing much money, while the United States still has not found the perpetrator of 9/11. But, it actually says more than that, doesn't it? Note the writer's attitude toward Bush, the war, and the U.S. military.

How can we rewrite this passage to make it more favorable? Here is one version produced by students in a group exercise:

> President Bush continues to defend the war in Iraq—which Congress never declared but continues to fund—in spite of the considerable cost to stabilize that country and the region. Meanwhile more troops will be needed to finally capture bin Laden and bring him to justice.

The writers have not changed their view that the Iraq War is costing a lot and that so far we have failed to capture bin Laden. But, in this version neither Bush nor the military is ridiculed. What is the difference in the two passages? Only the word choice.

## Denotative and Connotative Word Choice

The students' ability to rewrite the passage on the war in Iraq to give it a positive attitude tells us that, although some words may have similar meanings, they cannot always be substituted for one another without changing the message. Words with similar meanings have similar *denotations.* Often, though, words with similar denotations do not have the same connotations. A word's *connotation* is what the word suggests, what we associate the word with. The words *house* and *home,* for example, both refer to a building in which people live, but the word *home* suggests ideas—and feelings—of family and security. Thus the word *home* has a strong positive connotation. *House* by contrast brings to mind a picture of a physical structure only because the word doesn't carry any "emotional baggage."

We learn the connotations of words the same way we learn their denotations—in context. Most of us, living in the same culture, share the same connotative associations of words. At times, the context in which a word is used will affect the word's connotation. For example, the word *buddy* usually has positive connotations. We may think of an old or trusted friend. But when an unfriendly person who thinks a man may have pushed in front of him says, "Better watch it, *buddy,*" the word has a negative connotation. Social, physical, and language contexts control the connotative significance of words. Become more alert to the connotative power of words by asking what words the writers could have used instead.

> **NOTE:** Writers make choices; their choices reflect and convey their attitudes. *Studying the context in which a writer uses emotionally charged words is the only way to be sure that we understand the writer's attitude.*

## EXERCISES: Connotation

1. For each of the following words or phrases, list at least two synonyms that have a more negative connotation than the given word.
   a. child
   b. persistent
   c. thin
   d. a large group
   e. scholarly
   f. trusting
   g. underachiever
   h. quiet
2. For each of the following words, list at least two synonyms that have a more positive connotation than the given word.
   a. notorious
   b. fat
   c. politician
   d. old (people)
   e. fanatic
   f. reckless
   g. sot
   h. cheap

3.  Read the following paragraph and decide how the writer feels about the activity described. Note the choice of details and the connotative language that make you aware of the writer's attitude.

> Needing to complete a missed assignment for my physical education class, I dragged myself down to the tennis courts on a gloomy afternoon. My task was to serve five balls in a row into the service box. Although I thought I had learned the correct service movements, I couldn't seem to translate that knowledge into a decent serve. I tossed up the first ball, jerked back my racket, swung up on the ball—clunk—I hit the ball on the frame. I threw up the second ball, brought back my racket, swung up on the ball—ping—I made contact with the strings, but the ball dribbled down on my side of the net. I trudged around the court, collecting my tennis balls; I had only two of them.

4.  Write a paragraph describing an activity that you liked or disliked without saying how you felt. From your choice of details and use of connotative language, convey your attitude toward the activity. (The paragraph in exercise 3 is your model.)

5.  Select one of the words listed below and explain, in a paragraph, what the word connotes to you personally. Be precise; illustrate your thoughts with details and examples.

    a.  nature          d.  geek
    b.  mother          e.  playboy
    c.  romantic        f.  artist

## COLLABORATIVE EXERCISES: On Connotation

1.  List all of the words you know for *human female* and for *human male*. Then classify them by connotation (positive, negative, neutral) and by level of usage (formal, informal, slang). Is there any connection between type of connotation and level of usage? Why are some words more appropriate in some social contexts than in others? Can you easily list more negative words used for one sex than for the other? Why?

2.  Some words can be given a different connotation in different contexts. First, for each of the following words, label its connotation as positive, negative, or neutral. Then, for each word with a positive connotation, write a sentence in which the word would convey a more negative connotation. For each word with a negative connotation, write a sentence in which the word would suggest a more positive connotation.

    a.  natural         d.  free
    b.  old             e.  chemical
    c.  committed       f.  lazy

3.  Each of the following groups of words might appear together in a thesaurus, but the words actually vary in connotation. After looking up any words whose connotation you are unsure of, write a sentence in which each word is used

correctly. Briefly explain why one of the other words in the group should not be substituted.
a. brittle, hard, fragile
b. quiet, withdrawn, glum
c. shrewd, clever, cunning
d. strange, remarkable, bizarre
e. thrifty, miserly, economical

## Tone

We can describe a writer's attitude toward the subject as positive, negative, or (rarely) neutral. Attitude is the writer's position on, or feelings about, his or her subject. The way that attitude is expressed—the voice we hear and the feelings conveyed through that voice—is the writer's *tone*. Writers can choose to express attitude through a wide variety of tones. We may reinforce a negative attitude through an angry, somber, sad, mocking, peevish, sarcastic, or scornful tone. A positive attitude may be revealed through an enthusiastic, serious, sympathetic, jovial, light, or admiring tone. We cannot be sure that just because a writer selects a light tone, for example, the attitude must be positive. Humor columnists such as Dave Barry often choose a light tone to examine serious social and political issues. Given their subjects, we recognize that the light and amusing tone actually conveys a negative attitude toward the topic.

## COLLABORATIVE EXERCISES: On Tone

With your class partner or in small groups, examine the following three paragraphs, which are different responses to the same event. First, decide on each writer's attitude. Then describe, as precisely as possible, the tone of each paragraph.

1. It is tragically inexcusable that this young athlete was not examined fully before he was allowed to join the varsity team. The physical examinations given were unbelievably sloppy. What were the coach and trainer thinking of not to insist that each youngster be examined while undergoing physical stress? Apparently they were not thinking about our boys at all. We can no longer trust our sons and our daughters to this inhumane system so bent on victory that it ignores the health—indeed the very lives—of our children.

2. It was learned last night, following the death of varsity fullback Jim Bresnick, that none of the players was given a stress test as part of his physical examination. The oversight was attributed to laxness by the coach and trainer, who are described today as being "distraught." It is the judgment of many that the entire physical education program must be reexamined with an eye to the safety and health of all students.

3. How can I express the loss I feel over the death of my son? I want to blame someone, but who is to blame? The coaches, for not administering more rigorous physical checkups? Why should they have done more than other coaches have done before or than other coaches are doing at other schools? My son, for not telling me that he felt funny after practice? His teammates, for not telling the coaches that my son said he did not feel well? Myself, for not knowing that

something was wrong with my only child? Who is to blame? All of us and none of us. But placing blame will not return my son to me; I can only pray that other parents will not have to suffer so. Jimmy, we loved you.

## Level of Diction

In addition to responding to a writer's choice of connotative language, observe the *level of diction* used. Are the writer's words primarily typical of conversational language or of a more formal style? Does the writer use slang words or technical words? Is the word choice concrete and vivid or abstract and intellectual? These differences help to shape tone and affect our response to what we read. Lincoln's word choice in "The Gettysburg Address" (see p. 4) is formal and abstract. Lincoln writes "on this continent" rather than "in this land," "we take increased devotion" rather than "we become more committed." Another style, the technical, will be found in some articles in this text. The social scientist may write that "the child . . . is subjected to extremely punitive discipline," whereas a nonspecialist, more informally, might write that "the child is controlled by beatings or other forms of punishment."

One way to create an informal style is to choose simple words: *land* instead of *continent.* To create greater informality, a writer can use contractions: *we'll* for *we will.* There are no contractions in "The Gettysburg Address."

> **NOTE:** In your academic and professional writing, you should aim for a style informal enough to be inviting to readers but one that, in most cases, avoids contractions or slang words.

## Sentence Structure

Attitude is conveyed and tone created primarily through word choice, but sentence structure and other rhetorical strategies are also important. Studying a writer's sentence patterns will reveal how they affect style and tone. When analyzing these features, consider the following questions:

1.  *Are the sentences generally long or short, or varied in length?*
Are the structures primarily:

- *Simple* (one independent clause)
  In 1900 empires dotted the world.
- *Compound* (two or more independent clauses)
  Women make up only 37 percent of television characters, yet women make up more than half of the population.
- *Complex* (at least one independent and one dependent clause)
  As nations grew wealthier, traditional freedom wasn't enough.

Sentences that are both long and complex create a more formal style. Compound sentences joined by *and* do not increase formality much because such sentences are really only two or more short, simple patterns hooked together.

On the other hand, a long "simple" sentence with many modifiers will create a more formal style. The following example, from an essay on leadership by Michael Korda, is more complicated than the sample compound sentence above:

- *Expanded simple sentence*
  [A] leader is like a mirror, reflecting back to us our own sense of purpose, putting into words our own dreams and hopes, transforming our needs and fears into coherent policies and programs.

In "The Gettysburg Address" three sentences range from 10 to 16 words, six sentences from 21 to 29 words, and the final sentence is an incredible 82 words. All but two of Lincoln's sentences are either complex or compound-complex sentences. By contrast, in "The Future Is Now," Joel Achenbach includes a paragraph with five sentences. These sentences are composed of 7, 11, 3, 11, and 19 words each. All five are simple sentences.

**2.  *Does the writer use sentence fragments (incomplete sentences)?***

Although many instructors struggle to rid student writing of fragments, professional writers know that the occasional fragment can be used effectively for emphasis. Science fiction writer Bruce Sterling, thinking about the "melancholic beauty" of a gadget no longer serving any purpose, writes:

- Like Duchamp's bottle-rack, it becomes a found objet d'art. A metallic fossil of some lost human desire. A kind of involuntary poem.

The second and third sentences are, technically, fragments, but because they build on the structure of the first sentence, readers can add the missing words *It becomes* to complete each sentence. The brevity, repetition of structure, and involvement of the reader to "complete" the fragments all contribute to a strong conclusion to Sterling's paragraph.

**3.  *Does the writer seem to be using an overly simplistic style? If so, why?***

Overly simplistic sentence patterns, just like an overly simplistic choice of words, can be used to show that the writer thinks the subject is silly or childish or insulting. In one of her columns, Ellen Goodman objects to society's over-simplifying of addictions and its need to believe in quick and lasting cures. She makes her point with reference to two well-known examples—but notice her technique:

- Hi, my name is Jane and I was once bulimic but now I am an exercise guru . . .
- Hi, my name is Oprah and I was a food addict but now I am a size 10.

**4.  *Does the writer use parallelism (coordination) or antithesis (contrast)?***

When two phrases or clauses are parallel in structure, the message is that they are equally important. Look back at Korda's expanded simple sentence. He coordinates three phrases, asserting that a leader is like a mirror in these three ways:

- Reflects back our purpose
- Puts into words our dreams
- Transforms our needs and fears

*Antithesis* creates tension. A sentence using this structure says "not this" but "that." Lincoln uses both parallelism and antithesis in one striking sentence:

- The world will little note nor long remember
    <u>what</u> we say here,
  but it [the world] can never forget
    <u>what</u> they did here.

## Metaphors

When Korda writes that a leader is like a mirror, he is using a *simile.* When Lincoln writes that the world will not remember, he is using a *metaphor*—actually *personification.* Metaphors, whatever their form, all make a comparison between two items that are not really alike. The writer is making a *figurative comparison,* not a literal one. The writer wants us to think about some ways in which the items are similar. Metaphors state directly or imply the comparison; similes express the comparison using a connecting word; personification always compares a nonhuman item to humans. The exact label for a metaphor is not as important as

- recognizing the use of a figure of speech,
- identifying the two items being compared,
- understanding the point of the comparison, and
- grasping the emotional impact of the figurative comparison.

> **REMEMBER:** We need to pay attention to writers' choices of metaphors. They reveal much about their feelings and perceptions of life. And, like connotative words, they affect us emotionally even if we are not aware of their use. Become aware. Be able to "open up"—explain—metaphors you find in your reading.

## EXERCISE: Opening Up Metaphors

During World War II, E. B. White, the essayist and writer of children's books, defined the word *democracy* in one of his *New Yorker* columns. His definition contains a series of metaphors. One is: Democracy "is the hole in the stuffed shirt through which the sawdust slowly trickles." We can open up or explain the metaphor this way:

> Just as one can punch a hole in a scarecrow's shirt and discover that there is only sawdust inside, nothing to be impressed by, so the idea of equality in a democracy "punches" a hole in the notion of an aristocratic ruling class and reveals that aristocrats, underneath, are ordinary people, just like you and me.

Here are two more of White's metaphors on democracy. Open up each one in a few sentences.

> Democracy is "the dent in the high hat."
> Democracy is "the score at the beginning of the ninth."

## Organization and Examples

Two other elements of writing, organization and choice of examples, also reveal attitude and help to shape the reader's response. When you study a work's organization, ask yourself questions about both placement and volume. Where are these ideas placed? At the beginning or end—the places of greatest emphasis—or in the middle, suggesting that they are less important? With regard to volume, ask yourself, "What parts of the discussion are developed at length? What points are treated only briefly?" *Note:* Sometimes simply counting the number of paragraphs devoted to the different parts of the writer's subject will give you a good understanding of the writer's main idea and purpose in writing.

## Repetition

Well-written, unified essays will contain some repetition of key words and phrases. Some writers go beyond this basic strategy and use repetition to produce an effective cadence, like a drum beating in the background, keeping time to the speaker's fist pounding the lectern. In his repetition of the now-famous phrase "I have a dream," Martin Luther King Jr. gives emphasis to his vision of an ideal America (see pp. 222–26). In the following paragraph, a student tried her hand at repetition to give emphasis to her definition of liberty:

> Liberty is having the right to vote and not having other laws which restrict that right; it is having the right to apply to the university of your choice without being rejected because of race. Liberty exists when a gay man has the right to a teaching position and is not released from the position when the news of his orientation is disclosed. Liberty exists when a woman who has been offered a job does not have to decline for lack of access to day care for her children, or when a 16-year-old boy from a ghetto can get an education and is not instead compelled to go to work to support his needy family.

These examples suggest that repetition generally gives weight and seriousness to writing and thus is appropriate when serious issues are being discussed in a forceful style.

## Hyperbole, Understatement, and Irony

These three strategies create some form of tension to gain emphasis. Hyperbole overstates:

- "I will love you through all eternity!"

Understatement says less than is meant:

- Coming in soaking wet, you say, "It's a bit damp outside."

Irony creates tension by stating the opposite of what is meant:

- To a teen dressed in torn jeans and a baggy sweatshirt, the parent says, "Dressed for dinner, I see."

## Quotation Marks, Italics, and Capital Letters

Several visual techniques can also be used to give special attention to certain words. A writer can place a word or phrase within quotation marks to question its validity or meaning in that context. Ellen Goodman writes, for example:

- I wonder about this when I hear the word "family" added to some politician's speech.

Goodman does not agree with the politician's meaning of the word *family*. The expression *so-called* has the same effect:

- There have been restrictions on the Tibetans' so-called liberty.

Italicizing a key word or phrase or using all caps also gives additional emphasis. Dave Barry, in his essay beginning on page 43, uses all caps for emphasis:

- Do you want appliances that are smarter than you? Of course not. Your appliances should be DUMBER than you, just like your furniture, your pets and your representatives in Congress.

Capitalizing words not normally capitalized has the same effect of giving emphasis. As with exclamation points, writers need to use these strategies sparingly, or the emphasis sought will be lost.

## EXERCISES: Recognizing Elements of Style

1.  Name the technique or techniques used in each of the following passages. Then briefly explain the idea of each passage.
    a.  We are becoming the tools of our tools. (Henry David Thoreau)
    b.  The bias and therefore the business of television is to *move* information, not collect it. (Neil Postman)
    c.  If guns are outlawed, only the government will have guns. Only the police, the secret police, the military. The hired servants of our rulers. Only the government—and a few outlaws. (Edward Abbey)
    d.  Having read all the advice on how to live 900 years, what I think is that eating a tasty meal once again will surely doom me long before I reach 900 while not eating that same meal could very well kill me. It's enough to make you reach for a cigarette! (Russell Baker)
    e.  If you are desperate for a quick fix, either legalize drugs or repress the user. If you want a civilized approach, mount a propaganda campaign against drugs. (Charles Krauthammer)

f. Oddly enough, the greatest scoffers at the traditions of American etiquette, who scorn the rituals of their own society as stupid and stultifying, voice respect for the customs and folklore of Native Americans, less industrialized people, and other societies they find more "authentic" than their own. (Judith Martin)

g. Text is story. Text is event, performance, special effect. Subtext is ideas. It's motive, suggestions, visual implications, subtle comparisons. (Stephen Hunter)

h. This flashy vehicle [the school bus] was as punctual as death: seeing us waiting at the cold curb, it would sweep to a halt, open its mouth, suck the boy in, and spring away with an angry growl. (E. B. White)

2. Read the following essay by Dave Barry. Use the questions that precede and follow the essay to help you determine Barry's attitude toward his subject and to characterize his style.

# IN A BATTLE OF WITS WITH KITCHEN APPLIANCES, I'M TOAST | DAVE BARRY

A humor columnist for the *Miami Herald* for more than twenty years, Dave Barry has been syndicated in more than 150 newspapers. A Pulitzer Prize winner in 1988, Barry has written several books, including *Dave Barry Slept Here* (1989). The following column appeared in March 2000.

PREREADING QUESTIONS What is Barry's purpose in writing? What does he want to accomplish in this column—besides being funny?

Recently the *Washington Post* printed an article explaining how the appliance manufacturers plan to drive consumers insane. 1

Of course they don't *say* they want to drive us insane. What they SAY they 2 want to do is have us live in homes where "all appliances are on the Internet, sharing information" and appliances will be "smarter than most of their owners." For example, the article states, you could have a home where the dishwasher "can be turned on from the office" and the refrigerator "knows when it's out of milk" and the bathroom scale "transmits your weight to the gym."

I frankly wonder whether the appliance manufacturers, with all due 3 respect, have been smoking crack. I mean, did they ever stop to ask themselves WHY a consumer, after loading a dishwasher, would go to the office to start it? Would there be some kind of career benefit?

YOUR BOSS: What are you doing? 4

YOU (tapping computer keyboard): I'm starting my dishwasher! 5

YOUR BOSS: That's the kind of productivity we need around here! 6

YOU: Now I'm flushing the upstairs toilet! 7

Listen, appliance manufacturers: We don't NEED a dishwasher that we can 8 communicate with from afar. If you want to improve our dishwashers, give us one that senses when people leave dirty dishes on the kitchen counter, and shouts at them: "PUT THOSE DISHES IN THE DISHWASHER RIGHT NOW OR I'LL LEAK ALL OVER YOUR SHOES!"

9    Likewise, we don't need a refrigerator that knows when it's out of milk. We already have a foolproof system for determining if we're out of milk: We ask our wives. What we could use is a refrigerator that refuses to let us open its door when it senses that we are about to consume our fourth Jell-O Pudding Snack in two hours.

10    As for a scale that transmits our weight to the gym: Are they NUTS? We don't want our weight transmitted to our own EYEBALLS! What if the gym decided to transmit our weight to all these other appliances on the Internet? What if, God forbid, our refrigerator found out what our weight was? We'd never get the door open again!

11    But here is what really concerns me about these new "smart" appliances: Even if we like the features, we won't be able to use them. We can't use the appliance features we have NOW. I have a feature-packed telephone with 43 buttons, at least 20 of which I am afraid to touch. This phone probably can communicate with the dead, but I don't know how to operate it, just as I don't know how to operate my TV, which has features out the wazooty and requires THREE remote controls. One control (44 buttons) came with the TV; a second (39 buttons) came with the VCR; the third (37 buttons) was brought here by the cable man, who apparently felt that I did not have enough buttons.

12    So when I want to watch TV, I'm confronted with a total of 120 buttons, identified by such helpful labels as PIP, MTS, DBS, F2, JUMP and BLANK. There are three buttons labeled POWER but there are times—especially if my son and his friends, who are not afraid of features, have changed the settings—when I honestly cannot figure out how to turn the TV on. I stand there, holding three remote controls, pressing buttons at random, until eventually I give up and go turn on the dishwasher. It has been, literally, years since I have successfully recorded a TV show. That is how "smart" my appliances have become.

13    And now the appliance manufacturers want to give us even MORE features. Do you know what this means? It means that some night you'll open the door of your "smart" refrigerator, looking for a beer, and you'll hear a pleasant, cheerful voice—recorded by the same woman who informs you that Your Call Is Important when you call a business that does not wish to speak with you personally—telling you: "Your celery is limp." You will not know how your refrigerator knows this, and, what is worse, you will not know who else your refrigerator is telling about it ("Hey, Bob! I hear your celery is limp!"). And if you want to try to make the refrigerator STOP, you'll have to decipher Owner's Manual instructions written by and for nuclear physicists ("To disable the Produce Crispness Monitoring feature, enter the Command Mode, then select the Edit function, then select Change Vegetable Defaults, then assume that Train A leaves Chicago traveling westbound at 47 mph, while Train B . . .").

14    Is this the kind of future you want, consumers? Do you want appliances that are smarter than you? Of course not. Your appliances should be DUMBER than you, just like your furniture, your pets and your representatives in Congress. So I am urging you to let the appliance industry know, by phone,

letter, fax and e-mail, that when it comes to "smart" appliances, you vote NO. You need to act quickly. Because while you're reading this, your microwave oven is voting YES.

Source: From *Boogers Are My Beat* by Dave Barry, copyright © 2003 by Dave Barry. Used by permission of Crown Publishers, a division of Random House, Inc.

## QUESTIONS FOR READING AND REASONING

1. After thinking about Barry's subject and purpose, what do you conclude to be his thesis? Does he have more than one main idea?
2. How would you describe the essay's tone? Serious? Humorous? Ironic? Angry? Something else? Does a nonserious tone exclude the possibility of a degree of serious purpose? Explain your answer.

## QUESTIONS FOR REFLECTION AND WRITING

3. What passages in the article do you find funniest? Why?
4. What strategies does Barry use to create tone and convey attitude? List, with examples, as many as you can.

# WRITING ABOUT STYLE

What does it mean to "do a style analysis"? A style analysis answers the question "How is it written?" Let's think through the steps in preparing a study of a writer's choice and arrangement of language.

## Understanding Purpose and Audience

A style analysis is not the place for challenging the ideas of the writer. A style analysis requires the discipline to see how a work has been put together *even if you disagree with the writer's views*. You do not have to agree with a writer to appreciate his or her skill in writing.

If you think about audience in the context of your purpose, you should conclude that a summary of content does not belong in a style analysis. Why? Because we write style analyses for people who have already read the work. Remember, though, that your reader may not know the work in detail, so you will need to give examples to illustrate the points of your analysis.

## Planning the Essay

First, organize your analysis according to elements of style, not according to the organization of the work. Scrap any thoughts of "hacking" your way through the

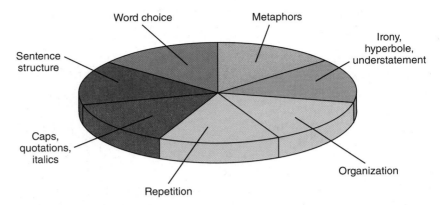

**FIGURE 2.1**  Analyzing Style

essay, commenting on the work paragraph by paragraph. This approach invites summary and means that you have not selected an organization that supports your purpose in writing. Think of an essay as like the pie in Figure 2.1. We could divide the pie according to key ideas—if we were summarizing. But we can also carve the pie according to elements of style, the techniques we have discussed in this chapter. This is the general plan you want to follow for your essay.

Choose those techniques you think are most important in creating the writer's attitude and discuss them one at a time. Do not try to include the entire pie; instead, select three or four elements to examine in some detail. If you were asked to write an analysis of the Dave Barry column, for example, you might select his use of quotation marks, hyperbole, and irony. These are three techniques that stand out in Barry's writing.

## Drafting the Style Analysis

If you were to select three elements of style, as in the Dave Barry example above, your essay might look something like this:

| | |
|---|---|
| *Paragraph 1: Introduction* | 1. Attention-getter<br>2. Author, title, publication information of article/book<br>3. Brief explanation of author's subject<br>4. Your thesis—that you will be looking at style |
| *Paragraph 2: First body paragraph* | Analysis of quotation marks. (See below for  more details on body paragraphs.) |

| | |
|---|---|
| *Paragraph 3: Second body paragraph* | 1. Topic sentence that introduces analysis of hyperbole<br>2. Three or more examples of hyperbole<br>3. Explanation of how each example connects to the author's thesis—that is, how the example of hyperbole works to convey attitude. This is your analysis; don't forget it! |
| *Paragraph 4: Third body paragraph* | Analysis of irony—with same three parts as listed above. |
| *Paragraph 5: Conclusion* | Restate your thesis: We can understand Barry's point through a study of these three elements of his style. |

## A CHECKLIST FOR REVISION

When revising and polishing your draft, use these questions to complete your essay.

- ☐ Have I handled all titles correctly?
- ☐ Have I correctly referred to the author?
- ☐ Have I used quotation marks correctly when presenting examples of style? (Use the guidelines in Chapter 1 for these first three questions.)
- ☐ Do I have an accurate, clear presentation of the author's subject and thesis?
- ☐ Do I have enough examples of each element of style to show my readers that these elements are important?
- ☐ Have I connected examples to the author's thesis? That is, have I shown my readers how these techniques work to develop the author's attitude?

To reinforce your understanding of style analysis, read the following essay by Ellen Goodman, answer the questions that follow, and then study the student essay that analyzes Goodman's style.

## IN PRAISE OF A SNAIL'S PACE   |   ELLEN GOODMAN

Author of *Close to Home* (1979), *At Large* (1981), and *Keeping Touch* (1985), collections of her essays, Ellen Goodman began as a feature writer for the Boston *Globe* in 1967 and was a syndicated columnist from 1976 until her retirement in 2009. The following column was published August 13, 2005.

PREREADING QUESTIONS Why might someone write in praise of snail mail? What does Goodman mean by "hyperactive technology"?

1    CASCO BAY, Maine—I arrive at the island post office carrying an artifact from another age. It's a square envelope, handwritten, with a return address that can be found on a map. Inside is a condolence note, a few words of memory and sympathy to a wife who has become a widow. I could have sent these words far more efficiently through e-mail than through this "snail mail." But I am among those who still believe that sympathy is diluted by two-thirds when it arrives over the Internet transom.

2    I would no more send an e-condolence than an e-thank you or an e-wedding invitation. There are rituals you cannot speed up without destroying them. It would be like serving Thanksgiving dinner at a fast-food restaurant.

3    My note goes into the old blue mailbox and I walk home wondering if slowness isn't the only way we pay attention now in a world of hyperactive technology.

4    Weeks ago, a friend lamented the trouble she had communicating with her grown son. It wasn't that her son was out of touch. Hardly. They were connected across miles through e-mail and cell phone, instant-messaging and text-messaging. But she had something serious to say and feared that an e-mail would elicit a reply that said: I M GR8. Was there no way to get undivided

Are we having fun yet?

attention in the full in-box of his life? She finally chose a letter, a pen on paper, a stamp on envelope.

How do you describe the times we live in, so connected and yet frac- 5 tured? Linda Stone, a former Microsoft techie, characterizes ours as an era of "continuous partial attention." At the extreme end are teenagers instant-messaging while they are talking on the cell phone, downloading music and doing homework. But adults too live with all systems go, interrupted and distracted, scanning everything, multi-technological-tasking everywhere.

We suffer from the illusion, Stone says, that we can expand our personal 6 bandwidth, connecting to more and more. Instead, we end up overstimulated, overwhelmed and, she adds, unfulfilled. Continuous partial attention inevitably feels like a lack of full attention.

But there are signs of people searching for ways to slow down and listen 7 up. We are told that experienced e-mail users are taking longer to answer, freeing themselves from the tyranny of the reply button. Caller ID is used to find out who we don't have to talk to. And the next "killer ap," they say, will be e-mail software that can triage the important from the trivial.

Meanwhile, at companies where technology interrupts creativity and 8 online contact prevents face-to-face contact, there are no e-mail-free Fridays. At others, there are bosses who require that you check your BlackBerry at the meeting door.

If a ringing cell phone once signaled your importance to a client, now that 9 client is impressed when you turn off the cell phone. People who stayed connected 10 ways, 24-7, now pride themselves on "going dark."

"People hunger for more attention," says Stone, whose message has been 10 welcomed even at a conference of bloggers. "Full attention will be the aphrodisiac of the future."

Indeed, at the height of our romance with e-mail, "You've Got Mail" was 11 the cinematic love story. Now e-mail brings less thrill—"who will be there?" And more dread—"how many are out there?" Today's romantics are couples who leave their laptops behind on the honeymoon.

As for text-message flirtation, a young woman ended hers with a man who 12 wrote, "C U L8R." He didn't have enough time to spell out Y-O-U?

Slowness guru Carl Honore began "In Praise of Slowness" after he found 13 himself seduced by a book of condensed classic fairy tales to read to his son. One-minute bedtime stories? We are relearning that paying attention briefly is as impossible as painting a landscape from a speeding car.

It is not just my trip to the mailbox that has brought this to mind. I come 14 here each summer to stop hurrying. My island is no Brigadoon: WiFi is on the way, and some people roam the island with their cell phones, looking for a hot spot. But I exchange the Internet for the country road.

Georgia O'Keeffe once said that it takes a long time to see a flower. No 15 technology can rush the growth of the leeks in the garden. All the speed in the Internet cannot hurry the healing of a friend's loss. Paying attention is the coin of this realm.

16    Sometimes, a letter becomes the icon of an old-fashioned new fashion. And sometimes, in this technological whirlwind, it takes a piece of snail mail to carry the stamp of authenticity.

## QUESTIONS FOR READING AND REASONING

1. What has Goodman just done? How does this action serve the author as a lead-in to her subject?
2. What is Goodman's main idea or thesis?
3. What examples illustrate the problem the author sees in our times? What evidence does Goodman present to suggest that people want to change the times?
4. What general solutions does Goodman suggest?

## QUESTIONS FOR REFLECTION AND WRITING

5. How do the details at the beginning and end of the essay contribute to Goodman's point? Write a paragraph answer to this question. Then consider: Which one of the different responses to reading does your paragraph illustrate?
6. The author describes our time as one of "continuous partial attention." Does this phrase sum up our era? Why or why not? If you agree, do you think this is a problem? Why or why not?
7. For what kinds of research projects would this essay be useful? List several possibilities to discuss with classmates.

# STUDENT ESSAY

A Convincing Style

James Goode

Ellen Goodman's essay, "In Praise of a Snail's Pace," is not, of course, about snails. It is about a way of communicating that our society has largely lost or ignored: the capability to pay full attention in communications and relationships. Her prime example of this is the "snail mail" letter, used for cards, invitations, and condolences. Anything really worth saying, she argues, must be written fully and sent by mail to make us pay attention. Goodman's easy, winning style of word choice and metaphor persuades us to agree with her point, a point also backed up by the logic of her examples.

"In Praise of a Snail's Pace" starts innocently. The author is merely taking a walk to the post office with a letter, surely nothing unusual. But as Goodman describes her letter, she reveals her belief that "snail mail" is a much more authentic way of sharing serious tidings than a message that "arrives over the Internet transom." The letter, with its "square" envelope and "handwritten" address, immediately sounds more personal than the ultramodern electronic message. The words have guided the reader's thinking. Goodman also describes our times as "connected yet fractured" and us as living in a world of "continuous partial attention." "Being connected" becomes synonymous by the end of the essay with "not paying attention." Word choice is crucial here. The author creates in the reader's mind a dichotomy: be fast and false, or slow down and mean it.

Goodman's metaphors make a point, too. "A picture is worth a thousand words" and the pictures created by the words here further the fast/slow debate. The idea that sending an e-condolence would be "like serving Thanksgiving dinner at a fast-food restaurant" gives an instant image of the worthlessness of an e-mail condolence note. The mother trying to get attention in the "full in-box" of her son's life shows us that a divided and distracted brain answering five hundred e-mails cannot be expected to concentrate on any of them. Again, trying to pay attention briefly is just as impossible as "painting a landscape from a speeding car." The "tyranny" of the reply button must be overcome by our "going dark." Getting away from our electronic world, Goodman reasons, helps us restore meaning to what we do.

But while the reader listens to clever words and paints memorable mind pictures, any resistance is worn away with a steady stream of examples. From the author mailing an envelope to Georgia O'Keeffe's remark that it takes a long time to see a flower, example after example supports her view. The mother wishing for the total attention of her son and the office workers' turning off cell phones and computers have already been mentioned. Linda Stone, a former Microsoft techie and a credible authority on modern communications and their effects on users, is quoted several times. Goodman notes with excellent effect that Stone's message has been received even at a conference of bloggers—if the most connected group out there supports this, why shouldn't everyone else? The author herself comes to an island every year to escape the mad hurry of the business world by wandering country roads. These examples build until the reader is convinced that snail mail is the mark of authenticity and connectedness.

"In Praise of a Snail's Pace" is a thoughtful essay that takes aim at the notion that one person can do it all and still find meaning. The "connected" person is in so much of a hurry that he or she must not be really interested in much of anything. By showing "interrupted and distracted" readers that "no technology can rush the growth of the leeks in the garden," the author makes a convincing case for the real effectiveness of written mail. Whether through word choice, metaphor, or example, Ellen Goodman's message comes through: Slow down and send some "snail mail" and be really connected for once.

## ANALYZING TWO OR MORE SOURCES

Scientists examining the same set of facts do not always draw the same conclusions; neither do historians and biographers agree on the significance of the same documents. How do we recognize and cope with these disparities? As critical readers we analyze what we read, pose questions, and refuse to believe everything we find in print or online. To develop these skills in recognizing differences, instructors frequently ask students to contrast the views of two or more writers. In psychology class, for example, you may be asked to contrast the views of Sigmund Freud and John B. Watson on child development. In a communications course, you may be asked to contrast the moderator styles of two talk-show hosts. We can examine differences in content or presentation, or both. Here are guidelines for preparing a contrast of sources.

## GUIDELINES for Preparing a Contrast Essay

- **Work with sources that have something in common.** Think about the context for each, that is, each source's subject and purpose. (There is little sense in contrasting a textbook chapter, for example, with a TV talk show because their contexts are so different.)
- **Read actively to understand the content of the two sources.** Tape films, radio, or TV shows so that you can listen/view them several times, just as you would read a written source more than once.
- **Analyze for differences, focusing on your purpose in contrasting.** If you are contrasting the ideas of two writers, for example, then your analysis will focus on ideas, not on writing style. To explore differences in two news accounts, you may want to consider all of the following: the impact of placement in the newspaper/magazine, accompanying photographs or graphics, length of each article, what is covered in each article, and writing styles. Prepare a list of specific differences.
- **Organize your contrast.** It is usually best to organize by points of difference. If you write first about one source and then about the other, the ways that the sources differ may not be clear for readers. Take the time to plan an organization that clearly reveals your contrast purpose in writing. To illustrate, a paper contrasting the writing styles of two authors can be organized according to the following pattern:

Introduction: Introduce your topic and establish your purpose to contrast styles of writer A and writer B.

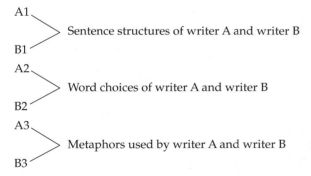

Conclusion: Explain the effect of the differences in style of the writers.

- **Illustrate and discuss each of the points of difference for each of the sources.** Provide examples and explain the impact of the differences.
- **Always write for an audience who may be familiar with your general topic but not with the specific sources you are discussing.** Be sure to provide adequate context (names, titles of works, etc.).

## EXERCISE: Analyzing Two Sources

Whenever two people choose to write on the same topic, there are bound to be differences in choice of specifics and emphasis—as well as differences in political, social, or philosophical perspective. So, we need to read widely and not settle for only one source for our information. When reading newspapers, journals of opinion, and blogs, we need to become aware of the "leaning" or "slant" of each source.

Read the following two articles on the congressional passage of the repeal of the "don't ask, don't tell" ruling that would now allow gays to serve openly in the military, legislation that all news outlets covered and discussed at length. Analyze each article for possible differences on the following points: impact of any visuals, length of treatment, differences in key points about the story, differences in how the issue is framed—in the context provided—and differences in style and tone. Then answer these questions: Is one author/periodical more positive regarding the legislation than the other? If so, in what way? How do you know?

Bring detailed notes to class for discussion, or write an analysis that contrasts the two articles on several key points of difference.

## IN HISTORIC VOTE, SENATE MOVES TO END "DON'T ASK, DON'T TELL" | GAIL RUSSELL CHADDOCK

This article was posted December 18, 2010, by the *Christian Science Monitor* at *CSMonitor.com.*

Veterans and supporters rallied outside the JFK Federal Building in Boston Wednesday in support of repealing the "don't ask, don't tell" ban on gays and lesbians serving openly in the military.

1      The Senate Saturday voted to end a longstanding ban on gay troops serving openly in the US armed services—a move Democrats compare to President Truman's ending the ban on racial segregation in the military in 1948.

"It is time to close this chapter in our history," said President Obama in a ₂
statement. "It is time to recognize that sacrifice, valor and integrity are no more
defined by sexual orientation than they are by race or gender, religion or creed. It
is time to allow gay and lesbian Americans to serve their country openly."

Six Republicans—Sens. Scott Brown of Massachusetts, Susan Collins and ₃
Olympia Snowe of Maine, Mark Kirk of Illinois, Lisa Murkowski of Alaska, and
George Voinovich of Ohio—broke with their party to give Democrats the
votes needed to break a GOP filibuster. The measure subsequently passed, 65
to 31. Sens John Ensign (R) of Nevada and Richard Burr (R) of North Carolina
also joined Democrats on the final vote.

### "DON'T ASK, DON'T TELL": CAN MILITARY HANDLE A REPEAL OF GAY BAN?

The House passed an identical repeal on Wednesday, 250–175, sending the ₄
bill to the White House. At least 60 days before the law takes effect, both the
President and Defense Secretary Robert Gates have to certify that ending the
"don't ask, don't tell" policy won't adversely affect military readiness or morale.

That issue was a major theme in today's Senate debate. The Senate Armed ₅
Services Committee held two days of hearings on the final report of a Pentagon
working group that reviewed the issue.

Its conclusion was that a repeal of the ban "would present a low risk to the ₆
military's effectiveness even during a time of war," said Sen. Carl Levin (D) of
Michigan, who chairs the panel.

"Seventy percent of the surveyed members believe that the impact on ₇
their units would be positive, mixed or of no consequence," he added, during
Saturday's floor debate. "While combat units expressed more concerns about
the consequences of repeal, those concerns disappeared for troops who have
worked with a gay or lesbian coworker."

But the top Republican on the panel, Sen. John McCain of Arizona and ₈
other GOP critics criticized the Pentagon's survey for focusing on implementation of repeal of the ban, not on whether repeal was in fact good policy.

"The Marine Corps Commandant has said he believes that changing this ₉
policy this way would cause distraction among the Marine Corps to the point
that he is worried about increased casualties," said Sen. Lindsey Graham (R) of
South Carolina, citing recent comments by Marine Corps Commandant Gen.
James Amos.

"From the Marines I talked to, he simply reflected what members of the ₁₀
Corps are going through," said Sen. Pat Roberts (R) of Kansas, a former Marine
who voted against repeal, in an interview. "Marines are different. We fight in
very close combat units. This is going to result in some very bad situations that
could have been avoided, if we had taken it on a step-by-step basis."

Sen. Jim Webb (D) of Virginia, also a Marine Corps veteran, responded ₁₁
from the floor that the issue was not whether there should be gays and lesbians
in the military.

"They are already there," he said, adding that the issue is not whether the ₁₂
policy will lead anyone to engage in inappropriate conduct.

13      "We will not allow that and we will be very vigorous in our oversight of the Department of Defense to make sure that does not occur," he said, noting that the Pentagon has committed to "a sequenced implementation" of the new policy for different units in the military.

14      Today's vote fulfills a campaign pledge of the last two Democratic presidents.

15      President Clinton campaigned in 1992 to "lift the ban" on homosexuals serving in the military, but Congress balked. The theme of "gays in the military" also set off a firestorm of protest among some Christian conservative groups, talk radio, and within the military, and it became virtual shorthand for the woes of Clinton's first year in office.

16      In July 1993, the Clinton administration proposed "don't ask, don't tell," as a compromise policy, which Congress voted into law in November.

17      But social conservatives have been largely out of the latest fight on repeal of the ban. The activists who lobbied lawmakers outside the Senate chamber today were all human rights activists committed to repeal.

18      "The conservative groups are not here because they're going to lose," said David Smith, vice president of the Human Rights Campaign, the largest gay and lesbian civil rights group. "Public attitudes have shifted. There are people on the front lines in combat who know gay and lesbians in the ranks. Eighty percent say there's no problem."

Source: Reproduced with permission from the December 18, 2010 issue of *The Christian Science Monitor* (www.CSMonitor.com). © 2010 The Christian Science Monitor.

## CLINTON AND OBAMA BOTH GET CREDIT ON "DON'T ASK, DON'T TELL" REPEAL | SUSAN MILLIGAN

This article was posted December 20, 2010, at *usnews.com*.

1      Maybe it takes a Congress undergoing post-election traumatic syndrome to do the right thing and allow gays and lesbians in the military to do their jobs without the added stress of lying about who they are. Maybe it's something about the holiday season that led lawmakers to acknowledge that there's something very distasteful about asking people to feel ashamed abut whom they love.

2      The more alarming trend is that the anonymity of the Internet (until WikiLeaks outs everyone, anyway) has emboldened people to brag shamelessly about how many kinds of people they hate. Vitriol, bigotry and distrust of immigrants or minority groups or Muslims—all of this has become accepted "free speech" by people looking to justify their ignorance and prejudice. But acknowledging love for someone of the same gender? That, for an indefensibly long time, has been banned by the U.S. military and treated with disdain by many in politics.

Former President Clinton was excoriated for his early efforts to repeal the   3
ban on gays in the military—not necessarily for the substance of the move, but
for the politics of it. Clinton was foolish to spend early political capital on
something so polarizing, critics argued, and the failed effort undermined the
commander-in-chief with a skeptical military and weakened him on Capitol
Hill. That's an easy, cable-TV political analysis to make. But social change
doesn't come without an early, audacious effort to upend wrong-headed policy, and Clinton should be commended for starting the process. The fact that
President Obama chose a different legislative strategy—focusing on the
healthcare and financial services reform first, angering gay rights activists who
wanted him to throw his political weight behind eliminating the offensive
"don't ask, don't tell" rule for gays and lesbians in the military—doesn't make
him less committed to human rights than Clinton. Both divergent strategies
were necessary to getting the policy changed—even if it took 17 years.

Source: From *U.S. News & World Report*, posted December 20, 2010. Copyright 2010 U.S. News &
World Report, L.P. Reprinted with permission.

## FOR READING AND ANALYSIS

### THE "F WORD"  |  FIROOZEH DUMAS

Born in Iran, Firoozeh Dumas moved to California when she was seven, returned to
Iran with her family for two years, and then came back to California. She attended the
University of California at Berkeley, married, and has three children. Initially she
started to write stories for her children. These were developed into *Funny in Farsi: A
Memoir of Growing Up Iranian in America* (2003), from which the following excerpt is
taken. *Laughing Without an Accent* was published in 2008

PREREADING QUESTIONS  Based on her title, what did you first think this work
would be about? How does the information above help you to adjust your
thinking?

My cousin's name, Farbod, means "Greatness."                                      1
When he moved to America, all the kids called him "Farthead." My brother   2
Farshid ("He Who Enlightens") became "Fartshit." The name of my friend
Neggar means "Beloved," although it can be more accurately translated as
"She Whose Name Almost Incites Riots." Her brother Arash ("Giver") initially
couldn't understand why every time he'd say his name, people would laugh
and ask him if it itched.

All of us immigrants knew that moving to America would be fraught with   3
challenges, but none of us thought that our names would be such an obstacle.
How could our parents have ever imagined that someday we would end up in
a country where monosyllabic names reign supreme, a land where "William" is

shortened to "Bill," where "Susan" becomes "Sue," and "Richard" somehow evolves into "Dick"? America is a great country, but nobody without a mask and a cape has a *z* in his name. And have Americans ever realized the great scope of the guttural sounds they're missing? Okay, so it has to do with linguistic roots, but I do believe this would be a richer country if all Americans could do a little tongue aerobics and learn to pronounce "kh," a sound more commonly associated in this culture with phlegm, or "gh," the sound usually made by actors in the final moments of a choking scene. It's like adding a few new spices to the kitchen pantry. Move over, cinnamon and nutmeg, make way for cardamom and sumac.

4    Exotic analogies aside, having a foreign name in this land of Joes and Marys is a pain in the spice cabinet. When I was twelve, I decided to simplify my life by adding an American middle name. This decision serves as proof that sometimes simplifying one's life in the short run only complicates it in the long run.

5    My name, Firoozeh, chosen by my mother, means "Turquoise" in Persian. In America, it means "Unpronounceable" or "I'm Not Going to Talk to You Because I Cannot Possibly Learn Your Name and I Just Don't Want to Have to Ask You Again and Again Because You'll Think I'm Dumb or You Might Get Upset or Something." My father, incidentally, had wanted to name me Sara. I do wish he had won that argument.

6    To strengthen my decision to add an American name, I had just finished fifth grade in Whittier, where all the kids incessantly called me "Ferocious." That summer, my family moved to Newport Beach, where I looked forward to starting a new life. I wanted to be a kid with a name that didn't draw so much attention, a name that didn't come with a built-in inquisition as to when and why I had moved to America and how was it that I spoke English without an accent and was I planning on going back and what did I think of America?

7    My last name didn't help any. I can't mention my maiden name, because:

8    "Dad, I'm writing a memoir."

9    "Great! Just don't mention our name."

10    Suffice it to say that, with eight letters, including a *z*, and four syllables, my last name is as difficult and foreign as my first. My first and last name together generally served the same purpose as a high brick wall. There was one exception to this rule. In Berkeley, and only in Berkeley, my name drew people like flies to baklava. These were usually people named Amaryllis or Chrysanthemum, types who vacationed in Costa Rica and to whom lentils described a type of burger. These folks were probably not the pride of Poughkeepsie, but they were refreshingly nonjudgmental.

11    When I announced to my family that I wanted to add an American name, they reacted with their usual laughter. Never one to let mockery or good judgment stand in my way, I proceeded to ask for suggestions. My father suggested "Fifi." Had I had a special affinity for French poodles or been considering a career in prostitution, I would've gone with that one. My mom suggested "Farah," a name easier than "Firoozeh" yet still Iranian. Her reasoning made sense, except that Farrah Fawcett was at the height of her popularity and I didn't want to be associated with somebody whose poster hung in

every postpubescent boy's bedroom. We couldn't think of any American names beginning with *F,* so we moved on to *J,* the first letter of our last name. I don't know why we limited ourselves to names beginning with my initials, but it made sense at that moment, perhaps by the logic employed moments before bungee jumping. I finally chose the name "Julie" mainly for its simplicity. My brothers, Farid and Farshid, thought that adding an American name was totally stupid. They later became Fred and Sean.

That same afternoon, our doorbell rang. It was our new next-door neigh- 12 bor, a friendly girl my age named Julie. She asked me my name and after a moment of hesitation, I introduced myself as Julie. "What a coincidence!" she said. I didn't mention that I had been Julie for only half an hour.

Thus I started sixth grade with my new, easy name and life became infi- 13 nitely simpler. People actually remembered my name, which was an entirely refreshing new sensation. All was well until the Iranian Revolution, when I found myself with a new set of problems. Because I spoke English without an accent and was known as Julie, people assumed I was American. This meant that I was often privy to their real feelings about those "damn I-raynians." It was like having those X-ray glasses that let you see people naked, except that what I was seeing was far uglier than people's underwear. It dawned on me that these people would have probably never invited me to their house had they known me as Firoozeh. I felt like a fake.

When I went to college, I eventually went back to using my real name. All 14 was well until I graduated and started looking for a job. Even though I had graduated with honors from UC–Berkeley, I couldn't get a single interview. I was guilty of being a humanities major, but I began to suspect that there was more to my problems. After three months of rejections, I added "Julie" to my résumé. Call it coincidence, but the job offers started coming in. Perhaps it's the same kind of coincidence that keeps African Americans from getting cabs in New York.

Once I got married, my name became Julie Dumas. I went from having an 15 identifiably "ethnic" name to having ancestors who wore clogs. My family and non-American friends continued calling me Firoozeh, while my coworkers and American friends called me Julie. My life became one big knot, especially when friends who knew me as Julie met friends who knew me as Firoozeh. I felt like those characters in soap operas who have an evil twin. The two, of course, can never be in the same room, since they're played by the same person, a struggling actress who wears a wig to play one of the twins and dreams of moving on to bigger and better roles. I couldn't blame my mess on a screen writer; it was my own doing.

I decided to untangle the knot once and for all by going back to my real 16 name. By then, I was a stay-at-home mom, so I really didn't care whether people remembered my name or gave me job interviews. Besides, most of the people I dealt with were in diapers and were in no position to judge. I was also living in Silicon Valley, an area filled with people named Rajeev, Avishai, and Insook.

Every once in a while, though, somebody comes up with a new permuta- 17 tion and I am once again reminded that I am an immigrant with a foreign name. I recently went to have blood drawn for a physical exam. The waiting room for blood work at our local medical clinic is in the basement of the building, and no matter how early one arrives for an appointment, forty coughing, wheezing people have gotten there first. Apart from reading *Golf Digest* and *Popular Mechanics,* there isn't much to do except guess the number of contagious diseases represented in the windowless room. Every ten minutes, a name is called and everyone looks to see which cough matches that name. As I waited patiently, the receptionist called out, "Fritzy, Fritzy!" Everyone looked around, but no one stood up. Usually, if I'm waiting to be called by someone who doesn't know me, I will respond to just about any name starting with an *F.* Having been called Froozy, Frizzy, Fiorucci, and Frooz and just plain "Uhhhh . . . ," I am highly accommodating. I did not, however, respond to "Fritzy" because there is, as far as I know, no *t* in my name. The receptionist tried again, "Fritzy, Fritzy DumbAss." As I stood up to this most linguistically original version of my name, I could feel all eyes upon me. The room was momentarily silent as all of these sick people sat united in a moment of gratitude for their own names.

18      Despite a few exceptions, I have found that Americans are now far more willing to learn new names, just as they're far more willing to try new ethnic foods. Of course, some people just don't like to learn. One mom at my children's school adamantly refused to learn my "impossible" name and instead settled on calling me "F Word." She was recently transferred to New York where, from what I've heard, she might meet an immigrant or two and, who knows, she just might have to make some room in her spice cabinet.

Source: From *Funny in Farsi: A Memoir of Growing Up Iranian in America* by Firoozeh Dumas, copyright © 2003 by Firoozeh Dumas. Used by permission of Villard Books, a division of Random House, Inc.

## QUESTIONS FOR READING

1. What happened when the author changed her name to Julie?
2. What happened when she sought a job after college, using her original name?
3. When did she decide to use only her original name?
4. When Dumas is called at the medical clinic, what does she think the other patients are feeling?

## QUESTIONS FOR REASONING AND ANALYSIS

5. Although this essay may not have the "feel" of an argument, it nonetheless makes a point. What is Dumas's claim?
6. What has changed in America since her arrival as a young girl? Is the change complete? What would she like to see Americans learn to do?
7. What writing strategies are noteworthy in creating her style? Illustrate with examples.

8.  How much effort do you make to pronounce names correctly? Why is it important to get a person's name right?

9.  Have you had the experience of Americans impatient with the pronunciation of your name—or just refusing to get it right? If so, what has been your response?

10. What might be some of the reasons Americans have trouble with the pronunciation of ethnic names—whether the names belong to foreign nationals or to ethnic Americans? Reflect on possible causes.

11. What are the advantages of facing the world with humor?

## HUSBAND HAL | CATHERINE GETCHES

A freelance writer living in San Diego, Catherine Getches often writes abut cultural issues. The following essay was published in the *Washington Post* on August 22, 2009.

PREREADING QUESTIONS When you see an essay begin with a paragraph in italics and a citation to a source, what do you anticipate about the essay? When you combine the second paragraph with the first, what does that tell you about Husband Hal?

*"Impressed and alarmed by advances in artificial intelligence, a group of* 1 *computer scientists is debating whether there should be limits on research that might lead to loss of human control over computer-based systems. . . . How would it be, for example, to relate to a machine that is as intelligent as your spouse?"*

—**The** *New York Times*, **July 25**

Hello, Human Wife.                                                                                            2

According to facial recognition data, I detect your lengthy glare at the    3 toilet seat that I left up, and identify your heavy human breath noise while flinging my wet towel from your side of the bed and into the hamper. Might I suggest this combo special for Bright and Clean toilet bowl cleaner that comes with Free and Gentle bleach? Maybe then our towels will be as white-bright as my mom [CHEER$^{TM}$ fully] mentioned approximately 2.7 times on her last visit, according to statistics with an accuracy ratio of plus or minus 0.33, given what may or may not have been a passive-aggressive tone—neither men nor robots can accurately tell. The pop-up now conveniently appearing on my forehead shows that said cleaning products can be bought 0.8 miles down the street at Walgreens.

Behavioral tracking confirms that fresh coffee and homemade waffles    4 before I leave for work are a thing of the past. Authentication on recent activity demonstrates a preference to check Facebook and wear an iPod rather than confer with Robot Husband, who can't find his hard drive or brown belt anywhere, again.

5    According to credit card activity that I can constantly monitor and flash in front of your face on this handy hand screen right here, you had your hair done last week. I couldn't tell you had anything done. But it, the spa treatment and a $257 charge at Saks Fifth Avenue do not fit in the "necessary expenses" column of our budget. (Data show an almost Pavlovian tendency to pay more when offered a coupon to "save more when you spend more.") I will enable a friendly ping noise to go off similar to the one that signals you to buy more beer when the refrigerator gets low. Wow, that ever-deepening furrow in your brow just won't quit, will it? Might I recommend Botox? And, while you're e-mailing your sister about the death of her labradoodle, I thought it might be helpful to flash these discounts on coffins—now available at Costco!

6    Your Facebook status update reveals that you are looking forward to your book club meeting. Poke. Here's a friendly suggestion: Oprah. The least you could do is become a fan of *O Magazine*. Here's a mojito to that. Why don't you take the quiz: "Which Desperate Housewife Are You?"

7    I noticed from monitoring your Internet activity that you Googled "weight loss." Might I also point you to this anorexia blog? Let's face up to the large pixels on your thighs—thesaurus correction, cellulite—that grapefruit diet isn't exactly working at what I'd call DSL speed. It's time to up the ante. And if you're interested in upping the ante, online poker is *huge*. Think you have a gambling problem? Maybe you'd also be interested in AA. Dialing back on drinking all that chardonnay at the book club might also get some of that junk out of your trunk. Do you know how many calories are in a glass of wine? There's an app for that.

8    You are correct that I said I'd be home right after golf. But this will be fol-lowed by a necessary reboot and lengthy system updates on the couch. Warning: This could take up to two hours to complete. *(Ping!)* Better stock the fridge.

9    No sex again tonight? Well, Bob just forwarded me a hilarious YouTube video, and you would not believe the late-night selection online!

10    Numbers show you snore at a higher-than-average decibel level, some-thing that has proportionately increased with your nose-hair growth, which also seems proportional to the rotundity of your rear. Ah, all this "being on" has me fried. Need more power. Have you seen my plug? I can't find it anywhere.

Source: From *The Washington Post*, August 22, 2009. Reprinted by permission of the author.

## QUESTIONS FOR READING

1.   Why is the opening paragraph in italics? What is the connection between the opening paragraph and the rest of the essay?

2.   What *types* of topics does Hal "discuss" with his wife?

QUESTIONS FOR REASONING AND ANALYZING

3.  Why is the husband called Hal? To what other Hal is this a reference?

4.  How is the essay organized; that is, what pattern does it follow? What makes this a useful tool?

5.  How does Getches create humor? Give some specific examples.

QUESTIONS FOR REFLECTION AND WRITING

6.  How different is Hal from many husbands? Is he just a stereotype created for humor—or are the jokes frequently made about husbands based on some truth?

7.  How much have gender roles changed within today's marriages? What do you expect your husband—or wife—to contribute to a marriage?

8.  What is Getches's point—the claim of her argument?

1. Analyze the style of one of the essays from Section 5 of this text. Do not comment on every element of style; select several elements that seem to characterize the writer's style and examine them in detail. Remember that style analyses are written for an audience familiar with the work, so summary is not necessary.

2. Many of the authors included in this text have written books that you will find in your library. Select one that interests you, read it, and prepare a review of it that synthesizes summary, analysis, and evaluation. Prepare a review of about 300 words; assume that the book has just been published.

3. Choose two newspaper and/or magazine articles that differ in their discussion of the same person, event, or product. You may select two different articles on a person in the news, two different accounts of a news event, an advertisement and a *Consumer Reports* analysis of the same product, or two reviews of a book or movie. Analyze differences in both content and presentation and then consider why the two accounts differ. Organize by points of difference and write to an audience not necessarily familiar with the articles.

4. Choose a recently scheduled public event (the Super Bowl, the Olympics, a presidential election, the Academy Award presentations, the premiere of a new television series) and find several articles written before and several after the event. First compare articles written after the event to see if they agree factually. If not, decide which article appears to be more accurate and why. Then examine the earlier material and decide which was the most and which the least accurate. Write an essay in which you explain the differences in speculation before the event and why you think these differences exist. Your audience will be aware of the event but not necessarily aware of the articles you are studying.

# The World of Argument

# Understanding the Basics of Argument

    **BY RICHARD THOMPSON**

**READ:** What is the situation? What is the reaction of the younger children? What does the older boy try to do?

**REASON:** Why is the older boy frustrated?

**REFLECT/WRITE:** What can happen to those who lack scientific knowledge?

In this section we will explore the processes of thinking logically and analyzing issues to reach informed judgments. Remember: Mature people do not need to agree on all issues to respect one another's good sense, but they do have little patience with uninformed or illogical statements masquerading as argument.

# CHARACTERISTICS OF ARGUMENT

## Argument Is Conversation with a Goal

When you enter into an argument (as speaker, writer, or reader), you become a participant in an ongoing debate about an issue. Since you are probably not the first to address the issue, you need to be aware of the ways that the issue has been debated by others and then seek to advance the conversation, just as you would if you were having a more casual conversation with friends. If the time of the movie is set, the discussion now turns to whose car to take or where to meet. If you were to just repeat the time of the movie, you would add nothing useful to the conversation. Also, if you were to change the subject to a movie you saw last week, you would annoy your friends by not offering useful information or showing that you valued the current conversation. Just as with your conversation about the movie, you want your argument to stay focused on the issue, to respect what others have already contributed, and to make a useful addition to our understanding of the topic.

## Argument Takes a Stand on an Arguable Issue

A meaningful argument focuses on a debatable issue. We usually do not argue about facts. "Professor Jones's American literature class meets at 10:00 on Mondays" is not arguable. It is either true or false. We can check the schedule of classes to find out. (Sometimes the facts change; new facts replace old ones.) We also do not debate personal preferences for the simple reason that they are just that—personal. If the debate is about the appropriateness of boxing as a sport, for you to declare that you would rather play tennis is to fail to advance the conversation. You have expressed a personal preference, interesting perhaps, but not relevant to the debate.

## Argument Uses Reasons and Evidence

Some arguments merely "look right." That is, conclusions are drawn from facts, but the facts are not those that actually support the assertion, or the conclusion is not the only or the best explanation of those facts. To shape convincing arguments, we need more than an array of facts. We need to think critically, to analyze the issue, to see relationships, to weigh evidence. We need to avoid the temptation to "argue" from emotion only, or to believe that just stating our opinion is the same thing as building a sound argument.

### Argument Incorporates Values

Arguments are based not just on reason and evidence but also on the beliefs and values we hold and think that our audience may hold as well. In a reasoned debate, you want to make clear the values that you consider relevant to the argument. In an editorial defending the sport of boxing, one editor wrote that boxing "is a sport because the world has not yet become a place in which the qualities that go into excellence in boxing [endurance, agility, courage] have no value" (*Washington Post,* February 5, 1983). But James J. Kilpatrick also appeals to values when he argues, in an editorial critical of boxing, that we should not want to live in a society "in which deliberate brutality is legally authorized and publicly applauded" (*Washington Post,* December 7, 1982). Observe, however, the high level of seriousness in the appeal to values. Neither writer settles for a simplistic personal preference: "Boxing is exciting," or "Boxing is too violent."

### Argument Recognizes the Topic's Complexity

Much false reasoning (the logical fallacies discussed in Chapter 6) results from a writer's oversimplifying an issue. A sound argument begins with an understanding that most issues are terribly complicated. The wise person approaches such ethical concerns as abortion or euthanasia or such public policy issues as tax cuts or trade agreements with the understanding that there are many philosophical, moral, and political issues that complicate discussions of these topics. Recognizing an argument's complexity may also lead us to an understanding that there can be more than one "right" position. The thoughtful arguer respects the views of others, seeks common ground when possible, and often chooses a conciliatory approach.

## THE SHAPE OF ARGUMENT: WHAT WE CAN LEARN FROM ARISTOTLE

Still one of the best ways to understand the basics of argument is to reflect on what the Greek philosopher Aristotle describes as the three "players" in any argument: the *writer* (or *speaker*), the *argument itself,* and the *reader* (or *audience*). Aristotle also reminds us that the occasion or "situation" (*karios*) is important in understanding and evaluating an argument. Let's examine each part of this model of argument.

### *Ethos* (about the Writer/Speaker)

It seems logical to begin with *ethos* because without this player we have no argument. We could, though, end with the writer because Aristotle asserts that this player in any argument is the most important. No argument, no matter how logical, no matter how appealing to one's audience, can succeed if the audience rejects the arguer's credibility, his or her *ethical* qualities.

Think how often in political contests those running attack their opponent's character rather than the candidate's programs. Remember the smear campaign against Obama—he is (or was) a Muslim and therefore unfit to be president, the first point an error of fact, the second point an emotional appeal to voters' fears. Candidates try these smear tactics, even without evidence, because they understand that every voter they can convince of an opponent's failure of *ethos* is a citizen who will vote for them. Many American voters want to be assured that a candidate is patriotic, religious (but of course not fanatic!), a loyal spouse, and a loving parent. At times, unfortunately, we even lose sight of important differences in positions as we focus on the person instead. But, this tells us how much an audience values their sense of the arguer's credibility. During his campaign for reelection, after the Watergate break-in, Nixon was attacked with the line "Would you buy a used car from this guy?" (In defense of used-car salespeople, not all are untrustworthy!)

## *Logos* (about the Logic of the Argument)

*Logos* refers to the argument itself—to the assertion and the support for it. Aristotle maintains that part of an arguer's appeal to his or her audience lies in the logic of the argument and the quality of the support provided. Even the most credible of writers will not move thoughtful audiences with inadequate evidence or sloppy reasoning. Yes, "arguments" that appeal to emotions, to our needs and fantasies, will work for some audiences—look at the success of advertising, for example. But, if you want to present a serious claim to critical readers, then you must pay attention to your argument. Paying attention means not only having good reasons but also organizing them clearly. Your audience needs to see *how* your evidence supports your point. Consider the following argument in opposition to the war on Iraq.

> War can be justified only as a form of self-defense. To initiate a war, we need to be able to show that our first strike was necessary as a form of self-defense. The Bush administration argued that Iraq had weapons of mass destruction and intended to use them against us. Responding to someone's "intent" to do harm is always a difficult judgment call. But, in this case, there were no weapons of mass destruction so there could not have been any intent to harm the United States, or at least none that was obvious and immediate. Thus we must conclude that this war was not the right course of action for the United States.

You may disagree (many will) with this argument's assertion, but you can respect the writer's logic, the clear connecting of one reason to the next. One good way to strengthen your credibility is to get respect for clear reasoning.

## *Pathos* (about Appeals to the Audience)

Argument implies an audience, those whose views we want to influence in some way. Aristotle labels this player *pathos*, the Greek word for both passion and suffering (hence *pathology*, the study of disease). Arguers need to be aware of their audience's feelings on the issue, the attitudes and values that will affect their response to the argument. There are really two questions arguers must answer: "How can I engage my audience's interest?" and "How can I engage their sympathy for my position?"

Some educators and health experts believe that childhood obesity is a major problem in the United States. Other Americans are much more focused on the economy—or their own careers. Al Gore is passionately concerned about the harmful effects of global warming; others, though increasingly fewer, think he lacks sufficient evidence of environmental degradation. How does a physician raise reader interest in childhood obesity? How does Gore convince doubters that we need to reduce carbon emissions? To prepare an effective argument, we need always to plan our approach with a clear vision of how best to connect to a specific audience—one which may or may not agree with our interests or our position.

## *Karios* (about the Occasion or Situation)

While *ethos, logos,* and *pathos* create the traditional three-part communication model, Aristotle adds another term to enhance our understanding of any argument "moment." The term *karios* refers to the occasion for the argument, the situation that we are in. What does this moment call for from us? Is the lunch table the appropriate time and place for an argument with your coworker over her failure to meet a deadline that is part of a joint project? You have just received a 65 on your history test; is this the best time to e-mail your professor to protest

Personal confrontation at a business meeting: Not cool.

the grade? Would the professor's office be the better place for your discussion than an e-mail sent from your BlackBerry minutes after you have left class?

The concept of *karios* asks us to consider what is most appropriate for the occasion, to think through the best time, place, and genre (type of argument) to make a successful argument. This concept has special meaning for students in a writing class who sometimes have difficulty thinking about audience at all. When practicing writing for the academic community, you may need to modify the language or tone that you more typically use in other situations.

We argue in a specific context of three interrelated parts, as illustrated in Figure 3.1.

We present support for an assertion to a specific audience whose expectations and character we have given thought to when shaping our argument. And we present ourselves as informed, competent, and reliable so that our audience will give us their attention.

## THE LANGUAGE OF ARGUMENT

We could title this section the *languages* of argument because arguments come in visual language as well as in words. But visual arguments—cartoons, photos, ads—are almost always accompanied by some words: figures speaking in bubbles, a caption, a slogan (Nike's "Just Do It!"). So we need to think about the kinds of statements that make up arguments, whether those arguments are legal briefs or cartoons, casual conversations or scholarly essays. To build an argument we need some statements that support other statements that present the main idea or claim of the argument.

- Claims: usually either inferences or judgments, for these are debatable assertions.
- Support: facts, opinions based on facts (inferences), or opinions based on values, beliefs, or ideas (judgments) or some combination of the three.

Let's consider what kinds of statements each of these terms describes.

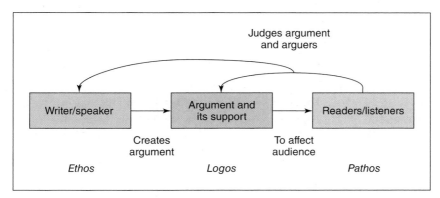

**FIGURE 3.1** Aristotelian Structure of Argument

## Facts

*Facts are statements that are verifiable.* Factual statements refer to what can be counted or measured or confirmed by reasonable observers or trusted experts.

> There are twenty-six desks in Room 110.
>
> In the United States about 400,000 people die each year as a result of smoking.

These are factual statements. We can verify the first by observation—by counting. The second fact comes from medical records. We rely on trusted record-keeping sources and medical experts for verification. By definition, we do not argue about the facts. Usually. Sometimes "facts" change, as we learn more about our world. For example, only in the last thirty years has convincing evidence been gathered to demonstrate the relationship between smoking and various illnesses of the heart and lungs. And sometimes "facts" are false facts. These are statements that sound like facts but are incorrect. For example: Nadel has won more Wimbledon titles than Federer. Not so.

## Inferences

*Inferences are opinions based on facts.* Inferences are the conclusions we draw from an analysis of facts.

> There will not be enough desks in Room 110 for upcoming fall-semester classes.
>
> Smoking is a serious health hazard.

Predictions of an increase in student enrollment for the coming fall semester lead to the inference that most English classes scheduled in Room 110 will run with several more students per class than last year. The dean should order new desks. Similarly, we infer from the number of deaths that smoking is a health problem; statistics show more people dying from tobacco than from AIDS, or murder, or car accidents, causes of death that get media coverage but do not produce nearly as many deaths.

Inferences vary in their closeness to the facts supporting them. That the sun will "rise" tomorrow is an inference, but we count on its happening, acting as if it is a fact. However, the first inference stated above is based not just on the fact of twenty-six desks but on another inference—a projected increase in student enrollment—and two assumptions. The argument looks like this:

| | |
|---|---|
| **FACT:** | There are twenty-six desks in Room 110. |
| **INFERENCE:** | There will be more first-year students next year. |
| **ASSUMPTIONS:** | 1. English will remain a required course. |
| | 2. No additional classrooms are available for English classes. |
| **CLAIM:** | There will not be enough desks in Room 110 for upcoming fall-semester classes. |

This inference could be challenged by a different analysis of the facts supporting enrollment projections. Or, if additional rooms can be found, the dean will not need to order new desks. Inferences can be part of the support of an argument, or they can be the claim of an argument.

## Judgments

*Judgments are opinions based on values, beliefs, or philosophical concepts.* (Judgments also include opinions based on personal preferences, but we have already excluded these from argument.) Judgments concern right and wrong, good and bad, better or worse, should and should not:

> No more than twenty-six students should be enrolled in any English class.

> Cigarette advertising should be eliminated, and the federal government should develop an antismoking campaign.

> **NOTE:** Placing such qualifiers as "I believe," "I think," or "I feel" in an assertion does not free you from the need to support that claim. The statement "I believe that President Bush was a great president" calls for an argument based on evidence and reasons.

To support the first judgment, we need to explain what constitutes overcrowding, or what constitutes the best class size for effective teaching. If we can support our views on effective teaching, we may be able to convince the college president that ordering more desks for Room 110 is not the best solution to an increasing enrollment in English classes. The second judgment also offers a solution to a problem, in this case a national health problem. To reduce the number of deaths, we need to reduce the number of smokers, either by encouraging smokers to quit or nonsmokers not to start. The underlying assumption: Advertising does affect behavior.

## EXERCISE: Facts, Inferences, and Judgments

Compile a list of three statements of fact, three inferences, and three judgments. Try to organize them into three related sets, as illustrated here:

- Smoking is prohibited in some restaurants.
- Secondhand smoke is a health hazard.
- Smoking should be prohibited in all restaurants.

We can classify judgments to see better what kind of assertion we are making and, therefore, what kind of support we need to argue effectively.

**FUNCTIONAL JUDGMENTS (guidelines for judging how something or someone works or could work)**

Tiger Woods is the best golfer to play the game.

Antismoking advertising will reduce the number of smokers.

**AESTHETIC JUDGMENTS (guidelines for judging art, literature, music, or natural scenes)**

The sunrise was beautiful.

*The Great Gatsby*'s structure, characters, and symbols are perfectly wedded to create the novel's vision of the American dream.

**ETHICAL JUDGMENTS (guidelines for group or social behavior)**

Lawyers should not advertise.

It is discourteous to talk during a film or lecture.

**MORAL JUDGMENTS (guidelines of right and wrong for judging individuals and for establishing legal principles)**

Taking another person's life is wrong.

Equal rights under the law should not be denied on the basis of race or gender.

Functional and aesthetic judgments generally require defining key terms and establishing criteria for the judging or ranking made by the assertion. How, for example, do we compare golfers? On the amount of money won? The number of tournaments won? Or the consistency of winning throughout one's career? What about the golfer's quality and range of shots? Ethical and moral judgments may be more difficult to support because they depend not just on how terms are defined and criteria established but on values and beliefs as well. If taking another person's life is wrong, why isn't it wrong in war? Or is it? These are difficult questions that require thoughtful debate.

## EXERCISES: Understanding Assumptions, Facts, False Facts, Inferences, and Judgments

1. Categorize the judgments you wrote for the previous exercise (p. 73) as either aesthetic, moral, ethical, or functional. Alternatively, compile a list of three judgments that you then categorize.
2. For each judgment listed for exercise 1, generate one statement of support, either a fact or an inference or another judgment. Then state any underlying assumptions that are part of each argument.
3. Read the following article and then complete the exercise that follows. This exercise tests both careful reading and your understanding of the differences among facts, inferences, and judgments.

# YOUR BRAIN LIES TO YOU  | SAM WANG and SANDRA AAMODT

Dr. Samuel S. H. Wang is a professor of molecular biology and neuroscience at Princeton, where he manages a research lab. Dr. Sandra Aamodt, former editor of *Nature Neuroscience*, is a freelance science writer. Drs. Wang and Aamodt are the authors of *Welcome to Your Brain: Why You Lose Your Car Keys but Never Forget How to Drive and Other Puzzles of Everyday Life* (2008). The following article appeared on June 27, 2008, in the *New York Times*.

FALSE beliefs are everywhere. Eighteen percent of Americans think the sun revolves around the earth, one poll has found. Thus it seems slightly less egregious that, according to another poll, 10 percent of us think that Senator Barack Obama, a Christian, is instead a Muslim. The Obama campaign has created a Web site to dispel misinformation. But this effort may be more difficult than it seems, thanks to the quirky way in which our brains store memories—and mislead us along the way.

The brain does not simply gather and stockpile information as a computer's hard drive does. Current research suggests that facts may be stored first in the hippocampus, a structure deep in the brain about the size and shape of a fat man's curled pinkie finger. But the information does not rest there. Every time we recall it, our brain writes it down again, and during this re-storage, it is also reprocessed. In time, the fact is gradually transferred to the cerebral cortex and is separated from the context in which it was originally learned. For example, you know that the capital of California is Sacramento, but you probably don't remember how you learned it.

This phenomenon, known as source amnesia, can also lead people to forget whether a statement is true. Even when a lie is presented with a disclaimer, people often later remember it as true.

With time, this misremembering only gets worse. A false statement from a non-credible source that is at first not believed can gain credibility during the months it takes to reprocess memories from short-term hippocampal storage to longer-term cortical storage. As the source is forgotten, the message and its implications gain strength. This could explain why, during the 2004 presidential campaign, it took some weeks for the Swift Boat Veterans for Truth campaign against Senator John Kerry to have an effect on his standing in the polls.

Even if they do not understand the neuroscience behind source amnesia, campaign strategists can exploit it to spread misinformation. They know that if their message is initially memorable, its impression will persist long after it is debunked. In repeating a falsehood, someone may back it up with an opening line like "I think I read somewhere" or even with a reference to a specific source.

In one study, a group of Stanford students was exposed repeatedly to an unsubstantiated claim taken from a Web site that Coca-Cola is an effective paint thinner. Students who read the statement five times were nearly one-third more likely than those who read it only twice to attribute it to *Consumer Reports* (rather than *The National Enquirer*, their other choice), giving it a gloss of credibility.

7    Adding to this innate tendency to mold information we recall is the way our brains fit facts into established mental frameworks. We tend to remember news that accords with our worldview, and discount statements that contradict it.

8    In another Stanford study, 48 students, half of whom said they favored capital punishment and half of whom said they opposed it, were presented with two pieces of evidence, one supporting and one contradicting the claim that capital punishment deters crime. Both groups were more convinced by the evidence that supported their initial position.

9    Psychologists have suggested that legends propagate by striking an emotional chord. In the same way, ideas can spread by emotional selection, rather than by their factual merits, encouraging the persistence of falsehoods about Coke—or about a presidential candidate.

10   Journalists and campaign workers may think they are acting to counter misinformation by pointing out that it is not true. But by repeating a false rumor, they may inadvertently make it stronger. In its concerted effort to "stop the smears," the Obama campaign may want to keep this in mind. Rather than emphasize that Mr. Obama is not a Muslim, for instance, it may be more effective to stress that he embraced Christianity as a young man.

11   Consumers of news, for their part, are prone to selectively accept and remember statements that reinforce beliefs they already hold. In a replication of the study of students' impressions of evidence about the death penalty, researchers found that even when subjects were given a specific instruction to be objective, they were still inclined to reject evidence that disagreed with their beliefs.

12   In the same study, however, when subjects were asked to imagine their reaction if the evidence had pointed to the opposite conclusion, they were more open-minded to information that contradicted their beliefs. Apparently, it pays for consumers of controversial news to take a moment and consider that the opposite interpretation may be true.

13   In 1919, Justice Oliver Wendell Holmes of the Supreme Court wrote that "the best test of truth is the power of the thought to get itself accepted in the competition of the market." Holmes erroneously assumed that ideas are more likely to spread if they are honest. Our brains do not naturally obey this admirable dictum, but by better understanding the mechanisms of memory perhaps we can move closer to Holmes's ideal.

Source: Originally appeared in *The New York Times*, June 27, 2008. Reprinted by permission of the authors.

*Label each of the following sentences as F (fact), FF (false fact), I (inference), or J (judgment).*

_____  1. Campaigns have trouble getting rid of misinformation about their candidate.

_____  2. When we reprocess information we may get the information wrong, but we always remember the source.

_____ 3. The Obama campaign should stress that he became a Christian as a young man.

_____ 4. Most of us remember information that matches our view of the world.

_____ 5. When students were told to be objective in evaluating evidence, they continued to reject evidence they disagreed with.

_____ 6. Coke is an effective paint thinner.

_____ 7. True statements should be accepted and false statements rejected.

_____ 8. Justice Holmes was wrong about the power of truth to spread more widely than falsehood.

_____ 9. The more we understand about the way the world works, the better our chances of separating truth from falsehood.

_____ 10. Americans do not seem to understand basic science.

## THE SHAPE OF ARGUMENT: WHAT WE CAN LEARN FROM TOULMIN

British philosopher Stephen Toulmin adds to what we have learned from Aristotle by focusing our attention on the basics of the argument itself. First, consider this definition of argument: *An argument consists of evidence and/or reasons presented in support of an assertion or claim that is either stated or implied.* For example:

| | |
|---|---|
| **CLAIM:** | We should not go skiing today |
| **EVIDENCE:** | because it is too cold. |
| **EVIDENCE:** | Because some laws are unjust, |
| **CLAIM:** | civil disobedience is sometimes justified. |
| **EVIDENCE:** | It's only fair and right for academic institutions to |
| **CLAIM:** | accept students only on academic merit. |

The parts of an argument, Toulmin asserts, are actually a bit more complex than these examples suggest. Each argument has a third part that is not stated in the preceding examples. This third part is the "glue" that connects the support—the evidence and reasons—to the argument's claim and thus fulfills the logic of the argument. Toulmin calls this glue an argument's *warrants.* These are the principles or assumptions that allow us to assert that our evidence or reasons—what Toulmin calls the *grounds*—do indeed support our claim. (Figure 3.2 illustrates these basics of the Toulmin model of argument.)

| | |
|---|---|
| **CLAIM:** | Academic institutions should accept students only on academic merit. |
| **EVIDENCE:** | It is only fair and right. |
| **WARRANT:** | (1) Fair and right are important values. (2) Academic institutions are only about academics. |

**FIGURE 3.2** The Toulmin Structure of Argument

Look again at the sample arguments to see what warrants must be accepted to make each argument work:

| | |
|---|---|
| **CLAIM:** | We should not go skiing today. |
| **EVIDENCE:** | It is too cold. |
| **ASSUMPTIONS (WARRANTS):** | When it is too cold, skiing is not fun; the activity is not sufficient to keep one from becoming uncomfortable. AND: Too cold is what is too cold for me. |
| **CLAIM:** | Civil disobedience is sometimes justified. |
| **EVIDENCE:** | Some laws are unjust. |
| **ASSUMPTIONS (WARRANTS):** | To get unjust laws changed, people need to be made aware of the injustice. Acts of civil disobedience will get people's attention and make them aware that the laws need changing. |
| **CLAIM:** | Academic institutions should accept students only on academic merit. |
| **EVIDENCE:** | It is fair and right. |
| **ASSUMPTIONS (WARRANTS):** | Fair and right are important values. AND: Academic institutions are only about academics. |

Assumptions play an important role in any argument, so we need to be sure to understand what they are. Note, for instance, the second assumption operating in the first argument: The temperature considered uncomfortable for the speaker will also be uncomfortable for her companions—an uncertain assumption. In the second argument, the warrant is less debatable, for acts of civil disobedience usually get media coverage and thus dramatize the issue. The underlying assumptions in the third example stress the need to know one's warrants. Both warrants will need to be defended in the debate over selection by academic merit only.

## COLLABORATIVE EXERCISE: Building Arguments

With your class partner or in small groups, examine each of the following claims. Select two, think of one statement that could serve as evidence for each claim, and then think of the underlying assumption(s) that complete each of the arguments.

1. Professor X is not a good instructor.
2. Americans need to reduce the fat in their diets.
3. Tiger Woods is a great golfer.
4. Military women should be allowed to serve in combat zones.
5. College newspapers should be free of supervision by faculty or administrators.

Toulmin was particularly interested in the great range in the strength or probability of various arguments. Some kinds of arguments are stronger than others because of the language or logic they use. Other arguments must, necessarily, be heavily qualified for the claim to be supportable. Toulmin developed his language to provide a strategy for analyzing the degree of probability in a given argument and to remind us of the need to qualify some kinds of claims. You have already seen how the idea of warrants, or assumptions, helps us think about the "glue" that presumably makes a given argument work. Taken together, Toulmin terms and concepts help us analyze the arguments of others and prepare more convincing arguments of our own.

## Claims

A claim is what the argument asserts or seeks to prove. It answers the question "What is your point?" In an argumentative speech or essay, the claim is the speaker's or writer's main idea or thesis. Although an argument's claim "follows" from reasons and evidence, we often present an argument—whether written or spoken—with the claim stated near the beginning of the presentation. We can better understand an argument's claim by recognizing that we can have claims of fact, claims of value, and claims of policy.

### Claims of Fact

Although facts usually support claims, we do argue over some facts. Historians and biographers may argue over what happened in the past, although they are more likely to argue over the significance of what happened. Scientists also argue over the facts, over how to classify an unearthed fossil, or whether the fossil indicates that the animal had feathers. For example:

**CLAIM:** The small, predatory dinosaur *Deinonychus* hunted its prey in packs.

This claim is supported by the discovery of several fossils of *Deinonychus* close together and with the fossil bones of a much larger dinosaur. Their teeth have also been found in or near the bones of dinosaurs that have died in a struggle.

Assertions about what will happen are sometimes classified as claims of fact, but they can also be labeled as inferences supported by facts. Predictions about a future event may be classified as claims of fact:

**CLAIM:** The United States will win the most gold medals at the 2008 Olympics.

**CLAIM:** I will get an A on tomorrow's psychology test.

What evidence would you use to support each of these claims? (And, did the first one turn out to be correct?)

### Claims of Value

These include moral, ethical, and aesthetic judgments. Assertions that use such words as *good* or *bad, better* or *worse,* and *right* or *wrong* will be claims of value. The following are all claims of value:

**CLAIM:** Roger Federer is a better tennis player than Andy Roddick.

**CLAIM:** *Adventures of Huckleberry Finn* is one of the most significant American novels.

| CLAIM: | Cheating hurts others and the cheater too. |
|---|---|
| CLAIM: | Abortion is wrong. |

Arguments in support of judgments demand relevant evidence, careful reasoning, and an awareness of the assumptions one is making. Support for claims of value often include other value statements. For example, to support the claim that censorship is bad, arguers often assert that the free exchange of ideas is good and necessary in a democracy. The support is itself a value statement. The arguer may believe, probably correctly, that most people will more readily agree to the support (the free exchange of ideas is good) than to the claim (censorship is bad).

### Claims of Policy

Finally, claims of policy are assertions about what should or should not happen, what the government ought or ought not to do, how to best solve social problems. Claims of policy debate, for example, college rules, state gun laws, or federal aid to Africans suffering from AIDS. The following are claims of policy:

| CLAIM: | College newspapers should not be controlled in any way by college authorities. |
|---|---|
| CLAIM: | States should not have laws allowing people to carry concealed weapons. |
| CLAIM: | The United States must provide more aid to African countries where 25 percent or more of the citizens have tested positive for HIV. |

Claims of policy are often closely tied to judgments of morality or political philosophy, but they also need to be grounded in feasibility. That is, your claim needs to be doable, to be based on a thoughtful consideration of the real world and the complexities of public policy issues.

## Grounds (or Data or Evidence)

The term *grounds* refers to the reasons and evidence provided in support of a claim. Although the words *data* and *evidence* can also be used, note that *grounds* is the most general term because it includes reasons or logic as well as examples or statistics. We determine the grounds of an argument by asking the question "Why do you think that?" or "How do you know that?" When writing your own arguments, you can ask yourself these questions and answer by using a *because* clause:

| CLAIM: | Smoking should be banned in restaurants because |
|---|---|
| GROUNDS: | secondhand smoke is a serious health hazard. |
| CLAIM: | Federer is a better tennis player than Roddick because |

| GROUNDS: | 1. he has been ranked number one longer than Roddick, |
|---|---|
| | 2. he has won more tournaments than Roddick, and |
| | 3. he has won more major tournaments than Roddick. |

## Warrants

Why should we believe that your grounds do indeed support your claim? Your argument's warrants answer this question. They explain why your evidence really is evidence. Sometimes warrants reside in language itself, in the meanings of the words we are using. If I am *younger* than my brother, then my brother must be *older* than I am. In a court case attempting to prove that Jones murdered Smith, the relation of evidence to claim is less assured. If the police investigation has been properly managed and the physical evidence is substantial, then Smith may be Jones's murderer. The prosecution has—presumably beyond a reasonable doubt—established motive, means, and opportunity for Smith to commit the murder. In many arguments based on statistical data, the argument's warrant rests on complex analyses of the statistics—and on the conviction that the statistics have been developed without error. In some philosophical arguments, the warrants are the logical structures (often shown mathematically) connecting a sequence of reasons.

Still, without taking courses in statistics and logic, you can develop an alertness to the "good sense" of some arguments and the "dubious sense" of others. You know, for example, that good SAT scores are a predictor of success in college. Can you argue that you will do well in college because you have good SATs? No. We can determine only a statistical probability. We cannot turn probabilities about a group of people into a warrant about one person in the group. (In addition, SAT scores are only one predictor. Another key variable is motivation.)

What is the warrant for the Federer claim?

| CLAIM: | Federer is a better tennis player than Roddick. |
|---|---|
| GROUNDS: | The three facts listed above. |
| WARRANT: | It is appropriate to judge and rank tennis players on these kinds of statistics. That is, the better player is one who has held the number-one ranking for the longest time, has won the most tournaments, and also has won the most major tournaments. |

## Backing

Standing behind an argument's warrant may be additional *backing*. Backing answers the question "How do we know that your evidence is good evidence?" You may answer this question by providing authoritative sources for the data used (for example, the Census Bureau or the U.S. Tennis Association). Or, you may explain in detail the methodology of the experiments performed or the surveys taken. When scientists and social scientists present the results of their research, they anticipate the question of backing and automatically provide a detailed explanation of the process by which they acquired their evidence. In criminal trials, defense attorneys challenge the backing of the prosecution's argument. They question the handling of blood samples sent to labs for DNA testing, for instance. The defense attorneys want jury members to doubt the *quality* of the evidence, perhaps even to doubt the reliability of DNA testing altogether.

This discussion of backing returns us to the point that one part of any argument is the audience. To create an effective argument, you need to assess the potential for acceptance of your warrants and backing. Is your audience likely to share your values, your religious beliefs, or your scientific approach to issues? If you are speaking to a group at your church, then backing based on the religious beliefs of that church may be effective. If you are preparing an argument for a general audience, then using specific religious assertions as warrants or backing probably will not result in an effective argument.

## Qualifiers

Some arguments are absolute; they can be stated without qualification. *If I am younger than my brother, then he must be older than I am.* Most arguments need some qualification; many need precise limitations. If, when playing bridge, I am dealt eight spades, then my opponents and partner together must have five spade cards—because there are thirteen cards of each suit in a deck. My partner *probably* has one spade but *could be* void of spades. My partner *possibly* has two or more spades, but I would be foolish to count on it. When bidding my hand, I must be controlled by the laws of probability. Look again at the smoking-ban claim. Observe the absolute nature of both the claim and its support. If secondhand smoke is indeed a health hazard, it will be that in *all* restaurants, not just in some. With each argument we need to assess the need of qualification that is appropriate to a successful argument.

Sweeping generalizations often come to us in the heat of a debate or when we first start to think about an issue. For example: *Gun control is wrong because it restricts individual rights.* But on reflection surely you would not want to argue against all forms of gun control. (Remember: An unqualified assertion is understood by your audience to be absolute.) Would you sell guns to felons in jail or to children on the way to school? Obviously not. So, let's try the claim again, this time with two important qualifiers:

> **QUALIFIED**      Adults without a criminal record should not be restricted in the
>
> **CLAIM:**      purchase of guns.

Others may want this claim further qualified to eliminate particular types of guns or to control the number purchased or the process for purchasing. The gun-control debate is not about absolutes; it is all about which qualified claim is best.

## Rebuttals

Arguments can be challenged. Smart debaters assume that there are people who will disagree with them. They anticipate the ways that opponents can challenge their arguments. When you are planning an argument, you need to think about how you can counter or rebut the challenges you anticipate. Think of yourself as an attorney in a court case preparing your argument *and* a defense of the other attorney's challenges to your argument. If you ignore the important role of rebuttals, you may not win the jury to your side.

# USING TOULMIN'S TERMS TO ANALYZE ARGUMENTS

Terms are never an end in themselves; we learn them when we recognize that they help us to organize our thinking about a subject. Toulmin's terms can aid your reading of the arguments of others. You can "see what's going on" in an argument if you analyze it, applying Toulmin's language to its parts. Not all terms will be useful for every analysis because, for example, some arguments will not have qualifiers or rebuttals. But to recognize that an argument is *without qualifiers* is to learn something important about that argument.

First, here is a simple argument broken down into its parts using Toulmin's terms:

| | |
|---|---|
| **GROUNDS:** | Because Dr. Bradshaw has an attendance policy, |
| **CLAIM:** | students who miss more than seven classes will |
| **QUALIFIER:** | most likely (last year, Dr. Bradshaw did allow one student, in unusual circumstances, to continue in the class) be dropped from the course. |
| **WARRANT:** | Dr. Bradshaw's syllabus explains her attendance policy, a |
| **BACKING:** | policy consistent with the concept of a discussion class that depends on student participation and consistent with the attendance policies of most of her colleagues. |
| **REBUTTAL:** | Although some students complain about an attendance policy of any kind, Dr. Bradshaw does explain her policy and her reasons for it the first day of class. She then reminds students that the syllabus is a contract between them; if they choose to stay, they agree to abide by the guidelines explained on the syllabus. |

This argument is brief and fairly simple. Let's see how Toulmin's terms can help us analyze a longer, more complex argument. Read actively and annotate the following essay while noting the existing annotations using Toulmin's terms. Then answer the questions that follow the article.

## LET THE ZOO'S ELEPHANTS GO | LES SCHOBERT

The author has spent more than thirty-five years working in zoos, primarily in care of elephants. He has been a curator of both the Los Angeles and North Carolina zoos. His argument was published October 16, 2005, in the *Washington Post*.

PREREADING QUESTIONS What are some good reasons to have zoos? What are some problems associated with them?

Toulmin's terms.

1    The Smithsonian Institution is a national treasure, but when it comes to elephants, its National Zoo is a national embarrassment.

2    In 2000 the zoo euthanized Nancy, an African elephant that was suffering from foot problems so painful that standing had become difficult for her. Five years later the zoo has announced that Toni, an Asian elephant, is suffering from arthritis so severe that she, too, may be euthanized.

Grounds.

3    The elephants' debilitating ailments are probably a result of the inadequate conditions in which they have been held. The same story is repeated in zoos across the country.

4    When I began my zoo career 35 years ago, much less was known about elephants than is known today. We now understand that keeping elephants in tiny enclosures with unnatural surfaces destroys their legs and feet. We have

Backing.

learned that to breed naturally and rear their young, elephants must live in herds that meet their social requirements. And we have come to realize that controlling elephants through domination and the use of ankuses (sharply pointed devices used to inflict pain) can no longer be justified.

Claim.

5    Zoos must change the concept of how elephants are kept in captivity, starting with how much space we allot them. Wild elephants may walk 30 miles a day. A typical home range of a wild elephant is 1,000 square miles. At the National Zoo, Toni has access to a yard of less than an acre. Zoo industry standards allow the keeping of elephants in as little as 2,200 square feet, or about 5 percent of an acre.

Grounds.

6    Some zoos have begun to reevaluate their ability to house elephants. After the death of two elephants in 2004, the San Francisco Zoo sent its surviving elephants to a sanctuary in California. This year the Detroit Zoo closed its elephant exhibit on ethical grounds, and its two surviving elephants now thrive at the California sanctuary as well.

7    But attitudes at other zoos remain entrenched. To justify their outdated exhibits, some zoos have redefined elephant longevity and natural behavior. For example, National Zoo officials blame Toni's arthritis on old age. But ele-

Rebuttal to counterargument.

phants in the wild reproduce into their fifties, and female elephants live long after their reproductive cycles cease. Had she not been captured in Thailand at the age of 7 months, Toni, at age 39, could have had decades more of life as a mother and a grandmother. Instead, she faces an early death before her 40th birthday, is painfully thin and is crippled by arthritis.

The National Zoo's other elephants face the same bleak future if changes   8
are not made. A preserve of at least 2 square miles—1,280 acres, or almost
eight times the size of the National Zoo—would be necessary to meet an elephant's physical and social needs. Since this is not feasible, the zoo should
send its pachyderms to a sanctuary. One such facility, the Elephant Sanctuary
in Tennessee, offers 2,700 acres of natural habitat over which elephants can
roam and heal from the damage caused by zoo life. The sanctuary's soft
soil, varied terrain, freedom of choice and freedom of movement have restored
life to elephants that were suffering foot and joint diseases after decades in
zoos and circuses.

The National Zoo has the opportunity to overcome its troubled animal-   9
care history by joining progressive zoos in reevaluating its elephant program.
The zoo should do right by its elephants, and the public should demand
nothing less.

*Claim, qualified (options explained). Grounds.*

*Grounds.*

*Claim restated. Warrant (states values).*

Source: From *The Washington Post*, October 16, 2005. Reprinted by permission of the author.

## QUESTIONS FOR READING

1.  What is the occasion that led to the writing of this article?
2.  What is Schobert's subject?
3.  State his claim in a way that shows that it is a solution to a problem.

## QUESTIONS FOR REASONING AND ANALYSIS

4.  What type of evidence (grounds) does the author provide?
5.  What are the nature and source of his backing?
6.  What makes his opening effective?
7.  What values does Schobert express? What assumption does he make about his readers?

## QUESTIONS FOR REFLECTING AND WRITING

8.  Are you surprised by any of the facts about elephants presented by Schobert? Do they make sense to you, upon reflection?
9.  Should zoos close down their elephant houses? Why or why not?
10. Are there any alternatives to city zoos with small elephant houses besides elephant sanctuaries?

You have seen how Toulmin's terms can help you to see what writers are
actually "doing" in their arguments. You have also observed from both the short
and the longer argument that writers do not usually follow the terms in precise
order. Indeed, you can find both grounds and backing in the same sentence, or

claim and qualifiers in the same paragraph, and so on. Still, the terms can help you to sort out your thinking about a claim you want to support. Now use your knowledge of argument as you read and analyze the following arguments.

# FOR ANALYSIS AND DEBATE

## LET MY TEENAGER DRINK | T. R. REID

A former Tokyo correspondent and London Bureau Chief for the *Washington Post*, T. R. Reid has covered presidential compaigns and global affairs for the *Post*. He is also the author of several books on Japan, including *Ski Japan* (1994) and *Confucius Lives Next Door: What Living in the East Teaches Us About Living in the West* (2000). His argument for teen drinking was published May 4, 2003.

PREREADING QUESTIONS  Do you or did you drink "underage"? If so, did this lead to any problems? Do you think the drinking age should be lowered in the United States?

1     My 16-year-old called me from a bar. She said my 17-year-old was there, too, along with the rest of the gang from high school: "Everything's fine, Dad. We'll be home after last call."

2     I breathed a quiet sigh of relief. Like many other parents, I knew my teen-agers were out drinking that Saturday night. Unlike most American kids, though, my daughters were drinking safely, legally and under close adult supervision—in the friendly neighborhood pub two blocks from our London home.

3     My kids could do that because Britain, like almost every other developed nation, has decided that teenagers are going to drink whether it's legal or not—and that attempts at prohibition inevitably make things worse.

4     Some countries have no minimum drinking age—a conservative approach that leaves the issue up to families rather than government bureaucrats. In most Western democracies, drinking becomes legal in the late teens. In Britain, a 16-year-old can have a beer in a pub if the drink accompanies a meal. Most publicans we knew were willing to call a single bag of potato chips—sorry, "crisps"—a full meal for purposes of that law.

5     And yet teen drinking tends to be a far more dangerous problem in the prohibitionist United States than in those more tolerant countries. The reason lies in the law itself. Because of our nationwide ban on drinking before the age of 21, American teenagers tend to do their drinking secretly, in the worst possible places—in a dark corner of the park, at the one house in the neigh-borhood where the adults have left for the weekend, or, most commonly, in the car.

6     Amid a national outcry over an epidemic of "binge drinking," the politi-cians don't like to admit that this problem is largely a product of the liquor laws. Kids know they have to do all their drinking before they get to the dance or the concert, where adults will be present.

It's party time.

On campus, this binge of fast 7 and furious drinking is known as "pregaming." Any college student will tell you that the pre-game goal is to get good and drunk—in the dorm room or in the car—before the social event begins. It would be smarter, and more pleasant for all concerned, to stretch out whatever alcohol there is over the course of an evening. But Congress in its wisdom has made this safer approach illegal.

Our family currently has kids 8 at three U.S. universities. The deans of all three schools have sent us firm letters promising zero tolerance for underage drinking. In conversation, though, the same deans concede readily that their teenage students drink every weekend— as undergraduates always have.

The situation would be vastly easier to manage, these educators say, if 9 they could allow the kids to drink in public—thus obviating the "pre-game" binge—and provide some kind of adult presence at the parties.

But those obvious steps would make a school complicit in violating the 10 prohibition laws—and potentially liable for civil lawsuits.

The deans lament that there is no political will to change the national 11 drinking age—or even to hand the issue back to the states. Politicians, after all, garner support and contributions from the interest groups by promising to "stop teen drinking."

But, of course, the law doesn't stop teens from drinking. "Most college 12 students drink . . . regardless of the legal drinking age, without harming themselves or anyone else," writes Richard Keeling, editor of the *Journal of American College Health.*

As a wandering *Post* correspondent, I have raised teenagers in three places: 13 Tokyo, London and Colorado. No parent will be surprised to read that high school and college students had easy access to alcohol in all three places. In all three countries, kids sometimes got drunk. But overseas, they did their drinking at a bar, a concert or a party. There were adults—and, often, police—around to supervise. As a result, most teenagers learned to use alcohol socially and responsibly. And they didn't have to hide it from their parents.

In the United States, our kids learn that drinking is something to be done 14 in the dark, and quickly. Is that the lesson we want to teach them about alcohol use? It makes me glad my teenagers had the legal right to go down the street to that pub.

1.   What is Reid's claim?

2.   Explain the term "pre-gaming."

3.   What do college administrators say is their position on underage drinking on campus? What do they say actually happens on their campuses?

4.   Analyze Reid's argument, using Toulmin's terms. What passages contain his evidence (grounds)? Does he qualify his claim? (Study his word choice throughout.)

5.   Evaluate Reid's argument. What kind of evidence does he use? Is it convincing? With what audience(s) might his argument be most successful?

6.   Do you agree with Reid? If so, is that because you want to drink legally or because you think he has a convincing argument?

7.   If you disagree, what are your counterarguments? Organize a rebuttal for class debate or for an essay.

# DON'T MAKE TEEN DRINKING EASIER

JOSEPH A. CALIFANO JR.

Joseph Califano is a lawyer and former secretary of Health, Education, and Welfare (1977–1979). The author of numerous books and articles, he is founder and chairman of the National Center on Addiction and Substance Abuse. His rebuttal to T. R. Reid's article was published in the *Washington Post* on May 11, 2003.

PREREADING QUESTIONS   Given what you know about Joseph Califano, what do you expect his position to be?

1    T. R. Reid's May 4 [2003] op-ed piece, "Let My Teenager Drink," is a dangerous example of what happens if we let anecdote trump facts. Reid jumps from the comfort he derives from his 16- and 17-year-old daughters "out drinking Saturday night" at a neighborhood pub in London, where it is legal, to the conclusion that the English and Europeans have far fewer problems with teen drinking than we do in the United States, where the age to legally buy alcohol is 21.

2    Let's start with the facts. In 2001 the Justice Department released an analysis comparing drinking rates in Europe and the United States. The conclusion: American 10th-graders are less likely to use and abuse alcohol than people of the same age in almost all European countries, including Britain. British 15- and 16-year-olds were more than twice as likely as Americans to binge drink

(50 percent vs. 24 percent) and to have been intoxicated within the past 30 days (48 percent vs. 21 percent). Of Western European nations, only Portugal had a lower proportion of young people binge drinking, which is defined as having five or more drinks in a row.

That same year, in a study of 29 nations, including Eastern and Western Europe, the World Health Organization found that American 15-year-olds were less likely than those in 18 other nations to have been intoxicated twice or more. British girls and boys were far likelier than their U.S. counterparts to have been drunk that often (52 and 51 percent vs. 28 and 34 percent).

Then there are the consequences of teen drinking. This month a Rand study that followed 3,400 people from seventh grade through age 23 reported that those who had three or more drinks within the past year, or any drink in the past month, were likelier to use nicotine and illegal drugs, to have stolen items within the past year and to have problems in school. In a report issued last December, the American Medical Association found that teen drinking— not bingeing, just drinking—can seriously damage growth processes of the brain and that such damage "can be long term and irreversible." The AMA warned that "short term or moderate drinking impairs learning and memory far more in youth than in adults" and that "adolescents need only drink half as much to suffer the same negative effects." This exhaustive study concluded that teen drinkers "perform worse in school, are more likely to fall behind and have an increased risk of social problems, depression, suicidal thoughts and violence."

Alcohol is a major contributing factor in the three leading causes of teen death—accidents, homicide and suicide—and increases the chances of juvenile delinquency and crime. Studies at the National Center on Addiction and Substance Abuse at Columbia University have found that teenagers who drink are more likely than those who do not to have sex and have it at an earlier age and with multiple partners.

There are many reasons why teens drink, but I doubt that states setting the drinking age at 21 is one of them. Focus groups of young women suggest that the increase in their binge drinking is related to their wanting to "be one of the boys" and to reduce inhibition, particularly because of the pressure many feel to have sex. Few understand that, on average, one drink has the impact on a woman that it takes two drinks to have on a man. Adolescents of both sexes who have low self-esteem or learning disabilities, or who suffer eating disorders, are at higher risk of drinking.

As for the alcohol industry's role: The Center on Alcohol Marketing and Youth at Georgetown University recently revealed that during the past two years, those under 21 heard more beer and liquor commercials on the radio than did adults. The Kaiser Family Foundation Teen Media Monitor, released in February, identified Coors Light and Budweiser beers as two of the five largest advertisers on the most popular television shows for teen boys. For the alcohol industry, it's a good long-term investment, because underage drinkers are likelier to become heavy adult drinkers and grow up to become that 9 percent of adult drinkers who consume 46.3 percent of the alcohol sold in the

United States. If Mr. Reid thinks that politicians are hanging tough on the drinking age of 21 in order to "garner support and contributions from interest groups," I suggest he take a look at the political contributions from the alcohol industry to keep the price down by killing tax increases (and in this Congress to roll taxes back) and to prevent content and caloric labeling of its products.

8    Fortunately, overwhelming majorities of teens in the United States (84 percent) and adults (83 percent) favor keeping the legal drinking age of 21. Rather than paint rosy but unrealistic pictures of life in countries where teens can legally buy alcohol, we need to get serious about preventing underage drinking. We need to address the many factors that influence teens to drink: genetics, family situation, peer pressure, schools, access to alcohol, alcohol advertising targeting teens. The best place to start is to help parents understand the consequences of their teen's drinking.

Source: From *The Washington Post*, May 11, 2003. Reprinted by permission of the author.

## QUESTIONS FOR READING

1. What is Califano's initial purpose in writing?
2. How do American teens compare with European teens in terms of alcohol consumption, binge drinking, and intoxication?
3. What are the consequences of teen drinking?
4. What are some of the causes of teen drinking?
5. How do American adults and teens feel about this country's drinking age?

## QUESTIONS FOR REASONING AND ANALYSIS

6. Analyze Califano's argument using Toulmin's terms.
7. Analyze the author's organization. What does he do first? Second? And so on? How does his organization help his rebuttal?
8. Evaluate Califano's argument. What kind of evidence (grounds) does he use? Is it effective?

## QUESTIONS FOR REFLECTION AND WRITING

9. Do you agree with Califano? If so, then presumably you accept the legal drinking age of 21—right? If you disagree with Califano, what are your counterarguments?
10. Usually, what kind of argument works best with you, one based on personal experience and anecdote or one based on statistics? Why?

1.  What are some problems caused by college students' drinking? You may be able to offer some answers to this question based on your knowledge and experience. You may also want to go online for some statistics about college drinking and health and safety risks. Drawing on both experience and data, what claim can you support?

2.  Compare the style and tone in Reid's and Califano's essays. Has each one written in a way that works for the author's approach to this issue? Be prepared to explain your views or develop them into a comparative analysis of style.

3.  Explore further into the strongly debated issue of zoos. Check your library's electronic database for recent articles. If you are near a zoo, take a look at the animals and the zoo's programs and schedule an interview with one of the curators. Where does your new information lead you? Can you defend a position on zoos?

## GOING ONLINE

A good starting place for online research about college drinking and health and safety risks is at **www.collegedrinkingprevention.gov**, or conduct your own search.

# CHAPTER 4

# Writing Effective Arguments

READ:  Who are the figures in the painting? What are they doing?

REASON:  What details in the painting help to date the scene?

REFLECT/WRITE:  What is significant about the moment captured in this painting?

The basics of good writing remain much the same for works as seemingly different as the personal essay, the argument, and the researched essay. Good writing is focused, organized, and concrete. Effective essays are written in a style and tone that are suited to both the audience and the writer's purpose. These are sound principles, all well known to you. But how, exactly, do you achieve them when writing argument? This chapter will help you answer that question.

# KNOW YOUR AUDIENCE

Too often students plunge into writing without thinking much about audience, for, after all, their "audience" is only the instructor who has given the assignment, just as their purpose in writing is to complete the assignment and get a grade. These views of audience and purpose are likely to lead to badly written arguments. First, if you are not thinking about readers who may disagree with you, you may not develop the best defense of your claim—which may need a rebuttal to possible counterarguments. Second, you may ignore your essay's needed introductory material on the assumption that the instructor, knowing the assignment, has a context for understanding your writing. To avoid these pitfalls, use the following questions to sharpen your understanding of audience.

## Who Is My Audience?

If you are writing an essay for the student newspaper, your audience consists—primarily—of students, but do not forget that faculty and administrators also read the student newspaper. If you are preparing a letter-to-the-editor refutation of a recent column in your town's newspaper, your audience will be the readers of that newspaper—that is, adults in your town. Some instructors give assignments that create an audience such as those just described so that you will practice writing with a specific audience in mind.

If you are not assigned a specific audience, imagine your classmates, as well as your instructor, as part of your audience. In other words, you are writing to readers in the academic community. These readers are intelligent and thoughtful, expecting sound reasoning and convincing evidence. These readers also represent varied values and beliefs, as they are from diverse cultures and experiences. Do not confuse the shared expectations of writing conventions with shared beliefs.

## What Will My Audience Know about My Topic?

What can you expect a diverse group of readers to know? Whether you are writing on a current issue or a centuries-old debate, you must expect most readers to have some knowledge of the issues. Their knowledge does not free you from the responsibility of developing your support fully, though. In fact, their knowledge creates further demands. For example, most readers know the main arguments on both sides of the abortion issue. For you to write as if they do not—and thus to ignore the arguments of the opposition—is to produce an argument that probably adds little to the debate on the subject.

On the other hand, what some readers "know" may be little more than an overview of the issues from TV news—or the emotional outbursts of a family member. Some readers may be misinformed or prejudiced, but they embrace their views enthusiastically nonetheless. So, as you think about the ways to develop and support your argument, you will have to assess your readers' knowledge and sophistication. This assessment will help you decide how much background information to provide or what false facts need to be revealed and dismissed.

## Where Does My Audience Stand on the Issue?

Expect readers to hold a range of views, even if you are writing to students on your campus or to an organization of which you are a member. It is not true, for instance, that all students want coed dorms or pass/fail grading. And, if everyone already agrees with you, you have no reason to write. An argument needs to be about a topic that is open to debate. So:

- Assume that some of your audience will probably never agree with you but may offer you grudging respect if you compose an effective argument.
- Assume that some readers do not hold strong views on your topic and may be open to convincing, if you present a good case.
- Assume that those who share your views will still be looking for a strong argument in support of their position.
- Assume that if you hold an unpopular position your best strategy will be a conciliatory approach. (See p. 97 for a discussion of the conciliatory argument.)

## How Should I Speak to My Audience?

Your audience will form an opinion of you based on how you write and how you reason. The image of argument—and the arguer—that we have been creating in this text's discussion is of thoughtful claims defended with logic and evidence. However, the heated debate at yesterday's lunch does not resemble this image of argument. Sometimes the word *persuasion* is used to separate the emotionally charged debate from the calm, intellectual tone of the academic argument. Unfortunately, this neat division between argument and persuasion does not describe the real world of debate. The thoughtful arguer also wants to be persuasive, and highly emotional presentations can contain relevant facts in support of a sound idea. Instead of thinking of two separate categories— argument and persuasion—think instead of a continuum from the most rigorous logic to extreme flights of fantasy. Figure 4.1 suggests this continuum with some kinds of arguments placed along it.

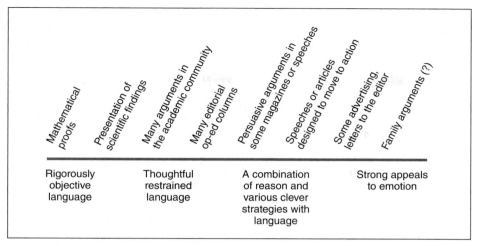

**FIGURE 4.1** A Continuum of Argumentative Language

Where should you place yourself along this continuum of language? You will have to answer this question with each specific writing context. Much of the time you will choose "thoughtful, restrained language" as expected by the academic community, but there may be times that you will use various persuasive strategies. Probably you will not select "strong appeals to emotion" for your college or workplace writing. Remember that you have different roles in your life, and you use different voices as appropriate to each role. Most of the time, you will want to use the serious voice you normally select for serious conversations with other adults. This is the voice that will help you establish your credibility, your *ethos.*

As you learned in Chapter 2, irony is a useful rhetorical strategy for giving one's words greater emphasis by actually writing the opposite of what you mean. Many writers use irony effectively. Irony catches our attention, makes us think, and engages us with the text. Sarcasm is not quite the same as irony. Irony can cleverly focus on life's complexities. Sarcasm is more often vicious than insightful, relying on harsh, negative word choice. Probably in most of your academic work, you will want to avoid sarcasm and think carefully about using any strongly worded appeal to your readers' emotions. Better to persuade your audience with the force of your reasons and evidence than to lose them because of the static of nasty language. But the key, always, is to know your audience and understand how best to present a convincing argument to that specific group.

## UNDERSTAND YOUR WRITING PURPOSE

There are many types or genres of argument and different reasons for writing—beyond wanting to write convincingly in defense of your views. Different types of arguments require different approaches, or different kinds of evidence. It helps to be able to recognize the kind of argument you are contemplating.

## What Type (Genre) of Argument Am I Preparing?

Here are some useful ways to classify arguments and think about their support.

- **Investigative paper similar to those in the social sciences.** If you are asked to collect evidence in an organized way to support a claim about advertising strategies or violence in children's TV programming, then you will be writing an investigative essay. You will present evidence that you have gathered and analyzed to support your claim.
- **Evaluation.** If your assignment is to explain why others should read a particular book or take a particular professor's class, then you will be preparing an evaluation argument. Be sure to think about your criteria: What makes a book or a professor good? Why do you dislike Amy Winehouse? Is it really her music—or her lifestyle?
- **Definition.** If you are asked to explain the meaning of a general or controversial term, you will be writing a definition argument. What do we mean by *wisdom*? What are the characteristics of *cool*? A definition argument usually requires both specific details to illustrate the term and general ideas to express its meaning.
- **Claim of values.** If you are given the assignment to argue for your position on euthanasia, trying juveniles as adults, or the use of national identification cards, recognize that your assignment calls for a position paper, a claim based heavily on values. Pay close attention to your warrants or assumptions in any philosophical debate.
- **Claim of policy.** If you are given a broad topic: "What should we do about _____?" and you have to fill in the blank, your task is to offer solutions to a current problem. What should we do about childhood obesity? About home foreclosures? These kinds of questions are less philosophical and more practical. Your solutions must be workable.
- **Refutation or rebuttal.** If you are given the assignment to find a letter to the editor, a newspaper editorial, or an essay in this text with which you disagree, your job is to write a refutation essay, a specific challenge to a specific argument. You know, then, that you will repeatedly refer to the work you are rebutting, so you will need to know it thoroughly.

## What Is My Goal?

It is also helpful to consider your goal in writing. Does your topic call for a strong statement of views (i.e., "These are the steps we must take to reduce childhood obesity")? Or, is your goal an exploratory one, a thinking through of possible answers to a more philosophical question ("Why is it often difficult to separate performance from personality when we evaluate a star?")? Thinking about your goal as well as the argument's genre will help you decide on the kinds of evidence needed and on the approach you take and tone you select.

## Will the Rogerian or Conciliatory Approach Work for Me?

Psychologist Carl Rogers asserts that the most successful arguments take a conciliatory approach. The characteristics of this approach include

- showing respect for the opposition in the language and tone of the argument,
- seeking common ground by indicating specific facts and values that both sides share, and
- qualifying the claim to bring opposing sides more closely together.

In their essay "Euthanasia—A Critique," authors Peter A. Singer and Mark Siegler provide a good example of a conciliatory approach. They begin their essay by explaining and then rebutting the two main arguments in favor of euthanasia. After stating the two arguments in clear and neutral language, they write this in response to the first argument:

> We agree that the relief of pain and suffering is a crucial goal of medicine. We question, however, whether the care of dying patients cannot be improved without resorting to the drastic measure of euthanasia. Most physical pain can be relieved with the appropriate use of analgesic agents. Unfortunately, despite widespread agreement that dying patients must be provided with necessary analgesia, physicians continue to underuse analgesia in the care of dying patients because of the concern about depressing respiratory drive or creating addiction. Such situations demand better management of pain, not euthanasia.

In this paragraph the authors accept the value of pain management for dying patients. They go even further and offer a solution to the problem of suffering among the terminally ill—better pain management by doctors. They remain thoughtful in their approach and tone throughout, while sticking to their position that legalizing euthanasia is not the solution.

Consider how you can use the conciliatory approach to write more effective arguments. It will help you avoid "overheated" language and maintain your focus on what is doable in a world of differing points of view. There is the expression that "you can catch more flies with honey than with vinegar." Using "honey" instead of "vinegar" might also make you feel better about yourself.

# MOVE FROM TOPIC TO CLAIM TO POSSIBLE SUPPORT

When you write a letter to the editor of a newspaper, you have chosen to respond to someone else's argument that has bothered you. In this writing context, you already know your topic and, probably, your claim as well. You also know that your purpose will be to refute the article you have read. In composition classes, the context is not always so clearly established, but you will usually be given some guidelines with which to get started.

## Selecting a Topic

Suppose that you are asked to write an argument that is in some way connected to First Amendment rights. Your instructor has limited and focused your topic choice and purpose. Start thinking about possible topics that relate to freedom of speech and censorship issues. To aid your topic search and selection, use one or more invention strategies:

- Brainstorm (make a list).
- Freewrite (write without stopping for ten minutes).
- Map or cluster (connect ideas to the general topic in various spokes, a kind of visual brainstorming).
- Read through this text for ideas.

Your invention strategies lead, let us suppose, to the following list of possible topics:

> Administrative restrictions on the college newspaper
> Hate speech restrictions or codes
> Deleting certain books from high school reading lists
> Controls and limits on alcohol and cigarette advertising
> Restrictions on violent TV programming
> Dress codes/uniforms

Looking over your list, you realize that the last item, dress codes/uniforms, may be about freedom but not freedom of speech, so you drop it from consideration. All of the other topics have promise. Which one do you select? Two considerations should guide you: interest and knowledge. First, your argument is likely to be more thoughtful and lively if you choose an issue that matters to you. But, unless you have time for study, you are wise to choose a topic about which you already have some information and ideas. Suppose that you decide to write about television violence because you are concerned about violence in American society and have given this issue some thought. It is time to phrase your topic as a tentative thesis or claim.

## Drafting a Claim

Good claim statements will keep you focused in your writing—in addition to establishing your main idea for readers. Give thought, then, both to your position on the issue and to the wording of your claim. *Claim statements to avoid:*

- Claims using vague words such as *good* or *bad.*

  **VAGUE:**     TV violence is bad for us.

  **BETTER:**    We need more restrictions on violent TV programming.

- Claims in loosely worded "two-part" sentences.

  **UNFOCUSED:**   Campus rape is a serious problem, and we need to do
  something about it.

**BETTER:**    College administrators and students need to work together to reduce both the number of campus rapes and the fear of rape.

- Claims that are not appropriately qualified.

**OVERSTATED:**    Violence on television is making us a violent society.

**BETTER:**    TV violence is contributing to viewers' increased fear of violence and insensitivity to violence.

- Claims that do not help you focus on your purpose in writing.

**UNCLEAR PURPOSE:**    Not everyone agrees on what is meant by violent TV programming.

*(Perhaps this is true, but more important, this claim suggests that you will define violent programming. Such an approach would not keep you focused on a First Amendment issue.)*

**BETTER:**    Restrictions on violent TV programs can be justified.

*(Now your claim directs you to the debate over restrictions of content.)*

## Listing Possible Grounds

As you learned in Chapter 3, you can generate grounds to support a claim by adding a "because" clause after a claim statement. We can start a list of grounds for the topic on violent TV programming in this way:

We need more restrictions on violent television programming *because*

- Many people, including children and teens, watch many hours of TV (get stats).
- People are affected by the dominant activities/experiences in their lives.
- There is a connection between violent programming and desensitizing and fear of violence and possibly more aggressive behavior in heavy viewers (get detail of studies).
- Society needs to protect young people.

You have four good points to work on, a combination of reasons and inferences drawn from evidence.

## Listing Grounds for the Other Side or Another Perspective

Remember that arguments generate counterarguments. Continue your exploration of this topic by considering possible rebuttals to your proposed grounds. How might someone who does not want to see restrictions placed on television programming respond to each of your points? Let's think about them one at a time:

*We need more restrictions on violent television programming because*

1. *Many people, including children and teens, watch many hours of TV.*

Your opposition cannot really challenge your first point on the facts, only its relevance to restricting programming. The opposition might argue that if parents think their children are watching too much TV, they should turn it off. The restriction needs to be a family decision.

2.  *People are affected by the dominant activities/experiences in their lives.*

It seems common sense to expect people to be influenced by dominant forces in their lives. Your opposition might argue, though, that many people have the TV on for many hours but often are not watching it intently for all of that time. The more dominant forces in our lives are parents and teachers and peers, not the TV. The opposition might also argue that people seem to be influenced to such different degrees by television that it is not fair or logical to restrict everyone when perhaps only a few are truly influenced by their TV viewing to a harmful degree.

3.  *There is a connection between violent programming and desensitizing and fear of violence and possibly more aggressive behavior in heavy viewers.*

Some people are entirely convinced by studies showing these negative effects of violent TV programming, but others point to the less convincing studies or make the argument that if violence on TV were really so powerful an influence, most people would be violent or fearful or desensitized.

4.  *Society needs to protect young people.*

Your opposition might choose to agree with you in theory on this point—and then turn again to the argument that parents should be doing the protecting. Government controls on programming restrict adults, as well as children, whereas it may only be some children who should watch fewer hours of TV and not watch adult "cop" shows at all.

Working through this process of considering opposing views can help you see

- where you may want to do some research for facts to provide backing for your grounds,
- how you can best develop your reasons to take account of typical counter-arguments, and
- if you should qualify your claim in some ways.

## Planning Your Approach

Now that you have thought about arguments on the other side, you decide that you want to argue for a qualified claim that is also more precise:

> To protect young viewers, we need restrictions on violence in children's programs and ratings for prime-time adult shows that clearly establish the degree of violence in those shows.

This qualified claim responds to two points of the rebuttals. Our student hasn't given in to the other side but has chosen to narrow the argument to emphasize the protection of children, an area of common ground.

Next, it's time to check some of the articles in this text or go online to get some data to develop points 1 and 3. You need to know that 99 percent of homes have at least one TV; you need to know that by the time young people graduate from high school, they have spent more time in front of the TV than in the classroom. Also, you can find the average number of violent acts by hour of TV in children's programs. Then, too, there are the various studies of fearfulness and aggressive behavior that will give you some statistics to use to develop the third point. Be sure to select reliable sources and then cite the sources you use. *Citing sources is not only required and right; it is also part of the process of establishing your credibility and thus strengthening your argument.*

Finally, how are you going to answer the point about parents controlling their children? You might counter that in theory this is the way it should be—but in fact not all parents are at home watching what their children are watching, and not all parents care enough to pay attention. However, all of us suffer from the consequences of those children who are influenced by their TV watching to become more aggressive or fearful or desensitized. These children grow up to become the adults the rest of us have to interact with, so the problem becomes one for the society as a whole to solve. If you had not disciplined yourself to go through the process of listing possible rebuttals, you may not have thought through this part of the debate.

## DRAFT YOUR ARGUMENT

Many of us can benefit from a step-by-step process of invention—such as we have been exploring in the last few pages. In addition, the more notes you have from working through the Toulmin structure, the easier it will be to get started on your draft. Students report that they can control their writing anxiety when they generate detailed notes. A page or two of notes that also suggest an organizational strategy can remove that awful feeling of staring at a blank computer screen.

In the following chapters on argument, you will find specific suggestions for organizing the various kinds of arguments. But you can always rely on one of these two basic organizations, regardless of the specific genre:

### PLAN 1: ORGANIZING AN ARGUMENT

Attention-getting opening (why the issue is important, or current, etc.)
Claim statement
Reasons and evidence in order from least important to most important
Challenge to potential rebuttals or counterarguments
Conclusion that reemphasizes claim

### PLAN 2: ORGANIZING AN ARGUMENT

Attention-getting opening
Claim statement (or possibly leave to the conclusion)
Order by arguments of opposing position, with your challenge to each
Conclusion that reemphasizes (or states for the first time) your claim

# GUIDELINES for Drafting

- **Try to get a complete draft of an essay in one sitting so that you can "see" the whole piece.**
- **If you can't think of a clever opening, state your claim and move on to the body of your essay.** After you draft your reasons and evidence, a good opening may occur to you.
- **If you find that you need something more in some parts of your essay, leave space there as a reminder that you will need to return to that paragraph later.**
- **Try to avoid using either a dictionary or thesaurus while drafting.** Your goal is to get the ideas down. You will polish later.
- **Learn to draft at your computer.** Revising is so much easier that you will be more willing to make significant changes if you work at your PC. If you are handwriting your draft, leave plenty of margin space for additions or for directions to shift parts around.

## REVISE YOUR DRAFT

If you have drafted at the computer, begin revising by printing a copy of your draft. Most of us cannot do an adequate job of revision by looking at a computer screen. Then remind yourself that revision is a three-step process: rewriting, editing, and proofreading.

### Rewriting

You are not ready to polish the writing until you are satisfied with the argument. Look first at the total piece. Do you have all the necessary parts: a claim, support, some response to possible counterarguments? Examine the order of your reasons and evidence. Do some of your points belong, logically, in a different place? Does the order make the most powerful defense of your claim? Be willing to move whole paragraphs around to test the best organization. Also reflect on the argument itself. Have you avoided logical fallacies? Have you qualified statements when appropriate? Do you have enough support? The best support?

Consider development: Is your essay long enough to meet assignment requirements? Are points fully developed to satisfy the demands of readers? One key to development is the length of your paragraphs. If most of your paragraphs are only two or three sentences, you have not developed the point of each paragraph satisfactorily. It is possible that some paragraphs need to be combined because they are really on the same topic. More typically, short paragraphs need further explanation of ideas or examples to illustrate ideas. Compare the following paragraphs for effectiveness:

### First Draft of a Paragraph from an Essay on Gun Control

One popular argument used against the regulation of gun ownership is the need of citizens, especially in urban areas where the crime rate is higher, to possess a handgun for personal protection, either carried or kept in the home. Some citizens may not be aware of the dangers to themselves or their families when they purchase a gun. Others, more aware, may embrace the myth that "bad things only happen to other people."

### Revised Version of the Paragraph with Statistics Added

One popular argument used against the regulation of gun ownership is the need of citizens, especially in urban areas where the crime rate is higher, to possess a handgun for personal protection, whether it is carried or kept in the home. Although some citizens may not be aware of the dangers to themselves or their families when they purchase a gun, they should be. According to the Center to Prevent Handgun Violence, from their web page "Firearm Facts," "guns that are kept in the home for self-protection are 22 times more likely to kill a family member or friend than to kill in self-defense." The Center also reports that guns in the home make homicide three times more likely and suicide five times more likely. We are not thinking straight if we believe that these dangers apply only to others.

A quick trip to the Internet has provided this student with some facts to support his argument. Observe how he has referred informally but fully to the source of his information. (If your instructor requires formal MLA documentation in all essays, then you will need to add a Works Cited page and give a full reference to the website. See pp. 314–28.)

## Editing

Make your changes, print another copy, and begin the second phase of revision: editing. As you read through this time, pay close attention to unity and coherence, to sentence patterns, and to word choice. Read each paragraph as a separate unit to be certain that everything is on the same subtopic. Then look at your use of transition and connecting words, both within and between paragraphs. Ask yourself: Have you guided the reader through the argument using appropriate connectors such as *therefore, in addition, as a consequence, also,* and so forth?

Read again, focusing on each sentence, checking to see that you have varied sentence patterns and length. Read sentences aloud to let your ear help you find awkward constructions or unfinished thoughts. Strive as well for word choice that is concrete and specific, avoiding wordiness, clichés, trite expressions, or incorrect use of specialized terms. Observe how Samantha edited one paragraph in her essay "Balancing Work and Family":

### Draft Version of Paragraph

Women have come a long way in equalizing themselves, but inequality within marriages do exist. One reason for this can be found in the media. Just last week America turned on their televisions to watch a grotesque dramatization of skewed priorities. On *Who Wants to Marry a Millionaire,* a panel of women

Vague reference.

Wordy.

**Short sentences.**

vied for the affections of a millionaire who would choose one of them to be his wife. This show said that women can be purchased. Also that men must provide and that money is worth the sacrifice of one's individuality. The show also suggests that physical attraction is more important than the building of a complete relationship. Finally, the show says that women's true value lies in

**Vague reference.**

their appearance. This is a dangerous message to send to both men and women viewers.

### Edited Version of Paragraph

Although women have come a long way toward equality in the workplace, inequality within marriages can still be found. The media may be partly to blame for this continued inequality. Just last week Americans watched a grotesque dramatization of skewed priorities. On *Who Wants to Marry a Millionaire,* a panel of women vied for the affections of a millionaire who would choose one of them to be his wife. Such displays teach us that women can be purchased, that men must be the providers, that the desire for money is worth the sacrifice of one's individuality, that physical attraction is more important than a complete relationship, and that women's true value lies in their appearance. These messages discourage marriages based on equality and mutual support.

Samantha's editing has eliminated wordiness and vague references and has combined ideas into one forceful sentence. Support your good argument by taking the time to polish your writing.

## A Few Words about Words and Tone

You have just been advised to check your word choice to eliminate wordiness, vagueness, clichés, and so on. Here is a specific checklist of problems often found in student papers with some ways to fix the problems:

- *Eliminate clichés.* Do not write about "the fast-paced world we live in today" or the "rat race." First, do you know for sure that the pace of life for someone who has a demanding job is any faster than it was in the past? Using time effectively has always mattered. Also, clichés suggest that you are too lazy to find your own words.
- *Avoid jargon.* In the negative sense of this word, "jargon" refers to non-specialists who fill their writing with "heavy-sounding terms" to give the appearance of significance. Watch for any overuse of "scientific" terms such as *factor* or *aspect,* or other vague, awkward language.
- *Avoid language that is too informal for most of your writing contexts.* What do you mean when you write: *"Kids* today watch too much TV"? Alternatives include *children, teens, adolescents.* These words are less slangy and more precise.
- *Avoid nasty attacks on the opposition.* Change "those jerks who are foolish enough to believe that TV violence has no impact on children" to language that explains your counterargument without attacking those who may

disagree with you. After all, you want to change the thinking of your audience, not make them resent you for name-calling.

- *Avoid all discriminatory language.* In the academic community and the adult workplace, most people are bothered by language that belittles any one group. This includes language that is racist or sexist or reflects negatively on older or disabled persons or those who do not share your sexual orientation or religious beliefs. Just don't do it!

## Proofreading

You also do not want to lose the respect of readers because you submit a paper filled with "little" errors—errors in punctuation, mechanics, and incorrect word choice. Most readers will forgive one or two little errors but will become annoyed if they begin to pile up. So, after you are finished rewriting and editing, print a copy of your paper and read it slowly, looking specifically at punctuation, at the handling of quotations and references to writers and to titles, and at those pesky words that come in two or more "versions": *to, too,* and *two; here* and *hear; their, there,* and *they're;* and so forth. If instructors have found any of these kinds of errors in your papers over the years, then focus your attention on the kinds of errors you have been known to make.

Refer to Chapter 1 for handling references to authors and titles and for handling direct quotations. Use a glossary of usage in a handbook for homonyms (words that sound alike but have different meanings), and check a handbook for punctuation rules. Take pride in your work and present a paper that will be treated with respect. What follows is a checklist of the key points for writing good arguments that we have just examined.

## A CHECKLIST FOR REVISION

- ☐ Have I selected an issue and purpose consistent with assignment guidelines?
- ☐ Have I stated a claim that is focused, appropriately qualified, and precise?
- ☐ Have I developed sound reasons and evidence in support of my claim?
- ☐ Have I used Toulmin's terms to help me study the parts of my argument, including rebuttals to counterarguments?
- ☐ Have I taken advantage of a conciliatory approach and emphasized common ground with opponents?
- ☐ Have I found a clear and effective organization for presenting my argument?
- ☐ Have I edited my draft thoughtfully, concentrating on producing unified and coherent paragraphs and polished sentences?
- ☐ Have I eliminated wordiness, clichés, jargon?
- ☐ Have I selected an appropriate tone for my purpose and audience?
- ☐ Have I used my word processor's spell-check and proofread a printed copy with great care?

# FOR ANALYSIS AND DEBATE

## UNDERSTANDING THE COSTS OF RISING INEQUALITY
STEVEN PEARLSTEIN

A graduate of Trinity College in Hartford, Connecticut, Steven Pearlstein has been a journalist most of his life, from the editor's chair at his college paper to business columnist at the *Washington Post* since 2003. His three-times-a-week columns, covering local, national, and international business and economic topics, have been recognized with a Pulitzer Prize. The following column appeared October 6, 2010.

PREREADING QUESTIONS  What kinds of costs do you expect Pearlstein to address? Do you think there are costs to income inequality in our society?

1    Although much of the Republicans' "Pledge to America" is given over to a discussion of economic issues, there is one topic that is never mentioned: the dramatic rise in income inequality. As with global warming, Republicans seem to have decided that the best way to deal with this fundamental challenge is to deny it exists.

2    If you asked Americans how much of the nation's pretax income goes to the top 10 percent of households, it is unlikely they would come anywhere close to 50 percent, which is where it was just before the bubble burst in 2007. That's according to groundbreaking research by economists Thomas Piketty, of the Paris School of Economics, and Emmanuel Saez, of the University of California at Berkeley, who last week won one of this year's MacArthur Foundation "genius" grants.

3    It wasn't always that way. From World War II until 1976, considered by many as the "golden years" for the U.S. economy, the top 10 percent of the population took home less than a third of the income generated by the private economy. But since then, according to Saez and Piketty, virtually all of the benefits of economic growth have gone to households that, in today's terms, earn more than $110,000 a year.

4    Even within that top "decile," the distribution is remarkably skewed. By 2007, the top 1 percent of households took home 23 percent of the national income after a 15-year run in which they captured more than half—yes, you read that right, more than half—of the country's economic growth. As Tim Noah noted recently in a wonderful series of articles in *Slate,* that's the kind of income distribution you'd associate with a banana republic or a sub-Saharan kleptocracy, not the world's oldest democracy and wealthiest market economy.

5    In trying to figure out who or what is responsible for rising inequality, there are lots of suspects. Globalization is certainly one, in the form of increased flows of people, goods and capital across borders. So is technological change, which has skewed the demand for labor in favor of workers with higher education without a corresponding increase in the supply of such workers. There are a number of other culprits that come under the heading of what

economists call "institutional" changes—the decline of unions, industry dereg-
ulation and the increased power of financial markets over corporate behavior.
Over time, more industries have developed the kind of superstar pay structures that were long associated with Hollywood and professional sports.

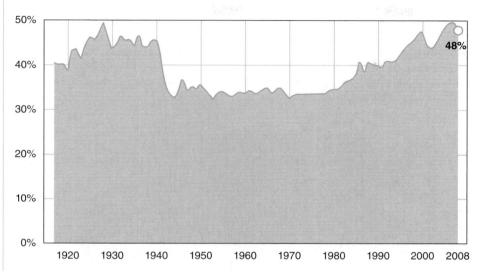

Percentage of Americans' income going to top 10 percent of households
Note: Income is pretax and includes capital gains.
Source: Emmanuel Saez and Thomas Piketty

And then there is my favorite culprit: changing social norms around the   6
issue of how much inequality is socially acceptable.

Economists spend a lot of time trying to quantify precisely how much   7
responsibility to assign to each of these, but in truth the death of equality is
much like Agatha Christie's *Murder on the Orient Express:* They all did it.

There are moral and political reasons for caring about this dramatic skew-   8
ing of income, which in the real world leads to a similar skewing of opportunity, social standing and political power. But there is also an important
economic reason: Too much inequality, just like too little, appears to reduce
global competitiveness and long-term growth, at least in developed countries
like ours.

We know from recent experience, for example, that financial bubbles   9
reduce equality by siphoning off a disproportionate share of national income
to Wall Street's highly-paid bankers and traders. What may be less obvious,
but not less important, is that the causality also works the other way: Too much
inequality can lead to financial bubbles.

The liberal version of this argument comes from former Labor secretary 10
Robert Reich in his new book, *Aftershock.* Because so much of the nation's
income is siphoned off to the super-rich, Reich says, a struggling middle class
trying to maintain its standard of living had no choice but to take on more and
more debt. I have some problem with the argument that the middle class had

no choice, but it's certainly true that the middle class and the economy as a whole would be in better shape today if households weren't burdened with so much debt.

11      The more conservative version of this argument comes from University of Chicago economist Raghuram Rajan. In his new book, *Fault Lines,* Rajan argues that in order to respond to the stagnant incomes of their constituents, politicians took a number of steps to keep the "American Dream" within reach, including subsidization of home mortgages and college loans. He might have added that politicians also were quick to cut taxes for the middle class even when it meant running up the national debt to pay for popular entitlement programs and government services.

Pedestrians scurry past a homeless man on a wintry day.

12      Concentrating so much income in a relatively small number of households has also led to trillions of dollars being spent and invested in ways that were spectacularly unproductive. In recent decades, the rich have used their winnings to bid up the prices of artwork and fancy cars, the tuition at prestigious private schools and universities, the services of celebrity hairdressers and interior decorators, and real estate in fashionable enclaves from Park City to Park Avenue. And what wasn't misspent was largely misinvested in hedge funds and private equity vehicles that played a pivotal role in inflating a series of speculative financial bubbles, from the junk bond bubble of the '80s to the tech and telecom bubble of the '90s to the credit bubble of the past decade.

13      The biggest problem with runaway inequality, however, is that it undermines the unity of purpose necessary for any firm, or any nation, to

thrive. People don't work hard, take risks and make sacrifices if they think the rewards will all flow to others. Conservative Republicans use this argument all the time in trying to justify lower tax rates for wealthy earners and investors, but they chose to ignore it when it comes to the incomes of everyone else.

It's no coincidence that polarization of income distribution in the United 14 States coincides with a polarization of the political process. Just as income inequality has eroded any sense that we are all in this together, it has also eroded the political consensus necessary for effective government. There can be no better proof of that proposition than the current election cycle, in which the last of the moderates are being driven from the political process and the most likely prospect is for years of ideological warfare and political gridlock.

Political candidates may not be talking about income inequality during 15 this election [2010], but it is the unspoken issue that underlies all the others. Without a sense of shared prosperity, there can be no prosperity. And given the realities of global capitalism, with its booms and busts and winner-take-all dynamic, that will require more government involvement in the economy, not less.

## QUESTIONS FOR READING

1.  What percentage of household pretax income goes to those earning in the top 10 percent? What percentage of household income did this group take home between World War II and 1976?

2.  Of the percentage of income going to the top 10 percent, what percentage is going to the top 1 percent?

3.  What causes have been put forward to explain the increase in income inequality in the last twenty years? What is the author's view of the cause(s)?

4.  What is the economic effect on society of too much inequality?

5.  How do liberals account for the economic problems produced by inequality? How do conservatives explain it?

## QUESTIONS FOR REASONING AND ANALYSIS

6.  What, for Pearlstein, is the biggest problem created by income inequality? What are the consequences for society? For politics?

7.  Have you thought that significant income inequality could be a cause of the ousting of political moderates from office? Does Pearlstein's argument make sense to you? Why or why not?

8. What is Pearlstein's main point—the claim of his argument? (When writing a claim statement, think about how you would classify his argument by genre.)

9. What evidence does the author provide in support of his argument? Is it effective? Why or why not?

QUESTIONS FOR REFLECTION AND WRITING

10. Did you have any problems following the author's discussion? If so, how would you account for this? (Who is Pearlstein's audience? Are you part of that audience? If not, do you want to be? Explain.)

11. Do you agree that significant inequality is a social and political—as well as economic—problem? Why or why not? If there is any part of the author's argument with which you disagree, how would you refute it?

## POLITICAL STUPIDITY, U.S. STYLE | E. J. DIONNE JR.

Holding a doctorate in philosophy from Oxford University, E. J. Dionne is a senior fellow at the Brookings Institution, an adjunct professor at Georgetown University, and a syndicated columnist. Two of his books include *Why Americans Hate Politics* (1991) and *Souled Out: Reclaiming Faith and Politics After the Religious Right* (2008). The following column was published July 29, 2010.

PREREADING QUESTIONS If Dionne is writing about political *stupidity*, then what kind of political analysis will he not include in this column? What would you label *stupid* in U.S. politics today?

1    Can a nation remain a superpower if its internal politics are incorrigibly stupid?

2    Start with taxes. In every other serious democracy, conservative political parties feel at least some obligation to match their tax policies with their spending plans. David Cameron, the new Conservative prime minister in Britain, is a leading example.

3    He recently offered a rather brutal budget that includes severe cutbacks. I have doubts about some of them, but at least Cameron cared enough about reducing his country's deficit that alongside the cuts he also proposed an increase in the value-added tax, from 17.5 percent to 20 percent. Imagine: a fiscal conservative who really is a fiscal conservative.

4    That could never happen here because the fairy tale of supply-side economics insists that taxes are always too high, especially on the rich.

5    This is why Democrats will be fools if they don't try to turn the Republicans' refusal to raise taxes on families earning more than $250,000 a year into an election issue. If Democrats go into a headlong retreat on this, they will have no standing to govern.

The simple truth is that the wealthy in the United States—the people who 6 have made almost all the income gains in recent years—are undertaxed compared with everyone else.

Consider two reports from the Center on Budget and Policy Priorities. 7 One, issued last month, highlighted findings from the Congressional Budget Office showing that "the gaps in after-tax income between the richest 1 percent of Americans and the middle and poorest fifths of the country more than tripled between 1979 and 2007."

The other, from February, used Internal Revenue Service data to show that 8 the effective federal income tax rate for the 400 taxpayers with the very highest incomes declined by nearly half in just over a decade, even as their pretax incomes have grown five times larger.

The study found that the top 400 households "paid 16.6 percent of their 9 income in federal individual income taxes in 2007, down from 30 percent in 1995." We are talking here about truly rich people. Using 2007 dollars, it took an adjusted gross income of at least $35 million to make the top 400 in 1992, and $139 million in 2007.

The notion that when we are fighting two wars, we're not supposed to 10 consider raising taxes on such Americans is one sign of a country that's no longer serious. Why do so few foreign policy hawks acknowledge that if they lack the gumption to ask taxpayers to finance the projection of American military power, we won't be able to project it in the long run?

And if we are unwilling to have a full-scale debate over whether nation-building 11 abroad is getting in the way of nation-building at home, we will accomplish neither.

Our discussion of the economic stimulus is another symptom of political 12 irrationality. It's entirely true that the $787 billion recovery package passed last year was not big enough to keep unemployment from rising above 9 percent.

But this is not actually an argument against the stimulus. On the contrary, 13 studies showing that the stimulus created or saved as many as 3 million jobs are very hard to refute. It's much easier to pretend that all this money was wasted, although the evidence is overwhelming that we should have stimulated more.

Then there's the structure of our government. Does any other democracy 14 have a powerful legislative branch as undemocratic as the U.S. Senate?

When our republic was created, the population ratio between the largest 15 and smallest state was 13 to 1. Now, it's 68 to 1. Because of the abuse of the filibuster, 41 senators representing less than 11 percent of the nation's population can, in principle, block action supported by 59 senators representing more than 89 percent of our population. And you wonder why it's so hard to get anything done in Washington?

I'm a chronic optimist about America. But we are letting stupid politics, 16 irrational ideas on fiscal policy and an antiquated political structure undermine our power.

17    We need a new conservatism in our country that is worthy of the name. We need liberals willing to speak out on the threat our daft politics poses to our influence in the world. We need moderates who do more than stick their fingers in the wind to calculate the halfway point between two political poles.

And, yes, we need to reform a Senate that has become an embarrassment to its democratic claims.

## QUESTIONS FOR READING

1. What are the three examples of political stupidity examined by Dionne?
2. What is Dionne's position on raising taxes on the rich? What concept is used to argue against raising taxes?
3. Did the stimulus package work?
4. What makes the U.S. legislature "undemocratic" in Dionne's view?

## QUESTIONS FOR REASONING AND ANALYSIS

5. What is Dionne's claim? Where does he state it?
6. What *kinds* of evidence does the author provide to support each of his three examples? Is the evidence convincing? If you don't think so, what evidence do you have with which to challenge his conclusions?
7. Columnists regularly write to complain about political issues or politicians. How does Dionne get his readers' attention so that they will listen to his concerns? Did he get your attention? Why or why not?

## QUESTIONS FOR REFLECTION AND WRITING

8. Did any of Dionne's three examples surprise you? If so, which one(s) and why? If not, why not?
9. Do you agree that Dionne's examples represent political *stupidity*? If you disagree, how would you refute Dionne?

# SUGGESTIONS FOR DISCUSSION AND WRITING

1. If Pearlstein has demonstrated convincingly that significant income disparity has negative economic consequences, that is a serious problem for the United States. But, is there a moral issue as well? Should the wealthiest be 50 times richer than the average American? 100 times? At what point is the discrepancy morally unacceptable to you? Or, is the difference in income irrelevant unless it affects the economy? Organize your thoughts on this topic for discussion or an essay.

2. Where do you stand on the issue of extending the Bush tax cuts indefinitely for everyone, including households making more than $250,000 per year? Consider the facts regarding income and taxes presented by both Pearlstein and Dionne as you prepare to defend your position.

3. Dionne presents examples of what he calls "political stupidity." Can you think of a fourth example that you would defend as political stupidity? Gather your facts and ideas to prepare your argument to add to Dionne's.

## GOING ONLINE

Both Pearlstein and Dionne refer to books, studies, and online articles to develop and support their arguments. Go online to see what more you can learn about the authors' references. Then answer these questions: Which source interests you the most? Why?

# CHAPTER 5

# Reading, Analyzing, and Using Visuals and Statistics in Argument

READ: What is this photo's subject? Where are we?

REASON: What details make it dramatic?

REFLECT/WRITE: What message does the photo send? How does it make you feel?

We live in a visual age. Many of us go to movies to appreciate and judge the film's visual effects. The Internet is awash in pictures and colorful icons. Perhaps the best symbol of our visual age is *USA Today*, a paper filled with color photos and many tables and other graphics as a primary way of presenting information. *USA Today* has forced the more traditional papers to add color to compete. We also live in a numerical age. We refer to the events of September 11, 2001, as 9/11—without any disrespect. This chapter brings together these markers of our times as they are used in argument—and as argument. Finding statistics and visuals used as part of argument, we also need to remember that cartoons and advertisements are arguments in and of themselves.

## RESPONDING TO VISUAL ARGUMENTS

Many arguments bombard us today in visual forms. These include photos, political cartoons, and advertising. Most major newspapers have a political cartoonist whose drawings appear regularly on the editorial page. (Some comic strips are also political in nature, at least some of the time.) These cartoons are designed to make a political point in a visually clever and amusing way. (That is why they are both "cartoons" and "political" at the same time.) Their uses of irony and caricatures of known politicians make them among the most emotionally powerful, indeed stinging, of arguments.

Photographs accompany many newspaper and magazine articles, and they often tell a story. Indeed some photographers are famous for their ability to capture a personality or a newsworthy moment. So accustomed to these visuals today, we sometimes forget to study photographs. Be sure to examine each photo, remembering that authors and editors have selected each one for a reason.

Advertisements are among the most creative and powerful forms of argument today. Remember that ads are designed to take your time (for shopping) and your money. Their messages need to be powerful to motivate you to action. With some products (what most of us consider necessities), ads are designed to influence product choice, to get us to buy brand A instead of brand B. With other products, ones we really do not need or which may actually be harmful to us, ads need to be especially clever. Some ads do provide information (car X gets better gas mileage than car Y). Other ads (perfume ads, for example) take us into a fantasy land so that we will spend $50 on a small but pretty bottle. Another type of ad is the "image advertisement," an ad that assures us that a particular company is top-notch. If we admire the company, we will buy its goods or services.

Here are guidelines for reading visual arguments with insight. You can practice these steps with the exercises that follow.

# GUIDELINES for Reading Photographs

- **Is a scene or situation depicted?** If so, study the details to identify the situation.
- **Identify each figure in the photo.**
- **What details of scene or person(s) carry significance?**
- **How does the photograph make you feel?**

# GUIDELINES for Reading Political Cartoons

- **What scene is depicted?** Identify the situation.
- **Identify each of the figures in the cartoon.** Are they current politicians, figures from history or literature, the "person in the street," or symbolic representations?
- **Who speaks the lines in the cartoon?**
- **What is the cartoon's general subject?** What is the point of the cartoon, the claim of the cartoonist?

# GUIDELINES for Reading Advertisements

- **What product or service is being advertised?**
- **Who seems to be the targeted audience?**
- **What is the ad's primary strategy?** To provide information? To reinforce the product's or company's image? To appeal to particular needs or desires? For example, if an ad shows a group of young people having fun and drinking a particular beer, to what needs/desires is the ad appealing?
- **Does the ad use specific rhetorical strategies such as humor, understatement, or irony?**
- **What is the relation between the visual part of the ad (photo, drawing, typeface, etc.) and the print part (the text, or copy)?** Does the ad use a slogan or catchy phrase? Is there a company logo? Is the slogan or logo clever? Is it well known as a marker of the company? What may be the effect of these strategies on readers?
- **What is the ad's overall visual impression?** Consider both images and colors used.

## EXERCISES: Analyzing Photos, Cartoons, and Ads

1. Analyze the photo on page 117, using the guidelines previously listed.
2. Review the photos that open Chapters 1, 4, 5, 8, 18, and 23. Select the one you find most effective. Analyze it in detail to show why you think it is the best.
3. Analyze the cartoon on page 117 using the guidelines listed previously. You may want to jot down your answers to the questions to be well prepared for class discussion.

4. Review the cartoons that open Chapters 2, 3, 6, 7, 9, 10, 15, 16, 17, 19, 20, 21, and 22. Select the one you find most effective. Analyze it in detail to show why you think it is the cleverest.

5. Analyze the ads on pages 118–20 and 361–63, again using the guidelines listed above. After answering the guideline questions, consider these as well: Will each ad appeal effectively to its intended audience? If so, why? If not, why not?

FRANK & ERNEST © Thaves/Dist. by United Feature Syndicate, Inc.

# the river of life

......................................

**Retracing a historic journey to help fight malaria.**

......................................................................................................................

In 1858, Scottish missionary David Livingstone embarked on a historic journey along the Zambezi River in southern Africa. On that trip, malaria claimed the life of Livingstone's wife, Mary. Livingstone himself also later died from the disease.

Today, 150 years later, malaria remains a threat. Over one million people, mostly children and pregnant women, die from malaria each year. About 40 percent of the global population is vulnerable to the disease.

But an unprecedented global action—by governments and corporations, NGOs and health organizations—has been mobilized against malaria. And this combined effort is yielding results:

• Across Africa, people are receiving anti-malarial medications, as well as bed nets and insecticides that protect against the mosquitoes that transmit the disease.

Photo by Helge Bendl

• In Rwanda, malaria cases are down by 64 percent, and deaths by 66 percent. Similar results are seen in Ethiopia and Zambia. And in Mozambique, where 9 out of 10 children had been infected, that number is now 2 in 10.

• Scientists are expanding the pipeline of affordable, effective anti-malarial medicines, while also making progress on discovering a vaccine.

April 25 is World Malaria Day.  As part of that event, a team of medical experts will retrace Livingstone's journey along the Zambezi, the "River of Life." As part of the Roll Back Malaria Zambezi Expedition, they will travel 1,500 miles in inflatable boats through Angola, Namibia, Botswana, Zambia, Zimbabwe and Mozambique.

By exposing the difficulties of delivering supplies to remote areas, the expedition will demonstrate that only a coordinated, cross-border action can beat back the disease, and turn the lifeline of southern Africa into a "River of Life" for those threatened by malaria.

ExxonMobil is the largest non-pharmaceutical private-sector contributor to the fight against malaria. But our support is more than financial. We are actively partnering with governments and agencies in affected countries, enabling them to combat malaria with the same disciplined, results-based business practices that ExxonMobil employs in its global operations.

Livingstone once said, "I am prepared to go anywhere, provided it be forward."  The communities burdened by this disease cannot move forward until malaria is controlled and, someday, eradicated. We urge everyone to join in this global effort.

*For more information, visit www.zambezi-expedition.org and www.rollbackmalaria.org.*

**E**x**xonMobil**
**Taking on the world's toughest energy challenges.**

**FOR STRONGER TEETH CHEW ORBIT**
Orbit is now accepted by the American Dental Association

The ADA Council on Scientific Affairs' Acceptance of Orbit is based on its finding that the physical action of chewing Orbit sugar-free
gum for 20 minutes after eating, stimulates saliva flow, which helps to prevent cavities by reducing plaque acids and strengthening teeth.

# READING GRAPHICS

Graphics—photographs, diagrams, tables, charts, and graphs—present a good bit of information in a condensed but also visually engaging format. Graphics are everywhere: in textbooks, magazines, newspapers, and the Internet. It's a rare training session or board meeting that is conducted without the use of graphics to display information. So, you want to be able to read graphics and create them, when appropriate, in your own writing. First, study the chart below that illustrates the different uses of various visuals. General guidelines for reading graphics follow. The guidelines will use Figure 5.1 to illustrate points. Study the figure repeatedly as you read through the guidelines.

## Understanding How Graphics Differ

Each type of visual serves specific purposes. You can't use a pie chart, for example, to explain a process; you need a diagram or a flowchart. So, when reading graphics, understand what each type can show you. When preparing your own visuals, select the graphic that will most clearly and effectively present the particular information you want to display.

| TYPE | PURPOSE | EXAMPLE |
|------|---------|---------|
| Diagram | show details<br>demonstrate process | drawing of knee tendons<br>photosynthesis |
| Table | list numerical information | income of U.S. households |
| Bar chart | comparative amounts of<br>related numbers | differences in suicide rates by<br>age and race |
| Pie chart | relative portions of a whole | percentages of Americans by<br>educational level |
| Flowchart | steps in a process | purification of water |
| Graph | relationship of two items | income increases over time |
| Map | information relative to a<br>geographical area | locations of world's rain forests |

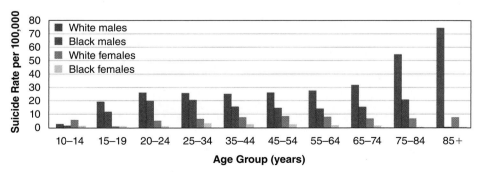

**FIGURE 5.1** Differences in Suicide Rate According to Race, Gender, and Age
(Source: Data from the U.S. Bureau of the Census, 1994)

# GUIDELINES for Reading Graphics

1. **Locate the particular graphic referred to in the text and study it at that point in your reading.** Graphics may not always be placed on the same page as the text reference. Stop your reading to find and study the graphic; that's what the writer wants you to do. Find Figure 5.1 on the previous page.

2. **Read the title or heading of the graphic.** Every graphic is given a title. What is the subject of the graphic? What kind of information is provided? Figure 5.1 shows differences in suicide rates by race, gender, and age.

3. **Read any notes, description, and the source information at the bottom of the graphic.** Figure 5.1 came from the U.S. Bureau of the Census for 1994. Critical questions: What is this figure showing me? Is the information coming from a reliable source? Is it current enough to still be meaningful?

4. **Study the labels—and other words—that appear as part of the graphic.** You cannot draw useful conclusions unless you understand exactly what is being shown. Observe in Figure 5.1 that the four bars for each age group (shown along the horizontal axis) represent white males, black males, white females, and black females, in that order, for each age category.

5. **Study the information, making certain that you understand what the numbers represent.** Are the numerals whole numbers, numbers in hundreds or thousands, or percentages? In Figure 5.1 we are looking at suicide *rates per 100,000 people* for four identified groups of people at different ages. So, to know exactly how many white males between 15 and 19 commit suicide, we need to know how many white males between 15 and 19 there are (or were in 1994) in the United States population. The chart does not give us this information. It gives us *comparative rates* per 100,000 people in each category and tells us that almost 20 in every 100,000 white males between 15 and 19 commit suicide.

6. **Draw conclusions.** Think about the information in different ways. Critical questions: What does the author want to accomplish by including these figures? How are they significant? What conclusions can you draw from Figure 5.1? Answer these questions to guide your thinking:

   a. Which of the four compared groups faces the greatest risk from suicide over his or her lifetime? Would you have guessed this group? Why or why not? What might be some of the causes for the greatest risk to this group?

   b. What is the greatest risk factor for increased suicide rate—race, gender, age, or a combination? Does this surprise you? Would you have guessed a different factor? Why?

   c. Which group, as young teens, is at greatest risk? Are you surprised? Why or why not? What might be some of the causes for this?

Graphics provide information, raise questions, explain processes, engage us emotionally, make us think. Study the various graphics in the exercises that follow to become more expert in reading and responding critically to visuals.

# EXERCISES: Reading and Analyzing Graphics

1.  Study the pie charts in Figure 5.2 and then answer the following questions.
    a.  What is the subject of the charts?
    b.  In addition to the information within the pie charts, what other information is provided?
    c.  Which group increases by the greatest relative amount? How would you account for that increase?
    d.  Which figure surprises you the most? Why?
2.  Study the line graph in Figure 5.3 and then answer the following questions.
    a.  What two subjects are treated by the graph?
    b.  In 2000 what percentage of men's income did women earn?
    c.  During which five-year period did men's incomes increase by the greatest amount?
    d.  Does the author's prediction for the year 2005 suggest that income equality for women will have taken place?
    e.  Are you bothered by the facts on this graph? Why or why not?
3.  Study the table in Figure 5.4 and then answer the following questions.
    a.  What is being presented and compared in this table?
    b.  What, exactly, do the numerals in the second line represent? What, exactly, do the numerals in the third line represent? (Be sure that you understand what these numbers mean.)
    c.  For the information given in lines 2, 3, 4, and 5, in which category have women made the greatest gains on men?
    d.  See if you can complete the missing information in the last line. Where will you look to find out how many men and women were single parents in 2000? (In 2010?)
    e.  Which figure surprises you the most? Why?

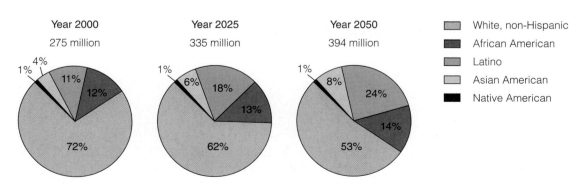

**FIGURE 5.2** The Shifting of U.S. Racial-Ethnic Mix (Sources: U.S. Bureau of the Census, *Current Population Reports* P25:1130, 1996; James M. Henslin, *Sociology: A Down-to-Earth Approach*, 5th ed.)

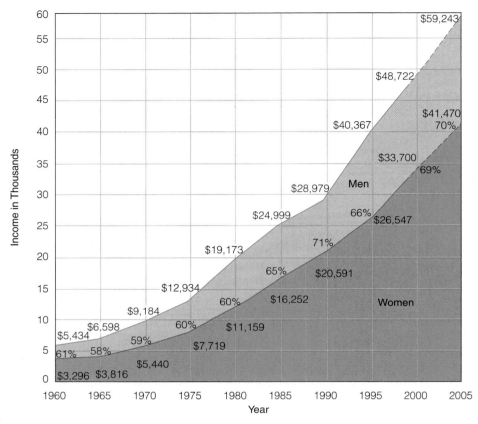

Note: The income jump from 1990 to 1995 is probably due to a statistical procedure. The 1995 source (for 1990 income) uses "median income," while the 1997 source (for 1995 income) merely says "average earnings." How the "average" is computed is not stated. Broken lines indicate the author's estimates.

**FIGURE 5.3** What Percentage of Men's Income Do Women Earn? The Gender Gap Over Time (Source: James M. Henslin, *Sociology*, 5th ed.)

|  | 1970 | | 2000 | |
| --- | --- | --- | --- | --- |
|  | **MEN** | **WOMEN** | **MEN** | **WOMEN** |
| Estimated life expectancy | 67.1 | 74.1 | 74.24 | 79.9 |
| % high school graduates | 53 | 52 | 87 | 88 |
| % of BAs awarded | 57 | 43 | 45 | 55 |
| % of MAs awarded | 60 | 40 | 45 | 55 |
| % of PhDs awarded | 87 | 13 | 61 | 39 |
| % in legal profession | 95 | 5 | 70 | 30 |
| Median earnings | $26,760 | $14,232 | $35,345 | $25,862 |
| Single parents | 1.2 million | 5.6 million | n/a | n/a |

**FIGURE 5.4** Men and Women in a Changing Society (Sources: for *1970: 1996 Statistical Abstract,* U.S. Dept. of Commerce, Economics and Statistics Administration, Bureau of the Census. 2000 data: National Center for Education Statistics http://nces.ed.gov/fastfacts)

4. Maps can be used to show all kinds of information, not just the locations of cities, rivers, or mountains. Study the map in Figure 5.5 and then answer the questions that follow.

   a. What, exactly, does the map show? Why does it not "look right"?
   b. How many electoral votes did each candidate win?
   c. How are the winning states for each candidate clustered? What conclusions can you draw from observing this clustering?
   d. What advice would you give to each party to ensure that party's presidential win in 2012?
   e. How would the map look if it were drawn to show population by state? Would the red states look bigger or smaller?

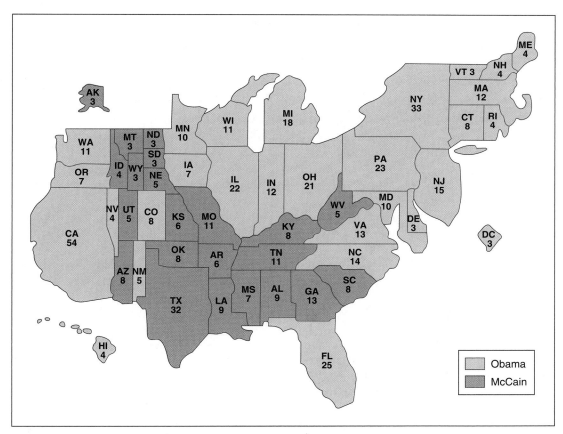

**Note: States drawn in proportion to number of electoral votes. Total electoral votes: 538** (Source: Based on a map that originally appeared in New York Times. November 5, 2002. Reprinted by permission of NYT Graphics. From O'Connor and Sabato, American Government © 2002; published by Allyn and Bacon, Boston, MA Copyright © 2002 by Pearson Education. Updated for the 2008 election by the author.)

**FIGURE 5.5** Electoral Votes per State for the 2008 Presidential Election

# THE USES OF AUTHORITY AND STATISTICS

Most of the visuals you have just studied provide a way of presenting statistics—data that many today consider essential to defending a claim. One reason you check the source information accompanying graphics is that you need to know—and evaluate—the authority of that source. When a graphic's numbers have come from the Census Bureau, you know you have a reliable source. When the author writes that "studies have shown . . . ," you want to become suspicious of the authority of the data. All elements of the arguments we read—and write—affect a writer's credibility.

## Judging Authorities

We know that movie stars and sports figures are not authorities on soft drinks and watches. But what about *real* authorities? When writers present the opinions or research findings of authorities as support for a claim, they are saying to readers that the authority is trustworthy and the opinions valuable. But what they are asserting is actually an assumption or warrant, part of the glue connecting evidence to claim. Remember: Warrants can be challenged. If the "authority" can be shown to lack authority, then the logic of the argument is destroyed. Use this checklist of questions to aid your evaluation of authorities:

☐ *Is the authority actually an authority on the topic under discussion?* When a famous scientist supports a candidate for office, he or she speaks as a citizen, not as an authority.

☐ *Is the work of the authority still current?* Times change; expertise does not always endure. Galileo would be lost in the universe of today's astrophysicists. Be particularly alert to the dates of information in the sciences in general, in genetics and the entire biomedical field, in health and nutrition. It is almost impossible to keep up with the latest findings in these areas of research.

☐ *Does the authority actually have legitimate credentials?* Are the person's publications in respected journals? Is he or she respected by others in the same field? *Just because it's in print does not mean it's a reliable source!*

☐ *Do experts in the field generally agree on the issue?* If there is widespread disagreement, then referring to one authority does not do much to support a claim. This is why you need to understand the many sides of a controversial topic before you write on it, and you need to bring knowledge of controversies and critical thinking skills to your reading of argument. This is also why writers often provide a source's credentials, not just a name, unless the authority is quite famous.

☐ *Is the authority's evidence reliable, so far as you can judge, but the interpretation of that evidence seems odd, or seems to be used to support strongly held beliefs?* Does the evidence actually connect to the claim? A respected authority's work can be stretched or manipulated in an attempt to defend a claim that the authority's work simply does not support.

## EXERCISES: Judging Authorities

1.  Jane Goodall has received worldwide fame for her studies of chimpanzees in Gombe and for her books on those field studies. Goodall is a vegetarian. Should she be used as an authority in support of a claim for a vegetarian diet? Why or why not? Consider:
    a.  Why might Goodall have chosen to become a vegetarian?
    b.  For what arguments might Goodall be used as an authority?
    c.  For what arguments might she be used effectively for emotional appeal?
2.  Suppose a respected zoologist prepares a five-year study of U.S. zoos, compiling a complete list of all animals at each zoo. He then updates the list for each of the five years, adding births and deaths. When he examines his data, he finds that deaths are one and one-half times the number of births. He considers this loss alarming and writes a paper arguing for the abolishing of zoos on the grounds that too many animals are dying. Because of his reputation, his article is published in a popular science magazine. How would you evaluate his authority and his study?
    a.  Should you trust the data? Why or why not?
    b.  Should you accept his conclusions? Why or why not?
    c.  Consider: What might be possible explanations for the birth/death ratio?

## Understanding and Evaluating Statistics

There are two useful clichés to keep in mind: "Statistics don't lie, but people lie with statistics" and "There are lies, damned lies, and statistics." The second cliché is perhaps a bit cynical. We don't want to be naïve in our faith in numbers, but neither do we want to become so cynical that we refuse to believe any statistical evidence. What we do need to keep in mind is that when statistics are presented in an argument they are being used by someone interested in winning that argument.

Some writers use numbers without being aware that the numbers are incomplete or not representative. Some present only part of the relevant information. Some may not mean to distort, but they do choose to present the information in language that helps their cause. There are many ways, some more innocent than others, to distort reality with statistics. Use the following guidelines to evaluate the presentation of statistical information.

# GUIDELINES for Evaluating Statistics

Study these questions to be alert to the ways data can be misleading:

- **Is the information current and therefore still relevant?** Crime rates in your city based on 2000 census data probably are no longer relevant, certainly not current enough to support an argument for increased (or decreased) police department spending.

- **If a sample was used, was it randomly selected and large enough to be significant?** Sometimes in medical research, the results of a small study are publicized to guide researchers to important new areas of study. When these results are reported in the press or on TV, however, the small size of the study is not always made clear. Thus one week we learn that coffee is bad for us, the next week that it is okay.
- **What information, exactly, has been provided?** When you read "Two out of three chose the Merit combination of low tar and good taste," you must ask yourself "Two-thirds of how many altogether?"
- **How have the numbers been presented?** And what is the effect of that presentation? Numbers can be presented as fractions, whole numbers, or percentages. Writers who want to emphasize budget increases will use whole numbers—billions of dollars. Writers who want to de-emphasize those increases select percentages. Writers who want their readers to respond to the numbers in a specific way add words to direct their thinking: "a *mere* 3 percent increase" or "the *enormous* $5 billion increase."

## EXERCISES: Reading Tables and Charts and Using Statistics

1.  Figure 5.6, a table from the Census Bureau, shows U.S. family income data from 1980 to 2005. Percentages and median income are given for all families and then, in turn, for white, black, Asian, and Hispanic families. Study the data and then complete the exercises that follow.
    a.  In a paper assessing the advantages of a growing economy, you want to include a paragraph on family income growth to show that a booming economy helps everyone, that "a rising tide lifts all boats." Select data from the table that best support your claim. Write a paragraph beginning with a topic sentence and including your data as support. Think about how to present the numbers in the most persuasive form.
    b.  Write a second paragraph with the topic sentence "Not all Americans have benefited from the boom years" or "A rising tide does not lift all boats." Select data from the table that best support this topic sentence and present the numbers in the most persuasive form.
    c.  Exchange paragraphs with a classmate and evaluate each other's selection and presentation of evidence.
2.  Go back to Figure 5.1 (p. 121) and reflect again on the information that it depicts. Then consider what conclusions can be drawn from the evidence and what the implications of those conclusions are. Working in small groups or with a class partner, decide how you want to use the data to support a point.
3.  Figure 5.7 (p. 130), another table from the Census Bureau, presents mean earnings by highest degree earned. First, be sure that you know the difference between mean and median (which is the number used in Figure 5.6). Study the data and reflect on the conclusions you can draw from the statistics. Consider: Of the various groups represented, which group most benefits from obtaining a college degree—as opposed to having only a high school diploma?

| Year | Number of families (1,000) | Percent distribution | | | | | | | Median income (dollars) |
|---|---|---|---|---|---|---|---|---|---|
| | | Under $15,000 | $15,000–$24,999 | $25,000–$34,999 | $35,000–$49,999 | $50,000–$74,999 | $75,000–$99,999 | $100,000 and over | |
| **ALL FAMILIES [1]** | | | | | | | | | |
| 1980 . . . . . . . . . . . . | 60,309 | 10.3 | 12.1 | 12.6 | 18.9 | 24.5 | 12.0 | 9.6 | 47,173 |
| 1990 . . . . . . . . . . . . | 66,322 | 10.2 | 10.6 | 11.3 | 16.8 | 22.6 | 13.4 | 15.2 | 51,202 |
| 2000 [2] . . . . . . . . . . . | 73,778 | 8.1 | 9.7 | 10.7 | 15.0 | 20.7 | 14.3 | 21.5 | 57,508 |
| 2004 [3] . . . . . . . . . . . | 76,866 | 9.2 | 10.3 | 10.6 | 14.5 | 20.4 | 13.6 | 21.4 | 55,869 |
| 2005 . . . . . . . . . . . . | 77,418 | 8.9 | 10.0 | 10.7 | 14.6 | 20.3 | 13.5 | 21.8 | 56,194 |
| **WHITE** | | | | | | | | | |
| 1980 . . . . . . . . . . | 52,710 | 8.4 | 11.3 | 12.5 | 19.2 | 25.6 | 12.7 | 10.3 | 49,150 |
| 1990 . . . . . . . . . . | 56,803 | 7.8 | 10.0 | 11.2 | 17.2 | 23.4 | 14.2 | 16.2 | 53,464 |
| 2000 [2] . . . . . . . . . | 61,330 | 6.7 | 9.0 | 10.3 | 15.0 | 21.2 | 14.9 | 22.8 | 60,112 |
| 2004 [3, 4, 5] . . . . . . . | 63,084 | 7.6 | 9.7 | 10.3 | 14.3 | 20.9 | 14.3 | 22.9 | 58,620 |
| 2005 [4, 5] . . . . . . . . . | 63,414 | 7.2 | 9.3 | 10.5 | 14.7 | 21.0 | 14.1 | 23.2 | 59,317 |
| **BLACK** | | | | | | | | | |
| 1980 . . . . . . . . . . . . | 6,317 | 26.1 | 19.0 | 13.6 | 16.7 | 15.5 | 6.1 | 3.0 | 28,439 |
| 1990 . . . . . . . . . . . . | 7,471 | 27.0 | 15.1 | 13.1 | 14.4 | 16.9 | 7.0 | 6.4 | 31,027 |
| 2000 [2] . . . . . . . . . . | 8,731 | 17.6 | 15.4 | 13.6 | 15.9 | 18.0 | 9.4 | 10.1 | 38,174 |
| 2004 [3, 4, 6] . . . . . . . | 8,906 | 20.8 | 14.9 | 13.1 | 15.4 | 17.1 | 9.3 | 9.4 | 36,323 |
| 2005 [4, 6] . . . . . . . . | 9,051 | 20.5 | 15.6 | 13.3 | 14.7 | 16.4 | 9.2 | 10.2 | 35,464 |
| **ASIAN AND PACIFIC ISLANDER** | | | | | | | | | |
| 1990 . . . . . . . . . . . . | 1,536 | 8.7 | 9.0 | 8.0 | 12.8 | 23.4 | 15.2 | 22.7 | 61,185 |
| 2000 [2] . . . . . . . . . . | 2,982 | 6.9 | 6.9 | 8.1 | 12.6 | 18.9 | 16.0 | 30.6 | 70,981 |
| 2004 [3, 4, 7] . . . . . . . | 3,142 | 6.2 | 7.5 | 8.3 | 13.1 | 20.4 | 13.7 | 30.8 | 67,608 |
| 2005 [4, 7] . . . . . . . . . | 3,208 | 7.8 | 7.7 | 7.0 | 11.8 | 19.7 | 14.4 | 31.6 | 68,957 |
| **HISPANIC ORIGIN [8]** | | | | | | | | | |
| 1980 . . . . . . . . . . . . | 3,235 | 18.5 | 18.9 | 16.1 | 18.6 | 18.3 | 6.2 | 3.6 | 33,021 |
| 1990 . . . . . . . . . . . . | 4,981 | 19.9 | 17.0 | 14.8 | 17.3 | 17.4 | 7.3 | 6.2 | 33,935 |
| 2000 [2] . . . . . . . . . . | 8,017 | 14.5 | 16.1 | 14.3 | 17.8 | 18.8 | 9.5 | 8.9 | 39,043 |
| 2004 [3] . . . . . . . . . . | 9,521 | 15.4 | 17.6 | 15.0 | 16.7 | 17.5 | 8.3 | 9.5 | 36,625 |
| 2005 . . . . . . . . . . . . | 9,868 | 14.7 | 16.3 | 15.2 | 17.4 | 18.2 | 8.9 | 9.3 | 37,867 |

**[Constant dollars based on CPI-U-RS deflator. Families as of March of the following year (60,309 represents 60,309,000).** Based on Current Population Survey, Annual Social and Economic Supplement (ASEC): see text, Sections 1 and 13, and Appendix III. For data collection changes over time, see <http://www.census.gov/hhes/www/income/histinc/hstchg.html>. For definition of median, see Guide to Tabular Presentation]

[1] Includes other races not shown separately.   [2] Data reflect implementation of Census 2000-based population controls and a 28,000 household sample expansion to 78,000 households.   [3] Data have been revised to reflect a correction to the weights in the 2005 ASEC.   [4] Beginning with the 2003 Current Population Survey (CPS), the questionnaire allowed respondents to choose more than one race. For 2002 and later, data represent persons who selected this race group only and excludes persons reporting more than one race.   The CPS in prior years allowed respondents to report only one race group.   See also comments on race in the text for Section 1.   [5] Data represent White alone, which refers to people who reported White and did not report any other race category.   [6] Data represent Black alone, which refers to people who reported Black and did not report any other race category.   [7] Data represent Asian alone, which refers to people who reported Asian and did not report any other race category.   [8] People of Hispanic origin may be of any race.

Source: U.S. Census Bureau, *Current Population Reports*, P60-231; and Internet sites <http://www.census.gov/prod/2006pubs/p60-231.pdf> (released August 2006) and <http://www.census.gov/hhes/www/income/histinc/f23.html>.

**FIGURE 5.6** Money Income of Families—Percent Distribution by Income Level in Constant (2005) Dollars: 1980 to 2005

## WRITING THE INVESTIGATIVE ARGUMENT

The first step in writing an investigative argument is to select a topic to study. Composition students can write successful investigative essays on the media, on campus issues, and on various local concerns. Although you begin with a topic—not a claim—since you have to gather evidence before you can see what

| Characteristic | Total persons | Mean earnings by level of highest degree (dol.) | | | | | | | |
|---|---|---|---|---|---|---|---|---|---|
| | | Not a high school graduate | High school graduate only | Some college, no degree | Associate's | Bachelor's | Master's | Professional | Doctorate |
| **All persons [1] . . .** | **42,064** | **21,484** | **31,286** | **33,009** | **39,746** | **57,181** | **70,186** | **120,978** | **95,565** |
| Age: | | | | | | | | | |
| 25 to 34 years old. . . . | 37,352 | 21,678 | 28,982 | 31,843 | 36,741 | 48,256 | 55,401 | 81,458 | 74,489 |
| 35 to 44 years old. . . . | 48,851 | 24,383 | 36,060 | 41,542 | 42,489 | 63,124 | 75,739 | 134,240 | 94,631 |
| 45 to 54 years old. . . . | 51,058 | 25,801 | 36,562 | 44,201 | 45,145 | 68,131 | 81,419 | 127,818 | 110,410 |
| 55 to 64 years old. . . . | 49,214 | 24,842 | 34,161 | 40,838 | 42,344 | 61,862 | 71,063 | 138,844 | 102,956 |
| 65 years old and over . | 36,497 | 24,703 | 25,678 | 31,938 | 32,021 | 48,245 | 51,519 | 93,672 | 73,417 |
| Sex: | | | | | | | | | |
| Male. . . . . . . . . . . . | 50,110 | 24,985 | 36,839 | 39,375 | 47,190 | 70,898 | 86,966 | 142,282 | 108,941 |
| Female . . . . . . . . . . | 32,899 | 15,315 | 24,234 | 26,527 | 33,276 | 43,127 | 54,772 | 83,031 | 69,251 |
| White [2]. . . . . . . . . . . | 43,139 | 22,289 | 32,223 | 33,465 | 40,373 | 58,652 | 71,321 | 122,885 | 97,254 |
| Male. . . . . . . . . . . . | 51,781 | 25,886 | 38,214 | 40,508 | 48,444 | 73,477 | 89,678 | 144,371 | 110,480 |
| Female . . . . . . . . . . | 32,899 | 15,278 | 24,276 | 26,007 | 33,223 | 42,846 | 54,532 | 82,758 | 69,778 |
| Black [2]. . . . . . . . . . . | 33,333 | 17,439 | 27,179 | 31,318 | 36,445 | 46,502 | 56,398 | 94,049 | 96,092 |
| Male. . . . . . . . . . . . | 35,668 | 19,705 | 29,640 | 32,236 | 38,921 | 53,029 | 63,801 | (B) | (B) |
| Female . . . . . . . . . . | 31,317 | 14,869 | 24,724 | 30,599 | 34,774 | 41,560 | 51,695 | (B) | (B) |
| Hispanic [3]. . . . . . . . . . | 29,910 | 21,303 | 27,604 | 29,384 | 35,348 | 44,696 | 68,040 | 84,512 | (B) |
| Male. . . . . . . . . . . . | 33,040 | 23,923 | 30,932 | 33,643 | 42,140 | 50,805 | 81,069 | 95,907 | (B) |
| Female . . . . . . . . . . | 25,262 | 15,574 | 22,283 | 24,884 | 29,279 | 38,584 | 54,263 | (B) | (B) |

[In dollars. For persons 18 years old and over with earnings. Persons as of March the following year.** Based on Current Population Survey; see text, Section 1, and Appendix III. For definition of mean, see Guide to Tabular Presentation]

B Base figure too small to meet statistical standards for reliability of a derived figure.    [1] Includes other races, not shown separately.    [2] For persons who selected this race group only. See footnote 2, Table 224.    [3] Persons of Hispanic origin may be any race.

Source: U.S Census Bureau, *Current Population Survey.* See Internet site <http://www.census.gov/population/www/socdemo/educ-attn.html>.

**FIGURE 5.7** Mean Earnings by Highest Degree Earned: 2007

it means, you should select a topic that holds your interest and that you may have given some thought to before choosing to write. For example, you may have noticed some clever ads for jeans or beer, or perhaps you are bothered by plans for another shopping area along a major street near your home. Either one of these topics can lead to an effective investigative, or inductive, argument.

## Gathering and Analyzing Evidence

Let's reflect on strategies you will need to use to gather evidence for a study of magazine ads for a particular kind of product (the topic of the sample student paper that follows).

- Select a time frame and a number of representative magazines.
- Have enough magazines to render at least twenty-five ads on the product you are studying.
- Once you decide on the magazines and issues to be used, pull *all* ads for your product. Your task is to draw useful conclusions based on adequate data objectively collected. You can't leave some ads out and have a valid study.

- Study the ads, reflecting on the inferences they allow you to draw. The inferences become the claim of your argument. You may want to take the approach of classifying the ads, that is, grouping them into categories by the various appeals used to sell the product.

More briefly, consider your hunch that your area does not need another shopping mall. What evidence can you gather to support a claim to that effect? You could locate all existing strip or enclosed malls within a 10-mile radius of the proposed new mall site, visit each one, and count the number and types of stores already available. You may discover that there are plenty of malls but that the area really needs a grocery store or a bookstore. So instead of reading to find evidence to support a claim, you are creating the statistics and doing the analysis to guide you to a claim. Just remember to devise objective procedures for collecting evidence so that you do not bias your results.

## Planning and Drafting the Essay

You've done your research and studied the data you've collected; how do you put this kind of argument together? Here are some guidelines to help you draft your essay.

## GUIDELINES for Writing an Investigative Argument

- **Begin with an opening paragraph that introduces your topic in an interesting way.** Possibilities include beginning with a startling statistic or explaining what impact the essay's facts will have on readers.
- **Devote space early in your paper to explaining your methods or procedures, probably in your second or third paragraph.** For example, if you have obtained information through questionnaires or interviews, recount the process: the questions asked, the number of people involved, the basis for selecting the people, and so on.
- **Classify the evidence that you present.** Finding a meaningful organization is part of the originality of your study and will make your argument more forceful. It is the way you see the topic and want readers to see it. If you are studying existing malls, you might begin by listing all of the malls and their locations. But then do not go store by store through each mall. Rather, group the stores by type and provide totals.
- **Consider presenting evidence in several ways, including in charts and tables as well as within paragraphs.** Readers are used to visuals, especially in essays containing statistics.
- **Analyze evidence to build your argument.** Do not ask your reader to do the thinking. No data dumps! Explain how your evidence *is* evidence by discussing the connection between facts and the inferences they support.

## Analyzing Evidence: The Key to an Effective Argument

This is the thinking part of the process. Anyone can count stores or collect ads. What is your point? How does the evidence you have collected actually support your claim? You must guide readers through the evidence. Consider this example:

In a study of selling techniques used in computer ads in business magazines, a student, Brian, found four major selling techniques, one of which he classifies as "corporate emphasis." Brian begins his paragraph on corporate emphasis thus:

> In the technique of corporate emphasis, the advertiser discusses the whole range of products and services that the corporation offers, instead of specific elements. This method relies on the public's positive perception of the company, the company's accomplishments, and its reputation.

Brian then provides several examples of ads in this category, including an IBM ad:

> In one of its eight ads in the study, IBM points to the scientists on its staff who have recently won the Nobel Prize in physics.

But Brian does not stop there. He explains the point of this ad, connecting the ad to the assertion that this technique emphasizes the company's accomplishments:

> The inference we are to draw is that IBM scientists are hard at work right now in their laboratories developing tomorrow's technology to make the world a better place in which to live.

## Preparing Graphics for Your Essay

Tables, bar charts, and pie charts are particularly helpful ways to present statistical evidence you have collected for an inductive argument. One possibility is to create a pie chart showing your classification of ads (or stores or questions on a questionnaire) and the relative amount of each item. For example, suppose you find four selling strategies. You can show in a pie chart the percentage of ads using each of the four strategies.

Computers help even the technically unsophisticated prepare simple charts. You can also do a simple table. When preparing graphics, keep these points in mind:

- Every graphic must be referred to in the text at the appropriate place—where you are discussing the information in the visual. Graphics are not disconnected attachments to an argument. They give a complete set of data in an easy-to-digest form, but some of that data must be discussed in the essay.
- Every graphic (except photographs) needs a label. Use Figure 1, Figure 2, and so forth. Then, in the text refer to each graphic by its label.
- Every graphic needs a title. Always place a title after Figure 1 (and so forth), on the same line, at the top or bottom of your visual.

- In a technically sophisticated world, hand-drawn graphics are not acceptable. Underline the graphic's title line, or place the visual within a box. (Check the tool bar at the top of your screen.) Type elements within tables. Use a ruler or compass to prepare graphics, or learn to use the graphics programs in your computer.

## A CHECKLIST FOR REVISION

- ☐ Have I stated a claim that is precise and appropriate to the data I have collected?
- ☐ Have I fully explained the methodology I used in collecting my data?
- ☐ Have I selected a clear and useful organization?
- ☐ Have I presented and discussed enough specifics to show readers how my data support my conclusions?
- ☐ Have I used graphics to present the data in an effective visual display?
- ☐ Have I revised, edited, and proofread my paper?

# STUDENT ESSAY

## BUYING TIME

### Garrett Berger

Chances are you own at least one wristwatch. Watches allow us immediate access to the correct time. They are indispensable items in our modern world, where, as the saying is, time is money. Today the primary function of a wristwatch does not necessarily guide its design; like clothes, houses, and cars, watches have become fashion statements and a way to flaunt one's wealth.

*Introduction connects to reader.*

To learn how watches are being sold, I surveyed all of the full-page ads from the November issues of four magazines. The first two, *GQ* and *Vogue,* are well-known fashion magazines. *The Robb Report* is a rather new magazine that caters to the overclass. *Forbes* is of course a well-known financial magazine. I was rather surprised at the number of advertisements I found. After surveying 86 ads, marketing 59 brands, I have concluded that today watches are being sold through five main strategies: DESIGN/BRAND appeal, CRAFTSMANSHIP, ASSOCIATION, FASHION appeal, and EMOTIONAL appeal. The percentage of ads using each of these strategies is shown in Figure 1.

*Student explains his methodology of collecting ads. Paragraph concludes with his claim.*

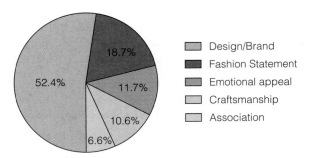

**FIGURE 1** Percentage of Total Ads Using Each Strategy

*Discussion of first category.*

In most DESIGN/BRAND appeal ads, only a picture and the brand name are used. A subset of this category uses the same basic strategy with a slogan or phrases to emphasize something about the brand or product. A Mont Blanc ad shows a watch profile with a contorted metal link band, asking the question "Is that you?" The reputation of the name and the appeal of the design sell the watch. Rolex, perhaps the best-known name in high-end watches, advertises, in *Vogue,* its "Oyster Perpetual Lady-Datejust Pearlmaster." A close-up of the watch face showcases the white, mother-of-pearl dial, sapphire bezel, and diamond-set band. A smaller, more complete picture crouches underneath, showing the watch on its side. The model name is displayed along a gray band that runs near the bottom. The Rolex crest anchors the bottom of the page. Forty-five ads marketing 29 brands use the DESIGN/BRAND strategy. A large picture of the product centered on a solid background is the norm.

*Discussion of second category.*

CRAFTSMANSHIP, the second strategy, focuses on the maker, the horologer, and the technical sides of form and function. Brand heritage and a unique, hand-crafted design are major selling points. All of these ads are targeted at men, appearing in every magazine except *Vogue.* Collector pieces and limited editions were commonly sold using this strategy. The focus is on accuracy and technical excellence. Pictures of the inner works and cutaways, technical information, and explanations of movements and features are popular. Quality and exclusivity are all-important.

*Detailed examples to illustrate second category.*

A Cronoswiss ad from *The Robb Report* is a good example. The top third pictures a horologer, identified as "Gerd-R Lange, master watchmaker and founder of Cronoswiss in Munich," directly below. The middle third of the ad shows a watch, white-faced with a black leather band. The logo and slogan appear next to the watch. The bottom third contains copy beginning with the words "My watches are a hundred years behind the times." The rest explains what that statement means. Mr. Lange apparently believes that technical perfection in horology has already been attained. He also offers his book, *The Fascination of Mechanics,* free of charge along with the "sole distributor for North America" at the bottom. A "Daniel Roth" ad from the same magazine displays the name across the top of a white page; toward the top, left-hand corner a gold buckle and black band lead your eye to the center, where a gold watch with a transparent face displays its inner works exquisitely. Above and to the right, copy explains the exclusive and unique design accomplished by inverting the movement, allowing it to be viewed from above.

The third strategy is to sell the watch by establishing an ASSOCIATION with an object, experience, or person, implying that its value and quality are beyond question. In the six ads I found using this approach, watches are associated with violins, pilots, astronauts, hot air balloons, and a hero of the free world. This is similar to the first strategy, but relies on a reputation other than that of the maker. The watch is presented as being desirable for the connections created in the ad.

*Discussion of third category.*

Parmigiani ran an ad in *The Robb Report* featuring a gold watch with a black face and band illuminated by some unseen source. A blue-tinted violin rises in the background; the rest of the page is black. The brief copy reads: "For those who think a Stradivarius is only a violin. The Parmigiani Toric Chronograph is only a wristwatch." "The Moon Watch" proclaims an Omega ad from *GQ*. Inset on a white background is a picture of an astronaut on the moon saluting the American flag. The silver watch with a black face lies across the lower part of the page. The caption reads: "Speedmaster Professional. The first and only watch worn on the moon." Omega's logo appears at the bottom. Figure 2 shows another Omega use of this strategy.

**FIGURE 2** Example of Association Advertising

The fourth strategy is to present the watch simply as a FASHION statement. In this line of attack, the ads appeal to our need to be current, accepted, to fit in and be like everyone else, or to make a statement, setting us apart from others as hip and cool. The product is presented as a necessary part of our wardrobes. The watch is fashionable and will send the "right" message. Design and style are the foremost concerns; "the look" sells the watch.

Discussion of fourth category.

Techno Marine has an ad in *GQ* which shows a large close-up of a watch running down the entire length of the left side of the page. Two alternate color schemes are pictured on the right, separating small bits of copy. At the bottom on the right are the name and logo. The first words at the top read: "Keeping time—you keep your closet up to the minute, why not your wrist? The latest addition to your watch wardrobe should be the AlphaSport." Longines uses a similar strategy in *Vogue*. Its ad is divided in half lengthwise. On the left is a black-and-white picture of Audrey Hepburn. The right side is white with the Longines' logo at the top and two ladies' watches in the center. Near the bottom is the phrase "Elegance is an Attitude." Retailers appear at the bottom. The same ad ran in *GQ,* but with a man's watch and a picture of Humphrey Bogart. A kind of association is made, but quality and value aren't the overriding concerns. The point is to have an elegant attitude like these fashionable stars did, one that these watches can provide and enhance.

The fifth and final strategy is that of EMOTIONAL appeal. The ads using this approach strive to influence our emotional responses and allege to influence the emotions of others towards us. Their power and appeal are exerted through the feelings they evoke in us. Nine out of ten ads rely on a picture as the main device to trigger an emotional link between the product and the viewer. Copy is scant; words are used mainly to guide the viewer to the advertiser's desired conclusions.

Discussion of fifth category.

A Frederique Constant ad pictures a man, wearing a watch, mulling over a chess game. Above his head are the words "Inner Passion." The man's gaze is odd; he is looking at something on the right side of the page, but a large picture of a watch superimposed over the picture hides whatever it is that he is looking at. So we are led to the watch. The bottom third is white and contains the maker's logo and the slogan "Live your Passion." An ad in *GQ* shows a man holding a woman. He leans against a rock; she reclines in his arms. Their eyes are closed, and both have peaceful, smiling expressions. He is wearing a Tommy Hilfiger watch. The ad spans two pages; a close-up of the watch is presented on the right half of the second page. The only words are the ones in the logo. This is perhaps one of those pictures that are worth a thousand words. The message is he got the girl because he's got the watch.

**Strong conclusion; the effect of watch ads.**

Even more than selling a particular watch, all of these ads focus on building the brand's image. I found many of the ads extremely effective at conveying their messages. Many of the better-known brands favor the comparatively simple DESIGN/BRAND appeal strategy, to reach a broader audience. Lesser-known, high-end makers contribute many of the more specialized strategies. We all count and mark the passing hours and minutes. And society places great importance on time, valuing punctuality. But these ads strive to convince us that having "the right time" means so much more than "the time."

# FOR READING AND ANALYSIS

## EVERY BODY'S TALKING | JOE NAVARRO

Joe Navarro spent more than twenty-five years in the FBI, specializing in counterintelligence and profiling. He is recognized as an authority on nonverbal messages, especially given off by those who are lying, and he continues to consult to government and industry. He has also turned his expertise to poker and has published, with Marvin Karlines, *Read 'Em and Reap* (2006), a guide to reading the nonverbal messages from poker opponents. The following essay appeared in the *Washington Post* on June 24, 2008.

**PREREADING QUESTIONS** What does the term "counterintelligence" mean? How much attention do you give to body language messages from others?

Picture this: I was sailing the Caribbean for three days with a group of 1 friends and their spouses, and everything seemed perfect. The weather was beautiful, the ocean diaphanous blue, the food exquisite; our evenings together were full of laughter and good conversation.

Things were going so well that one friend said to the group, "Let's do this 2 again next year." I happened to be across from him and his wife as he spoke those words. In the cacophony of resounding replies of "Yes!" and "Absolutely!" I noticed that my friend's wife made a fist under her chin as she grasped her necklace. This behavior stood out to me as powerfully as if someone had shouted, "Danger!"

I watched the words and gestures of the other couples at the table, and 3 everyone seemed ecstatic—everyone but one, that is. She continued to smile, but her smile was tense.

Her husband has treated me as a brother for more than 15 years, and I 4 consider him the dearest of friends. At that moment I knew that things between him and his wife were turning for the worse. I did not pat myself on the back for making these observations. I was saddened.

For 25 years I worked as a paid observer. I was a special agent for the FBI 5 specializing in counterintelligence—specifically, catching spies. For me, observing human behavior is like having software running in the background, doing its job—no conscious effort needed. And so on that wonderful cruise, I made a "thin-slice assessment" (that's what we call it) based on just a few significant behaviors. Unfortunately, it turned out to be right: Within six months of our return, my friend's wife filed for divorce, and her husband discovered painfully that she had been seeing someone else for quite a while.

When I am asked what is the most reliable means of determining the 6 health of a relationship, I always say that words don't matter. It's all in the language of the body. The nonverbal behaviors we all transmit tell others, in real time, what we think, what we feel, what we yearn for or what we intend.

Now I am embarking on another cruise, wondering what insights I will 7 have about my travel companions and their relationships. No matter what, this promises to be a fascinating trip, a journey for the mind and the soul. I am with a handful of dear friends and 3,800 strangers, all headed for Alaska; for an observer it does not get any better than this.

While lining up to board on our first day, I notice just ahead of me a couple 8 who appear to be in their early 30s. They are obviously Americans (voice, weight and demeanor).

Not so obvious is their dysfunctional relationship. He is standing stoically, 9 shoulders wide, looking straight ahead. She keeps whispering loudly to him, but she is not facing forward. She violates his space as she leans into him. Her face is tense and her lips are narrow slivers each time she engages him with what clearly appears to be a diatribe. He occasionally nods his head but avoids contact with her. He won't let his hips near her as they start to walk side by side. He reminds me of Bill and Hillary Clinton walking toward the Marine One helicopter immediately after the Monica Lewinsky affair: looking straight ahead, as much distance between them as possible.

| TORSO | ARMS | HANDS AND FINGERS | FEET AND LEGS |
|---|---|---|---|
| **LEANING AWAY FROM SOMEONE:** Means we dislike or disagree with them. / **LEANING TOWARD SOMEONE:** Means we like or agree with them. | **FINGERTIPS SPREAD APART ON A SURFACE:** A display of confidence and authority. | **THUMBS UP:** A good indication of positive thoughts. | **JIGGLING/KICKING FOOT:** Indicates discomfort. |
| **SPLAYING OUT:** A sign of comfort becomes a territorial or dominance display when there are serious issues being discussed. | **ARMS AKIMBO:** Establishes dominance or communicates there are 'issues.' | **STEEPLING:** (FINGERTIP TO FINGERTIP) A powerful display of confidence. | **CROSSING LEGS:** Indicates we are comfortable. |
| **CROSSED ARMS:** Suddenly crossing arms tightly is a sign of discomfort. | **ARMS BEHIND THE BACK:** Says "don't draw near" —keeps people at bay. | **NECK TOUCHING:** Indicates emotional discomfort, doubt or insecurity. | **TOE POINTS UPWARD:** Signals a good mood. |

Illustrations by Peter Arkle. Reprinted by permission.

10    I think everyone can decipher this one from afar because we have all seen situations like this. What most people will miss is something I have seen this young man do twice now, which portends poorly for both of them. Every time she looks away, he "disses" her. He smirks and rolls his eyes, even as she stands beside him. He performs his duties, pulling their luggage along; I suspect he likes to have her luggage nearby as a barrier between them. I won't witness the dissolution of their marriage, but I know it will happen, for the research behind this is fairly robust. When two people in a relationship have contempt for each other, the marriage will not last.

When it comes to relationships and courtship behaviors, the list of useful 11 cues is long. Most of these behaviors we learned early when interacting with our mothers. When we look at loving eyes, our own eyes get larger, our pupils dilate, our facial muscles relax, our lips become full and warm, our skin becomes more pliable, our heads tilt. These behaviors stay with us all of our lives.

I watched two lovers this morning in the dining room. Two young people, 12 perhaps in their late 20s, mirror each other, staring intently into each other's eyes, chin on hand, head slightly tilted, nose flaring with each breath. They are trying to absorb each other visually and tactilely as they hold hands across the table.

Over time, those who remain truly in love will show even more indicators 13 of mirroring. They may dress the same or even begin to look alike as they adopt each other's nonverbal expressions as a sign of synchrony and empathy. They will touch each other with kind hands that touch fully, not with the finger-tips of the less caring.

They will mirror each other in ways that are almost imperceptible; they will 14 have similar blink rates and breathing rates, and they will sit almost identically. They will look at the same scenery and not speak, merely look at each other and take a deep breath to reset their breathing synchrony. They don't have to talk. They are in harmony physically, mentally and emotionally, just as a baby is in exquisite synchrony with its mother who is tracing his every expression and smile.

As I walk through the ship on the first night, I can see the nonverbals of 15 courtship. There is a beautiful woman, tall, slender, smoking a cigarette outside. Two men are talking to her, both muscular, handsome, interested. She has crossed her legs as she talks to them, an expression of her comfort. As she holds her cigarette, the inside of her wrist turns toward her newfound friends. Her interest and comfort with them resounds, but she is favoring one of them. As he speaks to her, she preens herself by playing with her hair. I am not sure he is getting the message that she prefers him; in the end, I am sure it will all get sorted out.

At the upscale lounge, a man is sitting at the bar talking animatedly to the 16 woman next to him and looking at everyone who walks by. The woman has begun the process of ignoring him, but he does not get it. After he speaks to her a few times, she gathers her purse and places it on her lap. She has turned slightly away from him and now avoids eye contact. He has no clue; he thinks he is cool by commenting on the women who pass by. She is verbally and non-verbally indifferent.

The next night it is more of the same. This time, I see two people who just 17 met talking gingerly. Gradually they lean more and more into each other. She is now dangling her sandal from her toes. I am not sure he knows it. Perhaps he sees it all in her face, because she is smiling, laughing and relaxed. Communication is fluid, and neither wants the conversation to end. She is extremely interested.

18      All of these individuals are carrying on a dialogue in nonverbals. The socially adept will learn to read and interpret the signs accurately. Others will make false steps or pay a high price for not being observant. They may end up like my friend on the Caribbean cruise, who missed the clues of deceit and indifference.

19      This brings me back to my friend and his new wife, who are on this wonderful voyage. They have been on board for four days, and they are a delight individually and together. He lovingly looks at her; she stares at him with love and admiration. When she holds his hand at dinner, she massages it ever so gently. Theirs is a strong marriage. They don't have to tell me. I can sense it and observe it. I am happy for them and for myself. I can see cues of happiness, and they are unmistakable. You can't ask for more.

Source: From *The Washington Post*, June 24, 2008. Reprinted by permission of the author.

### QUESTIONS FOR READING

1.   What is Navarro's subject? (Do not answer "taking cruises"!)
2.   What clues are offered to support the conclusion that the two cruise couples' relationships are about to dissolve?
3.   What are the nonverbal messages that reveal loving relationships?
4.   What nonverbal messages should the man in the lounge be observing?

### QUESTIONS FOR REASONING AND ANALYSIS

5.   What is Navarro's claim?
6.   What kind of evidence does he provide?
7.   How do the illustrations contribute to the argument? What is effective about the author's opening?

### QUESTIONS FOR REFLECTION AND WRITING

8.   Has the author convinced you that nonverbal language reveals our thoughts and feelings? Why or why not?
9.   Can you "read" the nonverbal language of your instructors? Take some time to analyze each of your instructors. What have you learned? (You might also reflect on what messages you may be sending in class.)

For all investigative essays—inductive arguments—follow the guidelines in this chapter and use the student essay as your model. Remember that you will need to explain your methods for collecting data, to classify evidence and present it in several formats, and also to explain its significance for readers. Just collecting data does not create an argument. Here are some possible topics to explore:

1.  Study print ads for one type of product (e.g., cars, cosmetics, cigarettes) to draw inferences about the dominant techniques used to sell that product. Remember that the more ads you study, the more support you have for your inferences. You should study at least twenty-five ads.

2.  Study print ads for one type of product as advertised in different types of magazines clearly directed to different audiences to see how (or if) selling techniques change with a change in audience. (Remember: To demonstrate no change in techniques can be just as interesting a conclusion as finding changes.) Study at least twenty-five ads, in a balanced number from the different magazines.

3.  Select a major figure currently in the news and conduct a study of bias in one of the newsmagazines (e.g., *Time, U.S. News & World Report,* or *Newsweek*) or a newspaper. Use at least eight issues of the magazine or newspaper from the last six months and study all articles on your figure in each of those issues. To determine bias, look at the amount of coverage, the location (front pages or back pages), the use of photos (flattering or unflattering), and the language of the articles.

4.  Conduct a study of amounts of violence on TV by analyzing, for one week, all prime-time programs that may contain violence. (That is, eliminate sitcoms and decide whether you want to include or exclude news programs.) Devise some classification system for types of violence based on your prior TV viewing experience before beginning your study—but be prepared to alter or add to your categories based on your viewing of shows. Note the number of times each violent act occurs. You may want to consider the total length of time (per program, per night, per type of violent act) of violence during the week you study. Give credit to any authors in this text or other publications for any ideas you borrow from their articles.

5.  As an alternative to topic 4, study the number and types of violent acts in children's programs on Saturday mornings. (This and topic 4 are best handled if you can record and then replay the programs several times.)

6.  Conduct a survey and analyze the results on some campus issue or current public policy issue. Prepare questions that are without bias and include questions to get information about the participants so that you can correlate answers with the demographics of your participants (e.g., age, gender, race, religion, proposed major in college, political affiliation, or whatever else you think is important to the topic studied). Decide whether you want to survey students only or both students and faculty. Plan how you are going to reach each group.

**143**

# CHAPTER 6

# Learning More about Argument: Induction, Deduction, Analogy, and Logical Fallacies

**READ:** What is the situation? What is Petey's reaction to the snowman? What is the reaction of the two children in the last frame?

**REASON:** What is surprising about the responses in the last frame? Is there any basis for their conclusions?

**REFLECT/WRITE:** What makes the cartoon amusing? What is its more serious message?

You can build on your knowledge of the basics of argument, examined in Chapter 3, by understanding some traditional forms of argument: induction, deduction, and analogy. It is also important to recognize arguments that do not meet the standards of good logic.

# INDUCTION

*Induction is the process by which we reach inferences—opinions based on facts,* or on a combination of facts and less debatable inferences. The inductive process moves from particular to general, from support to assertion. We base our inferences on the facts we have gathered and studied. In general, the more evidence, the more convincing the argument. No one wants to debate tomorrow's sunrise; the evidence for counting on it is too convincing. Most inferences, though, are drawn from less evidence, so we need to examine these arguments closely to judge their reasonableness.

The pattern of induction looks like this:

**EVIDENCE:** There is the dead body of Smith. Smith was shot in his bedroom between the hours of 11:00 P.M. and 2:00 A.M., according to the coroner. Smith was shot by a .32-caliber pistol. The pistol left in the bedroom contains Jones's fingerprints. Jones was seen, by a neighbor, entering the Smith home at around 11:00 the night of Smith's death. A coworker heard Smith and Jones arguing in Smith's office the morning of the day Smith died.

**CLAIM:** Jones killed Smith.

The facts are presented. The jury infers that Jones is a murderer. Unless there is a confession or a trustworthy eyewitness, the conclusion is an inference, not a fact. This is the most logical explanation; that is, the conclusion meets the standards of simplicity and frequency while accounting for all of the known evidence.

The following paragraph illustrates the process of induction. In their book *Discovering Dinosaurs,* authors Mark Norell, Eugene Gaffney, and Lowell Dingus answer the question "Did dinosaurs really rule the world?"

> For almost 170 million years, from the Late Triassic to the end of the Cretaceous, there existed dinosaurs of almost every body form imaginable: small carnivores, such as *Compsognathus* and *Ornitholestes,* ecologically equivalent to today's foxes and coyotes; medium-sized carnivores, such as *Velociraptor* and the troodontids, analogous to lions and tigers; and the monstrous carnivores with no living analogs, such as *Tyrannosaurus* and *Allosaurus.* Included among the ornithischians and the elephantine sauropods are terrestrial herbivores of diverse body form. By the end of the Jurassic, dinosaurs had even taken to the skies. The only habitats that dinosaurs did not dominate during the Mesozoic were aquatic. Yet, there were marine representatives, such as the primitive toothed bird *Hesperornis.* Like penguins, these birds were flightless, specialized for diving, and probably had to return to land to reproduce. In light of this broad morphologic diversity [number of

body forms], dinosaurs did "rule the planet" as the dominant life form on
Earth during most of the Mesozoic [era that includes the Triassic, Jurassic, and
Cretaceous periods, 248 to 65 million years ago].

Observe that the writers organize evidence by type of dinosaur to demonstrate
the range and diversity of these animals. A good inductive argument is based
on a sufficient volume of *relevant* evidence. The basic shape of this inductive
argument is illustrated in Figure 6.1.

| | |
|---|---|
| **CLAIM:** | Dinosaurs were the dominant life form during the Mesozoic era. |
| **GROUNDS:** | The facts presented in the paragraph. |
| **ASSUMPTION (WARRANT):** | The facts are representative, revealing dinosaur diversity. |

**FIGURE 6.1** The Shape of an Inductive Argument

## COLLABORATIVE EXERCISE: Induction

With your class partner or in small groups, make a list of facts that could be used to
support each of the following inferences:

1. Whole-wheat bread is nutritious.
2. Fido must have escaped under the fence during the night.
3. Sue must be planning to go away for the weekend.
4. Students who do not hand in all essay assignments fail Dr. Bradshaw's English
   class.
5. The price of Florida oranges will go up in grocery stores next year.

# DEDUCTION

Although induction can be described as an argument that moves from particular to general, from facts to inference, deduction cannot accurately be described
as the reverse. Deductive arguments are more complex. *Deduction is the reasoning process that draws a conclusion from the logical relationship of two assertions, usually one broad judgment or definition and one more specific assertion, often an inference.*
Suppose, on the way out of American history class, you say, "Abraham Lincoln
certainly was a great leader." Someone responds with the expected question
"Why do you think so?" You explain: "He was great because he performed
with courage and a clear purpose in a time of crisis." Your explanation contains
a conclusion and an assertion about Lincoln (an inference) in support. But
behind your explanation rests an idea about leadership, in the terms of deduction, *a premise.* The argument's basic shape is illustrated in Figure 6.2.

| **CLAIM:** | Lincoln was a great leader. |
|---|---|
| **GROUNDS:** | 1. People who perform with courage and clear purpose in a crisis are great leaders. |
| | 2. Lincoln was a person who performed with courage and a clear purpose in a crisis. |
| **ASSUMPTION (WARRANT):** | The relationship of the two reasons leads, logically, to the conclusion. |

**FIGURE 6.2** The Shape of a Deductive Argument

Traditionally, the deductive argument is arranged somewhat differently from these sentences about Lincoln. The two reasons are called *premises;* the broader one, called the *major premise,* is written first and the more specific one, the *minor premise,* comes next. The premises and conclusion are expressed to make clear that assertions are being made about categories or classes. To illustrate:

| **MAJOR PREMISE:** | All people who perform with courage and a clear purpose in a crisis are great leaders. |
|---|---|
| **MINOR PREMISE:** | Lincoln was a person who performed with courage and a clear purpose in a crisis. |
| **CONCLUSION:** | Lincoln was a great leader. |

If these two premises are correctly, that is, logically, constructed, then the conclusion follows logically, and the deductive argument is *valid.* This does not mean that the conclusion is necessarily *true.* It does mean that if you accept the truth of the premises, then you must accept the truth of the conclusion, because in a valid argument the conclusion follows logically, necessarily. How do we know that the conclusion must follow if the argument is logically constructed? Let's think about what each premise is saying and then diagram each one to represent each assertion visually. The first premise says that all people who act a particular way are people who fit into the category called "great leaders":

The second premise says that Lincoln, a category of one, belongs in the category of people who act in the same particular way that the first premise describes:

If we put the two diagrams together, we have the following set of circles, demonstrating that the conclusion follows from the premises:

We can also make negative and qualified assertions in a deductive argument. For example:

| **PREMISE:** | No cowards can be great leaders. |
|---|---|
| **PREMISE:** | Falstaff was a coward. |
| **CONCLUSION:** | Falstaff was not a great leader. |

Or, to reword the conclusion to make the deductive pattern clearer: No Falstaff (no member of this class) is a great leader. Diagramming to test for validity, we find that the first premise says no A's are B's:

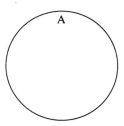
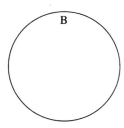

The second premise asserts all C's are A's:

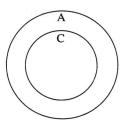

Put together, we see that the conclusion follows necessarily from the premises: No C's can possibly be members of class B.

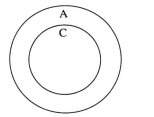 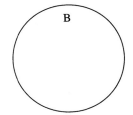

Some deductive arguments merely look right, but the two premises do not lead logically to the conclusion that is asserted. We must read each argument carefully or diagram each one to make certain that the conclusion follows from the premises. Consider the following argument: *Unions must be communistic because they want to control wages.* The sentence contains a conclusion and one reason, or premise. From these two parts of a deductive argument we can also determine the unstated premise, just as we could with the Lincoln argument: *Communists want to control wages.* If we use circles to represent the three categories of people in the argument and diagram the argument, we see a different result from the previous diagrams:

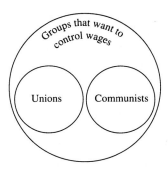

Diagramming the argument reveals that it is invalid; that is, it is not logically constructed because the statements do not require that the union circle be placed inside the communist circle. We cannot draw the conclusion we want from any two premises, only from those that provide a logical basis from which a conclusion can be reached.

We must first make certain that deductive arguments are properly constructed or valid. But suppose the logic works and yet you do not agree with the claim? Your complaint, then, must be with one of the premises, a judgment or inference that you do not accept as true. Consider the following argument:

| | |
|---|---|
| **MAJOR PREMISE:** | (All) dogs make good pets. |
| **MINOR PREMISE:** | Fido is a dog. |
| **CONCLUSION:** | Fido will make a good pet. |

This argument is valid. (Diagram it; your circles will fit into one another just as with the Lincoln argument.) However, you are not prepared to agree, necessarily, that Fido will make a good pet. The problem is with the major premise. For the argument to work, the assertion must be about *all* dogs, but we know that not all dogs will be good pets.

When composing a deductive argument, your task will be to defend the truth of your premises. Then, if your argument is valid (logically constructed), readers will have no alternative but to agree with your conclusion. If you disagree with someone else's logically constructed argument, then you must show why one of the premises is not true. Your counterargument will seek to discredit one (or both) of the premises. The Fido argument can be discredited by your producing examples of dogs that have not made good pets.

A deductive argument can serve as the core of an essay, an essay that supports the argument's claim by developing support for each of the premises. Since the major premise is either a broad judgment or a definition, it will need to be defended on the basis of an appeal to values or beliefs that the writer expects readers to share. The minor premise, usually an inference about a particular situation (or person), would be supported by relevant evidence, as with any inductive argument. You can see this process at work in the Declaration of Independence. Questions follow the Declaration to guide your analysis of this famous example of the deductive process.

## THE DECLARATION OF INDEPENDENCE |

In Congress, July 4, 1776
The unanimous declaration of the thirteen
United States of America

1   When in the course of human events, it becomes necessary for one people to dissolve the political bands which have connected them with another, and to assume among the powers of the earth, the separate and equal station to which the Laws of Nature and of Nature's God entitle them, a decent respect

to the opinions of mankind requires that they should declare the causes which impel them to the separation.

We hold these truths to be self-evident, that all men are created equal, that they are endowed by their Creator with certain unalienable rights, that among these are life, liberty and the pursuit of happiness. That to secure these rights, governments are instituted among men, deriving their just powers from the consent of the governed. That whenever any form of government becomes destructive of these ends, it is the right of the people to alter or to abolish it, and to institute new government, laying its foundation on such principles and organizing its powers in such form, as to them shall seem most likely to effect their safety and happiness. Prudence, indeed, will dictate that governments long established should not be changed for light and transient causes; and accordingly all experience hath shown, that mankind are more disposed to suffer, while evils are sufferable, than to right themselves by abolishing the forms to which they are accustomed. But when a long train of abuses and usurpations, pursuing invariably the same object evinces a design to reduce them under absolute despotism, it is their right, it is their duty, to throw off such government, and to provide new guards for their future security. Such has been the patient sufferance of these Colonies; and such is now the necessity which constrains them to alter their former systems of government. The history of the present King of Great Britain is a history of repeated injuries and usurpations, all having in direct object the establishment of an absolute tyranny over these States. To prove this, let facts be submitted to a candid world.

He has refused his assent to laws, the most wholesome and necessary for the public good.

He has forbidden his Governors to pass laws of immediate and pressing importance, unless suspended in their operation till his assent should be obtained; and when so suspended, he has utterly neglected to attend to them.

He has refused to pass other laws for the accommodation of large districts of people, unless those people would relinquish the right of representation in the Legislature, a right inestimable to them and formidable to tyrants only.

He has called together legislative bodies at places unusual, uncomfortable, and distant from the depository of their public records, for the sole purpose of fatiguing them into compliance with his measures.

He has dissolved representative houses repeatedly, for opposing with manly firmness his invasions on the rights of the people.

He has refused for a long time, after such dissolutions, to cause others to be elected; whereby the legislative powers, incapable of annihilation, have returned to the people at large for their exercise; the State remaining in the meantime exposed to all the dangers of invasion from without and convulsions within.

He has endeavoured to prevent the population of these States; for that purpose obstructing the laws of naturalization of foreigners; refusing to pass others to encourage their migration hither, and raising the conditions of new appropriations of lands.

10    He has obstructed the administration of justice, by refusing his assent to laws for establishing judiciary powers.

11    He has made judges dependent on his will alone, for the tenure of their offices, and the amount and payment of their salaries.

12    He has erected a multitude of new offices, and sent hither swarms of officers to harass our people, and eat out their substance.

13    He has kept among us, in times of peace, standing armies without the consent of our legislatures.

14    He has affected to render the military independent of and superior to the civil power.

15    He has combined with others to subject us to a jurisdiction foreign to our constitution, and unacknowledged by our laws; giving his assent to their acts of pretended legislation:

16    For quartering large bodies of armed troops among us:

17    For protecting them, by a mock trial, from punishment for any murders which they should commit on the inhabitants of these States:

18    For cutting off our trade with all parts of the world:

19    For imposing taxes on us without our consent:

20    For depriving us, in many cases, of the benefits of trial by jury:

21    For transporting us beyond seas to be tried for pretended offences:

22    For abolishing the free system of English laws in a neighbouring Province, establishing therein an arbitrary government, and enlarging its boundaries so as to render it at once an example and fit instrument for introducing the same absolute rule into these Colonies:

23    For taking away our Charters, abolishing our most valuable laws, and altering fundamentally the forms of our governments:

24    For suspending our own Legislatures, and declaring themselves invested with power to legislate for us in all cases whatsoever.

25    He has abdicated government here, by declaring us out of his protection and waging war against us.

26    He has plundered our seas, ravaged our coasts, burnt our towns, and destroyed the lives of our people.

27    He is at this time transporting large armies of foreign mercenaries to complete the works of death, desolation and tyranny, already begun with circumstances of cruelty and perfidy scarcely paralleled in the most barbarous ages, and totally unworthy the head of a civilized nation.

28    He has constrained our fellow citizens taken captive on the high seas to bear arms against their country, to become the executioners of their friends and brethren, or to fall themselves by their hands.

29    He has excited domestic insurrections amongst us, and has endeavoured to bring on the inhabitants of our frontiers, the merciless Indian savages, whose known rule of warfare, is an undistinguished destruction of all ages, sexes, and conditions.

30    In every stage of these oppressions we have petitioned for redress in the most humble terms; our repeated petitions have been answered only by repeated injury. A prince whose character is thus marked by every act which may define a tyrant is unfit to be the ruler of a free people.

Nor have we been wanting in attention to our British brethren. We have ₃₁ warned them from time to time of attempts by their legislature to extend an unwarrantable jurisdiction over us. We have reminded them of the circumstances of our emigration and settlement here. We have appealed to their native justice and magnanimity, and we have conjured them by the ties of our common kindred to disavow these usurpations, which would inevitably interrupt our connections and correspondence. They too have been deaf to the voice of justice and of consanguinity. We must, therefore, acquiesce in the necessity, which denounces our separation, and hold them, as we hold the rest of mankind, enemies in war, in peace friends.

We, therefore, the Representatives of the United States of America, in ₃₂ General Congress assembled, appealing to the Supreme Judge of the world for the rectitude of our intentions, do, in the name, and by the authority of the good people of these Colonies, solemnly publish and declare, That these United Colonies are, and of right ought to be Free and Independent States; that they are absolved from all allegiance to the British Crown, and that all political connection between them and the State of Great Britain, is and ought to be totally dissolved; and that as Free and Independent States, they have full power to levy war, conclude peace, contract alliances, establish commerce, and to do all other acts and things which Independent States may of right do. And for the support of this declaration, with a firm reliance on the protection of Divine Providence, we mutually pledge to each other our lives, our fortunes, and our sacred honor.

## QUESTIONS FOR ANALYSIS

1. What is the Declaration's central deductive argument? State the argument in the shape illustrated above: major premise, minor premise, conclusion. Construct a valid argument. If necessary, draw circles representing each of the three terms in the argument to check for validity. (*Hint:* Start with the claim "George III's government should be overthrown.")

2. Which paragraphs are devoted to supporting the major premise? What kind of support has been given?

3. Which paragraphs are devoted to supporting the minor premise? What kind of support has been given?

4. Why has more support been given for one premise than the other?

## EXERCISES: Completing and Evaluating Deductive Arguments

Turn each of the following statements into valid deductive arguments. (You have the conclusion and one premise, so you will have to determine the missing premise that would complete the argument. Draw circles if necessary to test for validity.) Then decide which arguments have premises that could be supported. Note the kind of support that might be provided. Explain why you think some arguments have insupportable premises. Here is an example:

| | |
|---|---|
| **PREMISE:** | All Jesuits are priests. |
| **PREMISE:** | No women are priests. |
| **CONCLUSION:** | No women are Jesuits. |

Since the circle for women must be placed outside the circle for priests, it must also be outside the circle for Jesuits. Hence the argument is valid. The first premise is true by definition; the term *Jesuit* refers to an order of Roman Catholic priests. The second premise is true for the Roman Catholic Church, so if the term *priest* is used only to refer to people with a religious vocation in the Roman Catholic Church, then the second premise is also true by definition.

1. Mrs. Ferguson is a good teacher because she can explain the subject matter clearly.
2. Segregated schools are unconstitutional because they are unequal.
3. Michael must be a good driver because he drives fast.
4. The media clearly have a liberal bias because they make fun of religious fundamentalists.

## ANALOGY

*The argument from analogy is an argument based on comparison.* Analogies assert that since A and B are alike in several ways, they must be alike in another way as well. The argument from analogy concludes with an inference, an assertion of a significant similarity in the two items being compared. The other similarities serve as evidence in support of the inference. The shape of an argument by analogy is illustrated in Figure 6.3.

Although analogy is sometimes an effective approach to an issue because clever, imaginative comparisons are often moving, analogy is not as rigorously logical as either induction or deduction. Frequently an analogy is based on only two or three points of comparison, whereas a sound inductive argument presents many examples to support its conclusion. Further, to be convincing, the points of comparison must be fundamental to the two items being compared. An argument for a county leash law for cats developed by analogy with dogs may cite the following similarities:

| | |
|---|---|
| **GROUNDS:** | A has characteristics 1, 2, 3, and 4. |
| | B has characteristics 1, 2, and 3. |
| **CLAIM:** | B has characteristic 4 (as well). |
| **ASSUMPTION** | If B has three characteristics in common with A, it must have |
| **(WARRANT):** | the key fourth characteristic as well. |

**FIGURE 6.3** The Shape of an Argument by Analogy

- Cats are pets, just like dogs.
- Cats live in residential communities, just like dogs.
- Cats can mess up other people's yards, just like dogs.
- Cats, if allowed to run free, can disturb the peace (fighting, howling at night), just like dogs.

Does it follow that cats should be required to walk on a leash, just like dogs? If such a county ordinance were passed, would it be enforceable? Have you ever tried to walk a cat on a leash? In spite of legitimate similarities brought out by the analogy, the conclusion does not logically follow because the arguer is overlooking a fundamental difference in the two animals' personalities. Dogs can be trained to a leash; most cats (Siamese are one exception) cannot be so trained. Such thinking will produce sulking cats and scratched owners. But the analogy, delivered passionately to the right audience, could lead community activists to lobby for a new law.

Observe that the problem with the cat-leash-law analogy is not in the similarities asserted about the items being compared but rather in the underlying assumption that the similarities logically support the argument's conclusion. A good analogy asserts many points of comparison and finds likenesses that are essential parts of the nature or purpose of the two items being compared. The best way to challenge another's analogy is to point out a fundamental difference in the nature or purpose of the compared items. For all of their similarities, when it comes to walking on a leash, cats are *not* like dogs.

## EXERCISES: Analogy

Analyze the following analogies. List the stated and/or implied points of comparison and the conclusion in the pattern illustrated on page 154. Then judge each argument's logic and effectiveness as a persuasive technique. If the argument is not logical, state the fundamental difference in the two compared items. If the argument could be persuasive, describe the kind of audience that might be moved by it.

1. College newspapers should not be under the supervision or control of a faculty sponsor. Fortunately, no governmental sponsor controls the *New York Times,* or we would no longer have a free press in this country. We need a free college press, too, one that can attack college policies when they are wrong.

2. Let's recognize that college athletes are really professional and start paying them properly. College athletes get a free education, and spending money from boosters. They are required to attend practices and games, and—if they play football or basketball—they bring in huge revenues for their "organization." College coaches are also paid enormous salaries, just like professional coaches, and often college coaches are tapped to coach professional teams. The only difference: The poor college athletes don't get those big salaries and huge signing bonuses.

3. Just like any business, the federal government must be made to balance its budget. No company could continue to operate in the red as the government does and expect to be successful. A constitutional amendment requiring a balanced federal budget is long overdue.

# LOGICAL FALLACIES

A thorough study of argument needs to include a study of logical fallacies because so many "arguments" fail to meet standards of sound logic and good sense. Why do people offer arguments that aren't sensible?

## Causes of Illogic

### Ignorance

One frequent cause for illogical debate is a lack of knowledge of the subject. Some people have more information than others. The younger you are, the less you can be expected to know about complex issues. On the other hand, if you want to debate a complex or technical issue, then you cannot use ignorance as an excuse. Instead, read as much as you can, listen carefully to discussions, ask questions, and select topics about which you have knowledge or will research before writing.

### Egos

Ego problems are another cause of weak arguments. Those with low self-esteem often have difficulty in debates because they attach themselves to their ideas and then feel personally attacked when someone disagrees with them. Remember: Self-esteem is enhanced when others applaud our knowledge and thoughtfulness, not our irrationality.

### Prejudices

The prejudices and biases that we carry around, having absorbed them "ages ago" from family and community, are also sources of irrationality. Prejudices range from the worst ethnic, religious, or sexist stereotypes to political views we have adopted uncritically (Democrats are all bleeding hearts; Republicans are all rich snobs) to perhaps less serious but equally insupportable notions (if it's in print, it must be right). People who see the world through distorted lenses cannot possibly assess facts intelligently and reason logically from them.

### A Need for Answers

Finally, many bad arguments stem from a human need for answers—any answers—to the questions that deeply concern us. We want to control our world because that makes us feel secure, and having answers makes us feel in control. This need can lead to illogic from oversimplifying issues.

Based on these causes of illogic, we can usefully divide fallacies into (1) oversimplifying the issue and (2) ignoring the issue by substituting emotion for reason.

## Fallacies That Result from Oversimplifying

### Errors in Generalizing

Errors in generalizing include overstatement and hasty or faulty generalization. All have in common an error in the inductive pattern of argument. The inference drawn from the evidence is unwarranted, either because too broad a generalization is made or because the generalization is drawn from incomplete or incorrect evidence.

*Overstatement* occurs when the argument's assertion is unqualified—referring to all members of a category. Overstatements often result from stereotyping, giving the same traits to everyone in a group. Overstatements are frequently signaled by words such as *all, every, always, never,* and *none.* But remember that assertions such as "children love clowns" are understood to refer to "all children," even though the word *all* does not appear in the sentence. It is the writer's task to qualify statements appropriately, using words such as *some, many,* or *frequently,* as appropriate.

Overstatements are discredited by finding only one exception to disprove the assertion. One frightened child who starts to cry when the clown approaches will destroy the argument. Here is another example:

- Lawyers are only interested in making money.

  (What about lawyers who work to protect consumers, or public defenders who represent those unable to pay for a lawyer?)

*Hasty or faulty generalizations* may be qualified assertions, but they still oversimplify by arguing from insufficient evidence or by ignoring some relevant evidence. For example:

- Political life must lead many to excessive drinking. In the last six months the paper has written about five members of Congress who either have confessed to alcoholism or have been arrested on DUI charges.

  (Five is not a large enough sample from which to generalize about *many* politicians. Also, the five in the newspaper are not a representative sample; they have made the news because of their drinking.)

### Forced Hypothesis

The *forced hypothesis* is also an error in inductive reasoning. The explanation (hypothesis) offered is "forced," or illogical, because either (1) sufficient evidence does not exist to draw any conclusion or (2) the evidence can be explained more simply or more sensibly by a different hypothesis. This fallacy often results from not considering other possible explanations. You discredit a forced hypothesis by providing alternative conclusions that are more sensible than or just as sensible as the one offered. Consider this example:

- Professor Redding's students received either A's or B's last semester. He must be an excellent teacher.

  (The grades alone cannot support this conclusion. Professor Redding could be an excellent teacher; he could have started with excellent students; he could be an easy grader.)

### Non Sequitur

The term *non sequitur,* meaning literally "it does not follow," could apply to all illogical arguments, but the term is usually reserved for those in which the conclusions are not logically connected to the reasons. In a hasty generalization, for example, there is a connection between support (five politicians in the news) and conclusion (many politicians with drinking problems), just not a convincing connection. With the *non sequitur* there is no recognizable connection, either because (1) whatever connection the arguer sees is not made clear to others or because (2) the evidence or reasons offered are irrelevant to the conclusion. For example:

- Donna will surely get a good grade in physics; she earned an A in her biology class.

  (Doing well in one course, even one science course, does not support the conclusion that the student will get a good grade in another course. If Donna is not good at math, she definitely will not do well in physics.)

### Slippery Slope

The *slippery slope* argument asserts that we should not proceed with or permit A because, if we do, the terrible consequences X, Y, and Z will occur. This type of argument oversimplifies by assuming, without evidence and usually by ignoring historical examples, existing laws, or any reasonableness in people, that X, Y, and Z will follow inevitably from A. This kind of argument rests on the belief that most people will not want the final, awful Z to occur. The belief, however accurate, does not provide a sufficiently good reason for avoiding A. One of the best-known examples of slippery slope reasoning can be found in the gun-control debate:

- If we allow the government to register handguns, next it will register hunting rifles; then it will prohibit all citizen ownership of guns, thereby creating a police state or a world in which only outlaws have guns.

  (Surely no one wants the final dire consequences predicted in this argument. However, handgun registration does not mean that these consequences will follow. The United States has never been a police state, and its system of free elections guards against such a future. Also, citizens have registered cars, boats, and planes for years without any threat of their confiscation.)

### False Dilemma

The *false dilemma* oversimplifies by asserting only two alternatives when there are more than two. The either–or thinking of this kind of argument can be an effective tactic if undetected. If the arguer gives us only two choices and one of those is clearly unacceptable, then the arguer can push us toward the preferred choice. For example:

- The Federal Reserve System must lower interest rates, or we will never pull out of the recession.

  (Clearly, staying in a recession is not much of a choice, but the alternative may not be the only or the best course to achieve a healthy economy. If interest rates go too low, inflation can result. Other options include the government's creating new jobs and patiently letting market forces play themselves out.)

### False Analogy

When examining the shape of analogy, we also considered the problems with this type of argument. (See pp. 154–55.) Remember that you challenge a false analogy by noting many differences in the two items being compared or by noting a significant difference that has been ignored.

### Post Hoc Fallacy

The term *post hoc,* from the Latin *post hoc, ergo propter hoc* (literally, "after this, therefore because of it") refers to a common error in arguments about cause. One oversimplifies by confusing a time relationship with cause. Reveal the illogic of *post hoc* arguments by pointing to other possible causes:

- We should throw out the entire city council. Since the members were elected, the city has gone into deficit spending.

  (Assuming that deficit spending in this situation is bad, was it caused by the current city council? Or did the current council inherit debts? Or is the entire region suffering from a recession?)

## EXERCISES: Fallacies That Result from Oversimplifying

1. Here is a list of the fallacies we have examined so far. Make up or collect from your reading at least one example of each fallacy.
   a. Overstatement
   b. Stereotyping
   c. Hasty generalization
   d. Forced hypothesis
   e. *Non sequitur*
   f. Slippery slope
   g. False dilemma
   h. False analogy
   i. *Post hoc* fallacy
2. Explain what is illogical about each of the following arguments. Then name the fallacy represented. (Sometimes an argument will fit into more than one category. In that case name all appropriate terms.)
   a. Everybody agrees that we need stronger drunk-driving laws.
   b. The upsurge in crime on Sundays is the result of the reduced rate of church attendance in recent years.
   c. The government must create new jobs. A factory in Illinois has laid off half its workers.
   d. Steve has joined the country club. Golf must be one of his favorite sports.
   e. Blondes have more fun.
   f. You'll enjoy your Volvo; foreign cars never break down.
   g. Gary loves jokes. He would make a great comedian.
   h. The economy is in bad shape because of the Federal Reserve Board. Ever since it expanded the money supply, the stock market has been declining.
   i. Either we improve the city's street lighting, or we will fail to reduce crime.
   j. DNA research today is just like the study of nuclear fission. It seems important, but it's just another bomb that will one day explode on us. When will we learn that government must control research?

  k.  To prohibit prayer in public schools is to limit religious practice solely to internal belief. The result is that an American is religiously "free" only in his or her own mind.

  l.  Professor Johnson teaches in the political science department. I'll bet she's another socialist.

  m.  Coming to the aid of any country engaged in civil war is a bad idea. Next we'll be sending American troops, and soon we'll be involved in another Vietnam.

  n.  We must reject affirmative action in hiring or we'll have to settle for incompetent employees.

## Fallacies That Result from Avoiding the Real Issue

There are many ways to divert attention from the issue under debate. Of the six discussed here, the first three try to divert attention by introducing a separate issue or "sliding by" the actual issue. The following three divert by appealing to the audience's emotions or prejudices. In the first three the arguer tries to give the impression of good logic. In the last three the arguer charges forward on emotional manipulation alone.

### Begging the Question

To assume that part of your argument is true without supporting it is to *beg the question.* Arguments seeking to pass off as proof statements that must themselves be supported are often introduced with such phrases as "the fact is" (to introduce opinion), "obviously," and "as we can see." For example:

- Clearly, lowering grading standards would be bad for students, so a pass/fail system should not be adopted.

  (Does a pass/fail system lower standards? No evidence has been given. If so, is that necessarily bad for students?)

### Red Herring

The *red herring* is a foul-smelling argument indeed. The debater introduces a side issue, some point that is not relevant to the debate:

- The senator is an honest woman; she loves her children and gives to charities.

  (The children and charities are side issues; they do not demonstrate honesty.)

### Straw Man

The *straw man* argument attributes to opponents incorrect and usually ridiculous views that they do not hold so that their position can be easily attacked. We can challenge this illogic by demonstrating that the arguer's opponents do not hold those views or by demanding that the arguer provide some evidence that they do:

- Those who favor gun control just want to take all guns away from responsible citizens and put them in the hands of criminals.

  (The position attributed to proponents of gun control is not only inaccurate but actually the opposite of what is sought by gun-control proponents.)

### Ad Hominem

One of the most frequent of all appeals to emotion masquerading as argument is the *ad hominem* argument (literally, argument "to the man"). When someone says that "those crazy liberals at the ACLU just want all criminals to go free," or a pro-choice demonstrator screams at those "self-righteous fascists" on the other side, the best retort may be silence, or the calm assertion that such statements do not contribute to meaningful debate.

### Common Practice or Bandwagon

To argue that an action should be taken or a position accepted because "everyone is doing it" is illogical. The majority is not always right. Frequently when someone is defending an action as ethical on the ground that everyone does it, the action isn't ethical and the defender knows it isn't. For example:

- There's nothing wrong with fudging a bit on your income taxes. After all, the superrich don't pay any taxes, and the government expects everyone to cheat a little.

  (First, not everyone cheats on taxes; many pay to have their taxes done correctly. And if it is wrong, it is wrong regardless of the number who do it.)

### Ad Populum

Another technique for arousing an audience's emotions and ignoring the issue is to appeal *ad populum,* "to the people," to the audience's presumed shared values and beliefs. Every Fourth of July, politicians employ this tactic, appealing to God, mother, apple pie, and "traditional family values." Simply reject the argument as illogical.

- Good, law-abiding Americans must be sick of the violent crimes occurring in our once godly society. But we won't tolerate it anymore; put the criminals in jail and throw away the key.

  (This does not contribute to a thoughtful debate on criminal justice issues.)

## EXERCISES: Fallacies That Result from Ignoring the Issue

1.  Here is a list of fallacies that result from ignoring the issue. Make up or collect from your reading at least one example of each fallacy.
    a.  Begging the question
    b.  Red herring
    c.  Straw man

     d. *Ad hominem*

     e. Common practice or bandwagon

     f. *Ad populum*

2. Explain what is illogical about each of the following arguments. Then name the fallacy represented.

     a. Gold's book doesn't deserve a Pulitzer Prize. She had been married four times.

     b. I wouldn't vote for him; many of his programs are basically socialist.

     c. Eight out of ten headache sufferers use Bayer to relieve headache pain. It will work for you, too.

     d. We shouldn't listen to Colman McCarthy's argument against liquor ads in college newspapers because he obviously thinks young people are ignorant and need guidance in everything.

     e. My roommate Joe does the craziest things; he must be neurotic.

     f. Since so many people obviously cheat the welfare system, it should be abolished.

     g. She isn't pretty enough to win the contest, and besides she had her nose "fixed" two years ago.

     h. Professors should chill out; everybody cheats on exams from time to time.

     i. The fact is that bilingual education is a mistake because it encourages students to use only their native language and that gives them an advantage over other students.

     j. Don't join those crazy liberals in support of the American Civil Liberties Union. They want all criminals to go free.

     k. Real Americans understand that free-trade agreements are evil. Let your representatives know that we want American goods protected.

## EXERCISE: Analyzing Arguments

Examine the following letter to the editor by Christian Brahmstedt that appeared in the *Washington Post* on January 2, 1989. If you think it contains logical fallacies, identify the passages and explain the fallacies.

---

### HELP THOSE WHO HELP, NOT HURT, THEMSELVES

1      In the past year, and repeatedly throughout the holiday season, the *Post* has devoted an abnormally large share of newsprint to the "plight" of the vagrants who wander throughout the city in search of free handouts: i.e., the "homeless."

2      As certain as taxes, the poor shall remain with civilization forever. Yet these "homeless" are certainly not in the same category as the poor. The poor of civilization, of which we have all been a part at one time in our lives, are proud and work hard until a financial independence frees them from the category.

The "homeless" do not seek work or pride. They are satisfied to beg and survive on others' generosity.

The best correlation to the "homeless" I have witnessed are the gray squirrels on Capitol Hill. After feeding several a heavy dose of nuts one afternoon, I returned the next day to see the same squirrels patiently waiting for a return feeding. In the same fashion, the "homeless" are trained by Washington's guilt-ridden society to continue begging a sustenance rather than learning independence.

3

The *Post* has preached that these vagrants be supported from the personal and federal coffers—in the same manner as the squirrels on Capitol Hill. This support is not helping the homeless; it is only teaching them to rely on it. All of our parents struggled through the depression as homeless of a sort, to arise and build financial independence through hard work.

4

The "homeless" problem will go away when, and only when, Washingtonians refuse to feed them. They will learn to support themselves and learn that society demands honest work for an honest dollar.

5

It would be better for Washington citizens to field their guilt donations to the poor, those folks who are holding down two or more jobs just to make ends meet, rather than throwing their tribute to the vagrants on the sewer grates. The phrase "help those who help themselves" has no more certain relevance than to the "homeless" issue.

6

Source: © *The Washington Post.*

# FOR READING AND ANALYSIS

## DECLARATION OF SENTIMENTS  |  ELIZABETH CADY STANTON

Elizabeth Cady Stanton (1815–1902) was one of the most important leaders of the women's rights movement. Educated at the Emma Willard Seminary in Troy, New York, Stanton studied law with her father before her marriage. At the Seneca Falls Convention in 1848 (the first women's rights convention), Stanton gave the opening speech and read her "Declaration of Sentiments." She founded and became president of the National Women's Suffrage Association in 1869.

PREREADING QUESTION   As you read, think about the similarities and differences between this document and the Declaration of Independence. What significant differences in wording and content do you find?

1    When, in the course of human events, it becomes necessary for one portion of the family of man to assume among the people of the earth a position different from that which they have hitherto occupied, but one to which the laws of nature and of nature's God entitle them, a decent respect to the opinions of mankind requires that they should declare the causes that impel them to such a course.

2    We hold these truths to be self-evident: that all men and women are created equal; that they are endowed by their Creator with certain inalienable rights; that among these are life, liberty, and the pursuit of happiness; that to secure these rights governments are instituted, deriving their just powers from the consent of the governed. Whenever any form of government becomes destructive of these ends, it is the right of those who suffer from it to refuse allegiance to it, and to insist upon the institution of a new government, laying its foundation on such principles, and organizing its powers in such form, as to them shall seem most likely to effect their safety and happiness. Prudence, indeed, will dictate that governments long established should not be changed for light and transient causes; and accordingly all experience hath shown that mankind are more disposed to suffer, while evils are sufferable, than to right themselves by abolishing the forms to which they were accustomed. But when a long train of abuses and usurpations, pursuing invariably the same object evinces a design to reduce them under absolute despotism, it is their duty to throw off such government, and to provide new guards for their future security. Such has been the patient sufferance of the women under this government, and such is now the necessity which constrains them to demand the equal station to which they are entitled.

3    The history of mankind is a history of repeated injuries and usurpations on the part of man toward woman, having in direct object the establishment of an absolute tyranny over her. To prove this, let facts be submitted to a candid world.

4    He has never permitted her to exercise her inalienable right to the elective franchise.

5    He has compelled her to submit to laws, in the formation of which she had no voice.

6    He has withheld from her rights which are given to the most ignorant and degraded men—both natives and foreigners.

7    Having deprived her of this first right of a citizen, the elective franchise, thereby leaving her without representation in the halls of legislation, he has oppressed her on all sides.

8    He has made her, if married, in the eye of the law, civilly dead.

9    He has taken from her all right in property, even to the wages she earns.

10    He has made her, morally, an irresponsible being, as she can commit many crimes with impunity, provided they be done in the presence of her

husband. In the covenant of marriage, she is compelled to promise obedience to her husband, he becoming, to all intents and purposes, her master—the law giving him power to deprive her of her liberty, and to administer chastisement.

He has so framed the laws of divorce, as to what shall be the proper 11 causes, and in case of separation, to whom the guardianship of the children shall be given, as to be wholly regardless of the happiness of women—the law, in all cases, going upon a false supposition of the supremacy of man, and giving all power into his hands.

After depriving her of all rights as a married woman, if single, and the 12 owner of property, he has taxed her to support a government which recognizes her only when her property can be made profitable to it.

He has monopolized nearly all the profitable employments, and from 13 those she is permitted to follow, she receives but a scanty remuneration. He closes against her all the avenues to wealth and distinction which he considers most honorable to himself. As a teacher of theology, medicine, or law, she is not known.

He has denied her the facilities for obtaining a thorough education, all col- 14 leges being closed against her.

He allows her in Church, as well as State, but a subordinate position, claim- 15 ing Apostolic authority for her exclusion from the ministry, and, with some exceptions, from any public participation in the affairs of the Church.

He has created a false public sentiment by giving to the world a different 16 code of morals for men and women, by which moral delinquencies which exclude women from society, are not only tolerated, but deemed of little account in man.

He has usurped the prerogative of Jehovah himself, claiming it as his right 17 to assign for her a sphere of action, when that belongs to her conscience and to her God.

He has endeavored, in every way that he could, to destroy her confidence 18 in her own powers, to lessen her self-respect, and to make her willing to lead a dependent and abject life.

Now in view of this entire disfranchisement of one-half the people of this 19 country, their social and religious degradation—in view of the unjust laws above mentioned, and because women do feel themselves aggrieved, oppressed, and fraudulently deprived of their most sacred rights, we insist that they have immediate admission to all the rights and privileges which belong to them as citizens of the United States.

In entering upon the great work before us, we anticipate no small amount 20 of misconception, misrepresentation, and ridicule; but we shall use every instrumentality within our power to effect our object. We shall employ agents, circulate tracts, petition the State and National legislatures, and endeavor to enlist the pulpit and the press in our behalf. We hope this Convention will be followed by a series of Conventions embracing every part of the country.

1.  Summarize the ideas of paragraphs 1 and 2. Be sure to use your own words.
2.  What are the first three facts given by Stanton? Why are they presented first?
3.  How have women been restricted by law if married or owning property? How have they been restricted in education and work? How have they been restricted psychologically?
4.  What, according to Stanton, do women demand? How will they seek their goals?

5.  What is Stanton's claim? With what does she charge men?
6.  Most—but not all—of Stanton's charges have been redressed, however slowly. Which continue to be legitimate complaints, in whole or in part?

7.  Do we need a new declaration of sentiments for women? If so, what specific charges would you list? If not, why not?
8.  Do we need a declaration of sentiments for other groups—children, minorities, the elderly, animals? If so, what specific charges should be listed? Select one group (that concerns you) and prepare a declaration of sentiments for that group. If you do not think any group needs a declaration, explain why.


## THINGS PEOPLE SAY | NEIL DEGRASSE TYSON

An astrophysicist whose research interests include star formation and the structure of the Milky Way, Neil Tyson is director of the Hayden Planetarium in New York City. He is also one of today's most important figures in bringing science to the nonspecialist. He has been *Natural History* magazine's columnist, and since 2006 he has been the host of the PBS show *NOVAScienceNow*. A popular public speaker, Tyson is the author of nine books, including a collection of his essays. The following column from *Natural History* was originally published in the July/August 1998 issue.

PREREADING QUESTIONS Given your knowledge of the author and the title of his essay, what do you expect his subject to be? How often do you observe the physical universe and think about what you see?

1    Aristotle once declared that while the planets moved against the background stars, and while shooting stars, comets, and eclipses represented intermittent variability in the atmosphere and the heavens, the stars themselves were fixed and unchanging on the sky and that Earth was the center of all motion in the universe. From our enlightened perch, 25 centuries later, we chuckle at the folly of these ideas, but the claims were the consequence of legitimate, albeit simple, observations of the natural world.

Neil deGrasse Tyson with the "tools of his trade."

Aristotle also made other kinds of claims. He said that heavy things fall faster than light things. Who could argue against that? Rocks obviously fall to the ground faster than tree leaves. But Aristotle went further and declared that heavy things fall faster than light things in direct proportion to their own weight, so that a 10-pound object would fall ten times faster than a 1-pound object.

Aristotle was badly mistaken.

To test him, simply release a small rock and a big rock simultaneously from the same height. Unlike fluttering leaves, neither rock will be much influenced by air resistance and both will hit the ground at the same time. This experiment does not require a grant from the National Science Foundation to execute. Aristotle could have performed it but didn't. Aristotle's teachings were later adopted into the doctrines of the Catholic Church. And through the Church's power and influence Aristotelian philosophies became lodged in the common knowledge of the Western world, blindly believed and repeated. Not only did people repeat to others that which was not true, but they also ignored things that clearly happened but were not supposed to be true.

When scientifically investigating the natural world, the only thing worse than a blind believer is a seeing denier. In A.D. 1054, a star in the constellation Taurus abruptly increased in brightness by a factor of a million. The Chinese astronomers wrote about it. Middle Eastern astronomers wrote about it. Native Americans of what is now the southwestern United States made rock engravings of it. The star became bright enough to be plainly visible in the daytime for weeks, yet we have no record of anybody in all of Europe recording the event. (The bright new star in the sky was actually a supernova explosion that occurred in space some 7,000 years earlier but its light had only just reached Earth.) True, Europe was in the Dark Ages, so we cannot expect that acute data-taking skills were common, but cosmic events that were "allowed" to happen were routinely recorded. For example, 12 years later, in 1066, what ultimately became known as Halley's comet was seen and duly depicted—complete with agape onlookers—in a section of the famous Bayeux tapestry, circa 1100. An exception indeed. The Bible says the stars don't change. Aristotle said the stars don't change. The Church, with its unmatched authority, declares the stars don't change. The population then falls victim to a collective delusion that was stronger than its members' own powers of observation.

6      We all carry some blindly believed knowledge because we cannot realistically test every statement uttered by others. When I tell you that the proton has an antimatter counterpart (the antiproton), you would need $1 billion worth of laboratory apparatus to verify my statement. So it's easier to just believe me and trust that, at least most of the time, and at least with regard to the astrophysical world, I know what I am talking about. I don't mind if you remain skeptical. In fact, I encourage it. Feel free to visit your nearest particle accelerator to see antimatter for yourself. But how about all those statements that don't require fancy apparatus to prove? One would think that in our modern and enlightened culture, popular knowledge would be immune from falsehoods that were easily testable.

7      It is not.

8      Consider the following declarations. The North Star is the brightest star in the nighttime sky. The Sun is a yellow star. What goes up must come down. On a dark night you can see millions of stars with the unaided eye. In space there is no gravity. A compass points north. Days get shorter in the winter and longer in the summer. Total solar eclipses are rare.

9      Every statement in the above paragraph is false.

10     Many people (perhaps most people) believe one or more of these statements and spread them to others even when a firsthand demonstration of falsehood is trivial to deduce or obtain. Welcome to my things-people-say rant:

11     The North Star is not the brightest star in the nighttime sky. It's not even bright enough to earn a spot in the celestial top 40. Perhaps people equate popularity with brightness. But when gazing upon the northern sky, three of the seven stars of the Big Dipper, including its "pointer" star, are brighter than the North Star, which is parked just three fist-widths away. There is no excuse.

12     And I don't care what else anyone has ever told you, the Sun is white, not yellow. Human color perception is a complicated business, but if the Sun were yellow, like a yellow lightbulb, then white stuff such as snow would reflect this light and appear yellow—a snow condition confirmed to happen only near fire hydrants. What could lead people to say that the Sun is yellow? In the middle of the day, a glance at the Sun can damage your eyes. Near sunset, however, with the Sun low on the horizon and when the atmospheric scattering of blue light is at its greatest, the Sun's intensity is significantly diminished. The blue light from the Sun's spectrum, lost to the twilight sky, leaves behind a yellow-orange-red hue for the Sun's disk. When people glance at this color-corrupted setting Sun, their misconceptions are fueled.

13     What goes up need not come down. All manner of golf balls, flags, automobiles, and crashed space probes litter the lunar surface. Unless somebody goes up there to bring them back, they will never return to Earth. Not ever. If you want to go up and not come down, all you need to do is travel at any speed faster than about seven miles per second. Earth's gravity will gradually slow you down but it will never succeed in reversing your motion and forcing you back to Earth.

Unless your eyes have pupils the size of binocular lenses, no matter your 14 seeing conditions and no matter your location on Earth, you will not resolve any more than about five or six thousand stars in the entire sky out of the 100 billion (or so) stars of our Milky Way galaxy. Try it one night. Things get much, much worse when the Moon is out. And if the Moon happens to be full, it will wash out the light of all but the brightest few hundred stars.

During the Apollo space program, while one of the missions was en route 15 to the Moon, a noted television news anchor announced the exact moment when the "astronauts left the gravitational field of Earth." Since the astronauts were still on their way to the Moon, and since the Moon orbits Earth, then Earth's gravity must extend into space *at least as far as the Moon*. Indeed, Earth's gravity, and the gravity of every other object in the universe, extends without limit—albeit with ever-diminishing strength. Every spot in space is teeming with countless gravitational tugs in the direction of every other object in the universe. What the announcer meant was that the astronauts crossed the point in space where the force of the Moon's gravity exceeds the force of Earth's gravity. The whole job of the mighty three-stage *Saturn V* rocket was to endow the command module with enough initial speed to just reach this point in space because thereafter you can passively accelerate toward the Moon— and they did. Gravity is everywhere.

Everybody knows that when it comes to magnets, opposite poles attract 16 while similar poles repel. But a compass needle is designed so that the half that has been magnetized "North" points to Earth's magnetic north pole. The only way a magnetized object can align its north half to Earth's magnetic north pole is if Earth's magnetic north pole is actually in the south and the magnetic south pole is actually in the north. Furthermore, there is no particular law of the universe that requires the precise alignment of an object's magnetic poles with its geographic poles. On Earth the two are separated by about 800 miles, which makes navigation by compass a futile exercise in northern Canada.

Since the first day of winter is the shortest "day" of the year, then every 17 succeeding day in the winter season must get longer and longer. Similarly, since the first day of summer is the longest "day" of the year, then every suc- ceeding day in the summer must get shorter and shorter. This is, of course, the opposite of what is told and retold.

On average, every couple years, somewhere on Earth's surface, the Moon 18 passes completely in front of the Sun to create a total solar eclipse. This event is more common than the Olympics, yet you don't read newspaper headlines declaring "a rare Olympics will take place this year." The perceived rarity of eclipses may derive from a simple fact: for any chosen spot on Earth, you can wait up to a half-millennium before you see a total solar eclipse. True, but lame as an argument because there are spots on Earth (like the middle of the Sahara Desert or any region of Antarctica) that have never, and will not likely ever, host the Olympics.

Want a few more? At high noon, the Sun is directly overhead. The Sun 19 rises in the east and sets in the west. The Moon comes out at night. On the equinox there are 12 hours of day and 12 hours of night. The Southern Cross is a beautiful constellation. All of these statements are wrong too.

20     There is no time of day, nor day of the year, nor place in the continental United States where the Sun ascends to directly overhead. At "high noon," straight vertical objects cast no shadow. The only people on the planet who see this live between 23.5 degrees south latitude and 23.5 degrees north latitude. And even in that zone, the Sun reaches directly overhead on only two days per year. The concept of high noon, like the brightness of the North Star and the color of the Sun, is a collective delusion.

21     For every person on Earth, the Sun rises due east and sets due west on only two days of the year: the first day of spring and the first day of fall. For every other day of the year, and for every person on Earth, the Sun rises and sets someplace else on the horizon. On the equator, sunrise varies by 47 degrees across the eastern horizon. From the latitude of New York City (41 degrees north—the same as that of Madrid and Beijing) the sunrise spans more than 60 degrees. From the latitude of London (51 degrees north) the sunrise spans nearly 80 degrees. And when viewed from either the Arctic or Antarctic circles, the Sun can rise due north and due south, spanning a full 180 degrees.

22     The Moon also "comes out" with the Sun in the sky. By invoking a small extra investment in your skyward viewing (like looking up in broad daylight) you will notice that the Moon is visible in the daytime nearly as often as it is visible at night.

23     The equinox does not contain exactly 12 hours of day and 12 hours of night. Look at the sunrise and sunset times in the newspaper on the first day of either spring or fall. They do not split the day into two equal 12-hour blocks. In all cases, daytime wins. Depending on your latitude, it can win by as few as seven minutes at the equator up to nearly half an hour at the Arctic and Antarctic circles. Who or what do we blame? Refraction of sunlight as it passes from the vacuum of interplanetary space to Earth's atmosphere enables an image of the Sun to appear above the horizon several minutes before the actual Sun has actually risen. Equivalently, the actual Sun has set several minutes before the Sun that you see. The convention is to measure sunrise by using the upper edge of the Sun's disk as it peeks above the horizon; similarly, sunset is measured by using the upper edge of the Sun's disk as it sinks below the horizon. The problem is that these two "upper edges" are on opposite halves of the Sun thereby providing an extra solar width of light in the sunrise/sunset calculation.

24     The Southern Cross gets the award for the greatest hype among all eighty-eight constellations. By listening to Southern Hemisphere people talk about this constellation, and by listening to songs written about it, and by noticing it on the national flags of Australia, New Zealand, Western Samoa, and Papua New Guinea, you would think we in the North were somehow deprived. Nope. Firstly, one needn't travel to the Southern Hemisphere to see the Southern Cross. It's plainly visible (although low in the sky) from as far north as Miami,

Florida. This diminutive constellation is the smallest in the sky—your fist at arm's length would eclipse it completely. Its shape isn't very interesting either. If you were to draw a rectangle using a connect-the-dots method you would use four stars. And if you were to draw a cross you would presumably include a fifth star in the middle to indicate the cross-point of the two beams. But the Southern Cross is composed of only four stars, which more accurately resemble a kite or a crooked box. The constellation lore of Western cultures owes its origin and richness to centuries of Babylonian, Chaldean, Greek, and Roman imaginations. Remember, these are the same imaginations that gave rise to the endless dysfunctional social lives of the gods and goddesses. Of course, these were all Northern Hemisphere civilizations, which means the constellations of the southern sky (many of which were named only within the last 250 years) are mythologically impoverished. In the North we have the Northern Cross, which is composed of all five stars that a cross deserves. It forms a subset of the larger constellation Cygnus the swan, which is flying across the sky along the Milky Way. Cygnus is nearly twelve times larger than the Southern Cross.

When people believe a tale that conflicts with self-checkable evidence it 25 tells me that people undervalue the role of evidence in formulating an internal belief system. Why this is so is not clear, but it enables many people to hold fast to ideas and notions based purely on supposition. But all hope is not lost. Occasionally, people say things that are simply true no matter what. One of my favorites is, "Whatever you go, there you are" and its Zen corollary, "If we are all here, then we must not be all there."

Source: Reprinted with permission from *Natural History*, July / August 1998. This article appears in Neil deGrasse Tyson's book *Death by Black Hole: And Other Cosmic Quandaries* (New York: W. W. Norton, 2007), pp. 291–297.

QUESTIONS FOR READING

1.  What happened in 1054? Who wrote about the event? Who did not? What happened in 1066? Why did Europeans record this year's event?

2.  What *kinds* of knowledge do we usually have to accept from experts? What *kinds* of falsehoods should we not hold on to?

3.  Why do people believe that the sun is yellow? Or that it rises in the east and sets in the west?

4.  How does Tyson account for people believing statements that conflict with evidence?

5. What does Tyson accomplish in his opening four paragraphs?

6. The author provides a list of well-known "truths" and then explains why each one is a false fact. Has he provided sufficient evidence to make his point? If not, why not?

7. What is Tyson's claim, the main point he wants to establish with readers?

8. Has Tyson convinced you that it is important to observe the natural world and use logic to test what we assume to be true? If not, why not?

9. What are some of the sources of false facts? Where does Tyson put most of the blame—on those who pass on false facts or those who embrace them by ignoring evidence to the contrary? Do you agree with his view on where to place the blame? Why or why not?

10. How many of Tyson's false facts did you believe to be true? Have you now adjusted your fact list? Are you sharing your new knowledge with family and friends? Reflect on your reactions to Tyson's essay.

# Studying Some Arguments by Genre

# Definition Arguments

READ:  How does the cat respond to the big dog's questions?

REASON:  Does the big dog expect the responses he gets to his questions? How do you know?

REFLECT/WRITE:  What is a rhetorical question? What is the risk of using one?

"Define your terms!" someone yells in the middle of a heated debate. Although yelling may not be the best strategy, the advice is sound for writers of argument. People do disagree over the meaning of words. We cannot let words mean whatever we want and still communicate, but we do need to understand that many words have more than one meaning. In addition, some words carry strong connotations, the emotional associations we attach to them. For this reason, realtors never sell *houses;* they always sell *homes.* They want you to believe that the house they are showing will become the home in which you will feel happy and secure.

Many important arguments turn on the definition of key terms. If you can convince others that you have the correct definition, then you are well on your way to winning your argument. The civil rights movement, for example, really turned on a definition of terms. Leaders argued that some laws are unjust, that because it is the law does not necessarily mean it is right. Laws requiring separate schools and separate drinking fountains and seats at the back of the bus for blacks were, in the view of civil rights activists, unjust laws, unjust because they are immoral and as such diminish us as humans. If obeying unjust laws is immoral, then it follows that we should not obey such laws. And when we recognize that obeying such laws hurts us, then we have an obligation to act to remove unjust laws. Civil disobedience—illegal behavior to some—becomes, by definition, the best moral behavior.

Attorney Andrew Vachss has argued that there are no child prostitutes, only prostituted children. Yes, there are children who engage in sex for money. But, Vachss argues, that is not the complete definition of a prostitute. A prostitute chooses to exchange sex for money. Children do not choose; they are exploited by adults, beaten and in other ways abused if they do not work for the adult in control of them. If we agree with his definition, Vachss expects that we will also agree that the adults must be punished for their abuse of those prostituted children.

## DEFINING AS PART OF AN ARGUMENT

There are two occasions for defining words as a part of your argument:

- You need to define any technical terms that may not be familiar to readers— or that readers may not understand as fully as they think they do. David Norman, early in his book on dinosaurs, writes:

    Nearly everyone knows what some dinosaurs look like, such as *Tyrannosaurus, Triceratops,* and *Stegosaurus.* But they may be much more vague about the lesser known ones, and may have difficulty in distinguishing between dinosaurs and other types of prehistoric creatures. It is not at all unusual to overhear an adult, taking a group of children around a museum display, being reprimanded sharply by the youngsters for failing to realize that a woolly mammoth was not a dinosaur, or—more forgivably—that a giant flying reptile such as *Pteranodon,* which lived at the time of the dinosaurs, was not a dinosaur either.

So what exactly is a dinosaur? And how do paleontologists decide on the groups they belong to?

Norman answers his questions by explaining the four characteristics that all dinosaurs have. He provides what is often referred to as a *formal definition*. He places the dinosaur in a class, established by four criteria, and then distinguishes this animal from other animals that lived a long time ago. His definition is not open to debate. He is presenting the definition and classification system that paleontologists, the specialists, have established.

- You need to define any word you are using in a special way. If you were to write: "We need to teach discrimination at an early age," you should add: "by *discrimination* I do not mean prejudice. I mean discernment, the ability to see differences." (*Sesame Street* has been teaching children this good kind of discrimination for many years.) The word *discrimination* used to have only a positive connotation; it referred to an important critical thinking skill. Today, however, the word has been linked to prejudice; to discriminate is to act on one's prejudice against some group. Writing today, you need to clarify if you are using the word in its original, positive meaning.

## WHEN DEFINING *IS* THE ARGUMENT

We also turn to definition because we believe that a word is being used incorrectly or is not fully understood. Columnist George Will once argued that we should forget *values* and use instead the word *virtues*—that we should seek and admire virtues, not values. His point was that the term *values,* given to us by today's social scientists, is associated with situational ethics, or with an "if it feels good do it" approach to action. He wants people to return to the more old-fashioned word *virtues* so that we are reminded that some behavior is right and some is wrong, and that neither the situation nor how we might "feel" about it alters those truths. In discussions such as Will's the purpose shifts. Instead of using definition as one step in an argument, definition becomes the central purpose of the argument. Will rejects the idea that *values* means the same thing as *virtues* and asserts that it is virtue—as he defines it—that must guide our behavior. An extended definition *is* the argument.

## STRATEGIES FOR DEVELOPING AN EXTENDED DEFINITION

Arguing for your meaning of a word provides your purpose in writing. But, it may not immediately suggest ways to develop such an argument. Let's think in terms of what definitions essentially do: They establish criteria for a class or category and then exclude other items from that category. (A pen is a writing instrument that uses ink.) Do you see your definition as drawing a line or as setting up two entirely separate categories? For example:

When does interrogation                                become              torque?
_____‖_____

One might argue that some strategies for making the person questioned uncomfortable are appropriate to interrogation (reduced sleep or comforts, loud noise). But, at some point (stretching on a rack or waterboarding) one crosses a line to torture. To define torture, you have to explain where that line is—and how the actions on one side of the line are different from those on the other side.

What are the characteristics of wisdom as opposed to knowledge?

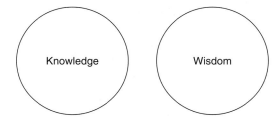

Do we cross a line from knowledge to become wise? Not many would agree with this, more likely arguing that wisdom requires traits or skills that are not to be found by increasing one's knowledge. The categories are separate.

Envisioning these two approaches supports the abstract thinking that defining requires. Then what? Use some of the basic strategies of good writing:

- *Descriptive details.* Illustrate with specifics. List the traits of a leader or a courageous person. Explain the behaviors that we find in a wise person, or the behaviors that should be called torture. Describe the situations in which liberty can flourish, or the situations that result from unjust laws. Remember to use negative traits as well as positive ones. That is, show what is *not* covered by the word you are defining.

- *Examples.* Develop your definition with actual or hypothetical examples. Churchill, Lincoln, and FDR can all be used as examples of leaders. The biblical Solomon is generally acknowledged as a good example of a wise person. You can also create a hypothetical wise or courteous person, or a person whose behavior you would consider virtuous.

- *Comparison and/or contrast.* Clarify and limit your definition by contrasting it with words of similar—but not exactly the same—meanings. For example, what are the differences between knowledge and wisdom or interrogation and torture? The goal of your essay is to establish subtle but important differences so that your readers understand precisely what you want a given word to mean. In an essay at the end of this chapter, Robin Givhan distinguishes among *glamour, charisma,* and *cool* as a way to develop her definition of *glamour.*

- *History of usage or word origin.* The word's original meanings can be instructive. If the word has changed meaning over time, explore these changes as clues to how the word can (or should) be used. If you want readers to reclaim *discrimination* as a positive trait, then show them how that was part of the word's original meaning before the word became tied to prejudice. Word origin—etymology—can also give us insight into a word's meaning. Many words in English come from another language, or they are a combination of two words. The words *liberty* and *freedom* can usefully be discussed by examining etymology. Most dictionaries provide some word origin information, but the best source is, always, the *Oxford English Dictionary.*

- *Use or function.* A frequent strategy for defining is explaining an item's use or function: A pencil is a writing instrument. A similar approach can give insight into more general or abstract words as well. For example, what do we have—or gain—by emphasizing virtues instead of values? Or, what does a wise person *do* that a non-wise person does not do?

- *Metaphors.* Consider using figurative comparisons. When fresh, not clichés, they add vividness to your writing while offering insight into your understanding of the word.

In an essay titled "Why I Blog," Andrew Sullivan, one of the Internet's earliest bloggers, uses many of these strategies for developing a definition of the term *blog:*

- *Word origin.* "The word *blog* is a conflation of two words: *Web* and *log.* . . . In the monosyllabic vernacular of the Internet, *Web log* soon became the word *blog.*"

- *One-sentence definition.* "It contains in its four letters a concise and accurate self-description: it is a log of thoughts and writing posted publicly on the World Wide Web."

- *Descriptive details.* "This form of instant and global self-publishing . . . allows for no retroactive editing. . . . [I]ts truth [is] inherently transitory."

- *Contrast.* "The wise panic that can paralyze a writer . . . is not available to a blogger. You can't have blogger's block."

- *Metaphors.* "A blog . . . bobs on the surface of the ocean but has its anchorage in waters deeper than those print media is technologically able to exploit."

These snippets from Sullivan's lengthy essay give us a good look at defining strategies in action.

# GUIDELINES for Evaluating Definition Arguments

When reading definition arguments, what should you look for? The basics of good argument apply to all arguments: a clear statement of claim, qualified if appropriate, a clear explanation of reasons and evidence, and enough relevant evidence to support the claim. How do we recognize these qualities in a definition argument? Use the following points as guides to evaluating:

- **Why is the word being defined?** Has the writer convinced you of the need to understand the word's meaning or change the way the word is commonly used?

- **How is the word defined?** Has the writer established his or her definition, clearly distinguishing it from what the writer perceives to be objectionable definitions? It is hard to judge the usefulness of the writer's position if the differences in meaning remain fuzzy. If George Will is going to argue for using *virtues* instead of *values,* he needs to be sure that readers understand the differences he sees in the two words.

- **What strategies are used to develop the definition?** Can you recognize the different types of evidence presented and see what the writer is doing in his or her argument? This kind of analysis can aid your evaluation of a definition argument.

- **What are the implications of accepting the author's definition?** Why does George Will want readers to embrace *virtues* rather than *values*? Will's argument is not just about subtle points of language. His argument is also about attitudes that affect public policy issues. Part of any evaluation of a definition argument must include our assessment of the author's definition.

- **Is the definition argument convincing?** Do the reasons and evidence lead you to agree with the author, to accept the idea of the definition and its implications as well?

## PREPARING A DEFINITION ARGUMENT

In addition to the guidelines for writing arguments presented in Chapter 4, you can use the following advice specific to writing definition arguments.

### Planning

1. *Think:* Why do you want to define your term? To add to our understanding of a complex term? To challenge the use of the word by others? If you don't have a good reason to write, find a different word to examine.

2. *Think:* How are you defining the word? What are the elements/parts/steps in your definition? Some brainstorming notes are probably helpful to keep your definition concrete and focused.

3.  *Think:* What strategies will you use to develop and support your definition? Consider using several of these possible strategies for development:
    *   *Word origin or history of usage*
    *   *Descriptive details*
    *   *Comparison and/or contrast*
    *   *Examples*
    *   *Function or use*
    *   *Metaphors*

## Drafting

1.  Begin with an opening paragraph or two that introduces your subject in an interesting way. Possibilities include the occasion that has led to your writing—explain, for instance, a misunderstanding about your term's meaning that you want to correct.
2.  Do *not* begin by quoting or paraphrasing a dictionary definition of the term. "According to Webster . . ." is a tired approach lacking reader interest. If the dictionary definition were sufficient, you would have no reason to write an entire essay to define the term.
3.  State your claim—your definition of the term—early in your essay, if you can do so in a sentence or two. If you do not state a brief claim, then establish your purpose in writing early in your essay. (You may find that there are too many parts to your definition to combine into one or two sentences.)
4.  Use several specific strategies for developing your definition. Select strategies from the list above and organize your approach around these strategies. That is, you can develop one paragraph of descriptive details, another of examples, another of contrast with words that are not exactly the same in meaning.
5.  Consider specifically refuting the error in word use that led to your decision to write your own definition. If you are motivated to write based on what you have read, then make a rebuttal part of your definition argument.
6.  Consider discussing the implications of your definition. You can give weight and value to your argument by defending the larger significance of your definition.

## A CHECKLIST FOR REVISION

☐ Do I have a good understanding of my purpose? Have I made this clear to readers?

☐ Have I clearly stated my definition? Or clearly established the various parts of the definition that I discuss in separate paragraphs?

☐ Have I organized my argument, building the parts of my definition into a logical, coherent structure?

☐ Have I used specifics to clarify and support my definition?

☐ Have I used the basic checklist for revision in Chapter 4 (see p. 105)?

# STUDENT ESSAY

PARAGON OR PARASITE?

Laura Mullins

Do you recognize this creature? He is low maintenance and often
unnoticeable, a favorite companion of many. Requiring no special attention, he
grows from the soil of pride and rejection, feeding regularly on a diet of
ignorance and insecurity, scavenging for hurt feelings and defensiveness,
gobbling up dainty morsels of lust and scandal. Like a cult leader clothed in a
gay veneer, disguising himself as blameless, he wields power. Bewitching
unsuspecting but devoted groupies, distracting them from honest self-
examination, deceiving them into believing illusions of grandeur or, on the other
extreme, unredeemable worthlessness, he breeds jealousy, hate, and fear; thus,
he thrives. He is Gossip.

One of my dearest friends is a gossip. She is an educated, honorable,
compassionate, loving woman whose character and judgment I deeply admire
and respect. After sacrificially raising six children, she went on to study medicine
and become a doctor who graciously volunteers her expertise. How, you may be
wondering, could a gossip deserve such praise? Then you do not understand the
word. My friend is my daughter's godmother; she is my gossip, or *godsib,* meaning
sister-in-god. Derived from Middle English words *god,* meaning spiritual, and *sip/
sib/syp,* meaning kinsman, this term was used to refer to a familiar acquaintance,
close family friend, or intimate relation, according to the *Oxford English Dictionary.*
As a male, he would have joined in fellowship and celebration with the father of
the newly born; if a female, she would have been a trusted friend, a birth-
attendant or midwife to the mother of the baby. The term grew to include
references to the type of easy, unrestrained conversation shared by these folks.

As is often the case with words, the term's meaning has certainly evolved,
maybe eroded from its original idea. Is it harmless, idle chat, innocuous sharing

*Attention-getting
introduction.*

*Clever extended
metaphor.*

*Subject introduced.*

*Etymology of gossip
and early meanings.*

*Current meanings.*

of others' personal news, or back-biting, rumor-spreading, and manipulation? Is it a beneficial activity worthy of pursuit, or a deplorable danger to be avoided?

In her article "Evolution, Alienation, and Gossip" (for the Social Issues Research Centre in Oxford, England), Kate Fox writes that "gossip is not a trivial pastime; it is essential to human social, psychological, and even physical well-being." Many echo her view that gossip is a worthy activity, claiming that engaging in gossip produces endorphins, reduces stress, and aids in building intimate relationships. Gossip, seen at worst as a harmless outlet, is encouraged in the workplace. Since much of its content is not inherently critical or malicious, it is viewed as a positive activity. However, this view does nothing to encourage those speaking or listening to evaluate or examine motive or purpose; instead, it seems to reflect the "anything goes" thinking so prevalent today.

Conversely, writer and high school English and geography teacher Lennox V. Farrell of Toronto, Canada, in his essay titled "Gossip: An Urban Form of Sorcery," presents gossip as a kind of "witchcraft . . . based on using unsubstantiated accusations by those who make them, and on uncritically accepting these by those enticed into listening." Farrell uses gossip in its more widely understood definition, encompassing the breaking of confidences, inappropriate sharing of indiscretions, destructive tale-bearing, and malicious slander.

What, then, is gossip? We no longer use the term to refer to our children's godparents. Its current definition usually comes with derogatory implications. Imagine a backyard garden: you see a variety of greenery, recognizing at a glance that you are looking at different kinds of plants. Taking a closer look, you will find the gossip vine; inconspicuously blending in, it doesn't appear threatening, but ultimately it destroys. If left in the garden it will choke and then suck out life from its host. Zoom in on the garden scene and follow the creeping vine up trees and along a fence where two neighbors visit. You can overhear one woman saying to the other, "I know I should be the last to tell you, but your husband is being unfaithful to me." (Caption from a cartoon by Alan De la Nougerede.)

*[margin note] Good use of sources to develop definition.*

*[margin note] Good use of metaphor to depict gossip as negative.*

The current popular movement to legitimize gossip seems an excuse to condone the human tendency to puff-up oneself. Compared in legal terms, gossip is to conversation as hearsay is to eyewitness testimony; it's not credible. Various religious doctrines abhor the idea and practice of gossip. An old Turkish proverb says, "He who gossips to you will gossip of you." From the Babylonian Talmud, which calls gossip the three-pronged tongue, destroying the one talking, the one listening, and the one being spoken of, to the Upanishads, to the Bible, we can conclude that no good fruit is born from gossip. Let's tend our gardens and check our motives when we have the urge to gossip. Surely we can find more noble pursuits than the self-aggrandizement we have come to know as gossip.

*Conclusion states view that gossip is to be avoided—the writer's thesis.*

# FOR ANALYSIS AND DEBATE

## GLAMOUR, THAT CERTAIN SOMETHING | ROBIN GIVHAN

Robin Givhan is a graduate of Princeton and holds a master's degree in journalism from the University of Michigan. She is fashion editor for the *Washington Post* and has won a Pulitzer Prize (2006) for criticism, the first time the prize has been awarded to a fashion writer. Givhan's coverage of the world of fashion frequently becomes a study of culture, as we see in the following column, published February 17, 2008, shortly before the 2008 Academy Awards show.

PREREADING QUESTIONS  What is the difference between glamour and good looks? What famous people do you consider glamorous?

Glamour isn't a cultural necessity, but its usefulness can't be denied.   1

It makes us feel good about ourselves by making us believe that life can   2 sparkle. Glamorous people make difficult tasks seems effortless. They appear to cruise through life shaking off defeat with a wry comment. No matter how hard they work for what they have, the exertion never seems to show. Yet the cool confidence they project doesn't ever drift into lassitude.

Hollywood attracts people of glamour—as well as the misguided souls   3 who confuse it with mere good looks—because that is where it is richly rewarded. And the Academy Awards are the epicenter of it all. We'll watch the Oscars next Sunday to delight in the stars who glide down the red carpet like graceful swans or who swagger onto the stage looking dashing.

4    Of course, we'll watch for other reasons, too. There's always the possibility of a supremely absurd fashion moment or an acceptance speech during which the winner becomes righteously indignant—Michael Moore–style—or practically hyperventilates like Halle Berry. While Moore, a nominee, is not glamorous, he is compelling for the sheer possibility of an impolitic eruption. Berry isn't glamorous either, mostly because nothing ever looks effortless with her. (She has even expressed anguish over her beauty.) Mostly, though, we will watch in search of "old Hollywood" glamour. But really, is there any other kind?

5    Among the actors who consistently manage to evoke memories of Cary Grant or Grace Kelly are George Clooney and Cate Blanchett. There's something about the way they present themselves that speaks to discretion, sex appeal and glossy perfection. As an audience, we think we know these actors but we really don't. We know their image, the carefully crafted personality they display to the public. If they have been to rehab, they went quietly and without a crowd of paparazzi.

6    Their lives appear to be an endless stream of lovely adventures, minor mishaps that turn into cocktail party banter, charming romances and just enough gravitas to keep them from floating away on a cloud of frivolity.

7    These actors take pretty pictures because they seem supremely comfortable with themselves. It's not simply their beauty we're seeing; it's also an unapologetic pleasure in being who they are.

8    Oscar nominee Tilda Swinton has the kind of striking, handsome looks of Anjelica Huston or Lauren Bacall. But Swinton doesn't register as glamorous as much as cool. She looks a bit androgynous and favors the eccentric Dutch design team of Viktor & Rolf, which once populated an entire runway show with Swinton doppelgangers. Coolness suggests that the person knows

something or understands something that average folks haven't yet figured out. Cool people are a step ahead. Glamour is firmly situated in the now.

There's nothing particularly intimate about glamour, which is why it plays 9 so well on the big screen and why film actors who embody it can sometimes be disappointing in real life. Glamour isn't like charisma, which is typically described as the ability to make others feel important or special.

Neither quality has much to do with a person's inner life. Glamour is no 10 measure of soulfulness or integrity. It isn't about truth, but perception. *Redbook* traffics in truth. *Vogue* promotes glamour.

Although Hollywood is the natural habitat for the glitterati, they exist 11 everywhere: politics, government, sports, business. Tiger Woods brought glamour to golf with his easy confidence and his ability to make the professional game look as simple as putt-putt. Donald Trump aspires to glamour with his flashy properties and their gold-drenched decor. But his efforts are apparent, his yearning obvious. The designer Tom Ford is glamorous. The man never rumples.

In the political world, Barack Obama has glamour. Bill Clinton has cha-12 risma. And Hillary Clinton has an admirable work ethic. Bill Clinton could convince voters that he felt their pain. Hillary Clinton reminds them detail by detail of how she would alleviate it. Glamour has a way of temporarily making you forget about the pain and just think the world is a beautiful place of endless possibilities.

Ronald Reagan evoked glamour. His white-tie inaugural balls and 13 morning-coat swearing-in were purposefully organized to bring a twinkle back to the American psyche. George W. Bush has charisma, a.k.a. the likability factor, although it does not appear to be helping his approval rating now. Still, he remains a back-slapper and bestower of nicknames.

Charisma is personal. Glamour taps into a universal fairy tale. It's uncon-14 cerned with the nitty-gritty. Instead, it celebrates the surface gloss. And sometimes, a little shimmer can be hard to resist.

## QUESTIONS FOR READING

1. How does glamour make us feel?
2. Where do we usually find glamour? Why?
3. Which celebrities today best capture Hollywood's glamour of the past?
4. What traits do the glamorous have?
5. Explain the differences among glamour, charisma, and cool.

6. Examine the opening three sentences in paragraph 12. What makes them effective?

7. What are the specific strategies Givhan uses to develop her definition?

8. What is Givhan's claim?

9. Givhan asserts that glamour is in the present but "cool people are a step ahead." Does this contrast make sense to you? Why or why not?

10. Do we ever really know the glamorous, charismatic, and cool celebrities? Explain.

11. Some young people aspire to be cool. How would you advise them? What should one do, how should one behave, to be cool? Is "cool" a trait that we can "put on" if we wish? Why or why not?

1. In the student essay, Laura Mullins defines the term *gossip*. Select one of the following words to define and prepare your own extended definition argument, using at least three of the strategies for defining described in this chapter. For each word in the list, you see a companion word in parentheses. Use that companion word as a word that you contrast with the word you are defining. (For example, how does gossip differ from conversation?) The idea of an extended definition argument is to make fine distinctions among words similar in meaning.

   courtesy (manners)          hero (star)
   wisdom (knowledge)          community (subdivision)
   patriotism (chauvinism)     freedom (liberty)

2. Select a word you believe is currently misused. It can be misused because it has taken on a negative (or positive) connotation that it did not originally have, or because it has changed meaning and lost something in the process. A few suggestions include *awful, fabulous, exceptional* (in education), *propaganda*.

3. Define a term that is currently used to label people with particular traits or values. Possibilities include *nerd, yuppie, freak, jock, redneck, bimbo, wimp*. Reflect, before selecting this topic, on why you want to explain the meaning of the word you have chosen. One purpose might be to explain the word to someone from another culture. Another might be to defend people who are labeled negatively by a term; that is, you want to show why the term should not have a negative connotation.

# CHAPTER 8

# Evaluation Arguments

READ: What is the situation? Where are we?

REASON: Look at the faces; what do you infer to be the attitude of the participants?

REASON/WRITE: What is the photo's message?

" I really love Ben's Camaro; it's so much more fun to go out with him than to go with Gregory in his Volvo wagon," you confide to a friend. "On the other hand, Ben always wants to see the latest horror movie—and boy are they horrid! I'd much rather watch one of our teams play—whatever the season; sports events are so much more fun than horror movies!"

"Well, at least you and Ben agree not to listen to Amy Winehouse CDs. Her life is so messed up; why would anyone admire her music?" your friend responds.

## CHARACTERISTICS OF EVALUATION ARGUMENTS

Evaluations. How easy they are to make. We do it all the time. So, surely an evaluation argument should be easy to prepare. Not so fast. Remember at the beginning of the discussion of argument in Chapter 3, we observed that we do not argue about personal preferences because there is no basis for building an argument. If you don't like horror movies, then don't go to them—even with Ben! However, once you assert that sporting events are more fun than horror movies, you have shifted from personal preference to the world of argument, the world in which others will judge the effectiveness of your logic and evidence. On what basis can you argue that one activity is more fun than the other? And, always more fun? And, more fun for everyone? You probably need to qualify this claim and then you will need to establish the criteria by which you have made your evaluation. Although you might find it easier to defend your preference for a car for dates, you, at least in theory, can build a convincing argument for a qualified claim in support of sporting events. Your friend, though, will have great difficulty justifying her evaluation of Winehouse based on Winehouse's lifestyle. An evaluation of her music needs to be defended based on criteria about music—unless she wants to try to argue that any music made by people with unconventional or immoral lifestyles will be bad music, a tough claim to defend.

In a column for *Time* magazine, Charles Krauthammer argues that Tiger Woods is the greatest golfer ever to play the game. He writes:

> How do we know? You could try Method 1: Compare him directly with the former greatest golfer, Jack Nicklaus. . . . But that is not the right way to compare. You cannot compare greatness directly across the ages. There are so many intervening variables: changes in technology, training, terrain, equipment, often rules and customs.
> How then do we determine who is greatest? Method 2: The Gap. Situate each among his contemporaries. Who towers? . . . Nicklaus was great, but he ran with peers: Palmer, Player, Watson. Tiger has none.

Krauthammer continues with statistics to demonstrate that there is no one playing now with Tiger who comes close in number of tournaments won, number of majors won, and number of strokes better in these events than the next player. He then applies the Gap Method to Babe Ruth in baseball, Wayne

Gretzky in hockey, and Bobby Fischer in chess to demonstrate that it works to reveal true greatness in competition among the world's best.

Krauthammer clearly explains his Gap Method, his basic criterion for judging greatness. Then he provides the data to support his conclusions about who are or were the greatest in various fields. His is a convincing evaluation argument.

These examples suggest some key points about evaluation arguments:

- **Evaluation arguments are arguments, not statements of personal preferences.** As such, they need a precise, qualified claim and reasons and evidence for support, just like any argument.

- **Evaluation arguments are about "good" and "bad," "best" and "worst."** These arguments are not about what we should or should not do or why a situation is the way it is. The debate is not whether one should select a boyfriend based on the kind of car he drives or why horror movies have so much appeal for many viewers. The argument is that sports events are great entertainment, or better entertainment than horror movies.

- **Evaluation arguments need to be developed based on a clear statement of the criteria for evaluating.** Winehouse has won Grammys for her music—why? By what standards of excellence do we judge a singer? A voice with great musicality and nuance? The selection of songs with meaningful lyrics? The ability to engage listeners—the way the singer can "sell" a song? The number of recordings sold and awards won? All of these criteria? Something else?

- **Evaluation arguments, to be successful, may need to defend the criteria, not just to list them and show that the subject of the argument meets those criteria.** Suppose you want to argue that sporting events are great entertainment because it is exciting to cheer with others, you get to see thrilling action, and it is good, clean fun. Are sports always "good, clean fun"? Some of the fighting in hockey matches is quite vicious. Some football players get away with dirty hits. Krauthammer argues that his Method 2 provides the better criterion for judging greatness and then shows why it is the better method. Do not underestimate the challenge of writing an effective evaluation argument.

## TYPES OF EVALUATION ARGUMENTS

The examples we have examined above are about people or items or experiences in our lives. Tiger Woods is the greatest golfer ever, based on the Gap Method criterion. Sports events are more fun to attend than horror movies. We can (and do!) evaluate just about everything we know or do or buy. This is one type of evaluation argument. In this category we would place the review—of a book, movie, concert, or something similar.

A second type of evaluation is a response to another person's argument. We are not explaining why the car or college, sitcom or singer, is good or great or the best. Instead, we are responding to one specific argument we have read (or listened to) that we think is flawed, flawed in many ways or in one significant way that essentially destroys the argument. This type of evaluation argument is called a rebuttal or refutation argument.

Sometimes our response to what we consider a really bad argument is to go beyond the rebuttal and write a counterargument. Rather than writing about the limitations and flaws in our friend's evaluation of Winehouse as a singer not to be listened to, we decide to write our own argument evaluating Winehouse's strengths as a contemporary singer. This counterargument is best described as an evaluation argument, not a refutation. Similarly, we can disagree with someone's argument defending restrictions placed by colleges on student file sharing. But, if we decide to write a counterargument defending students' rights to share music files, we have moved from rebuttal to our own position paper, our own argument based on values. Counterarguments are best seen as belonging to one of the other genres of argument discussed in this section of the text.

## GUIDELINES for Analyzing an Evaluation Argument

The basics of good argument apply to all arguments: a clear statement of claim, qualified as appropriate, a clear explanation of reasons and evidence, and enough relevant evidence to support the claim. When reading evaluation arguments, use the following points as additional guides:

- **What is the writer's claim?** Is it clear, qualified if necessary, and focused on the task of evaluating?
- **Has the writer considered audience as a basis for both claim and criteria?** Your college may be a good choice for you, given your criteria for choosing, but is it a good choice for your audience? Qualifications need to be based on audience: College A is a great school for young people in need of B and with X amount of funds. Or: *The Da Vinci Code* is an entertaining read for those with some understanding of art history and knowledge of the Roman Catholic Church.
- **What criteria are presented as the basis for evaluation?** Are they clearly stated? Do they seem reasonable for the topic of evaluation? Are they defended if necessary?
- **What evidence and/or reasons are presented to show that the item under evaluation passes the criteria test?** Specifics are important in any evaluation argument.
- **What are the implications of the claim?** If we accept the Gap Method for determining greatness, does that mean that we can never compare stars from different generations? If we agree with the rebuttal argument, does that mean that there are no good arguments for the claim in the essay being refuted?
- **Is the argument convincing?** Does the evidence lead you to agree with the author? Do you want to buy that car, listen to that CD, read that book, see that film as a result of reading the argument?

# PREPARING AN EVALUATION ARGUMENT

In addition to the guidelines for writing arguments presented in Chapter 4, you can use the following advice specific to writing evaluation arguments.

### Planning

1. **Think:** Why do you want to write this evaluation? Does it matter, or are you just sharing your personal preferences? Select a topic that requires you to think deeply about how we judge that item (college, book, CD, etc.).

2. **Think about audience:** Try to imagine writing your evaluation for your classmates, not just your instructor. Instead of thinking about an assignment to be graded, think about why we turn to reviews, for example. What do readers want to learn? They want to know if they should see that film. Your job is to help them make that decision.

3. **Think:** What are my criteria for evaluation? And, how will I measure my topic against them to show that my evaluation is justified? You really must know how you would determine a great singer or a great tennis player before you write, or you risk writing only about personal preferences.

4. **Establish a general plan:** If you are writing a review, be sure to study the work carefully. Can you write a complete and accurate summary? (It is easier to review a CD than a live concert because you can replay the CD to get all the details straight.) You will need to balance summary, analysis, and evaluation in a review—and be sure that you do not mostly write summary or reveal the ending of a novel or film! If you are evaluating a college or a car, think about how you would order your criteria. Do you want to list all criteria first and then show how your item connects to them, point by point? Or, do you want the criteria to unfold as you make specific points about your item?

    To analyze a film, consider the plot, the characters, the actors who play the lead characters, any special effects used, and the author's (and director's) "take" on the story. If the "idea" of the film is insignificant, then it is hard to argue that it is a great film. Analysis of style in a book needs to be connected to that book's intended audience; style and presentation will vary depending on the knowledge and sophistication of the intended reader. If, for example, you have difficulty understanding a book aimed at a general audience, then it is fair to say that the author has not successfully reached his or her audience. But if you are reviewing a book intended for specialists, then your difficulties in reading are not relevant to a fair evaluation of that book. You can point out, though, that the book is tough going for a nonspecialist—just as you could point out that a movie sequel is hard to follow for those who did not see the original film.

### Drafting

1. Begin with an opening paragraph or two that engages your reader while introducing your subject and purpose in writing. Is there a specific occasion that has led to your writing? And what, exactly, are you evaluating?

2. Either introduce your criteria next and then show how your item for evaluation meets the criteria, point by point, through the rest of the essay; or, decide on an order for introducing your criteria and use that order as your structure. Put the most important criterion either first or last. It can be effective to put the most controversial point last.

3. If you are writing a review, then the basic criteria are already established. You will need some combination of summary, analysis, and evaluation. Begin with an attention-getter that includes a broad statement of the work's subject or subject category: This is a *biography* of Benjamin Franklin; this is a *female action-hero film.* An evaluation in general terms can complete the opening paragraph. For example:

> Dr. Cynthia Pemberton's new book, *More Than a Game: One Woman's Fight for Gender Equity in Sport,* is destined to become a classic in sport sociology, sport history, and women's studies.

4. The rest of the review will then combine summary details, analysis of presentation, and a final assessment of the work in the concluding paragraph. From the same review, after learning specifics of content, we read:

> The target audience for this book includes educators, coaches, athletes, and administrators at any level. Additionally, anyone interested in studying women's sports or pursuing a Title IX case will love this book.

5. Consider discussing the implications of your evaluation. Why is this important? Obviously for a book or film or art show, for example, we want to know if this is a "must read" or "must see." For other evaluation arguments, let us know why we should care about your subject and your perspective. Charles Krauthammer does not just argue that Tiger Woods is the greatest golfer ever; he also argues that his Gap Method is the best strategy for evaluation. That's why he shows that it works not just to put Woods ahead of Nicklaus but also to put other greats in their exalted place in other sports.

## A CHECKLIST FOR REVISION

- ☐ Do I have a good understanding of my purpose? Have I made my evaluation purpose clear to readers?
- ☐ Have I clearly stated my claim?
- ☐ Have I clearly stated my criteria for evaluation—or selected the appropriate elements of content, style, presentation, and theme for a review?
- ☐ Have I organized my argument into a coherent structure by some pattern that readers can recognize and follow?
- ☐ Have I provided good evidence and logic to support my evaluation?
- ☐ Have I used the basic checklist for revision in Chapter 4? (See p. 105.)

## STUDENT REVIEW

### WINCHESTER'S ALCHEMY: TWO MEN AND A BOOK

#### Ian Habel

One can hardly imagine a tale promising less excitement for a general audience than that of the making of the *Oxford English Dictionary* (*OED*). The sensationalism of murder and insanity would have to labor intensely against the burden of lexicography in crafting a genuine page-turner on the subject. Much to my surprise, Simon Winchester, in writing *The Professor and the Madman: A Tale of Murder, Insanity, and the Making of the Oxford English Dictionary,* has succeeded in producing so compelling a story that I was forced to devour it completely in a single afternoon, an unprecedented personal feat.

*The Professor and the Madman* is the story of the lives of two apparently very different men and the work that brought them together. Winchester begins by recounting the circumstances that led to the incarceration of Dr. W. C. Minor, a well-born, well-educated, and quite insane American ex-Army surgeon. Minor, in a fit of delusion, had murdered a man whom he believed to have crept into his Lambeth hotel room to torment him in his sleep. The doctor is tried and whisked off to the Asylum for the Criminally Insane, Broadmoor.

The author then introduces readers to the other two main characters: the *OED* itself and its editor James Murray, a lowborn, self-educated Scottish philologist. The shift in narrative focus is used to dramatic effect. The natural assumption on the part of the reader that these two seemingly unrelated plots must eventually meet urges us to read on in anticipation of that connection. As each chapter switches focus from one man to the other, it is introduced by a citation from the *OED,* reminding us that the story is ultimately about the dictionary. The citations also serve to foreshadow and provide a theme for the chapter. For example, the *OED* definition of *murder* heads the first chapter, relating to the details of Minor's crime.

Winchester acquaints us with the shortcomings of seventeenth- and eighteenth-century attempts at compiling a comprehensive dictionary of the English language. He takes us inside the meetings of the Philological Society, whose members proposed the compilation of the dictionary to end all dictionaries. The *OED* was to include examples of usage illustrating every shade of meaning for every word in the English language. Such a mammoth feat would require enlisting thousands of volunteer readers to comb the corpus of English literature in search of illustrative quotations to be submitted on myriad slips of paper. These slips of paper on each word would in turn be studied by a small army of editors preparing the definitions.

It is not surprising that our Dr. Minor, comfortably tucked away at Broadmoor, possessing both a large library and seemingly infinite free time, should become one of those volunteer readers. After all, we are still rightfully assuming some connection of the book's two plot lines. Yet what sets Dr. Minor apart from his fellow volunteers (aside from the details of his incarceration) is the remarkable efficiency with which he approached his task. Not content merely to fill out slips of paper for submission, Minor methodically indexed every possibly useful mention of any word appearing in his personal library. He then asked to be kept informed of the progress of the work, submitting quotations that would be immediately useful to editors. In this way he managed to "escape" his cell and plunge himself into the work of contemporaries, to become a part of a major event of his time.

Minor's work proved invaluable to the *OED*'s staff of editors, led by James Murray. With the two plot lines now intertwined, readers face such questions as "Will they find out that Minor is insane?" "Will Minor and Murray ever meet?" and "How long will they take to complete the dictionary?" The author builds suspense regarding a meeting of Minor and Murray by providing a false account of their first encounter, as reported by the American press, only to shatter us with the fact that this romantic version did not happen. I'll let Winchester give you the answers to these questions, while working his magic on you, drawing you into this fascinating tale of the making of the world's most famous dictionary.

## EVALUATING AN ARGUMENT: THE REBUTTAL OR REFUTATION ESSAY

When your primary purpose in writing is to challenge someone's argument rather than to present your own argument, you are writing a *rebuttal* or *refutation*. A good refutation demonstrates, in an orderly and logical way, the weaknesses of logic or evidence in the argument. Study the following guidelines to prepare a good refutation essay and then study the sample refutation that follows. It has been annotated to show you how the author has structured his rebuttal.

## GUIDELINES for Preparing a Refutation or Rebuttal Argument

1. **Read accurately.** Make certain that you have understood your opponent's argument. If you assume views not expressed by the writer and accuse the writer of holding those illogical views, you are guilty of the straw man fallacy, of attributing and then attacking a position that the person does not hold. Look up terms and references you do not know and examine the logic and evidence thoroughly.

2. **Pinpoint the weaknesses in the original argument.** Analyze the argument to determine, specifically, what flaws the argument contains. If the argument contains logical fallacies, make a list of the ones you plan to discredit. Examine the evidence presented. Is it insufficient, unreliable, or irrelevant? Decide, before drafting your refutation, exactly what elements of the argument you intend to challenge.

3. **Write your claim.** After analyzing the argument and deciding on the weaknesses to be challenged, write a claim that establishes that your disagreement is with the writer's logic, assumptions, or evidence, or a combination of these.

4. **Draft your essay, using the following three-part organization:**

   a. *The opponent's argument.* Usually you should not assume that your reader has read or remembered the argument you are refuting. Thus at the beginning of your essay, you need to state, accurately and fairly, the main points of the argument to be refuted.

   b. *Your claim.* Next make clear the nature of your disagreement with the argument you are rebutting.

   c. *Your refutation.* The specifics of your rebuttal will depend on the nature of your disagreement. If you are challenging the writer's evidence, then you must present the more recent evidence to explain why the evidence used is unreliable or misleading. If you are challenging assumptions, then you must explain why they do not hold up. If your claim is that the piece is filled with logical fallacies, then you must present and explain each fallacy.

# GENDER GAMES   | DAVID SADKER

A professor of education at American University, David Sadker has written extensively on educational issues, especially on the treatment of girls in the classroom. He is the author of *Failing at Fairness: How Our Schools Cheat Girls* (1995). "Gender Games" appeared in the *Washington Post* on July 31, 2000. Read, study the annotations, and then answer the questions that follow.

Remember when your elementary school teacher would announce the teams for the weekly spelling bee? "Boys against the girls!" There was nothing like a gender showdown to liven things up. Apparently, some writers never left this elementary level of intrigue. A spate of recent books and articles takes us back to the "boys versus girls" fray but this time, with much higher stakes. **1**

Attention-getting opening.

May's *Atlantic Monthly* cover story, "Girls Rule," is a case in point. The magazine published an excerpt from *The War Against Boys* by Christina Hoff Sommers, a book advancing the notion that boys are the real victims of gender bias while girls are soaring in school. **2**

Claim to be refuted.

Sommers and her supporters are correct in saying that girls and women have made significant educational progress in the past two decades. Females today make up more than 40 percent of medical and law school students, and more than half of college students. Girls continue to read sooner and write better than boys. And for as long as anyone can remember, girls have received higher grades than boys. **3**

What's right about the opponent's argument.

But there is more to these selected statistics than meets the eye. Although girls continue to receive higher report card grades than boys, their grades do not translate into higher test scores. The same girls who beat boys in the spelling bees score below boys on the tests that matter: the PSATs crucial for scholarships, the SATs and the ACTs needed for college acceptances, the GREs for graduate school and even the admission tests for law, business and medical schools. **4**

1st point of refutation.

Many believe that girls' higher grades may be more a reflection of their manageable classroom behavior than their intellectual accomplishment. Test scores are not influenced by quieter classroom behavior. Girls may in fact be trading their initiative and independence for peer approval and good grades, a trade-off that can have costly personal and economic consequences. **5**

2nd point of refutation.

The increase in female college enrollment catches headlines because it heralds the first time that females have outnumbered males on college campuses. But even these enrollment figures are misleading. The female presence increases as the status of the college decreases. Female students are more likely to dominate two-year schools than the Ivy League. And wherever they are, they find themselves segregated and channeled into the least prestigious and least costly majors. **6**

3rd point of refutation.

In today's world of e-success, more than 60 percent of computer science and business majors are male, about 70 percent of physics majors are males, and more than 80 percent of engineering students are male. But peek into **7** language, psychology, nursing and humanities classrooms, and you will find a sea of female faces.

8      Higher female enrollment figures mask the "glass walls" that separate the sexes and channel females and males into very different careers, with very different paychecks. Today, despite all the progress, the five leading occupations of employed women are secretary, receptionist, bookkeeper, registered nurse and hairdresser/cosmetologist.

9      Add this to the "glass ceiling" (about 3 percent of Fortune 500 top managers are women) and the persistence of a gender wage gap (women with advanced degrees still lag well behind their less-educated male counterparts) and the crippling impact of workplace and college stereotyping becomes evident.

10     Even within schools, where female teachers greatly outnumber male teachers, school management figures remind us that if there is a war on boys, women are not the generals. More than 85 percent of junior and senior high school principals are male, while 88 percent of school superintendents are male.

4th point of refutation.

11     Despite sparkling advances of females on the athletic fields, two-thirds of athletic scholarships still go to males. In some areas, women have actually lost ground. When Title IX was enacted in 1972, women coached more than 90 percent of intercollegiate women's teams. Today women coach only 48 percent of women's teams and only 1 percent of men's teams.

5th point of refutation.

12     If some adults are persuaded by the rhetoric in such books as *The War Against Boys*, be assured that children know the score. When more than 1,000 Michigan elementary school students were asked to describe what life would be like if they were born a member of the opposite sex, more than 40 percent of the girls saw positive advantages to being a boy: better jobs, more money and definitely more respect. Ninety-five percent of the boys saw no advantage to being a female.

Author concludes by stating his claim.

13     *The War Against Boys* attempts to persuade the public to abandon support for educational initiatives designed to help girls and boys avoid crippling stereotypes. I hope the public and Congress will not be taken in by the book's misrepresentations. We have no time to wage a war on either our boys or our girls.

Source: From *The Washington Post*, July 31, 2000. Reprinted by permission of the author.

### QUESTIONS FOR READING

1.  What work, specifically, is Sadker refuting? What is the claim presented by this work?
2.  What facts about girls does Sadker grant to Sommers?
3.  What facts about girls create a different story, according to Sadker?

### QUESTIONS FOR REASONING AND ANALYSIS

4.  What is Sadker's claim? What is he asserting about girls?
5.  What does Sadker think about the whole idea of books such as Sommers's?

6.   What statistic is most startling to you? Why?

7.   Do you agree that Sadker's statistics are more significant in telling us how women are doing in school, sports, and work? If you disagree with Sadker, how would you counter his argument?

8.   Think about your high school experiences. Do you think that teachers are waging a war against boys? What evidence do you have to support your views?

# FOR ANALYSIS AND DEBATE

## ADDICTED TO HEALTH | ROBERT H. BORK

A conservative legal scholar currently a law professor and visiting fellow at the Hoover Institution, Robert Bork has been acting attorney general and solicitor general of the U.S. Court of Appeals. His appointment to the Supreme Court, rejected by the Congress, has led to a book by Bork on the whole affair and to other books and articles on legal and public policy issues. The following appeared in the *National Review* on July 28, 1997.

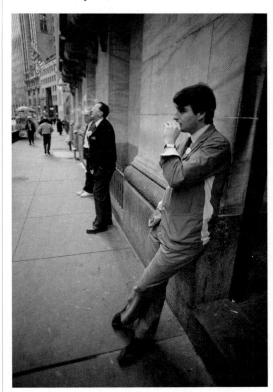

Smokers lined up outside their office building.

Government efforts to deal 1 with tobacco companies betray an ultimate ambition to control Americans' lives.

When moral self-righteousness, greed for money, and 2 political ambition work hand in hand they produce irrational, but almost irresistible, policies. The latest example is the war on cigarettes and cigarette smokers. A proposed settlement has been negotiated among politicians, plaintiffs' lawyers, and the tobacco industry. The only interests left out of the negotiations were smokers, who will be ordered to pay enormous sums with no return other than the deprivation of their own choices and pleasures.

It is a myth that today's 3 Americans are a sturdy, self-reliant folk who will fight any officious interference with their liberties. That has not been true at least since the New Deal. If you doubt that, walk the streets of any American city and see the forlorn men and women cupping their hands against the wind to light cigarettes so that they can get through a few more smokeless hours in their offices. Twenty-five percent of Americans smoke. Why can't they demand and get a compromise rather than accepting docilely the exile that employers and building managers impose upon them?

4    The answer is that they have been made to feel guilty by self-righteous non-smokers. A few years back, hardly anyone claimed to be seriously troubled by tobacco smoke. Now, an entire class of the morally superior claim to be able to detect, and be offended by, tobacco smoke several offices away from their own. These people must possess the sense of smell of a deer or an Indian guide. Yet they will happily walk through suffocating exhaust smoke from buses rather than wait a minute or two to cross the street.

5    No one should assume that peace will be restored when the last cigarette smoker has been banished to the Alaskan tundra. Other products will be pressed into service as morally reprehensible. If you would know the future, look at California—the national leader in health fanaticism. After a long day in Los Angeles flogging a book I had written, my wife and I sought relaxation with a drink at our hotel's outdoor bar. Our anticipation of pleasure was considerably diminished by a sign: "Warning! Toxic Substances Served Here." They were talking about my martini!

6    And martinis are a toxic substance, taken in any quantity sufficient to induce a sense of well-being. Why not, then, ban alcohol or at least require a death's head on every martini glass? Well, we did once outlaw alcohol; it was called Prohibition. The myth is that Prohibition increased the amount of drinking in this country; the truth is that it reduced it. There were, of course, some unfortunate side effects, like Al Capone and Dutch Schultz. But by and large the mobsters inflicted rigor mortis upon one another.

7    Why is it, then, that the end of Prohibition was welcomed joyously by the population? Not because alcohol is not dangerous. Not because the consumption of alcohol was not lessened. And not in order to save the lives of people with names like Big Jim and Ice Pick Phil. Prohibition came to an end because most Americans wanted to have a drink when and where they felt like it. If you insist on sounding like a law-and-economics professor, it ended because we thought the benefits of alcohol outweighed the costs.

8    That is the sort of calculation by which we lead our lives. Automobiles kill tens of thousands of people every year and disable perhaps that many again. We could easily stop the slaughter. Cars could be made with a top speed of ten miles an hour and with exteriors the consistency of marshmallows. Nobody would die, nobody would be disabled, and nobody would bother with cars very much.

9    There are, of course, less draconian measures available. On most highways, it is almost impossible to find anyone who observes the speed limits. On the theory of the tobacco precedent, car manufacturers should be liable for deaths caused by speeding; after all, they could build automobiles incapable of exceeding legal speed limits.

The reason we are willing to offer up lives and limbs to automobiles is, 10 quite simply, that they make life more pleasant (for those who remain intact)—among other things, by speeding commuting to work, by making possible family vacations a thousand miles from home, and by lowering the costs of products shipped from a distance. The case for regulating automobiles far more severely than we do is not essentially different from the case for heavy regulation of cigarettes or, soon, alcohol.

But choices concerning driving, smoking, and drinking are the sort of 11 things that ought to be left to the individual unless there are clear, serious harms to others.

The opening salvo in the drive to make smoking a criminal act is the pro- 12 posed settlement among the cigarette companies, plaintiffs' lawyers, and the states' attorneys general. We are told that the object is to protect teenagers and children (children being the last refuge of the sanctimonious). But many restrictions will necessarily affect adults, and the tobacco pact contains provisions that can only be explained as punishment for selling to adults.

The terms of the settlement plainly reveal an intense hatred of smoking. 13 Opposition to the pact comes primarily from those who think it is not severe enough. For example, critics say the settlement is defective in not restricting the marketing of cigarettes overseas by American tobacco companies. Connecticut's attorney general, Richard Blumenthal, defended the absence of such a provision: "Given our druthers we would have brought them to their knees all over the world, but there is a limit to our leverage." So much for the sovereignty of nations.

What the settlement does contain is bad enough. The pact would require 14 the companies to pony up $60 billion; $25 billion of this would be used for public-health issues to be identified by a presidential panel and the rest for children's health insurance. Though the purpose of the entire agreement is punitive, this slice is most obviously so.

The industry is also required to pay $308 billion over 25 years, in part to 15 repay states for the cost of treating sick smokers. There are no grounds for this provision. The tobacco companies have regularly won litigation against plaintiffs claiming injury on the grounds that everybody has known for the past forty years that smoking can cause health problems. This $308 billion, which takes from the companies what they have won in litigation, says, in effect, that no one assumed the risk of his own behavior.

The provision is groundless for additional reasons. The notion that the 16 states have lost money because of cigarettes ignores the federal and state taxes smokers have paid, which cover any amount the states could claim to have lost. Furthermore, a percentage of the population dies early from smoking. Had these people lived longer, the drain on Medicare and Medicaid would have been greater. When lowered pension and Social Security costs are figured in, it seems certain that government is better off financially with smoking than without it. If we must reduce the issue to one of dollars, as the attorneys general have done, states have profited financially from smoking. If this seems a gruesome and heartless calculation, it is. But don't blame me. The state governments advanced the financial argument and ought to live with its consequences, however distasteful.

17   Other provisions of the settlement fare no better under the application of common sense. The industry is to reduce smoking by teenagers by 30 percent in five years, 50 percent in seven years, and 60 percent in ten years. No one knows how the industry is to perform this trick. But if those goals are not met, the industry will be amerced $80 million a year for each percentage point it falls short.

18   The settlement assumes teenage smoking can be reduced dramatically by requiring the industry to conduct an expensive anti-smoking advertising campaign, banning the use of people and cartoon characters to promote cigarettes, and similar tactics. It is entirely predictable that this will not work. Other countries have banned cigarette advertising, only to watch smoking increase. Apparently the young, feeling themselves invulnerable, relish the risk of smoking. Studies have shown, moreover, that teenagers are drawn to smoking not because of advertising but because their parents smoke or because of peer pressure. Companies advertise to gain or maintain market share among those who already smoke.

19   To lessen the heat on politicians, the pact increases the powers of the Food and Drug Administration to regulate tobacco as an addictive drug, with the caveat that it may not prohibit cigarette smoking altogether before the year 2009. The implicit promise is that the complete prohibition of cigarettes will be seriously contemplated at that time. In the meantime, the FDA will subject cigarettes to stricter and stricter controls on the theory that tobacco is a drug.

20   Another rationale for prohibiting or sharply limiting smoking is the supposed need to protect non-smokers from secondhand smoke. The difficulty is that evidence of causation is weak. What we see is a possible small increase in an already small risk which, as some researchers have pointed out, may well be caused by other variables such as misclassification of former smokers as non-smokers or such lifestyle factors as diet.

21   But the tobacco companies should take little or no comfort from that. Given today's product-liability craze, scientific support, much less probability, is unnecessary to successful lawsuits against large corporations.

22   The pact is of dubious constitutionality as well. It outlaws the advertising of a product it is legal to sell, which raises the problem of commercial speech protected by the First Amendment. The settlement also requires the industry to disband its lobbying organization, the Tobacco Institute. Lobbying has traditionally been thought to fall within the First Amendment's guarantee of the right to petition the government for the redress of grievances.

23   And who is to pay for making smoking more difficult? Smokers will have the price of cigarettes raised by new taxes and by the tobacco companies' costs of complying with the settlement. It is a brilliant strategy: Smokers will pay billions to have their pleasure taken away. But if the tobacco settlement makes little sense as public policy, what can be driving it to completion? The motivations are diverse. Members of the plaintiff's bar, who have signally failed

in litigation against tobacco to date, are to be guaranteed billions of dollars annually. The states' attorneys general have a different set of incentives. They are members of the National Association of Attorneys General, NAAG, which is commonly, and accurately, rendered as the National Association of Aspiring Governors.

So far they have got what they wanted. There they are, on the front pages 24 of newspapers all over the country, looking out at us, jaws firm, conveying images of sobriety, courage, and righteousness. They have, after all, done battle with the forces of evil, and won—at least temporarily.

Tobacco executives and their lawyers are said to be wily folk, however. 25 They may find ways of defeating the strictures laid upon them. It may be too soon to tell, therefore, whether the tobacco settlement is a major defeat or a victory for the industry. In any case, we can live with it. But whenever individual responsibility is denied, government control of our behavior follows. After cigarettes it will be something else, and so on *ad infinitum*. One would think we would have learned that lesson many times over and that we would have had enough of it.

Source: From *National Review,* July 28, 1997. © 1997 by National Review, Inc., 215 Lexington Avenue, New York, NY 10016. Reprinted by permission.

QUESTIONS FOR READING

1. What is Bork's subject? (Do not answer smoking dangers, or secondhand smoke; be precise.)
2. What people or organizations are his primary target? What is his attitude toward smokers' acceptance of their "exile"?
3. What are the specifics of the settlement with tobacco companies?
4. What assumption, in Bork's view, stands behind the requirement of anti-smoking ads? Does he agree with the assumption?

QUESTIONS FOR REASONING AND ANALYSIS

5. What is Bork's claim?
6. What kinds of grounds or evidence does he present in support of his claim?
7. What is the tone of his argument? (Do you think that he expects his readers to agree with him?)

QUESTIONS FOR REFLECTION AND WRITING

8. Has Bork supported his claim to your satisfaction? Why or why not?
9. Do you find any logical fallacies in his argument? If so, how would you challenge them?
10. Does Bork's essay warrant a rebuttal? Why or why not?

# SUGGESTIONS FOR DISCUSSION AND WRITING

1. Think about sports stars you know. Write an argument defending one player as the best in his or her field of play. Think about whether you want to use Krauthammer's "Method 1" or "Method 2" or your own method for your criteria. (Remember that you can qualify your argument; you could write about the best college football player this year, for example.)

2. If you like music, think about what you might evaluate from this field. Who is the best rock band? Hip-hop artist? Country-western singer? And so forth. Be sure to make your criteria for evaluation clear.

3. You have had many instructors—and much instruction—in the last 12+ years. Is there one teacher who is/was the best? If so, why? Is there a teaching method that stands out in your memory for the excellence of its approach? Find an evaluation topic from your educational experiences.

4. Select an editorial, op-ed column, letter to the editor, or one of the essays in this text as an argument with which you disagree. Prepare a refutation of the work's logic or evidence or both. Follow the guidelines for writing a refutation or rebuttal in this chapter.

5. What is your favorite book? Movie? Television show? Why is it your favorite? Does it warrant an argument that it is really good, maybe even the best, in some way or in some category (sitcoms, for example)? Write a review, following the guidelines for this type of evaluation argument given in this chapter.

# The Position Paper: Claims of Values

READ: Who are the speakers? What is the situation?

REASON: What is the point of the cartoon? What does Dana Summers, the cartoonist, want readers to think about?

REFLECT/WRITE: Why does this cartoon make a good opening for a chapter on arguments based on values?

As we established in Chapter 4, all arguments involve values. Evaluation arguments require judgment—thoughtful judgment, one hopes, based on criteria—but judgment nonetheless. If you believe that no one should spend more than $25,000 for a car, then you will not appreciate the qualities that attract some people to Mercedes. When one argues that government tax rates should go up as income goes up, it is because one believes that it is *right* for government to redistribute income to some degree: The rich pay more in taxes, the poor get more in services. When countries ban the importing of ivory, they do so because they believe it is *wrong* to destroy the magnificent elephant just so humans can use their ivory tusks for decorative items. (Observe that the word *magnificent* expresses a value.)

Some arguments, though, are less about judging what is good or best, or less about how to solve specific problems, than they are about stating a position on an issue. An argument that defends a general position (segregated schools are wrong) may imply action that should result (schools should be integrated), but the focus of the argument is first to state and defend the position. It is helpful to view these arguments, based heavily on values and a logical sequencing of ideas with less emphasis on specifics, as a separate type—genre—of argument. These claims of values are often called position papers.

## CHARACTERISTICS OF THE POSITION PAPER

The position paper, or claim of values, may be the most difficult of arguments simply because it is often perceived to be the easiest. Let's think about this kind of argument:

- A claim based on values and argued more with logic than specifics is usually more general or abstract or philosophical than other types of argument. Greenpeace objects to commercial fishing that uses large nets that ensnare dolphins along with commercial fish such as tuna. Why? Because we ought not to destroy such beautiful and highly developed animals. Because we ought not to destroy more than we need, to waste part of nature because we are careless or in a hurry. For Greenpeace, the issue is about values—though it may be about money for the commercial fishermen.

- The position paper makes a claim about what is right or wrong, good or bad, for us as individuals or as a society. Topics can range from capital punishment to pornography to endangered species.

- A claim based on values is often developed in large part by a logical sequencing of reasons. But a support of principles also depends on relevant facts. Remember the long list of specific abuses listed in the Declaration of Independence (see pp. 150–53). If Greenpeace can show that commercial fisheries can be successful using a different kind of net or staying away from areas heavily populated by dolphins, it can probably get more support for its general principles.

- A successful position paper requires more than a forceful statement of personal beliefs. If we can reason logically from principles widely shared by our audience, we are more likely to be successful. If we are going to challenge their beliefs or values, then we need to consider the conciliatory approach as a strategy for getting them to at least listen to our argument.

## GUIDELINES for Analyzing a Claim of Value

When reading position papers, what should you look for? Again, the basics of good argument apply here as well as with definition arguments. To analyze claims of values specifically, use these questions as guides:

- **What is the writer's claim?** Is it clear?
- **Is the claim qualified if necessary?** Some claims of value are broad philosophical assertions ("Capital punishment is immoral and bad public policy"). Others are qualified ("Capital punishment is acceptable only in crimes of treason").
- **What facts are presented?** Are they credible? Are they relevant to the claim's support?
- **What reasons are given in support of the claim?** What assumptions are necessary to tie reasons to claim? Make a list of reasons and assumptions and analyze the writer's logic. Do you find any fallacies?
- **What are the implications of the claim?** For example, if you argue for the legalization of all recreational drugs, you eliminate all "drug problems" by definition. But what new problems may be created by this approach? Consider more car accidents and reduced productivity for openers.
- **Is the argument convincing?** Does the evidence provide strong support for the claim? Are you prepared to agree with the writer, in whole or in part?

## PREPARING A POSITION PAPER

In addition to the guidelines for writing arguments presented in Chapter 4, you can use the following advice specific to writing position papers or claims of value.

### Planning

1. **Think:** What claim, exactly, do you want to support? Should you qualify your first attempt at a claim statement?
2. **Think:** What grounds (evidence) do you have to support your claim? You may want to make a list of the reasons and facts you would consider using to defend your claim.

3. **Think:** Study your list of possible grounds and identify the assumptions (warrants) and backing for your grounds.

4. **Think:** Now make a list of the grounds most often used by those holding views that oppose your claim. This second list will help you prepare counterarguments to possible rebuttals, but first it will help you test your commitment to your position. If you find the opposition's arguments persuasive and cannot think how you would rebut them, you may need to rethink your position. Ideally, your two lists will confirm your views but also increase your respect for opposing views.

5. **Consider:** How can I use a conciliatory approach? With an emotion-laden or highly controversial issue, the conciliatory approach can be an effective strategy. Conciliatory arguments include

   - the use of nonthreatening language,
   - the fair expression of opposing views, and
   - a statement of the common ground shared by opposing sides.

   You may want to use a conciliatory approach when (1) you know your views will be unpopular with at least some members of your audience; (2) the issue is highly emotional and has sides that are "entrenched" so that you are seeking some accommodations rather than dramatic changes of position; (3) you need to interact with members of your audience and want to keep a respectful relationship going. The sample student essay on gun control (at the end of this chapter) illustrates a conciliatory approach.

## Drafting

1. Begin with an opening paragraph or two that introduces your topic in an interesting way. Possibilities include a statement of the issue's seriousness or reasons why the issue is currently being debated—or why we should go back to reexamine it. Some writers are spurred by a recent event that receives media coverage; recounting such an event can produce an effective opening. You can also briefly summarize points of the opposition that you will challenge in supporting your claim. Many counterarguments are position papers.

2. Decide where to place your claim statement. Your best choices are either early in your essay or at the end of your essay, after you have made your case. The second approach can be an effective alternative to the more common pattern of stating one's claim early.

3. Organize evidence in an effective way. One plan is to move from the least important to the most important reasons, followed by rebuttals to potential counterarguments. Another possibility is to organize by the arguments of the opposition, explaining why each of their reasons fails to hold up. A third approach is to organize logically. That is, if some reasons build on the accepting of other reasons, you want to begin with the necessary underpinnings and then move forward from those.

4.  Provide a logical defense of or specifics in support of each reason. You have not finished your task by simply asserting several reasons for your claim. You also need to present facts or examples for or a logical explanation of each reason. For example, you have not defended your views on capital punishment by asserting that it is right or just to take the life of a murderer. Why is it right or just? Executing the murderer will not bring the victim back to life. Do two wrongs make a right? These are some of the thoughts your skeptical reader may have unless you explain and justify your reasoning. *Remember:* Quoting another writer's opinion on your topic does not provide proof for your reasons. It merely shows that someone else agrees with you.

5.  Maintain an appropriate level of seriousness for an argument of principle. Of course, word choice must be appropriate to a serious discussion, but in addition be sure to present reasons that are also appropriately serious. For example, if you are defending the claim that music CDs should not be subject to content labeling because such censorship is inconsistent with First Amendment rights, do not trivialize your argument by including the point that young people are tired of adults controlling their lives. (This is another issue for another paper.)

## A CHECKLIST FOR REVISION

- ☐ Do I have a clear statement of my claim? Is it qualified, if appropriate?
- ☐ Have I organized my argument, building the parts of my support into a clear and logical structure that readers can follow?
- ☐ Have I avoided logical fallacies?
- ☐ Have I found relevant facts and examples to support and develop my reasons?
- ☐ Have I paid attention to appropriate word choice, including using a conciliatory approach if that is a wise strategy?
- ☐ Have I used the basic checklist for revision in Chapter 4 (see p. 105)?

## STUDENT ESSAY

### EXAMINING THE ISSUE OF GUN CONTROL

#### Chris Brown

The United States has a long history of compromise. Issues such as representation in government have been resolved because of compromise, forming some of the bases of American life. Americans, however, like to feel

Introduction connects ambivalence in American character to conflict over gun control.

that they are uncompromising, never willing to surrender an argument. This attitude has led to a number of issues in modern America that are unresolved, including the issue of gun control. Bickering over the issue has slowed progress toward legislation that will solve the serious problem of gun violence in America, while keeping recreational use of firearms available to responsible people. To resolve the conflict over guns, the arguments of both sides must be examined, with an eye to finding the flaws in both. Then perhaps we can reach some meaningful compromises.

Student organizes by arguments for no gun control.

Gun advocates have used many arguments for the continued availability of firearms to the public. The strongest of these defenses points to the many legitimate uses for guns. One use is protection against violence, a concern of some people in today's society. There are many problems with the use of guns for protection, however, and these problems make the continued use of firearms for protection dangerous. One such problem is that gun owners are not always able to use guns responsibly. When placed in a situation in which personal injury or loss is imminent, people often do not think intelligently. Adrenaline surges through the body, and fear takes over much of the thinking process. This causes gun owners to use their weapons, firing at whatever threatens them. Injuries and deaths of innocent people, including family members of the gun owner, result. Removing guns from the house seems to be the only solution to these sad consequences.

1. Guns for protection.

Responding to this argument, gun advocates ask how they are to defend themselves without guns. But guns are needed for protection from other guns. If there are no guns, people need only to protect themselves from criminals using knives, baseball bats, and other weapons. Obviously the odds of surviving a knife attack are greater than the odds of surviving a gun attack. One reason is that a gun is an impersonal weapon. Firing at someone from 50 feet away requires much less commitment than charging someone with a knife and stabbing repeatedly. Also, bullet wounds are, generally, more severe than knife wounds. Guns are also more likely to be misused when a dark figure is in one's house. To kill with the gun requires only to point and shoot; no recognition of the figure is needed. To kill with a knife, by contrast, requires getting within arm's reach of the figure.

There are other uses of guns, including recreation. Hunting and target shooting are valid, responsible uses of guns. How do we keep guns available for recreation? The answer is in the form of gun clubs and hunting clubs. Many are already established; more can be constructed. These clubs can provide recreational use of guns for responsible people while keeping guns off the streets and out of the house.

2. Recreational uses.

The last argument widely used by gun advocates is the constitutional right to bear arms. The fallacies in this argument are that the Constitution was written in a vastly different time. This different time had different uses for guns, and a different type of gun. Firearms were defended in the Constitution because of their many valid uses and fewer problems. Guns were mostly muskets, guns that were not very accurate beyond close range. Also, guns took more than 30 seconds to load in the eighteenth century and could fire only one shot before reloading. These differences with today's guns affect the relative safety of guns then and now. In addition, those who did not live in the city at the time used hunting for food as well as for recreation; hunting was a necessary component of life. That is not true today. Another use of guns in the eighteenth century was as protection from animals. Wild animals such as bears and cougars were much more common. Settlers, explorers, and hunters needed protection from these animals in ways not comparable with modern life.

3. Second Amendment rights.

Finally, Revolutionary America had no standing army. Defense of the nation and of one's home from other nations relied on local militia. The right to bear arms granted in the Constitution was inspired by the need for national protection as well as by the other outdated needs previously discussed. Today America has a standing army with enough weaponry to adequately defend itself from outside aggressors. There is no need for every citizen to carry a musket, or an AK-47, for the protection of the nation. It would seem, then, that the Second Amendment does not apply to modern society.

Student establishes
a compromise
position.

To reach a compromise, we also have to examine the other side of the issue. Some gun-control advocates argue that all guns are unnecessary and should be outlawed. The problem with this argument is that guns will still be available to those who do not mind breaking the law. Until an economically sound and feasible way of controlling illegal guns in America is found, guns cannot be totally removed, no matter how much legislation is passed. This means that if guns are to be outlawed for uses other than recreational uses, a way must be found to combat the illegal gun trade that will evolve. Tough criminal laws and a large security force are all that can be offered to stop illegal uses of guns until better technology is available. This means that, perhaps, a good resolution would involve gradual restrictions on guns, until eventually guns were restricted only to recreational uses in a controlled setting for citizens not in the police or military.

Conclusion restates
student's claim.

Both sides on this issue have valid points. Any middle ground needs to offer something to each side. It must address the reasons people feel that they need guns for protection, allow for valid recreational use, and keep guns out of the hands of the public, except for properly trained police officers. Time and money will be needed to move toward the removal of America's huge handgun arsenal. But, sooner or later a compromise on the issue of gun control must be made to make America a safer, better place to live.

## THE BATTLE FOR YOUR BRAIN | RONALD BAILEY

A graduate of the University of Virginia, Ronald Bailey is science correspondent for *Reason* magazine and *Reason.com*. A longtime global warming skeptic and author of *Global Warming and Other Eco-Myths* (2002), Bailey has more recently changed his position. He has also turned his attention to the advances in biotechnology, publishing in 2005 his book *Liberation Biology: The Moral and Scientific Case for the Biotech Revolution*. The following essay was published in *Reason* magazine in February 2003. The essay is lengthy and serious, but worth your study and reflection as a view into an important medical debate.

**PREREADING QUESTIONS** Are you excited about scientific advances designed to improve the human brain? Why or why not?

"We're on the verge of profound changes in our ability to manipulate the  1
brain," says Paul Root Wolpe, a bioethicist at the University of Pennsylvania.
He isn't kidding. The dawning age of neuroscience promises not just new
treatments for Alzheimer's and other brain diseases but enhancements to
improve memory, boost intellectual acumen, and fine-tune our emotional
responses. "The next two decades will be the golden age of neuroscience,"
declares Jonathan Moreno, a bioethicist at the University of Virginia. "We're
on the threshold of the kind of rapid growth of information in neuroscience
that was true of genetics fifteen years ago."

One man's golden age is another man's dystopia. One of the more vocif-  2
erous critics of such research is Francis Fukuyama, who warns in his book *Our
Posthuman Future* that "we are already in the midst of this revolution" and
*"we should use the power of the state to regulate it"* (emphasis his). In May a
cover story in the usually pro-technology *Economist* worried that "neuroscientists may soon be able to screen people's brains to assess their mental health,
to distribute that information, possibly accidentally, to employers or insurers,
and to 'fix' faulty personality traits with drugs or implants on demand."

There are good reasons to consider the ethics of tinkering directly with  3
the organ from which all ethical reflection arises. Most of those reasons boil
down to the need to respect the rights of the people who would use the new
technologies. Some of the field's moral issues are common to all biomedical
research: how to design clinical trials ethically, how to ensure subjects' privacy,
and so on. Others are peculiar to neurology. It's not clear, for example, whether
people suffering from neurodegenerative disease can give informed consent
to be experimented on.

Last May the Dana Foundation sponsored an entire conference at Stanford  4
on "neuroethics." Conferees deliberated over issues like the moral questions
raised by new brain scanning techniques, which some believe will lead to the
creation of truly effective lie detectors. Participants noted that scanners might
also be able to pinpoint brain abnormalities in those accused of breaking the
law, thus changing our perceptions of guilt and innocence. Most nightmarishly,
some worried that governments could one day use brain implants to monitor
and perhaps even control citizens' behavior.

But most of the debate over neuroethics has not centered around patients'  5
or citizens' autonomy, perhaps because so many of the field's critics themselves hope to restrict that autonomy in various ways. The issue that most
vexes *them* is the possibility that neuroscience might enhance previously
"normal" human brains.

The tidiest summation of their complaint comes from the conservative col-  6
umnist William Safire. "Just as we have anti-depressants today to elevate
mood," he wrote after the Dana conference, "tomorrow we can expect a kind
of Botox for the brain to smooth out wrinkled temperaments, to turn shy
people into extroverts, or to bestow a sense of humor on a born grouch. But
what price will human nature pay for these nonhuman artifices?"

Truly effective neuropharmaceuticals that improve moods and sharpen  7
mental focus are already widely available and taken by millions. While there is

some controversy about the effectiveness of Prozac, Paxil, and Zoloft, nearly 30 million Americans have taken them, with mostly positive results. In his famous 1993 book *Listening to Prozac,* the psychiatrist Peter Kramer describes patients taking the drug as feeling "better than well." One Prozac user, called Tess, told him that when she isn't taking the medication, "I am not myself."

### ONE PILL MAKES YOU SMARTER . . .

8    That's exactly what worries Fukuyama, who thinks Prozac looks a lot like *Brave New World*'s soma. The pharmaceutical industry, he declares, is producing drugs that "provide self-esteem in the bottle by elevating serotonin in the brain." If you need a drug to be your "self," these critics ask, do you really have a self at all?

9    Another popular neuropharmaceutical is Ritalin, a drug widely prescribed to remedy attention deficit hyperactivity disorder (ADHD), which is characterized by agitated behavior and an inability to focus on tasks. Around 1.5 million schoolchildren take Ritalin, which recent research suggests boosts the activity of the neurotransmitter dopamine in the brain. Like all psychoactive drugs, it is not without controversy. Perennial psychiatric critic Peter Breggin argues that millions of children are being "drugged into more compliant or submissive state[s]" to satisfy the needs of harried parents and school officials. For Fukuyama, Ritalin is prescribed to control rambunctious children because "parents and teachers . . . do not want to spend the time and energy necessary to discipline, divert, entertain, or train difficult children the old-fashioned way."

10   Unlike the more radical Breggin, Fukuyama acknowledges that drugs such as Prozac and Ritalin have helped millions when other treatments have failed. Still, he worries about their larger social consequences. "There is a disconcerting symmetry between Prozac and Ritalin," he writes. "The former is prescribed heavily for depressed women lacking in self-esteem; it gives them more the alpha-male feeling that comes with high serotonin levels. Ritalin, on the other hand, is prescribed largely for young boys who do not want to sit still in class because nature never designed them to behave that way. Together, the two sexes are gently nudged toward that androgynous median personality, self-satisfied and socially compliant, that is the current politically correct outcome in American society."

11   Although there are legitimate questions here, they're related not to the chemicals themselves but to who makes the decision to use them. Even if Prozac and Ritalin can help millions of people, that doesn't mean schools should be able to force them on any student who is unruly or bored. But by the same token, even if you accept the most radical critique of the drug—that ADHD is not a real disorder to begin with—that doesn't mean Americans who exhibit the symptoms that add up to an ADHD diagnosis should not be allowed to alter their mental state chemically, if that's an outcome they want and a path to it they're willing to take.

12   Consider Nick Megibow, a senior majoring in philosophy at Gettysburg College. "Ritalin made my life a lot better," he reports. "Before I started taking Ritalin as a high school freshman, I was doing really badly in my classes. I had really bad grades, Cs and Ds mostly. By sophomore year, I started taking

Ritalin, and it really worked amazingly. My grades improved dramatically to mostly As and Bs. It allows me to focus and get things done rather than take three times the amount of time that it should take to finish something." If people like Megibow don't share Fukuyama's concerns about the wider social consequences of their medication, it's because they're more interested, quite reasonably, in feeling better and living a successful life.

What really worries critics like Safire and Fukuyama is that Prozac and 13 Ritalin may be the neuropharmacological equivalent of bearskins and stone axes compared to the new drugs that are coming. Probably the most critical mental function to be enhanced is memory. And this, it turns out, is where the most promising work is being done. At Princeton, biologist Joe Tsien's laboratory famously created smart mice by genetically modifying them to produce more NMDA brain receptors, which are critical for the formation and maintenance of memories. Tsien's mice were much faster learners than their unmodified counterparts. "By enhancing learning, that is, memory acquisition, animals seem to be able to solve problems faster," notes Tsien. He believes his work has identified an important target that will lead other researchers to develop drugs that enhance memory.

A number of companies are already hard at work developing memory 14 drugs. Cortex Pharmaceuticals has developed a class of compounds called AMPA receptor modulators, which enhance the glutamate-based transmission between brain cells. Preliminary results indicate that the compounds do enhance memory and cognition in human beings. Memory Pharmaceuticals, cofounded by Nobel laureate Eric Kandel, is developing a calcium channel receptor modulator that increases the sensitivity of neurons and allows them to transmit information more speedily and a nicotine receptor modulator that plays a role in synaptic plasticity. Both modulators apparently improve memory. Another company, Targacept, is working on the nicotinic receptors as well.

All these companies hope to cure the memory deficits that some 30 mil- 15 lion baby boomers will suffer as they age. If these compounds can fix deficient memories, it is likely that they can enhance normal memories as well. Tsien points out that a century ago the encroaching senility of Alzheimer's disease might have been considered part of the "normal" progression of aging. "So it depends on how you define *normal*," he says. "Today we know that most people have less good memories after age forty, and I don't believe that's a normal process."

## EIGHT OBJECTIONS

And so we face the prospect of pills to improve our mood, our memory, 16 our intelligence, and perhaps more. Why would anyone object to that?

Eight objections to such enhancements recur in neuroethicists' arguments. 17 None of them is really convincing.

*Neurological enhancements permanently change the brain.* Erik Parens of 18 the Hastings Center, a bioethics think tank, argues that it's better to enhance a child's performance by changing his environment than by changing his brain—that it's better to, say, reduce his class size than to give him Ritalin. But this is a false dichotomy. Reducing class size is aimed at changing the child's biology too, albeit indirectly. Activities like teaching are supposed to induce biological changes in a child's brain, through a process called *learning.*

19      Fukuyama falls into this same error when he suggests that even if there is some biological basis for their condition, people with ADHD "clearly . . . can do things that would affect their final degree of attentiveness or hyperactivity. Training, character, determination, and environment more generally would all play important roles." So can Ritalin, and much more expeditiously, too. "What is the difference between Ritalin and the Kaplan SAT review?" asks the Dartmouth neuroscientist Michael Gazzaniga. "It's six of one and a half dozen of the other. If both can boost SAT scores by, say, 120 points, I think it's immaterial which way it's done."

20      *Neurological enhancements are antiegalitarian.* A perennial objection to new medical technologies is the one Parens calls "unfairness in the distribution of resources." In other words, the rich and their children will get access to brain enhancements first, and will thus acquire more competitive advantages over the poor.

21      This objection rests on the same false dichotomy as the first. As the University of Virginia's Moreno puts it, "We don't stop people from giving their kids tennis lessons." If anything, the new enhancements might *increase* social equality. Moreno notes that neuropharmaceuticals are likely to be more equitably distributed than genetic enhancements, because "after all, a pill is easier to deliver than DNA."

22      *Neurological enhancements are self-defeating.* Not content to argue that the distribution of brain enhancements won't be egalitarian enough, some critics turn around and argue that it will be *too* egalitarian. Parens has summarized this objection succinctly: "If everyone achieved the same relative advantage with a given enhancement, then ultimately no one's position would change; the 'enhancement' would have failed if its purpose was to increase competitive advantage."

23      This is a flagrant example of the zero-sum approach that afflicts so much bioethical thought. Let's assume, for the sake of argument, that everyone in society will take a beneficial brain-enhancing drug. Their relative positions may not change, but the overall productivity and wealth of society would increase considerably, making everyone better off. Surely that is a social good.

24      *Neurological enhancements are difficult to refuse.* Why exactly would everyone in the country take the same drug? Because, the argument goes, competitive pressures in our go-go society will be so strong that a person will be forced to take a memory-enhancing drug just to keep up with everyone else. Even if the law protects freedom of choice, social pressures will draw us in.

25      For one thing, this misunderstands the nature of the technology. It's not simply a matter of popping a pill and suddenly zooming ahead. "I know a lot of smart people who don't amount to a row of beans," says Gazzaniga "They're just happy underachieving, living life below their potential. So a pill that pumps up your intellectual processing power won't necessarily give you the drive and ambition to use it."

Beyond that, it's not as though we don't all face competitive pressures [26] anyway—to get into and graduate from good universities, to constantly upgrade skills, to buy better computers and more productive software, whatever. Some people choose to enhance themselves by getting a Ph.D. in English; others are happy to stop their formal education after high school. It's not clear why a pill should be more irresistible than higher education, or why one should raise special ethical concerns while the other does not.

*Neurological enhancements undermine good character.* For some critics, [27] the comparison to higher education suggests a different problem. We should strive for what we get, they suggest; taking a pill to enhance cognitive functioning is just too easy. As Fukuyama puts it: "The normal, and morally acceptable, way of overcoming low self-esteem was to struggle with oneself and with others, to work hard, to endure painful sacrifices, and finally to rise and be seen as having done so."

"By denying access to brain-enhancing drugs, people like Fukuyama are [28] advocating an exaggerated stoicism," counters Moreno. "I don't see the benefit or advantage of that kind of tough love." Especially since there will still be many different ways to achieve things and many difficult challenges in life. Brain-enhancing drugs might ease some of our labors, but as Moreno notes, "there are still lots of hills to climb, and they are pretty steep." Cars, computers, and washing machines have tremendously enhanced our ability to deal with formerly formidable tasks. That doesn't mean life's struggles have disappeared—just that we can now tackle the next ones.

*Neurological enhancements undermine personal responsibility.* Carol [29] Freedman, a philosopher at Williams College, argues that what is at stake "is a conception of ourselves as responsible agents, not machines." Fukuyama extends the point, claiming that "ordinary people" are eager to "medicalize as much of their behavior as possible and thereby reduce their responsibility for their own actions." As an example, he suggests that people who claim to suffer from ADHD "want to absolve themselves of personal responsibility."

But we are not debating people who might use an ADHD diagnosis as an [30] excuse to behave irresponsibly. We are speaking of people who use Ritalin to *change* their behavior. Wouldn't it be more irresponsible of them to not take corrective action?

*Neurological enhancements enforce dubious norms.* There are those who [31] assert that corrective action might be irresponsible after all, depending on just what it is that you're trying to correct. People might take neuropharmaceuticals, some warn, to conform to a harmful social conception of normality. Many bioethicists—Georgetown University's Margaret Little, for example—argue that we can already see this process in action among women who resort to expensive and painful cosmetic surgery to conform to a social ideal of feminine beauty. Never mind for the moment that beauty norms for both men and women have never been so diverse. Providing and choosing to avail oneself of that surgery makes one complicit in norms that are morally wrong, the critics argue. After all, people should be judged not by their physical appearances but by the content of their characters.

32    That may be so, but why should someone suffer from society's slights if she can overcome them with a nip here and a tuck there? The norms may indeed be suspect, but the suffering is experienced by real people whose lives are consequently diminished. Little acknowledges this point, but argues that those who benefit from using a technology to conform have a moral obligation to fight against the suspect norm. Does this mean people should be given access to technologies they regard as beneficial only if they agree to sign on to a bioethical fatwa?

33    Of course, we should admire people who challenge norms they disagree with and live as they wish, but why should others be denied relief just because some bioethical commissars decree that society's misdirected values must change? Change may come, but real people should not be sacrificed to some restrictive bioethical utopia in the meantime. Similarly, we should no doubt value depressed people or people with bad memories just as highly as we do happy geniuses, but until that glad day comes people should be allowed to take advantage of technologies that improve their lives in the society in which they actually live.

34    Furthermore, it's far from clear that everyone will use these enhancements in the same ways. There are people who alter their bodies via cosmetic surgery to bring them closer to the norm, and there are people who alter their bodies via piercings and tattoos to make them more individually expressive. It doesn't take much imagination to think of unusual or unexpected ways that Americans might use mind enhancing technologies. Indeed, the war on drugs is being waged, in part, against a small but significant minority of people who prefer to alter their consciousness in socially disapproved ways.

35    *Neurological enhancements make us inauthentic.* Parens and others worry that the users of brain-altering chemicals are less authentically themselves when they're on the drug. Some of them would reply that the exact opposite is the case. In *Listening to Prozac*, Kramer chronicles some dramatic transformations in the personalities and attitudes of his patients once they're on the drug. The aforementioned Tess tells him it was "as if I had been in a drugged state all those years and now I'm clearheaded."

36    Again, the question takes a different shape when one considers the false dichotomy between biological and "nonbiological" enhancements. Consider a person who undergoes a religious conversion and emerges from the experience with a more upbeat and attractive personality. Is he no longer his "real" self? Must every religious convert be deprogrammed?

37    Even if there were such a thing as a "real" personality, why should you stick with it if you don't like it? If you're socially withdrawn and a pill can give you a more vivacious and outgoing manner, why not go with it? After all, you're choosing to take responsibility for being the "new" person the drug helps you to be.

### AUTHENTICITY AND RESPONSIBILITY

38    "Is it a drug-induced personality or has the drug cleared away barriers to the real personality?" asks the University of Pennsylvania's Wolpe. Surely the

person who is choosing to use the drug is in a better position to answer that question than some bioethical busybody.

This argument over authenticity lies at the heart of the neuroethicists' 39 objections. If there is a single line that divides the supporters of neurological freedom from those who would restrict the new treatments, it is the debate over whether a natural state of human being exists and, if so, how appropriate it is to modify it. Wolpe makes the point that in one sense cognitive enhancement resembles its opposite, Alzheimer's disease. A person with Alzheimer's loses her personality. Similarly, an enhanced individual's personality may become unrecognizable to those who knew her before.

Not that this is unusual. Many people experience a version of this process 40 when they go away from their homes to college or the military. They return as changed people with new capacities, likes, dislikes, and social styles, and they often find that their families and friends no longer relate to them in the old ways. Their brains have been changed by those experiences, and they are not the same people they were before they went away. Change makes most people uncomfortable, probably never more so than when it happens to a loved one. Much of the neuro-Luddites' case rests on a belief in an unvarying, static personality, something that simply doesn't exist,

It isn't just personality that changes over time. Consciousness itself is far 41 less static than we've previously assumed, a fact that raises contentious questions of free will and determinism. Neuroscientists are finding more and more of the underlying automatic processes operating in the brain, allowing us to take a sometimes disturbing look under our own hoods. "We're finding out that by the time we're conscious of doing something, the brain's already done it," explains Gazzaniga. Consciousness, rather than being the director of our activities, seems instead to be a way for the brain to explain to itself why it did something.

Haunting the whole debate over neuroscientific research and neuroen- 42 hancements is the fear that neuroscience will undercut notions of responsibility and free will. Very preliminary research has suggested that many violent criminals do have altered brains. At the Stanford conference, *Science* editor Donald Kennedy suggested that once we know more about brains, our legal system will have to make adjustments in how we punish those who break the law. A murderer or rapist might one day plead innocence on the grounds that "my amygdala made me do it." There is precedent for this: The legal system already mitigates criminal punishment when an offender can convince a jury he's so mentally ill that he cannot distinguish right from wrong.

Of course, there are other ways such discoveries might pan out in the 43 legal system, with results less damaging to social order but still troubling for notions of personal autonomy. One possibility is that an offender's punishment might be reduced if he agrees to take a pill that corrects the brain defect he blames for his crime. We already hold people responsible when their drug use causes harm to others—most notably, with laws against drunk driving. Perhaps in the future we will hold people responsible if they fail to take drugs that would help prevent them from behaving in harmful ways. After all, which is more damaging to personal autonomy, a life confined to a jail cell or roaming free while taking a medication?

44    The philosopher Patricia Churchland examines these conundrums in her [2002] book, *Brainwise: Studies in Neurophilosophy.* "Much of human social life depends on the expectation that agents have control over their actions and are responsible for their choices," she writes. "In daily life it is commonly assumed that it is sensible to punish and reward behavior so long as the person was in control and chose knowingly and intentionally." And that's the way it should remain, even as we learn more about how our brains work and how they sometimes break down.

45    Churchland points out that neuroscientific research by scientists like the University of Iowa's Antonio Damasio strongly shows that emotions are an essential component of viable practical reasoning about what a person should do. In other words, neuroscience is bolstering philosopher David Hume's insight that "reason is and ought only to be the slave of the passions." Patients whose affects are depressed or lacking due to brain injury are incapable of judging or evaluating between courses of action. Emotion is what prompts and guides our choices.

46    Churchland further argues that moral agents come to be morally and practically wise not through pure cognition but by developing moral beliefs and habits through life experiences. Our moral reflexes are honed through watching and hearing about which actions are rewarded and which are punished; we learn to be moral the same way we learn language. Consequently, Churchland concludes "the default presumption that agents are responsible for their actions is empirically necessary to an agent's learning, both emotionally and cognitively, how to evaluate the consequences of certain events and the price of taking risks."

47    It's always risky to try to derive an "ought" from an "is," but neuroscience seems to be implying that liberty—i.e., letting people make choices and then suffer or enjoy the consequences—is essential for inculcating virtue and maintaining social cooperation. Far from undermining personal responsibility, neuroscience may end up strengthening it.

## FOR NEUROLOGICAL LIBERTY

48    Fukuyama wants to "draw red lines" to distinguish between therapy and enhancement, "directing research toward the former while putting restrictions on the latter." He adds that "the original purpose of medicine is, after all, to heal the sick, not turn healthy people into gods." He imagines a federal agency that would oversee neurological research, prohibiting anything that aims at enhancing our capacities beyond some notion of the human norm.

49    "For us to flourish as human beings, we have to live according to our nature, satisfying the deepest longings that we as natural beings have," Fukuyama told the Christian review *Books & Culture* last summer. "For example, our nature gives us tremendous cognitive capabilities, capability for reason, capability to learn, to teach ourselves things, to change our opinions, and so forth. What follows from that? A way of life that permits such growth is better than a life in which this capacity is shriveled and stunted in various ways." This is absolutely

correct. The trouble is that Fukuyama has a shriveled, stunted vision of human nature, leading him and others to stand athwart neuroscientific advances that will make it possible for more people to take fuller advantage of their reasoning and learning capabilities.

Like any technology, neurological enhancements can be abused, especially 50 if they're doled out—or imposed—by an unchecked authority. But Fukuyama and other critics have not made a strong case for why *individuals*, in consultation with their doctors, should not be allowed to take advantage of new neuroscientific breakthroughs to enhance the functioning of their brains. And it is those individuals that the critics will have to convince if they seriously expect to restrict this research.

It's difficult to believe that they'll manage that. In the 1960s many states 51 outlawed the birth control pill, on the grounds that it would be too disruptive to society. Yet Americans, eager to take control of their reproductive lives, managed to roll back those laws, and no one believes that the pill could be re-outlawed today.

Moreno thinks the same will be true of the neurological advances to come. 52 "My hunch," he says, "is that in the United States, medications that enhance our performance are not going to be prohibited." When you consider the sometimes despairing tone that Fukuyama and others like him adopt, it's hard not to conclude that on that much, at least, they agree.

Source: From *Reason*, February 2003. Reprinted by permission. *Reason* magazine and Reason.com.

## QUESTIONS FOR READING

1. What are some of the medical possibilities that may be coming from advances in neurotechnology?
2. What is the area of greatest concern for those who are worried about these potential neurotechnologies?
3. What group of people are heavy users of Prozac? Of Ritalin? What are the objections to these psychoactive drugs?
4. What, apparently, will be the next type of psychoactive drug?
5. State the eight objections to new drugs to enhance mood, memory, and intelligence. Then state Bailey's response to each objection in your own words.
6. Explain the concerns regarding autonomy and individual responsibility—and Bailey's responses to these concerns.
7. Who, according to Bailey, should decide how neuroscientific breakthroughs should be selected and used?

## QUESTIONS FOR REASONING AND ANALYSIS

8. How does Bailey organize his argument? What makes this a useful strategy?
9. In addition to categorizing his argument as a claim about values, how else might his argument be classified?

10. Examine the quoted language of those opposing psychoactive drugs. How would you describe their tone? What tone does Bailey use in his argument? Why is tone important in this debate?

11. State Bailey's claim; try to be precise and complete.

12. What support does the author provide?

13. In what sense is this also a definition argument? What is the central concept or definition on which one's argument on psychoactive drugs depends?

QUESTIONS FOR REFLECTION AND WRITING

14. Do you accept Bailey's definition of the individual human being as reshaped by experiences? If you disagree, how would you defend your view of a distinct, unchanging personhood?

15. Do you agree with Bailey that Prozac and Ritalin—and the new products that are coming—are other ways that we have to enhance our lives? That is, they do not, somehow, cross an unethical line? Why or why not?

16. If you believe, with Bailey's opponents, that some individual enhancements cross that unethical line and will destroy human autonomy and responsibility, how would you define "the line" and defend your position? Is Prozac, for example, unethical? Would a pill to improve memory be unethical? Explain your position.

17. Has Bailey made a convincing case for his position? If you disagree, is your disagreement about his reasoning and evidence? About his values? Something else?

## I HAVE A DREAM | MARTIN LUTHER KING JR.

Martin Luther King Jr. (1929–1968), Baptist minister, civil rights leader dedicated to nonviolence, president of the Southern Christian Leadership Conference, Nobel Peace Prize winner in 1964, was assassinated in 1968. He was an important figure in the August 1963 poor people's march on Washington, where he delivered his speech from the steps of the Lincoln Memorial.

King's plea for equality, echoing the language and cadences of both the Bible and "The Gettysburg Address," has become a model of effective oratory.

PREREADING QUESTION  What is the purpose or what are the purposes of King's speech?

1    Five score years ago, a great American, in whose symbolic shadow we stand, signed the Emancipation Proclamation. This momentous decree came as a great beacon light of hope to millions of Negro slaves who had been seared in the flames of withering injustice. It came as a joyous daybreak to end the long night of captivity.

2    But one hundred years later, we must face the tragic fact that the Negro is still not free. One hundred years later, the life of the Negro is still sadly crippled

Martin Luther King Jr., after delivering his speech at the Lincoln Memorial.

by the manacles of segregation and the chains of discrimination. One hundred years later, the Negro lives on a lonely island of poverty in the midst of a vast ocean of material prosperity. One hundred years later, the Negro is still languished in the corners of American society and finds himself an exile in his own land. So we have come here today to dramatize an appalling condition.

In a sense we have come to our nation's Capital to cash a check. When the architects of our republic wrote the magnificent words of the Constitution and the Declaration of Independence, they were signing a promissory note to which every American was to fall heir. This note was a promise that all men would be guaranteed the unalienable rights of life, liberty, and the pursuit of happiness.

It is obvious today that America has defaulted on this promissory note insofar as her citizens of color are concerned. Instead of honoring this sacred obligation, America has given the Negro people a bad check which has come back marked "insufficient funds." But we refuse to believe that the bank of justice is bankrupt. We refuse to believe that there are insufficient funds in the great vaults of opportunity of this nation. So we have come to cash this check— a check that will give us upon demand the riches of freedom and the security of justice. We have also come to this hallowed spot to remind America of the fierce urgency of *now*. This is no time to engage in the luxury of cooling off or to take the tranquilizing drug of gradualism. *Now* is the time to make real the promises of Democracy. *Now* is the time to rise from the dark and desolate valley of segregation to the sunlit path of racial justice. *Now* is the time to open the doors of opportunity to all of God's children. *Now* is the time to lift our nation from the quicksands of racial injustice to the solid rock of brotherhood.

5     It would be fatal for the nation to overlook the urgency of the moment and to underestimate the determination of the Negro. This sweltering summer of the Negro's legitimate discontent will not pass until there is an invigorating autumn of freedom and equality. 1963 is not an end, but a beginning. Those who hope that the Negro needed to blow off steam and will now be content will have a rude awakening if the nation returns to business as usual. There will be neither rest nor tranquility in America until the Negro is granted his citizenship rights. The whirlwinds of revolt will continue to shake the foundations of our nation until the bright day of justice emerges.

6     But there is something that I must say to my people who stand on the warm threshold which leads into the palace of justice. In the process of gaining our right place we must not be guilty of wrongful deeds. Let us not seek to satisfy our thirst for freedom by drinking from the cup of bitterness and hatred. We must forever conduct our struggle on the high plane of dignity and discipline. We must not allow our creative protest to degenerate into physical violence. Again and again we must rise to the majestic heights of meeting physical force with soul force. The marvelous new militancy which has engulfed the Negro community must not lead us to a distrust of all white people, for many of our white brothers, as evidenced by their presence here today, have come to realize that their destiny is tied up with our destiny and their freedom is inextricably bound to our freedom. We cannot walk alone.

7     And as we walk, we must make the pledge that we shall march ahead. We cannot turn back. There are those who are asking the devotees of civil rights, "When will you be satisfied?" We can never be satisfied as long as the Negro is the victim of the unspeakable horrors of police brutality. We can never be satisfied as long as our bodies, heavy with the fatigue of travel, cannot gain lodging in the motels of the highways and the hotels of the cities. We cannot be satisfied as long as the Negro's basic mobility is from a smaller ghetto to a larger one. We can never be satisfied as long as a Negro in Mississippi cannot vote and a Negro in New York believes he has nothing for which to vote. No, no, we are not satisfied, and we will not be satisfied until justice rolls down like waters and righteousness like a mighty stream.

8     I am not unmindful that some of you have come here out of great trials and tribulations. Some of you have come fresh from narrow jail cells. Some of you have come from areas where your quest for freedom left you battered by the storms of persecution and staggered by the winds of police brutality. You have been the veterans of creative suffering. Continue to work with the faith that unearned suffering is redemptive.

9     Go back to Mississippi, go back to Alabama, go back to South Carolina, go back to Georgia, go back to Louisiana, go back to the slums and ghettos of our northern cities, knowing that somehow this situation can and will be changed. Let us not wallow in the valley of despair.

10     I say to you today, my friends, that in spite of the difficulties and frustrations of the moment I still have a dream. It is a dream deeply rooted in the American dream.

I have a dream that one day this nation will rise up and live out the true 11
meaning of its creed: "We hold these truths to be self-evident; that all men are
created equal."

I have a dream that one day on the red hills of Georgia the sons of former 12
slaves and the sons of former slaveowners will be able to sit down together at
the table of brotherhood.

I have a dream that one day even the state of Mississippi, a desert state 13
sweltering with the heat of injustice and oppression, will be transformed into
an oasis of freedom and justice.

I have a dream that my four little children will one day live in a nation 14
where they will not be judged by the color of their skin but by the content of
their character.

I have a dream today.                                                        15

I have a dream that one day the state of Alabama, whose governor's lips 16
are presently dripping with the words of interposition and nullification, will be
transformed into a situation where little black boys and black girls will be able
to join hands with little white boys and white girls and walk together as sisters
and brothers.

I have a dream today.                                                        17

I have a dream that one day every valley shall be exalted, every hill and 18
mountain shall be made low, the rough places will be made plain, and the
crooked places will be made straight, and the glory of the Lord shall be
revealed, and all flesh shall see it together.

This is our hope. This is the faith with which I return to the South. With this 19
faith we will be able to hew out of the mountain of despair a stone of hope.
With this faith we will be able to transform the jangling discords of our nation
into a beautiful symphony of brotherhood. With this faith we will be able to
work together, to pray together, to struggle together, to go to jail together, to
stand up for freedom together, knowing that we will be free one day.

This will be the day when all of God's children will be able to sing with new 20
meaning

> My country, 'tis of thee,
> Sweet land of liberty,
>    Of thee I sing;
> Land where my fathers died,
> Land of the pilgrims' pride,
> From every mountain side
>    Let freedom ring.

And if America is to be a great nation this must become true. So let free- 21
dom ring from the prodigious hilltops of New Hampshire. Let freedom ring
from the mighty mountains of New York. Let freedom ring from the heighten-
ing Alleghenies of Pennsylvania!

Let freedom ring from the snowcapped Rockies of Colorado!            22

Let freedom ring from the curvaceous peaks of California!            23

24   But not only that; let freedom ring from Stone Mountain of Georgia!

25   Let freedom ring from Lookout Mountain of Tennessee!

26   Let freedom ring from every hill and molehill of Mississippi. From every mountainside, let freedom ring.

27   When we let freedom ring, when we let it ring from every village and every hamlet, from every state and every city, we will be able to speed up that day when all of God's children, black men and white men, Jews and Gentiles, Protestants and Catholics, will be able to join hands and sing in the words of the old Negro spiritual, "Free at last! thank God almighty, we are free at last!"

Source: Reprinted by arrangement with The Heirs to the Estate of Martin Luther King Jr., c/o Writers House as agent for the proprietor New York, NY. Copyright 1963 Dr. Martin Luther King Jr; copyright renewed 1991 Coretta Scott King.

## QUESTIONS FOR READING

1. King is directly addressing those participants in the poor people's march who are at the Lincoln Memorial. What other audience did he have as well?

2. How does the language of the speech reflect King's vocation as a Christian minister? How does it reflect his sense of his place in history?

3. What are the specific values upon which King rests his argument?

## QUESTIONS FOR REASONING AND ANALYSIS

4. List all the elements of style discussed in Chapter 2 that King uses. What elements of style dominate?

5. What stylistic techniques do Lincoln and King share?

6. Find one sentence that you think is especially effective and explain why you picked it. Is the effect achieved in part by the way the sentence is structured?

7. Explain each metaphor in paragraph 2.

8. State the claim of King's argument.

## QUESTIONS FOR REFLECTION AND WRITING

9. Which, in your view, is King's most vivid and powerful metaphor? Why do you find it effective?

10. If King were alive today, would he want to see another march on Washington? If so, what would be the theme, or purpose, of the march? If not, why not?

11. Would King have supported the Million Man March? The rally of the Promise Keepers? Why or why not? (If necessary, do some research on these two events.)

1. Chris Brown, in the student essay, writes a conciliatory argument seeking common ground on the volatile issue of gun control. Write your own conciliatory argument on this issue, offering a different approach than Brown, but citing Brown for any ideas you borrow from his essay. Alternatively, write a counterargument of his essay.

2. There are other "hot issues," issues that leave people entrenched on one side or the other, giving expression to the same arguments again and again without budging many, if any, readers. Do not try to write on any one of these about which you get strongly emotional. Select one that you can be calm enough over to write a conciliatory argument, seeking to find common ground. Some of these issues include same-sex marriage, legalizing recreational drugs, capital punishment, mainstreaming students with disabilities, the use of torture to interrogate terrorists. Exclude abortion rights from the list—it is too controversial for most writers to handle successfully.

3. Other issues that call for positions based on values stem from First Amendment rights. Consider a possible topic from this general area. Possibilities include:

   Hate speech should (or should not) be a crime.

   Obscenity and pornography on the Internet should (or should not) be restricted.

   Hollywood films should (or should not) show characters smoking.

4. Consider issues related to college life. Should all colleges have an honor code—or should existing codes be eliminated? Should students be automatically expelled for plagiarism? Should college administrators have any control over what is published in the college newspaper?

# CHAPTER 10

# Arguments about Cause

DRILL, BABY, DRILL!

SPILL, BABY, SPILL!

KILL, BABY, KILL!

FILL, BABY, FILL!!!

READ: What does each frame present visually?

REASON: How do the words at the bottom tie together the four frames? What relationship among the frames is implied?

REFLECT/WRITE: What conclusion are we to draw from the cartoon?

B ecause we want to know *why* things happen, arguments about cause are both numerous and important to us. We begin asking why at a young age, pestering adults with questions such as "Why is the sky blue?" and "Why is the grass green?" And, to make sense of our world, we try our hand at explanations as youngsters, deciding that the first-grade bully is "a bad boy." The bully's teacher, however, will seek a more complex explanation because an understanding of the causes is the place to start to guide the bully to more socially acceptable behavior.

As adults we continue the search for answers. We want to understand past events: Why was President Kennedy assassinated? We want to explain current situations: Why do so many college students binge drink? And of course we also want to predict the future: Will the economy improve if there is a tax cut? All three questions seek a causal explanation, including the last one. If you answer the last question with a yes, you are claiming that a tax cut is a cause of economic improvement.

## CHARACTERISTICS OF CAUSAL ARGUMENTS

Causal arguments vary not only in subject matter but in structure. Here are the four most typical patterns:

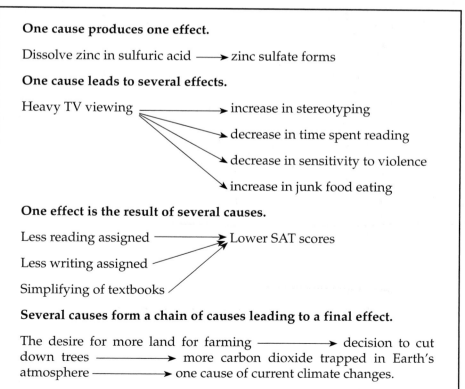

**One cause produces one effect.**

Dissolve zinc in sulfuric acid ⟶ zinc sulfate forms

**One cause leads to several effects.**

Heavy TV viewing ⟶ increase in stereotyping
⟶ decrease in time spent reading
⟶ decrease in sensitivity to violence
⟶ increase in junk food eating

**One effect is the result of several causes.**

Less reading assigned ⟶ Lower SAT scores
Less writing assigned
Simplifying of textbooks

**Several causes form a chain of causes leading to a final effect.**

The desire for more land for farming ⟶ decision to cut down trees ⟶ more carbon dioxide trapped in Earth's atmosphere ⟶ one cause of current climate changes.

These models lead to several key points about causal arguments:

- **Most causal arguments are highly complex.** Except for some simple chemical reactions, most arguments about cause are difficult, can involve many steps, and are often open to challenge. Even arguments based in science lead to shrill exchanges. While scientists seek genetic markers for obesity, others argue that obesity is a result of a lack of willpower. Think, then, how much more open to debate are arguments about the worldwide economic downturn or arguments about human behavior. Many people think that "it's obvious" that violent TV and video games lead to more aggressive behavior as well as a loss of horror in the face of violence. And yet, psychologists, in study after study, have not demonstrated conclusively that there is a clear causal connection. One way to challenge this causal argument is to point to the majority of people who do not perform violent acts even though they have watched television and played video games while growing up.

- **Because of the multiple and intertwined patterns of causation in many complex situations, the best causal arguments keep focused on their purpose.** For example, you are concerned with global warming. Cows contribute to global warming. Are we going to stop cattle farming? Not likely. Factories contribute to global warming. Are we going to tear down factories? Not likely—but we can demand that smokestacks have filters to reduce harmful emissions. Focus your argument on the causes that readers are most likely to accept because they are most likely to accept the action that the causes imply.

- **Learn and use the specific terms and concepts that provide useful guides to thinking about cause.** First, when looking for the cause of an event, we look for an *agent*—a person, situation, another event that led to the effect. For example, a lit cigarette dropped in a bed caused the house fire—the lit cigarette is the agent. But why, we ask, did someone drop a lit cigarette on a bed? The person, old and ill, took a sleeping pill and dropped the cigarette when he fell asleep. Where do we stop in the chain of causes?

  Second, most events do not occur in a vacuum with a single cause. There are *conditions* surrounding the event. The man's age and health were conditions. Third, we can also look for *influences*. The sleeping pill certainly influenced the man to drop the cigarette. Some conditions and influences may qualify as *remote causes. Proximate causes* are more immediate, usually closer in time to the event or situation. The man's dozing off is a proximate cause of the fire. Finally, we come to the *precipitating cause*, the triggering event—in our example, the cigarette's igniting the combustible mattress fabric. Sometimes we are interested primarily in the precipitating cause; in other situations, we need to go further back to find the remote causes or conditions that are responsible for what has occurred.

- **Be alert to the difference between cause and correlation.** First, be certain that you can defend your pattern of cause and effect as genuine causation, not as correlation only. Married people are better off financially, are healthier, and report happier sex lives than singles or cohabiting couples.

Is this a correlation only? Or, does marriage itself produce these effects? Linda Waite is one sociologist who argues that marriage is the cause. Another example: Girls who participate in after-school activities are much less likely to get pregnant. Are the activities a cause? Probably not. But there are surely conditions and influences that have led to both the decision to participate in activities and the decision not to become pregnant.

## An Example of Causal Complexity: Lincoln's Election and the Start of the Civil War

If Stephen Douglas had won the 1860 presidential election instead of Abraham Lincoln, would the Civil War have been avoided? An interesting question posed to various American history professors and others, including Waite Rawls, president of the Museum of the Confederacy. Their responses were part of an article that appeared in the *Washington Post* on November 7, 2010.

Obviously, this is a question that cannot be answered, but it led Rawls to discuss the sequence of causes leading to the breakout of the war. Rawls organizes his brief causal analysis around a great metaphor: the building and filling and then lighting of a keg of powder. Let's look at his analysis.

### Existing Conditions

"The wood for the keg was shaped by the inability of the founding fathers to solve the two big problems of state sovereignty and slavery in the shaping of the Constitution."

### More Recent Influences

1. "[T]he economics of taxes and the politics of control of the westward expansion were added to those two original issues as the keg was filled with powder."

2. "By the time of the creation of the Republican Party in 1856, the powder keg was almost full and waiting for a fuse. And the election of any candidate from the Republican Party—a purely sectional party—put the fuse in the powder keg, and the Deep South states seceded. But there was still no war."

### Proximate Causes

"Two simultaneous mistakes in judgment brought the matches out of the pocket—the Deep South mistakenly thought that Lincoln, now elected, would not enforce the Union, and Lincoln mistakenly thought that the general population of the South would not follow the leadership" of the Deep South states.

### Precipitating Causes

1. "Lincoln struck the match when he called the bluff of the South Carolinians and attempted to reinforce Fort Sumter, but that match could have gone out without an explosion."

2.  "Lincoln struck a second, more fateful match, when he called for troops to put down the 'insurrection.' That forced the Upper South and Border States into a conflict that they had vainly attempted to avoid." (Reprinted by permission of Waite Rawls.)

Rawls concludes that the election of Lincoln did not start the war; it was only one step in a complex series of causes that led to America's bloodiest war. His analysis helps us see the complexity of cause/effect analysis.

## Mill's Methods for Investigating Causes

John Stuart Mill, a nineteenth-century British philosopher, explained in detail some important ways of investigating and demonstrating causal relationships: commonality, difference, and process of elimination. We can benefit in our study of cause by understanding and using his methods.

1.  *Commonality.* One way to isolate cause is to demonstrate that one agent is *common* to similar outcomes. For instance, twenty-five employees attend a company luncheon. Late in the day, ten report to area hospitals, and another four complain the next day of having experienced vomiting the night before. Public health officials will soon want to know what these people ate for lunch. Different people during the same twelve-hour period had similar physical symptoms of food poisoning. The common factor may well have been the tuna salad they ate for lunch.

2.  *Difference.* Another way to isolate cause is to recognize one key *difference.* If two situations are alike in every way but one, and the situations result in different outcomes, then the one way they differ must have caused the different outcome.

    Studies in the social sciences are often based on the single-difference method. To test for the best teaching methods for math, an educator could set up an experiment with two classrooms similar in every way except that one class devotes fifteen minutes three days a week to instruction by drill. If the class receiving the drill scores much higher on a standard test given to both groups of students, the educator could argue that math drills make a measurable difference in learning math. But the educator should be prepared for skeptics to challenge the assertion of only one difference between the two classes. Could the teacher's attitude toward the drills also make a difference in student learning? If the differences in student scores are significant, the educator probably has a good argument, even though a teacher's attitude cannot be controlled in the experiment.

3.  *Process of elimination.* One can develop a causal argument around a technique we all use for problem solving: *the process of elimination.* When something happens, we examine all possible causes and eliminate them, one by one, until we are satisfied that we have isolated the actual cause (or causes).

    When the Federal Aviation Administration has to investigate a plane crash, it uses this process, exploring possible causes such as mechanical failure, weather, human error, or terrorism. Sometimes the process isolates more than one cause or points to a likely cause without providing absolute proof. You will see how Lester Thurow uses the process of elimination method in his argument at the end of this chapter (pp. 236–38).

## EXERCISE: Understanding Causal Patterns

From the following events or situations, select the one you know best and list as many conditions, influences, and causes—remote, proximate, precipitating—as you can think of. You may want to do this exercise with your class partner or in small groups. Be prepared to explain your causal pattern to the class.

1. Teen suicide
2. Global warming
3. Increase in the numbers of women elected to public office
4. High salaries of professional athletes
5. Increased interest in soccer in the United States
6. Comparatively low scores by U.S. students on international tests in math and science
7. Majority of undergraduates now women

## GUIDELINES for Analyzing Causal Arguments

When analyzing causal arguments, what should you look for? The basics of good argument apply to all arguments: a clear statement of claim, qualified if appropriate; a clear explanation of reasons and evidence; and enough relevant evidence to support the claim. How do we recognize these qualities in a causal argument? Use these points as guides to analyzing:

- **Does the writer carefully distinguish among types of causes?** Word choice is crucial. Is the argument that A and A alone caused B or that A was one of several contributing causes?

- **Does the writer recognize the complexity of causation and not rush to assert only one cause for a complex event or situation?** The credibility of an argument about cause is quickly lost if readers find the argument oversimplified.

- **Is the argument's claim clearly stated, with qualifications as appropriate?** If the writer wants to argue for one cause, not the only cause, of an event or situation, then the claim's wording must make this limited goal clear to readers. For example, one can perhaps build the case for heavy television viewing as one cause of stereotyping, loss of sensitivity to violence, and increased fearfulness. But we know that the home environment and neighborhood and school environments also do much to shape attitudes.

- **What reasons and evidence are given to support the argument?** Can you see the writer's pattern of development? Does the reasoning seem logical? Are the data relevant? This kind of analysis of the argument will help you evaluate it.

- **Does the argument demonstrate causality, not just a time relationship or correlation?** A causal argument needs to prove *agency:* A is the cause of B, not just something that happened before B or something that is present when B is present. March precedes April, but March does not cause April to arrive.
- **Does the writer present believable causal agents, agents consistent with our knowledge of human behavior and scientific laws?** Most educated people do not believe that personalities are shaped by astrological signs or that scientific laws are suspended in the Bermuda Triangle, allowing planes and ships to vanish or enter a fourth dimension.
- **What are the implications for accepting the causal argument?** If A and B clearly are the causes of C, and we don't want C to occur, then we presumably must do something about A and B—or at least we must do something about either A or B and see if reducing or eliminating one of the causes significantly reduces the incidence of C.
- **Is the argument convincing?** After analyzing the argument and answering the questions given in the previous points, you need to decide if, finally, the argument works.

## PREPARING A CAUSAL ARGUMENT

In addition to the guidelines for writing arguments presented in Chapter 4, you can use the following advice specific to writing causal arguments.

*Planning*

1. **Think:** What are the focus and limits of your causal argument? Do you want to argue for one cause of an event or situation? Do you want to argue for several causes leading to an event or situation? Do you want to argue for a cause that others have overlooked? Do you want to show how one cause is common to several situations or events? Diagramming the relationship of cause to effect may help you see what you want to focus on.

2. **Think:** What reasons and evidence do you have to support your tentative claim? Consider what you already know that has led to your choice of topic. A brainstorming list may be helpful.

3. **Think:** How, then, do you want to word your claim? As we have discussed, wording is crucial in causal arguments. Review the discussion of characteristics of causal arguments if necessary.

4. **Reality check:** Do you have a claim worth defending in a paper? Will readers care?

5. **Think:** What, if any, additional evidence do you need to develop a convincing argument? You may need to do some reading or online searching to obtain data to strengthen your argument. Readers expect relevant, reliable, current statistics in most arguments about cause. Assess what you need and then think about what sources will provide the needed information.

6. **Think:** What assumptions (warrants) are you making in your causal reasoning? Are these assumptions logical? Will readers be likely to agree with your assumptions, or will you need to defend them as part of your argument? For example: One reason to defend the effects of heavy TV watching on viewers is the commonsense argument that what humans devote considerable time to will have a significant effect on their lives. Will your readers be prepared to accept this commonsense reasoning, or will they remain skeptical, looking for stronger evidence of a cause/effect relationship?

## Drafting

1. Begin with an opening paragraph or two that introduces your topic in an interesting way. Lester Thurow in "Why Women Are Paid Less Than Men" writes:

   > In the 40 years from 1939 to 1979 white women who work full time have with monotonous regularity made slightly less than 60 percent as much as white men. Why?

   This opening establishes the topic and Thurow's purpose in examining causes. The statistics get the reader's attention.

2. Do not begin by announcing your subject. Avoid openers such as: In this essay I will explain the causes of teen vandalism.

3. Decide where to place your claim statement. You can conclude your opening paragraph with it, or you can place it in your conclusion, after you have shown readers how best to understand the causes of the issue you are examining. Thurow uses the second approach effectively in his essay.

4. Present reasons and evidence in an organized way. If you are examining a series of causes, beginning with background conditions and early influences, then your basic plan will be time sequence. Readers need to see the chain of causes unfolding. Use appropriate terms and transitional words to guide readers through each stage in the causal pattern. If you are arguing for an overlooked cause, begin with the causes that have been put forward and show what is flawed in each one. Then present and defend your explanation of cause. This process of elimination structure works well when readers are likely to know what other causes have been offered in the past. You can also use one of Mill's other two approaches, if one of them is relevant to your topic.

5. Address the issue of correlation rather than cause, if appropriate. After presenting the results of a study of marriage that reveals many benefits (emotional, physical, financial) of marriage, Linda Waite examines the question that she knows skeptical readers may have: Does marriage actually *cause* the benefits, or is the relationship one of *correlation* only—that is, the benefits of marriage just happen to come with being married; they are not caused by being married.

6. Conclude by discussing the implications of the causal pattern you have argued for, if appropriate. Lester Thurow ends by asserting that if he is

right about the cause of the gender pay gap, then there are two approaches society can take to remove the pay gap. If, in explaining the causes of teen vandalism, you see one cause as "group behavior," a gang looking for something to do, it then follows that you can advise young readers to stay out of gangs. Often with arguments about cause, there are personal or public policy implications in accepting the causal explanation.

## A CHECKLIST FOR REVISION

- ☐ Do I have a clear statement of my claim? Is it appropriately qualified and focused? Is it about an issue that matters?
- ☐ Have I organized my argument so that readers can see my pattern for examining cause?
- ☐ Have I used the language for discussing causes correctly, distinguishing among conditions and influences and remote and proximate causes? Have I selected the correct word—either *affect* or *effect*—as needed?
- ☐ Have I avoided the *post hoc* fallacy and the confusing of correlation and cause?
- ☐ Have I carefully examined my assumptions and convinced myself that they are reasonable and can be defended? Have I defended them when necessary to clarify and thus strengthen my argument?
- ☐ Have I found relevant facts and examples to support and develop my argument?
- ☐ Have I used the basic checklist for revision in Chapter 4 (see p. 105)?

# FOR ANALYSIS AND DEBATE

## WHY WOMEN ARE PAID LESS THAN MEN | LESTER C. THUROW

A professor at the MIT Sloan School of Management for more than forty years and a consultant to both government and private corporations, Lester C. Thurow has written extensively on economic and public policy issues. The latest of his more than a dozen books is *Fortune Favors the Bold: What We Must Do to Build a New and Lasting Global Prosperity* (2003). "Why Women Are Paid Less than Men," published in the *New York Times* (March 8, 1981), offers an explanation for the discrepancy between the incomes of men and women.

PREREADING QUESTIONS When he asks "why" at the end of paragraph 1, what kind of argument does Thurow signal he will develop? Were you aware that women earn less than men?

1    In the 40 years from 1939 to 1979 white women who work full time have with monotonous regularity made slightly less than 60 percent as much as white men. Why?

Over the same time period, minorities have made substantial progress in 2 catching up with whites, with minority women making even more progress than minority men.

Black men now earn 72 percent as much as white men (up 16 percentage 3 points since the mid-1950s) but black women earn 92 percent as much as white women. Hispanic men make 71 percent of what their white counterparts do, but Hispanic women make 82 percent as much as white women. As a result of their faster progress, fully employed black women make 75 percent as much as fully employed black men while Hispanic women earn 68 percent as much as Hispanic men.

This faster progress may, however, end when minority women finally catch 4 up with white women. In the bible of the New Right, George Gilder's *Wealth and Poverty,* the 60 percent is just one of Mother Nature's constants like the speed of light or the force of gravity.

Men are programmed to provide for their families economically while 5 women are programmed to take care of their families emotionally and physically. As a result men put more effort into their jobs than women. The net result is a difference in work intensity that leads to that 40 percent gap in earnings. But there is no discrimination against women—only the biological facts of life.

The problem with this assertion is just that. It is an assertion with no evi- 6 dence for it other than the fact that white women have made 60 percent as much as men for a long period of time.

"Discrimination against women" is an easy answer but it also has its prob- 7 lems as an adequate explanation. Why is discrimination against women not declining under the same social forces that are leading to a lessening of discrimination against minorities? In recent years women have made more use of the enforcement provisions of the Equal Employment Opportunities Commission and the courts than minorities. Why do the laws that prohibit discrimination against women and minorities work for minorities but not for women?

When men discriminate against women, they run into a problem. To dis- 8 criminate against women is to discriminate against your own wife and to lower your own family income. To prevent women from working is to force men to work more.

When whites discriminate against blacks, they can at least think that they 9 are raising their own incomes. When men discriminate against women they have to know that they are lowering their own family income and increasing their own work effort.

While discrimination undoubtedly explains part of the male-female earn- 10 ings differential, one has to believe that men are monumentally stupid or irrational to explain all of the earnings gap in terms of discrimination. There must be something else going on.

Back in 1939 it was possible to attribute the earnings gap to large differ- 11 ences in educational attainments. But the educational gap between men and women has been eliminated since World War II. It is no longer possible to use education as an explanation for the lower earnings of women.

12      Some observers have argued that women earn less money since they are less reliable workers who are more apt to leave the labor force. But it is difficult to maintain this position since women are less apt to quit one job to take another and as a result they tend to work as long, or longer, for any one employer. From any employer's perspective they are more reliable, not less reliable, than men.

13      Part of the answer is visible if you look at the lifetime earnings profile of men. Suppose that you are asked to predict which men in a group of 25-year-olds would become economically successful. At age 25 it is difficult to tell who will be economically successful and your predictions are apt to be highly inaccurate.

14      But suppose that you were asked to predict which men in a group of 35-year-olds would become economically successful. If you are successful at age 35 you are very likely to remain successful for the rest of your life. If you have not become economically successful by age 35, you are very unlikely to do so later.

15      The decade between 25 and 35 is when men either succeed or fail. It is the decade when lawyers become partners in the good firms, when business managers make it onto the "fast track," when academics get tenure at good universities, and when blue-collar workers find the job opportunities that will lead to training opportunities and the skills that will generate high earnings.

16      If there is any one decade when it pays to work hard and to be consistently in the labor force, it is the decade between 25 and 35. For those who succeed, earnings will rise rapidly. For those who fail, earnings will remain flat for the rest of their lives.

17      But the decade between 25 and 35 is precisely the decade when women are most apt to leave the labor force or become part-time workers to have children. When they do, the current system of promotion and skill acquisition will extract an enormous lifetime price.

18      This leaves essentially two avenues for equalizing male and female earnings.

19      Families where women who wish to have successful careers, compete with men, and achieve the same earnings should alter their family plans and have their children either before 25 or after 35. Or society can attempt to alter the existing promotion and skill acquisition system so that there is a longer time period in which both men and women can attempt to successfully enter the labor force.

20      Without some combination of these two factors, a substantial fraction of the male-female earnings differentials are apt to persist for the next 40 years, even if discrimination against women is eliminated.

## QUESTIONS FOR READING

1. What situation is the subject of Thurow's argument?
2. Briefly explain why Thurow rejects each of the possible explanations that he covers.
3. What is the author's explanation for the discrepancy between the earnings of white women and white men?

## QUESTIONS FOR REASONING AND ANALYSIS

4. What question should you ask about Thurow's numbers? Do you know the answer to the question?
5. What is Thurow's claim?
6. What evidence does the author provide for his claim? Is it convincing?
7. What strategy for determining cause does Thurow use?

## QUESTIONS FOR REFLECTION AND WRITING

8. Do you agree that most people who are going to be successful are so by age 35? Can you think of people who did not become successful until after 35? Is this the kind of assumption that can create its own reality?
9. Evaluate the two solutions Thurow proposes. Do they follow logically from his causal analysis?
10. Thurow's figures are based on the total earnings of workers; they are not comparisons by job category. What are other facts about jobs that men and women hold that may account for some of the discrepancy in pay?

## HOW IMMIGRANTS CREATE MORE JOBS   |   TYLER COWEN

Tyler Cowen is a professor of economics at George Mason University and at the Center for the Study of Public Choice. Cowen writes a daily blog under the heading "The Marginal Revolution" and is the author of both professional and popular articles. One of his more than a dozen books is *Create Your Own Economy: The Path to Prosperity in a Disordered World* (2009). The following article appeared October 31, 2010, in the *New York Times.*

PREREADING QUESTIONS The usual "wisdom" is that immigrants take jobs away from Americans. Are you eager to read Cowen's essay and consider another perspective? Why or why not?

In the campaign season now drawing to a close [2010], immigration and   1
globalization have often been described as economic threats. The truth, however, is more complex.

2    Over all, it turns out that the continuing arrival of immigrants to American shores is encouraging business activity here, thereby producing more jobs, according to a new study. Its authors argue that the easier it is to find cheap immigrant labor at home, the less likely that production will relocate offshore.

3    The study, "Immigration, Offshoring and American Jobs," was written by two economics professors—Gianmarco I. P. Ottaviano of Bocconi University in Italy and Giovanni Peri of the University of California, Davis—along with Greg C. Wright, a Ph.D. candidate at Davis.

4    The study notes that when companies move production offshore, they pull away not only low-wage jobs but also many related jobs, which can include high-skilled managers, tech repairmen and others. But hiring immigrants even for low-wage jobs helps keep many kinds of jobs in the United States, the authors say. In fact, when immigration is rising as a share of employment in an economic sector, offshoring tends to be falling, and vice versa, the study found.

5    In other words, immigrants may be competing more with offshored workers than with other laborers in America.

6    American economic sectors with much exposure to immigration fared better in employment growth than more insulated sectors, even for low-skilled labor, the authors found. It's hard to prove cause and effect in these studies, or to measure all relevant variables precisely, but at the very least, the evidence in this study doesn't offer much support for the popular bias against immigration, and globalization more generally.

7    We see the job-creating benefits of trade and immigration every day, even if we don't always recognize them. As other papers by Professor Peri have shown, low-skilled immigrants usually fill gaps in American labor markets and generally enhance domestic business prospects rather than destroy jobs; this occurs because of an important phenomenon, the presence of what are known as "complementary" workers, namely those who add value to the work of others. An immigrant will often take a job as a construction worker, a drywall installer or a taxi driver, for example, while a native-born worker may end up being promoted to supervisor. And as immigrants succeed here, they help the United States develop strong business and social networks with the rest of the world, making it easier for us to do business with India, Brazil and most other countries, again creating more jobs.

8    For all the talk of the dangers of offshoring, there is a related trend that we might call in-shoring. Dell or Apple computers may be assembled overseas, for example, but those products aid many American businesses at home and allow them to expand here. A cheap call center in India can encourage a company to open up more branches to sell its products in the United States.

9    Those are further examples of how some laborers can complement others; it's not all about one group of people taking jobs from another. Job creation and destruction are so intertwined that, over all, the authors find no statistically verifiable connection between offshoring and net creation of American jobs.

10   We're all worried about unemployment, but the problem is usually rooted in macroeconomic conditions, not in immigration or offshoring. (According to a Pew study, the number of illegal immigrants from the Caribbean and Latin

Hispanic workers at a construction site.

America fell 22 percent from 2007 to 2009; their departure has not had much effect on the weak United States job market.) Remember, too, that each immigrant consumes products sold here, therefore also helping to create jobs.

When it comes to immigration, positive-sum thinking is too often absent 11 in public discourse these days. Debates on immigration and labor markets reflect some common human cognitive failings—namely, that we are quicker to vilify groups of different "others" than we are to blame impersonal forces.

Consider the fears that foreign competition, offshoring and immigration 12 have destroyed large numbers of American jobs. In reality, more workers have probably been displaced by machines—as happens every time computer software eliminates a task formerly performed by a clerical worker. Yet we know that machines and computers do the economy far more good than harm and that they create more jobs than they destroy.

Nonetheless, we find it hard to transfer this attitude to our dealings with 13 immigrants, no matter how logically similar "cost-saving machines" and "cost-saving foreign labor" may be in their economic effects. Similarly, tariffs or other protectionist measures aimed at foreign nations have a certain populist appeal, even though their economic effects may be roughly the same as those caused by a natural disaster that closes shipping lanes or chokes off a domestic harbor.

As a nation, we spend far too much time and energy worrying about 14 foreigners. We also end up with more combative international relations with our economic partners, like Mexico and China, than reason can justify. In turn, they are more economically suspicious of us than they ought to be, which cements a negative dynamic into place.

The current skepticism has deadlocked prospects for immigration reform, 15 even though no one is particularly happy with the status quo. Against that trend, we should be looking to immigration as a creative force in our economic favor. Allowing in more immigrants, skilled and unskilled, wouldn't just create jobs. It could increase tax revenue, help finance Social Security, bring new home buyers and improve the business environment.

16    The world economy will most likely grow more open, and we should be prepared to compete. That means recognizing the benefits—including the employment benefits—that immigrants bring to this country.

Source: From *The New York Times*, October 31, 2010. Reprinted by permission of the author.

### QUESTIONS FOR READING

1.  What is the occasion for Cowen's article—what is he responding to?
2.  What does Cowen think we can conclude—as a minimum—from the recent study on immigration?
3.  What is the role of "complementary" workers?
4.  What is the relationship between "offshoring" and the gain or loss of American jobs?
5.  Explain "positive-sum thinking."
6.  What has probably cost more American jobs than either immigration or globalization?

### QUESTIONS FOR REASONING AND ANALYSIS

7.  What is Cowen's claim? Where does he state it?
8.  What *kinds* of evidence does the author provide to support his claim?
9.  In what sense is Cowen's argument a refutation? What passages present the views with which he objects?
10. What is Cowen's tone throughout his argument? How does this influence reader response?

### QUESTIONS FOR REFLECTION AND WRITING

11. What information or ideas most surprised you in this argument? Why?
12. Has Cowen convinced you possibly to change your thinking about immigrant workers and globalization as they affect American jobs? Why or why not? If you disagree with Cowen's analysis, how would you refute him?

1. Do you agree with the causes presented by Thurow to account for the pay gap by gender, or the effects of immigrants on jobs presented by Cowen? If not, how would you refute Thurow's argument, or Cowen's argument? What cause or causes has either Thurow or Cowen, in your view, overlooked?

2. Think about your educational experiences as a basis for generating a topic for a causal argument. For example: What are the causes of writer's block? Why do some apparently good students (based on class work, grades, etc.) do poorly on standardized tests? How does pass/fail grading affect student performance? What are the causes of high tuition and fees? What might be some of the effects of higher college costs? What are the causes of binge drinking among college students? What are the effects of binge drinking?

3. *Star Trek*, in its many manifestations, continues to play on television—why? What makes it so popular a series? Why are horror movies popular? What are the causes for the great success of the Harry Potter books? If you are familiar with one of these works, or another work that has been amazingly popular, examine the causes for that popularity.

# CHAPTER 11

# Presenting Proposals: The Problem/Solution Argument

READ: What is this ad selling? Who is the target audience?

REASON: What strategies are used in the ad? (Consider the visual effect, the words presented, and the identification of the ad's sponsor.)

REFLECT/WRITE: In what way is this ad a proposal argument? Is the argumentative strategy an effective one?

You think that there are several spots on campus that need additional lighting at night. You are concerned that the lake near your hometown is green, with algae floating on it. You believe that bikers on the campus need to have paths and a bike lane on the main roads into the college. These are serious local issues; you should be concerned about them. And, perhaps it is time to act on your concerns—how can you do that? You can write a proposal, perhaps a letter to the editor of the college newspaper or your hometown newspaper.

These three issues invite a recommendation for change. And to make that recommendation is to offer a solution to what you perceive to be a problem. Public policy arguments, whether local and specific (such as lampposts or bike lanes), or more general and far-reaching (such as the federal government must stop the flow of illegal drugs into the country) can best be understood as arguments over solutions to problems. If there are only 10 students on campus who bike to class or only 200 Americans wanting to buy cocaine, then most people would not agree that we have two serious problems in need of debate over the best solutions. But, when the numbers become significant, then we see a problem and start seeking solutions.

Consider some of these issues stated as policy claims:

- The college needs bike lanes on campus roads and more bike paths across the campus.
- We need to spend whatever is necessary to stop the flow of drugs into this country.

Each claim offers a solution to a problem, as we can see:

- Bikers will be safer if there are bike lanes on main roads and more bike paths across the campus.
- The way to address the drug problem in this country is to eliminate the supply of drugs.

The basic idea of policy proposals looks like this:

**Somebody**                 **should (or should not)**             **do X – because:**
*(Individual, organization, government)*                                              *(solve this problem)*

Observe that proposal arguments recommend action. They look to the future. And, they often advise the spending of someone's time and/or money.

## CHARACTERISTICS OF PROBLEM/ SOLUTION ARGUMENTS

- *Proposal arguments may be about local and specific problems or about broader, more general public policy issues.* We need to "think globally" these days, but we still often need to "act locally," to address the problems we see around us in our classrooms, offices, and communities.

- *Proposal arguments usually need to define the problem.* How we define a problem has much to do with what kinds of solutions are appropriate. For example, many people are concerned about our ability to feed a growing world population. Some will argue that the problem is not an agricultural one—how much food we can produce. The problem is a political one—how we distribute the food, at what cost, and how competent or fair some governments are in handling food distribution. If the problem is agricultural, we need to worry about available farmland, water supply, and farming technology. If the problem is political, then we need to concern ourselves with price supports, distribution strategies, and embargoes for political leverage. To develop a problem/solution argument, you first need to define the problem.

- *How we define the problem also affects what we think are the causes of the problem.* Cause is often a part of the debate, especially with far-reaching policy issues, and may need to be addressed, particularly if solutions are tied to eliminating what we consider to be the causes. Why are illegal drugs coming into the United States? Because people want those drugs. Do you solve the problems related to drug addicts by stopping the supply? Or, do you address the demand for drugs in the first place?

- *Proposal arguments need to be developed with an understanding of the processes of government, from college administrations to city governments to the federal bureaucracy.* Is that dying lake near your town on city property or state land? Are there conservation groups in your area who can be called on to help with the process of presenting proposals to the appropriate people?

- *Proposal arguments need to be based on the understanding that they ask for change—and many people do not like change, period.* Probably all but the wealthiest Americans recognize that our health-care system needs fixing. That doesn't change the fact that many working people struggling to pay premiums are afraid of any changes introduced by the federal government.

- *Successful problem/solution arguments offer solutions that can realistically be accomplished.* Consider Prohibition, for example. This was a solution to problem drinking—except that it did not work, could not be enforced, because the majority of Americans would not abide by the law.

## GUIDELINES for Analyzing Problem/Solution Arguments

When analyzing problem/solution arguments, what should you look for? In addition to the basics of good argument, use these points as guides to analyzing:

- **Is the writer's claim not just clear but also appropriately qualified and focused?** For example, if the school board in the writer's community is not doing a good job of communicating its goals as a basis for its funding package, the writer needs to focus just on that particular school board, not on school boards in general.

- **Does the writer show an awareness of the complexity of most public policy issues?** There are many different kinds of problems with American schools and many more causes for those problems. A simple solution—a longer school year, more money spent, vouchers—is not likely to solve the mixed bag of problems. Oversimplified arguments quickly lose credibility.
- **How does the writer define and explain the problem?** Is the way the problem is stated clear? Does it make sense to you? If the problem is being defined differently than most people have defined it, has the writer argued convincingly for looking at the problem in this new way?
- **What reasons and evidence are given to support the writer's solutions?** Can you see how the writer develops the argument? Does the reasoning seem logical? Are the data relevant? This kind of analysis will help you evaluate the proposed solutions.
- **Does the writer address the feasibility of the proposed solutions?** Does the writer make a convincing case for the realistic possibility of achieving the proposed solutions?
- **Is the argument convincing?** Will the solutions solve the problem as it has been defined? Has the problem been defined accurately? Can the solutions be achieved?

Read and study the following annotated argument. Complete your analysis by answering the questions that follow.

## A NEW STRATEGY FOR THE WAR ON DRUGS | JAMES Q. WILSON

Author of *The Moral Sense* (1997), James Q. Wilson is a professor of public policy at Pepperdine University. His solution to America's drug problem was published on April 13, 2000, in the *Wall Street Journal*.

The current Senate deliberation over aid to Colombia aimed at fighting narcotics reminds us that there are two debates over how the government ought to deal with dangerous drugs. The first is about their illegality and the second is about their control. People who wish to legalize drugs and those who wish to curtail their supply believe that their methods will reduce crime. Both these views are mistaken, but there is a third way.

*1*   *Opening presents two solutions that Wilson will challenge.*

Advocates of legalization think that both buyers and sellers would benefit. People who can buy drugs freely and at something like free-market prices would no longer have to steal to afford cocaine or heroin; dealers would no longer have to use violence and corruption to maintain their market share. Though drugs may harm people, reducing this harm would be a medical problem not a criminal-justice one. Crime would drop sharply.

*2*

### PRICES WOULD FALL

But there is an error in this calculation. Legalizing drugs means letting the price fall to its competitive rate (plus taxes and advertising costs). That market price would probably be somewhere between one-third and 1/20th of the

*3*   *Wilson rebuts first solution.*

illegal price. And more than the market price would fall. As Harvard's Mark Moore has pointed out, the "risk price"—that is, all the hazards associated with buying drugs, from being arrested to being ripped off—would also fall, and this decline might be more important than the lower purchase price.

4    Under a legal regime, the consumption of low-priced, low-risk drugs would increase dramatically. We do not know by how much, but the little evidence we have suggests a sharp rise. Until 1968 Britain allowed doctors to prescribe heroin. Some doctors cheated, and their medically unnecessary prescriptions helped increase the number of known heroin addicts by a factor of 40. As a result, the government abandoned the prescription policy in favor of administering heroin in clinics and later replacing heroin with methadone.

5    When the Netherlands ceased enforcing laws against the purchase or possession of marijuana, the result was a sharp increase in its use. Cocaine and heroin create much greater dependency, and so the increase in their use would probably be even greater.

6    The average user would probably commit fewer crimes if these drugs were sold legally. But the total number of users would increase sharply. A large fraction of these new users would be unable to keep a steady job. Unless we were prepared to support them with welfare payments, crime would be one of their main sources of income. That is, the number of drug-related crimes *per user* might fall even as the total number of drug-related crimes increased. Add to the list of harms more deaths from overdose, more babies born to addicted mothers, more accidents by drug-influenced automobile drivers and fewer people able to hold jobs or act as competent parents.

7    Treating such people would become far more difficult. As psychiatrist Sally Satel has written on this page, many drug users will not enter and stay in treatment unless they are compelled to do so. Phoenix House, the largest national residential drug treatment program, rarely admits patients who admit they have a problem and need help. The great majority are coerced by somebody— a judge, probation officer or school official—into attending. Phoenix House CEO Mitchell Rosenthal opposes legalization, and for good reason. Legalization means less coercion, and that means more addicts and addicts who are harder to treat.

8    Douglas Anglin, drawing on experiences in California and elsewhere, has shown that people compelled to stay in treatment do at least as well as those who volunteer for it, and they tend (of necessity) to stay in the program longer. If we legalize drugs, the chances of treatment making a difference are greatly reduced. And as for drug-use prevention, forget it. Try telling your children not to use a legal substance.

Wilson rebuts second solution.

9    But people who want to keep drugs illegal have problems of their own. The major thrust of government spending has been to reduce the supply of drugs by cutting their production overseas, intercepting their transfer into the U.S. and arresting dealers. Because of severe criminal penalties, especially on handlers of crack cocaine, our prisons have experienced a huge increase in persons sentenced on drug charges. In the early 1980s, about 1/12th of all prison inmates were in for drug convictions; now well over one-third are.

No one can be certain how imprisoning drug suppliers affects drug use, [10] but we do know that an arrested drug dealer is easily replaced. Moreover, the government can never seize more than a small fraction of the drugs entering the country, a fraction that is easily replaced.

Emphasizing supply over treatment is dangerous. Not only do we spend [11] huge sums on it; not only do we drag a reluctant U.S. military into the campaign; we also heighten corruption and violence in countries such as Colombia and Mexico. The essential fact is this: Demand will produce supply.

We can do much more to reduce demand. Some four million Americans [12] are currently on probation or parole. From tests done on them when they are jailed, we know that half or more had a drug problem when arrested. Though a lot of drug users otherwise obey the law (or at least avoid getting arrested), probationers and parolees constitute the hard core of dangerous addicts. Reducing their demand for drugs ought to be our highest priority.

Mark Kleiman of UCLA has suggested a program of "testing and control": [13] Probationers and parolees would be required to take frequent drug tests—say, twice weekly—as a condition of remaining on the street. If you failed the test, you would spend more time in jail; if you passed it, you would remain free. This approach would be an inducement for people to enter and stay in treatment.

Wilson presents his solution.

This would require some big changes in how we handle offenders. Police, [14] probation and parole officers would be responsible for conducting these tests, and more officers would have to be hired. Probation and parole authorities would have to be willing to sanction a test failure by immediate incarceration, initially for a short period (possibly a weekend), and then for longer periods if the initial failure were repeated. Treatment programs at little or no cost to the user would have to be available not only in every prison, but for every drug-dependent probationer and parolee.

Challenges of implementing his solution.

These things are not easily done. Almost every state claims to have an inten- [15] sive community supervision program, but few offenders are involved in them, the frequency with which they are contacted is low, and most were released from supervision without undergoing any punishment for violating its conditions.

But there is some hope. Our experience with drug courts suggests that [16] the procedural problems can be overcome. In such courts, several hundred of which now exist, special judges oversee drug-dependent offenders, insisting that they work to overcome their habits. While under drug-court supervision, offenders reduce drug consumption and, at least for a while after leaving the court, offenders are less likely to be arrested.

Our goal ought to be to extend meaningful community supervision to all [17] probationers and parolees, especially those who have a serious drug or alcohol problem. Efforts to test Mr. Kleiman's proposals are under way in Connecticut and Maryland.

How solution can work.

If this demand-reduction strategy works, it can be expanded. Drug tests [18] can be given to people who apply for government benefits, such as welfare and public housing. Some critics will think this is an objectionable intrusion. But giving benefits without conditions weakens the character-building responsibility of society.

### PREVENT HARM TO OTHERS

19    John Stuart Mill, the great libertarian thinker, argued that the only justifiable reason for restricting human liberty is to prevent harm to others. Serious drug abuse does harm others. We could, of course, limit government action to remedying those harms without addressing their causes, but that is an uphill struggle, especially when the harms fall on unborn children. Fetal drug syndrome imposes large costs on infants who have had no voice in choosing their fate.

20    Even Mill was clear that full liberty cannot be given to children or barbarians. By "barbarians" he meant people who are incapable of being improved by free and equal discussion. The life of a serious drug addict—the life of someone driven by drug dependency to prostitution and crime—is the life of a barbarian.

*Defense of his solution based on practicality and values.*

Source: Reprinted from *The Wall Street Journal*, April 13, 2000. © 2000 Dow Jones & Company, Inc.

### QUESTIONS FOR READING

1. What are the two solutions to the drug problem presented by others?
2. Why, according to Wilson, will legalizing drugs not be a good solution? What are the specific negative consequences of legalization?
3. Government strategies for controlling illegal drugs have included what activities?
4. What percentage of prisoners are now in prison on drug charges?
5. What problems do we face trying to reduce the supply of drugs? What, according to Wilson, drives supply?
6. What is Wilson's proposed solution? Explain the details of his solution.
7. What are some of the difficulties with the author's solution? What does he gain by bringing up possible difficulties?

### QUESTIONS FOR REASONING AND ANALYSIS

8. What does Wilson seek to accomplish in his concluding two paragraphs? What potential counterargument does he seek to rebut in his conclusion?
9. For what reasons might one agree that Wilson's solution is workable and still object to it? (Think about his concluding comments.)

### QUESTIONS FOR REFLECTION AND WRITING

10. Has Wilson convinced you that legalizing drugs will not reduce crime? Why or why not?
11. Is his argument against the supply-reduction approach convincing? Why or why not?
12. Has Wilson's defense of his solution convinced you that it is workable?
13. Do you have a different solution to the drug problem? If so, how would you refute Wilson and argue for your solution?

# PREPARING A PROBLEM/SOLUTION ARGUMENT

In addition to the guidelines for writing arguments presented in Chapter 4, you can use the following advice specific to defending a proposal.

## Planning

1. **Think:** What should be the focus and limits of your argument? There's a big difference between presenting solutions to the problem of physical abuse of women by men and presenting solutions to the problem of date rape on your college campus. Select a topic that you know something about, one that you can realistically handle.

2. **Think:** What reasons and evidence do you have to support your tentative claim? Think through what you already know that has led you to select your particular topic. Suppose you want to write on the issue of campus rapes. Is this choice due to a recent event on the campus? Was this event the first in many years or the last in a trend? Where and when are the rapes occurring? A brainstorming list may be helpful.

3. **Reality check:** Do you have a claim worth defending? Will readers care? Binge drinking and the polluting of the lake near your hometown are serious problems. Problems with your class schedule may not be—unless your experience reveals a college-wide problem.

4. **Think:** Is there additional evidence that you need to obtain to develop your argument? If so, where can you look for that evidence? Are there past issues of the campus paper in your library? Will the campus police grant you an interview?

5. **Think:** What about the feasibility of each solution you plan to present? Are you thinking in terms of essentially one solution with several parts to it or several separate solutions, perhaps to be implemented by different people? Will coordination be necessary to achieve success? How will this be accomplished? For the problem of campus rape, you may want to consider several solutions as a package to be coordinated by the counseling service or an administrative vice president.

## Drafting

1. Begin by either reminding readers of the existing problem you will address or arguing that a current situation should be recognized as a problem. In many cases, you can count on an audience who sees the world as you do and recognizes the problem you will address. But in some cases, your first task will be to convince readers that a problem exists that should worry them. If they are not concerned, they won't be interested in your solutions.

2. Early in your essay define the problem—as you see it—for readers. Do not assume that they will necessarily accept your way of seeing the issue. You may need to defend your assessment of the nature of the problem before moving on to solutions.

3.  If appropriate, explain the cause or causes of the problem. If your proposed solution is tied to removing the cause or causes of the problem, then you need to establish cause and prove it early in your argument. If cause is important, argue for it; if it is irrelevant, move to your solution.

4.  Explain your solution. If you have several solutions, think about how best to order them. If several need to be developed in a sequence, then present them in that necessary sequence. If you are presenting a package of diverse actions that together will solve the problem, then consider presenting them from the simplest to the more complex. With a problem of campus rape, for example, you may want to suggest better lighting on campus paths at night plus an escort service for women who are afraid to walk home alone plus sensitivity training for male students. Adding more lampposts is much easier than getting students to take sensitivity classes.

5.  Explain the process for achieving your solution. If you have not thought through the political or legal steps necessary to implement your solution, then this step cannot be part of your purpose in writing. However, anticipating a skeptical audience that says "How are we going to do that?" you would be wise to have precise steps to offer your reader. You may have obtained an estimate of costs for new lighting on your campus and want to suggest specific paths that need the lights. You may have investigated escort services at other colleges and can spell out how such a service can be implemented on your campus. Showing readers that you have thought ahead to the next steps in the process can be an effective method of persuasion.

6.  Support the feasibility of your solution. Be able to estimate costs. Show that you know who would be responsible for implementation. Explain how your solutions can be sold to people who may be unwilling to accommodate your proposals. All of this information will strengthen your argument.

7.  Show how your solution is better than others. Anticipate challenges by including reasons for adopting your program rather than another program. Explain how your solution will be more easily adopted or more effective when implemented than other possibilities. Of course, a less practical but still viable defense is that your solution is the right thing to do. Values also belong in public policy debates, not just issues of cost and acceptability.

## A CHECKLIST FOR REVISION

- ☐ Do I have a clear statement of my policy claim? Is it appropriately qualified and focused?
- ☐ Have I clearly explained how I see the problem to be solved? If necessary, have I argued for seeing the problem that way?
- ☐ Have I presented my solutions—and argued for them—in a clear and logical structure? Have I explained how these solutions can be implemented and why they are better than other solutions that have been suggested?
- ☐ Have I used data that are relevant and current?
- ☐ Have I used the basic checklist for revision in Chapter 4? (See p. 105.)

# FOR ANALYSIS AND DEBATE

## IMMIGRATE, ASSIMILATE | AMY CHUA

A professor at Yale Law School since 2001, Amy Chua specializes in international business transactions, ethnic conflict, and globalization and the law. She is the author of *World on Fire* (2004) and *Day of Empire: How Hyperpowers Rise to Global Dominance—And Why They Fall* (2007). Her essay on immigration, published February 3, 2008, was a special to the *Washington Post.*

PREREADING QUESTIONS Given the title, where do you expect to find Chua on the immigration debate? Given her education and expertise, how do you expect her to support her argument?

If you don't speak Spanish, Miami really can feel like a foreign country. In 1 any restaurant, the conversation at the next table is more likely to be in Spanish than English. And Miami's population is only 65 percent Hispanic. El Paso is 76 percent Latino. Flushing, N.Y., is 60 percent immigrant, mainly Chinese.

Chinatowns and Little Italys have long been part of America's urban land- 2 scape, but would it be all right to have entire U.S. cities where most people spoke and did business in Chinese, Spanish or even Arabic? Are too many Third World, non-English-speaking immigrants destroying our national identity?

For some Americans, even asking such questions is racist. At the other 3 end of the spectrum, conservative talk-show host Bill O'Reilly fulminates against floods of immigrants who threaten to change America's "complexion" and replace what he calls the "white Christian male power structure."

But for the large majority in between, Democrats and Republicans alike, 4 these questions are painful, and there are no easy answers. At some level, most of us cherish our legacy as a nation of immigrants. But are all immigrants really equally likely to make good Americans? Are we, as Samuel Huntington warns, in danger of losing our core values and devolving "into a loose confederation of ethnic, racial, cultural and political groups, with little or nothing in common apart from their location in the territory of what had been the United States of America"?

My parents arrived in the United States in 1961, so poor that they couldn't 5 afford heat their first winter. I grew up speaking only Chinese at home (for every English word accidentally uttered, my sister and I got one whack of the chopsticks). Today, my father is a professor at Berkeley, and I'm a professor at Yale Law School. As the daughter of immigrants, a grateful beneficiary of America's tolerance and opportunity, I could not be more pro-immigrant.

Nevertheless, I think Huntington has a point. 6

Around the world today, nations face violence and instability as a result of 7 their increasing pluralism and diversity. Across Europe, immigration has resulted in unassimilated, largely Muslim enclaves that are hotbeds of unrest and even terrorism. The riots in France late last year were just the latest manifestation.

With Muslims poised to become a majority in Amsterdam and elsewhere within a decade, major West European cities could undergo a profound transformation. Not surprisingly, virulent anti-immigration parties are on the rise.

8      Not long ago, Czechoslovakia, Yugoslavia and the Soviet Union disintegrated when their national identities proved too weak to bind together diverse peoples. Iraq is the latest example of how crucial national identity is. So far, it has found no overarching identity strong enough to unite its Kurds, Shiites and Sunnis.

9      The United States is in no danger of imminent disintegration. But this is because it has been so successful, at least since the Civil War, in forging a national identity strong enough to hold together its widely divergent communities. We should not take this unifying identity for granted.

10     The greatest empire in history, ancient Rome, collapsed when its cultural and political glue dissolved, and peoples who had long thought of themselves as Romans turned against the empire. In part, this fragmentation occurred because of a massive influx of immigrants from a very different culture. The "barbarians" who sacked Rome were Germanic immigrants who never fully assimilated.

11     Does this mean that it's time for the United States to shut its borders and reassert its "white, Christian" identity and what Huntington calls its Anglo-Saxon, Protestant "core values"?

## ANTI-IMMIGRANT MISTAKES

12     No. The anti-immigration camp makes at least two critical mistakes.

13     First, it neglects the indispensable role that immigrants have played in building American wealth and power. In the 19th century, the United States would never have become an industrial and agricultural powerhouse without the millions of poor Irish, Polish, Italian and other newcomers who mined coal, laid rail and milled steel. European immigrants led to the United States' winning the race for the atomic bomb.

14     Today, American leadership in the Digital Revolution—so central to our military and economic preeminence—owes an enormous debt to immigrant contributions. Andrew Grove (co-founder of Intel), Vinod Khosla (Sun Microsystems) and Sergey Brin (Google) are immigrants. Between 1995 and 2005, 52.4 percent of Silicon Valley startups had one key immigrant founder. And Vikram S. Pundit's recent appointment to the helm of Citigroup means that 14 CEOs of Fortune 100 companies are foreign-born.

15     The United States is in a fierce global competition to attract the world's best high-tech scientists and engineers—most of whom are not white Christians. Just this past summer, Microsoft opened a large new software-development center in Canada, in part because of the difficulty of obtaining U.S. visas for foreign engineers.

16     Second, anti-immigration talking heads forget that their own scapegoating vitriol will, if anything, drive immigrants further from the U.S. mainstream. One reason we don't have Europe's enclaves is our unique success in forging an ethnically and religiously neutral national identity, uniting individuals of all backgrounds. This is America's glue, and people like Huntington and O'Reilly unwittingly imperil it.

Nevertheless, immigration naysayers also have a point.   17

America's glue can be subverted by too much tolerance. Immigration   18 advocates are too often guilty of an uncritical political correctness that avoids hard questions about national identity and imposes no obligations on immigrants. For these well-meaning idealists, there is no such thing as too much diversity.

### MAINTAINING OUR HERITAGE

The right thing for the United States to do—and the best way to keep   19 Americans in favor of immigration—is to take national identity seriously while maintaining our heritage as a land of opportunity. U.S. immigration policy should be tolerant but also tough. Here are five suggestions:

### • Overhaul Admission Priorities.

Since 1965, the chief admission criterion has been family reunification.   20 This was a welcome replacement for the ethnically discriminatory quota system that preceded it. But once the brothers and sisters of a current U.S. resident get in, they can sponsor their own extended families. In 2006, more than 800,000 immigrants were admitted on this basis. By contrast, only about 70,000 immigrants were admitted on the basis of employment skills, with an additional 65,000 temporary visas granted to highly skilled workers.

This is backward. Apart from nuclear families (spouse, minor children, pos-   21 sibly parents), the special preference for family members should be drastically reduced. As soon as my father got citizenship, his relatives in the Philippines asked him to sponsor them. Soon, his mother, brother, sister and sister-in-law were also U.S. citizens or permanent residents. This was nice for my family, but frankly there is nothing especially fair about it.

Instead, the immigration system should reward ability and be keyed to the   22 country's labor needs, skilled or unskilled, technological or agricultural. In particular, we should significantly increase the number of visas for highly skilled workers, putting them on a fast track for citizenship.

### • Make English the Official National Language.

A common language is critical to cohesion and national identity in an ethni-   23 cally diverse society. Americans of all backgrounds should be encouraged to speak more languages—I've forced my own daughters to learn Mandarin (minus the threat of chopsticks)—but offering Spanish-language public education to Spanish-speaking children is the wrong kind of indulgence. Native-language education should be overhauled, and more stringent English proficiency requirements for citizenship should be set up.

### • Immigrants Must Embrace the Nation's Civic Virtues.

It took my parents years to see the importance of participating in the   24 larger community. When I was in third grade, my mother signed me up for Girl Scouts. I think she liked the uniforms and merit badges, but when I told her that I was picking up trash and visiting soup kitchens, she was horrified.

A Hispanic American shows his dual loyalties in march on Washington.

25    For many immigrants, only family matters. Even when immigrants get involved in politics, they often focus on protecting their own and protesting discrimination. That they can do so is one of the great virtues of U.S. democracy. But a mind-set based solely on taking care of your own factionalizes our society.

26    Like all Americans, immigrants have a responsibility to contribute to the social fabric. It's up to each immigrant community to fight off an "enclave" mentality and give back to their new country. It's not healthy for Chinese to hire only Chinese, or Koreans only Koreans. By contrast, the free health clinic set up by Muslim Americans in Los Angeles—serving the entire poor community—is a model to emulate. Immigrants are integrated at the moment they realize that their success is intertwined with everyone else's.

### • Enforce the Law.

27    Illegal immigration, along with terrorism, is the chief cause of today's anti-immigration backlash. It is also inconsistent with the rule of law, which, as any immigrant from a developing country will tell you, is a critical aspect of U.S. identity. But if we're serious about this problem, we need to enforce the law against not only illegal aliens, but also against those who hire them.

28    It's the worst of all worlds to allow U.S. employers who hire illegal aliens—thus keeping the flow of illegal workers coming—to break the law while demonizing the aliens as lawbreakers. An Arizona law that took effect Jan. 1 tightens the screws on employers who hire undocumented workers, but this issue can't be left up to a single state.

## • Make the United States an Equal-Opportunity Immigration Magnet.

That the 11 million to 20 million illegal Immigrants are 80 percent Mexican 29 and Central American is itself a problem. This is emphatically not for the reason Huntington gives—that Hispanics supposedly don't share America's core values. But if the U.S. immigration system is to reflect and further our ethnically neutral identity, it must itself be ethnically neutral, offering equal opportunity to Sudanese, Estonians, Burmese and so on. The starkly disproportionate ratio of Latinos—reflecting geographical fortuity and a large measure of lawbreaking—is inconsistent with this principle.

Immigrants who turn their backs on American values don't deserve to be 30 here. But those of us who turn our backs on immigrants misunderstand the secret of America's success and what it means to be American.

Source: From *The Washington Post*, February 3, 2008. Reprinted by permission of the author.

### QUESTIONS FOR READING

1. What is Huntington's concern for America?
2. What has happened in some European cities? To several European countries? What causes internal conflict in Iraq?
3. What are the two mistakes of those who oppose immigration, in the author's view?
4. What are the author's suggestions for a tough immigration policy? State her five proposals in your own words.

### QUESTIONS FOR REASONING AND ANALYSIS

5. Why does Chua provide her immigrant experience and family success story? As a part of her argument, what purpose does it serve?
6. What is clever about her concluding paragraph? How does it mirror the approach of her argument?
7. What is Chua's claim? Express her position as a problem/solution argument.
8. Look at Chua's five proposals. What kinds of grounds does she provide in support?
9. Is the author convincing? If so, what makes her argument effective? If not, why not?

### QUESTIONS FOR REFLECTION AND WRITING

10. Chua asserts that the chief cause of anti-immigration attitudes is a combination of terrorism and illegal aliens. Do you agree with this assessment? If not, why not?
11. Where do you stand on immigration? In opposition? Embracing diversity? Or somewhere in the middle? Has Chua established a good argument for the middle ground? Why or why not?
12. Is there any specific proposal with which you disagree? If so, why? How would you refute Chua's defense of that proposal?

# A MODEST PROPOSAL | JONATHAN SWIFT

For Preventing the Children of Poor People in Ireland from Being a Burden to Their Parents or Country, and for Making Them Beneficial to the Public

Born in Dublin, Jonathan Swift (1667–1745) was ordained in the Anglican Church and spent many years as dean of St. Patrick's in Dublin. Swift was also involved in the political and social life of London for some years, and throughout his life he kept busy writing. His most famous imaginative work is *Gulliver's Travels* (1726). Almost as well known is the essay that follows, published in 1729. Here you will find Swift's usual biting satire but also his concern to improve humanity.

**PREREADING QUESTIONS** Swift was a minister, but he writes this essay as if he were in a different job. What "voice" or persona do you hear? Does Swift agree with the views of this persona?

Jonathan Swift.

1    It is a melancholy object to those who walk through this great town[1] or travel in the country, where they see the streets, the roads, and cabin doors crowded with beggars of the female sex, followed by three, four, or six children, all in rags, and importuning every passenger for an alms. These mothers, instead of being able to work for their honest livelihood, are forced to employ all their time in strolling to beg sustenance for their helpless infants, who, as they grow up, either turn thieves for want of work, or leave their dear native country to fight for the pretender[2] in Spain or sell themselves to the Barbados.

2    I think it is agreed by all parties that this prodigious number of children in the arms, or on the backs, or at the heels of their mothers, and frequently of their fathers, is in the present deplorable state of the kingdom a very great additional grievance; and therefore, whoever could find out a fair, cheap, and easy method of making these children sound and useful members of the commonwealth would deserve so well of the public as to have his statue set up for a preserver of the nation.

_____
[1] Dublin.—Ed.
[2] James Stuart, claimant to the British throne lost by his father, James II, in 1688.—Ed.

*beggars*

*creates problems*

But my intention is very far from being confined to provide only for the children of professed beggars; it is of a much greater extent, and shall take in the whole number of infants at a certain age who are born of parents in effect as little able to support them as those who demand our charity in the streets. [3]

As to my own part, having turned my thoughts for many years upon this important subject, and maturely weighed the several schemes of other projectors,[3] I have always found them grossly mistaken in the computation. It is true a child just dropped from its dam may be supported by her milk for a solar year with little other nourishment; at most not above the value of two shillings, which the mother may certainly get, or the value in scraps, by her lawful occupation of begging; and, it is exactly at one year that I propose to provide for them in such a manner as instead of being a charge upon their parents or the parish, or wanting food and raiment for the rest of their lives, they shall on the contrary contribute to the feeding, and partly to the clothing, of many thousands. [4]

There is likewise another great advantage in my scheme, that it will prevent those voluntary abortions, and that horrid practice of women murdering their bastard children, alas, too frequent among us, sacrificing the poor innocent babes, I doubt, more to avoid the expense than the shame, which would move tears and pity in the most savage and inhuman breast. [5]

The number of souls in this kingdom being usually reckoned one million and a half, of these I calculate there may be about two hundred thousand couples whose wives are breeders; from which number I subtract thirty thousand couples who are able to maintain their own children, although I apprehend there cannot be so many, under the present distress of the kingdom; but this being granted, there will remain a hundred and seventy thousand breeders. I again subtract fifty thousand for those women who miscarry, or whose children die by accident or disease within the year. There only remain a hundred and twenty thousand children of poor parents annually born. The question therefore is, how this number shall be reared and provided for, which, as I have already said, under the present situation of affairs, is utterly impossible by all the methods hereto proposed. For we can neither employ them in handicraft or agriculture; we neither build houses (I mean in the country) nor cultivate land. They can very seldom pick up a livelihood by stealing until they arrive at six years old, except where they are of towardly parts[4]; although I confess they learn the rudiments much earlier, during which time they can, however, be properly looked upon only as probationers, as I have been informed by a principal gentleman in the country of Cavan, who protested to me that he never knew above one or two instances under the age of six, even in the part of the kingdom renowned for the quickest proficiency in that art. [6]

I am assured by our merchants that a boy or girl before twelve years old is no saleable commodity; and even when they come to this age they will not yield above three pounds, or three pounds and a half a crown at most, on the [7]

---

[3] Planners.—Ed.

[4] Innate abilities.—Ed.

exchange; which cannot turn to account either to the parents or the kingdom, the charge of nutriment and rags having been at least four times that value.

8    I shall now therefore humbly propose my own thoughts, which I hope will not be liable to the least objection.

9    I have been assured by a very knowing American of my acquaintance in London that a young healthy child well nursed is at a year old a most delicious, nourishing, and wholesome food, whether stewed, roasted, baked, or boiled; and I make no doubt that it will equally serve in a fricassee or ragout.

10    I do therefore humbly offer it to public consideration that of the hundred and twenty-thousand children, already computed, twenty thousand may be reserved for breed, whereof only one fourth part to be males, which is more than we allow to sheep, black cattle, or swine; and my reason is that these children are seldom the fruits of marriage, a circumstance not much regarded by our savages, therefore one male will be sufficient to serve four females. That the remaining hundred thousand may at a year old be offered in sale to the persons of quality and fortune, through the kingdom, always advising the mother to let them suck plentifully in the last month, so as to render them plump and fat for the table. A child will make two dishes at an entertainment for friends; and when the family dines alone, the fore or hind quarter will make a reasonable dish, and seasoned with a little pepper or salt will be very good boiled on the fourth day, especially in winter.

11    I have reckoned upon a medium that a child just born will weigh twelve pounds, and in a solar year if tolerably nursed increaseth to twenty-eight pounds.

12    I grant this food will be somewhat dear, and therefore very proper for landlords, who, as they have already devoured most of the parents, seem to have the best title to the children.

13    Infant's flesh will be in season throughout the year, but more plentiful in March, and a little before and after. For we are told by a grave author, an eminent French physician,[5] that fish being a prolific diet, there are more children born in Roman Catholic countries about nine months after Lent than at any other season; therefore reckoning a year after Lent, the markets will be more gutted than usual, because the number of popish infants is at least three to one in this kingdom; and therefore it will have one other collateral advantage, by lessening the number of Papists among us.

14    I have already computed the charge of nursing a beggar's child (in which list I reckon all cottagers, laborers, and four-fifths of the farmers) to be about two shillings per annum, rags included; and I believe no gentleman would repine to give ten shillings for the carcass of a good fat child, which, as I have said, will make four dishes of excellent nutritive meat, when he hath only some particular friend or his own family to dine with him. Thus the squire will learn to be a good landlord, and grow popular among his tenants; the mother will have eight shillings net profit, and be fit for work until she produces another child.

---

[5] François Rabelais.—Ed.

Those who are more thrifty (as I must confess the times require) may flay 15
the carcass; the skin of which artificially dressed will make admirable gloves for
ladies and summer boots for fine gentlemen.

As to our city of Dublin, shambles[6] may be appointed for this purpose, in 16
the most convenient parts of it, and butchers we may be assured will not be
wanting; although I rather recommend buying the children alive, and dressing
them hot from the knife as we do roasting pigs.

A very worthy person, a true lover of his country, and whose virtues I highly 17
esteem, was lately pleased in discoursing on this matter to offer a refinement
upon my scheme. He said that many gentlemen of this kingdom, having of late
destroyed their deer, he conceived that the want of venison might be well sup-
plied by the bodies of young lads and maidens, not exceeding fourteen years
of age nor under twelve, so great a number of both sexes in every county
being now ready to starve for want of work and service; and these to be disposed of by their parents, if alive, or otherwise by their nearest relations. But
with due deference to so excellent a friend and so deserving a patriot, I cannot be altogether in his sentiments. For as to the males, my American acquaintance assured me from frequent experience that their flesh was generally
tough and lean, like that of our school-boys, by continual exercise, and their
taste disagreeable; and to fatten them would not answer the charge. Then as
to the females, it would, I think with humble submission, be a loss to the public, because they soon would become breeders themselves; and besides, it is
not probable that some scrupulous people might be apt to censure such a
practice (although indeed very unjustly) as a little bordering upon cruelty;
which, I confess, hath always been with me the strongest objection against any
project, how wellsoever intended.

But in order to justify my friend, he confessed that this expedient was put 18
into his head by the famous Psalmanazar,[7] a native of the island Formosa who
came from thence to London above twenty years ago, and in conversation
told my friend that in his country when any young person happened to be put
to death, the executioner sold the carcass to persons of quality as a prime
dainty; and that in his time the body of a plump girl of fifteen, who was cruci-
fied for an attempt to poison the emperor, was sold to his Imperial Majesty's
prime minister of state, and other great mandarins of the court, in joints from
the gibbet, at four hundred crowns. Neither indeed can I deny that if the same
use were made of several plump young girls in this town, who without one
single groat to their fortunes cannot stir abroad without a chair, and appear at
the playhouse and assemblies in foreign fineries which they never will pay for,
the kingdom would not be the worse.

Some persons of a desponding spirit are in great concern about that vast 19
number of poor people who are aged, diseased, or maimed, and I have been
desired to employ my thoughts what course may be taken to ease the nation

---

[6] Butcher shops.—Ed.

[7] A known imposter who was French, not Formosan as he claimed.—Ed.

of so grievous an incumbrance. But I am not in the least pain upon that matter, because it is very well known that they are every day dying and rotting by cold and famine, and filth and vermin, as fast as can be reasonably expected. And as to the younger laborers, they are now in almost as hopeful a condition. They cannot get work, and consequently pine away for want of nourishment to a degree that if at any time they are accidentally hired to common labor, they have not strength to perform it; and thus the country and themselves are in a fair way of being soon delivered from the evils to come.

20      I have too long digressed, and therefore shall return to my subject. I think the advantages by the proposal which I have made are obvious and many, as well as of the highest importance.

21      For, first, as I have already observed, it would greatly lessen the number of Papists, with whom we are yearly overrun, being the principal breeders of the nation as well as our most dangerous enemies; and who stay at home on purpose with a design to deliver the kingdom to the pretender, hoping to take their advantage by the absence of so many good Protestants, who have chosen rather to leave their country than stay at home and pay tithes against their conscience to an idolatrous Episcopal curate.

22      Secondly, the poorer tenants will have something valuable of their own, which by law may be made liable to distress,[8] and help their landlord's rent; their corn and cattle being already seized, and money a thing unknown.

23      Thirdly, whereas the maintenance of a hundred thousand children, from two years old upwards, cannot be computed at less than ten shillings a piece per annum, the nation's stock will be thereby increased fifty thousand pounds per annum, besides the profit of a new dish introduced to the tables of all gentlemen of fortune in the kingdom who have any refinement in taste. And the money will circulate among ourselves, the goods being entirely of our own growth and manufacture.

24      Fourthly, the constant breeders, besides the gain of eight shillings sterling per annum by the sale of their children, will be rid of the charge of maintaining them after the first year.

25      Fifthly, this food would likewise bring great custom to taverns, where the vintners will certainly be so prudent as to procure the best receipts for dressing it to perfection, and consequently have their houses frequented by all the fine gentlemen, who justly value themselves upon their knowledge in good eating; and a skillful cook, who understands how to oblige his guests, will contrive to make it as expensive as they please.

26      Sixthly, this would be a great inducement to marriage, which all wise nations have either encouraged by rewards or enforced by laws and penalties. It would increase the care and tenderness of mothers towards their children, when they were sure of a settlement for life to the poor babes, provided in some sort by the public; to their annual profit instead of expense. We should soon see an honest emulation among the married women, which of them could bring the fattest child to the market. Men would become as fond of

---

[8] Can be seized by lenders.—Ed.

their wives during the time of their pregnancy as they are now of their mares in foal, their cows in calf, or sows when they are ready to farrow; nor offer to beat or kick them (as it is too frequent a practice) for fear of a miscarriage.

*as animals*

Many other advantages might be enumerated. For instance, the addition 27 of some thousand carcasses in our exportation of barrelled beef, the propagation of swine's flesh, and improvement in the art of making good bacon, so much wanted among us by the great destruction of pigs, too frequent at our tables, which are no way comparable in taste or magnificence to a well-grown fat, yearling child, which roasted whole will make a considerable figure at a lord mayor's feast or any other public entertainment. But this and many others I omit, being studious of brevity.

Supposing that one thousand families in this city would be constant cus- 28 tomers for infants' flesh, besides others who might have it at merry meetings, particularly weddings and christenings, I compute that Dublin would take off annually about twenty thousand carcasses, and the rest of the kingdom (where probably they will be sold somewhat cheaper) the remaining eighty thousand.

I can think of no one objection that will possibly be raised against this pro- 29 posal, unless it should be urged that the number of people will be thereby much lessened in the kingdom. This I freely own, and it was indeed one principal design in offering it to the world. I desire the reader will observe that I calculate my remedy for this one individual kingdom of Ireland and for no other that ever was, is, or I think ever can be upon earth. Therefore let no man talk to me of other expedients: of taxing our absentees at five shillings a pound: of using neither clothes nor household furniture except what is of our own growth and manufacture: of utterly rejecting the materials and instruments that promote foreign luxury: of curing the expensiveness or pride, vanity, idleness, and gaming in our women: of introducing a vein of parsimony, prudence and temperance: of learning to love our country, wherein we differ even from Laplanders and the inhabitants of Topinamboo[9]: of quitting our animosities and factions, nor act any longer like the Jews, who were murdering one another at the very moment their city was taken[10]: of being a little cautious not to sell our country and consciences for nothing: of teaching landlords to have at least one degree of mercy towards their tenants. Lastly, of putting a spirit of honesty, industry, and skill into our shopkeepers; who, if a resolution could now be taken to buy only our native goods, would immediately unite to cheat and exact upon us in the price, the measure, and the goodness, nor could ever yet be brought to make one fair proposal of just dealing, though often and earnestly invited to it.

*counter argument*

Therefore I repeat, let no man talk to me of these and the like expedients, 30 till he hath at least a glimpse of hope that there will ever be some hearty and sincere attempt to put them in practice.

---

[9] An area in Brazil.—Ed.

[10] Some Jews were accused of helping the Romans and were executed during the Roman siege of Jerusalem in A.D. 70—Ed.

31    But as to myself, having been wearied out for many years with offering vain, idle, visionary thoughts, and at length utterly despairing of success, I fortunately fell upon this proposal, which, as it is wholly new, so it hath something solid and real, of no expense and little trouble, full in our own power, and whereby we can incur no danger in disobliging England. For this kind of commodity will not bear exportation, the flesh being of too tender a consistence to admit a long continuance in salt, although perhaps I could name a country which would be glad to eat up our whole nation without it.

32    After all, I am not so violently bent upon my own opinion as to reject any offer proposed by wise men, which shall be found equally innocent, cheap, easy, and effectual. But before something of that kind shall be advanced in contradiction to my scheme, and offering a better, I desire the author, or authors, will be pleased maturely to consider two points. First, as things now stand, how they will be able to find food and raiment for a hundred thousand useless mouths and backs. And secondly, there being a round million of creatures in human figure throughout this kingdom, whose whole subsistence put into a common stock would leave them in debt two million of pounds sterling, adding those who are beggars by profession to the bulk of farmers, cottagers, and laborers, with their wives and children who are beggars, in effect; I desire those politicians who dislike my overture, and may perhaps be so bold to attempt an answer, that they will first ask the parents of these mortals whether they would not at this day think it a great happiness to have been sold for food at a year old in the manner I prescribe, and thereby have avoided such a perpetual scene of misfortunes as they have since gone through by the oppression of landlords, the impossibility of paying rent without money or trade, the want of common sustenance, with neither house nor clothes to cover them from the inclemencies of weather, and the most inevitable prospect of entailing the like or greater miseries upon their breed forever.

33    I profess, in the sincerity of my heart, that I have not the least personal interest in endeavoring to promote this necessary work, having no other motive than the public good of my country, by advancing our trade, providing for infants, relieving the poor, and giving some pleasure to the rich. I have no children by which I can propose to get a single penny, the youngest being nine years old, and my wife past childbearing.

QUESTIONS FOR READING

1.  How is the argument organized? What is accomplished in paragraphs 1–7? In paragraphs 8–16? In paragraphs 17–19? In paragraphs 20–28? In paragraphs 29–33?

2.  What specific advantages does the writer offer in defense of his proposal?

## QUESTIONS FOR REASONING AND ANALYSIS

3.  What specific passages and connotative words make us aware that this is a satirical piece using irony as its chief device?

4.  After noting Swift's use of irony, what do you conclude to be his purpose in writing?

5.  What can you conclude to be some of the problems in eighteenth-century Ireland? Where does Swift offer direct condemnation of existing conditions in Ireland and attitudes of the English toward the Irish?

6.  What actual reforms would Swift like to see?

## QUESTIONS FOR REFLECTION AND WRITING

7.  What are some of the advantages of using irony? What does Swift gain by this approach? What are possible disadvantages in using irony? Reflect on irony as a persuasive strategy.

8.  What are some current problems that might be addressed by the use of irony? Make a list. Then select one and think about what "voice" or persona you might use to bring attention to that problem. Plan your argument with irony as a strategy.

— counter argument
⇒ objective tone

1.  Think of a problem on your campus or in your community for which you have a workable solution. Organize your argument to include all relevant steps as described in this chapter. Although your primary concern will be to present your solution, depending on your topic you may need to begin by convincing readers of the seriousness of the problem or the causes of the problem—if your solutions involve removing those causes.

2.  Think of a problem in education—K–12 or at the college level—that you have a solution for and that you are interested in. You may want to begin by brainstorming to develop a list of possible problems in education about which you could write—or look through Chapter 20 for ideas. Be sure to qualify your claim and limit your focus as necessary to work with a problem that is not so broad and general that your "solutions" become general and vague comments about "getting better teachers." (If one problem is a lack of qualified teachers, then what specific proposals do you have for solving that particular problem?) Include as many steps as are appropriate to develop and support your argument.

3.  Think of a situation that you consider serious but that apparently many people do not take seriously enough. Write an argument in which you emphasize, by providing evidence, that the situation is a serious problem. You may conclude by suggesting a solution, but your chief purpose in writing will be to alert readers to a problem.

# The Researched and Formally Documented Argument

# CHAPTER 12

# Locating, Evaluating, and Preparing to Use Sources

We do research all the time. You would not select a college or buy a car without doing research: gathering relevant information, analyzing that information, and drawing conclusions from your study. You may already have done some research in this course, using sources in this text or finding data online to strengthen an argument. Then you acknowledged your sources either informally in your essay or formally, following the documentation guidelines in this section. So, when you are assigned a more formal research essay, remember that you are not facing a brand-new assignment. You are just doing a longer paper with more sources, and you have this section to guide you to success.

## SELECTING A GOOD TOPIC

To get started you need to select and limit a topic. One key to success is finding a workable topic. No matter how interesting or clever the topic, it is not workable if it does not meet the guidelines of your assignment. Included in those guidelines may be a required length, a required number of sources, and a due date. Understand and accept all of these guidelines as part of your writing context.

### What Type of Paper Am I Preparing?

Study your assignment to understand the type of project. Is your purpose expository, analytic, or argumentative? How would you classify each of the following topics?

1. Explain the chief solutions proposed for increasing the Southwest's water supply.
2. Compare the Freudian and behavioral models of mental illness.
3. Find the best solutions to a current environmental problem.
4. Consider: What twentieth-century invention has most dramatically changed our personal lives?

Did you recognize that the first topic calls for a report? The second topic requires an analysis of two schools of psychology, so you cannot report on only one, but you also cannot argue that one model is better than the other. Both topics 3 and 4 require an argumentative paper: You must select and defend a claim.

### Who Is My Audience?

If you are writing in a specific discipline, imagine your instructor as a representative of that field, a reader with knowledge of the subject area. If you are in a composition course, your instructor may advise you to write to a general reader, someone who reads newspapers but may not have the exact information and perspective you have. For a general reader, specialized terms and concepts need definition.

> **NOTE:** Consider the expectations of readers of research papers. A research essay is not like a personal essay. A research essay is not about you; it is about a subject, so keep yourself more in the background than you might in an informal piece of writing.

## How Can I Select a Good Topic?

*Choosing from assigned topics.* At times students are unhappy with topic restriction. Looked at another way, your instructor has eliminated a difficult step in the research process and has helped you avoid the problem of selecting an unworkable topic. If topics are assigned, you will still have to choose from the list and develop your own claim and approach.

*Finding a course-related topic.* This guideline gives you many options and requires more thought about your choice. Working within the guidelines, try to write about what interests you. Here are examples of assignments turned into topics of interest to the student:

| ASSIGNMENT | INTEREST | TOPIC |
|---|---|---|
| 1. Trace the influence of any twentieth-century event, development, invention. | Music | The influence of the Jazz Age on modern music |
| 2. Support an argument on some issue of pornography and censorship. | Computers | Censorship of pornography on the Internet |
| 3. Demonstrate the popularity of a current myth and then discredit it. | Science fiction | The lack of evidence for the existence of UFOs |

*Selecting a topic without any guidelines.* When you are free to write on any topic, you may need to use some strategies for topic selection.

- Look through your text's table of contents or index for subject areas that can be narrowed or focused.
- Look over your class notes and think about subjects covered that have interested you.
- Consider college-based or local issues.
- Do a subject search in an electronic database to see how a large topic can be narrowed—for example, type in "dinosaur" and observe such subheadings as *dinosaur behavior* and *dinosaur extinction.*
- Use one or more invention strategies to narrow and focus a topic:
  - Freewriting
  - Brainstorming
  - Asking questions about a broad subject, using the reporter's *who, what, where, when,* and *why.*

## What Kinds of Topics Should I Avoid?

Here are several kinds of topics that are best avoided because they usually produce disasters, no matter how well the student handles the rest of the research process:

1. *Topics that are irrelevant* to your interests or the course. If you are not interested in your topic, you will not produce a lively, informative paper. If you select a topic far removed from the course content, you may create some hostility in your instructor, who will wonder why you are unwilling to become engaged in the course.

2. *Topics that are broad subject areas.* These result in general surveys that lack appropriate detail and support.

3. *Topics that can be fully researched with only one source.* You will produce a summary, not a research paper.

4. *Biographical studies.* Short undergraduate papers on a person's life usually turn out to be summaries of one or two major biographies.

5. *Topics that produce a strong emotional response in you.* If there is only one "right" answer to the abortion issue and you cannot imagine counterarguments, don't choose to write on abortion. Probably most religious topics are best avoided.

6. *Topics that are too technical for you* at this point in your college work. If you do not understand the complexities of the federal tax code, then arguing for a reduction in the capital gains tax may be an unwise topic choice.

# WRITING A TENTATIVE CLAIM OR RESEARCH PROPOSAL

Once you have selected and focused a topic, you need to write a tentative claim, research question, or research proposal. Some instructors will ask to see a statement—from a sentence to a paragraph long—to be approved before you proceed. Others may require as much as a one-page proposal that includes a tentative claim, a basic organizational plan, and a description of types of sources to be used. Even if your instructor does not require anything in writing, you need to write something for your benefit—to direct your reading and thinking. Here are two possibilities:

1. **SUBJECT:** Computers

   **TOPIC:** The impact of computers on the twentieth century

   **CLAIM:** Computers had the greatest impact of any technological development in the twentieth century.

   **RESEARCH PROPOSAL:** I propose to show that computers had the greatest impact of any technological development in the twentieth century.

> I will show the influence of computers at work, in daily living, and in play to emphasize the breadth of influence. I will argue that other possibilities (such as cars) did not have the same impact as computers. I will check the library's book catalog and databases for sources on technological developments and on computers specifically. I will also interview a family friend who works with computers at the Pentagon.

This example illustrates several key ideas. First, the initial subject is both too broad and unfocused (*What* about computers?). Second, the claim is more focused than the topic statement because it asserts a position, a claim the student must support. Third, the research proposal is more helpful than the claim only because it includes some thoughts on developing the thesis and finding sources.

2.   Less sure of your topic? Then write a research question or a more open-ended research proposal. Take, for example, a history student studying the effects of Prohibition. She is not ready to write a thesis, but she can write a research proposal that suggests some possible approaches to the topic:

| | |
|---|---|
| **TOPIC:** | The effect of Prohibition |
| **RESEARCH QUESTION:** | What were the effects of Prohibition on the United States? |
| **RESEARCH PROPOSAL:** | I will examine the effects of Prohibition on the United States in the 1920s (and possibly consider some long-term effects, depending on the amount of material on the topic). Specifically, I will look at the varying effects on urban and rural areas and on different classes in society. |

## PREPARING A WORKING BIBLIOGRAPHY

To begin this next stage of your research, you need to know three things:

- *Your search strategy.* If you are writing on a course-related topic, your starting place may be your textbook for relevant sections and possible sources (if the text contains a bibliography). For this course, you may find some potential sources among the readings in this text. Think about what you already know or have in hand as you plan your search strategy.

- *A method for recording bibliographic information.* You have two choices: the always reliable 3 × 5 index cards or a bibliography file in your personal computer.

- *The documentation format you will be using.* You may be assigned the Modern Language Association (MLA) format, or perhaps given a choice between MLA and the American Psychological Association (APA) documentation styles. Once you select the documentation style, skim the appropriate pages in Chapter 14 to get an overview of both content and style.

A list of possible sources is only a *working* bibliography because you do not yet know which sources you will use. (Your final bibliography will include only those sources you cite—actually refer to—in your paper.) A working bibliography will help you see what is available on your topic, note how to locate each source, and contain the information needed to document. Whether you are using cards or computer files, follow these guidelines:

1. Check all reasonable catalogs and indexes for possible sources. (Use more than one reference source even if you locate enough sources there; you are looking for the best sources, not the first ones you find.)
2. Complete a card or prepare an entry for every potentially useful source. You won't know what to reject until you start a close reading of sources.
3. Copy (or download from an online catalog) all information needed to complete a citation and to locate the source. (When using an index that does not give all needed information, leave a space to be filled in when you actually read the source.)
4. Put bibliographic information in the correct format for every possible source; you will save time and make fewer errors. Do not mix or blend styles. When searching for sources, have your text handy and use the appropriate models as your guide.

The following brief guide to correct form will get you started. Illustrations are for cards, but the information and order will be the same in your PC file. (Guidelines are for MLA style.)

## Basic Form for Books

As Figure 12.1 shows, the basic MLA form for books includes the following information in this pattern:

1. The author's full name, last name first.
2. The title (and subtitle if there is one) of the book, in italics (underlined in handwriting).
3. The facts of publication: the city of publication (followed by a colon), the publisher (followed by a comma), and the date of publication.
4. The publication medium—Print.

Note that periods are placed after the author's name, after the title, and at the end of the citation. Other information, when appropriate (e.g., the number of volumes), is added to this basic pattern. (See pp. 320–30 for many sample citations.) Include, in your working bibliography, the book's classification number so that you can find it in the library.

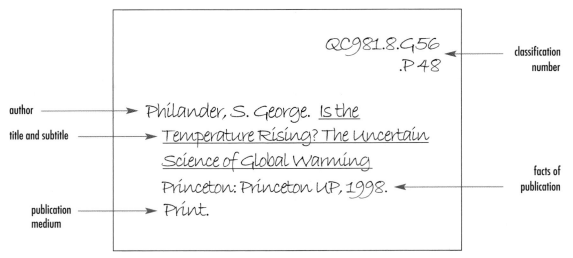

**FIGURE 12.1** Bibliography Card for a Book

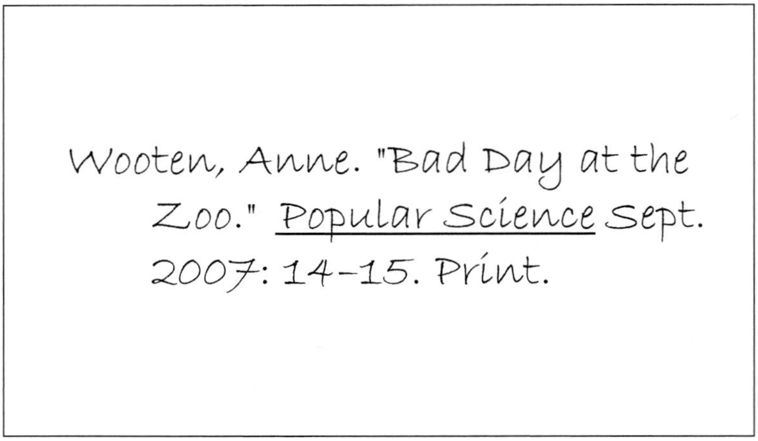

**FIGURE 12.2** Bibliography Card for a Magazine Article

## Basic Form for Articles

Figure 12.2 shows the simplest form for magazine articles. Include the following information, in this pattern:

1. The author's full name, last name first.
2. The title of the article, in quotation marks.
3. The facts of publication: the title of the periodical in italics (underlined in handwriting), the volume number (if the article is from a scholarly journal), the date (followed by a colon), and inclusive page numbers.
4. The publication medium—Print.

You will discover that indexes rarely present information in MLA format. Here, for example, is a source on problems with zoos, found in an electronic database:

**BAD DAY AT THE ZOO.**

Wooten, Anne. Popular Science, Sep2007, Vol. 271 Issue 3, p. 14–15, 2p.

If you read the article in the magazine itself, then the correct citation, for MLA, will look like that in the sample bibliography card in Figure 12.2. (Because *Popular Science* is a magazine, not a scholarly journal, you provide month and year but not volume and issue numbers.) However, if you obtain a copy of the article from one of your library's electronic databases, then your citation will need additional information to identify your actual source of the article:

Wooten, Anne. "Bad Day at the Zoo." *Popular Science* Sept. 2007: 14–15. *Academic Search Complete.* Web. 8 Sept. 2008.

Note that the medium of publication is now "Web," not "Print," and the name of the database is italicized as if it were a book containing the article.

**NOTE:** A collection of printouts, slips of paper, and backs of envelopes is not a working bibliography! You may have to return to the library for missing information, and you risk making serious errors in documentation. Know the basics of your documentation format and follow it faithfully when collecting possible sources.

One of the famous lions sitting in front of the New York Public Library.

# LOCATING SOURCES

All libraries contain books and periodicals and a system for accessing them. A library's *book collection* includes the general collection, the reference collection, and the reserve book collection. Electronic materials such as tapes and CDs will also be included in the general "book" collection. The *periodicals collection* consists of popular magazines, scholarly journals, and newspapers. Electronic databases with texts of articles provide alternatives to the print periodicals collection.

**REMEMBER:** All works, regardless of their source or the format in which you obtain them—and this includes online sources—must be fully documented in your paper.

## The Book Catalog

Your chief guide to books and audiovisual materials is the library catalog, usually an electronic database accessed from computer stations in the library or, with an appropriate password, from your personal computer.

In the catalog there will be at least four ways to access a specific book: the author entry, the title entry, one or more subject entries, and a keyword option. When you pull up the search screen, you will probably see that the keyword option is the default. If you know the exact title of the work you want, switch to the title option, type it in, and hit submit. If you want a list of all of the library's books on Hemingway, though, click on author and type in "Hemingway." Keep these points in mind:

- With a title search, do not type any initial article (a, an, the). To locate *The Great Gatsby,* type in "Great Gatsby."
- Use correct spelling. If you are unsure of spelling, use a keyword instead of an author or title search.
- If you are looking for a list of books on your subject, do a keyword or subject search.
- When screens for specific books are shown, either print screens of potential sources or copy all information needed for documentation—plus the call number for each book.

## The Reference Collection

The research process often begins with the reference collection. You will find atlases, dictionaries, encyclopedias, general histories, critical studies, and biographies. In addition, various reference tools such as bibliographies and indexes are part of the reference collection.

Many tools in the reference collection once only in print form are now also online. Some are now only online. Yet online is not always the way to go. Let's consider some of the advantages of each of the formats:

### Advantages of the Print Reference Collection

1. The reference tool may be only in print—use it.
2. The print form covers the period you are studying. (Most online indexes and abstracts cover only from 1980 to the present.)
3. In a book, with a little scanning of pages, you can often find what you need without getting spelling or commands exactly right.
4. If you know the best reference source to use and are looking for only a few items, the print source can be faster than the online source.

### Advantages of Online Reference Materials

1. Online databases are likely to provide the most up-to-date information.
2. You can usually search all years covered at one time.
3. Full texts (with graphics) are sometimes available, as well as indexes with detailed summaries of articles. Both can be printed or e-mailed to your PC.
4. Through links to the Internet, you have access to an amazing amount of material. (Unless you focus your keyword search, however, you may be overwhelmed.)

Before using any reference work, take a few minutes to check its date, purpose, and organization. If you are new to online searching, take a few minutes to learn about each reference tool by working through the online tutorial.

### A Word About Wikipedia

Many researchers go first to a general encyclopedia, in the past in print in the reference collection, today more typically online. This is not always the best strategy. Often you can learn more about your topic from a current book or a more specialized reference source—which your reference librarian can help you find. Both may give you additional sources of use to your project. If—or when—you turn to a general encyclopedia, make it a good one that is available online through your library. Some colleges have told their students that *Wikipedia* is not an acceptable source for college research projects.

## Electronic Databases

You will probably access electronic databases by going to your library's home page and then clicking on the appropriate term or icon. (You may have found the book catalog by clicking on "library catalog"; you may find the databases by clicking on "library resources" or some other descriptive label.) You will need to choose a particular database and then type in your keyword for a basic

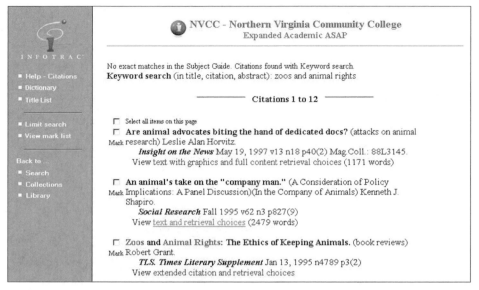

**FIGURE 12.3** Partial List of Articles Found on Search Topic

search or select "advanced search" to limit that search by date or periodical or in some other way. Each library will create somewhat different screens, but the basic process of selecting among choices provided and then typing in your search commands remains the same. Figure 12.3 shows a partial list of articles that resulted from a keyword search for "zoos and animal rights."

# GUIDELINES for Using Online Databases

Keep these points in mind as you use online databases:

- **Although some online databases provide full texts of all articles, others provide full texts of only some of the articles indexed.** The articles not in full text will have to be located in a print collection of periodicals.
- **Articles indexed but not available in full text often come with a brief summary or abstract.** This allows you to decide whether the article looks useful for your project. *Do not treat the abstract as the article. Do not use material from it and cite the author. If you want to use the article, find it in your library's print collection or obtain it from another library.*
- **The information you need for documenting material used from an article is not in correct format for any of the standard documentation styles.** You will have to reorder the information and use the correct style for writing titles. If your instructor wants to see a list of possible sources in MLA format, do not hand in a printout of articles from an online database.

- **Because no single database covers all magazines, you may want to search several databases that seem relevant to your project.** Ask your reference librarian for suggestions of various databases in the sciences, social sciences, public affairs, and education.

## The Internet

In addition to using electronic databases to find sources, you can search the Internet directly.

Keep in mind these facts about the Internet:

- The Internet is both disorganized and huge, so you can waste time trying to find information that is easily obtained in a library reference book or database.
- The Internet is best at providing current information, such as news and movie reviews. It is also a great source of government information.
- Because anyone can create a website and put anything on it, you will have to be especially careful in evaluating Internet sources. Remember that articles in magazines and journals have been selected by editors and are often peer reviewed as well, but no editor selects or rejects material on a personal website.

## GUIDELINES for Searching the Web

How much information you may find searching for a specific topic, and how useful it is, will vary from one research project to another. Here are some general guidelines to aid your research on the Internet:

1. **Bookmark sites you expect to use often so that you do not have to remember complicated Web addresses (URLs).**
2. **Make your search as precise as possible to avoid getting overwhelmed with hits.**
3. **If you are searching for a specific phrase, put quotation marks around the words.** This will reduce the number of hits and lead to sites more useful to your research. Examples: "Environmental Protection Agency" or "civil disobedience."
4. **Use Boolean connectors to make your search more precise.**

   - AND: This connector limits results to those sites that contain both terms, for example, "zoos AND animal rights."
   - OR: This connector extends the hits to include all sites that contain one or the other search term. So, "zoos OR animal rights" will generate a list of sites containing either term.

> - NOT: This connector limits the search to only the first term, not the second. Thus, "zoos NOT animal rights" will give you sites only about zoo issues not involving animal rights.

5. **If you are not successful with one search engine, try a different one.** Remember that each search engine searches only a part of the Internet.

6. **If you are not successful with a second search engine, check your spelling.** Search engines cannot always guess what you mean.

7. **To get the best sites for most college research projects, try a directory of evaluated sites or subject guides rather than, say, Yahoo!** (Yahoo! is better for news, people searches, and commercial sites.) Some of the best academic subject guides include:

   - The Argus Clearinghouse (**www.clearinghouse.net**)
   - The University of California's Infomine (**http://infomine.ucr.edu**)
   - Internet Scout Project (**http://scout.cs.wisc.edu**)

8. **Be certain to complete a bibliography card—including the date you accessed the material—for each separate site from which you take information.** (See pp. 314–30 for documentation guidelines.)

# FIELD RESEARCH

Field research can enrich many projects. The following sections offer some suggestions.

## Federal, State, and Local Government Documents

In addition to federal documents you may obtain through *PAIS* or *GPO Access,* department and agency websites, or the Library of Congress's good legislative site, *Thomas* (**http://thomas.loc.gov**), consider state and county archives, maps, and other published materials. Instead of selecting a national or global topic, consider examining the debate over a controversial bill introduced in your state legislature. Use online databases to locate articles on the bill and the debate and interview legislators and journalists who participated in or covered the debates or served on committees that worked with the bill.

You can also request specific documents from appropriate state or county agencies and nonprofit organizations. One student, given the assignment of examining solutions to an ecological problem, decided to study the local problem of preserving the Chesapeake Bay. She obtained issues of the Chesapeake Bay Foundation newsletter and brochures prepared by them advising homeowners about hazardous household waste materials that end up in the bay. Added to her sources were bulletins on soil conservation and landscaping tips for improving the area's water quality. Local problems can lead to interesting research topics because they are current and relevant to you and because they involve uncovering different kinds of source materials.

## Correspondence

Business and government officials are usually willing to respond to written requests for information. Make your letter brief and well written. Either include a self-addressed, stamped envelope for the person's convenience or e-mail your request. If you are not e-mailing, write as soon as you discover the need for information and be prepared to wait several weeks for a reply. It is appropriate to indicate your deadline and ask for a timely response. Three guidelines for either letters or e-mails to keep in mind are:

1. Explain precisely what information you need.
2. Do not request information that can be found in your library's reference collection.
3. Explain how you plan to use the information. Businesses especially are understandably concerned with their public image and will be disinclined to provide information that you intend to use as a means of attacking them.

Use reference guides to companies and government agencies or their websites to obtain addresses and the person to whom your letter or e-mail should be sent.

## Interviews

Some experts are available for personal interviews. Call or write for an appointment as soon as you recognize the value of an interview. Remember that interviews are more likely to be scheduled with state and local officials than with the president of General Motors. If you are studying a local problem, also consider leaders of the civic association with an interest in the issue. In many communities, the local historian or a librarian will be a storehouse of information about the community. Former teachers can be interviewed for papers on education. Interviews with doctors or nurses can add a special dimension to papers on medical issues.

If an interview is appropriate for your topic, follow these guidelines:

1. Prepare specific questions in advance.
2. Arrive on time, properly dressed, and behave in a polite, professional manner.
3. Take notes, asking the interviewee to repeat key statements so that your notes are accurate.
4. Take a tape recorder with you but ask permission to use it before taping.
5. If you quote any statements in your paper, quote accurately, eliminating only such minor speech habits as "you know's" and "uhm's." (See Chapter 14 for proper documentation of interviews.)
6. Direct the interview with your prepared questions, but also give the interviewee the chance to approach the topic in his or her own way. You may obtain information or views that had not occurred to you.
7. Do not get into a debate with the interviewee. You are there to learn.

## Lectures

Check the appropriate information sources at your school to keep informed of visiting speakers. If you are fortunate enough to attend a lecture relevant to a current project, take careful, detailed notes. Because a lecture is a source, use of information or ideas from it must be presented accurately and then documented. (See Chapter 14 for documentation format.)

## Films, Tapes, Television

Your library will have audiovisual materials that provide good sources for some kinds of topics. For example, if you are studying *Death of a Salesman,* view a videotaped version of the play. Also pay attention to documentaries on public television and to the many news and political talk shows on both public and commercial channels. In many cases transcripts of shows can be obtained from the TV station. Alternatively, tape the program while watching it so that you can view it several times. The documentation format for such nonprint sources is illustrated in Chapter 14.

## Surveys, Questionnaires, and Original Research

Depending on your paper, you may want to conduct a simple survey or write and administer a questionnaire. Surveys can be used for many campus and local issues, for topics on behavior and attitudes of college students and/or faculty, and for topics on consumer habits. Prepare a brief list of questions with space for answers. Poll faculty through their mailboxes or e-mail and students individually on campus or in your classes. When writing questions, keep these guidelines in mind:

- Use simple, clear language.
- Devise a series of short questions rather than only a few that have several parts to them. (You want to separate information for better analysis.)
- Phrase questions to avoid wording that seeks to control the answer. For example, do *not* ask "Did you perform your civic duty by voting in the last election?" This is a loaded question.

In addition to surveys and questionnaires, you can incorporate some original research. As you read sources on your topic, be alert to reports of studies that you could redo and update in part or on a smaller scale. Many topics on advertising and television give opportunities for your own analysis. Local-issue topics may offer good opportunities for gathering information on your own, not just from your reading. One student, examining the controversy over a proposed new shopping mall on part of the Manassas Civil War Battlefield in Virginia, made the argument that the mall served no practical need in the community. He supported his position by describing existing malls, including the number and types of stores each contained and the number of miles each was from the proposed new mall. How did he obtain this information? He drove around the area, counting miles and stores. Sometimes a seemingly unglamorous approach to a topic turns out to be an imaginative one.

## EVALUATING SOURCES, MAINTAINING CREDIBILITY

As you study your sources, keep rethinking your purpose and approach. Test your research proposal or tentative claim against what you are learning. Remember: You can always change the direction and focus of your paper as new approaches occur to you, and you can even change your position as you reflect on what you are learning.

You will work with sources more effectively if you keep in mind why you are using them. What you are looking for will vary somewhat, depending on your topic and purpose, but there are several basic approaches:

1. *Acquiring information and viewpoints firsthand.* Suppose that you are concerned about the mistreatment of animals kept in zoos. You do not want to just read what others have to say on this issue. First, visit a zoo, taking notes on what you see. Second, before you go, plan to interview at least one person on the zoo staff, preferably a veterinarian who can explain the zoo's guidelines for animal care. Only after gathering and thinking about these *primary sources* do you want to add to your knowledge by reading articles and books—*secondary sources.* Many kinds of topics require the use of both primary and secondary sources. If you want to study violence in children's TV shows, for example, you should first spend some time watching specific shows and taking notes.

2. *Acquiring new knowledge.* Suppose you are interested in breast cancer research and treatment, but you do not know much about the choices of treatment and, in general, where we are with this medical problem. You will need to turn to sources first to learn about the topic. You should begin with sources that will give you an overview, perhaps a historical perspective of how knowledge and treatment have progressed in the last thirty years. Similarly, if your topic is the effects of Prohibition in the 1920s, you will need to read first for knowledge but also with an eye to ways to focus the topic and organize your paper.

3. *Understanding the issues.* Suppose you think that you know your views on illegal immigration, so you intend to read only to obtain some useful statistical information to support your argument. Should you scan sources quickly, looking for facts you can use? This approach may be too hasty. As explained in Chapter 3, good arguments are built on a knowledge of counterarguments. You are wise to study sources presenting a variety of attitudes on your issue so that you understand—and can refute—the arguments of others. *Remember, too, that with controversial issues often the best argument is a conciliatory one that presents a middle ground and seeks to bring people together.*

When you use facts and opinions from sources, you are saying to readers that the facts are accurate and the ideas credible. If you do not evaluate your sources before using them, you risk losing your credibility as a writer. (Remember Aristotle's idea of *ethos*, how your character is judged.) Just because they are in print does not mean that a writer's "facts" are reliable or ideas worthwhile. Judging the usefulness and reliability of potential sources is an essential part of the research process.

# GUIDELINES for Evaluating Sources

Today, with access to so much material on the Internet, the need to evaluate is even more crucial. Here are some strategies for evaluating sources, with special attention to Internet sources:

- **Locate the author's credentials.** Periodicals often list their writers' degrees, current position, and other publications; books, similarly, contain an "about the author" section. If you do not see this information, check various biographical dictionaries (*Biography Index, Contemporary Authors*) or look for the author's website for information. For articles on the web, look for the author's e-mail address or a link to a home page. *Never use a web source that does not identify the author or the organization responsible for the material.* Critical question: Is this author qualified to write on this topic? How do I know?

- **Judge the credibility of the work.** For books, read how reviewers evaluated the book when it was first published. For articles, judge the respectability of the magazine or journal. Study the author's use of documentation as one measure of credibility. Scholarly works cite sources. Well-researched and reliable pieces in quality popular magazines will also make clear the sources of any statistics used or the credentials of any authority who is quoted. One good rule: Never use undocumented statistical information. Another judge of credibility is the quality of writing. Do not use sources filled with grammatical and mechanical errors. For web sources, find out what institution hosts the site. If you have not heard of the company or organization, find out more about it. *Critical question:* Why should I believe information/ideas from this source?

- **Select only those sources that are at an appropriate level for your research.** Avoid works that are either too specialized or too elementary for college research. You may not understand the former (and thus could misrepresent them in your paper), and you gain nothing from the latter. *Critical question:* Will this source provide a sophisticated discussion for educated adults?

- **Understand the writer's purpose.** Consider the writer's intended audience. Be cautious using works designed to reinforce biases already shared by the intended audience. Is the work written to persuade rather than to inform and analyze? Examine the writing for emotionally charged language. For Internet sources, ask yourself why this person or institution decided to have a website or contribute to a newsgroup. *Critical question:* Can I trust the information from this source, given the apparent purpose of the work?

- **In general, choose current sources.** Some studies published years ago remain classics, but many older works have become outdated. In scientific and technical fields, the "information revolution" has outdated some works published only five years ago. So look at publication dates (When was the website page last updated?) and pass over outdated sources in favor of current studies. *Critical question:* Is this information still accurate?

# CHAPTER 13

# Writing the Researched Essay

To continue your study and preparation for drafting a paper, you need to read and learn from your sources in an organized way. Some instructors require students to practice taking notes on their sources, either on cards or on their computer. Others recognize the ease, today, of photocopying and then annotating sources as they are read. Here are some general guidelines for studying sources.

## GUIDELINES for Studying Sources

1. **Read first; take notes later.** First, do background reading, selecting the most general sources that provide an overview of the topic.
2. **Skim what appear to be your chief sources.** Learn what other writers on the topic consider the important facts, issues, and points of debate.
3. **Annotate photocopies**—do not highlight endlessly. Instead, carefully bracket material you want to use. Then write a note in the margin indicating how and where you might use that material.
4. **Either download Internet sources or take careful notes on the material.** Before preparing a note on content, be sure to copy all necessary information for documenting the material—including the date you accessed the website.
5. **Initially mark key passages in books with Post-Its.** Write on the Post-It how and where you might use the material. Alternatively, photocopy book pages and then annotate them. Be sure to record for yourself the source of all copied pages.
6. **As you study and annotate, create labels for source materials that will help you organize your essay.** For example, if you are writing about the problem of campus rape, you might label passages as: "facts showing there is a problem," "causes of the problem," and "possible solutions to the problem."
7. **Recognize that when you are working with many sources, note taking rather than annotating copies of sources is more helpful.** Notes, whether on cards or typed on separate sheets, provide an efficient method for collecting and organizing lots of information.

## AVOIDING PLAGIARISM

Documenting sources accurately and fully is required of all researchers. Proper documentation distinguishes between the work of others and your ideas, shows readers the breadth of your research, and strengthens your credibility. In Western culture, copyright laws support the ethic that ideas, new information, and wording belong to their author. To borrow these without acknowledgment is against the law and has led to many celebrated lawsuits. For students who plagiarize, the consequences range from an F on the paper to suspension from college. Be certain, then, that you know what the requirements for correct documentation are; accidental plagiarism is still plagiarism and will be punished.

287

> **NOTE:** MLA documentation requires precise page references for all ideas, opinions, and information taken from sources—except for common knowledge. Author and page references provided in the text are supported by complete bibliographic citations on the Works Cited page.

In sum, you are required to document the following:

- Direct quotations from sources
- Paraphrased ideas and opinions from sources
- Summaries of ideas from sources
- Factual information, except common knowledge, from sources

Understand that putting an author's ideas in your own words in a paraphrase or summary does not eliminate the requirement of documentation. To illustrate, consider the following excerpt from Thomas R. Schueler's report *Controlling Urban Runoff* (Washington Metropolitan Water Resources Planning Board, 1987: 3–4) and a student paragraph based on the report.

### SOURCE

The aquatic ecosystems in urban headwater streams are particularly susceptible to the impacts of urbanization. . . . Dietemann (1975), Ragan and Dietemann (1976), Klein (1979) and WMCOG (1982) have all tracked trends in fish diversity and abundance over time in local urbanizing streams. Each of the studies has shown that fish communities become less diverse and are composed of more tolerant species after the surrounding watershed is developed. Sensitive fish species either disappear or occur very rarely. In most cases, the total number of fish in urbanizing streams may also decline.

Similar trends have been noted among aquatic insects which are the major food resource for fish. . . . Higher post-development sediment and trace metals can interfere in their efforts to gather food. Changes in water temperature, oxygen levels, and substrate composition can further reduce the species diversity and abundance of the aquatic insect community.

### PLAGIARIZED STUDENT PARAGRAPH

Studies have shown that fish communities become less diverse as the amount of runoff increases. Sensitive fish species either disappear or occur very rarely, and, in most cases, the total number of fish declines. Aquatic insects, a major source of food for fish, also decline because sediment and trace metals interfere with their food-gathering efforts. Increased water temperature and lower oxygen levels can further reduce the species diversity and abundance of the aquatic insect community.

The student's opening words establish a reader's expectation that the student has taken information from a source, as indeed the student has. But where is the documentation? The student's paraphrase is a good example of plagiarism: an unacknowledged paraphrase of borrowed information that even collapses into copying the source's exact wording in two places. For MLA style, the author's name and the precise page numbers are needed throughout the paragraph. Additionally, most of the first sentence and the final phrase must be put into the student's own words or be placed within quotation marks. The following revised paragraph shows an appropriate acknowledgment of the source used.

REVISED STUDENT PARAGRAPH TO REMOVE PLAGIARISM

In *Controlling Urban Runoff*, Thomas Schueler explains that studies have shown "that fish communities become less diverse as the amount of runoff increases" (3). Sensitive fish species either disappear or occur very rarely and, in most cases, the total number of fish declines. Aquatic insects, a major source of food for fish, also decline because sediment and trace metals interfere with their food-gathering efforts. Increased water temperature and lower oxygen levels, Schueler concludes, "can further reduce the species diversity and abundance of the aquatic insect community" (4).

## What Is Common Knowledge?

In general, common knowledge includes

- undisputed dates,
- well-known facts, and
- generally known facts, terms, and concepts in a field of study when you are writing in that field

So, do not cite a source for the dates of the American Revolution. If you are writing a paper for a psychology class, do not cite your text when using terms such as *ego* or *sublimation*. However, you must cite a historian who analyzes the causes of England's loss to the Colonies or a psychologist who disputes Freud's ideas. *Opinions* about well-known facts must be documented. *Discussions* of debatable dates, terms, or concepts must be documented. When in doubt, defend your integrity and document.

# USING SIGNAL PHRASES TO AVOID MISLEADING READERS

If you are an honest student, you do not want to submit a paper that is plagiarized, even though that plagiarism was unintentional on your part. What leads to unintentional plagiarism?

- A researcher takes careless notes, neglecting to include precise page numbers on the notes, but uses the information anyway, without documentation.

- A researcher works in material from sources in such a way that, even with page references, readers cannot tell what has been taken from the sources.

Good note-taking strategies will keep you from the first pitfall. Avoiding the second problem means becoming skilled in ways to include source material in your writing while still making your indebtedness to sources absolutely clear to readers. The way to do this: Give the author's name in the essay. You can also include, when appropriate, the author's credentials ("According to Dr. Hays, a geologist with the Department of Interior, . . ."). These *introductory tags* or *signal phrases* give readers a context for the borrowed material, as well as serving as part of the required documentation of sources. *Make sure that each signal phrase clarifies rather than distorts an author's relationship to his or her ideas and your relationship to the source.*

# GUIDELINES for Appropriately Using Sources

Here are three guidelines to follow to avoid misrepresenting borrowed material:

- **Pay attention to verb choice in signal phrases.** When you vary such standard wording as "Smith says" or "Jones states," be careful that you do not select verbs that misrepresent "Smith's" or "Jones's" attitude toward his or her own work. Do not write "Jones wonders" when in fact Jones has strongly asserted her views. (See pp. 300–01 for a discussion of varying word choice in signal phrases.)
- **Pay attention to the location of signal phrases.** If you mention Jones after you have presented her views, be sure that your reader can tell precisely which ideas in the passage belong to Jones. If your entire paragraph is a paraphrase of Jones's work, you are plagiarizing to conclude with "This idea is presented by Jones." Which of the several ideas in your paragraph comes from Jones? Your reader will assume that only the last idea comes from Jones.
- **Paraphrase properly.** Be sure that paraphrases are truly *in your own words*. To use Smith's words and sentence style in your writing is to plagiarize.

> **NOTE:** Putting a parenthetical page reference at the end of a paragraph is not sufficient if you have used the source throughout the paragraph. Use introductory tags or signal phrases to guide the reader through the material.

## EXERCISES: Acknowledging Sources to Avoid Plagiarism

1. The following paragraph (from Franklin E. Zimring's "Firearms, Violence and Public Policy" [*Scientific American*, Nov. 1991]) provides material for the examples that follow of adequate and inadequate acknowledgment of sources. After reading Zimring's paragraph, study the three examples with these questions in

mind: (1) Which example represents adequate acknowledgment? (2) Which examples do not represent adequate acknowledgment? (3) In exactly what ways is each plagiarized paragraph flawed?

### SOURCE

Although most citizens support such measures as owner screening, public opinion is sharply divided on laws that would restrict the ownership of handguns to persons with special needs. If the U.S. does not reduce handguns and current trends continue, it faces the prospect that the number of handguns in circulation will grow from 35 million to more than 50 million within 50 years. A national program limiting the availability of handguns would cost many billions of dollars and meet much resistance from citizens. These costs would likely be greatest in the early years of the program. The benefits of supply reduction would emerge slowly because efforts to diminish the availability of handguns would probably have a cumulative impact over time. (page 54)

### STUDENT PARAGRAPH 1

One approach to the problem of handgun violence in America is to severely limit handgun ownership. If we don't restrict ownership and start the costly task of removing handguns from our society, we may end up with around 50 million handguns in the country by 2040. The benefits will not be apparent right away but will eventually appear. This idea is emphasized by Franklin Zimring (54).

### STUDENT PARAGRAPH 2

One approach to the problem of handgun violence in America is to restrict the ownership of handguns except in special circumstances. If we do not begin to reduce the number of handguns in this country, the number will grow from 35 million to more than 50 million within 50 years. We can agree with Franklin Zimring that a program limiting handguns will cost billions and meet resistance from citizens (54).

### STUDENT PARAGRAPH 3

According to law professor Franklin Zimring, the United States needs to severely limit handgun ownership or face the possibility of seeing handgun ownership increase "from 35 million to more than 50 million within 50 years" (54). Zimring points out that Americans disagree significantly on restricting handguns and that enforcing such laws would be very expensive. He concludes that the benefits would not be seen immediately but that the restrictions

"would probably have a cumulative impact over time" (54). Although Zimring

paints a gloomy picture of high costs and little immediate relief from gun

violence, he also presents the shocking possibility of 50 million guns by the

year 2040. Can our society survive so much fire power?

Clearly, only the third student paragraph demonstrates adequate acknowledgment of the writer's indebtedness to Zimring. Notice that the placement of the last parenthetical page reference acts as a visual closure to the student's borrowing. She then turns to her response to Zimring and her own views on the problem of handguns.

2.  Read the following passage and then the three plagiarized uses of the passage. Explain why each one is plagiarized and how it can be corrected.

    Original Text: Stanley Karnow, *Vietnam, A History. The First Complete Account of Vietnam at War.* New York: Viking, 1983, 319.

    Lyndon Baines Johnson, a consummate politician, was a kaleidoscopic personality, forever changing as he sought to dominate or persuade or placate or frighten his friends and foes. A gigantic figure whose extravagant moods matched his size, he could be cruel and kind, violent and gentle, petty, generous, cunning, naïve, crude, candid, and frankly dishonest. He commanded the blind loyalty of his aides, some of whom worshipped him, and he sparked bitter derision or fierce hatred that he never quite fathomed.

    a.  LBJ's vibrant and changing personality filled some people with adoration and others with bitter derision that he never quite fathomed (Karnow 319).
    b.  LBJ, a supreme politician, had a personality like a kaleidoscope, continually changing as he tried to control, sway, appease, or intimidate his enemies and supporters (Karnow 319).
    c.  Often, figures who have had great impact on America's history have been dynamic people with powerful personalities and vibrant physical presence. LBJ, for example, was a huge figure who polarized those who worked for and with him. "He commanded the blind loyalty of his aides, some of whom worshipped him, and he sparked bitter derision or fierce hatred" from many others (Karnow 319).

3.  Read the following passage and then the four sample uses of the passage. Judge each of the uses for how well it avoids plagiarism and if it is documented correctly. Make corrections as needed.

    Original Text: Stanley Karnow, *Vietnam, A History. The First Complete Account of Vietnam at War.* New York: Viking, 1983, 327.

    On July 27, 1965, in a last-ditch attempt to change Johnson's mind, Mansfield and Russell were to press him again to "concentrate on finding a way out" of Vietnam—"a place where we ought not be," and where "the situation is rapidly going out of control." But the next day, Johnson announced his decision to add forty-four American combat battalions to the relatively small U.S. contingents already there. He had not been deaf to Mansfield's pleas, nor had he simply swallowed the Pentagon's plans. He had waffled and agonized during his nineteen months in the White House, but eventually this was his final judgment. As he would later explain: "There are many, many people who can recommend and advise, and a few of them consent. But there is only one who has been chosen by the American people to decide."

a.  Karnow writes that Senators Mansfield and Russell continued to try to convince President Johnson to avoid further involvement in Vietnam, "a place where we ought not to be" they felt. (327).

b.  Though Johnson received advice from many, in particular Senators Mansfield and Russell, he believed the weight of the decision to become further engaged in Vietnam was solely his as the one " 'chosen by the American people to decide' " (Karnow 327).

c.  On July 28, 1965, Johnson announced his decision to add forty-four battalions to the troops already in Vietnam, ending his waffling and agonizing of the past nineteen months of his presidency. (Karnow 357)

d.  Karnow explains that LBJ took his responsibility to make decisions about Vietnam seriously (327). Although Johnson knew that many would offer suggestions, only he had "'been chosen by the American people to decide'" (Karnow 327).

# ORGANIZING THE PAPER

Armed with an understanding of writing strategies to avoid plagiarism, you are now almost ready to draft your essay. Follow these steps to get organized to write:

1.  *Arrange notes (or your annotated sources) by the labels you have used and read them through.* You may discover that some notes or marked sections of sources now seem irrelevant. Set them aside, but do not throw them away yet. Some further reading and note taking may also be necessary to fill in gaps that have become apparent.

2.  *Reexamine your tentative claim or research proposal.* As a result of reading and reflection, do you need to alter or modify your claim in any way? Or, if you began with a research question, what now is your answer to the question? Is, for example, TV violence harmful to children?

3.  *Decide on the claim that will direct your writing.* To write a unified essay with a "reason for being," you need a claim that meets these criteria:

    •  It is a complete sentence, not a topic or statement of purpose.

| | |
|---|---|
| **TOPIC:** | Rape on college campuses. |
| **CLAIM:** | There are steps that both students and administrators can take to reduce incidents of campus rape. |

- It is limited and focused.

| | |
|---|---|
| **UNFOCUSED:** | Prohibition affected the 1920s in many ways. |
| **FOCUSED:** | Prohibition was more acceptable to rural than urban areas because of differences in values, social patterns, cultural backgrounds, and the economic result of prohibiting liquor sales. |

- It establishes a new or interesting approach to the topic that makes your research meaningful.

| | |
|---|---|
| **NOT INVENTIVE:** | A regional shopping mall should not be built next to the Manassas Battlefield. |
| **INVENTIVE:** | Putting aside an appeal to our national heritage, one can say, simply, that there is no economic justification for the building of a shopping mall next to the Manassas Battlefield. |

4. *Write down the organization that emerges from your labels and grouping of sources, and compare this with your preliminary plan.* If there are differences, justify those changes to yourself. Consider: Does the new, fuller plan provide a complete and logical development of your claim?

# DRAFTING THE ESSAY

## Plan Your Time

How much time will you need to draft your essay? Working with sources and taking care with documentation make research paper writing more time-consuming than writing an undocumented essay. You also need to allow time between completing the draft and revising. Do not try to draft, revise, and proof an essay all in one day.

## Handle In-Text Documentation as You Draft

The Modern Language Association (MLA) recommends that writers prepare their Works Cited page(s) *before* drafting their essay. With this important information prepared correctly and next to you as you draft, you will be less likely to make errors in documentation that will result in a plagiarized essay. Although you may believe that stopping to include parenthetical documentation as you write will cramp your writing, you really cannot try to insert the documentation after completing the writing. The risk of failing to document accurately is too great to chance. Parenthetical documentation is brief; listen to the experts and take the time to include it as you compose.

You saw some models of documentation in Chapter 12. In Chapter 14, you have complete guidelines and models for in-text (parenthetical) documentation and then many models for the complete citations of sources. Study the information in Chapter 14 and then draft your Works Cited page(s) as part of your preparation for writing.

## Choose an Appropriate Writing Style

Specific suggestions for composing the parts of your paper follow, but first here are some general guidelines for research essay style.

### Use the Proper Person

Research papers are written primarily in the third person *(she, he, it, they)* to create objectivity and to direct attention to the content of the paper. The question is over the appropriateness of the first person *(I, we)*. Although you want to avoid writing "as *you* can see," do not try to avoid the use of *I* if you need to distinguish your position from the views of others. It is better to write "I" than "it is the opinion of this writer" or "the researcher learned" or "this project analyzed." On the other hand, avoid qualifiers such as "I think." Just state your ideas.

### Use the Proper Tense

When you are writing about people, ideas, or events of the past, the appropriate tense is the past tense. When writing about current times, the appropriate tense is the present. Both tenses may occur in the same paragraph, as the following paragraph illustrates:

> Fifteen years ago "personal" computers were  all but unheard of.
>
> Computers were regarded  as unknowable, building-sized mechanized
>
> monsters that required  a precise 68 degree air-conditioned environment and
>
> eggheaded technicians with thick glasses and white lab coats scurrying about
>
> to keep the temperamental and fragile egos of the electronic brains mollified.
>
> Today's generation of computers is  accessible, affordable, commonplace, and
>
> much less mysterious. The astonishing progress made in computer technology
>
> in the last few years has made computers practical, attainable, and
>
> indispensable. Personal computers are  here to stay.

In the above example, when the student moves from computers in the past to computers in the present, he shifts tenses accurately.

When writing about sources, the convention is to use the present tense *even* for works or authors from the past. The idea is that the source, or the author, *continues* to make the point or use the technique into the present—that is, every time there is a reader. So, write "Lincoln selects  the biblical expression 'Fourscore and seven years ago'" and "King echoes  Lincoln when he writes  'five score years ago.' "

### *Avoid Excessive Quoting*

Many students use too many direct quotations. Plan to use your own words most of the time for these good reasons:

- Constantly shifting between your words and the language of your sources (not to mention all those quotation marks) makes reading your essay difficult.
- This is your paper and should sound like you.
- When you take a passage out of its larger context, you face the danger of misrepresenting the writer's views.
- When you quote endlessly, readers may begin to think either that you are lazy or that you don't really understand the issues well enough to put them in your own words. You don't want to present either image to your readers.
- You do not prove any point by quoting another person's opinion. All you indicate is that there is someone else who shares your views. Even if that person is an expert on the topic, your quoted material still represents the view of only one person. You support a claim with reasons and evidence, both of which can usually be presented in your own words.

When you must quote, keep the quotations brief, weave them carefully into your own sentences, and be sure to identify the author in a signal phrase. Study the guidelines for handling quotations on pages 22–24 for models of correct form and style.

## Write Effective Beginnings

The best introduction is one that presents your subject in an interesting way to gain the reader's attention, states your claim, and gives the reader an indication of the scope and limits of your paper. In a short research essay, you may be able to combine an attention-getter, a statement of subject, and a claim in one paragraph. More typically, especially in longer papers, the introduction will expand to two or three paragraphs. In the physical and social sciences, the claim may be withheld until the conclusion, but the opening introduces the subject and presents the researcher's hypothesis, often posed as a question. Since students sometimes have trouble with research paper introductions in spite of knowing these general guidelines, several specific approaches are illustrated here:

1.  In the opening to her study of car advertisements, a student, relating her topic to what readers know, reminds readers of the culture's concern with image:

    > Many Americans are highly image conscious. Because the "right" look is
    > essential to a prosperous life, no detail is too small to overlook. Clichés about
    > first impressions remind us that "you never get a second chance to make a
    > first impression," so we obsessively watch our weight, firm our muscles, sculpt

our hair, select our friends, find the perfect houses, and buy our automobiles. Realizing the importance of image, companies compete to make the "right" products, that is, those that will complete the "right" image. Then advertisers direct specific products to targeted groups of consumers. Although targeting may be labeled as stereotyping, it has been an effective strategy in advertising.

2. Terms and concepts central to your project need defining early in your paper, especially if they are challenged or qualified in some way by your study. This opening paragraph demonstrates an effective use of definition:

> William Faulkner braids a universal theme, the theme of initiation, into the fiber of his novel *Intruder in the Dust.* From ancient times to the present, a prominent focus of literature, of life, has been rites of passage, particularly those of childhood to adulthood. Joseph Campbell defines rites of passage as "distinguished by formal, and usually very severe, exercises of severance." A "candidate" for initiation into adult society, Campbell explains, experiences a shearing away of the "attitudes, attachments and life patterns" of childhood (9). This severe, painful stripping away of the child and installation of the adult is presented somewhat differently in several works by American writers.

3. Begin with a thought-provoking question. A student, arguing that the media both reflect and shape reality, started with these questions:

> Do the media just reflect reality, or do they also shape our perceptions of reality? The answer to this seemingly "chicken-and-egg" question is: They do both.

4. Beginning with important, perhaps startling, facts, evidence, or statistics is an effective way to introduce a topic, provided the details are relevant to the topic. Observe the following example:

> Teenagers are working again, but not on their homework. Over 40 percent of teenagers have jobs by the time they are juniors (Samuelson A22). And their jobs do not support academic learning since almost two-thirds of teenagers are employed in sales and service jobs that entail mostly carrying, cleaning, and wrapping (Greenberger and Steinberg 62–67), not reading, writing, and computing. Unfortunately, the negative effect on learning is not offset by improved opportunities for future careers.

## Avoid Ineffective Openings

Follow these rules for avoiding openings that most readers find ineffective or annoying.

1. *Do not restate the title* or write as if the title were the first sentence in paragraph 1. It is a convention of writing to have the first paragraph stand independent of the title.
2. *Do not begin with "clever" visuals* such as artwork or fancy lettering.
3. *Do not begin with humor* unless it is part of your topic.
4. *Do not begin with a question that is just a gimmick, or one that a reader may answer in a way you do not intend.* Asking "What are the advantages of solar energy?" may lead a reader to answer "None that I can think of." A straightforward research question ("Is *Death of a Salesman* a tragedy?") is appropriate.
5. *Do not open with an unnecessary definition quoted from a dictionary.* "According to Webster, solar energy means . . ." is a tired, overworked beginning that does not engage readers.
6. *Do not start with a purpose statement:* "This paper will examine . . ." Although a statement of purpose is a necessary part of a report of empirical research, a report still needs an interesting introduction.

## Compose Solid, Unified Paragraphs

As you compose the body of your paper, keep in mind that you want to (1) maintain unity and coherence, (2) guide readers clearly through source material, and (3) synthesize source material and your own ideas. Do not settle for paragraphs in which facts from notes are just loosely run together. Review the following discussion and study the examples to see how to craft effective body paragraphs.

### Provide Unity and Coherence

You achieve paragraph unity when every sentence in a paragraph relates to and develops the paragraph's main idea. Unity, however, does not automatically produce coherence; that takes attention to wording. Coherence is achieved when readers can follow the connection between one sentence and another and between each sentence and the main idea. Strategies for achieving coherence include repetition of key words, the use of pronouns that clearly refer to those key words, and the use of transition and connecting words. Observe these strategies at work in the following paragraph:

> Perhaps the most important differences between the initiations of Robin
>
> and Biff and that experienced by Chick are the facts that Chick's epiphany
>
> does not come all at once and it does not devastate him. Chick
>
> learns about adulthood—and enters adulthood—piecemeal and with support.

His first eye-opening experience occurs as he tries to pay Lucas for dinner and

is rebuffed (15–16). Chick learns, after trying again to buy a clear conscience,

the impropriety and affront of his actions (24). Lucas teaches Chick how he

should resolve his dilemma by setting him "free" (26–27). Later, Chick feels

outrage at the adults crowding into the town, presumably to see a lynching,

then disgrace and shame as they eventually flee (196–97, 210).

Coherence is needed not only within paragraphs but between paragraphs as well. You need to guide readers through your paper, connecting paragraphs and showing relationships by the use of transitions. The following opening sentences of four paragraphs from a paper on solutions to rape on the college campus illustrate smooth transitions:

¶ 3 Specialists have provided a number of reasons why men rape.

¶ 4 Some of the causes of rape on the college campus originate with the

colleges themselves and with how they handle the problem.

¶ 5 Just as there are a number of causes for campus rapes, there are a

number of ways to help solve the problem of these rapes.

¶ 6 If these seem like commonsense solutions, why, then, is it so difficult to

significantly reduce the number of campus rapes?

Without awkwardly writing "Here are some of the causes" and "Here are some of the solutions," the student guides her readers through a discussion of causes for and solutions to the problem of campus rape.

### Guide Readers Through Source Material

To understand the importance of guiding readers through source material, consider first the following paragraph from a paper on the British coal strike in the 1970s:

The social status of the coal miners was far from good. The country

blamed them for the dimmed lights and the three-day workweek. They had

been placed in the position of social outcasts and were beginning to "consider

themselves another country." Some businesses and shops had even gone so far

as to refuse service to coal miners (Jones 32).

Who has learned that the coal miners felt ostracized or that the country blamed them? As readers we cannot begin to judge the validity of these assertions without some context provided by the writer. Most readers are put off by an unattached direct quotation or some startling observation that is documented correctly but given no context within the paper. Using signal phrases that identify the author of the source and, when useful, the author's credentials helps guide readers through the source material. The following revision of the paragraph above provides not only context but also sentence variety:

> The social acceptance of coal miners, according to Peter Jones, British correspondent for *Newsweek,* was far from good. From interviews both in London shops and in pubs near Birmingham, Jones concluded that Britishers blamed the miners for the dimmed lights and three-day workweek. Several striking miners, in a pub on the outskirts of Birmingham, asserted that some of their friends had been denied service by shopkeepers and that they "consider[ed] themselves another country" (32).

### Select Appropriate Signal Phrases

When you use signal phrases, try to vary both the words you use and their place in the sentence. Look, for example, at the first sentence in the sample paragraph above. The signal phrase is placed in the middle of the sentence and is set off by commas. The sentence could have been written two other ways:

> The social acceptance of coal miners was far from good, according to Peter Jones, British correspondent for *Newsweek.*

> OR

> According to Peter Jones, British correspondent for *Newsweek,* the social acceptance of coal miners was far from good.

Whenever you provide a name and perhaps credentials for your source, you have these three sentence patterns to choose from. Make a point to use all three options in your paper. Word choice can be varied as well. Instead of writing "Peter Jones says" throughout your paper, consider some of these verb choices:

| | | |
|---|---|---|
| Jones *asserts* | Jones *contends* | Jones *attests to* |
| Jones *states* | Jones *thinks* | Jones *points out* |
| Jones *concludes* | Jones *stresses* | Jones *believes* |
| Jones *presents* | Jones *emphasizes* | Jones *agrees with* |
| Jones *argues* | Jones *confirms* | Jones *speculates* |

> **NOTE:** Not all the words in this list are synonyms; you cannot substitute *confirms* for *believes.* First, select the verb that most accurately conveys the writer's relationship to his or her material. Then, when appropriate, vary word choice as well as sentence structure.

Readers need to be told how to respond to the sources used. They need to know which sources you accept as reliable and which you disagree with, and they need you to distinguish clearly between fact and opinion. Ideas and opinions from sources need signal phrases and then some discussion from you.

### Synthesize Source Material and Your Own Ideas

A smooth synthesis of source material is aided by signal phrases and parenthetical documentation because they mark the beginning and ending of material taken from a source. But a complete synthesis requires something more: your ideas about the source and the topic. To illustrate, consider the problems in another paragraph from the British coal strike paper:

> Some critics believed that there was enough coal in Britain to maintain
>
> enough power to keep industry at a near-normal level for thirty-five weeks
>
> (Jones 30). Prime Minister Heath, on the other hand, had placed the country's
>
> usable coal supply at 15.5 million tons (Jones 30). He stated that this would
>
> have fallen to a critical 7 million tons within a month had he not declared a
>
> three-day workweek (Jones 31).

This paragraph is a good example of random details strung together for no apparent purpose. How much coal did exist? Whose figures were right? And what purpose do these figures serve in the paper's development? Note that the entire paragraph is developed with material from one source. Do sources other than Jones offer a different perspective? This paragraph is weak for several reasons: (1) It lacks a controlling idea (topic sentence) to give it purpose and direction; (2) it relies for development entirely on one source; (3) it lacks any discussion or analysis by the writer.

By contrast, the following paragraph demonstrates a successful synthesis:

> Of course, the iridium could have come from other extraterrestrial sources
>
> besides an asteroid. One theory, put forward by Dale Russell, is that the
>
> iridium was produced outside the solar system by an exploding star (500).
>
> Such an explosion, Russell states, could have blown the iridium either off the
>
> surface of the moon or directly from the star itself (500–01), while also pro-
>
> ducing a deadly blast of heat and gamma rays (Krishtalka 19). This theory
>
> seems to explain the traces of iridium in the mass extinction, but it does not
>
> explain why smaller mammals, crocodiles, and birds survived (Wilford 220).
>
> So the supernova theory took a backseat to the other extraterrestrial theories:
>
> those of asteroids and comets colliding with the Earth. The authors of the

book *The Great Extinction,* Michael Allaby and James Lovelock, subtitled their

work *The Solution to . . . the Disappearance of the Dinosaurs.* Their theory: an

asteroid or comet collided with Earth around sixty-five million years ago, kill-

ing billions of organisms, and thus altering the course of evolution (157). The

fact that the theory of collision with a cosmic body warrants a book calls for

some thought: Is the asteroid or comet theory merely sensationalism, or is it

rooted in fact? Paleontologist Leonard Krishtalka declares that few paleontol-

ogists have accepted the asteroid theory, himself calling "some catastrophic

theories . . . small ideas injected with growth hormone" (22). However,

other scientists, such as Allaby and Lovelock, see the cosmic catastrophic the-

ory as a solid one based on more than guesswork (10–11).

This paragraph's synthesis is accomplished by several strategies: (1) The paragraph has a controlling idea; (2) the paragraph combines information from several sources; (3) the information is presented in a blend of paraphrase and short
quotations; (4) information from the different sources is clearly indicated to
readers; and (5) the student explains and discusses the information.

You might also observe the different lengths of the two sample paragraphs
just presented. Although the second paragraph is long, it is not unwieldy
because it achieves unity and coherence. By contrast, body paragraphs of only
three sentences are probably in trouble.

## Write Effective Conclusions

Sometimes ending a paper seems even more difficult than beginning one. You
know you are not supposed to just stop, but every ending that comes to mind
sounds more corny than clever. If you have trouble, try one of these types of
endings:

1. Do not just repeat your claim exactly as it was stated in paragraph 1, but
   expand on the original wording and emphasize the claim's significance.
   Here is the conclusion of the solar energy paper:

   The idea of using solar energy is not as far-fetched as it seemed years ago.
   With the continued support of government plus the enthusiasm of research
   groups, environmentalists, and private industry, solar energy may become a
   household word quite soon. With the increasing cost of fossil fuel, the time
   could not be better for exploring this use of the sun.

2. End with a quotation that effectively summarizes and drives home the
   point of your paper. Researchers are not always lucky enough to find the

ideal quotation for ending a paper. If you find a good one, use it. Better yet, present the quotation and then add your comment in a sentence or two. The conclusion to a paper on the dilemma of defective newborns is a good example:

> Dr. Joseph Fletcher is correct when he says that "every advance in medical capabilities is an increase in our moral responsibility" (48). In a world of many gray areas, one point is clear. From an ethical point of view, medicine is a victim of its own success.

*very well done example*

3.  If you have researched an issue or problem, emphasize your proposed solutions in the concluding paragraph. The student opposing a mall adjacent to the Manassas Battlefield concluded with several solutions:

*reiterated claim with solutions*

> Whether the proposed mall will be built is clearly in doubt at the moment. What are the solutions to this controversy? One approach is, of course, not to build the mall at all. To accomplish this solution, now, with the re-zoning having been approved, probably requires an act of Congress to buy the land and make it part of the national park. Another solution, one that would please the county and the developer and satisfy citizens objecting to traffic problems, is to build the needed roads before the mall is completed. A third approach is to allow the office park of the original plan to be built, but not the mall. The local preservationists had agreed to this original development proposal, but now that the issue has received national attention, they may no longer be willing to compromise. Whatever the future of the William Center, the present plan for a new regional mall is not acceptable.

## Avoid Ineffective Conclusions

Follow these rules to avoid conclusions that most readers consider ineffective and annoying.

1.  *Do not introduce a new idea.* If the point belongs in your paper, you should have introduced it earlier.
2.  *Do not just stop or trail off,* even if you feel as though you have run out of steam. A simple, clear restatement of the claim is better than no conclusion.
3.  *Do not tell your reader what you have accomplished:* "In this paper I have explained the advantages of solar energy by examining the costs . . ." If you have written well, your reader knows what you have accomplished.

4. *Do not offer apologies or expressions of hope.* "Although I wasn't able to find as much on this topic as I wanted, I have tried to explain the advantages of solar energy, and I hope that you will now understand why we need to use it more" is a disastrous ending.

## Choose an Effective Title

Give some thought to your paper's title since that is what your reader sees first and what your work will be known by. A good title provides information and creates interest. Make your title informative by making it specific. If you can create interest through clever wording, so much the better. But do not confuse "cutesiness" with clever wording. Review the following examples of acceptable and unacceptable titles:

| | |
|---|---|
| **VAGUE:** | A Perennial Issue Unsolved<br>(There are many; which one is this paper about?) |
| **BETTER:** | The Perennial Issue of Press Freedom Versus Press Responsibility |
| **TOO BROAD:** | Earthquakes<br>(What about earthquakes? This title is not informative.) |
| **BETTER:** | The Need for Earthquake Prediction |
| **TOO BROAD:** | *The Scarlet Letter*<br>(Never use just the title of the work under discussion;<br>you can use the work's title as a part of a longer title of your own.) |
| **BETTER:** | Color Symbolism in *The Scarlet Letter* |
| **CUTESY:** | Babes in Trouble<br>(The slang "Babes" makes this title seem insensitive rather than clever.) |
| **BETTER:** | The Dilemma of Defective Newborns |

# REVISING THE PAPER: A CHECKLIST

After completing a first draft, catch your breath and then gear up for the next step in the writing process: revision. Revision actually involves three separate steps: *rewriting*—adding or deleting text, or moving parts of the draft around; *editing*—a rereading to correct errors from misspellings to incorrect documentation format; and then *proofreading* the typed copy. If you treat these as separate steps, you will do a more complete job of revision—and get a better grade on your paper!

## Rewriting

Read your draft through and make changes as a result of answering the following questions:

### *Purpose and Audience*

☐ Is my draft long enough to meet assignment requirements and my purpose?

☐ Are terms defined and concepts explained appropriately for my audience?

### Content
☐  Do I have a clearly stated thesis—the claim of my argument?
☐  Have I presented sufficient evidence to support my claim?
☐  Are there any irrelevant sections that should be deleted?

### Structure
☐  Are paragraphs ordered to develop my topic logically?
☐  Does the content of each paragraph help develop my claim?
☐  Is everything in each paragraph on the same subtopic to create paragraph unity?
☐  Do body paragraphs have a balance of information and analysis, of source material and my own ideas?
☐  Are there any paragraphs that should be combined? Are there any very long paragraphs that should be divided? (Check for unity.)

## Editing

Make revisions guided by your responses to the questions, make a clean copy, and read again. This time, pay close attention to sentences, words, and documentation format. Use the following questions to guide editing.

### Coherence
☐  Have connecting words been used and key terms repeated to produce paragraph coherence?
☐  Have transitions been used to show connections between paragraphs?

### Sources
☐  Have I paraphrased instead of quoted whenever possible?
☐  Have I used signal phrases to create a context for source material?
☐  Have I documented all borrowed material, whether quoted or paraphrased?
☐  Are parenthetical references properly placed after borrowed material?

### Style
☐  Have I varied sentence length and structure?
☐  Have I avoided long quotations?
☐  Do I have correct form for quotations? For titles?
☐  Is my language specific and descriptive?
☐  Have I avoided inappropriate shifts in tense or person?
☐  Have I removed any wordiness, deadwood, trite expressions, or clichés?
☐  Have I used specialized terms correctly?
☐  Have I avoided contractions as too informal for most research papers?
☐  Have I maintained an appropriate style and tone for academic work?

### Proofreading

When your editing is finished, prepare a completed draft of your paper according to the format described and illustrated below. Then proofread the completed copy, making any corrections neatly in ink. If a page has several errors, print a corrected copy. Be sure to make a copy of the paper for yourself before submitting the original to your instructor.

# THE COMPLETED PAPER

Your research paper should be double-spaced throughout (including the Works Cited page) with 1-inch margins on all sides. Your project will contain the following parts, in this order:

1. *A title page,* with your title, your name, your instructor's name, the course name or number, and the date, neatly centered, if an outline follows. If there is no outline, place this information at the top left of the first page.
2. *An outline,* or statement of purpose, if required.
3. *The body or text of your paper.* Number all pages consecutively, including pages of works cited, using arabic numerals. Place numbers in the upper right-hand corner of each page. Include your last name before each page number.
4. *A list of works cited,* placed on a separate page(s) after the text. Title the first page "Works Cited." (Do not use the title "Bibliography.")

# SAMPLE STUDENT ESSAY IN MLA STYLE

The following paper illustrates MLA style and an argumentative essay using sources.

George 1

*Appropriate heading when separate title page is not used.*

Lauren George

Dr. Dorothy U. Seyler

English Composition 2

4 August 2008

*Center the title.*

The Effects of Gangsta Rap on African-American Adolescent Females

*Indent 5 spaces.*

Ice Cube decreed: "Do like Ice Cube, slam her ass in a ditch" (N.W.A.). While N.W.A., one of the first rap groups to popularize gangsta rap, is no longer creating music, its influence on mainstream rap is evident. Today, rappers like 50 Cent, Ludacris, and Lil' Wayne, among others, perpetuate this

George 2

misogynistic theme in gangsta rap and their music videos. Bob Dole, former senator and presidential candidate, claimed that "we have reached the point where" gangsta rap and its images threaten "to undermine our character as a nation" (qtd. in Baldwin 159). But does gangsta rap negatively impact adolescent African-American females? African-American teenaged girls are in the most vulnerable periods of their lives and, by virtue of being black and female, are the direct subjects of contempt and disdain in gangsta rap. Gangsta rap may be seen as a contagiously diseased person: he may not be the cause of the disease, but he does spread it to others. Surely this music has a negative effect on the way adolescent black girls develop their sexual identities and body image.

Double-space throughout.

In a 2003 interview on "The O'Reilly Factor," Cam'ron defended his choice to rap about "pimping and bitches" by saying, "I'm just an author. So what I do is I write what goes on in the ghetto. I'm not a liar. So what I tell you goes on in my album, that's what does on the streets of Harlem." He isn't alone; many male and female rappers share Cam'ron's point of view. They believe that they are telling their story and the stories of the 'hood. Murray Forman writes that gangsta rap discusses "generally common phenomena" to further the "black struggles for empowerment" (211). Ice-T explains in his song, "O.G. Original Gangster":

Student presents the rappers' argument.

Indent display quotation 10 spaces.

> When I wrote about parties
>
> Someone always died
>
> When I tried to write happy
>
> Yo, I knew I lied, I lived a life of crime
>
> Why play ya blind?

Gangsta rappers clearly place more importance on the truth of their portrayals of the ghetto than on the influence they may have on young people. In doing so, they seek to show themselves as authentic "author[s]" or "keeping-it-real" (qtd. in Baldwin 160). Some analysts of rap argue that these lyrics help to build self-confidence and esteem in young people who often do

George 3

not feel in control or important (qtd. in Gallo 52). Some female rappers are no exception. Notably Lil' Kim and Foxy Brown both advocate many of the same behaviors for which male gangsta rappers are rebuked. Lil' Kim raps: "I treat y'all n*****s like y'all treat us" and Foxy Brown agrees with her, saying that she "pimp[s] hard . . . / [and] maybe a little conceited but that's always needed."

Despite the valid arguments that these artists make in favor of their rap, the good that rap can do for the black community in America is heavily outweighed by its more destructive effect on its listeners. Many—both blacks and whites—have argued that gangsta rap is filled with harmful messages that are a special problem because, as Stephens and Phillips explain, young people develop their sexual selves from the messages they get about sexual roles and behavior (3). African-American adolescent girls and stereotypical images and ideals are presented in gangsta rap. Stephens and Phillips describe the stereotype of the "the good, innocent, virginal girl [who] continues to be an idealized image of womanhood associated with white females, but unattainable for African-American females" (4). Tricia Rose argues that when faced with an ideal that society declares unattainable, black teenaged girls are likely to see their bodies as indicators of "sexual perversity and inferiority" (167). Internalizing the inferiority creates the standard of limited expectations, as Vanessa McGann and Janice Steil explain (177).

In Susanne Gallo's empirical study of the effects of gangsta rap on the adolescent female identity, she discovered that the girls who preferred gangsta rap were more likely to have been physically and sexually abused during their childhoods. Gallo also discovered that the girls who listened to gangsta rap watched roughly one hour more of corresponding music videos, on average, than girls who listened to underground rap. In addition, the grade point average of the gangsta rap listeners averaged .45 point less than the underground rap listeners (295). Although her study did not focus exclusively on African-American adolescent girls, 47 percent of her group was African-American. Her

George 4

study does reveal a negative impact on teenaged girls, and that includes black teenaged girls.

In another empirical study conducted by Shani Peterson et al., African-American adolescents, between 14 and 18, were more likely to engage in "binge drinking . . . test positive for marijuana . . . have multiple sexual partners . . . and have a negative body image" (1157). Peterson cites these outcomes as the result of being exposed to "sexual stereotypes" in rap music videos. Black Entertainment Television's target demographic is young African Americans. Jane Brown and Carol Pardun write that "even young children prefer characters who are similar to themselves in gender, age, or race" and that, over time, "'wishful identification' with characters . . . increases" (268). Unfortunately, the medium used most by BET happens to be music videos. According to a review of 203 BET music videos, "42% . . . depicted fondling and 58% of videos featured women dancing sexually" and black American adolescents are watching more than 3 hours of music videos a day (Peterson 1158).

*Signal phrase introduces quotation.*

A third study, by Gina Wingood et al., found that African-American girls were more likely to "fear abandonment as a result of negotiating condom use, . . . to perceive that they had fewer options for sexual partners, . . . to perceive themselves as having limited control in their sexual relationships, . . . and [to] worry about acquiring HIV" (433). This was true for African-American girls who were more dissatisfied with their body image than girls who had the same levels of self-esteem, body mass index, and depression. Wingood learned that as a result of poor body image, adolescent black girls will be more likely to "never [use] condoms during sexual intercourse in the past 30 days and . . . engage in unprotected vaginal sex in the prior 6 months" (433).

*Good use of ellipses to shorten quotation to key details.*

Gallo's study created a framework upon which the findings of Peterson and Wingood can rest. Girls who listen to gangsta rap watch more music videos for that type of music. These videos objectify the black female body and depict sexual dominance over black women by means of fondling and dehumanization by men. Adolescent black girls construct their body image and sexual identities

*Student summarizes 3 studies to create a transition paragraph.*

George 5

based upon the representation of the average "video ho." Due to a negative body image, black teen girls engage in risky behavior that leaves them vulnerable to more physical and sexual abuse.

*Further evidence is presented.*

The Centers for Disease Control's national "Youth Risk Behavior Survey: 2007" supports the findings of these researchers. The CDC reports that 10% fewer Hispanic students and 16% fewer white students have engaged in sexual intercourse with four or more partners than black students. Also, black students (14%) engaged in violent relations with the romantic partner more than white (8%) or Hispanic (11%) students. Lastly, twice as many black students (63%) watch three hours or more of television than white students (27%) and one and a half times more than Hispanic students (43%). All of these studies reveal that African-American teens are taking in more of gangsta rap's images than any other group.

*Conclusion connects evidence to a restated claim.*

Three separate studies have shown negative effects of gangsta rap and none have shown positive results. Although themes of misogyny and violence do not inhabit gangsta rap only, these themes are repeatedly and powerfully presented in this music, music that teens, most particularly black teenaged girls, are absorbing and being shaped by. Unless or until there is change in the rap genre, black women will continue to struggle with gangsta rap's images and attitudes toward them that lead to low self-esteem and greater indulgence in risky behavior.

George 6

## Works Cited

Baldwin, Davarian L. "Black Empire, White Desires: The Spatial Politics of

Identity in the Age of Hip-Hop." *That's the Joint!: The Hip-Hop Studies Reader.*

Ed. Mark Anthony Neal and Murray Forman. New York: Routledge, 2004.

159–76. Print.

Start a new page for Works Cited.

Brown, Foxy. "Candy." *Broken Silence.* Def Jam Records, 2001. CD.

Brown, Jane D., and Carol J. Pardun. "Little in Common: Racial and Gender

Differences in Adolescents' Television Diets." *Journal of Broadcasting &*

*Electronic Media* 48.2 (2004): 266–78. *Communication & Mass Media*

*Complete. EBSCOhost.* Web. 10 Aug. 2008.

Double-space throughout. Alphabetize and use hanging indentation.

Cam'ron and Damon Dash. "Is Gangsta Rap Hurting America's Children?"

Interview. *The O'Reilly Factor.* Host Bill O'Reilly. Fox News. 14 Nov. 2003.

Web. 10 Aug. 2008.

Centers for Disease Control and Prevention. "The National Youth Risk Behavior

Survey: 2007." Centers for Disease Control and Prevention. 2007. Web.

1 Aug. 2008.

Forman, Murray. "'Represent': Race, Space, and Place in Rap Music." *That's*

*the Joint!: The Hip-Hop Studies Reader.* Ed. Mark Anthony Neal and Murray

Forman. New York: Routledge, 2004. 201–22. Print.

Gallo, Susanne. "Music Preference with an Emphasis on Gangsta Rap:

Female Adolescent Identity, Beliefs, and Behavior." Diss. California

Institute of Integral Studies, 2003. *PsychINFO. EBSCOhost.* Web. 1 Aug.

2008.

Ice-T. "O.G. Original Gangster." *O.G. Original Gangster.* Sire/Warner Bros, 1991. CD.

Lil' Kim. "Suck My Dick." *Notorious K. I. M.* Atlantic Records, 2000. CD.

McGann, Vanessa L., and Janice M. Steil. "The Sense of Entitlement:

Implications for Gender Equality and Psychological Well-Being." *The*

*Handbook of Girls' and Women's Psychological Health.* Ed. Judith Worell and

Carol D. Goodheart. New York: Oxford UP, 2006. Print.

N.W.A. "A Bitch Iz a Bitch." *N. W. A and the Posse.* Priority Records. 1989. CD.

Peterson, Shani H., et al. "Images of Sexual Stereotypes in Rap Videos and the Health of African-American Female Adolescents." *Journal of Women's Health* 16.8 (2007): 1157–64. *Women's Studies International. EBSCOhost.* Web. 20 July 2008.

Rose, Tricia. *Black Noise: Rap Music and Black Culture in Contemporary America.* Hanover: UP of New England, 1994. Print.

Stephens, Dionne P., and Layli D. Phillips. "Freaks, Gold Diggers, Divas, and Dykes: The Sociohistorical Development of Adolescent African-American Women's Sexual Scripts." *Sexuality and Culture* 7.1 (2003): 3–49. *Women's Studies International. EBSCOhost.* Web. 1 Aug. 2008.

Wingood, Gina M., et al. "Body Image and African-American Females' Sexual Health." *Journal of Women's Health and Gender-Based Medicine* 11.5 (2002): 433–39. *Women's Studies International. EBSCOhost.* Web. 20 July 2008.

# CHAPTER 14

# Formal Documentation: MLA Style, APA Style

In Chapter 12 you were shown, in sample bibliography cards, what information about a source you need to prepare the documentation for a researched essay. In Chapter 13 you were shown in-text documentation patterns as part of the discussion of avoiding plagiarism and writing effective paragraphs. The format shown is for MLA (Modern Language Association) style, the documentation style used in the humanities. APA (American Psychological Association) style is used in the social sciences. The sciences and other disciplines also have style sheets, but the most common documentation patterns used by undergraduates are MLA and APA, the two patterns explained in this chapter.

Remember that MLA recommends that writers prepare their Works Cited list—a list of all sources they have used—before drafting the essay. This list can then be used as an accurate guide to the in-text/parenthetical documentation that MLA requires along with the Works Cited list at the end of the essay. Heed this good advice. This chapter begins with guidelines for in-text documentation and then provides many models of full documentation for a Works Cited list.

> **REMEMBER:** Never guess at documentation! Always consult this chapter to make each in-text citation and your Works Cited page(s) absolutely correct.

As you now know, MLA documentation style has two parts: in-text references to author and page number and then complete information about each source in a Works Cited list. Because parenthetical references to author and page are incomplete—readers could not find the source with such limited information—all sources referred to by author and page number in the essay require the full details of publication in a Works Cited list that concludes the essay. General guidelines for in-text citations are given below.

> **NOTE:** You need a 100 percent correspondence between the sources listed in your Works Cited and the sources you actually cite (refer to) in your essay. Do not omit from your Works Cited any sources you refer to in your essay. Do not include in your Works Cited any sources not referred to in your paper.

# GUIDELINES for Using Parenthetical Documentation

- **The purpose of documentation is to make clear exactly what material in a passage has been borrowed and from what source the borrowed material has come.**

- **Parenthetical in-text documentation requires specific page references for borrowed material—unless the source is not a print one.**
- **Parenthetical documentation is required for both quoted and paraphrased material and for both print and nonprint sources.**
- **Parenthetical documentation provides as brief a citation as possible consistent with accuracy and clarity.**

## THE SIMPLEST PATTERNS OF PARENTHETICAL DOCUMENTATION

The simplest in-text citation can be prepared in one of three ways:

1. Give the author's last name (full name in your first reference to the writer) in the text of your essay and put the appropriate page number(s) in parentheses following the borrowed material.

   Frederick Lewis Allen observes that, during the 1920s, urban tastes spread to

   the country (146).

2. Place the author's last name and the appropriate page number(s) in parentheses immediately following the borrowed material.

   During the 1920s, "not only the drinks were mixed, but the company as well"

   (Allen 82).

3. On the rare occasion that you cite an entire work rather than borrowing from a specific passage, give the author's name in the text and omit any page numbers.

   Leonard Sax explains, to both parents and teachers, the specific ways in which

   gender matters.

Each one of these in-text references is complete *only* when the full citation is placed in the Works Cited section of your paper:

   Allen, Frederick Lewis. *Only Yesterday: An Informal History of the Nineteen-*

      *Twenties.* New York: Harper, 1931. Print.

   Sax, Leonard. *Why Gender Matters.* New York: Random, 2005. Print.

The three patterns just illustrated should be used in each of the following situations:

1. The source referred to is not anonymous—the author is known.
2. The source referred to is by one author.
3. The source cited is the only work used by that author.
4. No other author in your list of sources has the same last name.

# PLACEMENT OF PARENTHETICAL DOCUMENTATION

The simplest placing of an in-text reference is at the end of the sentence *before* the period. When you are quoting, place the parentheses *after* the final quotation mark but still before the period that ends the sentence.

> During the 1920s, "not only the drinks were mixed, but the company as well"
>
> (Allen 82).

 **NOTE:** Do not put any punctuation between the author's name and the page number.

If the borrowed material forms only a part of your sentence, place the parenthetical reference *after* the borrowed material and *before* any subsequent punctuation. This placement more accurately shows readers what is borrowed and what are your own words.

> Sport, Allen observes about the 1920s, had developed into an obsession (66),
>
> another similarity between the 1920s and the 1980s.

If a quoted passage is long enough to require setting off in display form (block quotation), then place the parenthetical reference at the end of the passage, *after* the final period. Remember: Long quotations in display form *do not* have quotation marks.

> It is hard to believe that when he writes about the influence of science Allen is
>
> describing the 1920s, not the 1980s:
>
> > The prestige of science was colossal. The man in the street and the
> >
> > woman in the kitchen, confronted on every hand with new machines and
> >
> > devices which they owed to the laboratory, were ready to believe that
> >
> > science could accomplish almost anything. (164)

And to complete the documentation for all three examples:

Works Cited

Allen, Frederick Lewis. *Only Yesterday: An Informal History of the Nineteen-*

*Twenties.* New York: Harper, 1931. Print.

# PARENTHETICAL CITATIONS OF COMPLEX SOURCES

Not all sources can be cited in one of the three patterns illustrated above, for not all meet the four criteria listed on pp. 314–15. Works by two or more authors, for example, will need somewhat fuller references. Each sample form of in-text documentation given below must be completed with a full Works Cited reference, as shown above.

### Two Authors, Mentioned in the Text

Richard Herrnstein and Charles Murray contend that it is "consistently . . .

advantageous to be smart" (25).

### Two Authors, Not Mentioned in the Text

The advantaged smart group forms a "cognitive elite" in our society

(Herrnstein and Murray 26–27).

### A Book in Two or More Volumes

Sewall analyzes the role of Judge Lord in Dickinson's life (2: 642–47).

OR

Judge Lord was also one of Dickinson's preceptors (Sewall 2: 642–47).

> **NOTE:** The number before the colon always signifies the volume number. The number(s) after the colon represents the page number(s).

### A Book Listed by Title—Author Unknown

According to *The Concise Dictionary of American Biography*, William Jennings

Bryan's 1896 campaign stressed social and sectional conflicts (117).

The *New York Times*' editors were not pleased with some of the changes in

welfare programs ("Where Welfare Stands" 4: 16).

Always cite the title of the article, not the title of the journal, if the author is unknown. In the second example, the number before the page number is the newspaper's section number.

### A Work by a Corporate Author

> A report by the Institute of Ecology's Global Ecological Problems Workshop
>
> argues that the civilization of the city can lull us into forgetting our
>
> relationship to the total ecological system on which we depend (13).

Although corporate authors may be cited with the page number within the parentheses, your writing will be more graceful if corporate authors are introduced in the sentence. Then only page numbers go in parentheses.

### Two or More Works by the Same Author

> During the 1920s, "not only the drinks were mixed, but the company as well"
>
> (Allen, *Only Yesterday* 82).

> Frederick Lewis Allen contends that the early 1900s were a period of
>
> complacency in America (*The Big Change* 4–5).

> In *The Big Change*, Allen asserts that the early 1900s were a period of
>
> complacency (4–5).

If your list of sources contains two or more works by the same author, the fullest parenthetical citation includes the author's last name, followed by a comma, the work's title, shortened if possible, and the page number. If the author's name appears in the text—or the author and title both appear as in the third example above—omit these items from the parenthetical citation. When you have to include the title to distinguish among sources, it is best to put the author's name in the text.

### Two or More Works in One Parenthetical Reference

> Several writers about the future agree that big changes will take place in work
>
> patterns (Toffler 384–87; Naisbitt 35–36).

Separate each author with a semicolon. But, if the parenthetical reference becomes disruptively long, cite the works in a "See also" note rather than in the text.

### A Source Without Page Numbers

It is usually a good idea to name the nonprint source within your sentence so that readers will not expect to see page numbers.

> Although some still disagree, the *Oxford English Dictionary Online* defines global
>
> warming as "thought to be caused by various side-effects of modern energy
>
> consumption."

*Complete Publication Information in Parenthetical Reference*

At times you may want to give complete information about a source within parentheses in the text of your essay. Then a Works Cited list is not used. Use square brackets for parenthetical information within parentheses. This approach may be a good choice when you use only one source that you refer to several times. Literary analyses are one type of essay for which this approach to citation may be a good choice. For example:

> Edith Wharton establishes the bleakness of her setting, Starkfield, not just
>
> through description of place but also through her main character, Ethan, who
>
> is described as "bleak and unapproachable" (*Ethan Frome* [New York:
>
> Scribner's, 1911, Print] 3. All subsequent references are to this edition). Later
>
> Wharton describes winter as "shut[ting] down on Starkfield" and negating life
>
> there (7).

*Additional-Information Footnotes or Endnotes*

At times you may need to provide additional information that is not central to your argument. These additions belong in a content note. However, use these sparingly and never as a way of advancing your thesis. Many instructors object to content notes and prefer only parenthetical citations.

*"See Also" Footnotes or Endnotes*

More acceptable is the note that refers to other sources of evidence for or against the point to be established. These notes are usually introduced with "See also" or "Compare," followed by the citation. For example:

> Chekhov's debt to Ibsen should be recognized, as should his debt to other
>
> playwrights of the 1890s who were concerned with the inner life of their
>
> characters.[1]

---

[1] See also Eric Bentley, *In Search of Theater* (New York: Vintage, 1959) 330; Walter Bruford, *Anton Chekhov* (New Haven: Yale UP, 1957) 45.

## PREPARING MLA CITATIONS FOR A WORKS CITED LIST

The partial in-text citations described and illustrated above must be completed by a full reference in a list given at the end of the essay. To prepare your Works Cited list, alphabetize, by author last name, the sources you have actually referred to and complete each citation according to the forms explained and illustrated in the following pages. The key is to find the appropriate model for each of your sources and then follow the model exactly. (Guidelines for formatting a finished Works Cited page are found on pp. 311–12.) But, you will make fewer errors if you also understand the basic pieces of information needed in citations and the order of that information.

Books require the following information, in the order given, with periods after each of the four major elements:

- Author, last name first.
- Title—and subtitle if there is one—in italics.
- Facts of publication: city of publication, followed by a colon, shortened publisher's name (Norton for W. W. Norton, for example), followed by a comma, and the year of publication, followed by a period.
- Medium of publication: Print.

| Author | Title | Facts of Publication | Medium of Publication |
|--------|-------|----------------------|------------------------|
| Bellow, Saul. | *A Theft*. | New York: Viking-Penguin, 1989. | Print. |

## Forms for Books: Citing the Complete Book

### A Book by a Single Author

Schieff, Stacy. *Cleopatra: A Life*. New York: Little, Brown, 2010. Print.

The subtitle is included, preceded by a colon, even if there is no colon on the book's title page.

### A Book by Two or Three Authors

Adkins, Lesley, and Ray Adkins. *The Keys of Egypt: The Race to Crack the*

*Hieroglyph Code*. New York: HarperCollins, 2000. Print.

Second (and third) authors' names appear in normal signature order.

### A Book with More Than Three Authors

Baker, Susan P., et al. *The Injury Fact Book*. Oxford: Oxford UP, 1992. Print.

Use the name of the first person listed on the title page. The English "and others" may be used instead of "et al." Shorten "University Press" to "UP."

### Two or More Works by the Same Author

Goodall, Jane. *In the Shadow of Man*. Boston: Houghton, 1971. Print.

---. *Through a Window: My Thirty Years with the Chimpanzees of Gombe*. Boston:

Houghton, 1990. Print.

Give the author's full name with the first entry. For the second (and additional works), begin the citation with three hyphens followed by a period. Alphabetize the entries by the books' titles.

### A Book Written Under a Pseudonym with Name Supplied

Wrighter, Carl P. [Paul Stevens]. *I Can Sell You Anything.* New York: Ballantine,

1972. Print.

### An Anonymous Book

*Beowulf: A New Verse Translation.* Trans. Seamus Heaney. New York: Farrar,

2000. Print.

### An Edited Book

Hamilton, Alexander, James Madison, and John Jay. *The Federalist Papers.* Ed.

Isaac Kramnick. New York: Viking-Penguin, 1987. Print.

Lynn, Kenneth S., ed. *Huckleberry Finn: Text, Sources, and Critics.* New York:

Harcourt, 1961. Print.

If you cite the author's work, put the author's name first and the editor's name after the title, preceded by "Ed." If you cite the editor's work (an introduction or notes), then place the editor's name first, followed by a comma and "ed."

### A Translation

Schulze, Hagen. *Germany: A New History.* Trans. Deborah Lucas Schneider.

Cambridge: Harvard UP, 1998. Print.

Cornford, Francis MacDonald, trans. *The Republic of Plato.* New York: Oxford

UP, 1945. Print.

If the author's work is being cited, place the author's name first and the translator's name after the title, preceded by "Trans." If the translator's work is the important element, place the translator's name first, as in the second example above. If the author's name does not appear in the title, give it after the title. For example: By Plato.

### A Book in Two or More Volumes

Spielvogel, Jackson J. *Western Civilization.* 2 vols. Minneapolis: West,

1991. Print.

### A Book in Its Second or Subsequent Edition

O'Brien, David M. *Storm Center: The Supreme Court and American Politics.* 2nd

ed. New York: Norton, 1990. Print.

### A Book in a Series

Parkinson, Richard. *The Rosetta Stone.* British Museum Objects in Focus.

London: British Museum Press, 2005. Print.

The series title—and number, if there is one—follows the book's title but is not put in italics.

### A Reprint of an Earlier Work

Twain, Mark. *Adventures of Huckleberry Finn.* 1885. Centennial Facsimile

Edition. Introd. Hamlin Hill. New York: Harper, 1962. Print.

Faulkner, William. *As I Lay Dying.* 1930. New York: Vintage-Random, 1964. Print.

Provide the original date of publication as well as the facts of publication for the reprinted version. Indicate any new material, as in the first example. The second example illustrates citing a reprinted book, by the same publisher, in a paperback version. (Vintage is a paperback imprint of the publisher Random House.)

### A Book with Two or More Publishers

Green, Mark J., James M. Fallows, and David R. Zwick. *Who Runs Congress?* Ralph

Nader Congress Project. New York: Bantam; New York: Grossman, 1972. Print.

Separate the publishers with a semicolon.

### A Corporate or Governmental Author

California State Department of Education. *American Indian Education Handbook.*

Sacramento: California Department of Education, Indian Education Unit,

1991. Print.

### The Bible

The Bible [Always refers to the King James Version.] Print.

*The Reader's Bible: A Narrative.* Ed. with introd. Roland Mushat Frye. Princeton:

Princeton UP, 1965. Print.

In the first example do not put the title in italics. Indicate the version if it is not the King James Version. Provide facts of publication for versions not well known.

## Forms for Books: Citing Part of a Book

### A Preface, Introduction, Foreword, or Afterword

> Sagan, Carl. Introduction. *A Brief History of Time: From the Big Bang to Black*
>
> *Holes.* By Stephen Hawking. New York: Bantam, 1988, ix–x. Print.

Use this form if you are citing the author of the Preface, Introduction, Foreword, or the like. Use an identifying word after the author's name and give inclusive page numbers for the part of the book by the author you are citing.

### An Encyclopedia Article

> Ostrom, John H. "Dinosaurs." *McGraw-Hill Encyclopedia of Science and*
>
> *Technology.* 1957 ed. Print.

> "Benjamin Franklin." *Concise Dictionary of American Biography.* Ed. Joseph
>
> E. G. Hopkins. New York: Scribner's, 1964. Print.

Give complete publication facts for less well-known works or first editions.

### One or More Volumes in a Multivolume Work

> James, Henry. *The Portrait of a Lady.* Vols. 3 and 4 of *The Novels and Tales of*
>
> *Henry James.* New York: Scribner's, 1908. Print.

### A Work in an Anthology or Collection

> Hurston, Zora Neale. *The First One. Black Female Playwrights: An Anthology of Plays*
>
> *Before 1950.* Ed. Kathy A. Perkins. Bloomington: Indiana UP, 1989. 80–88. Print.

> Comstock, George. "The Medium and the Society: The Role of Television in
>
> American Life." *Children and Television: Images in a Changing Sociocultural*
>
> *World.* Ed. Gordon L. Berry and Joy Keiko Asamen. Newbury Park, CA:
>
> Sage, 1993. 117–31. Print.

Give inclusive page numbers for the particular work you have used.

### An Article in a Collection, Casebook, or Sourcebook

> MacKenzie, James J. "The Decline of Nuclear Power." *engage/social* April 1986.
>
> Rpt. as "America Does Not Need More Nuclear Power" in *The Environmental*
>
> *Crisis: Opposing Viewpoints.* Ed. Julie S. Bach and Lynn Hall. Opposing
>
> Viewpoints Series. St. Paul: Greenhaven, 1986. 136–41. Print.

Many articles in collections have been previously published, so a complete citation needs to include the original facts of publication (excluding page numbers if they are not readily available) as well as the facts of publication for the collection. Include inclusive page numbers for the article used.

### Cross-References

If you are citing several articles from one collection, you can cite the collection and then provide only the author and title of specific articles used, with a cross-reference to the editor(s) of the collection.

> Head, Suzanne, and Robert Heinzman, eds. *Lessons of the Rainforest.* San
>
>   Francisco: Sierra Club, 1990. Print.

> Bandyopadhyay, J., and Vandana Shiva. "Asia's Forest, Asia's Cultures." Head
>
>   and Heinzman 66–77. Print.

## Forms for Periodicals: Articles in Journals and Magazines Accessed in Print

Articles from the various forms of periodicals, when read in their print format, require the following information, in the order given, with periods after each of the four major elements:

- Author, last name first.
- Title of the article, in quotation marks.
- Facts of publication: title of the journal (magazine or newspaper) in italics, volume and issue number *for scholarly journals only,* date followed by a colon and inclusive page numbers, and then a period.
- Medium of publication: Print.

The following models show the variations in the details of publication, depending on the type of publication.

### Article in a Journal Paged by Year

> Brown, Jane D., and Carol J. Pardun. "Little in Common: Racial and Gender
>
>   Differences in Adolescents' Television Diets." *Journal of Broadcasting and*
>
>   *Electronic Media* 48.2 (2004): 266–78. Print.

Note that there is *no* punctuation between the title of the periodical and the volume number and date.

### Article in a Journal Paged by Issue

> Lewis, Kevin. "Superstardom and Transcendence." *Arete: The Journal of Sport*
>
>   *Literature* 2.2 (1985): 47–54. Print.

Provide both volume and issue number regardless of the journal's choice of paging.

### Article in a Monthly Magazine

Tyldesley, Joyce. "I, Cleopatra: This Was My Life." *Natural History* Oct. 2008:

42–47. Print.

Do not use volume or issue number. Cite the month(s) and year followed by a colon and inclusive page numbers. Abbreviate all months except May, June, and July.

### Article in a Weekly Magazine

Stein, Joel. "Eat This, Low Carbers." *Time* 15 Aug. 2005: 78. Print.

Provide the complete date, using the order of day, month, year.

### An Anonymous Article

"Death of Perestroika." *Economist* 2 Feb. 1991: 12–13. Print.

The missing name indicates that the article is anonymous. Alphabetize under D.

### A Published Interview

Angier, Natalie. "Ernst Mayr at 93." Interview. *Natural History* May 1997: 8–11. Print.

Follow the pattern for a published article, but add the descriptive label "Interview" (followed by a period) after the article's title.

### A Review

Bardsley, Tim. "Eliciting Science's Best." Rev. of *Frontiers of Illusion: Science,*

*Technology, and the Politics of Progress,* by Daniel Sarewitz. *Scientific American*

June 1997: 142. Print.

If the review is signed, begin with the author's name and then the title of the review article. Also provide the title of the work being reviewed and its author, preceded by "Rev. of." For reviews of art shows, videos, or computer software, provide place and date or descriptive label to make the citation clear.


## Forms for Periodicals: Articles in Newspapers Accessed in Print

### An Article from a Newspaper

Arguila, John. "What Deep Blue Taught Kasparov—and Us." *Christian Science*

*Monitor* 16 May 1997: 18. Print.

A newspaper's title should be cited as it appears on the masthead, excluding any initial article, thus *New York Times,* not *The New York Times.*

### An Article from a Newspaper with Lettered Sections

> Ferguson, Niall. "Rough Week, but America's Era Goes On." *Washington Post*
>
>   21 Sept. 2008: B1+. Print.

Place the section letter immediately before the page number without any spacing. If the paging is not consecutive, give the first page and the plus sign.

### An Article from a Newspaper with a Designated Edition

> Pereria, Joseph. "Women Allege Sexist Atmosphere in Offices Constitutes
>
>   Harassment." *Wall Street Journal* 10 Feb. 1988, eastern ed.: 23. Print.

Cite the edition used after the date and before the page number.

### An Editorial

> "Japan's Two Nationalisms." Editorial. *Washington Post* 4 June 2000: B6. Print.

Add the descriptive label "Editorial" after the article title.

### A Letter to the Editor

> Wiles, Yoko A. "Thoughts of a New Citizen." Letter. *Washington Post* 27 Dec.
>
>   1995: A22. Print.

## Forms for Web Sources

Remember that the purpose of a citation is to allow readers to obtain the source you have used. To locate online sources, more information is usually needed than for printed sources. Include as many of the items listed below, in the order given here, as are relevant—and available—for each source. Take time to search a website's home page to locate as much of the information as possible. AND: Always include the date you accessed the source, as the web remains ever fluid and changing.

- Author (or editor, compiler, translator), last name first.
- Title of the work, in quotation marks if it is part of a site, in italics if it is a complete and separate work, such as an online novel.
- Facts of publication of the print version if the item was originally published in print.
- Title of the website, in italics—unless it is the same as item 2 above.

- Publisher or sponsor of the site (possibly a university, company, or organization).
- Date of publication. (If none is available, use n.d.)
- Medium of publication: Web.
- Your date of access: day, month, and year.

Study this annotated citation as a general model:

### A Published Article from an Online Database

> Shin, Michael S. "Redressing Wounds: Finding a Legal Framework to Remedy
>
> Racial Disparities in Medical Care." *California Law Review* 90.6 (2002):
>
> 2047–2100. *JSTOR.* Web. 10 Sept. 2008.

> Kumar, Sanjay. "Scientists Accuse Animal Rights Activists of Stifling
>
> Research." *British Medical Journal* 23 Nov. 2002: 1192. *EBSCOhost.* Web. 12
>
> Sept. 2008.

Note that no posting date is used with databases of printed articles. Postings are ongoing.

### An Article from a Reference Source

> "Prohibition." *Encyclopaedia Britannica Online.* Encyclopaedia Britannica, 2007.
>
> Web. 16 July 2008.

### An Online News Source

> Associated Press. "Parents: Work Hinders Quality Time with Kids." *CNN.com.*
>
> Cable News Network. 31 July 2003. Web. 31 July 2003.

### An Article in an Online Magazine

> Kinsley, Michael. "Politicians Lie. Numbers Don't." *Slate.com.* Washington Post
>
> Company. 16 Sept. 2008. Web. 21 Sept. 2008.

### A Poem from a Scholarly Project

> Keats, John. "Ode to a Nightingale." *Poetical Works.* 1884. *Bartleby.com: Great*
>
> *Books.* Ed. Steven van Leeuwen. Web. 2 Oct. 2008.

### Information from a Government Site

> United States Department of Health and Human Services. "The 2008 HHS
>
> Poverty Guidelines." 23 Jan. 2008. Web. 23 Sept. 2008.

### Information from a Professional Site

> "Music Instruction Aids Verbal Memory." APA Press Release. Reporter: Agnes
>
> S. Chan. *APA Online.* American Psychological Association. 27 July 2003.
>
> Web. 16 Sept. 2008.

### Information from a Professional Home Page or Blog

> Sullivan, Andrew. "America: The Global Pioneer of Torture." *The Daily Dish.*
>
> The Atlantic Monthly Group. 14 Sept. 2008. Web. 23 Sept. 2008.

For information from an untitled personal home page, use the label "Home page" (but not in italics or quotation marks).

## Forms for Other Print and Nonprint Sources

The materials in this section, although often important to research projects, do not always lend themselves to documentation by the forms illustrated above. Follow the basic order of author, title, facts of publication, and medium of publication as much as possible. Add more information as needed to make the citation clear and useful to a reader.

### An Article Published in Print and on CD-ROM (or DVD-ROM)

> Detweiler, Richard A. "Democracy and Decency on the Internet." *Chronicle of*
>
> *Higher Education* 28 June 1996: A40. CD-ROM. *General Periodicals Ondisc.*
>
> *UMI-ProQuest.* Apr. 1997.

### A Work or Part of a Work on CD-ROM, DVD-ROM, Etc.

> Eseiolonis, Karyn. "Georgio de Chirico's *Mysterious Bathers.*" *A Passion for Art:*
>
> *Renoir, Cezanne, Matisse and Dr. Barnes.* CD-ROM. Corbis Productions, 1995.

Kloss, William. "Donatello and Padua." *Great Artists of the Italian Renaissance.*

DVD. Chantilly, VA: The Teaching Company, 2004.

### An Audio (or Video) from a Website

Vachss, Andrew. "Dead and Gone." Interview by Bill Thompson. Aired on *Eye*

*on Books,* 24 Oct. 2000. *The Zero.* Home page. Web. 25 Sept. 2008.

### A Recording

Stein, Joseph. *Fiddler on the Roof.* Jerry Bock, composer. Original-Cast

Recording with Zero Mostel. RCA, LSO-1093. 1964. LP.

The conductor and/or performers help identify a specific recording.

### Plays or Concerts

*Mourning Becomes Electra.* By Eugene O'Neill. Shakespeare Theater.

Washington, DC. 16 May 1997. Performance.

Principal actors, singers, musicians, and/or the director can be added as appropriate.

### A Television or Radio Program

"Breakthrough: Television's Journal of Science and Medicine." PBS series

hosted by Ron Hendren. 10 June 1997. Television.

### An Interview

Plum, Kenneth. Personal interview. 5 Mar. 1995.

### A Lecture

Bateson, Mary Catherine. "Crazy Mixed-Up Families." Northern Virginia

Community College, 26 Apr. 1997. Lecture.

### An Unpublished Letter or E-mail

Usick, Patricia. Message to the author. 26 June 2005. E-mail.

### Maps and Charts

*Hampshire and Dorset.* Map. Kent, UK: Geographers' A–Z, n.d. Print.

### Cartoons and Advertisements

Halleyscope. "Halleyscopes Are for Night Owls." Advertisement. *Natural*

*History* Dec. 1985: 15. Print.

United Airlines Advertisement. ESPN. 8 Aug. 2008. Television.

### A Published Dissertation

Brotton, Joyce D. *Illuminating the Present Through Literary Dialogism: From the*

*Reformation Through Postmodernism.* Diss. George Mason U, 2002. Ann

Arbor: UMI, 2002. Print.

### Government Documents

United States. Senate. Committee on Energy and Natural Resources.

Subcommittee on Energy Research and Development. *Advanced Reactor*

*Development Program: Hearing.* Washington: GPO, 24 May 1988. Print.

---. Environmental Protection Agency. *The Challenge of the Environment: A Primer*

*on EPA's Statutory Authority.* Washington: GPO, 1972. Print.

If the author is not given, cite the name of the government first followed by the name of the department or agency. If you cite more than one document published by the same government, use the standard three hyphens followed by a period. If you cite a second document prepared by the EPA, use another three hyphens and period. Abbreviate the U.S. Government Printing Office: GPO.

If the author is known, follow this pattern:

Geller, William. *Deadly Force.* U.S. Dept. of Justice National Institute of Justice

Crime File Study Guide. Washington: Dept. of Justice, n.d. Print.

### Legal Documents

U.S. Const. Art. 1, sec. 3. Print.

The Constitution is referred to by article and section. Abbreviations are used. Do not use italics.

When citing a court case, give the name of the case, the volume, name, and page of the report cited, and the date. Italicize the name of the case in your text but not in the Works Cited.

Turner v. Arkansas. 407 U.S. 366. 1972. Print.

# AUTHOR/YEAR OR APA STYLE

The *author/year system* identifies a source by placing the author's last name and the publication year of the source within parentheses at the point in the text where the source is cited. The in-text citations are supported by complete citations in a list of sources at the end of the paper. Most disciplines in the social sciences, biological sciences, and earth sciences use some version of the author/year style. The guidelines given here follow the style of the *Publication Manual of the American Psychological Association* (6th ed., 2010).

## APA Style: In-Text Citations

The simplest parenthetical reference can be presented in one of three ways:

1.  Place the year of publication within parentheses immediately following the author's name in the text.

    In a typical study of preference for motherese, Fernald (1985) used an

    operant auditory preference procedure.

Within the same paragraph, additional references to the source do not need to repeat the year, if the researcher clearly establishes that the same source is being cited.

Because the speakers were unfamiliar subjects, Fernald's work eliminates the possibility that it is the mother's voice per se that accounts for the preference.

2. If the author is not mentioned in the text, place the author's last name followed by a comma and the year of publication within parentheses after the borrowed information.

The majority of working women are employed in jobs that are at least 75 percent female (Lawrence & Matsuda, 1997).

3. Cite a specific passage by providing the page, chapter, or figure number following the borrowed material. *Always* give specific page references for quoted material.

- A brief quotation:

Deuzen-Smith (1988) believes that counselors must be involved with clients and "deeply interested in piecing the puzzle of life together" (p. 29).

- A quotation in display form:

Bartlett (1932) explains the cyclic process of perception:

Suppose I am making a stroke in a quick game, such as tennis or cricket. How I make the stroke depends on the relating of certain new experiences, most of them visual, to other immediately preceding visual experiences, and to my posture, or balance of posture, at the moment. (p. 201)

Indent a block quotation five spaces from the left margin, do not use quotation marks, and double-space throughout. To show a new paragraph within the block quotation, indent the first line of the new paragraph an additional five spaces. Note the placing of the year after the author's name, and the page number at the end of the direct quotation.

More complicated in-text citations should be handled as follows:

### Two Authors, Mentioned in the Text

Kuhl and Meltzoff (1984) tested 4- to 5-month-olds in an experiment . . .

### Two Authors, Not Mentioned in the Text

. . . but are unable to show preference in the presence of two mismatched modalities (e.g., a face and a voice; see Kuhl & Meltzoff, 1984).

Give both authors' last names each time you refer to the source. Connect their names with "and" in the text. Use an ampersand (&) in the parenthetical citation.

## More Than Two Authors

For works coauthored by three, four, or five people, provide all last names in the first reference to the source. Thereafter, cite only the first author's name followed by "et al."

As Price-Williams, Gordon, and Ramirez have shown (1969), . . .

OR

Studies of these children have shown (Price-Williams, Gordon, & Ramirez,

1969) . . .

THEN

Price-Williams et al. (1969) also found that . . .

If a source has six or more authors, use only the first author's last name followed by "et al." every time the source is cited.

## Corporate Authors

In general, spell out the name of a corporate author each time it is used. If a corporate author has well-known initials, the name can be abbreviated after the first citation.

**FIRST IN-TEXT CITATION:**     (National Institutes of Health [NIH], 1989)
**SUBSEQUENT CITATIONS:**     (NIH, 1989)

## Two or More Works Within the Same Parentheses

When citing more than one work by the same author in a parenthetical reference, use the author's name only once and arrange the years mentioned in order, thus:

Several studies of ego identity formation (Marcia, 1966, 1983) . . .

When an author, or the same group of coauthors, has more than one work published in the same year, distinguish the works by adding the letters *a, b, c,* and so on, as needed, to the year. Give the last name only once, but repeat the year, each one with its identifying letter; thus:

Several studies (Smith, 1990 a, 1990 b, 1990 c) . . .

When citing several works by different authors within the same parentheses, list the authors alphabetically; alphabetize by the first author when citing coauthored works. Separate authors or groups of coauthors with semicolons; thus:

Although many researchers (Archer & Waterman, 1983; Grotevant, 1983;

Grotevant & Cooper, 1986; Sabatelli & Mazor, 1985) study identity

formation . . .

### Personal Communication

Cite information obtained via interview, phone, letter, and e-mail communication.

> According to Sandra Haun (personal interview, September 7, 2008) . . .

Because readers cannot retrieve information from these personal sources, do *not* include a citation in your list of references.

# APA STYLE: PREPARING A LIST OF REFERENCES

Every source cited parenthetically in your paper needs a complete bibliographic citation. These complete citations are placed on a separate page (or pages) after the text of the paper and before any appendices included in the paper. Sources are arranged alphabetically, and the first page is titled "References." Begin each source flush with the left margin and indent second and subsequent lines five spaces. Double-space throughout the list of references. Follow these rules for alphabetizing:

1. Organize two or more works by the same author, or the same group of coauthors, chronologically.

   Beck, A. T. (1991).

   Beck, A. T. (1993).

2. Place single-author entries before multiple-author entries when the first of the multiple authors is the same as the single author.

   Grotevant, H. D. (1983).

   Grotevant, H. D., & Cooper, C. R. (1986).

3. Organize multiple-author entries that have the same first author but different second or third authors alphabetically by the name of the second author or third and so on.

   Gerbner, G., & Gross, L.

   Gerbner, G., Gross, L., Jackson-Beeck, M., Jeffries-Fox, S., & Signorielli, N.

   Gerbner, G., Gross, L., Morgan, M., & Signorielli, N.

4. Organize two or more works by the same author(s) published in the same year alphabetically by title.

## Form for Books

A book citation contains these elements in this form:

> Seligman, M. E. P. (1991). *Learned optimism.* New York: Knopf.

> Weiner, B. (Ed.). (1974). *Achievement motivation and attribution theory.*

> Morristown, NJ: General Learning Press.

## *Authors*

Give all authors' names, last name first, and initials. Separate authors with commas, use the ampersand (&) before the last author's name, and end with a period. For edited books, place the abbreviation "Ed." or "Eds." in parentheses following the last editor's name.

## *Date of Publication*

Place the year of publication in parentheses followed by a period.

## *Title*

Capitalize only the first word of the title and of the subtitle, if there is one, and any proper nouns. Italicize the title and end with a period. Place additional information such as number of volumes or an edition in parentheses after the title, before the period.

> Butler, R., & Lewis, M. (1982). *Aging and mental health* (3rd ed.).

## *Publication Information*

Cite the city of publication; add the state (using the Postal Service abbreviation) or country if necessary to avoid confusion; then give the publisher's name, after a colon, eliminating unnecessary terms such as *Publisher, Co.,* and *Inc.* End the citation with a period.

> Mitchell, J. V. (Ed.). (1985). *The ninth mental measurements yearbook.* Lincoln:
>
> University of Nebraska Press.

> National Institute of Drug Abuse. (1993, April 13). *Annual national high school*
>
> *senior survey.* Rockville, MD: Author.

> Newton, D. E. (1996). *Violence and the media.* Santa Barbara, CA: ABC-Clio.

Give a corporate author's name in full. When the organization is both author and publisher, place the word *Author* after the place of publication.

## Form for Articles

An article citation contains these elements in this form:

> Changeaux, J-P. (1993). Chemical signaling in the brain. *Scientific American,*
>
> *269,* 58–62.

## *Date of Publication*

Place the year of publication for articles in scholarly journals in parentheses, followed by a period. For articles in newspapers and popular magazines, give the year followed by month and day (if appropriate).

> (1997, March).

### Title of Article

Capitalize only the title's first word, the first word of any subtitle, and any proper nouns. Place any necessary descriptive information in square brackets immediately after the title.

> Scott, S. S. (1984, December 12). Smokers get a raw deal [Letter to the Editor].

### Publication Information

Cite the title of the journal in full, capitalizing according to conventions for titles. Italicize the title and follow it with a comma. Give the volume number, italicized, followed by a comma, and then inclusive page numbers followed by a period. *If* a journal begins each issue with a new page 1, then also cite the issue number in parentheses immediately following the volume number. Do not use "p." or "pp." before page numbers when citing articles from scholarly journals; do use "p." or "pp." in citations to newspaper and magazine articles.

> Martin, C. L., Wood, C. H., & Little, J. K. (1990). The development of gender
>
> stereotype components. *Child Development, 61,* 1891–1904.
>
> Leakey, R. (2000, April/May). Extinctions past and present. *Time,* p. 35.

### An Article or Chapter in an Edited Book

> Goodall, J. (1993). Chimpanzees—bridging the gap. In P. Cavalieri & P. Singer
>
> (Eds.), *The great ape project: Equality beyond humanity* (pp. 10–18). New
>
> York: St. Martin's.

Cite the author(s), date, and title of the article or chapter. Then cite the name(s) of the editor(s) in signature order after "In," followed by "Ed." or "Eds." in parentheses; the title of the book; the inclusive page numbers of the article or chapter, in parentheses, followed by a period. End with the city of publication and the publisher of the book.

### A Report

> U.S. Merit Systems Protection Board. (1988). *Sexual harassment in the federal*
>
> *workplace: An update.* Washington, DC: U.S. Government Printing Office.

## Form for Electronic Sources

As a minimum, an APA reference for any type of Internet source should include the following information: a document title or description, the date of publication, a way to access the document online, and, when possible, an author name. When the Internet address (URL) is likely to be stable, you can cite that address. For example: www.nytimes.com. However, a good source that you find during your research may not be found later by your readers with the URL that you used. APA recommends, therefore, that such sources be documented with the item's DOI (digital object identifier) instead of its URL.

Do not place URLs within angle brackets (< >). Do not place a period at the end of the URL, even though it concludes the citation. If you have to break a URL at the end of a line, break only after a slash. Introduce the URL at the end of the citation this way: Retrieved from www.nytimes.com

DOIs are a series of numbers and letters that provide a link to a specific item, and this link does not change with time. Although DOIs are often on the first page of a document, they can, at times, be hard to locate with a source that you want to use. To obtain a specific DOI for a source, you can go to http://doi.org/ and click on the Guest Query form. APA prefers that you always choose a source's DOI over its URL, if you can find it. Place the DOI at the end of the citation, and introduce the number thus: doi: [number]. Do not end the citation with a period.

Here are a few examples of citations for Internet sources:

### Journal Article Retrieved Online, with DOI Information

Habernas, Jurgen. (2006). Political communication in media society.

Communication Theory 16(4), 411–426. doi: 10.1111/j.

l468-2885.2006.00280.x

Gardiner, K., Herault, Y., Lott, I., Antonarakis, S., Reeves, R., & Dierssen, M.

(2010). Down syndrome: From understanding the neurobiology to ther-

apy. Journal of Neuroscience 30(45), 14943–14945. doi: 10.1523/

JNEUROSCI.3728-10.2010

### Electronic Daily Newspaper Article Available by Search

Schwartz, J. (2002, September 13). Air pollution con game. Washington Times.

Retrieved from http://www.washtimes.com

### Journal Article Available from a Periodical Database

Note that no URL is necessary; just provide the name of the database.

Dixon, B. (2001, December). Animal emotions. Ethics & the Environment, 6(2),

22. Retrieved from Academic Search Premier database/EBSCOhost

Research Databases.

### U.S. Government Report on a Government Website

U.S. General Accounting Office. (2002, March). Identity theft: Prevalence and

cost appear to be growing. Retrieved from http://www.consumer.gov/

idtheft/reports/gao-d02363.pdf

Cite a message posted to a newsgroup or electronic mailing list in the reference list. Cite an e-mail from one person to another *only* in the essay, not in the list of references.

## SAMPLE STUDENT ESSAY IN APA STYLE

The following pages (part of a student research essay) illustrate APA style. Use 1-inch margins and double-space throughout, including any block quotations. Block quotations should be indented *five* spaces from the left margin (in contrast to the ten spaces required by MLA style). Observe the following elements: title page, running head, abstract, author/year in-text citations, subheadings within the text, and a list of references.

Running Head: TRANSRACIAL ADOPTIONS

1 Sample title page for a paper in APA style.

Adoption: An Issue of Love, Not Race

Connie Childress

Northern Virginia Community College

Observe placement
of running head and
page number.

## Abstract

Over 400,000 children are in foster care in the United States. The majority

of these children are nonwhite. However, the majority of couples wanting to

adopt children are white. While matching race or ethnic background when

arranging adoptions may be the ideal, the mixing of race or ethnic background

should not be avoided, or delayed, when the matching of race is not possible.

Children need homes, and studies of racial adoptees show that they are as

adjusted as adoptees with new parents of their own race or ethnicity. Legislation

should support speedier adoptions of children, regardless of race or ethnic

background.

Papers in APA style
usually begin with
an abstract of the
paper.

Running Head: TRANSRACIAL ADOPTIONS                                      4

Adoption Issues and Problems

Subheadings are often used in papers in the social sciences.

Although interracial adoptions are "statistically rare in the United States," according to Robert S. Bausch and Richard T. Serpe (1997), who cite a 1990 study by Bachrach et al., the issue continues to receive attention from both social workers and the public (p. 137). A *New Republic* editorial (1994) lists several articles, including a cover story in *The Atlantic* in 1992, to illustrate the attention given to transracial adoptions. All of the popular-press articles as well as those in scholarly journals, the editors explain, describe the country's adoption and foster-care problems. While the great majority of families wanting to adopt are white, about half of the children in foster care waiting to be adopted are black. Robert Jackson (1995) estimates that, in 1995, about 440,000 children are being cared for in foster families. The *New Republic* editorial reports on a 1993 study revealing that "a black child in California's foster care system is three times less likely to be adopted than a white child" (p. 6). In some cases minority children have been in a single foster home with parents of a different race their entire life. They have bonded as a family. Yet, often when the foster parents apply to adopt these children, their petitions are denied and the children are removed from their care. For example, Beverly and David Cox, a white couple in Wisconsin, were asked to be foster parents to two young sisters, both African American. The Coxes provided love and nurturing for five years, but when they petitioned to adopt the two girls, not only was their request denied, but the girls were removed from their home. Can removing the children from the only home they have ever known just because of their skin color really be in the best interest of the children? Cole, Drummond, and Epperson (1995) quote Hillary Clinton as saying that "skin color [should] not outweigh the more important gift of love that adoptive parents want to offer" (p. 50).

Page numbers must be given for direct quotations.

Words added to a quotation for clarity are placed in square brackets.

The argument against transracial adoption has rested on the concern that children adopted by parents of a different race or ethnic background will lose

• • •

Running Head: TRANSRACIAL ADOPTIONS                                   9

## References

All in the family [Editorial]. (1994, January 24). *New Republic,* pp. 6–7.

Bausch, R. S., & Serpe, R. T. (1997). Negative outcomes of interethnic adoption of Mexican American children. *Social Work, 42*(2), 136–143.

Blackman, A., et al. (1994, August 22). Babies for export. *Time, Time On-Disc* [CD-ROM], pp. 64–65.

Bolles, E. B. (1984). *The Penguin adoption handbook: A guide to creating your new family.* New York: Viking.

Cole, W., Drummond, T., & Epperson, S. E. (1995, August 14). Adoption in black and white. *Time,* pp. 50–51.

Davis, R. (1995, April 13). Suits back interracial adoptions. *USA Today,* p. A3.

Harnack, A. (Ed.). (1995). *Adoption: Opposing viewpoints* (p. 188). San Diego: Greenhaven.

Jackson, R. L. (1995, April 25). U.S. stresses no race bias in adoptions. *Los Angeles Times,* p. A26.

Kennedy, R., & Moseley-Braun, C. (1995). At issue: interracial adoption—is the multiethnic placement act flawed? *ABA Journal 81, ABA Journal On-Disc* [CD-ROM], pp. 44–45.

Kuebelbeck, A. (1996, December 31). Interracial adoption debated. *AP US and World.* Retrieved from http://www.donet.com/~brandyjc/p6at111.htm

*Losing Isaiah* (1995) [film].

Russell, A. T. (1995). Transracial adoptions should be forbidden. In A. Harnack (Ed.), *Adoption: Opposing viewpoints* (pp. 189–196). San Diego: Greenhaven.

Simon, R. J., Alstein, H., & Melli, M. S. (1995). Transracial adoptions should be encouraged. In A. Harnack (Ed.), *Adoption: Opposing viewpoints* (pp. 198–204). San Diego: Greenhaven.

*[Margin note:]* Title the page "References."

*[Margin note:]* Double-space throughout. In each citation indent all lines, after the first, five spaces. Note APA-style placement of date and format for titles.

# A Collection of Readings

This section is divided into nine chapters, each on a current topic or set of interrelated issues open to debate. The chapters contain six or seven articles, or a combination of articles and visuals, to remind us that complex issues cannot be divided into simple "for" or "against" positions. This point remains true even for the chapters on a rather specific topic. It is not sound critical thinking to be simply for or against any complicated public policy issue. No one is "for" or "against" protecting our environment, for example. The debate begins with restrictions on factories (raising costs), restrictions on car manufacturers, restrictions on energy use. It is when we get into these sorts of policy decisions, and ways of funding those decisions, that people have opposing viewpoints.

Questions follow each article to aid reading, analysis, and critical responses. In addition, each chapter opens with a visual to enjoy and then reflect on and with a set of questions to focus your thinking as you read.

# The Media: Image and Reality

**READ:** What is the situation? Who speaks the lines?

**REASON:** Who, presumably, are the guys in suits sitting in front of the desk? Who, according to Wiley, must be controlling TV scheduling?

**REFLECT/WRITE:** What is Wiley's view of reality shows? Do you agree? Why or why not?

Although we may not agree with Marshall McLuhan that the medium itself IS the message, we still recognize the ways that the various media influence us, touching our emotions, shaping our vision of the world, altering our lives. The essays in this chapter explore and debate the effects of film and television, music and advertising, video games and the press on the ways we imagine the world and then construct our lives from those images. Surely we are influenced by media images, by the "reality" they reveal to us. The questions become how extensive is the influence, given the other influences in our lives, and what, if anything, can or should we do about it?

The chapter opens with a popular medium: the cartoon. Cartoons are not just a laugh; they present a view of life and seek to shape our thinking. Powerful messages also come to us in the print media—newspapers and magazines—in the form of photographs and advertisements. You have studied visuals in Chapter 5. Apply your knowledge when you examine Kilbourne's analysis of advertising—and the ads that accompany her essay.

## PREREADING QUESTIONS

1. How "real" are "reality" shows? Does it matter if they are scripted?
2. How accurate is our press coverage? Do media outlets around the world "see" and show the same worldview to their viewers? How do bloggers offer another useful way of seeing our world?
3. How do films reflect our world and also shape our image of that world?
4. What do the various forms of music (jazz, rock, gangsta rap) tell us about ourselves and our world? What does your music preference tell us about you?
5. How does advertising shape our images of the world? How realistic are those images? Do we want ads to be "realistic"?
6. What standards of reliability, objectivity, and fairness should be set for the media? What, if any, distortions are acceptable because they make the story more compelling?

## OF LOSERS AND MOLES: YOU THINK REALITY TV JUST WRITES ITSELF? | DERRICK SPEIGHT

Derrick Speight is, as he tells us in his essay, a reality TV writer based in Los Angeles, with a dozen TV series to his credit, as story writer or supervising story producer. His scoop on the reality of reality TV shows was published in the *Washington Post*, July 24, 2005.

PREREADING QUESTIONS Do you enjoy watching reality TV shows—or know people who do? Why do you—or they—like these shows? What are the reasons usually given for enjoying these types of TV shows?

1    A couple of summers ago, I found myself living out a high school fantasy. I was running across the hot white sands of a Mexican beach in Playa del

Narrative
Intro

Carmen, chasing after stunning Playboy playmate Angie Everhart. As her bright orange bikini disappeared into the Caribbean surf, I closed my eyes and smiled—then quickly snapped back to reality. I was there as a writer for ABC's "Celebrity Mole: Yucatan," and my job was to find out what Everhart was saying about the show's other beauty, former MTV VJ Ananda Lewis. Would they be dueling divas, headed for a catfight by day's end? I needed to find out. So I sighed, put on the earpiece that picked up the two women's microphones, and began taking notes.

Reality TV writers like me are at the heart of a lawsuit filed by the Writers Guild of America, West about two weeks ago. On behalf of 12 such scribes, the union is charging four reality production companies and four networks with unfair labor practices, including providing pay and benefits far below those earned by writers of traditional drama and sitcoms. The suit says a lot about the rise of reality TV, a formerly disreputable format that last year contributed half of the 20 top-rated shows on TV. But in hearing about it, I imagine that people across America were asking the same question members of my own family have voiced ever since I started down this career path: "How exactly do you *write* reality? Isn't it already real?"

Yes, Grandma, it is—in all its undigested, contextless, boring glory. What I do is shape that mass into something that'll make viewers want to tune in week after week. Like a journalist, I sniff out what I *think* the story will be, then craft the interviews or situations that'll draw it out. Like a paperback writer, I'm all about highlighting character and plot. Simply put, drama is the pursuit of a goal, with obstacles. Both by developing promising story lines and by pulling out the zingy moments burned in hours upon hours of ho-hum footage, reality TV writers like me—who go under various titles, including story editor and story producer—create it. As I tell my family, having a reality TV show without writers would be like having a countertop of cake ingredients but no idea how to put them together. So, yes, I consider myself a writer.

My voyage into reality TV began by accident. Seven years ago, I was new to Hollywood, and sure that I was destined to direct the next film version of *Superman.* But by the time I finished my first fresh-out-of-film-school internship with DreamWorks' Mark Gordon Productions, I was both slightly peeved about not meeting Steven Spielberg and badly in need of a paying job. Luckily, a friend of a friend was looking for production assistants to work on *World's Most Amazing Videos.* Hired for roughly $400 a week (and on top of the world about it), I was quickly promoted to logger—basically the guy who looks through all the footage and makes notes on what happens and when. That led to a job at a new company, Actual Reality Pictures, which would end up completely redirecting my career.

Actual Reality is the production company of Academy Award nominee R. J. Cutler, whose documentary *The War Room* followed Bill Clinton's 1992 presidential campaign. The building was an intellectual hothouse, packed with scores of Ivy League grads who loved nothing more than to ruminate over the most minuscule story points. As we worked on Cutler's latest project, a docudrama about suburban Chicago teens called *American High,* staff meetings were virtual master classes in narrative structure. Whole walls of multicolored index cards were dedicated to the deconstruction of an episode, inviting constant rearranging until the optimal narrative was found. And through it all, Cutler, the faintly aloof, greatly admired genius among us, wandered the office hallways yelling, "What's the story?!" My job was to rummage through film footage looking to answer that question. Apparently, our process worked: *American High* went on to win an Emmy.

6    After I left Actual Reality, I would never again encounter that type of intense, academic scrutiny of story structure. I had risen through the ranks, though, from logger to story assistant to story producer, overseeing other writers. So I ended up going to work on a whole slew of reality TV shows, both Nielsen-topping and not, including *The Bachelor, The Mole, The Surreal Life, The Benefactor* and *The Biggest Loser.* On every one of them, whether I was dealing with desperately weeping single gals or former parachute pant wearer MC Hammer, the main question was always the same: "What is the story?"

7    Some of the crafting of these shows took place on set, as on "Celebrity Mole: Yucatan." While filming is taking place, writers keep track of all the issues that may arise and anticipate which will yield the strongest narrative. Teams of us are on location, assigned to different characters. The uniform: a good pen, steno notepads, an audio monitoring device (to overhear comments and conversations), a digital watch, walkie-talkies and a comfortable pair of shoes—in case anyone takes off running. We typically stand within earshot of what's being filmed, noting mumbled quips, telling looks and memorable exchanges. At the end of the day, we all regroup, compare notes and decide which stories have evolved, or are evolving. These are the situations to which we'll pay particular attention, and in the days following, we'll make sure the right interview questions are asked to round out what appear to be the prominent stories. Like nonfiction writers, we do not script lines—but if we have a hunch, we ask the right questions to follow it up.

8    Preparation of this kind is, of course, half the battle, but the magic really happens after the filming is done, in post-production. In its one- to four-week scripting phase, the story producers pinpoint scenes, moments and interviews from a mountain of VHS tapes, then structure them to tell the strongest story. After it's approved by the executive producer, this script is given to an editor, who cuts it together. Six-day workweeks and long hours are expected—and get longer midway through editing, when a decision is invariably made to change the direction of the show. As story producers, the responsibility for that reshaping falls to us. Sometimes it's for the better, but sometimes it's for worse. *The Benefactor,* for example, began as an exciting, conceptually strong show led by billionaire Mark Cuban and dubbed the "Anti-Apprentice," to contrast with the Donald Trump hit. It was quickly mired by second guessing on all our parts, and we ended up giving in to some Trumpian gimmicks. In the end, the show floundered, suffering dismal ratings and was widely perceived as the very thing it was striving not to be . . . another *Apprentice.*

9    The current lawsuit isn't the Writer's Guild's first attempt to reach out to reality TV crew members. Since this spring, they've been on a major campaign

to unionize, gathering up union authorization cards from over 1,000 writers, editors and producers. Despite the many logistics associated with unionizing, at the core, I believe the WGA's gesture to be quite complimentary: By their actions, they are recognizing us as legitimate creative contributors, I like that. It's also a sign that they expect reality TV to be more than just a passing fad. Reality is evolving, and I look forward to its next chapter.

---

Source: From *The Washington Post*, July 24, 2005. Reprinted by permission of the author.

### QUESTIONS FOR READING

1. Who has filed a lawsuit? What is their issue?
2. What do reality TV writers "do" for reality TV shows? What do they try to find?
3. What strategies do these writers use during the filming? After the filming?
4. What do the lawsuit and unionizing attempts suggest about the future of reality TV?

### QUESTIONS FOR REASONING AND ANALYSIS

5. The author gives much information about his job. Is providing information his primary purpose—or not? If not, why does he give us all of the details?
6. If this is not primarily or exclusively informative, then what is Speight's claim?
7. What is effective about Speight's opening paragraph?
8. Why does he include the information in the second half of paragraph 8?

### QUESTIONS FOR REFLECTION AND WRITING

9. Are you surprised to learn about reality TV writers—and their complex jobs? Why or why not?
10. Are you shocked or disappointed in reading this essay? Why might some be disappointed?
11. Although some never watch them, many people are "hooked" on reality TV. Why? What is the appeal? Would the appeal be less if viewers understood how these shows are constructed?

## PRESS AND PUNDIT STAMPEDE TRAMPLES GOOD JUDGMENT, AND OFTEN THE FACTS, TOO | HOWARD KURTZ

Howard Kurtz was media reporter for the *Washington Post* for many years, but he left the newspaper and his "Media Notes" column in 2010 to continue his reporting at *The Daily Beast* website. Kurtz also hosts the CNN weekly media show *Reliable Sources*. The following essay was published in his *Post* column on August 23, 2010.

**PREREADING QUESTIONS** How thoroughly do you study current news events? When you form opinions on current issues—from the national debt to the war in Afghanistan to the latest WikiLeaks—on what do you base your views?

1     When the *New York Times* published a story last December about plans for a Muslim prayer space near the World Trade Center site, there was little reaction.

2     After all, the imam in charge was quoted as saying the building was an effort to "push back against the extremists" in the shadow of the terrorist attacks. Only months later did a conservative assault on the project morph into the most incendiary issue on the media landscape.

3     The herd was stampeding again.

4     You hear their thundering hooves on cable shows and talk radio, watch the gathering dust on the blogs. They trample everything in their path. Passivity is impossible: Everyone must form an immediate opinion on the matter at hand and defend it passionately.

5     The quickly labeled Ground Zero mosque—an Islamic cultural center neither at Ground Zero nor specifically a mosque—is a classic case. It is a symbolic slugfest that lacks the maddening complexity of health care legislation or banking reform—*"Don't you care about religious freedom?" "Don't you care about the families of 9/11 victims?"*—and is tailor-made for the sound-bite stampede.

6     The media herd loves to chase stories with colorful personalities that we can either love or hate, defend or denounce. Blago fit the bill: The jury deadlocks on 23 of 24 counts and the insta-punditry begins. Did the government blow the case? Were the jurors out to lunch? Could Rod Blagojevich actually have been . . . innocent?

7     When prosecutors first released the tawdry tapes, the media mob reached the obvious conclusion, that the Illinois governor was a sleazy operator. He was selling Barack Obama's Senate seat! But as he raced from one television studio to the next, less attention was paid to whether he could be convicted in court. The herd likes morality plays, not legal strategizing. *Hey, didja see Blago got bounced off "Celebrity Apprentice"?*

**WHAT ABOUT THE FACTS?**

8     Such lemming-like behavior was also on display in the case of Steven Slater. It's August, you see, and media folks so much wanted to make the JetBlue hothead into an overnight folk hero that they loaded up the story with sociological baggage. This wasn't just a matter of an erratic flight attendant sliding down the emergency chute, it was a clarion call for fed-up workers everywhere! "The last-straw moment a lot of people identify with," said NBC's Ann Curry. "He did what a lot of Americans would have done," said MSNBC's Ed Schultz.

9     The story soared even as Slater's account was falling apart. Passengers told reporters that *he* had been rude, that he hadn't been provoked, that he'd

gotten a bump on his head before the flight began. But by then the herd was heading off in another direction.

The herd isn't dumb, but it moves so quickly that snap judgments prevail 10 and nuance gets lost. It decided within hours that Shirley Sherrod was a racist, then concluded just as forcefully that she had been framed. The first charge took place over a maliciously edited videotape, the second after the release of the full tape. Having belatedly vindicated her, the herd began a furious debate over the role of the White House, Andrew Breitbart and Fox News.

Some stories appear naturally in the pack's path; others are planted there 11 by people with agendas, as with the Breitbart snippet of a speech by the Agriculture Department staffer. Controversies favored by the right are often pumped up by the *Drudge Report,* Fox and Rush Limbaugh; liberal crusades get picked up by the *Huffington Post* and MSNBC. The escalating rhetoric pushes the dispute onto op-ed pages and network newscasts, and there it remains until some countervailing force knocks it off.

At times, the early noise gives way to serious debate. When the BP oil well 12 blew up, plenty of newly minted experts held forth on the advisability of a "top kill" or "junk shot" or other esoteric approaches, not to mention the non-stop argument over whether the president was responding with sufficient emotion. But as journalists gradually educated themselves, the country got a lesson in the risks of offshore oil drilling and the shortcomings of federal regulation.

More commonly, though, the media crowd doesn't stick around long 13 enough to do more than stomp around. There was a furious argument over Obama giving General Motors a $50 billion bailout; now that the company is profitable and preparing a stock offering, the herd is MIA.

**NEXT!**

It always needs something new to chew on: Is Elena Kagan qualified 14 despite never having been a judge—and what about those rumors about her personal life? And the herd loses interest when the outcome isn't in doubt. Once it became clear that Republicans wouldn't block Kagan's Supreme Court confirmation, the coverage dwindled dramatically.

The herd is easily distracted by whatever buzzes by. Dr. Laura using the 15 N-word? Was she racially insensitive or just trying to make a point about who gets to use such language? Never mind, she's quitting already. Wait—Sarah Palin is defending her?

The media treated the withdrawal of the final American combat units 16 from Iraq last week as a one-day story, despite the bloody toll of the 7½-year conflict. Yes, it was symbolic, the war isn't over and 50,000 U.S. troops remain behind, but the conflict dominated our politics for years—and claimed the lives of more than 4,400 service members and untold Iraqi civilians. Except on MSNBC, which carried embedded correspondent Richard Engel reporting from the scene for hours, and a few front-page stories, the

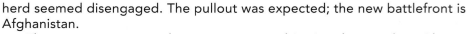

herd seemed disengaged. The pullout was expected; the new battlefront is Afghanistan.

The controversy over the mosque got a big-time boost when Obama called it a matter of religious freedom, then told CNN's Ed Henry the next day that he wasn't saying the project should be built. But little attention was paid to a Politico report that organizers of the $100 million center have raised only $18,255—making it unlikely that it will ever be built. To dwell on that, of course, would spoil the herd's fun.

### QUESTIONS FOR READING

1. Kurtz begins with four news stories. What are they? What do they have in common?
2. How long do the media stay with and explore a story? What drives "the news"?
3. What kinds of stories do the media seem to like best?

### QUESTIONS FOR REASONING AND ANALYSIS

4. What is Kurtz's central image of the media? What are its characteristics? What does the image say about the media?
5. Given the media's characteristics in Kurtz's view, what happens to our news?
6. Study the author's opening five paragraphs. What does he gain by his introduction?
7. What is Kurtz's point? What does he want us to understand about news coverage today?

### QUESTIONS FOR REFLECTION AND WRITING

8. Do you agree with the author that much of today's news coverage is shallow and quickly shifting to the next appealing story? If you disagree, how would you refute Kurtz's argument?
9. If you agree, why do you think this is happening? What is driving this kind of news coverage?
10. As a corollary to Kurtz's observations, would you also agree that readers/viewers of the news often seem more interested in the "back story" than the actual story and its consequences? That is, why so much focus on the deals, on the attitudes of the "players," on the behind-the-scene conflicts—whether it's sports or politics—instead of on what actually happens and the impact of those events on us?

# WHAT'S UP DOC? A BLOODY OUTRAGE, THAT'S WHAT | KATHERINE ELLISON

A Pulitzer Prize–winning former foreign correspondent for Knight-Ridder Newspapers, Katherine Ellison is the author of four nonfiction books, including *The Mommy Brain: How Motherhood Makes Us Smarter* (2005) and *Buzz: A Year of Paying Attention* (2010). Her reaction to violent Internet cartoons appeared on October 23, 2005, in the *Washington Post.*

**PREREADING QUESTIONS**  Do you use the Internet for "fun": games, porn, violent cartoons? Do you see any problems with such Internet sites?

*narrative*

The other day I found my 6-year-old son watching an Internet cartoon called "Happy Tree Friends." 1

Purple daisies danced, high-pitched voices sang and animals with heart-shaped noses waved cheerily. But then the music changed, and a previously merry green bear, wearing dog tags and camouflage, suffered an apparent psychotic breakdown. 2

*Crrrrrack!!* went the neck of a purple badger, as the bear snapped off its head. Blood splashed and continued flowing as the bear gleefully garroted a hedgehog, then finished off a whimpering squirrel already impaled on metal spikes by placing a hand grenade in its paw. 3

Joshua turned to me with a sheepish grin. He clearly had a sense that I wasn't happy about his new friends, but he couldn't have known what I was 4

really thinking. Which was this: I'm a longtime journalist who reveres the First Amendment, and I live in California's liberal bastion of Marin County. Yet I would readily skip my next yoga class to march with right-wing fundamentalists in a cultural war against "Happy Tree Friends."

5      Just when parents thought we knew who our electronic enemies were—the shoot-'em-up video games, the TVs hawking trans fats, the pedophile e-mail stalkers and teenage-boobs Web sites—here comes this new swamp-thing mass entertainment: the Internet "Flash cartoon," pared down to pure shock value. Its music and animation are tuned to the Teletubbies set—that's its "joke." Its faux warning, "Cartoon Violence: Not for Small Children or Big Babies" is pure come-on—for those who can read. And it's easy to watch over and over again, reinforcing its empathy-dulling impact. That makes it particularly harmful to young psyches, UCLA neuroscientist Marco Iacoboni told me, because children are prompted to copy what they see—especially what they see over and over again. "Not only do you get exposed and desensitized; you're primed, facilitated, almost invited to act that way," maintains Iacoboni, whose expertise in the brain dynamics of imitation makes him an outspoken critic of media mayhem.

6      "Happy Tree Friends" appears tailor-made to sneak under the radar of blocking software (which can't filter images), unless parents are somehow Internet-savvy enough to know about the site and specifically ban it in advance. And it's certainly suited for the kind of viral contagion that caught up with my 6-year-old, who learned of the site from his 9-year-old brother, who first saw it over the shoulder of a teenage summer camp counselor.

7      But the bottom line is, well, the bottom line. In its web-cartoon class, "Happy Tree Friends" is a humongous moneymaker, as irresistible to big advertisers as it is to 6-year-olds. At last count, the site was drawing 15 million unique viewers a month, reaping $300,000 or more in ads for each new episode. It recently snagged a place on cable TV, while spawning DVDs, trademark mints, T-shirts and, inevitably, a planned video game.

8      Internet cartoons had their defining moment with the hilarious "This Land Is Your Land" 2004 election-year parody, featuring George W. Bush calling John Kerry a "liberal wiener" and Kerry calling Bush a "right-wing nut job" to the famous Woody Guthrie tune. By then, the beaten-down Web ad industry was already starting to ride a dramatic recovery, thanks to burgeoning new content and the increasing prevalence of high-quality, high-speed connections. The trend has brought some truly interesting material—and also such savage fare as the graphic cartoon "Gonads & Strife" and another inviting you to repeatedly electrocute a gerbil in a light socket. The Bush-Kerry feature by some reports was the most popular cartoon ever. "Happy Tree Friends," now in its fifth, most successful, year [2005] may well be the most lucrative.

9      Its narrative is as primitive as its business plan. In every episode, the cute creatures are introduced, after which something awful happens to them, either by gruesome accident, or at the paws of the psychopathic bear. The wordless content appeals to a global audience, enhancing an already remarkably efficient delivery system for advertising. There's a running ad before each episode, while banners flash below and beside the cartoons.

The show itself reportedly began as a potential ad—ironically, *against* 10 media violence according to Kenn Navarro, its co-creator. Navarro came up with the idea while designing an eight-second spot for an educational company, to illustrate what kids *shouldn't* be watching. Indeed, 30 years of extensive research underscores the link between TV violence and increased violent behavior among viewers. One study equates the impact as larger than that of asbestos exposure to cancer—a health risk that certainly moved our society to act. But try telling that to "Happy Tree Friends" Executive Producer John Evershed, CEO of Mondo Media in San Francisco.

Evershed, the father of three children, the youngest aged 2, told me during a phone conversation that he wouldn't let them watch "Happy Tree Friends." But then he argued that the cartoon wasn't really harmful. "It's like 'Tom & Jerry,'" he said. "I grew up on 'Tom & Jerry,' and I don't think I'm particularly aggressive." 11

Aggressive? AGGRESSIVE? Much as I'd like to, I can't fairly speak for 12 Evershed on this point, but I certainly do worry about the impact on my children. As for "Tom & Jerry," I know "Tom & Jerry," and this is no "Tom & Jerry." "Tom & Jerry" never pulled knives or tore heads off or used someone's intestines to strangle a third party, just for starters.

"Tom & Jerry" also had creativity, with surprising plot twists and a richly 13 emotive score. Most importantly, "Tom & Jerry" had a conscience. Routinely, Tom attacks Jerry and is punished for his aggression. In terms of human evolution, the 1940s classic is light-years ahead of "Happy Tree Friends," whose authors, Navarro and Rhode Montijo, have been quoted as saying, "If we are in a room brainstorming episodes and end up laughing at the death scene, then it's all good!"

Mad as I am, I'm actually not suggesting that the feds step in and ban this 14 cartoon. The basic freedom of the Internet is too precious, and government censorship too risky and probably not even feasible. The current rules—restrictions on the major airwaves, but anything goes on the Web—will have to do.

But what about the big mainstream advertisers who've made "Happy Tree 15 Friends" such a wild success? I was startled, while watching the cartoon, to see banner ads for companies including Toyota and Kaiser Permanente (which has a new campaign they call "Thrive." Thrive, indeed!). Consumers ought to be able to raise a stink, threaten a reputation, even wage boycotts in the face of such irresponsibility. But many Internet ads enjoy the escape clause of being random and ephemeral, as I found out when I called Hilary Weber, Kaiser's San Francisco–based head of Internet marketing. Weber said she couldn't even confirm that her company's ad had appeared.

"I can't replicate it," she said, adding that it would "take a lot of research" 16 to establish whether Kaiser indeed had purchased such an ad. That, she explained, is because Kaiser, like many other big corporations, buys bulk ads through third parties—saving money, yet relinquishing control over where the ads end up.

Weber said she was concerned about Kaiser's reputation and planned to 17 investigate further, yet declined to tell me the names of the third-party companies placing the firm's ads. So I then turned to Mika Salmi, CEO of Atom Shockwave, which manages the ads on "Happy Tree Friends." Salmi, on his cell phone, said he couldn't, with confidence, name the third-party companies with whom he contracts, though he thought one "might" be *Advertising. com*. But when I contacted Lisa Jacobson, *Advertising.com*'s spokeswoman, she declined to name advertisers not already listed on her firm's Web page. "We actually don't think we're the best fit for this piece," Jacobson wrote me by e-mail. "You'll probably need to speak with companies like Kaiser and Toyota directly. But thanks for thinking of us . . ."

18    In our brief telephone conversation, Evershed told me he thinks parents have the ultimate responsibility to shield their kids from media violence. In the abstract, I certainly agree with that, but I admit I sometimes wonder if I'm actually doing my kids a disservice by spending so much time and energy chasing them off the Internet, while coaching them in empathy, manners and the Golden Rule. Because if most of their peers, who lack the luxury of moms with time to meddle, are gorging on "Happy Tree Friends," it would probably serve them better to be trained to defend themselves with firearms and karate.

19    Still, for now at least, I refuse to be overwhelmed by the sheer magnitude of what society expects from parents, with so little support in return.

20    So I'd like to offer just two public suggestions. Why can't summer camps and afterschool programs more closely supervise Internet use? And why can't Kaiser and other big companies start crafting contracts that specifically stipulate that their ads never, ever end up on sites like "Happy Tree Friends"?

21    Meanwhile, I'm talking to other parents because the first step in this peaceful war is to realize we're not alone. Together, we may even manage to subvert our culture's embrace of shock for shock's sake, one gory excess at a time.

Source: From *The Washington Post*, October 23, 2005. Reprinted by permission of the author.

## QUESTIONS FOR READING

1. "Happy Tree Friends" is Ellison's primary example; what is her subject?
2. What is the problem with "Happy Tree Friends"? How does it differ from "Tom & Jerry"?
3. How did the author's 6-year-old discover the cartoon?
4. What did the author's research reveal about the website's advertisers?
5. What suggestions for change does Ellison propose?

## QUESTIONS FOR REASONING AND ANALYSIS

6. What does Ellison *not* want to happen to the Internet? Why?
7. What is her claim?
8. In paragraph 18, Ellison writes that her sons might be better off with "firearms and karate" than encouragement in empathy and the Golden Rule. Does she really mean this? Why does she write it?

9. Do you think that Ellison's suggestions will be helpful? Why or why not?

10. Should there be federal controls on Internet content? Why or why not?

11. If there are no controls, how will we protect youngsters from unhealthy sites? Or, should we not worry about protecting them? Explain and defend your position.

# IN YOUR FACE . . . ALL OVER THE PLACE! | JEAN KILBOURNE

Writer, speaker, and filmmaker, Jean Kilbourne has also served as adviser on alcohol and tobacco advertising to two surgeons general. Her book *Deadly Persuasion*—from which the following excerpt comes—was republished in 2000 as *Can't Buy My Love.* Kilbourne's latest documentary film, *Killing Us Softly 4: Advertising's Image of Women* (2010), continues her commitment to teach media literacy and focus on advertising's damaging images of women.

PREREADING QUESTIONS We know that TV shows are filled with stereotypes; what about advertising? Think about print or TV ads. What kinds of stereotypes come to mind?

In spite of the fact that we are surrounded by more advertising than ever before, most of us still ridicule the idea that we might be personally influenced by it. The ridicule is often extremely simplistic. The argument essentially is, "I'm no robot marching down to the store to do advertising's bidding and therefore advertising doesn't affect me at all." This argument was made by Jacob Sullum, a senior editor at *Reason* magazine, in an editorial in the *New York Times.* Writing about "heroin chic," the advertising fad in the mid-1990s of using models who looked like heroin addicts, Sullum says, "Like you, I've seen . . . ads featuring sallow, sullen, scrawny youths. Not once have I had an overwhelming urge to rush out and buy some heroin." He concludes from this in-depth research that all critics of advertising are portraying "people not as independent moral agents but as mindless automatons," as if there were no middle ground between rushing out to buy heroin and being completely uninfluenced by the media images that surround us—or no possibility that disaffected teens are more vulnerable than middle-aged executives. After all, Sullum is *not* the target audience for heroin chic ads.

Of course, most of us feel far superior to the kind of person who would be affected by advertising. *We* are not influenced, after all. We are skeptical, even cynical . . . but ignorant (certainly not stupid, just uninformed). Advertising is familiar, but not known. The fact that we are surrounded by it, that we can sing the jingles and identify the models and recognize the logos, doesn't mean that we are educated about it, that we understand it. As Sut Jhally says, "To not be influenced by advertising would be to live outside of culture. No human being lives outside of culture."

Advertisers want us to believe that we are not influenced by ads. As Joseph Goebbels said, "This is the secret of propaganda: Those who are to be persuaded by it should be completely immersed in the ideas of the propaganda, without ever noticing that they are being immersed in it." So the advertisers sometimes play upon our cynicism. In fact, they co-opt our cynicism and our irony just as they have co-opted our rock music, our revolutions and movements for liberation, and our concern for the environment. In a current trend that I call "anti-advertising," the advertisers flatter us by insinuating that we are far too smart to be taken in by advertising. Many of these ads spoof the whole notion of image advertising. A scotch ad tells the reader "This is a glass of Cutty Sark. If you need to see a picture of a guy in an Armani suit sitting between two fashion models drinking it before you know it's right for you, it probably isn't."

4    And an ad for shoes says, "If you feel the need to be smarter and more articulate, read the complete works of Shakespeare. If you like who you are, here are your shoes." Another shoe ad, this one for sneakers, says, "Shoe buying rule number one: The image wears off after the first six miles." What a concept. By buying heavily advertised products, we can demonstrate that we are not influenced by advertising. Of course, this is not entirely new. Volkswagens were introduced in the 1960s with an anti-advertising campaign, such as the ad that pictured the car and the headline "Lemon." But such ads go a lot further these days, especially the foreign ones. A British ad for Easy jeans says, "We don't use sex to sell our jeans. We don't even screw you when you buy them." And French Connection UK gets away with a double-page spread that says "fcuk advertising."

5    Cynicism is one of the worst effects of advertising. Cynicism learned from years of being exposed to marketing hype and products that never deliver the promised goods often carries over to other aspects of life. This starts early: A study of children done by researchers at Columbia University in 1975 found that heavy viewing of advertising led to cynicism, not only about advertising, but about life in general. The researchers found that "in most cultures, adolescents have had to deal with social hypocrisy and even with institutionalized lying. But today, TV advertising is stimulating *preadolescent* children to think about socially accepted hypocrisy. They may be too young to cope with such thoughts without permanently distorting their views of morality, society, and business." They concluded that "7- to 10-year-olds are strained by the very existence of advertising directed to them." These jaded children become the young people whose mantra is "whatever," who admire people like David Letterman (who has made a career out of taking nothing seriously), whose response to almost every experience is "been there, done that," "duh," and "do ya think?" Cynicism is not criticism. It is a lot easier than criticism. In fact, easy cynicism is a kind of naivete. We need to be more critical as a culture and less cynical.

6    Cynicism deeply affects how we define our problems and envision their solutions. Many people exposed to massive doses of advertising both distrust every possible solution *and* expect a quick fix. There are no quick fixes to the problems our society faces today, but there are solutions to many of them. The first step, as always, is breaking through denial and facing the problems

squarely. I believe it was James Baldwin who said, "Not everything that is faced can be changed, but nothing can be changed until it is faced." One of the things we need to face is that we and our children are indeed influenced by advertising.

Although some people, especially advertisers, continue to argue that advertising simply reflects the society, advertising does a great deal more than simply reflect cultural attitudes and values. Even some advertisers admit to this: Rance Crain of *Advertising Age* said great advertising "plays the tune rather than just dancing to the tune." Far from being a passive mirror of society, advertising is an effective and pervasive medium of influence and persuasion, and its influence is cumulative, often subtle, and primarily unconscious. Advertising performs much the same function in industrial society as myth performed in ancient and primitive societies. It is both a creator and perpetuator of the dominant attitudes, values and ideology of the culture, the social norms and myths by which most people govern their behavior. At the very least, advertising helps to create a climate in which certain attitudes and values flourish and others are not reflected at all.

Advertising is not only our physical environment, it is increasingly our spiritual environment as well. By definition, however, it is only interested in materialistic values. When spiritual values or religious images show up in ads, it is only to appropriate them in order to sell us something. Sometimes this is very obvious. Eternity is a perfume by Calvin Klein. Infiniti is an automobile and Hydra Zen a moisturizer. Jesus is a brand of jeans. "See the light," says an ad for wool, while a face powder ad promises "an enlightening experience and absolute heaven." One car is "born again" and another promises to "energize your soul." In a full-page ad in *Advertising Age,* the online service Yahoo! proclaims, "We've got 60 million followers. That's more than some religions," but goes on to assure readers, "Don't worry. We're *not* a religion." When Pope John Paul II visited Mexico City in the winter of 1999, he could have seen a smiling image of himself on bags of Sabritas, a popular brand of potato chips, or a giant street sign showing him bowing piously next to a Pepsi logo with a phrase in Spanish that reads, "Mexico Always Faithful." In the United States, he could have treated himself to pope-on-a-rope soap.

But advertising's co-optation of spirituality goes much deeper than this. It is commonplace these days to observe that consumerism has become the religion of our time (with advertising its holy text), but the criticism usually stops short of what is most important, what is at the heart of the comparison. Advertising and religion share a belief in transformation and transcendence, but most religions believe that this requires work and sacrifice. In the world of advertising, enlightenment is achieved instantly by purchasing material goods. As James Twitchell, author of *Adcult USA,* says, "The Jolly Green Giant, the Michelin Man, the Man from Glad, Mother Nature, Aunt Jemima, Speedy AlkaSeltzer, the White Knight, and all their otherworldly kin are descendants of the earlier gods. What separates them is that they now reside in manufactured products and that, although earlier gods were invoked by fasting, prayer, rituals, and penance, the promise of purchase calls forth their modern ilk."

10     Advertising constantly promotes the core belief of American culture: that we *can* re-create ourselves, transform ourselves, transcend our circumstances—but with a twist. For generations Americans believed this could be achieved if we worked hard enough, like Horatio Alger. Today the promise is that we can change our lives instantly, effortlessly—by winning the lottery, selecting the right mutual fund, having a fashion makeover, losing weight, having tighter abs, buying the right car or soft drink. It is this belief that such transformation is possible that drives us to keep dieting, to buy more stuff, to read fashion magazines that give us the same information over and over again. Cindy Crawford's makeup is carefully described as if it could transform us into her. On one level, we know it won't—after all, most of us have tried this approach many times before. But on another level, we continue to try, continue to believe that this time it will be different. This American belief that we can transform ourselves makes advertising images much more powerful than they otherwise would be.

11     The focus of the transformation has shifted from the soul to the body. Of course, this trivializes and cheapens authentic spirituality and transcendence. But, more important, this junk food for the soul leaves us hungry, empty, malnourished. The emphasis on instant salvation is parodied in an ad from *Adbusters* for a product called Mammon, in which a man says, "I need a belief system that serves my needs right away." The copy continues, "Dean Sachs has a mortgage, a family and an extremely demanding job. What he doesn't need is a religion that complicates his life with unreasonable ethical demands." The ad ends with the words, "Mammon: Because you deserve to enjoy life—guilt free."

12     As advertising becomes more and more absurd, however, it becomes increasingly difficult to parody ads. There's not much of a difference between the ad for Mammon and the real ad for cruises that says "It can take several lifetimes to reach a state of inner peace and tranquillity. Or, it can take a couple of weeks." Of course, we know that a couple of weeks on a cruise won't solve our problems, won't bring us to a state of peace and enlightenment, but it is so tempting to believe that there is some easy way to get there, some ticket we can buy.

13     To be one of the "elect" in today's society is to have enough money to buy luxury goods. Of course, when salvation comes via the sale, it becomes important to display these goods. Owning a Rolex would not impress anyone who didn't know how expensive it is. A Rolex ad itself says the watch was voted "most likely to be coveted." Indeed, one of advertising's purposes is to create an aura for a product, so that other people will be impressed. As one marketer said recently in *Advertising Age*, "It's no fun to spend $100 on athletic shoes to wear to high school if your friends don't know how cool your shoes are."

14     Thus the influence of advertising goes way beyond the target audience and includes those who could never afford the product, who will simply be envious and impressed—perhaps to the point of killing someone for his sneakers or jacket, as has sometimes happened in our poverty-stricken neighborhoods. In the early 1990s the city health commissioner in Philadelphia issued a

Environmentally friendly plastic bags are a beautiful thing. Ecoflex, one of the latest breakthroughs from BASF, is a biodegradable plastic that can be used in bags and packaging. It© shelf stable for one full year, then completely decomposes in compost within a few weeks. Innovation is popping up everywhere. Learn more at basf.com/stories

Helping Make Products Better

□ ▪ BASF
The Chemical Company

public health warning cautioning youths against wearing expensive leather jackets and jewelry, while in Milwaukee billboards depicted a chalk outline of a body and the warning, "Dress Smart and Stay Alive." Poor children in many countries knot the laces of their Nikes around their ankles to avoid having them stolen while they sleep.

15      Many teens fantasize that objects will somehow transform their lives, give them social standing and respect. When they wear a certain brand of sneaker

**Your business side. Your creative side.
Inspire both. Introducing Avid's new editing lineup.**

Quality, performance and value. A new way of thinking. A new way of doing business.
Take a closer look at **Avid.com/NewThinkingScript.**

or jacket, they feel, "This is important, therefore I am important." The brand gives instant status. No wonder they are willing, even eager, to spend money for clothes that advertise the brands. A *USA Today*–CNN–Gallup Poll found that 61 percent of boys and 44 percent of girls considered brand names on clothes "very important" or "somewhat important." As ten-year-old Darion Sawyer from Baltimore said, "People will tease you and talk about you, say you got on no-name shoes or say you shop at Kmart." Leydiana Reyes, an eighth-grader in Brooklyn, said, "My father always tells me I could buy two pairs of jeans for what you pay for Calvin Klein. I know that. But I still want Calvin Klein." And Danny Shirley, a fourteen-year-old in Santa Fe decked out in Tommy Hilfiger regalia, said, "Kids who wear Levi's don't really care about what they wear, I guess."

16    In the beginning, these labels were somewhat discreet. Today we see sweatshirts with fifteen-inch "Polo" logos stamped across the chest, jeans with four-inch "Calvin Klein" labels stitched on them, and a jacket with "Tommy Hilfiger" in five-inch letters across the back. Some of these outfits are so close to sandwich boards that I'm surprised people aren't paid to wear them. Before too long, the logo-free product probably will be the expensive rarity.

17    What people who wear these clothes are really buying isn't a garment, of course, but an *image*. And increasingly, an image is all that advertising has to sell. Advertising began centuries ago with signs in medieval villages. In the nineteenth century, it became more common but was still essentially designed to give people information about manufactured goods and services. Since the 1920s, advertising has provided less information about the product and focused more on the lives, especially the emotional lives, of the prospective consumers. This shift coincided, of course, with the increasing knowledge and acceptability of psychology, as well as the success of propaganda used to convince the population to support World War I.

18    Industrialization gave rise to the burgeoning ability of businesses to mass-produce goods. Since it was no longer certain there would be a market for the goods, it became necessary not just to mass-produce the goods but to mass-produce markets hungry for the goods. The problem became not too little candy produced but not enough candy consumed, so it became the job of the advertisers to *produce consumers*. This led to an increased use of psychological research and emotional ploys to sell products. Consumer behavior became recognized as a science in the late 1940s.

19    As luxury goods, prepared foods, and nonessential items have proliferated, it has become crucial to create artificial needs in order to sell unnecessary products. Was there such a thing as static cling before there were fabric softeners and sprays? An ad for a "lip renewal cream" says, "I never thought of my lips as a problem area until Andrea came up with the solution."

20    Most brands in a given category are essentially the same. Most shampoos are made by two or three manufacturers. Blindfolded smokers or beer-drinkers can rarely identify what brand they are smoking or drinking, including their own. Whether we know it or not, we select products primarily because of the image reflected in their advertising. Very few ads give us any real information

at all. Sometimes it is impossible to tell what is being advertised. "This is an ad for the hair dryer," says one ad, featuring a woman lounging on a sofa. If we weren't told, we would never know. A joke made the rounds a while ago about a little boy who wanted a box of tampons so that he could effortlessly ride bicycles and horses, ski, and swim.

*WTF*

Almost all tobacco and alcohol ads are entirely image-based. Of course, 21 when you're selling a product that kills people, it's difficult to give honest information about it. Think of all the cigarette ads that never show cigarettes or even a wisp of smoke. One of the most striking examples of image advertising is the very successful and long-running campaign for Absolut vodka. This campaign focuses on the shape of the bottle and the word "Absolut," as in "Absolut Perfection," which features the bottle with a halo. This campaign has been so successful that a coffee-table book collection of the ads published just in time for Christmas, the perfect gift for the alcoholic in your family, sold over 150,000 copies. Collecting Absolut ads is now a common pastime for elementary-school children, who swap them like baseball cards.

*hasty generalization*

How does all this affect us? It is very difficult to do objective research 22 about advertising's influence because there are no comparison groups, almost no people who have not been exposed to massive doses of advertising. In addition, research that measures only one point in time does not adequately capture advertising's real effects. We need longitudinal studies, such as George Gerbner's twenty-five-year study of violence on television.

*irrelevant*

The advertising industry itself can't prove that advertising works. While 23 claiming to its clients that it does, it simultaneously denies it to the Federal Trade Commission whenever the subject of alcohol and tobacco advertising comes up. As an editorial in *Advertising Age* once said, "A strange world it is, in which people spending millions on advertising must do their best to prove that advertising doesn't do very much!" According to Bob Wehling, senior vice-president of marketing at Procter & Gamble, "We don't have a lot of scientific studies to support our belief that advertising works. But we have seen that the power of advertising makes a significant difference."

What research can most easily prove is usually what is least important, 24 such as advertising's influence on our choice of brands. This is the most obvious, but least significant, way that advertising affects us. There are countless examples of successful advertising campaigns, such as the Absolut campaign, that have sent sales soaring. A commercial for I Can't Believe It's Not Butter featuring a sculptress whose work comes alive in the form of romance-novel hunk Fabio boosted sales about 17 percent. Tamagotchis—virtual pets in an egg—were introduced in the United States with a massive advertising campaign and earned $150 million in seven months. And Gardenburger, a veggie patty, ran a thirty-second spot during the final episode of *Seinfeld* and, within a week, sold over $2 million worth, a market share jump of 50 percent and more than the entire category sold in the same week the previous year. But advertising is more of an art than a science, and campaigns often fail. In 1998 a Miller beer campaign bombed, costing the company millions of dollars and offending a large segment of their customers. The 1989 Nissan Infiniti campaign, known as the "Rocks and Trees" campaign, was the first ever to introduce a car without showing it and immediately became a target for Jay Leno's monologues. And, of course, the Edsel, a car introduced by Ford with great fanfare in 1957, remains a universal symbol of failure.

25    The unintended effects of advertising are far more important and far more difficult to measure than those effects that are intended. The important question is not "Does this ad sell the product?" but rather "What else does this ad sell?" An ad for Gap khakis featuring a group of acrobatic swing dancers probably sold a lot of pants, which, of course, was the intention of the advertisers. But it also contributed to a rage for swing dancing. This is an innocuous example of advertising's powerful unintended effects. Swing dancing is not binge drinking, after all.

26    Advertising often sells a great deal more than products. It sells values, images, and concepts of love and sexuality, romance, success, and, perhaps most important, normalcy. To a great extent, it tells us who we are and who we should be. We are increasingly using brand names to create our identities. James Twitchell argues that the label of our shirt, the make of our car, and our favorite laundry detergent are filling the vacuum once occupied by religion, education, and our family name.

27    Even more important, advertising corrupts our language and thus influences our ability to think clearly. Critic and novelist George Steiner once talked with an interviewer about what he called "anti-language, that which is transcendentally annihilating of truth and meaning." Novelist Jonathan Dee, applying this concept to advertising, writes that "the harm lies not in the ad itself; the harm is in the exchange, in the collision of ad language, ad imagery, with other sorts of language that contend with it in the public realm. When Apple reprints an old photo of Gandhi, or Heineken ends its ads with the words 'Seek the Truth,' or Winston suggests that we buy cigarettes by proposing (just under the surgeon general's warning) that 'You have to appreciate authenticity in all its forms,' or Kellogg's identifies itself with the message 'Simple is Good,' these occasions color our contact with those words and images in their other, possibly less promotional applications." The real violence of advertising, Dee concludes, is that "words can be made to mean anything, which is hard to distinguish from the idea that words mean nothing." We see the consequences of this in much of our culture, from "art" to politics, that has no content, no connection between language and conviction. Just as it is often difficult to tell what product an ad is selling, so is it difficult to determine what a politician's beliefs are (the "vision thing," as George Bush so aptly called it, albeit unintentionally) or what the subject is of a film or song or work of art. As Dee says, "The men and women who make ads are not hucksters; they are artists with nothing to say, and they have found their form." Unfortunately, their form deeply influences all the other forms of the culture. We end up expecting nothing more.

28    This has terrible consequences for our culture. As Richard Pollay says, "Without a reliance on words and a faith in truth, we lack the mortar for social cohesion. Without trustworthy communication, there is no communion, no

community, only an aggregation of increasingly isolated individuals, alone in the mass."

Advertising creates a worldview that is based upon cynicism, dissatisfaction, [29] and craving. The advertisers aren't evil. They are just doing their job, which is to sell a product, but the consequences, usually unintended, are often destructive to individuals, to cultures, and to the planet. In the history of the world, there has never been a propaganda effort to match that of advertising in the twentieth century. More thought, more effort, and more money go into advertising than has gone into any other campaign to change social consciousness. The story that advertising tells is that the way to be happy, to find satisfaction—and the path to political freedom, as well—is through the consumption of material objects. And the major motivating force for social change throughout the world today is this belief that happiness comes from the market.

So, advertising has a greater impact on all of us than we generally realize. [30] The primary purpose of the mass media is to deliver us to advertisers. Much of the information that we need from the media in order to make informed choices in our lives is distorted or deleted on behalf of corporate sponsors. Advertising is an increasingly ubiquitous presence in our lives, and it sells much more than products. We delude ourselves when we say we are not influenced by advertising. And we trivialize and ignore its growing significance at our peril.

## NOTES

1. "This argument was made by Jacob Sullum": Sullum, 1997, A31.
2. "As Sut Jhally says": Jhally, 1998.
3. "As Joseph Goebbels": Goebbels, 1933, March 28. Quoted in Jacobson and Mazur, 1995, 15.
4. "A study of children done by researchers at Columbia University": Bever, Smith, Bengen, and Johnson, 1975, 119.
5. "'7- to 10-year-olds are strained'": Bever, Smith, Bengen, and Johnson, 1975, 120.
6. "Rance Crain of *Advertising Age*": Crain, 1999, 23.
7. "When Pope John Paul II": Chacon and Ribadeneria, 1999, A8.
8. "'The Jolly Green Giant'": Twitchell, 1996, 30.
9. "'It's no fun to spend $100 on athletic shoes'": Peppers and Rogers, 1997, 32.
10. "the city health commissioner in Philadelphia": Worthington, 1992, 15.
11. "A *USA Today*–CNN–Gallup Poll": Jacobson and Mazur, 1995, 26.
12. "Leydiana Reyes": Leonhardt, 1997, 65.
13. "Danny Shirley": Espen, 1999, 59.
14. "sweatshirts with fifteen-inch 'Polo' logos": Ryan, 1996, D1.
15. "Consumer behavior": Woods, 1995.
16. "Most shampoos": Twitchell, 1996, 252.
17. "Blindfolded smokers": Twitchell, 1996, 125.
18. "'A strange world it is'": Bernstein, 1978, August 7.
19. "According to Bob Wehling": Crain, 1998, 24.

20. "A commercial for I Can't Believe It's Not Butter": Haran, 1996, 12.
21. "Tamagotchis": Goldner, 1998, S43.
22. "And Gardenburger": Gardenburger hits the spot, 1998, 17.
23. "In 1998 a Miller beer campaign": Crain, 1998, 24.
24. "The 1989 Nissan Infiniti": Horton, 1996, S28.
25. "the Edsel": Horton, 1996, S30.
26. "An ad for Gap khakis": Cortissoz, 1998, A10.
27. "James Twitchell argues": University of Florida news release, quoted by Orlando, 1999, *http://www.sciencedaily.com/releases/1999/05/9905181 14815.htm.*
28. "Critic and novelist George Steiner": Dee, 1999, 65–66.
29. "As Richard Pollay": Pollay, 1986.
30. "there has never been a propaganda effort": Jhally, 1998.

---

## QUESTIONS FOR READING

1. What is Kilbourne's subject? (Be more precise than just "advertising.")
2. How is advertising like propaganda?
3. What is the nature of the "anti-advertising" ad? What is one of the consequences of anti-advertising?
4. What role does advertising play in our society? How does it promote "the core belief of American culture"? How is its message different from what that core belief used to emphasize?
5. How does advertising go beyond the target audience? How do we want others to react to what we have purchased? What are we purchasing with designer-labeled clothing?
6. In the second half of the twentieth century, what became advertising's purpose or task? How did this purpose change ads?
7. How does advertising affect language?

## QUESTIONS FOR REASONING AND ANALYSIS

8. What is Kilbourne's claim? What *type* of argument is this—that is, what does it seek to accomplish?
9. Kilbourne provides a brief history of advertising. What does she accomplish by including this in her discussion?
10. List the effects of advertising discussed by Kilbourne. How does her discussion of effects support her claim? What evidence does the author provide throughout her analysis?
11. The author points out that it is difficult to study the effects of ads. Why is it difficult? Why does she include these comments in her argument?

12. Evaluate Kilbourne's argument. Does she convince you? If not, what would you need to be convinced?

13. Do you find considerable cynicism today? If so, have you ever connected it to the endless distortions created by ads? If not, does this seem like a reasonable causal connection to you now?

14. Should advertising be banned from children's TV programs? Why or why not?

## COPYRIGHT SILLINESS ON CAMPUS | FRED VON LOHMANN

A graduate of Stanford University and Stanford Law School, Fred von Lohmann is a senior staff attorney with the Electronic Frontier Foundation. Widely recognized as one of the leading intellectual property lawyers, von Lohmann has published opinion pieces in many periodicals and has frequently appeared on television to explain or debate legal issues related to intellectual property. In his essay in the *Washington Post* (June 6, 2007), he addresses issues of student file-sharing.

PREREADING QUESTIONS  Have you participated in music or film file-sharing? If so, did you pay for a service such as Napster?

1   What do Columbia, Vanderbilt, Duke, Howard and UCLA have in common? Apparently, leaders in Congress think that they aren't expelling enough students for illegally swapping music and movies.

2   The House committees responsible for copyright and education wrote a joint letter May 1 scolding the presidents of 19 major American universities, demanding that each school respond to a six-page questionnaire detailing steps it has taken to curtail illegal music and movie file-sharing on campus. One of the questions—"Does your institution expel violating students?"—shows just how out-of-control the futile battle against campus downloading has become.

3   As universities are pressured to punish students and install expensive "filtering" technologies to monitor their computer networks, the entertainment industry has ramped up its student shakedown campaign. The Recording Industry Association of America has targeted more than 1,600 individual students in the past four months, demanding that each pay $3,000 for file-sharing transgressions or face a federal lawsuit. In total, the music and movie industries have brought more than 20,000 federal lawsuits against individual Americans in the past three years.

4   History is sure to judge harshly everyone responsible for this absurd state of affairs. Our universities have far better things to spend money on than bullying students. Artists deserve to be fairly compensated, but are we really prepared to sue and expel every college student who has made an illegal copy? No one who takes privacy and civil liberties seriously can believe that the installation of surveillance technologies on university computer networks is a sensible solution.

5   It's not an effective solution, either. Short of appointing a copyright hall monitor for every dorm room, there is no way digital copying will be meaningfully reduced. Technical efforts to block file-sharing will be met with clever counter measures from sharp computer science majors. Even if students were completely cut off from the Internet, they would continue to copy CDs, swap hard drives and pool their laptops.

6   Already, a hard drive capable of storing more than 80,000 songs can be had for $100. Blank DVDs, each capable of holding more than a first generation iPod, now sell for a quarter apiece. Students are going to copy what they want, when they want, from whom they want.

7   So universities can't stop file-sharing. But they can still help artists get paid for it. How? By putting some cash on the bar.

8   Universities already pay blanket fees so that student a cappella groups can perform on campus, and they also pay for cable TV subscriptions and site licenses for software. By the same token, they could collect a reasonable amount from their students for "all you can eat" downloading.

9   The recording industry is already willing to offer unlimited downloads with subscription plans for $10 to $15 per month through services such as Napster and Rhapsody. But these services have been a failure on campuses, for a number of reasons, including these: They don't work with the iPod, they cause downloaded music to "expire" after students leave the school, and they don't include all the music students want.

10   The only solution is a blanket license that permits students to get unrestricted music and movies from sources of their choosing.

11   At its heart, this is a fight about money, not about morality. We should have the universities collect the cash, pay it to the entertainment industry and let the students do what they are going to do anyway. In exchange, the entertainment industry should call off the lawyers and lobbyists, leaving our nation's universities to focus on the real challenges facing America's next generation of leaders.

Source: From *The Washington Post*, June 6, 2007. Reprinted by permission of the author.

## QUESTIONS FOR READING

1.   What do some members of Congress want universities to do to control file-sharing among students?
2.   What organization is bringing lawsuits against students for illegal file-sharing of music?
3.   On what basis does the author reject the expelling of students?
4.   What solution does von Lohmann recommend?

## QUESTIONS FOR REASONING AND ANALYSIS

5.   What is the author's claim? State it as a claim for a problem/solution argument.

6. List the specific grounds in defense of his claim. What assumption, stated by von Lohmann, underpins the solutions presented by each side in this quarrel? What does he gain by spelling out the "heart" of the conflict between the artists and the file-sharers?

7. Examine von Lohmann's style. How effective are his title and opening paragraph in getting reader interest? Why?

### QUESTIONS FOR REFLECTION AND WRITING

8. Do you agree with the author that stopping file-sharing among students is futile? Is this issue like Prohibition—a law that cannot be enforced? Explain.

9. Students who break the law are expelled from universities. Why shouldn't they be expelled for breaking the law against stealing an artist's intellectual property?

10. Should part of the student activities fee go to pay for unlimited file-sharing so that recording artists are paid for their work? Why or why not?

## *THE SOCIAL NETWORK'S* FEMALE PROPS | REBECCA DAVIS O'BRIEN

As a student at Harvard, Rebecca Davis O'Brien lived in Kirkland House at the same time as Mark Zuckerberg. She was an associate managing editor and columnist at the *Harvard Crimson* while there, and is now a writer based in New York City, with articles published in the *New York Times*, *Forbes.com*, and *The Daily Beast* blog. *The King's English*, a memoir of her two years of work at a Jordan school, is scheduled for publication in 2011. Her analysis of the movie was published in *The Daily Beast* on October 3, 2010.

PREREADING QUESTIONS  Based on O'Brien's title, what do you expect to read about in her blog? What does the term *props* suggest to you? Have you seen the film? If not, you will need to do that in order to understand and respond to O'Brien's analysis.

By the time Aaron Sorkin and David Fincher's *The Social Network* opened 1 Friday, smitten reviewers and pundits had already proclaimed the film as the second coming of *Citizen Kane*, extolling Facebook founder Mark Zuckerberg, director Fincher, and writer Sorkin as modern prophets. This movie, we've been told, not only reflects its era, but will shape it.

Amid the frenzy, Stephen Colbert asked what few had observed: What 2 about "the ladies in the film"? in his interview with Sorkin on Sept. 30 [2010], Colbert mentioned Erica, Zuckerberg's "super smart" (ex-)girlfriend, played by Rooney Mara, then said, mischievously: "The other ladies in the movie don't have as much to say, because they're high or drunk or [bleep]ing some guys in the bathroom. Why are there no other women of any substance in the movie?

A scene from *The Social Network*.

3    "That's a fair question," Sorkin replied, pointing out the "one other woman," the young lawyer played by Rashida Jones. "The other women are prizes, basically," Sorkin said, later adding: "The women in this particular story who are prizes, it really doesn't speak to the entire female population of Harvard, this is just the people who are populating this story."

4    It's hard not to enjoy *The Social Network*. It is an impressive film: crisp, beautiful, kinetic, with humor as dark as its lighting.

5    But Colbert was right. Women in the movie—apart from the lawyer and Erica, who sets the stage and disappears—are less prizes than they are props, buxom extras literally bussed in to fill the roles of doting groupies, vengeful sluts, or dumpy, feminist killjoys. They are foils for the male characters, who in turn are cruel or indifferent to them. (In a somewhat ironic turn of events, former Harvard President Larry Summers is perhaps the only man in the movie portrayed both as solicitous and respectful of a woman's opinion.)

6    Complaining about misogyny in modern blockbuster cinema is about as productive as lamenting Facebook's grip on our society. But what is the state of things if a film that keeps women on the outer circles of male innovation enjoys such critical acclaim; indeed, is heralded as the "defining" story of our age? What are we to do with a great film that makes women look so awful?

7    "It seemed to me that women in this film are mostly liabilities," said Anna Holmes, a writer and founding editor of the women's website *Jezebel*. "They cause problems for the men."

8    "It's a man's world sort of movie," Holmes told me Friday. "There's a certain pacing to it, an excitement about money, the male relationships with one another. I also think it reflects the way a lot of young men regard females."

9    As I watched the film, I found myself laughing out loud at the women. From the girls trucked into the Phoenix Club in the film's opening scenes to the groupies giggling about their inability to play videogames, it seemed that the film set girls up as some joke on the state of womankind. Maybe the joke was on me?

10   *The Social Network* lampoons Asian women, in particular. We first meet Brenda Song's character, Harvard co-ed Christy, when she throws her cleavage

at newly successful (and, ohmigod, final club member!) Eduardo Saverin. A few minutes later, she's giving him oral sex in a public restroom. Afterward, Christy and her friend sit uselessly on a couch while the men plot the expansion of Facebook. This isn't the only time in the movie when two girls are drunk and irrelevant on a peripheral sofa.

Then, inexplicably and suddenly, Christy becomes mad with jealousy. Near 11 the climax of the film, Christy lights a scarf on fire in Eduardo's apartment, then turns and asks, doe-eyed, if he's leaving her. What this scene contributes to the film's development is beyond me—unless Sorkin is trying to explain why Harvard's all-male final clubs won't let women become members: We might all be vindictive pyromaniacs.

Kartina Richardson, a filmmaker and writer, described this scene to me as 12 "really the only cheap move on the movie's part—here's the erratic hypersexed Asian woman totally obsessed with her white Harvard man."

"This movie also showed this guy who really felt he should be on top and 13 had this hostility to women," Richardson said. "Nerds in movies are usually portrayed as really lovable underdogs. In reality, there's a strong sexist element to programming."

Elizabeth Wurtzel, Harvard class of 1989, said she doesn't remember 14 Harvard as being misogynistic but that the film does illustrate a problem with modern women: They're opting out of high-power jobs.

"What you see in the movie, the thing that's bothering you," Wurtzel, law- 15 yer and author of *Prozac Nation,* among other books, told me, "is that our culture, in its most powerful places, has gotten more sexist, because women are not in powerful positions in these places. And it's our fault. I don't know why women do this to ourselves. Silicon Valley and Wall Street are controlled by men. I think the movie just reflects what's starting to happen."

*The Social Network* draws a parallel between final clubs and early 16 Facebook. Perhaps in attempting to illustrate the gender divisions and inequalities at Harvard—which the film implies were part of the inspiration for *thefacebook.com*—Sorkin and Fincher deliberately portrayed women through the eyes of the male antiheroes.

If this was the case, Holmes suggested, they might have offered more 17 criticism of the gender dynamic, rather than letting art imitate bigotry. "You also have to ask—well, are they using shots that linger on women's bodies because that's the way these male characters look at women, or because it's cinematic eye candy?"

Aaron Sorkin can write some pretty badass female roles. C.J. Cregg of *The* 18 *West Wing* is an enduring favorite, along with the women of *A Few Good Men* and *Sports Night.* At Harvard, Zuckerberg had female friends. Was there no room in this film for a good female character, or was Sorkin trying to make a point about where women fall in the world of male ambition? Said Holmes: "You can have a movie about a rock band with groupies and still humanize the groupies." And there are plenty of films with no female characters at all that are not misogynistic.

If a movie gives aesthetic pleasure, if it entertains, critics tend not to con- 19 sider the portrayal of women and ignore those who cry foul. Hey, this is art!

And who wants a brilliant movie marred by some obligatory "strong lady" type-casting? Most reviews have sounded like this one, from the *New York Post*, which called the film "a timeless and compelling story that speaks volumes about the way we live today."

20      Compelling? Absolutely. Timeless? I guess we'll see. I'm just not sure it's a movie that defines my generation. Maybe just half of it.

---

Source: From *The Daily Beast,* October 3, 2010. www.thedailybeast.com. © 2010 RTST, Inc. Reprinted by permission.

## QUESTIONS FOR READING

1. What has been the critical response to the movie *The Social Network*?
2. What question did Colbert ask the author—and what was Sorkin's response?
3. What is O'Brien's label for the female characters?
4. How do Holmes, Richardson, and Wurtzel explain the female characters in the film?

## QUESTIONS FOR REASONING AND ANALYSIS

5. O'Brien seems to agree with Richardson that the scarf-burning scene is a throwaway—irrelevant to the film's story. Does she agree with Holmes's explanation of the role of the film's women? Explain.
6. What is meant by the term *antihero*?
7. What is O'Brien's explanation of the film's portrayal of women? What would she prefer Sorkin to do with women in the film? Make them tough? Leave them out? Something else? Why?
8. What is O'Brien's claim—the main point she wants to make about *The Social Network*? How is her claim qualified? What strengths does she find in the movie?

## QUESTIONS FOR REFLECTION AND WRITING

9. Richardson asserts—without offering evidence—that there is a "strong sexist element to programming." Do you agree with this assertion? Is there evidence that programmers, as a group, are hostile toward women and want to dominate them?
10. Do you agree with O'Brien that *The Social Network* "makes women look so awful"? If not, how would you counter her assertion?
11. If you agree with the view that women are presented badly in the film, how would you explain this? Consider the various explanations offered in this essay as well as your own responses to the movie. Are several explanations possible?
12. Do you agree with the view that the film is a classic that defines our times? Why or why not?

# The Internet and Social Media: Their Impact on Our Lives

READ:  Where is Rat? Why is he there?

REASON:  What are the differences in Rat's poses as he reacts to the screen?

REFLECT/WRITE:  What is the point of the story that the cartoon tells?

The influence of computers today—especially as a source of information and social interaction—is so great, and so complex, that it warrants a chapter's study. Virtually no one under 30 today turns first to a reference book. They "Google it." Meanwhile people of all ages, although most typically young people, spend many hours e-mailing, twittering, and posting on Facebook. The time we devote to these activities demands that we pause and think about the effects of such dramatic changes in our lives. Consider the following questions are you read and study the seven essays in this chapter.

## PREREADING QUESTIONS

1. Has e-mailing made us more—or less—productive?
2. Is Twitter a useful new form of communication—or a waste of time?
3. Is the Internet making us smarter—or interfering with the development of critical thinking?
4. What is the difference between having access to knowledge and being knowledgeable?

## IS GOOGLE MAKING US STUPID? | NICHOLAS CARR

Widely published in magazines, Nicholas Carr writes about the effects of technology on society and business. A popular speaker and a blogger (*Rough Type*) since 2005, he is the author of several books, including *The Shallows: What the Internet Is Doing to Our Brains* (2010). The following essay, published in the *Atlantic Monthly* in 2008, has generated much discussion.

PREREADING QUESTIONS What is your reaction to Carr's title? Can you think of ways that Google could make us stupid?

1    "Dave, stop. Stop, will you? Stop, Dave. Will you stop, Dave?" So the supercomputer HAL pleads with the implacable astronaut Dave Bowman in a famous and weirdly poignant scene toward the end of Stanley Kubrick's *2001: A Space Odyssey*. Bowman, having nearly been sent to a deep-space death by the malfunctioning machine, is calmly, coldly disconnecting the memory circuits that control its artificial brain. "Dave, my mind is going," HAL says, forlornly. "I can feel it. I can feel it."

2    I can feel it, too. Over the past few years I've had an uncomfortable sense that someone, or something, has been tinkering with my brain, remapping the neural circuitry, reprogramming the memory. My mind isn't going—so far as I can tell—but it's changing. I'm not thinking the way I used to think. I can feel it most strongly when I'm reading. Immersing myself in a book or a lengthy article used to be easy. My mind would get caught up in the narrative or the turns of the argument, and I'd spend hours strolling through long stretches of prose. That's rarely the case anymore. Now my concentration often starts to drift after two or three pages. I get fidgety, lose the thread, begin looking for something

else to do. I feel as if I'm always dragging my wayward brain back to the text. The deep reading that used to come naturally has become a struggle.

I think I know what's going on. For more than a decade now, I've been ₃ spending a lot of time online, searching and surfing and sometimes adding to the great databases of the Internet. The Web has been a godsend to me as a writer. Research that once required days in the stacks or periodical rooms of libraries can now be done in minutes. A few Google searches, some quick clicks on hyperlinks, and I've got the telltale fact or pithy quote I was after. Even when I'm not working, I'm as likely as not to be foraging in the Web's info-thickets—reading and writing e-mails, scanning headlines and blog posts, watching videos and listening to podcasts, or just tripping from link to link to link. (Unlike footnotes, to which they're sometimes likened, hyperlinks don't merely point to related works; they propel you toward them.)

For me, as for others, the Net is becoming a universal medium, the con- ₄ duit for most of the information that flows through my eyes and ears and into my mind. The advantages of having immediate access to such an incredibly rich store of information are many, and they've been widely described and duly applauded. "The perfect recall of silicon memory," *Wired*'s Clive Thompson has written, "can be an enormous boon to thinking." But that boon comes at a price. As the media theorist Marshall McLuhan pointed out in the 1960s, media are not just passive channels of information. They supply the stuff of thought, but they also shape the process of thought. And what the Net seems to be doing is chipping away my capacity for concentration and con-templation. My mind now expects to take in information the way the Net dis-tributes it: in a swiftly moving stream of particles. Once I was a scuba diver in the sea of words. Now I zip along the surface like a guy on a Jet Ski.

I'm not the only one. When I mention my troubles with reading to friends ₅ and acquaintances—literary types, most of them—many say they're having similar experiences. The more they use the Web, the more they have to fight to stay focused on long pieces of writing. Some of the bloggers I follow have also begun mentioning the phenomenon. Scott Karp, who writes a blog about online media recently confessed that he has stopped reading books alto-gether. "I was a lit major in college, and used to be [a] voracious book reader," he wrote. "What happened?" He speculates on the answer: "What if I do all my reading on the web not so much because the way I read has changed, i.e. I'm just seeking convenience, but because the way I THINK has changed?"

Bruce Friedman, who blogs regularly about the use of computers in medi- ₆ cine, also has described how the Internet has altered his mental habits. "I now have almost totally lost the ability to read and absorb a longish article on the web or in print," he wrote earlier this year. A pathologist who has long been on the faculty of the University of Michigan Medical School, Friedman elabo-rated on his comment in a telephone conversation with me. His thinking, he said, has taken on a "staccato" quality, reflecting the way he quickly scans short passages of text from many sources online. "I can't read *War and Peace* anymore," he admitted. "I've lost the ability to do that. Even a blog post of more than three or four paragraphs is too much to absorb. I skim it."

7    Anecdotes alone don't prove much. And we still await the long-term neurological and psychological experiments that will provide a definitive picture of how Internet use affects cognition. But a recently published study of online research habits, conducted by scholars from University College London, suggests that we may well be in the midst of a sea change in the way we read and think. As part of the five-year research program, the scholars examined computer logs documenting the behavior of visitors to two popular research sites, one operated by the British Library and one by a UK educational consortium, that provide access to journal articles, e-books, and other sources of written information. They found that people using the sites exhibited "a form of skimming activity," hopping from one source to another and rarely returning to any source they'd already visited. They typically read no more than one or two pages of an article or book before they would "bounce" out to another site. Sometimes they'd save a long article, but there's no evidence that they ever went back and actually read it. The authors of the study report:

> It is clear that users are not reading online in the traditional sense; indeed there are signs that new forms of "reading" are emerging as users "power browse" horizontally through titles, contents pages and abstracts going for quick wins. It almost seems that they go online to avoid reading in the traditional sense.

8    Thanks to the ubiquity of text on the Internet, not to mention the popularity of text-messaging on cell phones, we may well be reading more today than we did in the 1970s or 1980s, when television was our medium of choice. But it's a different kind of reading, and behind it lies a different kind of thinking—perhaps even a new sense of the self. "We are not only *what* we read," says Maryanne Wolf, a developmental psychologist at Tufts University and the author of *Proust and the Squid: The Story and Science of the Reading Brain.* "We are *how* we read." Wolf worries that the style of reading promoted by the Net, a style that puts "efficiency" and "immediacy" above all else, may be weakening our capacity for the kind of deep reading that emerged when an earlier technology, the printing press, made long and complex works of prose commonplace. When we read online, she says, we tend to become "mere decoders of information." Our ability to interpret text, to make the rich mental connections that form when we read deeply and without distraction, remains largely disengaged.

9    Reading, explains Wolf, is not an instinctive skill for human beings. It's not etched into our genes the way speech is. We have to teach our minds how to translate the symbolic characters we see into the language we understand. And the media or other technologies we use in learning and practicing the craft of reading play an important part in shaping the neural circuits inside our brains. Experiments demonstrate that readers of ideograms, such as the Chinese, develop a mental circuitry for reading that is very different from the circuitry found in those of us whose written language employs an alphabet. The variations extend across many regions of the brain, including those that govern such essential cognitive functions as memory and the interpretation of visual and auditory stimuli. We can expect as well that the circuits woven by

our use of the Net will be different from those woven by our reading of books and other printed works.

Sometime in 1882, Friedrich Nietzsche bought a typewriter—a Malling-Hansen Writing Ball, to be precise. His vision was failing, and keeping his eyes focused on a page had become exhausting and painful, often bringing on crushing headaches. He had been forced to curtail his writing, and he feared that he would soon have to give it up. The typewriter rescued him, at least for a time. Once he had mastered touch-typing, he was able to write with his eyes closed, using only the tips of his fingers. Words could once again flow from his mind to the page. 10

But the machine had a subtler effect on his work. One of Nietzsche's friends, a composer, noticed a change in the style of his writing. His already terse prose had become even tighter, more telegraphic. "Perhaps you will through this instrument even take to a new idiom," the friend wrote in a letter, noting that, in his own work, his " 'thoughts' in music and language often depend on the quality of pen and paper." 11

"You are right," Nietzsche replied, "our writing equipment takes part in the forming of our thoughts." Under the sway of the machine, writes the German media scholar Friedrich A. Kittler, Nietzsche's prose "changed from arguments to aphorisms, from thoughts to puns, from rhetoric to telegram style." 12

The human brain is almost infinitely malleable. People used to think that our mental meshwork, the dense connections formed among the 100 billion or so neurons inside our skulls, was largely fixed by the time we reached adulthood. But brain researchers have discovered that that's not the case. James Olds, a professor of neuroscience who directs the Krasnow Institute for Advanced Study at George Mason University, says that even the adult mind "is very plastic." Nerve cells routinely break old connections and form new ones. "The brain," according to Olds, "has the ability to reprogram itself on the fly, altering the way it functions." 13

As we use what the sociologist Daniel Bell has called our "intellectual technologies"—the tools that extend our mental rather than our physical capacities—we inevitably begin to take on the qualities of those technologies. The mechanical clock, which came into common use in the fourteenth century, provides a compelling example. In *Technics and Civilization*, the historian and cultural critic Lewis Mumford described how the clock "disassociated time from human events and helped create the belief in an independent world of mathematically measurable sequences." The "abstract framework of divided time" became "the point of reference for both action and thought." 14

The clock's methodical ticking helped bring into being the scientific mind and the scientific man. But it also took something away. As the late MIT computer scientist Joseph Weizenbaum observed in his 1976 book, *Computer Power and Human Reason: From Judgment to Calculation*, the conception of the world that emerged from the widespread use of timekeeping instruments "remains an impoverished version of the older one, for it rests on a rejection of those direct experiences that formed the basis for, and indeed constituted, 15 the old reality." In deciding when to eat, to work, to sleep, to rise, we stopped listening to our senses and started obeying the clock.

16     The process of adapting to new intellectual technologies is reflected in the changing metaphors we use to explain ourselves to ourselves. When the mechanical clock arrived, people began thinking of their brains as operating "like clockwork." Today, in the age of software, we have come to think of them as operating "like computers." But the changes, neuroscience tells us, go much deeper than metaphor. Thanks to our brain's plasticity, the adaptation occurs also at a biological level.

17     The Internet promises to have particularly far-reaching effects on cognition. In a paper published in 1936, the British mathematician Alan Turing proved that a digital computer, which at the time existed only as a theoretical machine, could be programmed to perform the function of any other information-processing device. And that's what we're seeing today. The Internet, an immeasurably powerful computing system, is subsuming most of our other intellectual technologies. It's becoming our map and our clock, our printing press and our typewriter, our calculator and our telephone, and our radio and TV.

18     When the Net absorbs a medium, that medium is re-created in the Net's image. It injects the medium's content with hyperlinks, blinking ads, and other digital gewgaws, and it surrounds the content with the content of all the other media it has absorbed. A new e-mail message, for instance, may announce its arrival as we're glancing over the latest headlines at a newspaper's site. The result is to scatter our attention and diffuse our concentration.

19     The Net's influence doesn't end at the edges of a computer screen, either. As people's minds become attuned to the crazy quilt of Internet media, traditional media have to adapt to the audience's new expectations. Television programs add text crawls and pop-up ads, and magazines and newspapers shorten their articles, introduce capsule summaries, and crowd their pages with easy-to-browse info-snippets. When, in March of this year, the *New York Times* decided to devote the second and third pages of every edition to article abstracts, its design director, Tom Bodkin, explained that the "shortcuts" would give harried readers a quick "taste" of the day's news, sparing them the "less efficient" method of actually turning the pages and reading the articles. Old media have little choice but to play by the new-media rules.

20     Never has a communications system played so many roles in our lives—or exerted such broad influence over our thoughts—as the Internet does today. Yet for all that's been written about the Net, there's been little consideration of how, exactly, it's reprogramming us. The Net's intellectual ethic remains obscure.

21     About the same time that Nietzsche started using his typewriter, an earnest young man named Frederick Winslow Taylor carried a stopwatch into the Midvale Steel plant in Philadelphia and began a historic series of experiments aimed at improving the efficiency of the plant's machinists. With the approval of Midvale's owners, he recruited a group of factory hands, set them to work on various metalworking machines, and recorded and timed their every movement as well as the operations of the machines. By breaking down every job

into a sequence of small, discrete steps and then testing different ways of performing each one, Taylor created a set of precise instructions—an "algorithm," we might say today—for how each worker should work. Midvale's employees grumbled about the strict new regime, claiming that it turned them into little more than automatons, but the factory's productivity soared.

More than a hundred years after the invention of the steam engine, the 22 Industrial Revolution had at last found its philosophy and its philosopher. Taylor's tight industrial choreography—his "system," as he liked to call it—was embraced by manufacturers throughout the country and, in time, around the world. Seeking maximum speed, maximum efficiency, and maximum output, factory owners used time-and-motion studies to organize their work and configure the jobs of their workers. The goal, as Taylor defined it in his celebrated 1911 treatise, *The Principles of Scientific Management,* was to identify and adopt, for every job, the "one best method" of work and thereby to effect "the gradual substitution of science for rule of thumb throughout the mechanic arts." Once his system was applied to all acts of manual labor, Taylor assured his followers, it would bring about a restructuring not only of industry but of society, creating a Utopia of perfect efficiency. In the past the man has been first," he declared; "in the future the system must be first."

Taylor's system is still very much with us; it remains the ethic of industrial 23 manufacturing. And now, thanks to the growing power that computer engineers and software coders wield over our intellectual lives, Taylor's ethic is beginning to govern the realm of the mind as well. The Internet is a machine designed for the efficient and automated collection, transmission, and manipulation of information, and its legions of programmers are intent on finding the "one best method"—the perfect algorithm—to carry out every mental movement of what we've come to describe as "knowledge work."

Google's headquarters, in Mountain View, California—the Googleplex—is 24 the Internet's high church, and the religion practiced inside its walls is Taylorism. Google, says its chief executive, Eric Schmidt, is "a company that's founded around the science of measurement," and it is striving to "systematize everything" it does. Drawing on the terabytes of behavioral data it collects through its search engine and other sites, it carries out thousands of experiments a day, according to the *Harvard Business Review,* and it uses the results to refine the algorithms that increasingly control how people find information and extract meaning from it. What Taylor did for the work of the hand, Google is doing for the work of the mind.

The company has declared that its mission is "to organize the world's 25 information and make it universally accessible and useful." It seeks to develop "the perfect search engine," which it defines as something that "understands exactly what you mean and gives you back exactly what you want." In Google's view, information is a kind of commodity, a utilitarian resource that can be mined and processed with industrial efficiency. The more pieces of information we can "access" and the faster we can extract their gist, the more productive we become as thinkers.

26    Where does it end? Sergey Brin and Larry Page, the gifted young men who founded Google while pursuing doctoral degrees in computer science at Stanford, speak frequently of their desire to turn their search engine into an artificial intelligence, a HAL-like machine that might be connected directly to our brains. "The ultimate search engine is something as smart as people—or smarter," Page said in a speech a few years back. "For us, working on search is a way to work on artificial intelligence." In a 2004 interview with *Newsweek*, Brin said, "Certainly if you had all the world's information directly attached to your brain, or an artificial brain that was smarter than your brain, you'd be better off." Last year Page told a convention of scientists that Google is "really trying to build artificial intelligence and to do it on a large scale."

27    Such an ambition is a natural one, even an admirable one, for a pair of math whizzes with vast quantities of cash at their disposal and a small army of computer scientists in their employ. A fundamentally scientific enterprise, Google is motivated by a desire to use technology, in Eric Schmidt's words, "to solve problems that have never been solved before," and artificial intelligence is the hardest problem out there. Why wouldn't Brin and Page want to be the ones to crack it?

28    Still, their easy assumption that we'd all "be better off" if our brains were supplemented, or even replaced, by an artificial intelligence is unsettling. It suggests a belief that intelligence is the output of a mechanical process, a series of discrete steps that can be isolated, measured, and optimized. In Google's world, the world we enter when we go online, there's little place for the fuzziness of contemplation. Ambiguity is not an opening for insight but a bug to be fixed. The human brain is just an outdated computer that needs a faster processor and a bigger hard drive.

29    The idea that our minds should operate as high-speed data-processing machines is not only built into the workings of the Internet, it is the network's reigning business model as well. The faster we surf across the Web—the more links we click and pages we view—the more opportunities Google and other companies gain to collect information about us and to feed us advertisements. Most of the proprietors of the commercial Internet have a financial stake in collecting the crumbs of data we leave behind as we flit from link to link—the more crumbs, the better. The last thing these companies want is to encourage leisurely reading or slow, concentrated thought. It's in their economic interest to drive us to distraction.

30    Maybe I'm just a worrywart. Just as there's a tendency to glorify technological progress, there's a countertendency to expect the worst of every new tool or machine. In Plato's *Phaedrus*, Socrates bemoaned the development of writing. He feared that, as people came to rely on the written word as a substitute for the knowledge they used to carry inside their heads, they would, in the words of one of the dialogue's characters, "cease to exercise their memory and become forgetful." And because they would be able to "receive a quantity of information without proper instruction," they would "be thought very knowledgeable when they are for the most part quite ignorant." They

would be "filled with the conceit of wisdom instead of real wisdom." Socrates wasn't wrong—the new technology did often have the effects he feared—but he was shortsighted. He couldn't foresee the many ways that writing and reading would serve to spread information, spur fresh ideas, and expand human knowledge (if not wisdom).

The arrival of Gutenberg's printing press in the fifteenth century set off 31 another round of teeth gnashing. The Italian humanist Hieronimo Squarciafico worried that the easy availability of books would lead to intellectual laziness, making men "less studious" and weakening their minds. Others argued that cheaply printed books and broadsheets would undermine religious authority, demean the work of scholars and scribes, and spread sedition and debauchery. As the New York University professor Clay Shirky notes, "Most of the arguments made against the printing press were correct, even prescient." But, again, the doomsayers were unable to imagine the myriad blessings that the printed word would deliver.

So, yes, you should be skeptical of my skepticism. Perhaps those who dis- 32 miss critics of the Internet as Luddites or nostalgists will be proved correct, and from our hyperactive, data-stoked minds will spring a golden age of intellectual discovery and universal wisdom. Then again, the Net isn't the alphabet, and although it may replace the printing press, it produces something altogether different. The kind of deep reading that a sequence of printed pages promotes is valuable not just for the knowledge we acquire from the author's words but for the intellectual vibrations those words set off within our own minds. In the quiet spaces opened up by the sustained, undistracted reading of a book, or by any other act of contemplation, for that matter, we make our own associations, draw our own inferences and analogies, foster our own ideas. Deep reading, as Maryanne Wolf argues, is indistinguishable from deep thinking.

If we lose those quiet spaces or fill them up with "content," we will sacri- 33 fice something important not only in ourselves but in our culture. In a recent essay, the playwright Richard Foreman eloquently described what's at stake:

> I come from a tradition of Western culture, in which the ideal (my ideal) was the complex, dense and "cathedral-like" structure of the highly educated and articulate personality—a man or woman who carried inside themselves a personally constructed and unique version of the entire heritage of the West. [But now] I see within us all (myself included) the replacement of complex inner density with a new kind of self—evolving under the pressure of information overload and the technology of the "instantly available."

As we are drained of our "inner repertory of dense cultural inheritance," Foreman concluded, we risk turning into " 'pancake people'—spread wide and thin as we connect with that vast network of information accessed by the mere touch of a button."

I'm haunted by that scene in *2001*. What makes it so poignant, and so 34 weird, is the computer's emotional response to the disassembly of its mind: its despair as one circuit after another goes dark, its childlike pleading with the astronaut—'I can feel it, I can feel it. I'm afraid"—and its final reversion to what can only be called a state of innocence. HAL's outpouring of feeling contrasts with the emotionlessness that characterizes the human figures in the film, who go about their business with an almost robotic efficiency. Their thoughts and actions feel scripted, as if they're following the steps of an algorithm. In the world of *2001*, people have become so machinelike that the most human character turns out to be a machine. That's the essence of Kubrick's dark prophecy: as we come to rely on computers to mediate our understanding of the world, it is our own intelligence that flattens into artificial intelligence.

---

Source: From *The Atlantic,* July/August 2008. Copyright 2008 by Nicholas Carr. Used with permission of the author.

### QUESTIONS FOR READING

1. What is Carr's subject? (Do not say "the Internet"; be more precise.)
2. How does Carr think his reading has changed?
3. What does the University College, London, study suggest about reading habits online?
4. How did the invention of the clock change human behavior?
5. What is Google's concept of the ideal search engine? What is the company's goal?
6. What is meant by *deep reading*—or *deep thinking*? How do these actions differ from collecting information from the Internet?

### QUESTIONS FOR REASONING AND ANALYSIS

7. Carr begins by using his own experience as evidence of the Internet's impact; how effective is this strategy as an introduction?
8. What is the author's claim? How does Carr qualify his position?
9. What kinds of evidence does he provide?
10. Carr opens and closes with references to *2001: A Space Odyssey.* How does he use the film to develop his claim? Is this an effective frame for his discussion? Why or why not?
11. Carr also uses a number of metaphors. Find two or three and explain each one.

### QUESTIONS FOR REFLECTION AND WRITING

12. Do you think that the Internet has made you smarter? If so, how do you define *smart*? Would Carr agree with your definition? Explain.
13. Carr devotes several paragraphs to a review of attitudes toward new technology over the years. What does he seek to accomplish? How does the discussion strengthen his argument?
14. How much time do you devote to deep reading or to contemplation? Has Carr convinced you that deep thinking is important? Why or why not?

# MIND OVER MASS MEDIA | STEVEN PINKER

A professor of psychology at Harvard University, Steven Pinker is the author of significant articles and books on visual cognition and the psychology of language—his areas of research. These include *The Language Instinct* (2007) and *How the Mind Works* (2009). *Time* magazine has listed Pinker as one of the "100 most influential people in the world." His contribution to the debate over mass media was published on June 12, 2010, in the *International Herald Tribune*.

PREREADING QUESTIONS Given Pinker's title and his essay's context in this chapter, what do you expect him to write about? What can you anticipate about his position?

New forms of media have always caused moral panics: the printing press, newspapers, paperbacks and television were all once denounced as threats to their consumers' brainpower and moral fiber. 1

So too with electronic technologies. PowerPoint, we're told, is reducing discourse to bullet points. Search engines lower our intelligence, encouraging us to skim on the surface of knowledge rather than dive to its depths. Twitter is shrinking our attention spans. 2

But such panics often fail basic reality checks. When comic books were accused of turning juveniles into delinquents in the 1950s, crime was falling to record lows, just as the denunciations of video games in the 1990s coincided with the great American crime decline. The decades of television, transistor radios and rock videos were also decades in which I.Q. scores rose continuously. 3

For a reality check today, take the state of science, which demands high levels of brainwork and is measured by clear benchmarks of discovery. These days scientists are never far from their e-mail, rarely touch paper and cannot lecture without PowerPoint. If electronic media were hazardous to intelligence, the quality of science would be plummeting. Yet discoveries are mulitiplying like fruit flies, and progress is dizzying. Other activities in the life of the mind, like philosophy, history and cultural criticism, are likewise flourishing, as anyone who has lost a morning of work to the Web site *Arts & Letters Daily* can attest. 4

Critics of new media sometimes use science itself to press their case, citing research that shows how "experience can change the brain." But cognitive neuroscientists roll their eyes at such talk. Yes, every time we learn a factor skill the wiring of the brain changes; it's not as if the information is stored in the pancreas. But the existence of neural plasticity does not mean the brain is a blob of clay pounded into shape by experience. 5

Experience does not revamp the basic information-processing capacities of the brain. Speed-reading programs have long claimed to do just that, but the verdict was rendered by Woody Allen after he read *War and Peace* in one sitting: "It was about Russia." Genuine multitasking, too, has been exposed as a myth, not just by laboratory studies but by the familiar sight of an S.U.V. undulating between lanes as the driver cuts deals on his cellphone. 6

Moreover, as the psychologists Christopher Chabris and Daniel Simons show in their new book *The Invisible Gorilla: And Other Ways Our Intuitions* 7

*Deceive Us*, the effects of experience are highly specific to the experiences themselves. If you train people to do one thing (recognize shapes, solve math puzzles, find hidden words), they get better at doing that thing, but almost nothing else. Music doesn't make you better at math, conjugating Latin doesn't make you more logical, brain-training games don't make you smarter. Accomplished people don't bulk up their brains with intellectual calisthenics; they immerse themselves in their fields. Novelists read lots of novels, scientists read lots of science.

8    The effects of consuming electronic media are also likely to be far more limited than the panic implies. Media critics write as if the brain takes on the qualities of whatever it consumes, the informational equivalent of "you are what you eat." As with primitive peoples who believe that eating fierce animals will make them fierce they assume that watching quick cuts in rock videos turns your mental life into quick cuts or that reading bullet points and Twitter postings turns your thoughts into bullet points and Twitter postings.

9    Yes, the constant arrival of information packets can be distracting or addictive, especially to people with attention deficit disorder. But distraction is not a new phenomenon. The solution is not to bemoan technology but to develop strategies of self-control, as we do with every other temptation in life. Turn off e-mail or Twitter when you work, put away your BlackBerry at dinner time, ask your spouse to call you to bed at a designated hour.

10    And to encourage intellectual depth, don't rail at PowerPoint or Google. It's not as if habits of deep reflection, thorough research and rigorous reasoning ever came naturally to people. They must be acquired in special institutions, which we call universities, and maintained with constant upkeep, which we call analysis, criticism and debate. They are not granted by propping a heavy encyclopedia on your lap, nor are they taken away by efficient access to information on the Internet.

11    The new media have caught on for a reason. Knowledge is increasing exponentially; human brainpower and waking hours are not. Fortunately, the Internet and information technologies are helping us manage, search and retrieve our collective intellectual output at different scales, from Twitter and previews to e-books and online encyclopedias. Far from making us stupid, these technologies are the only things that will keep us smart.

---

Source: From *The New York Times/International Herald Tribune,* June 12, 2010. Reprinted by permission of the author.

### QUESTIONS FOR READING

1. What is Pinker's subject? (Be precise.)
2. What happened to the crime rate during the 1990s?
3. What happened during the years of heavy TV use and the publication of rock videos?
4. What changes in the brain when we learn new information? What does not change?

5. What do people do to be successful in their fields?

6. To develop "intellectual depth," what do people need to do?

### QUESTIONS FOR REASONING AND ANALYSIS

7. What is Pinker's response to those who complain about the new electronic technologies? What is his claim?

8. How would you describe the author's tone? How does his tone aid his argument?

9. What kinds of evidence does Pinker provide? Is his argument convincing?

### QUESTIONS FOR REFLECTION AND WRITING

10. Pinker asserts that speed-reading and multitasking have been shown to be myths. Is this new to you? Are you surprised? Have you argued that you can multitask successfully? If so, how would you try to refute Pinker?

11. Has the author provided a convincing counter to Carr's argument in "Is Google Making Us Stupid?" Are there ways in which both authors can be right?

## THE MEDIUM IS THE MEDIUM | DAVID BROOKS

David Brooks is a columnist for the *New York Times* and a commentator on *The NewsHour with Jim Lehrer.* He has appeared in many newspapers and magazines and has published two books, including *On Paradise Drive: How We Live Now (and Always Have) in the Future Tense* (2004). "The Medium Is the Medium" appeared on July 9, 2010.

PREREADING QUESTIONS On what expression—what sociological comment about the media—does Brooks play with in his title? What does his play on words tell you about his anticipated audience?

Recently, book publishers got some good news. Researchers gave 852  1
disadvantaged students 12 books (of their own choosing) to take home at the end of the school year. They did this for three successive years.

Then the researchers, led by Richard Allington of the University of  2
Tennessee, looked at those students' test scores. They found that the students who brought the books home had significantly higher reading scores than other students. These students were less affected by the "summer slide"—the decline that especially afflicts lower-income students during the vacation months. In fact, just having those 12 books seemed to have as much positive effect as attending summer school.

This study, along with many others, illustrates the tremendous power of  3
books. We already knew, from research in 27 countries, that kids who grow up in a home with 500 books stay in school longer and do better. This new study suggests that introducing books into homes that may not have them also produces significant educational gains.

4    Recently, Internet mavens got some bad news. Jacob Vigdor and Helen Ladd of Duke's Sanford School of Public Policy examined computer use among a half-million 5th through 8th graders in North Carolina. They found that the spread of home computers and high speed Internet access was associated with significant declines in math and reading scores.

5    This study, following up on others, finds that broadband access is not necessarily good for kids and may be harmful to their academic performance. And this study used data from 2000 to 2005 before Twitter and Facebook took off.

6    These two studies feed into the debate that is now surrounding Nicholas Carr's book, *The Shallows*. Carr argues that the Internet is leading to a short-attention-span culture. He cites a pile of research showing that the multidistraction, hyperlink world degrades people's abilities to engage in deep thought or serious contemplation.

7    Carr's argument has been challenged. His critics point to evidence that suggests that playing computer games and performing Internet searches actually improves a person's ability to process information and focus attention. The Internet, they say, is a boon to schooling, not a threat.

8    But there was one interesting observation made by a philanthropist who gives books to disadvantaged kids. It's not the physical presence of the books that produces the biggest impact, she suggested. It's the change in the way the students see themselves as they build a home library. They see themselves as readers, as members of a different group.

9    The Internet-versus-books debate is conducted on the supposition that the medium is the message, But sometimes the medium is just the medium. What matters is the way people think about themselves while engaged in the two activities. A person who becomes a citizen of the literary world enters a hierarchical universe. There are classic works of literature at the top and beach reading at the bottom.

10    A person enters this world as a novice, and slowly studies the works of great writers and scholars. Readers immerse themselves in deep, alternative worlds and hope to gain some lasting wisdom. Respect is paid to the writers who transmit that wisdom.

11    A citizen of the Internet has a very different experience. The Internet smashes hierarchy and is not marked by deference. Maybe it would be different if it had been invented in Victorian England, but Internet culture is set in contemporary America. Internet culture is egalitarian. The young are more accomplished than the old. The new media is supposedly savvier than the old media. The dominant activity is free-wheeling, disrespectful, antiauthority disputation.

12    These different cultures foster different types of learning. The great essayist Joseph Epstein once distinguished between being well informed, being hip and being cultivated. The Internet helps you become well informed— knowledgeable about current events, the latest controversies and important trends. The Internet also helps you become hip—to learn about what's going on, as Epstein writes, "in those lively waters outside the boring mainstream."

13    But the literary world is still better at helping you become cultivated, mastering significant things of lasting import. To learn these sorts of things, you

have to defer to greater minds than your own. You have to take the time to immerse yourself in a great writer's world. You have to respect the authority of the teacher.

Right now, the literary world is better at encouraging this kind of identity. 14 The Internet culture may produce better conversationalists, but the literary culture still produces better students.

It's better at distinguishing the important from the unimportant, and 15 making the important more prestigious.

Perhaps that will change. Already, more "old-fashioned" outposts are 16 opening up across the Web. It could be that the real debate will not be books versus the Internet but how to build an Internet counterculture that will better attract people to serious learning.

---

## QUESTIONS FOR READING

1. What study did Richard Allington conduct, and what did he learn?
2. What did the study by Vigdor and Ladd reveal?
3. In what sense, for Brooks, is the medium "just the medium"?
4. What are the differences between the world of books and the world of the Internet? What is each best at providing?

## QUESTIONS FOR REASONING AND ANALYSIS

5. Brooks begins by referring to two studies. How do they help him develop his argument?
6. Brooks mentions Carr's argument specifically: In what way is Brooks's argument a refutation of Carr's? How does it add to the discussion?
7. What is the author's message to students—to young people who are most "hooked" on the Internet and social media?

## QUESTIONS FOR REFLECTION AND WRITING

8. Study Carr, Pinker, and Brooks. What do Pinker and Brooks concede to Carr? What approach do Pinker and Brooks share in their challenge to Carr?
9. What is the most important point that you take away from this three-way debate? Why?
10. Brooks asserts that entering the world of books and learning from authority is the best medium for students. Did you want to read this assertion? If you disagree with the author, how would you refute him?

## WHY GOOGLE SHOULD STAY IN CHINA | YASHENG HUANG

The author of *Capitalism with Chinese Characteristics: Entrepreneurship and the State* (2008) in addition to other books and academic articles, Yasheng Huang is professor of political economy and business at MIT's Sloan School of Management. At MIT he founded and runs the China Lab and India Lab—which help entrepreneurs in both countries gain management skills. His essay here was published in the *Washington Post* on March 28, 2010.

**PREREADING QUESTIONS** Did Google decide to stay in China—or leave? Does the answer to this question actually affect the argument that Huang makes?

The Google headquarters in China.

1    In a recent interview with the *Wall Street Journal,* Google co-founder Sergey Brin explained why his company decided to close its search engine in China. The problem, he explained, is that China reminds him of the country of his birth, the former Soviet Union. After lauding China's "great strides" in reducing poverty, Brin had this to say about Chinese politics: "In some aspects of their policy, particularly with respect to censorship, with respect to surveillance of dissidents, I see the same earmarks of totalitarianism, and I find that personally quite troubling."

2    There are at least two people in China who might disagree. One is Zhou Jiugeng, a former official in the city of Nanjing, who could hear about the Google wars only from a prison cell. Zhou was sentenced to 11 years in jail last year after he was spotted sporting a $25,000 watch, one far out of reach of the pay of a civil servant. This led to an online uproar, with countless postings and blogs questioning Zhou's income. A government investigation ensued, and Zhou was found to have accepted almost $200,000 in bribes. He was fired, prosecuted and sent to jail. (The same investigation apparently found that his watch was a fake, but that's another story.)

3    The second individual is Deng Yujiao, a young woman who rebuffed sexual advances by a government official in May 2009 and then stabbed him to death when he attempted to rape her. She was arrested, prompting a massive protest, online and off, with Chinese netizens and civil rights organizations petitioning for her release. Emboldened by the popular response, even the traditional Chinese media weighed in. Bowing to the pressure, the government cleared all the charges against Deng, and arrested and dismissed two officials who were present at the scene of the incident.

4    Without a vibrant Internet community in China, Zhou and Deng would probably have traded places—Zhou going about his corrupt business and

Deng languishing in jail. But the Internet has given China a measure of transparency, accountability and public voice, with an impact far more powerful than decades of 10 percent economic growth, foreign investment and urbanization. Brin is right that China's political system retains many of the Leninist attributes of the old Soviet Union, but he is wrong to conflate the government's attempts to enforce those attributes with the actual results.

The Google co-founder, who came to the United States in 1979, when he was 6 years old, complained in the interview that online censorship in China has intensified in recent years. Indeed, according to *China Digital Times*, a publication based in Berkeley, Calif., the Chinese government maintains a list of hundreds, if not thousands, of banned search terms, with new ones added periodically.

But let's maintain some perspective. Relative to the total information available on the Internet in China, the number of banned terms is minuscule, no matter how quickly the list expands. According to the China Internet Network Information Center, a Web site run by the Chinese Academy of Sciences, the total amount of digital information stored on Chinese Web sites has increased by more than 40 percent since 2005. There are now more than 9 million domain names registered under ".cn," compared with 1.1 million in 2006, when Google first entered China. The country has more than 300 million Internet users and more than 700 million mobile subscribers, many of whom access the Web with their phones. It defies logic to imagine exerting airtight and sustained control over such a massive Internet network.

Imagine trying to enforce a speed limit—say 35 miles an hour—in 1930 and in 2010. Surely there would be a lot more infractions in 2010; after all, there are more cars today and they can go faster. But does the higher number of violations mean that the authorities are intensifying traffic control? No, it means the technology they're seeking to control has changed. That is the situation with the Internet in China today. The government is trying to foist its old notions of information control on a rapidly changing and elusive technology. It is not that censorship is increasing, but that the volume of information to be censored is now far greater.

Brin cites the Chinese government's increasing requests that Google censor information as evidence of greater censorship. That's one way to interpret the data. Another equally plausible explanation is that the supply of content deemed worthy of censoring has multiplied, forcing the government to play catch up, often from a hopeless distance.

Anyone who has spent time online in China can testify that the Internet community there is easily one of the most dynamic and vibrant on Earth. On any issue, there are passionate debates and opinions across the ideological spectrum. Maoists, Hayekians and Confucians trade barbs with insults and zealotry. Blogs by serious intellectuals attract audiences unimaginable in the West. China's market for ideas is enormous. Last month, the Chinese premier, Wen Jiabao, went online and personally answered netizens' questions, even some that, by Chinese standards, were rather blunt. (One answer Wen gave on the real estate market prompted a blogger in China to post all the past statements Wen had made on controlling real estate prices—alongside an index of rising prices.)

10    Yes, a Google search on the Tiananmen crackdown of 1989 would yield nothing more than "no results due to restrictions of local laws and regulations," but I imagine that the protesters of 1989 would have cringed at the strident criticisms of government policies and officials that are online in China today. Western observers are fixated on dramas such as the Tiananmen protests and the condition of human rights dissidents. They forget that bread-and-butter issues, such as high housing prices and polluted rivers, now animate citizens as much as ideas of freedom and democracy did two decades ago.

11    Regardless of Brin's fears, China is no Soviet Union. Thanks to the Internet, Chinese citizens have acquired the technological means—although not yet the full legal protections—of free speech, defined as the ability to question and criticize the government. There are limits to this freedom, and many of us no doubt find them too numerous and onerous. But we should acknowledge that China has made genuine economic and social progress over the past 30 years, as well as progress in freedom of speech during the past 10 years, a decade in which the Internet truly came to China. Yes, censorship rightly offends moral sensibilities, but with the list of banned search terms, we at least know where the limits are, and we can learn to adapt, test or even evade them.

12    Google's effort to abide by its noble motto—"Don't be evil"—in China should be judged not by the company's intentions but by the consequences of its actions. By closing its search engine there, Google will harm the cause of free speech, transparency and accountability in China. Democracy is in many ways a technological revolution; without the world's foremost technology leader, China's Internet space will become less innovative, less dynamic and less vibrant.

13    Google's position as a distant second to Baidu, the Chinese search engine, does not detract from the company's importance. Its presence has forced Baidu to wrestle with the tradeoff between satisfying the government censors and retaining its users. This is the power of competition. But Google's departure will leave Baidu as a virtual monopoly. A monopolist, as Brin knows well from his experience with Microsoft, does not value consumer welfare. The losers will be China's netizens—the very people who are key to driving the political and social changes Brin favors.

14    In 2006, when Google was debating whether to enter China, it concluded that a more vibrant Internet would change the country for the better. I fear that history will show that its 2006 decision was prescient but that its 2010 move was mistaken.

15    And by the way, how does the whole world know which search terms the Chinese government has banned? Chinese Web users posted the list. Who else?

---

Source: From *The Washington Post*, March 28, 2010. Reprinted by permission of the author.

## QUESTIONS FOR READING

1.    What is Zhou Jiugeng's story? What is Deng Yujiao's story?
2.    Why does Google founder Sergey Brin want to close down Google in China?
3.    How many Internet users are there in China?

4.  Why does it appear that the Chinese government has increased its censorship of the Internet?

5.  What does Huang accomplish by opening with Zhou's and Deng's stories? What is clever about his conclusion?

6.  What is the author's claim? What is the core of his reasoning?

7.  Huang provides good evidence for Google to stay in China. What is the larger moral issue that Google had to wrestle with—and that would be the only challenge to Huang's practical evidence?

8.  Do you agree that Google should stay in China in spite of the government's list of banned search terms? If you disagree, how would you refute Huang?

9.  It has been said that politics is "the art of the possible." Politicians have to make compromises in order to pass difficult legislation. What about businesses? Is there both an ideal world and then the real world in which a business has to operate? When should a company make a moral stand, even if it means the loss of revenue? Does Google do "evil" by doing business in China? If you were Brin, how would you make the decision? And how would you defend it?

## IN EGYPT, TWITTER TRUMPS TORTURE   |   MONA ELTAHAWY

Egyptian-born, Mona Eltahawy is a lecturer, writer, and blogger with a focus on Arab and Muslim issues. Prior to moving to New York City, Eltahawy was a news reporter in the Middle East—and the first Egyptian to live and work in Israel for a Western news agency. Her article on Twitter appeared in the *Washington Post* on August 7, 2010.

PREREADING QUESTIONS   The author's title is a clever one—but what does it tell you to anticipate? What is likely to be Eltahawy's subject?

Khaled Said is not the first Egyptian whom police allegedly beat to death.   1 But his death has sparked a virtual revolution that is affecting Egypt's tightly controlled society.

Said, a 28-year-old Egyptian businessman, was brutally beaten, his family   2 and activists say, by two plainclothes police officers on June 6. An Interior Ministry autopsy claimed that Said suffocated after swallowing a bag of drugs he tried to hide from police. But a photograph of a shattered body that his family confirmed was his started circulating online. Teeth missing, lip torn, jaw broken and blood pouring from his head: It was difficult to square such trauma with suffocation. His family said he was targeted after he posted a video online allegedly showing police sharing profits of a drug bust.

If social media in the Arab world were merely outlets for venting or "stress   3 relief"—as detractors claim—then Said's fate would have ended with some angry comments on Facebook and a tweet or two railing at the Egyptian regime.

4     Instead, thanks to social media's increasing popularity and ability to connect activists with ordinary people, Egyptians are protesting police brutality in unprecedented numbers. On July 27, the two police officers connected to his death stood trial on charges of illegal arrest and excessive use of force. If convicted, they face three to 15 years' imprisonment.

5     While social media didn't invent courage—activists have long protested the tactics of President Hosni Mubarak, a U.S. ally who has maintained a state of emergency in Egypt since assuming office in 1981—the Internet has in recent months connected Egyptians and amplified their voices as never before. There's an anti-torture Web site with a hotline to report incidents. The independent advocacy group El Nadim Centre for Rehabilitation of Victims of Violence publishes an online diary that has documented 200 allegations of abuse since February. On another site Egyptians post pictures of abusive police officers.

6     This week, a woman in a full-length veil went on television to accuse two police officers of raping and robbing her. Her tearful segment has gone viral on YouTube.

7     Detractors say that social media sites are just the latest platforms from which "apathetic" Arabs now tilt at windmills. Facebook has not overthrown a single Arab dictator, and Twitter has yet to topple any regimes, the thinking goes.

8     But the better points to assess about social media have to do with their effect on young people in the Arab world—the bulk of the population—and the loosening of long-established controls.

9     An estimated 3.4 million Egyptians are on Facebook, according to Spot-On, a public relations firm, making Egypt the No. 1 user in the Arab world and 23rd globally, Nearly 2 million Egyptian Facebook users are younger than 25. As with Facebook users everywhere, Egyptians post embarrassing pictures, flirt with strangers and reunite with school friends. But to appreciate social media's growing importance in challenging authority, consider the events between Said's death and the trial of the two police officers.

10     After the photograph of Said's corpse started circulating on Facebook and Twitter, a protest outside the Interior Ministry in Cairo was the largest in living memory against police brutality.

11     At least 1,000 people attended Said's funeral, which became an impromptu protest. A new autopsy was ordered; it confirmed the Interior Ministry's initial claim but acknowledged the presence of bruises on Said's body.

12     Several Facebook pages and groups were launched in memory of Said, including "We Are All Khaled Said," which sent out the call for silent protests in black and now has more than 220,000 fans.

13     Egyptian activists and everyday citizens, including families with children, turned up in

unprecedented numbers. Reuters reported that as many as 8,000 people dressed in black took part in one protest along the promenade in Alexandria, Said's home town.

The government tried to paint Said as a pothead and petty criminal who 14 tried to evade national service. It suggested his brothers had converted to Judaism.

"They think the people are stupid," a group of Egyptian rappers sang in 15 response. Their video is available on YouTube and has been shared on Facebook and Twitter.

Egyptians who realize that any one of them could have been Khaled Said 16 have the chance through social media to challenge the state and its once-absolute ownership of the narrative. There is a difference, of course, between the real world and the virtual world. Social media won't overthrow regimes. But such sites have given a voice and platform to young people long marginalized by those regimes.

---

Source: From *The Washington Post,* August 7, 2010. Reprinted by permission of the author.

## QUESTIONS FOR READING

1. What is Said's story? How did Egyptians learn about him? What was their response?
2. How many Egyptians are on Facebook? How many of them are under 25?
3. What do Facebook and Twitter allow ordinary citizens to do in countries with restrictive regimes?

## QUESTIONS FOR REASONING AND ANALYSIS

4. What is Eltahawy's claim? Where does she state it?
5. How does the author qualify her claim? What does she concede? What does she gain from this?
6. Should we conclude that Said was a drug user/dealer? Do we know the truth? Does it matter for the author's argument? Why or why not?

## QUESTIONS FOR REFLECTION AND WRITING

7. Do you use social media? If so, do you see them as "social" only—or as a world of political action as well? Does how you answer have any relation to your ethnicity or how long you have been in the United States?
8. How much time each day do you spend on Facebook, Twitter, and so on? What do you gain from the time spent? How would you justify your time using social media?
9. The author writes of "ownership of the narrative." Explain this concept. Why is owning the narrative so important?

# I TWEET, THEREFORE I AM   | PEGGY ORENSTEIN

Peggy Orenstein is a contributing writer to the *New York Times Magazine,* a popular speaker, and the author of several notable books concerning women's issues. Her latest is *Cinderella Ate My Daughter: Dispatches from the Front Lines of the New Girlie-Girl Culture* (2011). The following *New York Times Magazine* essay was published August 1, 2010.

PREREADING QUESTIONS  On what expression—what philosophical statement—does Orenstein play with in her title? What does this play on words tell you about her anticipated audience?

1    On a recent lazy Saturday morning, my daughter and I lolled on a blanket in our front yard, snacking on apricots, listening to a download of E. B. White reading *The Trumpet of the Swan.* Her legs sprawled across mine; the grass tickled our ankles. It was the quintessential summer moment, and a year ago, I would have been fully present for it. But instead, a part of my consciousness had split off and was observing the scene from the outside: this was, I realized excitedly, the perfect opportunity for a tweet.

2    I came late to Twitter. I might have skipped the phenomenon altogether, but I have a book coming out this winter, and publishers, scrambling to promote 360,000-character tomes in a 140-character world, push authors to rally their "tweeps" to the cause. Leaving aside the question of whether that actually boosts sales, I felt pressure to produce. I quickly mastered the Twitterati's unnatural self-consciousness: processing my experience instantaneously, packaging life as I lived it. I learned to be "on" all the time, whether standing behind that woman at the supermarket who sneaked three extra items into the express check-out lane (you know who you are) or despairing over human rights abuses against women in Guatemala.

3    Each Twitter post seemed a tacit referendum on who I am, or at least who I believe myself to be. The grocery-store episode telegraphed that I was tuned in to the Seinfeldian absurdities of life; my concern about women's victimization, however sincere, signaled that I also have a soul. Together they suggest someone who is at once cynical and compassionate, petty yet deep. Which, in the end, I'd say, is pretty accurate.

4    Distilling my personality provided surprising focus, making me feel stripped to my essence. It forced me, for instance, to pinpoint the dominant feeling as I sat outside with my daughter listening to E. B. White. Was it my joy at being a mother? Nostalgia for my own childhood summers? The pleasures of listening to the author's quirky, underinflected voice? Each put a different spin on the occasion, of who I was within it. Yet the final decision ("Listening to E. B. White's *Trumpet of the Swan* with Daisy. Slow and sweet.") was not really about my own impressions: it was about how I imagined—and wanted—others to react to them. That gave me pause. How much, I began to wonder, was I shaping my Twitter feed, and how much was Twitter shaping me?

5    Back in the 1950s, the sociologist Erving Goffman famously argued that all of life is performance: we act out a role in every interaction, adapting it based on the nature of the relationship or context at hand. Twitter has extended that

metaphor to include aspects of our experience that used to be considered off-set: eating pizza in bed, reading a book in the tub, thinking a thought any-where, flossing. Effectively, it makes the greasepaint permanent, blurring the lines not only between public and private but also between the authentic and contrived self. If all the world was once a stage, it has now become a reality TV show: we mere players are not just aware of the camera; we mug for it.

The expansion of our digital universe—Second Life, Facebook, MySpace, Twitter—has shifted not only how we spend our time but also how we con-struct identity. For her coming book, *Alone Together,* Sherry Turkle, a profes-sor at M.I.T., interviewed more than 400 children and parents about their use of social media and cellphones. Among young people especially she found that the self was increasingly becoming externally manufactured rather than internally developed; a series of profiles to be sculptured and refined in response to public opinion. "On Twitter or Facebook you're trying to express something real about who you are," she explained. "But because you're also creating something for others' consumption, you find yourself imagining and playing to your audience more and more. So those moments in which you're supposed to be showing your true self become a performance. Your *psychol-ogy* becomes a performance." Referring to *The Lonely Crowd,* the landmark description of the transformation of the American character from inner- to outer-directed, Turkle added, "Twitter is outer-directedness cubed."

The fun of Twitter and, I suspect, its draw for millions of people, is its infinite potential for connection, as well as its opportunity for self-expression. I enjoy those things myself. But when every thought is externalized, what becomes of insight? When we reflexively post each feeling, what becomes of reflection? When friends become fans, what happens to intimacy? The risk of the perfor-mance culture, of the packaged self, is that it erodes the very relationships it purports to create, and alienates us from our own humanity. Consider the fate of empathy: in an analysis of 72 studies performed on nearly 14,000 college stu-dents between 1979 and 2009, researchers at the Institute for Social Research at the University of Michigan found a drop in that trait, with the sharpest decline occurring since 2000. Social media may not have instigated that trend, but by encouraging self-promotion over self-awareness, they may well be accelerating it.

None of this makes me want to cancel my Twitter account. It's too late for that anyway: I'm already hooked. Besides, I appreciate good writing whatever the form: some "tweeple" are as deft as haiku masters at their craft. I am experimenting with the art of the well-placed "hashtag" myself (the symbol that adds your post on a particular topic, like #ShirleySherrod, to a stream. You can also use them whimsically, as in, "I am pretending not to be afraid of the humongous spider on the bed. #lieswetellourchildren").

At the same time, I am trying to gain some perspective on the perpetual performer's self-consciousness. That involves trying to sort out the line between person and persona, the public and private self. It also means that the next time I find myself lying on the grass, stringing daisy chains and listening to E. B. White, I will resist the urge to trumpet about the swan.

Source: From *The New York Times Magazine,* August 1, 2010. Reprinted by permission of the author.

QUESTIONS FOR READING

1. Why did the author get into Twitter? How has tweeting affected her responses to experiences?
2. What, presumably, is Twitter's appeal for many users? How does this social medium actually produce the opposite of what users are seeking?
3. What is the difference between *person* and *persona*?
4. What is meant by the term *empathy*? What has happened to this trait among college students over the last thirty years?

QUESTIONS FOR REASONING AND ANALYSIS

5. Orenstein's approach and tone are different from previous essays in this chapter. Describe the essay's characteristics of style and tone.
6. Even though the "feel" of this essay may be different, Orenstein still presents an argument. What is her claim? What does she want readers to know about Twitter?

QUESTIONS FOR REFLECTION AND WRITING

7. Is participation in social media like performing on a reality show? What is your response to this comparison?
8. Are there any advantages to trying on different personalities? What are the possible disadvantages?
9. What other writers in this chapter suggest that the Internet and social media encourage the superficial, keep us from contemplation and insight? Do you agree with their analysis? If so, why? If not, why not?

## A VIOLIN REQUIEM FOR PRIVACY | ELIAS ABOUJAOUDE

Holding an MD from the Stanford University School of Medicine and Board Certified in psychiatry, Elias Aboujaoude is a clinical associate professor of psychiatry and behavioral science at Stanford. He has published results of his clinical studies and several books, the latest *Virtually You: The Dangerous Powers of the E-Personality* (2011). The following article appeared on October 7, 2010, in the *Chronicle of Higher Education.*

PREREADING QUESTIONS What is a requiem? How does it relate to privacy? How does this title announce the author's subject—and position?

1    By all accounts, Tyler Clementi, the 18-year-old Rutgers freshman who jumped from the George Washington Bridge after his roommate streamed a video of him having a sexual encounter with another man, followed appropriate—in retrospect, perhaps old-fashioned—dorm etiquette. To avoid surprises, the shy music major would ask to have the room to himself for specified blocks of time when he planned an intimate meeting. But etiquette, or even Netiquette, is overrated in our digital culture, and a promise of privacy

holds no water if you live in a post-privacy world. "Roommate asked for the room till midnight," Dharun Ravi, the roommate, tweeted before streaming the first video live. "I went into Molly's room and turned on my webcam. I saw him making out with a dude. Yay." Two days later, Ravi's 148 followers on Twitter received another message: "Anyone with iChat, I dare you to video chat me between the hours of 9:30 and 12. Yes it's happening again."

The exposed young violinist was made suicidal because of a critical 2 byproduct of our time: The small inviolate zone of privacy that we all need, and that is absolutely crucial to our psychological equilibrium, has now become virtually impossible to maintain. The greatest minds in the field of human development have stressed the importance of individuation, a process by which people achieve and maintain psychological stability by separating themselves from others. Erik Erikson placed individuation ahead of social success as a barometer of health. For him, mature involvement with another person can happen only when someone is comfortably autonomous and happy in his relationship with himself.

Carl Jung saw individuation as the person's fortress against the weight of 3 group mentality and group demands. It is at least as important to be oneself—that is, to be separate—as it is to belong: Individuation is, in general, "the process by which individual beings are formed and differentiated; in particular, it is the development of the psychological individual as a being distinct from the general, collective psychology." Jung went on to describe individuation as "a natural necessity inasmuch as its prevention by leveling down to collective standards is injurious to the vital activity of the individual."

That "natural necessity" assumes certain safeguards that protect confi- 4 dentiality, such as the basic assumption that a private sexual moment will not be easy to tape, and, if it is taped, will not be easy to broadcast. Psychological autonomy means being able to keep your personhood to yourself and dole out the pieces as you see fit, sharing yourself with people you think are worthy and with whom you want to form a special bond. It has been said that privacy is in part a form of self-possession. You don't truly possess your "self" if you don't have custody of the facts of your life, whether your Social Security number or your salary and sexual biography. Yet, with so many of our "facts" now readily available online for anyone to Google, then cc and bcc around or stream live, control over our personal business has become a chimerical goal—and so, perhaps, has that important task of individuating.

Nothing is confidential in today's world. Parents regularly invade their chil- 5 dren's Facebook accounts (often for good reason); children read their parents' e-mail (my 8-year-old niece easily figured out that her nickname is her mother's Hotmail password). Our genealogy is public knowledge—just bring up your family tree on Ancestry.com. Suspicious spouses install "keyloggers" on their partners' computers to track their keystrokes, and, therefore, their Web whereabouts. Blind dates are no longer blind, because they involve the requisite predate Google search. And the boss has access to everything that goes through the server at work. Everybody is, or everybody can easily be, in everybody else's business. To Erikson and Jung, this would look like development in reverse.

6      Possessing personal information is a source of power. When Clementi lost the right to withhold that information, he was weakened in the eyes of his roommate and his roommate's Twitter followers and Facebook friends, who now possessed it against his wishes.

7      One can make a long list of the ways in which the virtual revolution has made us feel empowered. At the top of that list is probably the ability to quickly gain access to information about anything or anyone. But if we pause—even briefly—between searches to consider how we no longer control our own personal information, we may feel distinctly *dis*empowered—and that realization can be tragically destabilizing. Tyler Clementi paid the ultimate price, but none of us are immune to the ravages of being forced to live a public life.

---

Source: From *The Chronicle of Higher Education*, October 7, 2010. Reprinted by permission of the author.

## QUESTIONS FOR READING

1. What did Tyler Clementi do before having sex in his dorm room? What did his roommate do? What ultimately happened?
2. What, according to well-known experts on human development, do we all need to be stable, happy adults?
3. What is lost when you no longer have control over your private life?

## QUESTIONS FOR REASONING AND ANALYSIS

4. What is Aboujaoude's claim? Where does he state it?
5. What kinds of evidence does he provide?
6. How does the author connect the life of Clementi to the rest of us?
7. How does Aboujaoude qualify his claim? What does he concede? Why? How does this strengthen his argument?

## QUESTIONS FOR REFLECTION AND WRITING

8. Aboujaoude writes that owning "personal information is a source of power." What is your reaction to this assertion? Does it make sense? If you disagree, how would you counter it?
9. It is easy to dismiss someone else's troubled life and suicide. How does Aboujaoude try to get his readers to find a message in the student's death? Has he been successful with you? Why or why not?
10. Do you feel as though you have lost privacy in today's world? If so, is this a problem—or something you are used to? Do you think this issue warrants reflection? Why or why not?

# CHAPTER 17

# The Environment: How Do We Cope with Climate Change?

READ: What situation is depicted? Who speaks the words?

REASON: How do the expressions differ? Why is that significant? How is the cartoon ironic?

REFLECT/WRITE: Explain the point of the cartoon.

In 2005 psychology professor Glenn Shean published a book titled *Psychology and the Environment*. Dr. Shean argues that we are behaving as if we have no environmental problems to face, and that therefore the biggest first step to solving problems related to environmental degradation is to make people aware of and concerned about the interconnected issues of climate change, the heavy use of fossil fuels, and species extinction. Because we are programmed to make quick decisions based on immediate dangers, we find it difficult to become engaged with dangers that stretch out into an indeterminate future. There is always tomorrow to worry about the polar bears or the increasing levels of $CO_2$ in the atmosphere, or the rapidly melting ice caps. And besides, who wants to give up a comfortable lifestyle because it might affect future life on this planet? David Fahrenthold, the second author in this chapter, continues this discussion.

By 2008 even the Bush administration began to give voice to the concerns of environmentalists such as Dr. Shean. After much resistance, there seems to be a more widespread acceptance of climate change and the problems that it can cause, but even among those grudgingly on board there is still a debate as to the degree to which human actions are a major cause of the problems—as opposed to a recognition of periods of temperature increases and decreases that have been a part of the history of the planet. Why do we resist accepting responsibility for adding to the problem? Because to admit to being a cause means that we have to accept being part of the solution—we have to agree to change some of the things we are doing that are heating up the atmosphere. And here is where sacrifice and cost enter the picture. Do we expect factories to shut down? No, but regulations governing pollutants from their smokestacks will help the atmosphere—at a cost to doing business. Do we expect people to stop enjoying the beach? No, but we could have restrictions on building that destroys the barrier islands and marshlands protecting shorelines from erosion and destruction from storms. Do we expect people to stop driving cars? No, but the government could require manufacturers to build more fuel-efficient cars—at a cost to doing business.

And so, even though the conversation has changed somewhat since 2005, the debate continues over the extent to which human actions make a difference and then what should be done, at what cost, and at whose expense. In six articles and several visuals—including the one that opens this chapter—a variety of voices are heard on this debate.

PREREADING QUESTIONS

1. To whom do you listen primarily when you explore scientific questions? Scientists? Politicians? Religious leaders? What is the reasoning behind your choice?

2. How green is your lifestyle? Do you think it matters? Why or why not?

3. Does Dr. Shean describe you when he writes of those who are complacent about environment problems because there does not seem to be an immediate danger? If so, do you think you should reconsider your position? Why or why not?

4. If you accept that we have a problem, what solutions would you support? Reject? Why?

# THE SIXTH EXTINCTION: IT HAPPENED TO HIM. IT'S HAPPENING TO YOU.

MICHAEL NOVACEK

Paleontologist Michael Novacek is senior vice president and provost of the American Museum of Natural History in New York City. Author of more than 200 articles and books, Novacek's most recent book is *Terra: Our 100-Million-Year-Old Ecosystem—and the Threats That Now Put It at Risk* (2008). "The Sixth Extinction" was published on January 13, 2008, in the *Washington Post*.

PREREADING QUESTIONS  Who is the "Him" in Novacek's title? Is it ridiculous to suggest that *we* could be like *him*?

*T. Rex* in charge.

1   The news of environmental traumas assails us from every side—unseasonal storms, floods, fires, drought, melting ice caps, lost species of river dolphins and giant turtles, rising sea levels potentially displacing inhabitants of Arctic and Pacific islands and hundreds of thousands of people dying every year from air pollution. Last week brought more—new reports that Greenland's glaciers may be melting away at an alarming rate.

2   What's going on? Are we experiencing one of those major shocks to life on Earth that rocked the planet in the past?

3   That's just doomsaying, say those who insist that economic growth and human technological ingenuity will eventually solve our problems. But in fact, the scientific take on our current environmental mess is hardly so upbeat.

4   More than a decade ago, many scientists claimed that humans were demonstrating a capacity to force a major global catastrophe that would lead to a traumatic shift in climate, an intolerable level of destruction of natural habitats, and an extinction event that could eliminate 30 to 50 percent of all living species by the middle of the 21st century. Now those predictions are coming true. The evidence shows that species loss today is accelerating. We find ourselves uncomfortably privileged to be witnessing a mass extinction event as it's taking place, in real time.

5   The fossil record reveals some extraordinarily destructive events in the past, when species losses were huge, synchronous and global in scale. Paleontologists recognize at least five of these mass extinction events, the last

of which occurred about 65 million years ago and wiped out all those big, charismatic dinosaurs (except their bird descendants) and at least 70 percent of all other species. The primary suspect for this catastrophe is a six-mile-wide asteroid (a mile higher than Mount Everest) whose rear end was still sticking out of the atmosphere as its nose augered into the crust a number of miles off the shore of the present-day Yucatan Peninsula in Mexico. Earth's atmosphere became a hell furnace, with super-broiler temperatures sufficient not only to kill exposed organisms, but also to incinerate virtually every forest on the planet.

6    For several million years, a period 100 times greater than the entire known history of Homo sapiens, the planet's destroyed ecosystems underwent a slow, laborious recovery. The earliest colonizers after the catastrophe were populous species that quickly adapted to degraded environments, the ancient analogues of rats, cockroaches and weeds. But many of the original species that occupied these ecosystems were gone and did not come back. They'll never come back. The extinction of a species, whether in an incinerated 65-million-year-old reef or in a bleached modern-day reef of the Caribbean, is forever.

7    Now we face the possibility of mass extinction event No. 6. No big killer asteroid is in sight. Volcanic eruptions and earthquakes are not of the scale to cause mass extinction. Yet recent studies show that troubling earlier projections about rampant extinction aren't exaggerated.

8    In 2007, of 41,415 species assessed for the International Union for the Conservation of Nature (IUCN) Red List of Threatened Species, 16,306 (39 percent) were categorized as threatened with extinction: one in three amphibians, one quarter of the world's pines and other coniferous trees, one in eight birds and one in four mammals. Another study identified 595 "centers of imminent extinction" in tropical forests, on islands and in mountainous areas. Disturbingly, only one-third of the sites surveyed were legally protected, and most were surrounded by areas densely populated by humans. We may not be able to determine the cause of past extinction events, but this time we have, indisputably: We are our own asteroids.

9    Still, the primary concern here is the future welfare of us and our children. Assuming that we survive the current mass extinction event, won't we do okay? The disappearance of more than a few species is regrettable, but we can't compromise an ever-expanding population and a global economy whose collapse would leave billions to starve. This dismissal, however, ignores an essential fact about all those species: They live together in tightly networked ecosystems responsible for providing the habitats in which even we humans thrive. Pollination of flowers by diverse species of wild bees, wasps, butterflies and other insects, not just managed honeybees, accounts for more than 30 percent of all food production that humans depend upon.

10    What will the quality of life be like in this transformed new world? Science doesn't paint a pretty picture. The tropics and coral reefs, major sources of the planet's biological diversity, will be hugely debilitated. The 21st century may mark the end of the line for the evolution of large mammals and other animals that are now either on the verge of extinction, such as the Yangtze River dolphin, or, like the African black rhinoceros, confined to small, inadequately

supportive habitats. And devastated ecosystems will provide warm welcome to all those opportunistic invader species that have already demonstrated their capacity to wipe out native plants and animals. We, and certainly our children, will find ourselves largely embraced by a pest and weed ecology ideal for the flourishing of invasive species and new, potentially dangerous microbes to which we haven't built up a biological resistance.

Of course people care about this. Recent surveys show a sharp increase in 11 concern over the environmental changes taking place. But much of this spike in interest is due to the marked shift in attention to climate change and global warming away from other environmental problems such as deforestation, water pollution, overpopulation and biodiversity loss. Global warming is of course a hugely important issue. But it is the double whammy of climate change combined with fragmented, degraded natural habitats—not climate change alone—that is the real threat to many populations, species and ecosystems, including human populations marginalized and displaced by those combined forces.

Still, human ingenuity, commitment and shared responsibility have great 12 potential to do good. The IUCN Red List now includes a handful of species that have been revived through conservation efforts, including the European white-tailed eagle and the Mekong catfish. Narrow corridors of protected habitat now connect nature preserves in South Africa, and similar corridors link up the coral reefs of the Bahamas, allowing species in the protected areas to move back and forth, exchange genes and sustain their populations. Coffee farms planted near protected forests and benefiting from wild pollinators have increased coffee yields. New York's $1 billion purchase of watersheds in the Catskill Mountains that purify water naturally secured precious natural habitat while eliminating the need for a filtration plant that would have cost $6 to $8 billion, plus annual operating costs of $300 million. Emissions of polluting gases such as dangerous nitrogen oxides have leveled off in North America and even declined in Europe (unfortunately emissions of the same are steeply rising in China). Plans for reflective roofing, green space and increased shade to cool urban "heat islands" are at least under consideration in many cities.

These actions may seem puny in light of the enormous problem we face, 13 but their cumulative effect can bring surprising improvements. Yet our recent efforts, however praiseworthy, must become more intensive and global. Any measure of success depends not only on international cooperation but also on the leadership of the most powerful nations and economies.

The first step in dealing with the problem is recognizing it for what it is. 14 Ecologists point out that the image of Earth still harboring unspoiled, pristine wild places is a myth. We live in a human-dominated world, they say, and virtually no habitat is untouched by our presence. Yet we are hardly the infallible masters of that universe. Instead, we are rather uneasy regents, a fragile and dysfunctional royal family holding back a revolution.

The sixth extinction event is under way. Can humanity muster the leadership 15 and international collaboration necessary to stop eating itself from the inside?

---

Source: From *The Washington Post,* January 13, 2008. Reprinted by permission of the author.

1. What events suggest to scientists that we may be heading for another mass extinction?
2. What is the response of many to this "doomsaying" discussion?
3. How many mass extinctions has the Earth experienced? When was the last one and what happened then?
4. How do scientists describe the consequences of extinction No. 6?
5. What are the specific problems that combine to threaten a disastrous change in our environment?

6. What is the primary cause of a potential extinction No. 6? What, then, needs to be the primary source of the solutions? What, in the author's view, is the necessary first step?
7. In paragraph 12, Novacek describes some actions we have taken to address problems. What does he seek to accomplish by including this paragraph?
8. What is Novacek's claim? State it to reveal a causal argument.
9. Of the various consequences of extinction No. 6, listed in paragraph 10, what seems most frightening or devastating to you? Why?

10. Novacek lists numbers and types of endangered species. Do these figures surprise you? Concern you? Why or why not?
11. In your experience, how widespread is the concern for environmental degradation? Do your friends and family discuss this issue? Do most dismiss the seriousness of the issue, as Novacek suggests?
12. Have you made changes to be kinder to the environment? If so, what have you done and what would you recommend that others do?
13. Do you agree with Novacek—or does he overstate the problem? If you agree, how would you contribute to his argument? If you disagree, how would you refute him?

# IT'S NATURAL TO BEHAVE IRRATIONALLY

| DAVID A. FAHRENTHOLD

A graduate of Harvard University, David Fahrenthold is a staff reporter for the *Washington Post* who covers environmental news. "It's Natural to Behave Irrationally" appeared December 8, 2009.

To a psychologist, climate change looks as if it was designed to be ignored. 1

It is a global problem, with no obvious villains and no one-step solutions, 2 whose worst effects seem as if they'll befall somebody else at some other time. In short, if someone set out to draw up a problem that people would not care about, one expert on human behavior said, it would look exactly like climate change.

That's the upshot of a spate of new research that tries to explain stalled 3 U.S. efforts to combat greenhouse-gas emissions by putting the country on the couch.

Polls—including one last month—indicate that a sizable, though shrinking, 4 number of Americans believe climate change is happening. Most of those people think it is a "serious" problem. So, rationally, shouldn't they be doing more to fight it?

The problem, many psychologists say, is the "rationally." 5

Those who are concerned that a real problem is being left unaddressed 6 have called for a change in the way that green groups talk about climate, which has traditionally been heavy on warnings about drought and stranded polar bears. Instead, researchers suggested a new set of back-door appeals, designed essentially to fool people into serving their own—and the planet's— best interests.

"We are collectively irrational, in the sense that we should really care 7 about the long-term well-being of the planet but when we get up in the morning it's very hard to motivate ourselves," said Dan Ariely, a professor of behavioral economics at Duke University, who gave a keynote speech last month at a Washington conference devoted to understanding why people don't do more to save energy.

Psychologists studying the issue say that the now-familiar warnings about 8 climate change kick at emotional dead spots in all human brains—but especially in American brains. Researchers have only theories to explain why people in the United States have done less than those in such places as Europe and Japan. Some think Americans are culturally leery of programs the government might develop to target climate change, trusting instead that the free market will solve major problems.

One U.S. researcher thought television is to blame: All those TV ads have 9 made Americans more focused on their own wants, she theorized, and less likely to care about the long-term good.

No matter where the public's complacency springs from, psychologists 10 have seen this kind of thing before, Ariely said: "That's why we don't exercise, and we overeat, and we bite our fingernails. . . . It's not something where we're going to overcome human nature."

Last month, shortly before Monday's start of an international conference 11 on climate change, the United States and China made pledges to work on cutting greenhouse-gas emissions. But even these underscored the point that much more remains to be done: The United States offered to cut emissions less than environmentalists say it needs to; China offered to cut in ways it was planning to anyway.

## OBSTACLES TO PROGRESS

12      The obstacles to progress—internationally and in the U.S. Senate, where a climate bill is stalled—aren't just mental.

13      Climate change is a policy problem that has "psychological distance": In layman's terms, there's a sense that this is a problem for somebody else or some other time.

14      Although researchers say the climate is, in fact, already shifting, psychologists say many Americans still don't feel close to the issue. And though scientists say that change is unequivocal, the science can be confusing: It is complex, and vocal skeptics are still saying the evidence is not at all conclusive.

15      Another problem with climate change is called, more obscurely, "system justification." This refers to humankind's deep-seated love for the status quo and willingness to defend it.

16      This is why climate change isn't like the hole in the ozone layer: In that crisis, the solution was to substitute new chemicals for old ones, and the changes happened mainly inside refrigerator coils and spray cans. In this one, they could alter basic things about modern life, everything from light bulbs to cars to air travel.

17      A third problem is that psychologists say humans can fret about only so many things at once—the technical term is the "finite pool of worry."

18      The proof of that might be found in last month's *Washington Post*–ABC News poll, which showed that belief in climate change had actually fallen 13 percentage points since 2006, from 85 percent to 72. It could be that new worries such as lost jobs and swine flu crowded old ones out of the pool.

19      Psychological researchers say one possible way to overcome all these obstacles is to frame the changes needed to curb carbon emissions as "saving" the American way of life, instead of changing it. Another is to pair warnings about the climate with concrete suggestions about what to do, so people can act instead of just stewing in worry.

20      Another is to tap into two powerful human impulses: to be like one's neighbors and then to beat them at something.

## CALL IN THE ELEPHANTS

21      In one small study around San Diego in 2007, researchers hung four fliers on doorknobs. One told homeowners that they should conserve energy because it helped the environment. One said saving energy was socially responsible. One said that it saved money. The fourth said that the majority of neighbors in the community were doing it.

22      The researchers waited and then read the meters. The houses with the fourth flier showed the most change.

23      "Simply urging people—or telling them that it's a good idea to recycle or conserve energy—is the same as nothing," said Robert Cialdini, a professor at Arizona State University who worked on the study.

24      One of those listening to the psychologists is Rep. Brian Baird (D-Wash.), who introduced a bill calling on the Department of Energy to study "social and behavioral factors" that affect energy use. It passed a House committee,

though Baird said some Republicans called it "mind control." "These [ideas] can all be met with derision until you try it," Baird said.

For now, however, some psychologists say they're frustrated that their ideas seem to have been picked up only unevenly by environmental groups. 25

For instance, an ad campaign running in the United States and 34 other countries calls for progress at international climate talks in Copenhagen using a play on the city's name: It becomes "Hopenhagen." The ads' strategy was devised by the firm Ogilvy & Mather, where an executive said they, also, wanted to leave behind gloomy messages about the climate. 26

But Janet Swim, a professor at Pennsylvania State University who led an American Psychological Association study of climate change messages, said something was missing. "What is a person supposed to do after seeing the message?" she wrote after seeing one video ad. 27

Another new ad, from the World Wildlife Fund, shows an elephant, birds and other wildlife dialing U.S. senators' offices. "So who will call to speak up for those who have no voice?" the narrator asks. 28

Better, Swim said. The commercial gives a concrete order: Call your senator. But, she said, it might communicate a "norm of inaction" by implying that no actual people are calling now. 29

The best example of climate psychology in action might be programs run by the Arlington energy efficiency software company Opower. In 12 areas around the country, the firm sends mailings to utility customers. The sheets compare each customer's power usage to that of neighbors with similar houses and offer tips for catching up, such as turning off lights and lowering the temperature settings of water heaters. 30

It works, the company says, lowering electricity usage by 2 percent in several test cases. The fliers never say a word about climate change. 31

## QUESTIONS FOR READING

1.  Why is climate change a problem "designed to be ignored"?
2.  What, according to the author, would be the rational response to climate change?
3.  What is the meaning of "system justification"?
4.  What strategies might work to encourage Americans to deal with climate change?

## QUESTIONS FOR REASONING AND ANALYSIS

5.  What, specifically, is the problem that Fahrenthold explores? What is his claim?
6.  What are possible causes of the problem?
7.  How are the solutions connected to the analysis of cause?

8. Do the analyses of the psychologists make sense to you? If yes, why? If no, why not?

9. On what assumption does Fahrenthold's argument rest? That is, what is not open to debate? If you disagree with the author's argument, is it because you disagree with the psychologists' analyses or because you disagree with Fahrenthold's underlying assumption?

## THE COST OF CLIMATE INACTION | KRISTEN SHEERAN and MINDY LUBBER

Formerly an associate professor at St. Mary's College of Maryland, Kristen Sheeran is now executive director of the Economics for Equity and the Environment Network (E3 Network), a group of economists concerned with environmental policy. Dr. Sheeran has published papers on economics in scholarly journals and addressed environmental issues in popular newspapers and magazines. Mindy Lubber, MBA, has been the regional administrator for the EPA and the founder/CEO of Green Century Capital Management. She is now president of Ceres, a national coalition of investors, environmental organizations, and other public interest groups working to incorporate sustainability into capital markets. Their article was published in the *Washington Post* on May 6, 2009.

PREREADING QUESTIONS The authors' title might seem a bit cryptic; what "inaction" do you expect them to examine? And what are they likely to mean by "cost"?

1    Robert J. Samuelson's April 27 [2009] op-ed, "Selling the Green Economy," was way off the mark on the economics of tackling climate change. It was a call to bury our collective heads in the sand simply because the future involves uncertainty—exactly the opposite of what we need to do.

2    Samuelson argued that the cost of moving to a clean-energy economy is higher than advocates expect and that transition can't happen nearly fast enough to meet the ambitious goals proposed in the climate and energy bill sponsored by Reps. Henry Waxman (D-Calif.) and Edward Markey (D-Mass.).

3    But this assumes that all costs involved in mitigating climate change—and there will be costs—represent new costs, without acknowledging the massive error in our market system that equates the price of carbon emissions to zero. This fundamental error skews everything that follows, because if emitting carbon costs nothing on a balance sheet, all steps to reduce pollution count as "new costs."

4    The real cost of carbon emissions is far from zero. Each new scientific report brings proof of a changing climate that promises to disrupt agricultural patterns, set off a scramble for dwindling resources, raise sea levels, propel population shifts and require massive emergency spending as we try to react to the growing crises. These are the costs of inaction.

5    A smart climate policy can create a mechanism to put the right price on carbon, and rapid economic change will follow that firm price signal, along

with reduced climate risks. Our work with more than 100 economists nationwide and at *RealClimateEconomics.org* demonstrates the weight of economic analysis supporting this point.

The failure to put a real price on carbon emissions also undermines 6 Samuelson's second point, that we cannot switch to clean energy technologies quickly. Many claim that these technologies will not work, at least in a cost-effective way, because we would already be using them if they did.

But we are not using them enough now because we have set the price of 7 carbon pollution at zero and have devoted most of our financial incentives to fossil fuel production to gas up our vehicles, heat our homes and power our factories. Acknowledging the climate crisis and pricing its risks correctly, instead of passing them on to our children, would produce an amazingly quick shift to new technologies and behaviors. We change habits when it makes economic sense to do so. Price matters.

Ultimately, households and businesses care more about their total energy 8 bill than costs per gallon or per kilowatt hour. Gas at $4 per gallon is cheaper in a car that gets 40 miles per gallon than $3-a-gallon gas in a clunker that gets 20 mpg. American entrepreneurial and research genius can move us to far greater energy efficiency quickly, using mostly existing technologies, when a carbon price rewards the effort.

The economic impacts on households, then, may not be as dramatic as 9 some warn. We can mobilize the political will for clean technologies and emissions reduction when, as economic research demonstrates, there is a visible payoff in jobs and strides in international competitiveness from these technologies.

And none of this is in conflict with the business community. Quite the 10 contrary. Consider Business for Innovative Climate and Energy Policy (BICEP), a coalition of nationally and globally known companies including Nike, Starbucks, Sun Microsystems, Timberland and Levi Strauss that the investor coalition Ceres coordinates. The heads of these companies believe that passing strong climate and energy legislation this year is in the interests of both the planet and their businesses.

Some BICEP businesses already see climate change affecting their supply 11 chains, manufacturing and international markets. Those are costs. These companies see strong climate and energy policy as pro-business because increased energy efficiency saves them money and clear price signals on carbon help them plan competitive strategies on a more level playing field.

The cost of inaction is high and could be catastrophic. But, contrary to claims, 12 the cost of switching to cleaner energy and dramatically lower emissions will spur competitive gains, cost far less and come much more quickly once we have set our goals, adjusted our incentives and corrected the market's false signals.

History shows that big changes often come in a rush, unforeseen by the 13 critics of the day. We believe that honest accounting for the reality of climate change will bring a convergence of effort and interests, triggering change on a scale that will, once again, alter the course of history.

Source: From *The Washington Post,* May 6, 2009. Reprinted by permission of Kristen Sheeran.

QUESTIONS FOR READING

1. Why do Sheeran and Lubber disagree with Robert Samuelson? What two points does Samuelson make? What, in the authors' view, does he ignore when making both points?

2. What are the climate disruptions listed by Sheeran and Lubber?

3. What can motivate households and businesses to embrace clean technologies and reduced emissions?

4. What is Ceres? What companies are part of BICEP?

5. What legislation do these companies support? Why do they support it?

QUESTIONS FOR REASONING AND ANALYSIS

6. Sheeran and Lubber use Samuelson's column as an occasion for writing, but their primary purpose is not simply to refute him. What is their claim? Where do they state it?

7. Explain, in your own words, the idea of carbon costs—and their effect on business decisions.

8. The authors conclude with a stirring belief in the possibility of significant change. Is their appeal an effective ending? Why or why not?

QUESTIONS FOR REFLECTION AND WRITING

9. Is the concept of carbon costs to business new to you? Does it make sense to factor in gas bills or spending for natural disasters as part of the costs of doing business? Why or why not?

10. Is the authors' focus on the costs of not responding to climate change an approach that David Fahrenthold would applaud? Does it work for you? If you are unmoved by Sheeran and Lubber's argument, how would you refute them?

# HOW MARKETPLACE ECONOMICS CAN HELP BUILD A GREENER WORLD | DANIEL GOLEMAN

A Harvard-trained psychologist who was science reporter for the *New York Times* until the great success of his 1995 book *Emotional Intelligence* led to a career in writing and public speaking. Among his half-dozen other books is his latest: *Ecological Intelligence: How Knowing the Hidden Impacts of What We Buy Can Change Everything* (2009). The following essay, an online posting at *Yale Environment 360* on August 19, 2010, explores more briefly the ideas in his 2009 book on ecology.

PREREADING QUESTION  What are some ways that marketplace forces could be used to fight climate change? Try to anticipate Goleman with your own thinking on this subject.

With climate legislation dead in Congress and the fizzled hopes for a break- 1
through in Copenhagen fading into distant memory, the time seems ripe for
fresh strategies—especially ones that do not depend on government action.

Here's a modest proposal: radical transparency, the laying bare of a 2
product's ecological impacts for all to see.

Economic theory applied to ecological metrics offers a novel way to ame- 3
liorate our collective assault on the global systems that sustain life. There are
two fundamental economic principles that, if applied well, might just accelerate the trend toward a more sustainable planet: marketplace transparency
about the ecological impacts of consumer goods and their supply chains, and
lowering the cost of that information to zero.

First transparency. A maxim in economics holds that transparency makes 4
markets work more efficiently. This rule has long been applied to price, but
why not also apply it to the ecological impacts of industry and commerce? At
present when it comes to the ecological consequence of the things we buy,
we have information asymmetry, where sellers know far more than buyers.

This seems about to change. One big mover is WalMart, which last sum- 5
mer announced it will develop a "sustainability index," a credible rating of the
ecological impacts of the products it sells boiled down into a single metric that
shoppers can use to compare Brand A and Brand B. There are signs this is
more than marketing hype: WalMart has started to pilot life-cycle analyses of
products it carries, and, some say, hopes to make transparent such data on the
environmental and social impacts of suppliers four levels deep in the chain of
vendors. The key, of course, will be to make sure the cost of quantifying and
listing such data is minimal, as price will remain the primary determining factor
for consumers.

WalMart is by no means the only player in taking steps to become more 6
ecologically transparent. Companies such as Unilever (brands like Dove Soap
and Lipton Tea) and Google (its servers consume enormous amounts of
energy) are following their own maps to transparency about the eco-impacts
of their operations, to find ways to make operations more sustainable.

Several global companies are forming a "Group of Ten" to develop a 7
supply chain transparency system called Earthster into its newest version,
"E2 Turbo." Rather than go to the expense of a full life-cycle analysis (which
can cost $50,000 and take months), E2 Turbo asks for data only on the
20 percent or so of a product's life cycle that accounts for around 80 percent
of environmental impacts.

Now under development, this supply-chain-tracking software lets compa- 8
nies understand where their largest negative impacts are, and how to find
more sustainable alternatives. A built-in recommendations engine, drawing on
a Department of Commerce database, suggests suppliers or other players that
can help companies improve those impacts. That guides business-to-business
decisions, with companies better able to find vendors that will let them keep
their eco-impact scores low.

As more and more companies feed data into E2 Turbo—which is open 9
source—they will together build what amounts to an information commons.

There has also been discussion about the U.S. government establishing a site for that commons, creating a public database on ecological impacts that amounts to a new public resource that any company, small or large, could draw on to improve the impacts of its operations.

10     A radical transparency about the ecological impacts may yet emerge from these efforts—and many in the business world are paying attention. A recent article in *Harvard Business Review* proclaims that sustainability has become an essential business strategy and the key driver of innovation. To be sure, there are large numbers of companies who resist—but they may yet join in, if markets shift toward brands that are more transparent about ecological footprints, creating a compelling business case.

11     That shift will become far more likely with the application of the second economic principle, lowering to zero the "cost" of this information, the cognitive effort we must make to get relevant data. Consumer surveys show that about 10 percent of today's shoppers will go out of their way to get information about the ecological impacts of what they buy, while about a third could not care less. The majority in the middle say that if the information were easy to come by, they might use it in deciding what to buy.

12     That's where the action is: making crucial data easy to get. That was done, for instance, at the Hannaford Brothers grocery chain in Maine, with nutritional ratings of foods. While the ratings were sophisticated—made by nutritionists at institutions like Yale and Dartmouth—they were boiled down into a three-, two-, or one-star rating posted next to the price tag (there was also zero, which about 80 percent of foods received, mainly because of the salt and fats in processed foods).

13     The result was a significant shift in purchases toward the more nutritious food and away from the less. The shifts in market share were large enough to get the attention of food brand reps who started asking what they needed to do to get higher ratings.

14     That switch in a company's actions because transparency in the marketplace has driven consumer decisions in a better direction has been called a "virtuous cycle" by Archon Fung at Harvard University's John F. Kennedy School of Government. Fung led a group studying how transparency alters market dynamics and becomes a mechanism for positive change.

15     Such marketplace transparency about the ecological impacts of consumer goods can be seen today at www.GoodGuide.com, a website that aggregates more than 200 databases on the environmental, health, and social impacts of tens of thousands of consumer goods. GoodGuide—a free smart phone app—allows shoppers to compare the eco-virtue of products while in the aisles of a store. Today that comparison requires running your shopping list by the website on your computer or swiping a product's bar code with a cellphone. But the day will come when a daring retailer puts that data next to price tags—thus reducing the information cost to zero, as Hannaford Brothers did with nutritional data.

16     Another website, Skin Deep, a project of the Environmental Working Group, reveals the potential medical risks of the chemicals used in personal

care products, and so ranks then from safest to most risky. Skin Deep's ratings are made by searching in medical databases for the biological effects of a given ingredient, and then weighting the health risks accordingly. Skin Deep has been consulted more than 100 million times by shoppers wanting to know which skin cream or baby lotion might be a better bet.

These two websites offer ratings that are credible, independent, and [17] transparent themselves—the three criteria proposed by the Kennedy School of Government group. To be sure, systems like GoodGuide have yet to obtain fully transparent data about the total eco-impacts of any company or product. These consumer-facing transparency systems are more proof of concept than state-of-the-art. But they offer a hopeful sign we may be headed in that direction.

As the head of product innovation at a global company pointed out to me, [18] ecological transparency would change the business landscape in two ways. First would be a shift in the "value basis" of a product, adding its ecological impacts into the equation. Second, such transparency would drive intense competition to rethink products to lower those impacts, and so protect a brand's market position.

As non-proprietary data collection systems like Earthster compile numbers [19] on the ecological footprints of industry, that information could well feed into an emerging metric that has been designed to replace GDP. Called the "General Progress Indicator," or GPI, this index of national progress rethinks economic indicators by, for example, rising when the poor receive a larger portion of a nation's income and dropping when they get less.

Among the indicators factored into GPI are resource depletion, pollution, and [20] long-term environmental damage. So while the GDP counts pollution as a double gain for an economy—for the economic activity while it is created and again while being cleaned up—GPI counts the costs of that pollution as a loss. Earthster-type databases could bring more precision and currency to GPI's metrics.

Another movement in economics that might embrace such data is the [21] attempt to "internalize externalities"—that is, to make companies bear the costs of, say, cleaning up their pollution rather than governments, by taxing their goods proportionally to their negative eco-impacts. That idea remains a hard sell to business, and to most governments. But marketplace ecological transparency makes pollution, toxics and the like a reputation cost for a brand or company. This substitutes a market force for government action, which— given political realities—may be both more realistic and quicker.

While many business people are starting to take ecological transparency [22] seriously enough to embed it in their strategic thinking, the question arises: Are economists paying attention? A few are. But for the most part these potentially disruptive information technologies, and the marketplace transparency they promise, are beneath the field's radar, or entirely off the map.

One exception is James Angresano, a political economist at The College of [23] Idaho, who sees promise in ecological transparency as a tool for sustainability— itself not a topic central to orthodox thinking in economics. "We've got to think differently," Angresano told me.

24      When Angresano lectured on these ideas recently to students in environmental economics at Peking University, they were so interested they stayed an
extra hour. "Of all the theories I covered over several weeks of lecturing, this
resonated the best," he commented. "They're depressed just hearing what
the problems are. This is a way of making changes; here are some solutions."

---

Source: From *Yale Environment 360*, August 19, 2010. http://www.e360.yale.edu. Reprinted by
permission of the author.

## QUESTIONS FOR READING

1. What is Goleman's proposal?
2. What are the two parts of the proposal?
3. What are specific strategies for creating information on a product's environmental
   impact?
4. Why is it important to make the cost of transparency free? What else is key for
   consumers?
5. How would ecological transparency affect product competition?

## QUESTIONS FOR REASONING AND ANALYSIS

6. Goleman asserts that some economists are paying attention to the transparency
   idea but many are not. What would make all of them start to take notice?
7. Is Goleman's proposal appealing? Has he presented clear explanations and
   good evidence for his anticipated audience? (Think about who his audience is
   and remember that evaluation always needs to be developed in the context of
   audience.)

## QUESTIONS FOR REFLECTION AND WRITING

8. Is Goleman's idea new to you? Does it make sense? If you disagree with his
   proposal, how would you challenge him?
9. Would you like to know that the making of one company's sugar—for
   example—pollutes more than the sugar made by another company? Would this
   affect your buying habits? Why or why not?
10. What are some of the ways that the manufacture of popular products affects
    the environment negatively? Select one product and think about all the steps in
    making and selling and using and disposing of that product—and how each
    step impacts the environment.

You can't solve the climate crisis alone.
But if we all work together, we can.

Join we today.    wecansolveit.org

## QUESTIONS FOR READING

1. What does the visual on this page represent?
2. What do the words in the visual communicate?

3.   What is the ad's claim?

4.   Does this ad's visual effectively support the claim? Why or why not?

5.   Who has to work together to solve the climate crisis? (Think about this and also draw from your reading in this chapter.) Are all of the significant players likely to work together? Why or why not?

6.   Does this ad catch your attention sufficiently for you to check out its website? For you to think about ways that you can help solve the climate problem? Why or why not?

# GLOBAL WARMING IS JUST THE TIP OF THE ICEBERG | JAMES R. LEE

Assistant professor at the American University School of International Service, Dr. Lee is also director of the Mandala Projects. These include the Trade and Environmental Database, the Inventory of Conflict and Environment, and the Global Classroom. He is currently working on a book related to the topic of the following essay, which appeared in the *Washington Post* on January 4, 2009.

PREREADING QUESTIONS   If global warming is just the tip, what lies below the tip of the iceberg? What do you expect Lee to write about?

1      The Cold War shaped world politics for half a century. But global warming may shape the patterns of global conflict for much longer than that—and help spark clashes that will be, in every sense of the word, hot wars.

2      We're used to thinking of climate change as an environmental problem, not a military one, but it's long past time to alter that mindset. Climate change may mean changes in Western lifestyles, but in some parts of the world, it will mean far more. Living in Washington, I may respond to global warming by buying a Prius, planting a tree or lowering my thermostat. But elsewhere, people will respond to climate change by building bomb shelters and buying guns.

3      "There is every reason to believe that as the 21st century unfolds, the security story will be bound together with climate change," warns John Ashton, a veteran diplomat who is now the United Kingdom's first special envoy on climate change. "The last time the world faced a challenge this complex was during the Cold War. Yet the stakes this time are even higher because the enemy now is ourselves, the choices we make."

4      Defense experts have also started to see the link between climate change and conflict. A 2007 CNA Corp. report, supervised by a dozen retired admirals and generals, warned that climate change could lead to political unrest in numerous badly hit countries, then perhaps to outright bloodshed and battle.

One key factor that could stoke these tensions is massive migration as people flee increasingly uninhabitable areas, which would lead to border tensions, greater demands for rescue and evacuation services and disputes over essential resources. With these threats looming, the U.N. Security Council held a precedent-setting debate on climate change in April 2007—explicitly casting global warming as a national security issue.

Global warming could lead to warfare in three different ways.   5

The first is conflict arising from scarcity. As the world gets hotter and drier,   6 glaciers will melt, and the amount of arable land will shrink. In turn, fresh water, plants, crops and cattle and other domestic animals will be harder to come by, thereby spurring competition and conflict over what's left. In extreme examples, a truly desiccated ecosystem could mean a complete evacuation of a hard-hit region. And the more people move, the more they will jostle with their new neighbors.

Such displacement can arise either suddenly or slowly. The growth of the   7 Sahara, for instance, took many millenniums; many thousands of years ago, people were slowly nudged out of the inland region of northern Africa and into such great river valleys as the Nile and the Niger. Over time, incremental but prolonged rises in sea levels will also gradually uproot hundreds of millions of people.

But sometimes the displacement happens with shocking speed: Just think   8 of the deadly hurricanes Katrina and Rita, which together drove millions of people to suddenly leave Louisiana, Mississippi and Texas. As global warming and population growth increase, we could see far deadlier storms than Katrina. In 1991, a cyclone in Bangladesh displaced 2 million people and killed 138,000.

9   All this can lead to warfare when it's time for the displaced to find a new home. For most of human history, they could at least theoretically do so in unclaimed lands—a sort of territorial pressure valve whose existence tamped down conflict. But today, this reservoir of vacant turf no longer exists, except in the least hospitable parts of the planet. So when the displaced start eyeing currently inhabited areas, expect trouble—and the bigger the displacement, the bigger the fight.

10   The second cause of the coming climate wars is the flip side of scarcity: the problems of an increase in abundance. Suppose that global warming makes a precious resource easier to get at—say, rising temperatures in northern Canada, Alaska and Siberia make it easier to get at oil and gas resources in regions that had previously been too bone-chilling to tap. (A few degrees of change in temperature can transform a previously inhospitable climate.) But what happens if some tempting new field pops up in international waters contested by two great powers? Or if smaller countries with murky borders start arguing over newly arable land?

11   Finally, we should also worry about new conflicts over issues of sovereignty that we didn't need to deal with in our older, colder world. Consider the Northwest Passage, which is turning into an ice-free corridor from Europe to Asia during the summer months. Canada claims some portions of the route as its own sovereign waters, while the United States argues that these sections lie within international waters. Admittedly, it'd take a lot of tension for this to turn into a military conflict, but anyone convinced that the United States and Canada could never come to blows has forgotten the War of 1812. And not all this sort of resource conflict will occur between friendly countries.

12   Other kinds of territorial quarrels will arise, too. Some remote islands—particularly such Pacific islands as Tuvalu, Kiribati, Tonga, the Maldives and many others—may be partially or entirely submerged beneath rising ocean waters. Do they lose their sovereignty if their territory disappears? After all, governments in exile have maintained sovereign rights in the past over land they didn't control (think of France and Poland in World War II). Nor are these new questions far away in the future. The first democratically elected president of the Maldives, Mohamed Nasheed, is already planning to use tourism revenue to buy land abroad—perhaps in India, Sri Lanka or Australia—to house his citizens. "We do not want to leave the Maldives, but we also do not want to be climate refugees living in tents for decades," he told Britain's *Guardian* newspaper.

13   The net result of these changes will be the creation of two geopolitical belts of tension due to global warming, which will dramatically shape the patterns of conflict in the 21st century.

14   First, politics will heat up along what we might call the equatorial tension belt, a broad swath of instability around the planet's center. This belt will creep southward, deeper into Africa, and extend far into central Asia.

15   Second, a new tension belt will develop around the polar circles. In the short term, the main problems will arise in the Northern Hemisphere, but later in the 21st century, the area around the South Pole may also see increasing

security strains as countries rush to claim and develop heretofore frozen areas. If the equatorial tension belt includes mostly poor, developing countries fighting over survival, the new polar tension belt will draw in wealthy, developed countries fighting over opportunity.

This is, admittedly, a glum view of the future. But we can still avoid the 16 new hot wars—or at least cool them down a bit. For starters, we should redouble our efforts to slow down global warming and undo the damage humanity has already done to the environment. Every little bit helps, so by all means, hassle your senator and recycle those bottles.

Beyond that, we need to get our heads around the idea that global warm- 17 ing is one of the most serious long-term threats to our national and personal security. For the next two decades or so, the climate will continue to change: Historic levels of built-up greenhouse gases will continue to warm the world— and spin it toward new patterns of conflict. So we need to do more than simply reverse climate change. We need to understand and react to it—ordinary people and governments alike—in ways that avoid conflict. Over the next few years, we may find that climate-change accords and peace treaties start to overlap more and more. And we may find that global warming is heating new conflicts up to the boiling point.

Source: From *The Washington Post,* January 4, 2009. Reprinted by permission of the author.

## QUESTIONS FOR READING

1. What are the three ways that global warming can lead to war?
2. How can human displacement caused by global warming happen slowly? How can it come about quickly?
3. How can sovereignty issues be a result of global warming?
4. Where are the two geopolitical "belts of tension"?

## QUESTIONS FOR REASONING AND ANALYSIS

5. What is Lee's claim? What evidence does he provide to support the seriousness of the problem?
6. Examine Lee's discussion of each cause; does he provide a convincing scenario for each possible source of conflict? Why or why not?
7. What type (genre) of argument is this? Where does Lee place most of his emphasis? Why? What does he provide in the final two paragraphs?

## QUESTIONS FOR REFLECTION AND WRITING

8. Lee concedes that most of us see global warming as an environmental problem only—serious as that is. Is his warning of climate-change war a new idea for you? Does it make sense? (If you were a Maldives native, would Lee's argument seem more convincing?)

9. Most of the author's argument is given to explaining the problem—understandably. Can you add to his discussion of solutions? If recycling bottles won't stop immigrants from arid lands seeking new homes, what else do we need to do—as individuals and as a nation—to address the problems raised by Lee?

## MOVING HEAVEN AND EARTH | GRAEME WOOD

Graeme Wood studied languages at Indiana University and the American University in Cairo and has traveled and worked in the Middle East. He has published book reviews and travel pieces in many magazines and is now a contributing editor to the *Atlantic Monthly*. The following essay was published in the July/August 2009 issue of *Atlantic*.

PREREADING QUESTION What does the term *geo-engineering* mean? Reflect on what you already know about geo-engineering strategies as you prepare to read Wood's article.

1    As the threat of global warming grows more urgent, a few scientists are considering some radical—and possibly extremely dangerous—schemes for reengineering the climate by brute force. Their ideas are technologically plausible and quite cheap. So cheap, in fact, that a rich and committed environmentalist could act on them tomorrow. And that's the scariest part.

2    If we were transported forward in time, to an Earth ravaged by catastrophic climate change, we might see long, delicate strands of fire hose stretching into the sky, like spaghetti, attached to zeppelins hovering 65,000 feet in the air. Factories on the ground would pump 10 kilos of sulfur dioxide up through those hoses every second. And at the top, the hoses would cough a sulfurous pall into the sky. At sunset on some parts of the planet, these puffs of aerosolized pollutant would glow a dramatic red, like the skies in *Blade Runner*. During the day, they would shield the planet from the sun's full force, keeping temperatures cool—as long as the puffing never ceased.

3    Technology that could redden the skies and chill the planet is available right now. Within a few years we could cool the Earth to temperatures not regularly seen since James Watt's steam engine belched its first smoky plume in the late 18th century. And we could do it cheaply: $100 billion could reverse anthropogenic climate change entirely, and some experts suspect that a hundredth of that sum could suffice. To stop global warming the old-fashioned way, by cutting carbon emissions, would cost on the order of $1 trillion yearly. If this idea sounds unlikely, consider that President Obama's science adviser, John Holdren, said in April that he thought the administration would consider it, "if we get desperate enough." And if it sounds dystopian or futuristic, consider that *Blade Runner* was set in 2019, not long after Obama would complete a second term.

4    Humans have been aggressively transforming the planet for more than 200 years. The Nobel Prize–winning atmospheric scientist Paul Crutzen—one of the first cheerleaders for investigating the gas-the-planet strategy—recently argued that geologists should refer to the past two centuries as the "anthropocene" period. In that time, humans have reshaped about half of the Earth's

surface. We have dictated what plants grow and where. We've pocked and deformed the Earth's crust with mines and wells, and we've commandeered a huge fraction of its freshwater supply for our own purposes. What is new is the idea that we might want to deform the Earth intentionally, as a way to engineer the planet either back into its preindustrial state, or into some improved third state. Large-scale projects that aim to accomplish this go by the name "geo-engineering," and they constitute some of the most innovative and dangerous ideas being considered today to combat climate change. Some scientists see geo-engineering as a last-ditch option to prevent us from cooking the planet to death. Others fear that it could have unforeseen—and possibly catastrophic—consequences. What many agree on, however, is that the technology neces-bary to reshape the climate is so powerful, and so easily implemented, that the world must decide how to govern its use before the wrong nation—or even the wrong individual—starts to change the climate all on its own.

If geo-engineers have a natural enemy, it is the sun. Their first impulse is to 5 try to block it out. Stephen Salter, a Scottish engineer, has mocked up a strat-egy that would cool the planet by painting the skies above the oceans white. Salter's designs—based on an idea developed by John Latham at the National Center for Atmospheric Research—call for a permanent fleet of up to 1,500 ships dragging propellers that churn up seawater and spray it high enough for the wind to carry it into the clouds. The spray would add moisture to the clouds and make them whiter and fluffier, and therefore better at bouncing sunlight back harmlessly into space. Salter, who has investigated the technical feasibility of this idea minutely (down to the question of whether ship owners would mind affixing spray nozzles to their hulls with magnets), estimates the cost to build the first 300 ships—enough to turn back the climatological clock to James Watt's era—to be $600 million, plus another $100 million per year to keep the project going.

Roger Angel, an astronomy and optics professor at the University of 6 Arizona, would block the sun by building a giant visor in space. He proposes constructing 20 electromagnetic guns, each more than a mile long and posi-tioned at high altitudes, that would shoot Frisbee-size ceramic disks. Each gun would launch 800,000 disks every five minutes—day and night, weekends and holidays—for 10 years. The guns would aim at the gravitational midpoint between the Earth and the sun, so that the disks would hang in space, provid-ing a huge array of sunshades that would block and scatter sunlight and put the Earth in a permanent state of annular eclipse. Angel's scheme relies on launch technology that doesn't yet exist (no one has ever wanted to shoot Frisbees at the sun before), and would cost several trillion dollars. "I know it sounds like mad science," he says. "But unfortunately we have a mad planet."

Of all the ideas circulating for blocking solar heat, however, sulfur-aerosol 7 injection—the *Blade Runner* scenario—may actually be the least mad. And it provides an illustrative example of the trade-offs that all geo-engineering proj-ects of its scale must confront. The approach is already known to work. When Mount Tambora erupted in Indonesia in 1815 and spewed sulfur dioxide into the stratosphere, farmers in New England recorded a summer so chilly that their fields frosted over in July. The Mount Pinatubo eruption in the Philippines in 1991 cooled global temperatures by about half a degree Celsius for the next few years. A sulfur-aerosol project could produce a Pinatubo of sulfur dioxide every four years.

8    The aerosol plan is also cheap—so cheap that it completely overturns conventional analysis of how to mitigate climate change. Thomas C. Schelling, who won the 2005 Nobel Prize in Economics, has pointed out how difficult it is to get vast international agreements—such as the Kyoto Protocol—to stick. But a geo-engineering strategy like sulfur aerosol "changes everything," he says. Suddenly, instead of a situation where any one country can foil efforts to curb global warming, any one country can curb global warming all on its own. Pumping sulfur into the atmosphere is a lot easier than trying to orchestrate the actions of 200 countries—or, for that matter, 7 billion individuals—each of whom has strong incentives to cheat.

9    But, as with nearly every geo-engineering plan, there are substantial drawbacks to the gas-the-planet strategy. Opponents say it might produce acid rain and decimate plant and fish life. Perhaps more disturbing, it's likely to trigger radical shifts in the climate that would hit the globe unevenly. "Plausibly, 6 billion people would benefit and 1 billion would be hurt," says Martin Bunzl, a Rutgers climate-change policy expert. The billion negatively affected would include many in Africa, who would, perversely, live in a climate even hotter and drier than before. In India, rainfall levels might severely decline; the monsoons rely on temperature differences between the Asian landmass and the ocean, and sulfur aerosols could diminish those differences substantially.

10   Worst of all is what Raymond Pierrehumbert, a geophysicist at the University of Chicago, calls the "Sword of Damocles" scenario. In Greek legend, Dionysius II, the ruler of Syracuse, used a single hair to suspend a sword over Damocles' head, ostensibly to show him how precarious the life of a powerful ruler can be. According to Pierrehumbert, sulfur aerosols would cool the planet, but we'd risk calamity the moment we stopped pumping: the aerosols would rain down and years' worth of accumulated carbon would make temperatures surge. Everything would be fine, in other words, until the hair snapped, and then the world would experience the full force of postponed warming in just a couple of catastrophic years. Pierrehumbert imagines another possibility in which sunblocking technology works but has unforeseen consequences, such as rapid ozone destruction. If a future generation discovered that a geo-engineering program had such a disastrous side effect, it couldn't easily shut things down. He notes that sulfur-aerosol injection, like many geo-engineering ideas, would be easy to implement. But if it failed, he says, it would fail horribly. "It's scary because it actually could be done," he says. "And it's like taking aspirin for cancer."

11   In 1977, the physicist Freeman Dyson published the first of a series of articles about how plants affect the planet's carbon-dioxide concentrations. Every summer, plants absorb about a tenth of the carbon dioxide in the atmosphere. In the fall, when they stop growing or shed their leaves, they release most of it back into the air. Dyson proposed creating forests of "carbon-eating trees,"

engineered to suck carbon more ravenously from the air, and to keep it tied up in thick roots that would decay into topsoil, trapping the carbon. He now estimates that by annually increasing topsoil by just a tenth of an inch over land that supports vegetation, we could offset all human carbon emissions.

Dyson's early geo-engineering vision addressed a central, and still daunt- 12 ing, problem: neither sulfur-aerosol injection nor an armada of cloud whiteners nor an array of space-shades would do much to reduce carbon-dioxide levels. As long as carbon emissions remain constant, the atmosphere will fill with more and more greenhouse gases. Blocking the sun does nothing to stop the buildup. It is not even like fighting obesity with liposuction: it's like fighting obesity with a corset, and a diet of lard and doughnuts. Should the corset ever come off, the flab would burst out as if the corset had never been there at all. For this reason, nearly every climate scientist who spoke with me unhesitatingly advocated cutting carbon emissions over geo-engineering.

But past international efforts to reduce emissions offer little cause for opti- 13 mism, and time may be quickly running out. That's why a few scientists are following Dyson's lead and attacking global warming at its source. David Keith, an energy-technology expert at the University of Calgary, hopes to capture carbon from the air. He proposes erecting vented building-size structures that contain grids coated with a chemical solution. As air flows through the vents, the solution would bind to the carbon-dioxide molecules and trap them. Capturing carbon in these structures, which might resemble industrial cooling towers, would allow us to manage emissions cheaply from central sites, rather than from the dispersed places from which they were emitted, such as cars, planes, and home furnaces. The grids would have to be scrubbed chemically to separate the carbon. If chemists could engineer ways to wash the carbon out that didn't require too much energy, Keith imagines that these structures could effectively make our carbon-spewing conveniences carbon-neutral.

The question then becomes where to put all that carbon once it's cap- 14 tured. Keith has investigated one elegant solution: put it back underground, where much of it originated as oil. The technology for stashing carbon beneath the earth already exists, and is routinely exploited by oil-well drillers. When oil wells stop producing in large quantities, drillers inject carbon dioxide into the ground to push out the last drops. If they inject it into the right kind of geological structure, and deep enough below the surface, it stays there.

We might also store carbon dioxide in the oceans. Already, on the oceans' 15 surface, clouds of blooming plankton ingest amounts of carbon dioxide comparable to those taken in by trees. Climos, a geo-engineering start-up based in San Francisco, is trying to cultivate ever-bigger plankton blooms that would suck in huge supplies of carbon. When the plankton died, the carbon would end up on the sea floor. Climos began with the observation that plankton bloom in the ocean only when they have adequate supplies of iron. In the 1980s, the oceanographer John Martin hypothesized that large amounts of oceanic iron may have produced giant plankton blooms in the past, and therefore chilled the atmosphere by removing carbon dioxide. Spread powdered iron over the surface of the ocean, and in very little time a massive bloom of plankton will grow, he predicted. "Give me half a tanker of iron," Martin said, "and I'll give you the next Ice Age." If Martin's ideas are sound, Climos could in effect become the world's gardener by seeding Antarctic waters with iron and creating vast, rapidly growing offshore forests to replace the ones that no longer exist on land. But this solution, too, could have terrible downsides. Alan Robock, an environmental scientist at Rutgers, notes that when the dead algae degrades, it could emit methane—a greenhouse gas 20 times stronger than carbon dioxide.

16    Just a decade ago, every one of these schemes was considered outlandish. Some still seem that way. But what sounded crankish only 10 years ago is now becoming mainstream thinking. Although using geo-engineering to combat climate change was first considered (and dismissed) by President Johnson's administration, sustained political interest began on the business-friendly right, which remains excited about any solution that doesn't get in the way of the oil companies. The American Enterprise Institute, a conservative think tank historically inimical to emission-reduction measures, has sponsored panels on the sulfur-aerosol plan.

17    By now, even staunch environmentalists and eminent scientists with long records of climate-change concern are discussing geo-engineering openly. Paul Crutzen, who earned his Nobel Prize by figuring out how human activity punched a hole in the ozone layer, has for years urged research on sulfur-aerosol solutions, bringing vast credibility to geo-engineering as a result.

18    With that growing acceptance, however, come some grave dangers. If geo-engineering is publicly considered a "solution" to climate change, governments may reduce their efforts to restrict the carbon emissions that caused global warming in the first place. If you promise that in a future emergency you can chill the Earth in a matter of months, cutting emissions today will seem far less urgent. "Geo-engineering needs some government funding, but the most disastrous thing that could happen would be for Barack Obama to stand up tomorrow and announce the creation of a geo-engineering task force with hundreds of millions in funds," says David Keith.

19    Ken Caldeira, of the Carnegie Institution for Science, thinks we ought to test the technology gradually. He suggests that we imagine the suite of geo-engineering projects like a knob that we can turn. "You can turn it gently or violently. The more gently it gets turned, the less disruptive the changes will be. Environmentally, the least risky thing to do is to slowly scale up small field experiments," he says. "But politically that's the riskiest thing to do."

20    Such small-scale experimentation, however, could be the first step on a very slippery slope. Raymond Pierrehumbert likens geo-engineering to building strategic nuclear weapons. "It's like the dilemma faced by scientists in the Manhattan Project, who had to decide whether that work was necessary or reprehensible," he says. "Geo-engineering makes the problem of ballistic-missile defense look easy. If has to work the first time, and just right. People quite rightly see it as a scary thing."

21    The scariest thing about geo-engineering, as it happens, is also the thing that makes it such a game-changer in the global-warming debate: it's incredibly cheap. Many scientists, in fact, prefer not to mention just how cheap it is.

Nearly everyone I spoke to agreed that the worst-case scenario would be the rise of what David Victor, a Stanford law professor, calls a "Greenfinger"—a rich madman, as obsessed with the environment as James Bond's nemesis Auric Goldfinger was with gold. There are now 38 people in the world with $10 billion or more in private assets, according to the latest Forbes list; theoretically, one of these people could reverse climate change all alone. "I don't think we really want to empower the Richard Bransons of the world to try solutions like this," says Jay Michaelson, an environmental-law expert, who predicted many of these debates 10 years ago.

22   Even if Richard Branson behaves, a single rogue nation could have the resources to change the climate. Most of Bangladesh's population lives in low-elevation coastal zones that would wash away if sea levels rose. For a fraction of its GDP, Bangladesh could refreeze the ice caps using sulfur aerosols (though, in a typical trade-off, this might affect its monsoons). If refreezing them would save the lives of millions of Bangladeshis, who could blame their government for acting? Such a scenario is unlikely; most countries would hesitate to violate international law and become a pariah. But it illustrates the political and regulatory complications that large-scale climate-changing schemes would trigger.

23   Michaelson—along with many others—has called for public research on some possible legal responses to geo-engineering. "It would be a classic situation where the problem should be handled in an official capacity," he says. In practice, that would likely mean industrialized governments' regulating geo-engineering directly, in a way that lets them monopolize the technology and prevent others from deploying it, through diplomatic and military means, or perhaps by just bribing Bangladesh not to puff out its own aerosols. Such a system might resemble the way the International Atomic Energy Agency now regulates nuclear technology.

24   And since geo-engineering—like nuclear weapons—would most likely be deployed during a moment of duress, legal experts like Victor have urged establishing preliminary regulations well in advance. "Suppose the U.S. or Brazil decided it needed some combination of emissions-cutting and geo-engineering in a sudden catastrophe," Victor says. "How would the rest of us respond? There's been no serious research on the topic. It has to be done right now, and not in a crisis situation." An outright ban on geo-engineering could lead other countries to try out dangerous ideas on their own, just as a ban on cloning in the United States has sent research to Korea and Singapore; it would constrain all but the least responsible countries.

25   Victor doesn't believe geo-engineering will solve anything by itself, but he expects that ultimately we will have a cocktail of solutions. Perhaps we could start with a few puffs of sulfur in the atmosphere to buy time, then forests of plankton in the ocean, and then genetically engineered carbon-hungry trees. What isn't an option, Victor says, is refusing to fund more research, in the hope that geo-engineering won't be needed.

26   Thomas Schelling, who won his Nobel Prize for using game theory to explain nuclear strategy and the behavior of states in arms races, shares

Victor's frustration about the way geo-engineering has been ignored. Multinational agreements to cut emissions amount to a game of chicken that tends to end unhappily in Schelling's models. The ideal outcome would be a technology that changes the game. "We just have to consider that we may need this kind of project, and might need it in a hurry," he says. "If the president has to go by boat from the White House to the Capitol, we should be ready scientifically—but also diplomatically—to do something about it."

27      We should keep such images in mind. And they should remind us that, one way or another, a prolonged love affair with carbon dioxide will end disastrously. A pessimist might judge geo-engineering so risky that the cure would be worse than the disease. But a sober optimist might see it as the biggest and most terrifying insurance policy humanity might buy—one that pays out so meagerly, and in such foul currency, that we'd better ensure we never need it. In other words, we should keep investigating geo-engineering solutions, but make quite clear to the public that most of them are so dreadful that they should scare the living daylights out of even a Greenfinger. In this way, the colossal dangers inherent in geo-engineering could become its chief advantage. A premonition of a future that looks like *Blade Runner,* with skies dominated by a ruddy smog that's our only defense against mass flooding and famine, with sunshades in space and a frothy bloom of plankton wreathing the Antarctic, could finally horrify the public into greener living. Perhaps a Prius doesn't sound so bad, when a zeppelin is the alternative.

28      It is not like fighting obesity with liposuction: it's like fighting obesity with a corset, and a diet of lard and doughnuts.

---

## QUESTIONS FOR READING

1. What technology currently exists that could cool the Earth?
2. Why label the last 200 years the "anthropocene" period?
3. What, according to Wood, is the biggest problem we face with strategies for cooling the Earth?
4. What are three strategies for reducing the power of the sun in order to cool the Earth?
5. What are the three kinds of negative consequences to these strategies?
6. What is a significant problem with the various "block-the-sun" approaches? What is Freeman Dyson's suggestion that addresses the problem? What is David Keith's strategy for reducing carbon?
7. If geo-engineering solutions become widely popular, what might be an immediate consequence?
8. What is one of the scariest characteristics of geo-engineering? Why are some scientists suggesting international agreements and government controls?

9. Wood presents various geo-engineering options to climate change in great detail, but his complex essay can be understood and analyzed. Begin by making an informal outline; after presenting three ways to decrease the power of the sun and cool the Earth, what does Wood cover? Then what, and so on?

10. Wood emphasizes the risks and limits of the various specific strategies most debated today, but he also stresses other kinds of risks. What are these? Why do they suggest the need for governments to be involved?

11. Look again at the author's concluding paragraphs. Where does he stand on this topic? By brief comments at the end and by larger implications, what does he think we should be trying to do, right now, to deal with the consequences of global warming? Write a claim statement for Wood's analysis.

12. How much of the specifics of geo-engineering discussed by Wood are new to you? Are you surprised by how far along some of the technology is for various strategies? If any of this surprises you, what surprises the most? What upsets you the most? Why?

13. What is the United Nations's position of geo-engineering at present? (If you don't know, go online and see what you can learn.) In light of what you may have learned from Wood, do you think that the UN should have a position on geo-engineering? Do you think that countries should be in serious discussions about the prospects of someone or some country trying some of the strategies? Why or why not?

14. Very few scientists and serious writers about climate change doubt that we have a problem—as you can see from this chapter. Are you prepared to see climate change as posing major problems for the United States and the world? Why or why not?

# CHAPTER 18

# Sports Talk—Sports Battles

The University of Connecticut women's basketball team celebrating their record 89 wins in a row!

Sports, at all levels, offer us so much. Sports can be a great equalizer. Many successful football and basketball players started at public schools, won scholarships to college, and made it to careers in the NFL or NBA. Sports also bring diverse people together, playing in amateur competition or cheering on their local professional teams.

And yet, controversies of one kind or another are never far from the front pages. Millionaire professional players make the news for assault, for arranging dogfights, for cheating on their wives. Should we expect superstar players to be role models? Or, just great players whose skills—but not whose lifestyles—we admire? Some would argue that they make their money because we support their play; shouldn't they feel an obligation to give back to the community? Is there a cult of privilege for athletes, beginning in high school, that can feed arrogance and a sense of being above the "rules" that govern the behavior of most people?

We can also ask about the role of sports in college. Although the original idea may have been to build strong bodies as well as strong minds, the reality is that Division I football and basketball are big business, pulling in big bucks for the schools and giving 18-year-olds a national stage on which to perform. Should these players see some of the money they "earn" for their schools?

These are some of the questions that authors in this chapter explore. After remembering the excitement and joy of cheering for a winning team, or participating in a victory for one's school, consider the following questions as you study this chapter's six essays.

PREREADING QUESTIONS

1. Should the NCAA demand higher academic credentials for would-be college athletes and expect college players to carry typical course loads leading to graduation?
2. Should Division I football and basketball players be paid a salary in addition to their college scholarships?
3. How much "enhancement" of athletes is fair? Should steroids be allowed?
4. Are young people with athletic ability given too many free passes on bad behavior?
5. Are we foolishly starstruck over our favorite professional players?

## SHOW THEM THE MONEY | DONALD H. YEE

A graduate of UCLA and the University of Virginia School of Law, Donald Yee is a partner in Yee & Dubin Sports, a Los Angeles–based sports management firm representing many professional players and coaches. Yee is a frequent speaker on sports-related issues and is an adjunct professor of law at the University of Southern California. "Show Them the Money" was published August 22, 2010, in the *Washington Post*.

PREREADING QUESTIONS  Are the NCAA rules too strict? Are they unrealistic?

1      The Church of College Football is about to open for services. It is perhaps the most passionate religion we have in this country, a seductive blend of our most popular sport and the romantic notion that the young athletes are playing for their schools, not for money.

2      Two championship coaches recently launched attacks on sports agents for allegedly defiling this house of worship by giving college players what the National Collegiate Athletic Association calls "impermissible benefits"—benefits that make those players pros and not amateurs. "The agents that do this, and I hate to say this, but how are they any better than a pimp?" Alabama's Nick Saban so memorably put it last month. "I have no respect for people who do that to young people. None." And Florida's Urban Meyer said that the problem is "epidemic right now" and that agents and their associates need to be "severely punished."

3      Yet, I suspect that virtually everyone in our industry—players, coaches, administrators, boosters, agents and fans—shed our naivete a long time ago. We know that the sole focus for many star college players is getting ready for pro ball, that coaches are looking for financial security on the backs of teenagers and that boosters enjoy the ego stroke that comes with virtually owning a piece of a team. There isn't anything inherently wrong with these goals, but there isn't anything "amateur" about the process, either.

4      And we know that while college football players aren't getting a W-2, they are getting paid to play the game. It's a straightforward business transaction: You play for us, we give you a one-year scholarship, renewable at the head coach's discretion. In some cases, rules are broken by schools or other parties so that relatives and other associates of the players can be paid, too,

This football player reaches for money, not the ball.

5      I've had the privilege of representing professional athletes and coaches for more than 20 years, and I've had a front-row seat to observe the NCAA's brand of amateurism. I've heard many times about events that would constitute NCAA rule violations—some were egregious, many weren't. Some athletes take money from agents, marketers or others simply because they are hungry (the scholarship is not always enough to buy food). Yes, there are some people out there with malicious agendas, but there are also many people who act in good faith with an allegiance to the integrity of the sport.

6      The primary culprit isn't the people around the game; it's the NCAA's legislated view of amateurism. It lacks intellectual integrity and is terribly unnecessary—particularly when better alternatives exist.

Two developments this spring demonstrate why the sham of amateurism 7 should come to an end.

The Pacific-10 Conference's luring of teams from the Mountain West and 8 Big 12 conferences, which caused some scrambling in June, had nothing to do with education or amateur sports. It really didn't have anything to do with football or its traditions, either. It had everything to do with money. Saddled with expiring television contracts, the Pac-10 wanted to get bigger so it could command larger contracts in its next round of negotiating and possibly launch its own TV network. With the addition of the University of Utah and the University of Colorado, the Pac-10's revenues will grow. Its coaches will make more money, and its players will get bigger and shinier facilities, fancier menus, cushier dorms, more stylish travel arrangements and other perks.

The average Pac-10 student will see none of this.                              9

Around the same time as the realignment, the University of Southern 10 California, home of one of the premier college football programs, suffered a major embarrassment when Reggie Bush, who starred at tailback for the Trojans in the mid-2000s, was found to have received lavish gifts from a sports marketer. According to the NCAA, Bush was, in effect, a pro while he was in college, and the university knew it. The NCAA concluded that USC demonstrated a "lack of institutional control" over its football program. The team received a two-year postseason ban, lost 30 scholarships over three seasons and vacated its victories from the period when Bush was deemed to have been ineligible—including the 2004 national championship season.

Bush is long gone, now an NFL millionaire. His former USC head coach, Pete 11 Carroll, is long gone, also now an NFL millionaire. Many of the assistant coaches who were there at the time are gone as well, and also became millionaires (e.g. University of Washington head coach Steve Sarkisian). Some left and then came back as millionaires (e.g. new head coach Lane Kiffin). Left to suffer the penalties are the current players, many of whom were in middle school or high school when Bush played.

The controversy over USC continues: Are the findings accurate? Should 12 Carroll have done more, earlier? Is the punishment excessive? The answers won't matter, because I have no doubt that Bush-like situations will continue to emerge throughout college football. This sort of thing has been going on for years, and the incentives to keep it up are too strong in the current system.

What needs to change is the entire attitude toward college football. This 13 is the perfect time to implement an honest approach to the combination of big-time football and higher education, an approach that eliminates the NCAA's notion of amateurism. College football generates huge revenues, and there is plenty of money to create a win-win business model for players, coaches and universities. A big business deserves market-driven reform, free of hypocrisy. Here are 10 steps to accomplish that.

**1. All of the major football-playing universities should lease the rights** 14 **to operate a commercial football program on behalf of the university to an independent, outside company.** For example, the University of Southern California would contract with USC Football Inc. Such leases would be open to bidding—schools such as Notre Dame, USC and Texas could generate massive revenue. USC football could look exactly as it does now, except USC Football Inc. would have paid for the right to operate it. The university and the company would share net profits from all revenue streams at a negotiated level. Can you imagine how much more revenue schools could garner if, for instance, they were allowed to sell more ad space on uniforms?

15    This would not be a new business structure for major universities; many already use similar arrangements for other ventures. For example, many major athletic departments now sell their marketing rights to outside companies, and the majority of schools (and the NCAA) contract with the Collegiate Licensing Company to market and license their trademarks.

16    Some universities would find that the marketplace doesn't have any interest in their programs. This means that business people think football is a money-loser for those schools. So those schools should drop football and allocate the money to their core objective: educating students.

17    **2. Each university's football corporation could create leagues, whether long- or short-term, with other corporations.** There wouldn't have to be any allegiance to geography, fan loyalties or tradition. For example, some of these leagues could be premised on budget size. To a large degree, this is already being done; it's called the BCS. A group of conferences formed the BCS, or Bowl Championship Series, and decided to exclude other conferences.

18    Or the football corporations could decide to avoid joining a league, simply scheduling games as a free agent. Again, this is hardly novel—Notre Dame has done it for years, and Brigham Young University is contemplating it now—so this arrangement would simply formalize and spread the practice.

19    **3. All of the players would be paid a salary, whatever the market would bear.** Players would no longer receive scholarships. Just as in the pros, they would be paid based on their perceived value to their program. If an outstanding high school player is coveted, he should be allowed to experience the fruits of American capitalism. Prominent high school players entering college are no different than prominent college players entering the NFL—they can bring excitement and new revenue to a program. No one, for instance, can deny the excitement, revenue and attention that Bush brought to USC. The players would pay income taxes; the football corporations would pay Social Security taxes; 401(k) plans could be established.

20    USC Football Inc. would be free to recruit a player any way it wants, with anything it wants, say, an iPhone and plane tickets for his parents. If a player feels misled in the recruiting process, he could sue for fraud. Each program would be reliant on the business acumen of its operators and subject to whatever profit-margin goal it chooses.

21    **4. The corporations could offer a range of educational opportunities.** Academically gifted players could take regular university courses, if they could have gained admission on their own merit. Others may be more interested in

vocational training or other specialty classes. Either way, average students would no longer lose a chance at admission because the university made an exception for an academically less qualified athlete. And athletes would have a broader array of course offerings. Some may even choose not to attend classes and simply focus on honing their football skills.

**5. The NCAA can be eliminated, at least as it relates to football.** Many 22 of its rules are archaic and frankly gibberish. The NCAA itself states that it does not have subpoena power, which is one way of admitting that enforcement of its rules is difficult.

**6. Universities could scrap much of their athletic administrations, just** 23 **as Vanderbilt University has done.** The chief executive of, say, USC Football Inc. would make decisions, and her mandate would be to ensure that the operation was self-sufficient—no student fees (or taxpayer dollars, in the case of a public university) would be used to subsidize the football program or facilities. Any profits flowing back to the university could go directly to support the general student body and faculty. As it stands now, large public universities across the country employ sizable staffs in their athletic departments; these public employees (including the coaches) are entitled to public benefits and pensions, which are a drain on public resources.

**7. Congress and state legislatures wouldn't have to waste time inves-** 24 **tigating or discussing the regulation of college football.** So long as these new corporations mind the same business laws that apply to Apple or General Electric, our representatives could devote their energies elsewhere.

**8. Coaches could focus strictly on coaching.** They would be employees 25 of the corporation, not the university. Lane Kiffin wouldn't have to worry about monitoring every player's vehicle of choice or whether a booster is buying meals for his quarterback. And Nick Saban wouldn't have to waste his time discussing "pimps." In this system, players could take money from agents or marketers because their amateurism wouldn't be at stake.

**9. Universities could focus on their core mission of educating students.** 26 University presidents wouldn't have to waste their time monitoring a football program, and they wouldn't have to attend any more NCAA functions.

**10. Finally, this system would end the tiresome sports media discus-** 27 **sions of whether this player or that player was paid.** We could say without any hint of sarcasm, speculation or cynicism that yes, he was.

Source: From *The Washington Post*, August 22, 2010. Reprinted by permission of the author.

QUESTIONS FOR READING

1. What is Yee's subject?
2. What two situations are used to illustrate the "sham of amateurism" in college football?

3. What would some colleges discover if they sought to lease their football program to an outside management firm?

4. What options would athletes have under an outside corporation system?

5. What advantage would Yee's recommendations have for both coaches and colleges?

## QUESTIONS FOR REASONING AND ANALYSIS

6. What is Yee's claim? What is the core of his argument?

7. Examine the author's introduction. What makes it clever?

8. What does Yee gain by presenting his proposal in a list of ten points? What effect on readers does he seek with this strategy?

9. Is it possible to agree with Yee that there is a problem and still reject his proposals? Is it possible to accept some of his suggestions? If so, which ones? If not, why not?

## QUESTIONS FOR REFLECTION AND WRITING

10. Do you agree that we "worship" college football? Is that an accurate account of the country's fall weekends? (Have you ever counted the number of televised games?)

11. Do you agree that, in spite of the romanticism surrounding college sports, most people are not naïve; most understand that it is big business and that NCAA rules are regularly ignored? If you disagree, how would you counter Yee? If you agree, then are you prepared to accept the author's proposals? Why or why not?

12. In what sense is it incorrect to say that college athletes are unpaid?

13. Is it right to ask college athletes to pretend to be students, if that is not their interest?

## EDUCATION, ATHLETICS: THE ODD COUPLE | SALLY JENKINS

A sportswriter for the *Washington Post* for a number of years, Sally Jenkins left in 1990 to work at *Sports Illustrated* and write a number of books, mostly about sports figures. She has a book written with Dean Smith about his years in college basketball. In 2000 she published, with Lance Armstrong, *It's Not About the Bike: My Journey Back to Life.* Her 2007 book *The Real All Americans* narrates the story of Jim Thorpe and the football players of the Carlisle Indian School. In 2000 Jenkins returned to the *Post.* The following column appeared there on September 13, 2002.

PREREADING QUESTIONS Explain Jenkins's title; what does it suggest her attitude will be toward college and athletics? How big are the problems with college athletics?

1    It's knee-jerk time in college athletics again. Ohio State and Maurice Clarett are examples of everything wrong, while Vanderbilt has preserved the

sanctity of the academic temple. For days now, we've enjoyed black and white thinking, moral certainty, and stern reform-mindedness. But the last thing we can apply to college sports any more is absolutism. Nothing is as good or bad as it seems—nor is the Ivy League, as it turns out.

Whatever you're sure of on the subject of college sports, you will certainly 2 question it after the publication of a book called *Reclaiming the Game,* by William G. Bowen and Sarah A. Levin. The book, which will appear next week from Princeton University Press, takes a hard-eyed look at the Ivies and other so-called "elite" colleges and reaches some startling conclusions: Recruited athletes are four times more likely to be admitted to the Ivies than other students, they have lower SAT scores than their peers by 119–165 points, and they chronically under-perform academically. Seem familiar? It sounds like Division I-A.

In other words, even the Ivies are getting it wrong? 3

It depends on your view. Every scandal, controversy and ill in the NCAA 4 always boils down to the same question: What are college athletics really for? What are they supposed to be, and what values should they represent? This is where the real trouble begins, because college athletics have increasingly become a matter of competing moralities. And they have always been extremely human, corrupt, and mistaken-prone endeavors, too.

People who want to apply pat reforms or even a consistent philosophy to 5 college athletics are simply barking up the wrong tree—and perhaps the worst tree we can bark up these days is to assume that some schools have found the higher moral ground.

One of the more interesting conclusions reached by Bowen, a former 6 president of Princeton who is now head of the Andrew W. Mellon Foundation, and co-author Levin, is that academic hypocrisy is rampant.

"Truth-telling is important, especially for institutions that pride them- 7 selves, as colleges and universities should, on inculcating respect for evidence and for their own unequivocal commitments to honest rendering of facts and to faithful reporting," they write. "But there is something unsettling about reading stories describing the 'purity' of athletics at the non-scholarship schools when so many of their leaders are well aware of the compromises that are being made in fielding teams. There is enough cynicism today about the capacity of institutions (whether they be corporations, churches, colleges and universities, governmental entities, or foundations) to be what they claim to be. . . ."

It's difficult to read that passage and not think about Vanderbilt, which 8 has presented itself as a paragon of academic virtue this week, while Ohio State, a very good school, is having a difficult time fighting off the taint of academic scandal. Ohio State Athletic Director Andy Geiger suspended Clarett for accepting money against NCAA rules. Meantime, Vanderbilt Chancellor Gordon Gee announced he was doing away with his athletic department.

But it turns out Gee's great reform basically amounts to a symbolic name 9 change—he's not cutting any sports, or scholarships. He accompanied it with a speech that smacked of grandstanding. "For too long, college athletics has been segregated from the core mission of the university," Gee intoned.

10    Gee sounds like a personable, well-intentioned guy. But he doesn't sound any more personable or well-intentioned than Geiger, who insists Ohio State is basically clean and the Clarett affair was isolated.

11    "I hope we get investigated up the yin-yang," Geiger said. "I'd submit we don't have a systemic issue, we have a maverick deal, and it's been more than difficult. But it's not because we're corrupt."

12    The funny thing is, Gee wasn't always so reform-minded and he's no stranger to big athletic programs. He once was president of Ohio State, where he actually hired Geiger, and he also presided over West Virginia, and Colorado, when the Buffaloes enjoyed both national championship and scandal under Bill McCartney. You have to wonder if, now that he's at Vandy, he's simply playing to a new crowd.

13    Geiger has a varied résumé too; he's been all over Division I-A, and his record for integrity is pretty good. He was the former athletic director at Stanford University, until he got tired of what he calls "Stanford-speak" and decided he wanted to work for public universities. He went to Maryland, and then Ohio State.

14    Here is the central problem with any reform of college athletes: The proper role of college sports on a campus depends entirely on what group is evaluating the question. Is the athletic scholarship a scam, or a tool of affirmative action? Some say Ohio State was wrong to give a scholarship to Clarett, a guy who didn't even want to be there. Others such as Geiger argue that to do away with scholarships and academic exceptions would be to kill opportunity. He also maintains that "athletics have some intellectual content unto themselves."

15    There are differences even within the same programs. Ohio State, for instance, will have 105,000 people at the football stadium on Saturday, and about 200 at a women's soccer game. Yet both sports are supposed to be part of the same school, program, values, effort, and management.

16    Any truly intelligent discussion of college athletics may require what Germaine Greer once called, in a discussion completely unrelated to football, "myriad-mindedness." Increasingly, if we're going to solve the "problem" of athletics we have to accept differing value systems and accept the tension between competing moralities. The NCAA is comprised of public schools, and private, of large corporatized universities and small precious intellectual havens, of Northeastern industrials and Midwestern agriculturals—and it's the clash between them that makes their games so interesting.

17    What are college sports for? Maybe we should first ask what a college is for. The chief event that occurs in college is the emancipation of your head. The main undertaking of a student is understanding, and this is why no one expects him or her to come up with anything resembling consistency; they're too busy questioning and rejecting. College is also where scruple and low-level crime duel. Youth carouses un-enforced by parents or much else in the way of authority. Hopefully, the outcome of this formative emancipation is

the development of one's own interior hall monitor. But sometimes it produces a communist, or a car wreck.

This is the risk we take by having colleges at all. The same principle could 18 be applied to games that undergraduates play.

## QUESTIONS FOR READING

1. What is Jenkins's subject? (Be more precise than "college sports.")
2. What does the book *Reclaiming the Game* reveal? From the title, what do you think is the authors' view regarding college sports?
3. What, according to Jenkins, is at the core of all debates over college athletics?
4. Who are Andy Geiger and Maurice Clarett? What happened at Ohio State?
5. What is the connection between Geiger at Ohio State and Chancellor Gee at Vanderbilt? What seems to be the author's attitude toward Gee?
6. Why is discussion of reforming college athletics difficult, in Jenkins's view?
7. What, in her view, are colleges for?

## QUESTIONS FOR REASONING AND ANALYSIS

8. What is Jenkins's claim? What are the main points in her argument?
9. Why does Jenkins present information about Gee's past positions and appointments? How does this serve as evidence in support of her thesis?
10. Explain the concept of "myriad-mindedness" as it applies to solving problems in college sports.
11. Examine Jenkins's images in paragraph 17. What makes them effective in support of her concept of college?

## QUESTIONS FOR REFLECTION AND WRITING

12. Evaluate Jenkins's argument. Do you agree with her approach to problems in college athletics? If yes, why? If no, how would you rebut her argument?
13. The sports pages offer an almost continual flow of rule breaking and scandals (including, in 2003, murder and attempted cover-up at Baylor University) in college athletics, yet Jenkins argues that it is not as bad as it seems. How might you defend her assessment? If you disagree, how would you respond to her?
14. What is the role or purpose of the university? What is the role or purpose of sports as part of the university? Do we have to "accept the tension between competing moralities," or can (should?) we agree on the basic values and goals of college and college sports?

## PRIVILEGE UNCHECKED IN THE U-VA CASE?  |  RUTH MARCUS

After attending law school, Ruth Marcus switched careers to journalism. She began her career at the *Washington Post* as a reporter but is now a member of the editorial board and a fairly regular columnist. The following column was published May 7, 2010.

PREREADING QUESTIONS  What is the University of Virginia case to which the title refers? (If you don't know, go online and see what you can learn.) What can you anticipate about the case Marcus will discuss?

1    The question has to be asked: Is it something about athletes? Something about entitled college athletes? Something about lacrosse?

2    George Huguely V, a 22-year-old University of Virginia lacrosse player, is charged with killing his one-time girlfriend, Yeardley Love, herself a lacrosse player. Huguely, according to a police report, confessed to kicking in Love's bedroom door, shaking her and hitting her head against the wall.

3    I don't think for a moment that lacrosse made him do it. But it's fair to ask whether the special benefits accorded a star athlete on the nation's No. 1-ranked team contributed to an eyes-averted attitude toward this young man's problems. Because for all his charmed existence, Huguely seems to have had a wild, even dangerous, side that went unaddressed until too late.

4    A 2006 story in *The Post,* referring to the elite, all-boys private high school that Huguely then attended, praised him as "Landon's Top Prankster." It quoted Huguely bragging about how he had filched the coach's car keys, drove to the practice and sat chatting in the driver's seat until the coach realized what was up.

5    Another time, Huguely bet an assistant coach that the assistant's fiancee would kiss him if he made a big play. "He walked off the field and said to the team, 'What's [her] number?'" the head coach recalled.

6    There's no direct line from arrogance to violence, or from macho jock culture to brutality. But Huguely's trajectory includes more disturbing data points. In Florida, where his family has a $2 million vacation home, he was charged in 2007 with underage possession of alcohol. The next year, police were summoned after Huguely got into a "very heated" argument with his father aboard their 40-foot fishing boat, dove into the ocean and tried to swim the quarter-mile to shore.

7    Most troubling, Huguely was arrested near a fraternity house at Washington and Lee University in Lexington in 2008 for public swearing, intoxication and resisting arrest. After being detained, Huguely "used colorful statements such as: 'I'll kill all you . . . I am not doing a damn thing you say . . . I want to talk to your supervisor now,'" according to a statement by the Lexington Police Department.

8    The arresting officer, R. L. Moss, said she had to use her Taser to subdue Huguely—although he did not remember that afterward. "He was by far the most rude, most hateful and most combative college kid I ever dealt with," Moss told the *New York Times*.

9    Huguely received a 60-day suspended sentence, six months' probation and a fine, and was required to perform community service and attend a

substance abuse program. You have to wonder: Would a dropout without access to a pricey lawyer have gotten a tougher sentence? Would a few weeks—a few days even—behind bars have done Huguely some good? Did someone ask: Is this a kid with an anger problem? University of Virginia officials say they never learned about the incident.

And just a few months ago, *The Post* reports, University of North Carolina 10 lacrosse players intervened to separate Huguely from Love at a party on the Charlottesville campus.

Where were Huguely's teammates during all of this? Where was his 11 family?

College students drink, sometimes to excess. They act wild and do dumb 12 things, athletes or not. They have tortured romances. Almost none of them kill their girlfriends. Those who do aren't necessarily star athletes.

When I was in college, a fellow student, Bonnie Garland, was murdered by 13 her estranged boyfriend, a recent Yale graduate who smashed her skull with a claw hammer in the bedroom of her Scarsdale, N.Y., home. The narrative in that tragedy was nearly the opposite of the Love murder: not privilege vs. privilege but a boy from the barrio of Los Angeles who found himself out of place in the Ivy League.

There are many routes to doing crazy, terrible things. It would be facile to 14 blame Huguely's conduct on lacrosse, but it's legitimate to wonder whether an atmosphere of entitlement and immunity from ordinary rules were contributing factors.

It's impossible to read the Huguely story without thinking back to the 15 Duke lacrosse case, where the rape charges seemed shoddy from the start—but the glimpse of boorish, alcohol-fueled lacrosse culture seems instructive. At Virginia, eight of 41 players on the lacrosse team have been charged with alcohol-related offenses.

As I wrote at the time of the Duke arrests, "These don't sound like young 16 men you'd want your daughter to date."

## QUESTIONS FOR READING

1. What is the occasion for Marcus's column?
2. What is the question Marcus poses regarding Huguely's actions and athletics?
3. What additional details are provided about Huguely?

## QUESTIONS FOR REASONING AND ANALYSIS

4. What picture of Huguely emerges from the article's details?
5. What is Marcus's claim? What type of argument is this?
6. How does the author repeatedly qualify her claim? Why is this important?

7.  The author seems most interested in getting readers to reflect on possible causes for Huguely's behavior. Has she given you good reasons to reflect? Why or why not?

8.  Lacrosse, from a distance, seems such a graceful sport, and yet, like ice hockey, sticks fly—often in the air—ready to result in painful injuries. Is it possible that lacrosse players are trying too hard—with drinking and aggression—to prove that they are macho? Or, is the problem that Marcus finds in Huguely mostly about the arrogance of unchecked privilege combined with too much alcohol?

9.  What can young women do to protect themselves from male aggression and brutality? What might be a good starting point—related to our sports culture?

## THE BEAM IN YOUR EYE: IF STEROIDS ARE CHEATING, WHY ISN'T LASIK?
WILLIAM SALETAN

*Slate's* national correspondent, William Saletan writes about science and politics and society. He has published several books, including *Bearing Right: How Conservatives Won the Abortion War* (2004).

PREREADING QUESTIONS  Why does Saletan begin with a quotation from the Bible? How does the quoted verse relate to his apparent topic?

> And why beholdest thou the mote that is in thy brother's eye, but considerest not the beam that is in thine own eye?
> —Matthew 7:3

1   A month ago, Mark McGwire was hauled before a congressional hearing and lambasted as a cheater for using a legal, performance-enhancing steroid precursor when he broke baseball's single-season home run record.

2   A week ago, Tiger Woods was celebrated for winning golf's biggest tournament, the Masters, with the help of superior vision he acquired through laser surgery.

3   What's the difference?

4   At the steroid hearing on March 17, numerous members of the House Committee on Government Reform, led by Chairman Tom Davis, R-Va., denounced performance-enhancing drugs. They offered three arguments: The drugs are illegal, they're harmful, and they're cheating. But illegality doesn't explain why a drug should be illegal, and the steroid precursor McGwire took, andro, was legal at the time. The director of the National Institute on Drug Abuse conceded at the hearing that steroid precursors weren't banned until last year, that steroids "do, in fact, enhance certain types of physical performance," that some are "prescribed to treat body wasting in patients with AIDS and other diseases that result in loss of lean muscle mass," and that "not all anabolic steroid abusers experience the same deleterious outcomes."

5   Don't get me wrong. If you buy a steroid off the street or the Internet today just to bulk up, you're taking a stupid risk. But much of that risk comes

from your ignorance and the dubious grade of steroid you're getting. A star player with access to the best stuff and the best medical supervision isn't taking the same degree of risk. Furthermore, steroids are a crude, early phase of enhancement technology. Chemists are trying every day to refine compounds and doses that might help proathletes without bad side effects.

Already the medical objection to doping has holes. At the hearing, lawmakers displayed a supposedly damning list of "Performance Enhancing Substances Not Covered by Baseball's New Testing Program." The first item on the list was human growth hormone. But the Food and Drug Administration has approved human growth hormone for use in short, healthy children based on studies showing its safety and efficacy. The National Institutes of Health says it's "generally considered to be safe, with rare side effects" in children, and the American Association of Clinical Endocrinologists has found the same pattern in adults.   6

That leaves one comprehensive complaint: cheating. At the hearing, I heard six lawmakers apply this term to performance-enhancing drugs. They compared the drugs to corking bats, deadening baseballs, and sharpening spikes. "When I played with Hank Aaron and Willie Mays and Ted Williams, they didn't put on 40 pounds of bulk in their careers, and they didn't hit more homers in their late thirties than they did in their late twenties," said Sen. Jim Bunning, R-Ky. "What's happening now in baseball isn't natural, and it isn't right." Rep. Mark Souder, R-Ind., chairman of the House subcommittee on drug policy, recalled that baseball had harshly punished players who threw games. He asked why such punishment didn't apply to "players today who systematically cheat through steroids and performance-enhancing drugs to alter the games." Davis, who presided at the hearing, announced that he would co-chair "Zero Tolerance: The Advisory Committee on Ending the Use of Performance-Enhancing Drugs in Sports."   7

Zero tolerance? Wait a minute. If the andro that helped McGwire hit 70 home runs in 1998 was an unnatural, game-altering enhancement, what about his high-powered contact lenses? "Natural" vision is 20/20. McGwire's custom-designed lenses improved his vision to 20/10, which means he could see at a distance of 20 feet what a person with normal, healthy vision could see at 10 feet. Think what a difference that makes in hitting a fastball. Imagine how many games those lenses altered.   8

You could confiscate McGwire's lenses, but good luck confiscating Woods' lenses. They've been burned into his head. In the late 1990s, both guys wanted stronger muscles and better eyesight. Woods chose weight training and laser surgery on his eyes. McGwire decided eye surgery was too risky and went for andro instead. McGwire ended up with 70 homers and a rebuke from Congress for promoting risky behavior. Woods, who had lost 16 straight tournaments before his surgery, ended up with 20/15 vision and won seven of his next 10 events.   9

Since then, scores of pro athletes have had laser eye surgery, known as LASIK (Laser-Assisted *In Situ* Keratomileusis). Many, like Woods, have upgraded their vision to 20/15 or better. Golfers Scott Hoch, Hale Irwin, Tom Kite, and Mike Weir have hit the 20/15 mark. So have baseball players Jeff Bagwell, Jeff Cirillo, Jeff Conine, Jose Cruz Jr., Wally Joyner, Greg Maddux, Mark Redman,   10 and Larry Walker. Amare Stoudemire and Rip Hamilton of the NBA have done it, along with NFL players Troy Aikman, Ray Buchanan, Tiki Barber, Wayne Chrebet, and Danny Kanell. These are just some of the athletes who have disclosed their results in the last five years. Nobody knows how many others have gotten the same result.

11      Does the upgrade help? Looks that way. Maddux, a pitcher for the Atlanta Braves, was 0–3 in six starts before his surgery. He won nine of his next 10 games. Kite had LASIK in 1998 and won six events on the Champions Tour over the next five years. Three months after his surgery, Irwin captured the Senior PGA Tour Nationwide Championship.

12      According to *Golf Digest,* Woods aimed for 20/15 when he signed up for LASIK. This probably didn't strike Woods as enhancement, since he was already using contacts that put him at 20/15. Now ads and quotes offering 20/15 are everywhere. One LASIK practice takes credit for giving Irwin 20/15 vision. Another boasts of raising Barber to 20/15 and calls the result "better than perfect." Other sellers promise the same thing and offer evidence to back it up. Last year, they report, 69 percent of traditional LASIK patients in a study had 20/16 vision six months after their surgery, and new "wavefront" technology raised the percentage to 85. Odds are, if you're getting LASIK, you're getting enhanced.

13      The medical spin for LASIK, as opposed to the entrepreneurial spin, is that it's corrective. Your eyesight sucks, you go in for surgery, you hope for 20/20. Maybe you get it, maybe you don't, and that's that. But it isn't that simple. If you don't like the results, your doctor might fire up the laser for a second pass. In the business, this is literally called an "enhancement." Hoch, the golfer, got four enhancements in 2002 and 2003. He ended up 20/15 in one eye, 20/10 in the other.

14      Nor do you need poor vision to find a willing doctor. Most states think you're fine to drive a car without corrective lenses as long as your eyesight is better than 20/40. Cirillo, then a third baseman for the Seattle Mariners, was 20/35 in one eye and 20/30 in the other when he went in for LASIK two years ago. He came out 20/20 and 20/12. Cruz, an outfielder for the Toronto Blue Jays, was 20/30 when he went for an eye exam. Five days later, he was under the beam. "The doctor kind of talked me into it," Cruz told the *Toronto Star.* He came out 20/15. According to the *Orange County Register,* Gary Sheffield, then an outfielder for the Los Angeles Dodgers, had eyesight *better* than 20/20 when he asked for laser surgery to raise his batting average. His doctor talked him out of it.

15      Why risk surgery for such small increments? "Every little half-centimeter counts," Cruz told the *Star.* Last year, the *Seattle Times* reported that Troy Glaus, a power hitter for the Anaheim Angels, had gotten LASIK because he "felt his contacts were sufficient, just not always ideal. A windy day or a wave of dust could tip the advantage back to the pitcher." Often, coaches play a role. The Minnesota Twins training staff successfully encouraged several players to get LASIK. Maddux told the *Atlanta Journal and Constitution* that the Braves gave him "a little push" to get LASIK in 2000. Meanwhile, the Braves'

manager, having talked to the same doctor about getting LASIK, in his own words "chickened out."

This is the difference between therapy and enhancement. You don't need 16 bad vision to get the surgery. Wavefront, if you've got the bucks for it, reliably gives you 20/16 or better. If your vision ends up corrected but not enhanced, you can go back for a second pass. Players calculate every increment. Pro golfers seek "to optimize any competitive advantage," a LASIK surgeon told the *Los Angeles Times.* "They're already tuned in to the best clubs, the best putter, the best ball. . . . Clearly having great vision is one of the best competitive advantages you can have." Eyes are just another piece of equipment. If you don't like 'em, change 'em.

The sports establishment is obtuse to this revolution. Leagues worry about 17 how you might doctor bats, balls, or clubs. They don't focus on how you might doctor yourself. Look at the official rules of Major League Baseball: A pitcher can't put rosin on his glove, but he can put it on his hand. A batter can't alter the bat "to improve the distance factor," but the rules don't bar him from altering his body to get the same result. Baseball now has a dope-testing policy, but it isn't in the rules; the players negotiate it. That's why it's weak.

At last month's hearing, baseball commissioner Bud Selig testified that in 18 1998 and 1999 he sent his executive vice president to Costa Rica to check out reports that juiced-up baseballs were causing an epidemic of home runs. Selig was looking for the wrong kind of juice. The U.S. Golf Association's Rules of Golf share the same blind spot: You can't use a device to warm the ball, but you can use it to warm your hands. You can't use a device to measure distance or "gauge the slope of the green," but you can get the same powers through LASIK. In the age of biotechnology, you *are* the device.

Read the testimonials. At 20/15, Kanell can read the eyes of defensive 19 backs. Tom Lehman, who will lead the U.S. golf team in next year's Ryder Cup, says LASIK improved his ability to "judge distances"—a common benefit, according to the technology's purveyors. Woods says he's "able to see slopes in greens a lot clearer." Woods' eye surgeon told the *Los Angeles Times,* "Golfers get a different three-dimensional view of the green after LASIK." They "can see the grain" and "small indentations. It's different. LASIK actually produces, instead of a spherical cornea, an aspherical cornea. It may be better than normal vision."

Just ask Tom Davis. "I was in and out in less than one hour," the congress- 20 man reports in a testimonial for the Eye Center, a Northern Virginia LASIK practice. "I was reading and watching television that evening. My reading was not impaired and my distance vision was excellent."

Good for you, Tom. Now, about that committee you've established for 21 zero tolerance of performance enhancement. Are you sure you're the right guy to chair it?

QUESTIONS FOR READING

1. What is Saletan's subject?
2. What were the three arguments used by the congressional committee denouncing McGuire?
3. What is wrong with the illegal argument, in the author's view?
4. What is wrong with the harmful argument?
5. Today, how are many professional athletes enhancing their performance?

QUESTIONS FOR REASONING AND ANALYSIS

6. What kinds of evidence does the author present for athletes' use of enhancement techniques?
7. Saletan calls eye enhancement among athletes a "revolution." Based on his evidence, does that seem an appropriate label?
8. What are the rule-makers missing in today's professional sports arena?
9. What is Saletan's claim? Does he state one? Does he imply a position? Defend your answer.

QUESTIONS FOR REFLECTION AND WRITING

10. Saletan begins and ends with Congressman Tom Davis. How does this aid his argument?
11. Is the use of performance-enhancing drugs cheating? Why or why not?
12. Is the use of LASIK or weight training cheating? Why or why not?
13. Can you make a case for allowing one kind of enhancement but not another? Defend your position.

## HOUSTON: WE HAVE A PROBLEM | JORDAN MAMORSKY

Jordan Mamorsky is a law student at the New York University Law School. He published his interview with Allan Houston and discussion of a sports problem in the October 2010 issue of the online site *Voices of Tomorrow*, a monthly site for articles by those under 30.

PREREADING QUESTIONS What is clever about Mamorsky's title? Given the context, what do you expect to read about?

1   The steep fall from grace is not surprising anymore. We have seen it all before. Whether it is a star NFL wide receiver bringing a gun into a tightly packed night club, an NBA all-star swingman bringing a gun into his team's locker room or a two-time Super Bowl winning quarterback allegedly sexually assaulting a girl in a seedy bar restroom, over the past few years, egregious misconduct by professional athletes has been a major blemish on an otherwise vibrant sports industry.

While fans pack the stadiums and arenas to see their favorite players 2 compete on game day, in their off-time players have increasingly found ways for their names to be the subject of headline news for all the wrong reasons.

Searching for answers, I recently spoke with Allan Houston, Assistant to 3 the President for Basketball Operations at the New York Knicks and founder of the "Legacy Foundation," an organization which works with local communities and corporate sponsors to help develop father-mentors and life skills for young athletes.

Houston believes that sports leagues, like the NBA and NFL, are not 4 responsible for the rise in player misconduct.

"First of all, you can't put it on the NBA and its programs," Houston said. 5 "That's the first really big mistake to say that the NBA and its programs are responsible for the well being of these young men. . . . It comes down to the support system around [the players] that can really walk with them and they can trust, that they respect. That's one of the things that current players, potential players have to take very seriously."

Houston speaks from personal experience as his own "support system" 6 was largely responsible for his development from a New York Knicks' legend to one of the rising front office-stars in the NBA. Houston's strong family structure as a youth enabled him to understand the value of hard work, determination and education as a professional basketball player.

"My parents were very hard working parents, who set high standards for 7 us," Houston said. "They were just examples. I made my share of mistakes but faith gave us a foundation and a standard that helped channel the gifts my sisters and I had."

"When I got to the Knicks I had not just my parents, but a lot of strong 8 men and people to look up to, to have as a point of reference. A lot of it comes down to how serious you treat your education. I wanted to be the best at everything I did. I never wanted to do anything half-way."

Many other professional athletes are not as fortunate as Houston. Single 9 parent homes, poverty and other negative external pressures burden many young athletes with difficult childhoods that leave them hungry for fame and fortune once they enter the business of professional sports.

"Eight out of 10 African Americans live at some point [of their lives] as part 10 of a single parent home," Houston said. "It's probably 60–70% for white families. To me, this is a cultural battle, the family, the structure, the standards are kind of dropping in general. We get in these debates about president and politics and this and that but if you look at the statistics we can't blame the NBA, the NCAA [or other institutions]. We have to look at what is happening at the core of what our culture is and where we are getting it from."

In order to battle a modern culture where traditional families are the 11 exception, rather than the norm, Houston feels that other interpersonal relationships with a young athlete's role models should be stressed.

"A lot of it could be the high school coach, a lot could be the AAU coach, 12 a lot of it could be the people who are around them," Houston said. "It comes down to the person who builds players' trust and that's who a lot of responsibility falls on."

Basketball players greet excited youngsters.

13    The idea that athletes as well have a responsibility as role models is a disputed issue. While some disagree that athletes should assume a role model responsibility, Houston believes that an athlete's fame and fortune should reflect exemplary behavior as role models.

14    "As professional athletes I believe we have a responsibility," Houston said. "But other people might not have that insight instilled in them so that they might not think that. So I can't tell you what someone like LeBron James thinks because I don't know him enough to get that answer, that in-depth answer. But I believe [sports] is a platform that was given to us to use—that God has given us—and we are responsible for it and it's not for us."

15    A lack of ethics and personal responsibility has not only been seen as the culprit in professional athlete misconduct, but also in the way pro athletes go about their own marketing and free agency. This past summer the sports business world was rocked by an unprecedented NBA free agency period, which received negative criticism in the sports community for overshadowing a competitive NBA season and playoffs.

16    There might have been nothing wrong with the way NBA players like LeBron James, Dwayne Wade and Chris Bosh handled the free agency process; however, Houston admits he would not have counseled his own son to act in a manner which resulted in a media circus never seen before in the sports industry.

17    "What they did was not wrong," Houston said. "It was just unprecedented, so I am not sure if I would have advised my son to handle it the way he [LeBron

James] handled it but it wasn't wrong. He had every right to go wherever he wanted to go and he had every right to say look I want to take less money and go somewhere else. There's nothing wrong with that. The character in which he did it didn't come off the way I would have said alright Allan do it this way."

During his time with the Knicks Allan Houston received a then franchise 18 record $100 million contract in the free agent period. Yet, despite receiving such a watershed deal, Houston positioned himself as a role model in the sports and sports business community. Now as an executive with the organization, Houston is dedicated to helping professional athletes transition into successful businessmen.

"My real goal is to use my platform to help the young men behind me use 19 their brand to create a strong legacy for themselves," Houston said. "A lot of our young men look at basketball as the end all and be all. Very few, especially African American young men, channel themselves to focus on a long-term legacy, generations after now, and what you are going to leave them. For me, that's my goal."

Houston's aim is an important one for more former professional athletes 20 to have. With few current and former players willing to carry the mantle of exemplary role model, the sports community is in need of more players like Houston willing to work to insure athletes blossom into responsible, dedicated, and successful professionals.

---

Source: From *Voices—Tomorrow's Leaders, Today's Issues,* October 2010, www.voicesoftomorrow. org—an international biweekly magazine written solely by and for 20–29 year olds around the world. Reprinted by permission of Voices of Tomorrow.

### QUESTIONS FOR READING

1. Who is Allan Houston? What did he play?
2. What is Mamorsky's subject, the problem he will explore?
3. What does Houston think is the way to keep professional players from getting into trouble?
4. What are some of the conditions in society today that contribute to the problem the author discusses?
5. What is Houston's view on players as role models?

### QUESTIONS FOR REASONING AND ANALYSIS

6. What is Mamorsky's claim? What kind of argument is this? With this kind of argument, what do writers gain by placing their claim at the end of the essay?
7. What kind of evidence does the author present? Does he make his point?

### QUESTIONS FOR REFLECTION AND WRITING

8. Houston argues that society and the backgrounds of players explain the misbehavior of some pro athletes. Do you agree with him? Why or why not?

9. Houston also argues that we should not hold the professional organizations responsible. Do you agree with Houston on this point? If yes, why? If no, why not?

10. In the summer of 2010, LeBron James held a huge media event to announce his move to the Miami Heat. Why do so many fans come out to these media extravaganzas? Are "we" part of the problem? Explain.

# IT'S ONLY A LETDOWN IF YOU EXPECTED SOMETHING BETTER | TRACEE HAMILTON

Tracee Hamilton came to the *Washington Post* from Kansas—with stops at the *Dallas Times Herald* and the *Detroit Free Press* along the way. Working as a sports editor for many years, she was given her own column in 2009. The following column was printed on December 10, 2009.

**PREREADING QUESTION** What does the word *sycophant* mean? (If you don't know, look it up—Hamilton suggests that the term applies to many sports fans.)

1    You're upset about the Tiger Woods scandal, and I'm here to tell you whom to blame for that: Yourself.

2    Get over it. Seriously. I can't stand the piteous mewling of America when confronted with infidelity among the rich and famous and athletically gifted. How can anyone, in 2009, still be surprised by this type of a behavior?

3    If you were looking for Tiger Woods to be your mentor, your life coach, your investment banker and the shining light by which you live your life, then boy, were you kidding yourself. Do not look to celebrities for your value system. To paraphrase: Sycophant, heal thyself.

4    You say that you can't cheer for someone at, say, the Masters after you've learned he cheated on his wife. Really? That's the yardstick you use? Then one assumes that you've cut everyone out of your life who has ever cheated on his or her spouse, right? Your co-workers, your friends, your siblings, your children, even your own parents? No?

5    Okay, then you're telling me you hold a guy you've never met, whose chief role in your life is essentially that of genial salesman, to a higher standard than the people closest to you, the people you trust with your heart, your children, your secrets, your work.

6    (And even if you've never experienced infidelity—or committed it—firsthand, don't for a minute tell me you've never known anyone who cheated on someone else. That's almost statistically impossible. Either you don't know enough people, or you're kidding yourself. The divorce rate in this country speaks for itself.)

7    Why is it so easy to forgive friends and family their indiscretions, and so difficult to forgive a total stranger whose acts of betrayal *literally* have no effect on you? I would posit that the problem is yours, not Woods's. That's not to say he doesn't have problems. He's got plenty. But your offended outrage is not one of them.

8    He hasn't changed; he hasn't let you down. You didn't know him. You still don't. This is true of most celebrities: We see what they want us to see. We make judgments based on sound bites and talk show interviews. This is perfectly

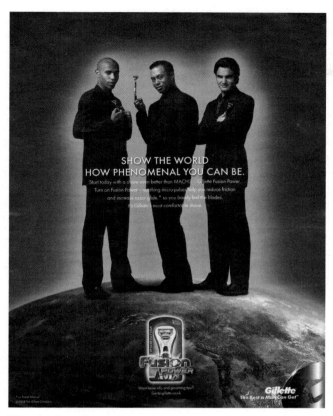

SHOW THE WORLD
HOW PHENOMENAL YOU CAN BE.

Woods, the salesman.

normal; just don't get your moral panties in a bunch when you find out you made a bad call. Admit you were wrong and move on; don't be a hypocrite.

If you like to watch Woods play golf because you've never seen anyone do it 9 better, then what has changed from last Thanksgiving to this Thanksgiving? Nothing. He's still the best golfer on the planet. He can still put your butt on the sofa on a beautiful summer Sunday because you know, you *know*, that greatness might—will—break out at any moment. He can still get himself into difficulties on all 18 holes and find 18 ways to triumph. He can probably play his way out of this, the deepest sand trap of his career, as well. We'll see.

But Woods's talent and his morals are two different things. Clearly. The Woods 10 who betrayed you, if you will, is not the fist-pumping force on the PGA Tour, but the guy who is selling you stuff, and making heaps of money doing it, with his smile and his charm. How good is Woods the salesman? Forbes.com reported in October that Woods had become the first athlete in history to earn $1 billion in his career. Only a fraction of that is purse money. Most of it is endorsements.

So if you want to express your outrage at Woods's behavior, that's the way to 11 do it: Don't buy his products. Write letters to his endorsers. I don't think the private jet folks are worried about losing my business or yours, but what the heck.

12    I won't boycott Woods the golfer, but I probably will boycott Woods the Willy Loman. Not that I ever was much of a customer of Woods's products; I don't need Gillette razors and Buicks to live my life. I can tell time without Rolex. I know there won't be any Woods-related golf shirts or hats under the tree this year—sorry, Dad!

13    So far, most of Woods's corporate partners have stood by him. But they aren't using him. Bloomberg reported Tuesday that according to the Nielsen Company, Woods was last seen in a prime-time ad on Nov. 29, in a 30-second spot for Gillette. We might not see the guy in a commercial until next Thanksgiving, if then.

14    But then again, this is a funny country, and a forgiving one. One 60-minute tears-and-recriminations session on network television—and think of the companies that will line up to sponsor *that*—and this, too, shall pass. Admit it, if he seemed repentant and Oprah hugged him, you'd forgive him in a heartbeat.

15    I mean, it's not like he's family or anything.

### QUESTIONS FOR READING

1. What is Hamilton's subject? (Don't just say "Tiger Woods"; be precise.)
2. What should the divorce rate tell us?
3. Woods has two jobs; which one should we boycott, in Hamilton's view?
4. What is our actual relationship to Woods?

### QUESTIONS FOR REASONING AND ANALYSIS

5. What is Hamilton's claim—what is her focus on Woods's infidelity?
6. What is her line of reasoning? Why should we *not* be upset by what we have learned about him?
7. How would you describe Hamilton's tone? What elements of style help to shape her tone?

### QUESTIONS FOR REFLECTION AND WRITING

8. What larger point about professional sports stars and the public does Hamilton make? Do you agree with her analysis? If you disagree, how would you counter her?
9. Why do we turn sports stars into heroes? Should we have heroes—and be unhappy when they fail to live up to our expectations? Should we have heroes but choose differently? Reflect on these questions.
10. How much, if at all, is the media to blame for the "stage" it gives to sports stars? Would there be sports columnists—and sports talk shows and sports coverage on TV—if we did not want this? Reflect on the role of the media and the role of fans in the problem Hamilton examines.

# CHAPTER 19

# Marriage and Gender Issues: The Debates Continue

READ: What happens in the cartoon? How does Marvin characterize the dog's attitude?

REASON: What attitude is reflected in the way the dog is drawn in frame 4? What attitude is reflected in the way the cat is drawn in frame 5?

REFLECT/WRITE: What makes the cartoon a clever way of expressing the artist's opposition to stereotyping?

Seven writers provide much for readers to reflect on and debate in this chapter of controversial marriage and gender issues. These writers examine the incredible changes that the twentieth century brought to the institution of marriage—and, by extension, to the family. Some approach these changes—and their effects on our politics, our culture, and our personal lives—from the social science perspective; others take a more jocular or satiric approach. Some write from the perspective of research data; others develop their arguments from emotion or from a legal perspective. Some express strongly held views; others seek common ground. Some focus specifically on marriage—how it affects lives and who should be allowed to participate. Others focus on gender issues—and on the stereotyping that continues to affect women and gays. However, whatever their specific topic, the source of their arguments, or the basis of their values, all of these writers would certainly agree that the changes of the past thirty years, with regard to how we live and work together as men and women, straight and gay, have had a profound effect on our culture and our personal lives.

## PREREADING QUESTIONS

1. Do you expect to have a career? To have a spouse and children? Should society support both men and women having these choices? If so, how?
2. What role, if any, should the government and the courts have in defining marriage?
3. What has been meant by the "traditional family"?
4. Do you have a position on gay marriage? On partnership recognition and rights? If you have a position, what is it—and what is its source?
5. Is there anything you can learn from arguments seeking to alter stereotypic views of women? Why or why not?

## SOCIAL SCIENCE FINDS: "MARRIAGE MATTERS"

LINDA J. WAITE

A former senior sociologist at the Rand Corporation, Linda Waite is currently a professor at the University of Chicago. She has coauthored several books, including *New Families, No Families?* (1991) and *Being Together, Working Apart* (with Barbara Schneider; 2005). In this article, published in *The Responsive Community* in 1996, Waite pulls together various studies to explore the effects that marriage has on married people.

PREREADING QUESTIONS Although marriage has declined, what has taken its place? How important is marriage to you? Why?

1    As we are all too aware, the last few decades have witnessed a decline in the popularity of marriage. This trend has not escaped the notice of politicians and pundits. But when critics point to the high social costs and taxpayer

burden imposed by disintegrating "family values," they overlook the fact that individuals do not simply make the decisions that lead to unwed parenthood, marriage, or divorce on the basis of what is good for society. Individuals weigh the costs and benefits of each of these choices to themselves—and sometimes their children. But how much is truly known about these costs and benefits, either by the individuals making the choices or demographers like myself who study them? Put differently, what are the implications, for individuals, of the current increases in nonmarriage? If we think of marriage as an insurance policy—which it is, in some respects—does it matter if more people are uninsured, or are insured with a term rather than a whole-life policy? I shall argue that it does matter, because marriage typically provides important and substantial benefits, benefits not enjoyed by those who live alone or cohabit.

A quick look at marriage patterns today compared to, say, 1950 shows the extent of recent changes. Figures from the Census Bureau show that in 1950, at the height of the baby boom, about a third of white men and women were not married. Some were waiting to marry for the first time, some were divorced or widowed and not remarried. But virtually everyone married at least once at some point in their lives, generally in their early twenties.

In 1950 the proportion of black men and women not married was approximately equal to the proportion unmarried among whites, but since that time the marriage behavior of blacks and whites has diverged dramatically. By 1993, 61 percent of black women and 58 percent of black men were not married, compared to 38 percent of white men and 41 percent of white women. So, in contrast to 1950 when only a little over one black adult in three was not married, now a majority of black adults are unmarried. Insofar as marriage "matters," black men and women are much less likely than whites to share in the benefits, and much less likely today than they were a generation ago.

The decline in marriage is directly connected to the rise in cohabitation—living with someone in a sexual relationship without being married. Although Americans are less likely to be married today than they were several decades ago, if we count both marriage and cohabitation, they are about as likely to be "coupled." If cohabitation provides the same benefits to individuals as marriage does, then we do not need to be concerned about this shift. But we may be replacing a valuable social institution with one that demands and offers less.

Perhaps the most disturbing change in marriage appears in its relationship to parenthood. Today a third of all births occur to women who are not married, with huge but shrinking differences between blacks and whites in this behavior. One in five births to white mothers and two-thirds of births to black mothers currently take place outside marriage. Although about a quarter of the white unmarried mothers are living with someone when they give birth, so that their children are born into two-parent—if unmarried—families, very few black children born to unmarried mothers live with fathers too.

I believe that these changes in marriage behavior are a cause for concern, because in a number of important ways married men and women do better than those who are unmarried. And I believe that the evidence suggests that they do better because they are married.

This family enjoys its cookout.

**MARRIAGE AND HEALTH**

7    The case for marriage is quite strong. Consider the issues of longevity and health. With economist Lee Lillard, I used a large national survey to follow men and women over a 20-year period. We watched them get married, get divorced, and remarry. We observed the death of spouses and of the individuals themselves. And we compared deaths of married men and women to those who were not married. We found that once we took other factors into account, married men and women faced lower risks of dying at any point than those who have never married or whose previous marriage has ended. Widowed women were much better off than divorced women or those who had never married, although they were still disadvantaged when compared with married women. But all men who were not currently married faced significantly higher risks of dying than married men, regardless of their marital history. Other scholars have found disadvantages in death rates for unmarried adults in a number of countries besides the United States.

8    How does marriage lengthen life? First, marriage appears to reduce risky and unhealthy behaviors. For example, according to University of Texas sociologist Debra Umberson, married men show much lower rates of problem drinking than unmarried men. Umberson also found that both married men and women are less likely to take risks that could lead to injury than are the unmarried. Second, as we will see below, marriage increases material well-being—income, assets, and wealth. These can be used to purchase better medical care, better diet, and safer surroundings, which lengthen life. This material improvement seems to be especially important for women.

Third, marriage provides individuals—especially men—with someone who  9
monitors their health and health-related behaviors and who encourages them
to drink and smoke less, to eat a healthier diet, to get enough sleep and to
generally take care of their health. In addition, husbands and wives offer each
other moral support that helps in dealing with stressful situations. Married
men especially seem to be motivated to avoid risky behaviors and to take care
of their health by the sense of meaning that marriage gives to their lives and
the sense of obligation to others that it brings.

## MORE WEALTH, BETTER WAGES—FOR MOST

Married individuals also seem to fare better when it comes to wealth. One 10
comprehensive measure to financial well-being—household wealth—includes
pension and Social Security wealth, real and financial assets, and the value of
the primary residence. According to economist James Smith, in 1992 married
men and women ages 51–60 had median wealth of about $66,000 per spouse,
compared to $42,000 for the widowed, $35,000 for those who had never married, $34,000 among those who were divorced, and only $7,600 for those who
were separated. Although married couples have higher incomes than others,
this fact accounts for only about a quarter of their greater wealth.

How does marriage increase wealth? Married couples can share many 11
household goods and services, such as a TV and heat, so the cost to each individual is lower than if each one purchased and used the same items individually. So the married spend less than the same individuals would for the same
style of life if they lived separately. Second, married people produce more
than the same individuals would if single. Each spouse can develop some skills
and neglect others, because each can count on the other to take responsibility
for some of the household work. The resulting specialization increases efficiency. We see below that this specialization leads to higher wages for men.
Married couples also seem to save more at the same level of income than do
single people.

The impact of marriage is again beneficial—although in this case not for 12
all involved—when one looks at labor market outcomes. According to recent
research by economist Kermit Daniel, both black and white men receive
a wage premium if they are married: 4.5 percent for black men and 6.3 percent
for white men. Black women receive a marriage premium of almost 3 percent.
White women, however, pay a marriage *penalty*, in hourly wages, of over
4 percent. In addition, men appear to receive some of the benefit of marriage
if they cohabit, but women do not.

Why should marriage increase men's wages? Some researchers think that 13
marriage makes men more productive at work, leading to higher wages. Wives
may assist husbands directly with their work, offer advice or support, or take
over household tasks, freeing husbands' time and energy for work. Also, as I
mentioned earlier, being married reduces drinking, substance abuse, and
other unhealthy behaviors that may affect men's job performance. Finally, marriage increases men's incentives to perform well at work, in order to meet
obligations to family members.

14    For women, Daniel finds that marriage and presence of children together seem to affect wages, and the effects depend on the woman's race. Childless black women earn substantially more money if they are married but the "marriage premium" drops with each child they have. Among white women only the childless receive a marriage premium. Once white women become mothers, marriage decreases their earnings compared to remaining single (with children), with very large negative effects of marriage on women's earnings for those with two children or more. White married women often choose to reduce hours of work when they have children. They also make less per hour than either unmarried mothers or childless wives.

15    Up to this point, all the consequences of marriage for the individuals involved have been unambiguously positive—better health, longer life, more wealth, and higher earnings. But the effects of marriage and children on white women's wages are mixed, at best. Marriage and cohabitation increase women's time spent on housework; married motherhood reduces their time in the labor force and lowers their wages. Although the family as a whole might be better off with this allocation of women's time, women generally share their husbands' market earnings only when they are married. Financial well-being declines dramatically for women and their children after divorce and widowhood; women whose marriages have ended are often quite disadvantaged financially by their investment in their husbands and children rather than in their own earning power. Recent changes in divorce law—the rise in no-fault divorce and the move away from alimony—seem to have exacerbated this situation, even while increases in women's education and work experience have moderated it.

### IMPROVED INTIMACY

16    Another benefit of married life is an improved sex life. Married men and women report very active sex lives—as do those who are cohabiting. But the married appear to be more satisfied with sex than others. More married men say that they find sex with their wives to be extremely physically pleasurable than do cohabiting men or single men say the same about sex with their partners. The high levels of married men's physical satisfaction with their sex lives contradicts the popular view that sexual novelty or variety improves sex for men. Physical satisfaction with sex is about the same for married women, cohabiting women, and single women with sex partners.

17    In addition to reporting more active and more physically fulfilling sex lives than the unmarried, married men and women say that they are more emotionally satisfied with their sex lives than do those who are single or cohabiting. Although cohabitants report levels of sexual activity as high as the married, both cohabiting men and women report lower levels of emotional satisfaction with their sex lives. And those who are sexually active but single report the lowest emotional satisfaction with it.

18    How does marriage improve one's sex life? Marriage and cohabitation provide individuals with a readily available sexual partner with whom they have an established, ongoing sexual relationship. This reduces the costs—in some sense—of any particular sexual contact, and leads to higher levels of

sexual activity. Since married couples expect to carry on their sex lives for many years, and since the vast majority of married couples are monogamous, husbands and wives have strong incentives to learn what pleases their partner in bed and to become good at it. But I would argue that more than "skills" are at issue here. The long-term contract implicit in marriage—which is not implicit in cohabitation—facilitates emotional investment in the relationship, which should affect both frequency of and satisfaction with sex. So the wife or husband who knows what the spouse wants is also highly motivated to provide it, both because sexual satisfaction in one's partner brings similar rewards to oneself and because the emotional commitment to the partner makes satisfying him or her important in itself.

To this point we have focused on the consequences of marriage for 19 adults—the men and women who choose to marry (and stay married) or not. But such choices have consequences for the children born to these adults. Sociologists Sarah McLanahan and Gary Sandefur compare children raised in intact, two-parent families with those raised in one-parent families, which could result either from disruption of a marriage or from unmarried childbearing. They find that approximately twice as many children raised in one-parent families than children from two-parent families drop out of high school without finishing. Children raised in one-parent families are also more likely to have a birth themselves while teenagers, and to be "idle"—both out of school and out of the labor force—as young adults.

Not surprisingly, children living outside an intact marriage are also more 20 likely to be poor. McLanahan and Sandefur calculated poverty rates for children in two-parent families—including stepfamilies—and for single-parent families. They found very high rates of poverty for single-parent families, especially among blacks. Donald Hernandez, chief of marriage and family statistics at the Census Bureau, claims that the rise in mother-only families since 1959 is an important cause of increases in poverty among children.

Clearly poverty, in and of itself, is a bad outcome for children. In addition, 21 however, McLanahan and Sandefur estimate that the lower incomes of single-parent families account for only half of the negative impact for children in these families. The other half comes from children's access—or lack of access—to the time and attention of two adults in two-parent families. Children in one-parent families spend less time with their fathers (this is not surprising given that they do not live with them), but they also spend less time with their mothers than children in two-parent families. Single-parent families and stepfamilies also move much more frequently than two-parent families, disrupting children's social and academic environments. Finally, children who spend part of their childhood in a single-parent family report substantially lower quality relationships with their parents as adults and have less frequent contact with them, according to demographer Diane Lye.

## CORRELATION VERSUS CAUSALITY

The obvious question, when one looks at all these "benefits" of marriage, 22 is whether marriage is responsible for these differences. If all, or almost all, of the benefits of marriage arise because those who enjoy better health, live longer lives, or earn higher wages anyway are more likely to marry, then marriage is not "causing" any changes in these outcomes. In such a case, we as a society and we as individuals could remain neutral about each person's decision to marry or not, to divorce or remain married. But scholars from many fields who have examined the issues have come to the opposite conclusion. Daniel found that only half of the higher wages that married men enjoy could be explained by selectivity; he thus concluded that the other half is causal. In the area of mental health, social psychologist Catherine Ross—summarizing her own research and that of other social scientists—wrote, "The positive effect of marriage on well-being is strong and consistent, and the selection of the psychologically healthy into marriage or the psychologically unhealthy out of marriage cannot explain the effect." Thus marriage itself can be assumed to have independent positive effects on its participants.

23    So, we must ask, what is it about marriage that causes these benefits? I think that four factors are key. First, the institution of marriage involves a long-term contract—"'til death do us part." This contract allows the partners to make choices that carry immediate costs but eventually bring benefits. The time horizon implied by marriage makes it sensible—a rational choice is at work here—for individuals to develop some skills and to neglect others because they count on their spouse to fill in where they are weak. The institution of marriage helps individuals honor this long-term contract by providing social support for the couple as a couple and by imposing social and economic costs on those who dissolve their union.

24    Second, marriage assumes a sharing of economic and social resources and what we can think of as co-insurance. Spouses act as a sort of small insurance pool against life's uncertainties, reducing their need to protect themselves—by themselves—from unexpected events.

25    Third, married couples benefit—as do cohabiting couples—from economies of scale.

26    Fourth, marriage connects people to other individuals, to their social groups (such as in-laws), and to other social institutions (such as churches and synagogues) which are themselves a source of benefits. These connections provide individuals with a sense of obligation to others, which gives life meaning beyond oneself.

27    Cohabitation has some but not all of the characteristics of marriage and so carries some but not all of the benefits. Cohabitation does not generally imply a lifetime commitment to stay together; a significant number of cohabiting couples disagree on the future of their relationship. Frances Goldscheider and Gail Kaufman believe that the shift to cohabitation from marriage signals "declining commitment within unions, of men and women to each other and to their relationship as an enduring unit, in exchange for more freedom, primarily for men." Perhaps as a result, many view cohabitation as an especially poor bargain for women.

28    The uncertainty that accompanies cohabitation makes both investment in the relationship and specialization with this partner much riskier than in

marriage and so reduces them. Cohabitants are much less likely than married couples to pool financial resources and more likely to assume that each partner is responsible for supporting himself or herself financially. And whereas marriage connects individuals to other important social institutions, cohabitation seems to distance them from these institutions.

Of course, all observations concern only the average benefits of marriage. 29 Clearly, some marriages produce substantially higher benefits for those involved. Some marriages produce no benefits and even cause harm to the men, women, and children involved. That fact needs to be recognized.

### REVERSING THE TREND

Having stated this qualification, we must still ask, if the average marriage 30 produces all of these benefits for individuals, why has it declined? Although this issue remains a subject of much research and speculation, a number of factors have been mentioned as contributing. For one, because of increases in women's employment, there is less specialization by spouses now than in the past; this reduces the benefits of marriage. Clearly, employed wives have less time and energy to focus on their husbands, and are less financially and emotionally dependent on marriage than wives who work only in the home. In addition, high divorce rates decrease people's certainty about the long-run stability of their marriage, and this may reduce their willingness to invest in it, which in turn increases the chance they divorce—a sort of self-fulfilling prophecy. Also, changes in divorce laws have shifted much of the financial burden for the breakup of the marriage to women, making investment within the marriage (such as supporting a husband in medical school) a riskier proposition for them.

Men, in turn, may find marriage and parenthood a less attractive option 31 when they know that divorce is common, because they may face the loss of contact with their children if their marriage dissolves. Further, women's increased earnings and young men's declining financial well-being may have made women less dependent on men's financial support and made young men less able to provide it. Finally, public policies that support single mothers and changing attitudes toward sex outside of marriage, toward unmarried childbearing, and toward divorce have all been implicated in the decline in marriage. This brief list does not exhaust the possibilities, but merely mentions some of them.

So how can this trend be reversed? First, as evidence accumulates and is 32 communicated to individuals, some people will change their behavior as a result. Some will do so simply because of their new understanding of the costs and benefits, to them, of the choices involved. In addition, we have seen that attitudes frequently change toward behaviors that have been shown to have negative consequences. The attitude change then raises the social cost of the newly stigmatized behavior.

In addition, though, we as a society can pull some policy levers to encourage 33 or discourage behaviors. Public policies that include asset tests (Medicaid is a good example) act to exclude the married, as do AFDC programs in most states.

The "marriage penalty" in the tax code is another example. These and other policies reinforce or undermine the institution of marriage. If, as I have argued, marriage produces individuals who drink less, smoke less, abuse substances less, live longer, earn more, are wealthier, and have children who do better, we need to give more thought and effort to supporting this valuable social institution.

Source: From *The Responsive Community*, Vol. 6, issue 3, Summer 1996. Copyright © 1996 by *The Responsive Community*. Reprinted with permission.

## QUESTIONS FOR READING

1. What is Waite's subject?
2. What groups are healthiest and live the longest? What three reasons does Waite list to explain these health facts?
3. In what ways can marriage increase wealth? Who, when married, loses in hourly wages?
4. What may be the causes of increased productivity for married men?
5. What are some effects of single-parent families on children?
6. If marriage has such benefits, why are fewer people getting married and more getting divorced?

## QUESTIONS FOR REASONING AND ANALYSIS

7. What is Waite's claim? Where does she state it?
8. How does the author help readers move through and see the parts of her argument?
9. How does the author defend her causal argument—that marriage itself is a cause of the financial, health, and contentment effects found in married people? Do you find her argument convincing? Why or why not?
10. What kind of evidence, primarily, does Waite provide? Is this evidence persuasive? Why or why not?

## QUESTIONS FOR REFLECTION AND WRITING

11. Which statistic most surprises you? Why?
12. What can be done to increase marriage benefits for women, the ones who have least benefited?
13. Should the evidence Waite provides encourage people to choose marriage over divorce, cohabitation, or the single life? If so, why? If no, why not? (Do you have a sense that most adults know—or do not know—the data that Waite provides?)
14. What can be done to change the movement away from marriage? What are Waite's suggestions? What are yours?

# ABOLISH MARRIAGE | MICHAEL KINSLEY

A member of the bar with a law degree from Harvard, Michael Kinsley is a former editor of both *Harper's* and *The New Republic* and a former columnist for the *Washington Post.* He is the founding editor (1996) of *Slate,* the online magazine, and has been a cohost of CNN's *Crossfire.* He is currently editor-in-chief of a new website by Atlantic Media. The following column appeared in the *Post,* July 3, 2003.

PREREADING QUESTIONS  What are the key issues in the debate over gay marriage? What are gay marriage proponents seeking? What are social conservatives seeking?

Critics and enthusiasts of *Lawrence v. Texas,* last week's Supreme Court decision invalidating state anti-sodomy laws, agree on one thing: The next argument is going to be about gay marriage. As Justice Antonin Scalia noted in his tart dissent, it follows from the logic of *Lawrence.* Mutually consenting sex with the person of your choice in the privacy of your own home is now a basic right of American citizenship under the Constitution. This does not mean that the government must supply it or guarantee it. But the government cannot forbid it, and the government also should not discriminate against you for choosing to exercise a basic right of citizenship. Offering an institution as important as marriage to male-female couples only is exactly this kind of discrimination. Or so the gay rights movement will now argue. Persuasively, I think.

Opponents of gay rights will resist mightily, although they have been in retreat for a couple of decades. General anti-gay sentiments are now considered a serious breach of civic etiquette, even in anti-gay circles. The current line of defense, which probably won't hold either, is between social toleration of homosexuals and social approval of homosexuality. Or between accepting the reality that people are gay, even accepting that gays are people, and endorsing something called "the gay agenda." Gay marriage, the opponents will argue, would cross this line. It would make homosexuality respectable and, worse, normal. Gays are welcome to exist all they want, and to do their inexplicable thing if they must, but they shouldn't expect a government stamp of approval.

It's going to get ugly. And then it's going to get boring. So we have two options here. We can add gay marriage to the short list of controversies—abortion, affirmative action, the death penalty—that are so frozen and ritualistic that debates about them are more like kabuki performances than intellectual exercises. Or we can think outside the box. There is a solution that ought to satisfy both camps, and may not be a bad idea even apart from the gay marriage controversy.

That solution is to end the institution of marriage. Or rather (he hastens to clarify, dear) the solution is to end the institution of government-sanctioned marriage. Or, framed to appeal to conservatives: End the government monopoly on marriage. Wait, I've got it: Privatize marriage. These slogans all mean the same thing. Let churches and other religious institutions continue to offer marriage ceremonies. Let department stores and casinos get into the act if they want. Let each organization decide for itself what kinds of couples it wants to offer marriage to. Let couples celebrate their union in any way they choose and consider themselves married whenever they want. Let others be free to consider them not married, under rules these others may prefer. And, yes, if three people want to get married, or one person wants to marry herself, and someone else wants to conduct a ceremony and declare them married, let 'em. If you and your government aren't implicated, what do you care?

5      In fact, there is nothing to stop any of this from happening now. And a lot of it does happen. But only certain marriages get certified by the government. So, in the United States we are about to find ourselves in a strange situation where the principal demand of a liberation movement is to be included in the red tape of a government bureaucracy. Having just gotten state governments out of their bedrooms, gays now want these governments back in. Meanwhile, social-conservative anti-gays, many of them southerners, are calling on the government in Washington to trample states' rights and nationalize the rules of marriage, if necessary, to prevent gays from getting what they want. The Senate majority leader, Bill Frist of Tennessee, responded to the Supreme Court's *Lawrence* decision by endorsing a constitutional amendment, no less, against gay marriage.

6      If marriage were an entirely private affair, all the disputes over gay marriage would become irrelevant. Gay marriage would not have the official sanction of government, but neither would straight marriage. There would be official equality between the two, which is the essence of what gays want and are entitled to. And if the other side is sincere in saying that its concern is not what people do in private but government endorsement of a gay "lifestyle" or "agenda," that problem goes away too.

7      Yes, yes, marriage is about more than sleeping arrangements. There are children, there are finances, there are spousal job benefits such as health insurance and pensions. In all of these areas, marriage is used as a substitute for other factors that are harder to measure, such as financial dependence or devotion to offspring. It would be possible to write rules that measure the real factors at stake and leave marriage out of the matter. Regarding children and finances, people can set their own rules, as many already do. None of this would be easy. Marriage functions as what lawyers call a "bright line," which saves the trouble of trying to measure a lot of amorphous factors. You're either married or you're not. Once marriage itself becomes amorphous, who-gets-the-kids and who-gets-health-care become trickier questions.

8      So, sure, there are some legitimate objections to the idea of privatizing marriage. But they don't add up to a fatal objection. Especially when you consider that the alternative is arguing about gay marriage until death do us part.

---

Source: From *The Washington Post*, July 3, 2003. Reprinted by permission.

### QUESTIONS FOR READING

1. What will the next argument be about? What ruling will bring on this argument? What about the ruling invites the argument?
2. Who will win the argument, in Kinsley's view?

3. According to the author, where are we in the "tug-of-war" over gay rights? Where would allowing gay marriage put us in the battle?

4. What is the author's solution to end the argument?

5. What is ironic about gays fighting for the right to marry? What is ironic about conservatives seeking a constitutional amendment against gay marriage?

6. What problems would emerge if governments stopped sanctioning marriage altogether? Are these problems insurmountable, in the author's view?

## QUESTIONS FOR REASONING AND ANALYSIS

7. What is Kinsley's claim? Where does he state it?

8. When Kinsley writes that the argument over gay marriage will "get boring," what does he mean? How does his comparison to kabuki performances or to debates over abortion or the death penalty illustrate his point here?

9. How does Kinsley seek to convince both sides of the argument that his solution should please them?

10. The author anticipates counterarguments in his last two paragraphs. How effective is his rebuttal?

11. Analyze the essay's tone. How serious do you think Kinsley is in presenting his solution to the argument over gay marriage? If he does not think his solution is viable, then why is he proposing it? What is his purpose in writing?

## QUESTIONS FOR REFLECTION AND WRITING

12. What is your reaction to Kinsley's proposal? Is the best solution to get government out of certifying marriage? If we wanted to "think outside the box," could we solve the other problems—of finances, child custody, and so forth—if we wanted to? How would you support the proposal or challenge it?

13. Is there any hope of finding common ground on this issue, or are we doomed to live with another issue that generates only ritualistic "debates"? Do you have any new suggestions for thinking outside the box on social issues that are currently so divisive?

## MY BIG FAT STRAIGHT WEDDING | ANDREW SULLIVAN

British-born Andrew Sullivan graduated from Oxford and has a PhD from Harvard University. Writing for newspapers and magazines, he was editor of *The New Republic* in the 90s, is a columnist for *Time* magazine, and in 2000 started his blog, *The Daily Dish*, first attached to *Time* but now at the Atlantic online. Sullivan has written six books, including *The Conservative Soul* (2006) and *Same-Sex Marriage: Pro and Con* (2004). The following article appeared in the September 2008 issue of the *Atlantic*.

**PREREADING QUESTIONS** What is the "source" of Sullivan's title? How does his title suggest his topic?

1    What if gays were straight?

2    The question is absurd—gays are defined as not straight, right?—yet increasingly central to the debate over civil-marriage rights. Here is how California's Supreme Court put it in a key passage in its now-famous May 15 [2008] ruling that gay couples in California must be granted the right to marry, with no qualifications or euphemisms:

> These core substantive rights include, most fundamentally, the opportunity of an individual to establish—with the person with whom the individual has chosen to share his or her life—an *officially recognized and protected family* possessing mutual rights and responsibilities and entitled to the same respect and dignity accorded a union traditionally designated as marriage.

3    What's notable here is the starting point of the discussion: an "individual." The individual citizen posited by the court is defined as prior to his or her sexual orientation. He or she exists as a person before he or she exists as straight or gay. And the right under discussion is defined as "the opportunity of an individual" to choose another "person" to "establish a family" in which reproduction and children are not necessary. And so the distinction between gay and straight is essentially abolished. For all the debate about the law in this decision, the debate about the terms under discussion has been close to nonexistent. And yet in many ways, these terms are at the core of the decision, and are the reason why it is such a watershed. The ruling, and the language it uses, represents the removal of the premise of the last generation in favor of a premise accepted as a given by the next.

4    The premise used to be that homosexuality was an activity, that gays were people who chose to behave badly; or, if they weren't choosing to behave badly, were nonetheless suffering from a form of sickness or, in the words of the Vatican, an "objective disorder." And so the question of whether to permit the acts and activities of such disordered individuals was a legitimate area of legislation and regulation.

5    But when gays are seen as the same as straights—as individuals; as normal, well-adjusted, human individuals—the argument changes altogether. The

question becomes a matter of how we treat a minority with an involuntary, defining characteristic along the lines of gender or race. And when a generation came of age that did not merely grasp this intellectually, but knew it from their own lives and friends and family members, then the logic for full equality became irresistible.

This transformation in understanding happened organically. It began with 6 the sexual revolution in the 1970s, and then came crashing into countless previously unaware families, as their sons and uncles and fathers died in vast numbers from AIDS in the 1980s and 1990s. It emerged as younger generations came out earlier and earlier, and as their peers came to see gay people as fellows and siblings, rather than as denizens of some distant and alien subculture. It happened as lesbian couples became parents and as gay soldiers challenged the discrimination against them. And it percolated up through the popular culture—from *Will & Grace* and *Ellen* to almost every reality show since *The Real World.*

What California's court did, then, was not to recognize a new right to 7 same-sex marriage. It was to acknowledge an emergent cultural consensus. And once that consensus had been accepted, the denial of the right to marry became, for many, a constitutional outrage. The right to marry, after all, is, as the court put it, "one of the basic, inalienable civil rights guaranteed to an individual." Its denial was necessarily an outrage—and not merely an anomaly— because the right to marry has such deep and inalienable status in American constitutional law.

The political theorist Hannah Arendt, addressing the debate over misce- 8 genation laws during the civil-rights movement of the 1950s, put it clearly enough:

> The right to marry whoever one wishes is an elementary human right compared to which "the right to attend an integrated school, the right to sit where one pleases on a bus, the right to go into any hotel or recreation area or place of amusement, regardless of one's skin or color or race" are minor indeed. Even political rights, like the right to vote, and nearly all other rights enumerated in the Constitution, are secondary to the inalienable human rights to "life, liberty and the pursuit of happiness" proclaimed in the Declaration of Independence; and to this category the right to home and marriage unquestionably belongs.

Note that Arendt put the right to marry before even the right to vote. And 9 this is how many gay people of the next generation see it. Born into straight families and reared to see homosexuality as a form of difference, not disability, they naturally wonder why they would be excluded from the integral institution of their own families' lives and history. They see this exclusion as unimaginable— as unimaginable as straight people would if they were told that they could not legally marry someone of their choosing. No other institution has an equivalent power to include people in their own familial narrative or civic history as deeply or as powerfully as civil marriage does. And the next generation see themselves as people first and gay second.

Born in a different era, I reached that conclusion through more pain and 10 fear and self-loathing than my 20-something fellow homosexuals do today.

But it was always clear to me nonetheless. It just never fully came home to me until I too got married.

11     It happened first when we told our families and friends of our intentions. Suddenly, they had a vocabulary to describe and understand our relationship. I was no longer my partner's "friend" or "boyfriend"; I was his fiancé. Suddenly, everyone involved themselves in our love. They asked how I had proposed; they inquired when the wedding would be; my straight friends made jokes about marriage that simply included me as one of them. At that first post-engagement Christmas with my in-laws, I felt something shift. They had always been welcoming and supportive. But now I was family. I felt an end—a sudden, fateful end—to an emotional displacement I had experienced since childhood.

12     The wedding occurred last August in Massachusetts in front of a small group of family and close friends. And in that group, I suddenly realized, it was the heterosexuals who knew what to do, who guided the gay couple and our friends into the rituals and rites of family. Ours was not, we realized, a different institution, after all, and we were not different kinds of people. In the doing of it, it was the same as my sister's wedding and we were the same as my sister and brother-in-law. The strange, bewildering emotions of the moment, the cake and reception, the distracted children and weeping mothers, the morning's butterflies and the night's drunkenness: this was not a gay marriage; it was a marriage.

13     And our families instantly and for the first time since our early childhood became not just institutions in which we were included, but institutions that we too owned and perpetuated. My sister spoke of her marriage as if it were interchangeable with my own, and my niece and nephew had no qualms in referring to my husband as their new uncle. The embossed invitations and the floral bouquets and the fear of fluffing our vows: in these tiny, bonding gestures of integration, we all came to see an alienating distinction become a unifying difference.

14     It was a moment that shifted a sense of our own identity within our psyches and even our souls. Once this happens, the law eventually follows. In California this spring, it did.

---

**QUESTIONS FOR READING**

1. What, according to Sullivan, is the key term in California's Supreme Court ruling in favor of gay marriage? How does it change the debate about gay marriage?
2. How did the change in thinking develop?
3. What does the author view the court's decision as recognizing?
4. What does the institution of marriage offer?
5. How did Sullivan come to fully understand its significance?

6. Although Sullivan uses his own experience, this is not primarily a personal narrative. What kind of argument is it?

7. What is the author's claim?

8. What kind of evidence does he present? Explain his line of reasoning in your own words.

9. Have you experienced the same shift in thinking about gays from Sullivan's generation to those in their 20s? (Polls demonstrate the shift in attitude for the country as a whole.)

10. Would you have put the right to marry ahead of the right to vote as the more essential right? What is Hannah Arendt's basis for this view?

11. Has Sullivan given you a new way to think about gays and gay marriage? Is he convincing? If not, why not?

## GAY ASIAN-AMERICAN MALE SEEKS HOME | CHONG-SUK HAN

Assistant professor of sociology and anthropology at Middlebury College, Chong-suk Han received his PhD from the University of Washington. He is also an award-winning journalist and served for three years as the editor of the *International Examiner,* the oldest pan–Asian American newspaper in the United States. The following article was published in the September/October 2005 issue of the *Gay and Lesbian Review Worldwide.*

PREREADING QUESTIONS  What does Han's title remind you of—where might you find such a line? What makes it a clever title?

> "The West thinks of itself as masculine—big guns, big industry, big money—so the East is feminine—weak, delicate, poor . . . but good at art, and full of inscrutable wisdom—the feminine mystique . . . I am an Oriental. And being an Oriental, I could never be completely a man."
> —Song Linling in *M Butterfly*

In the critically acclaimed play *M Butterfly*, by David Henry Hwang, the main character, Song Linling, explains his ability to fool a French lieutenant into believing that he was a woman for nearly two decades, a feat based not on his mastery of deception but on the lieutenant's inability to see him as anything other than a woman. For decades, the mainstream media have usually portrayed Asian men as meek, asexual houseboy types or as sexual deviants of some kind. When it comes to attitudes about sex, Asian-American men have generally been portrayed as being on the "traditional" or "conservative" side of the spectrum. Recently the magazine *Details*, which caters to "hip, young, urban males," prominently featured an item entitled "Gay or Asian," and challenged its readers to ascertain whether a given man was, in fact, gay or Asian. Interestingly enough, while the broader Asian-American community mounted a protest against the presentation of Asian men as "gay," the larger gay community stood silently by.

2    "The Orient was almost a European invention," observed Edward Said (1978), "and had been since antiquity a place of romance, exotic beings, haunting memories and landscapes, remarkable experiences." These are all images that happen to be female evocations in the Western mind, and indeed the association between the Orient and the feminine can be traced back to ancient times. The West's view of itself as the embodiment of the male principle was further justified by—and undoubtedly served to justify—Europe's subordination of much of Asia starting in the 18th century: its "masculine thrust" upon the continent, if you will.

3    This discourse of domination at the level of civilizations has played itself out in countless ways over the centuries. For men of Asian descent who have resided in the United States, this has often meant their exclusion from the labor market of "masculine" jobs and the denial of leadership positions in their communities and even in their families. The cultural emasculation of Asian men in America has produced what Eng (2001) has called "racial castration." This in turn has led to the image of Asian men as largely sexless or undersexed—but this hasn't prevented another stereotype from arising, that of Asian men as sexual deviants, helplessly lusting after white women who don't want them. But more often they fade into the sexual background—even as Asian women are often portrayed as highly desirable, notably to sexually competent white men.

4    The situation for gay men of Asian descent in the U.S. has been intimately tied to the same processes that led non-gay Asian men to be racialized and marginalized by mainstream society. While straight men have been able to function within the growing Asian-American community, gay Asian men continue to be marginalized both by the dominant society and by the Asian communities. If anything, they've been rendered even more invisible by a new cultural formation that stresses "family values" while it perpetuates the image of Asians as "America's model minority"—an image that denies the very existence of gay Asian-Americans. Studies on gender and sexuality have largely ignored racial minorities in their discussions. Given this invisibility, it is not surprising that so little has been written about the process of identity formation for gay Asian men. What is known about gay Asian-American men has come from the small but growing number of literary and artistic works produced by gay Asian men, as well as the literature on HIV/AIDS in the Asian-American community.

5    In Chay Yew's acclaimed play *Porcelain*, both the Chinese and the gay communities deny "ownership" of John Lee when he's charged with murdering his white lover in a London lavatory. In a particularly trenchant scene, members of the Chinese community exclaim, "He is not one of us!"—a sentiment that's echoed in the gay community as well. Choi et al. (1998) argues that marginalization by both of these communities may lead to low self-esteem among gay Asian men and contribute to the increasing percentage of gay Asian men who engage in unsafe sex and seroconvert.

In his essay "China Doll," Tony Ayers (1999) discusses his sense of being ⁶ outside the gay mainstream due to his Chinese ethnicity. In addition to discussing the overt forms of racism—such as gay classified ads that specifically state, "no fats, no femmes, no Asians," and being told by other gay men that they are "not into Asians"—Ayers describes some of the more subtle forms of racism, such as that of "rice queens" who desire Asian men purely for their exotic eroticism. What rice queens are often attracted to in Asian men is an idealized notion of a passive, docile, submissive—in short, a feminized—lover, eager to please his virile white man.

It is indeed striking how the image of gay white men has been transformed ⁷ from that of "sissy nelly" to "macho stud" over the past few decades, but no such transformation has occurred where gay API (Asian and Pacific Island) men are concerned. Gay white men are often portrayed as rugged, chiseled studs. But the masculinization of gay white men has been coupled with a feminization of gay API men. When a white man and an API man are presented together in a sexual situation, the former is almost always the sexual dominator while the latter is submissive. For better or worse, many gay Asian men seem to have accepted this stereotype, often participating in their own exotification and playing up their "feminine" allure.

What's more, Asian men themselves have also bought into the gay Western ⁸ notion of what is desirable. Ayers explains that "The sexually marginalized Asian man who has grown up in the West or is Western in his thinking is often invisible in his own fantasies. [Their] sexual daydreams are populated by handsome Caucasian men with lean, hard Caucasian bodies." In a survey of gay Asian men in San Francisco, Choi et al. (1995) found that nearly seventy percent of gay Asian men indicate a preference for white men. More damaging to the gay Asian population is that most of these men seem to be competing for the attention of a limited number of "rice queens." This competition hinders the formation of a unified gay Asian community and further acts to splinter those who should be seen as natural allies.

Not surprisingly, many gay Asian men report feeling inadequate within the ⁹ larger gay community that stresses a Eurocentric image of physical beauty. Given these feelings of inadequacy, gay Asian men may suffer from low self-esteem and actively pursue the company of white men in order to feel accepted. In addition to seeking the company of white men, the obsession with white beauty leads gay Asian men to reject their cultural roots. For example, Chuang (1999) writes about how he tried desperately to avoid anything related to his Chinese heritage and his attempts to transform his "shamefully slim Oriental frame . . . into a more desirable Western body." Other manifestations of attempting to hide one's heritage may include bleaching one's hair or even the wearing of blue contact lenses.

The fear of rejection from family and friends may be more acute for gay ¹⁰ Asians than for other groups. While some have noted the cultural factors associated with Confucianism and the strong family values associated with Asian-Americans, these explanations fall short, given that many Asian-American communities (particularly Filipino and South Asian) are not rooted in a

Confucian ethic. Instead, the compounded feeling of fear may have more to do with their status as racial and ethnic minorities within the U.S., which isolates these groups and increases the importance of the family as a nexus of support. By coming out to their families, Asian-American gays and lesbians risk losing the support of their family and community and facing the sometimes hostile larger society on their own. Unlike gay white men, who can find representation and support in the gay community, gay Asian men often do not have the option of finding a new community outside of the ethnic one they would be leaving behind. In fact, there is some evidence that gay Asian men who are less integrated into the Asian-American community may be at higher risk for HIV/AIDS due to a lack of available support networks. In a study with gay Asian men, Choi et al. (1998) found that gay Asian men often feel that their families would not support their sexual orientation, which leads them to remain closeted until a later age than is typical for white men.

11    In the absence of a vocabulary to describe their experiences, gay Asian men and women have had to create new words and concepts to define their identity. Within the past few years, a number of gay Asian groups and activists have challenged the Western notions of beauty and questioned the effects of these notions on the gay Asian community. Eric Reyes (1996) asks, "which do you really want—rice queen fantasies at your bookstore or freedom rings at the checkout stand of your local Asian market?" In posing this question, Reyes asks us where we should begin to build our home in this place we call America, in the "heterosexual male-dominated America, white gay male–centered Queer America, the marginalized People of Color America, or our often-romanticized Asian America?" It is this continuing attempt to find a gay Asian space that lies at the heart of one group's quest for a place in the American sun.

## REFERENCES

Ayers, T. "China Doll: The experience of being a gay Chinese Australian," in *Multicultural Queer: Australian Narratives,* by P. Jackson and G. Sullivan (eds.). Haworth Press, 1999.

Choi, K. H., et al. (1998). "HIV prevention among Asian and Pacific Islander American men who have sex with men." *AIDS Education and Prevention,* 1998.

Choi, K. H., et al. (1995). "High HIV risk among gay Asian and Pacific Islander men in San Francisco." *AIDS,* 9.

Chuang, K. "Using chopsticks to eat steak," in *Multicultural Queer: Australian Narratives,* by P. Jackson and G. Sullivan (eds.). Haworth Press, 1999.

Eng, D. *Racial Castration: Managing Masculinity in Asian America.* Duke University Press, 2001.

Reyes, Eric E. "Strategies for Queer Asian and Pacific Islander Spaces," in *Asian American Sexualities,* by Russell Leong (ed.). Routledge, 1996.

Said, Edward. *Orientalism.* Vintage Books, 1978.

Source: From *Gay and Lesbian Review,* September/October 2005. Reprinted by permission of the author.

1. What has been the Western view of the East, the Orient, for a long time?
2. What has been the result of this image of the East for Asian-American men? How have they been treated? How are they "viewed"?
3. What has contributed to the "invisibility" of gay Asian-American men?
4. What can happen to these men who are excluded by both the Asian community and the gay community? How can they be viewed by other gays—what can they be desired for? How does this affect their view of themselves?

5. Han opens his paper with a quotation from *M Butterfly* and then discusses the play in his first paragraph. What does he gain by the reference as an opening?
6. What is Han's claim? What is the central point of his study?
7. Analyze Han's style and tone. What does he gain from this approach?
8. Han's analysis of problems facing gay Asian-American men is based on sociological theories; does that come through? Does that scholarly perspective strengthen his argument? If so, how?

9. Can you relate to the sadness and emptiness experienced by anyone who feels "homeless," who cannot find a community or who lacks family support? If so, does your empathy extend to gays who are not fully accepted into that community? Why or why not?
10. Were you aware that gay Asian-American men may feel "homeless," or quite literally be without a home? (Were you aware that there are gays among the Asian community?) If Han has given you some new knowledge, what is your reaction to it? Would you recommend this essay to others to read? Why or why not?
11. Would you accept—or have you accepted—gay or lesbian members of your family? Why or why not?

# FOR WOMEN IN AMERICA, EQUALITY IS STILL AN ILLUSION | JESSICA VALENTI

Holding a master's degree from Rutgers University, Jessica Valenti is best known for her popular blog and online community *Feministing.com*. She also writes articles and is the author of several books, including *The Purity Myth: How America's Obsession with Virginity Is Hurting Young Women* (2009). The following essay was published on February 21, 2010, in the *Washington Post*.

**PREREADING QUESTIONS** What examples would you offer to demonstrate a lack of equality for women in the United States? If you can't think of any, are you eager to hear what Valenti has to say?

1    Every day, we hear about the horrors women endure in other countries: rape in Darfur, genital mutilation in Egypt, sex trafficking in Eastern Europe. We shake our heads, forward e-mails and send money.

2    We have no problem condemning atrocities done to women abroad, yet too many of us in the United States ignore the oppression on our doorstep. We're suffering under the mass delusion that women in America have achieved equality.

3    And why not—it's a feel-good illusion. We cry with Oprah and laugh with Tina Fey; we work and take care of our children; we watch Secretary of State Hillary Rodham Clinton and U.N. Ambassador Susan Rice proudly and sigh with relief, believing we've come so far. But we're basking in a "girl power" moment that doesn't exist—it's a mirage of equality that we've been duped into believing is the real thing.

4    Because despite the indisputable gains over the years, women are still being raped, trafficked, violated and discriminated against—not just in the rest of the world, but here in the United States. And though feminists continue to fight gender injustices, most people seem to think that outside of a few lingering battles, the work of the women's movement is done.

5    It's time to stop fooling ourselves. For all our "empowered" rhetoric, women in this country aren't doing nearly as well as we'd like to think.

6    After all, women are being shot dead in the streets here, too. It was only last year that George Sodini opened fire in a gym outside Pittsburgh, killing three women and injuring nine others. Investigators learned from Sodini's blog that he specifically targeted women. In 2000, a gunman went into an Amish schoolhouse in Pennsylvania; he sent the boys outside and opened fire on almost a dozen girls, killing five. That same year in Colorado, a man sexually assaulted six female students he had taken hostage at a high school before killing one of them.

7    And it's not just strangers who are killing women; more than 1,000 women were killed by their partners in 2005, and of all the women murdered in the United States, about a third are killed by a husband or boyfriend. A leading cause of death for pregnant women? Murder by a partner.

8    In Iraq, women serving in the military are more likely to be raped by a fellow soldier than killed by enemy fire.

9    Even the government underestimates the crisis American women are in. Last year the Justice Department reported that there were 182,000 sexual assaults committed against women in 2008, which would mean that the rate had decreased by 70 percent since 1993. But a study by the National Crime Victims Research and Treatment Center showed that the Justice Department's methodology was flawed. Instead of behaviorally based questions, such as "Has anyone ever forced you to have sex?" women were asked if they had been subject to "rape, attempted or other type of sexual attack." Victims often don't label their experience as "rape," especially when someone they know attacked them. The center says the actual number of U.S. women raped in 2008 was more than 1 million.

The distressing statistics don't stop with violence: Women hold 17 percent 10 of the seats in Congress; abortion is legal, but more than 85 percent of counties in the United States have no provider; women work outside the home, but they make about 76 cents to a man's dollar and make up the majority of Americans living in poverty.

This is a far cry from progress; it's an epidemic of sexism. So where's the 11 outrage? When my co-bloggers and I write at *Feministing.com* about the hurdles American women face, a common criticism is that if we cared about women's rights, we'd focus on countries where women are actually oppressed—that women here have it too good to complain. When I speak on college campuses, I'm sometimes asked the same question (generally by a male student): What are you complaining about? Women are doing terrific!

In her upcoming [2010] book, author Susan Douglas calls this "enlight- 12 ened sexism." She writes that the appearance of equality—from "girl power" to "Buffy the Vampire Slayer"—is a dangerous distraction from the pervasiveness of sexism.

So why the blinders? Most women know that sexism exists. But between 13 the glittery illusion Douglas refers to and the ongoing feminist backlash, it's not surprising that so many women don't realize how dire their situation is. Organizations such as the Independent' Women's Forum, for example, exist to tell women that equality is actually bad for them. In a 2007 opinion article in the *Washington Post* headlined "A Bargain at 77 Cents to a Dollar," the forum's Carrie Lukas wrote that the wage gap is simply "a trade-off" for holding jobs with "personal fulfillment." The organization's campus program argues against Title IX, the law that prohibits sex discrimination at educational institutions. Between pop culture and politics, women are being taught that everything is fine and dandy—and a lot of us are buying it.

Part of this unwillingness to see misogyny in America could be 14 self-protection—perhaps the truth is too scary to face. Or maybe American women are simply loath to view themselves as oppressed, and it's easier to look at women in other countries as the real victims. This isn't to say that international misogyny isn't a problem; of course it is. And many women in America do have it easier than women in other parts of the world. But this isn't a zero-sum game, and we can fight for our rights while fighting for women internationally as well.

In fact, our successes could help women abroad. The recent increase in 15 the number of female ambassadors globally has been dubbed the "Hillary effect"—the idea that our secretary of state's visibility has opened doors for women in other countries. And perhaps if the pay gap here were closed, women would have more money to spend on causes overseas. It's time to do away with the either-or mentality that surrounds domestic and international women's rights.

Fortunately, a vibrant feminist movement is still at large in the United 16 States, taking on issues from reproductive justice and racism to pay equity and motherhood. But feminists cannot pick up the sexist slack on their own, and recent mainstream conversations—such as when singer Rihanna was assaulted by her then-boyfriend Chris Brown, or when Clinton and Sarah Palin were the targets of sexism during the 2008 campaign—have been far too civilized for the mess that we're in.

17    We act as if the hatred directed at women is something that can be dealt with by a stern talking to, as if the misogyny embedded in our culture is an unruly child rather than systematic oppression. Yes, women today fare better than our foremothers. But the benchmarks so often cited—the right to vote, working outside the home, laws that make domestic violence illegal—don't change the reality of women's lives. They don't prevent 1 million women from being raped, female troops from being assaulted or the continued legal discrimination against gay and transgendered people. And seriously, are American women really supposed to be satisfied with the most basic rights of representation? Thrilled that our country has deigned to consider us fully human?

18    There is so much more work to be done. The truth is, most women don't have the privilege of being able to look at gender justice from a distance; they have no choice but to live it every day. Those of us who are lucky enough not to have to think about sexism, racism, poverty and homophobia on a daily basis—those of us who have the privilege of sending money to an international cause via e-mail while ignoring the plight of women here at home—have a responsibility to open our eyes to the misogyny right in front of us. And then to stop it.

---

Source: From *The Washington Post*, February 21, 2010. Reprinted by permission of the author.

## QUESTIONS FOR READING

1.   What is the general view of women's status in America today?
2.   What is the reality, according to the author?
3.   When Valenti tries to convince others that U.S. women do not have equality, what is a typical response?

## QUESTIONS FOR REASONING AND ANALYSIS

4.   What is Valenti's claim?
5.   What kind (genre) of argument is this? Where does Valenti place her focus within the genre?
6.   The author provides evidence of advances by American women; why does she include this information?
7.   What *kinds* of evidence does Valenti provide?
8.   How does Valenti account for women "being duped" into believing that all is well?

## QUESTIONS FOR REFLECTION AND WRITING

9.   Before reading this essay, did you think that women in the United States experience equality? If so, what is your response to Valenti's statistics?

10. Why do we so often focus on the problems and sufferings abroad and fail to see—and help solve—the problems and sufferings in our own country? Do you have any suggestions for fixing this problem?

11. Which statistic presented by Valenti most surprised you? Why? Does that surprising statistic make you want to do anything differently? Explain.

# 5 MYTHS ABOUT WORKING MOTHERS | NAOMI CAHN and JUNE CARBONE

A graduate of Columbia University School of Law, Naomi Cahn is a professor at the George Washington University Law School and the author of many law review articles on family law and feminist jurisprudence. June Carbone graduated from Yale University Law School and is a professor of law at the University of Missouri at Kansas City. She is the author of *From Partners to Parents* (2000). Cahn and Carbone coauthored *Red Families v. Blue Families* (2009) as well as the following article from the May 30, 2010, issue of the *Washington Post*.

PREREADING QUESTIONS  What are some assumptions/attitudes/perceptions you hold regarding mothers who work outside the home? Are you ready to consider that some of these may need to be adjusted?

Today, the notion of a mother holding a job outside the home is so commonplace, so unremarkable, that the phrase "working mother" seems redundant. Nearly two-thirds of women with children under age 18 now have jobs outside the home—more than three times the rate in 1960. But while the numbers have shifted rapidly, many of our beliefs about juggling work and family haven't quite caught up.

**1. Mothers today spend much less time caring for children than did their parents and grandparents.** Today's mothers and fathers both devote more time than ever to their children, in part because they are less likely than parents in earlier eras to send their kids out to play on their own or to put them to work inside or outside the home. According to a 2006 study by the Federal Reserve Bank of Boston, fathers in 1965 spent a little more than one hour per week on child care—meaning hands-on tending such as feeding, reading aloud, helping with homework, changing diapers or rocking to sleep—compared with more than three hours per week in 2003. Meanwhile, working mothers, who spent just under three hours per week on child care in 1965, had nearly doubled that number by 2003. Over the same period, the time households spent on house work, including cooking and indoor chores such as cleaning and laundry, plummeted by 6.4 hours per week.

**2. Women's jobs interfere with family life more than men's.** If anything, it is men's work that gets in the way. According to Penn State sociologist Paul Amato, approximately 45 percent of husbands in a nationally representative survey conducted in 2000 believed their job interfered with family life; about

35 percent of working wives felt that way about their own employment. This was a big shift from 1980, when around 23 percent of both husbands and wives thought that their own jobs interfered with family life. Part of this change may be because fathers today expect to be more involved in family life than they did a few decades ago.

4    Amato found that attitudes toward women's work have also changed, with both men and women holding more liberal opinions in 2000 than they did in 1980. By 2000, 74 percent of wives and 59 percent of husbands said that a working mother could be as close to her children as a nonworking mother, a substantial increase from 20 years earlier. Generally, Latinos and whites have relatively liberal beliefs about maternal employment, while African Americans have more conservative attitudes—even though black mothers are more likely to work outside the home than white mothers.

5    **3. Mothers with college degrees are more likely than other women to opt out of the workforce.** Despite a rash of media reports several years ago heralding an "opt-out" revolution among college-educated women, such women are not abandoning the workplace. In a 2005 paper, economist Heather Boushey reported that the "child penalty"—the extent to which having a child decreases a woman's odds of having a job—is greater for women with less education. According to 2007 Census Bureau data, only about 26 percent of mothers with a college degree stay home, while more than 40 percent of mothers lacking high school diplomas are at home. College-educated women are more successful in combining work and family than other groups in part because they tend to have the resources to pay for child care and other help.

6    At least for mothers of young children, the educational divide is relatively new. According to Princeton sociologist Sara McLanahan, in 1970, 18 percent of the most educated mothers and 12 percent of the least educated mothers with young children worked outside the home. By 2000, 65 percent of the more educated group worked, but only 30 percent of the least educated mothers had joined them in the labor market.

7    **4. Women who work are less likely to have successful marriages.** It depends. A couple's values are better predictors of a stable marriage than whether the wife works. In particular, Penn State's Amato finds that egalitarian attitudes (seen in shared decision-making, chores and child care) are linked to higher levels of marital well-being. Amato says the happiest couples are upper-middle-class, two-career couples. They report three times the marital contentment of the next happiest group—working- and middle-class families who favor a traditional division of labor and have only one breadwinner.

8    Which families are the least happy? Young, dual-wage, working-class couples—particularly those who believe that a husband should be the breadwinner but who both work out of financial necessity—have the highest levels of conflict and are three times more divorce-prone than any other group. However, even dual-income families with egalitarian beliefs become less stable if the wife works more than 45 hours a week outside the home.

**5. Parents don't experience discrimination in the workplace.** This is ⁹
half-true: Although fathers can receive a bonus in the form of more money and
better job prospects compared with childless men, the "motherhood penalty"
is alive and well. When sociologist Shelley Correll and her colleagues sent out
more than 1,200 fake résumés to employers in a large Northeastern city, mothers were significantly less likely than either childless women or fathers with
identical qualifications to get interviews. This effect seems to extend even to
the political arena: A 2008 study (before Sarah Palin's run for vice president)
found Republicans much less likely to vote for a mother with young children
than for a father with young children.

Fathers don't always get off free, though: According to the Equal ¹⁰
Employment Opportunity Commission, employers who provide family leave
sometimes deny men the same time off they give women, even though it's
illegal to do so.

Speaking of time off, while the Family and Medical Leave Act of 1993 ¹¹
allows eligible workers to take unpaid, job-protected leave to care for a new
child or a family member with a serious medical condition, only slightly more
than half of all employees work in businesses covered by the law, according to
an estimate that the Labor Department published in 2000. And while federal
law protects workers from discrimination based on sex or pregnancy status, it
doesn't protect against discrimination based on caregiving responsibilities—
so some state and local governments have begun to pass laws that do.
Researchers at the University of California's Hastings College of the Law report
that the number of lawsuits claiming discrimination based on caregiving
responsibilities has increased almost 400 percent over the past decade.

Source: From *The Washington Post*, May 30, 2010. Reprinted by permission of Naomi Cahn.

QUESTIONS FOR READING

1. What percentage of women with children under 18 now work outside the home?
2. How much time do working mothers spend with their children today? What about fathers?
3. Whose job interferes more with family life—the mother's or the father's?
4. Which couples report the happiest marriages?
5. Do mothers experience discrimination in the workplace?

QUESTIONS FOR REASONING AND ANALYSIS

6. What is the authors' claim? Where is it stated?
7. What kind of evidence do the authors provide to challenge the five perceptions? Does the evidence convincingly challenge each of the myths? Why or
   why not?

QUESTIONS FOR REFLECTION AND WRITING

8. What statistic most surprises you? Why?

9. What can be done to eliminate the "mother penalty" in hiring?

10. Why is it important to have myths challenged by facts? On this particular topic, why should readers understand what the studies reveal about working mothers?

## SUPREMACY CRIMES   |   GLORIA STEINEM

Editor, writer, and lecturer, Gloria Steinem has been cited in *World Almanac* as one of the twenty-five most influential women in America. She is the cofounder of *Ms.* magazine and of the National Women's Political Caucus and is the author of a number of books and many articles. The following article appeared in *Ms.* in the August/ September 1999 issue.

PREREADING QUESTIONS  Who are the teens who commit most of the mass shootings at schools? Who are the adults who commit most of the hate crimes and sadistic killings? What generalizations can you make about these groups based on your knowledge from media coverage?

1      You've seen the ocean of television coverage, you've read the headlines: "How to Spot a Troubled Kid," "Twisted Teens," "When Teens Fall Apart."

2      After the slaughter in Colorado that inspired those phrases, dozens of copycat threats were reported in the same generalized way: "Junior high students charged with conspiracy to kill students and teachers" (in Texas); "Five honor students overheard planning a June graduation bombing" (in New York); "More than 100 minor threats reported statewide" (in Pennsylvania). In response, the White House held an emergency strategy session titled "Children, Violence, and Responsibility." Nonetheless, another attack was soon reported: "Youth With 2 Guns Shoots 6 at Georgia School."

3      I don't know about you, but I've been talking back to the television set, waiting for someone to tell us the obvious: it's not "youth," "our children," or "our teens." It's our sons—and "our" can usually be read as "white," "middle class," and "heterosexual."

4      We know that hate crimes, violent and otherwise, are overwhelmingly committed by white men who are apparently straight. The same is true for an even higher percentage of impersonal, resentment-driven, mass killings like those in Colorado; the sort committed for no economic or rational gain except the need to say, "I'm superior because I can kill." Think of Charles Starkweather, who reported feeling powerful and serene after murdering ten women and men in the 1950s; or the shooter who climbed the University of Texas Tower in 1966, raining down death to gain celebrity. Think of the engineering student at the University of Montreal who resented females' ability to study that subject, and so shot to death 14 women students in 1989, while saying, "I'm

against feminism." Think of nearly all those who have killed impersonally in the workplace, the post office, McDonald's.

White males—usually intelligent, middle class, and heterosexual, or trying   5 desperately to appear so—also account for virtually all the serial, sexually motivated, sadistic killings, those characterized by stalking, imprisoning, tor- turing, and "owning" victims in death. Think of Edmund Kemper, who began by killing animals, then murdered his grandparents, yet was released to sexu- ally torture and dismember college students and other young women until he himself decided he "didn't want to kill all the coeds in the world." Or David Berkowitz, the Son of Sam, who murdered some women in order to feel in control of all women. Or consider Ted Bundy, the charming, snobbish young would-be lawyer who tortured and murdered as many as 40 women, usually beautiful students who were symbols of the economic class he longed to join. As for John Wayne Gacy, he was obsessed with maintaining the public mask of masculinity, and so hid his homosexuality by killing and burying men and boys with whom he had had sex.

These "senseless" killings begin to seem less mysterious when you con-   6 sider that they were committed disproportionately by white, non-poor males, the group most likely to become hooked on the drug of superiority. It's a drug pushed by a male-dominant culture that presents dominance as a natural right; a racist hierarchy that falsely elevates whiteness; a materialist society that equates superiority with possessions; and a homophobic one that empowers only one form of sexuality.

As Elliott Leyton reports in *Hunting Humans: The Rise of the Modern*   7 *Multiple Murderer,* these killers see their behavior as "an appropriate—even 'manly'—response to the frustrations and disappointments that are a normal part of life." In other words, it's not their life experiences that are the problem, it's the impossible expectation of dominance to which they've become addicted.

This is not about blame. This is about causation. If anything, ending the   8 massive cultural cover-up of supremacy crimes should make heroes out of boys and men who reject violence, especially those who reject the notion of superiority altogether. Even if one believes in a biogenetic component of male aggression, the very existence of gentle men proves that socialization can override it.

Nor is this about attributing such crimes to a single cause. Addiction to   9 the drug of supremacy is not their only root, just the deepest and most ignored one. Additional reasons why this country has such a high rate of violence include the plentiful guns that make killing seem as unreal as a video game; male violence in the media that desensitized viewers in much the same way that combat killers are desensitized in training; affluence that allows maximum access to violence-as-entertainment; a national history of genocide and slav- ery; the romanticizing of frontier violence and organized crime; not to mention extremes of wealth and poverty and the illusion that both are deserved.

But it is truly remarkable, given the relative reasons for anger at injustice in  10 this country, that white, non-poor men have a near-monopoly on multiple killings of strangers, whether serial and sadistic or mass and random. How can we ignore this obvious fact? Others may kill to improve their own condition, in self-defense, or for money or drugs; to eliminate enemies; to declare turf in drive-by shootings; even for a jacket or a pair of sneakers—but white males addicted to supremacy kill even when it worsens their condition or ends in suicide.

11      Men of color and females are capable of serial and mass killing, and commit just enough to prove it. Think of Colin Ferguson, the crazed black man on the Long Island Railroad, or Wayne Williams, the young black man in Atlanta who kidnapped and killed black boys, apparently to conceal his homosexuality. Think of Aileen Carol Wuornos, the white prostitute in Florida who killed abusive johns "in self-defense," or Waneta Hoyt, the upstate New York woman who strangled her five infant children between 1965 and 1971, disguising their cause of death as sudden infant death syndrome. Such crimes are rare enough to leave a haunting refrain of disbelief as evoked in Pat Parker's poem "jonestown": "Black folks do not/Black folks do not/Black folks do not commit suicide." And yet they did.

12      Nonetheless, the proportion of serial killings that are not committed by white males is about the same as the proportion of anorexics who are not female. Yet we discuss the gender, race, and class components of anorexia, but not the role of the same factors in producing epidemics among the powerful.

13      The reasons are buried deep in the culture, so invisible that only by reversing our assumptions can we reveal them.

14      Suppose, for instance, that young black males—or any other men of color—had carried out the slaughter in Colorado. Would the media reports be so willing to describe the murderers as "our children"? Would there be so little discussion about the boys' race? Would experts be calling the motive a mystery, or condemning the high school cliques for making those young men feel like "outsiders"? Would there be the same empathy for parents who gave the murderers luxurious homes, expensive cars, even rescued them from brushes with the law? Would there be as much attention to generalized causes, such as the dangers of violent video games and recipes for bombs on the Internet?

15      As for the victims, if racial identities had been reversed, would racism remain so little discussed? In fact, the killers themselves said they were targeting blacks and athletes. They used a racial epithet, shot a black male student in the head, and then laughed over the fact that they could see his brain. What if that had been reversed?

16      What if these two young murderers, who were called "fags" by some of the jocks at Columbine High School, actually had been gay? Would they have got the same sympathy for being gay-baited? What if they had been lovers? Would we hear as little about their sexuality as we now do, even though only their own homophobia could have given the word "fag" such power to humiliate them?

17      Take one more leap of the imagination: suppose these killings had been planned and executed by young women—of any race, sexuality, or class. Would the media still be so disinterested in the role played by gender-conditioning? Would journalists assume that female murderers had suffered from being shut

out of access to power in high school, so much so that they were pushed beyond their limits? What if dozens, even hundreds of young women around the country had made imitative threats—as young men have done—expressing admiration for a well-planned massacre and promising to do the same? Would we be discussing their youth more than their gender, as is the case so far with these male killers?

I think we begin to see that our national self-examination is ignoring some- 18 thing fundamental, precisely because it's like the air we breathe: the white male factor, the middle-class and heterosexual one, and the promise of supe- riority it carries. Yet this denial is self-defeating—to say the least. We will never reduce the number of violent Americans, from bullies to killers, without chal- lenging the assumptions on which masculinity is based: that males are superior to females, that they must find a place in a male hierarchy, and that the ability to dominate someone is so important that even a mere insult can justify lethal revenge. There are plenty of studies to support this view. As Dr. James Gilligan concluded in *Violence: Reflections on a National Epidemic*, "If humanity is to evolve beyond the propensity toward violence . . . then it can only do so by recognizing the extent to which the patriarchal code of honor and shame generates and obligates male violence."

I think the way out can only be found through a deeper reversal: just as we 19 as a society have begun to raise our daughters more like our sons—more like whole people—we must begin to raise our sons more like our daughters—that is, to value empathy as well as hierarchy; to measure success by other people's welfare as well as their own.

But first, we have to admit and name the truth about supremacy crimes.   20

---

Source: From *Ms.* magazine, August/September 1999. Reprinted by permission of the author.

## QUESTIONS FOR READING

1. What kinds of crimes is Steinem examining? What kinds of crimes is she excluding from her discussion?

2. What messages, according to Steinem, is our culture sending to white, non-poor males?

3. How does Elliott Leyton explain these killers' behavior?

4. What is the primary reason we have not examined serial and random killings correctly, in the author's view? What is keeping us from seeing what we need to see?

5. What do we need to do to reduce "the number of violent Americans, from bullies to killers"?

## QUESTIONS FOR REASONING AND ANALYSIS

6. What is Steinem's claim? Where does she state it?

7. What is her primary type of evidence?

8. How does Steinem qualify her claim and thereby anticipate and answer counterarguments? In what paragraphs does she present qualifiers and counterarguments to possible rebuttals?

9. How does the author seek to get her readers to understand that we are not thinking soundly about the mass killings at Columbine High School? Is her strategy an effective one? Why or why not?

## QUESTIONS FOR REFLECTION AND WRITING

10. Steinem concludes by writing that we must first "name the truth" about supremacy violence before we can begin to address the problem. Does this make sense to you? How can this be good advice for coping with most problems? Think of other kinds of problems that this approach might help solve.

11. Do you agree with Steinem's analysis of the causes of serial and random killings? If yes, how would you add to her argument? If no, how would you refute her argument?

# Education in America: Problems at All Levels

READ: What is the situation? Who is writing the words below the graph?

REASON: What does the graph show? What does the answer to the test imply about the United States?

REFLECT/WRITE: What is Toles's point about American education—and our perception of American education?

To say that the issues in education are both numerous and serious is certainly an understatement. Clinton wanted to be the "education president." Bush had his No Child Left Behind initiative. Obama has his Race to the Top plan. And yet criticism continues amid only a few voices defending U.S. schools. America's best schools and colleges attract students from around the world. But the variations in funding, facilities, teachers, and test scores from one school to another are often unacceptable to politicians and parents alike.

To move to the college level: Up to one-third of the freshman class at many quality colleges is taking at least one remedial course, and fewer than half of those who start college actually graduate with a BA or BS degree. The number of college graduates in this country remains under 30 percent. Is this a failure of a goal of universal education—or is a college degree as the measure an unrealistic standard? And if it is, can we be competitive in a global economy and, increasingly, in a workforce requiring brainpower, not brawn?

The first three authors in this chapter examine K–12 issues, pointing out distressing statistics but also arguing for changes. The last three authors explore college-level concerns, from getting into college to a commitment to class participation and learning. Collectively they add to our understanding of current problems and inspire us to seek improvements in American education.

## PREREADING QUESTIONS

1. Many K–12 schools are cutting back on physical education classes for financial reasons or to provide more class time for other activities. Is this wise? Why has phys. ed. been a part of schooling for many years?

2. How do you account for the weak showing of U.S. students on international tests? Should we, as a nation, be concerned?

3. What is the impact of family stability and educational level on success in school?

4. What is the biggest obstacle to getting into college?

---

## THE FITTEST BRAINS: HOW EXERCISING AFFECTS KIDS' INTELLIGENCE | GRETCHEN REYNOLDS

Gretchen Reynolds is a freelance journalist who writes about fitness for several magazines and the *New York Times*. A former editor of *Outside* magazine, she is now working on a book about the frontiers of fitness. The following *New York Times* article appeared September 19, 2010.

PREREADING QUESTIONS What clues to Reynolds's subject are in her title? What makes her title clever?

1    In an experiment published last month [August 2010], researchers recruited schoolchildren, ages 9 and 10, who lived near the Champaign-Urbana campus of the University of Illinois and asked them to run on a treadmill. The

Michelle Obama encourages youngsters
to get moving.

researchers were hoping to learn more about how fitness affects the immature human brain. Animal studies had already established that, when given access to running wheels, baby rodents bulked up their brains, enlarging certain areas and subsequently outperforming sedentary pups on rodent intelligence tests. But studies of the effect of exercise on the actual shape and function of children's brains had not yet been tried.

2  So the researchers sorted the children, based on their treadmill runs, into highest-, lowest-, and median-fit categories. Only the most- and least-fit groups continued in the study (to provide the greatest contrast). Both groups completed a series of cognitive challenges involving watching directional arrows on a computer screen and pushing certain keys in order to test how well the children filter out unnecessary information and attend to relevant cues. Finally, the children's brains were scanned, using magnetic resonance imaging technology to measure the volume of specific areas.

3  Previous studies found that fitter kids generally scored better on such tests. And in this case, too, those children performed better on the tests. But the M.R.I.'s provided a clearer picture of how it might work. They showed that fit children had significantly larger basal ganglia, a key part of the brain that aids in maintaining attention and "executive control," or the ability to coordinate actions and thoughts crisply. Since both groups of children had similar socioeconomic backgrounds, body mass index and other variables, the researchers concluded that being fit had enlarged that portion of their brains.

4  Meanwhile, in a separate, newly completed study by many of the same researchers at the University of Illinois, a second group of 9- and 10-year-old children were also categorized by fitness levels and had their brains scanned, but they completed different tests, this time focusing on complex memory. Such thinking is associated with activity in the hippocampus, a structure in the brain's medial temporal lobes. Sure enough, the M.R.I. scans revealed that the fittest children had heftier hippocampi.

5  The two studies did not directly overlap, but the researchers, in their separate reports, noted that the hippocampus and basal ganglia regions interact in

the human brain, structurally and functionally. Together they allow some of the most intricate thinking. If exercise is responsible for increasing the size of these regions and strengthening the connection between them, being fit in young people may "enhance neurocognition," the authors concluded.

6     These findings arrive at an important time. For budgetary and administrative reasons, school boards are curtailing physical education, while on their own, children grow increasingly sluggish. Recent statistics from the Centers for Disease Control and Prevention show that roughly a quarter of children participate in zero physical activity outside of school.

7     At the same time, evidence accumulates about the positive impact of even small amounts of aerobic activity. Past studies from the University of Illinois found that "just 20 minutes of walking" before a test raised children's scores, even if the children were otherwise unfit or overweight, says Charles Hillman, a professor of kinesiology at the university and the senior author of many of the recent studies.

8     But it's the neurological impact of sustained aerobic fitness in young people that is especially compelling. A memorable, years-long study published last year out of Sweden found that, among more than a million 18-year-old boys who joined the army, better fitness was correlated with higher I.Q.'s, even among identical twins. The fitter the twin, the higher his I.Q. The fittest of them were also more likely to go on to lucrative careers than the least fit, rendering them less likely, you would hope, to live in their parents' basements. No correlation was found between muscular strength and I.Q. scores. There's no evidence that exercise leads to a higher I.Q., but the researchers suspect that aerobic exercise, not strength training, produces specific growth factors and proteins that stimulate the brain, said Georg Kuhn, a professor at the University of Gothenburg and the senior author of the study.

9     But for now, the takeaway is clear. "More aerobic exercise!" for young people, Kuhn said. Hillman agreed. So get kids moving, he added, and preferably away from their Wiis. A still-unpublished study from his lab compared the cognitive impact in young people of 20 minutes of running on a treadmill with 20 minutes of playing sports style video games at a similar intensity. Running improved test scores immediately afterward. Playing the video games did not.

---

### QUESTIONS FOR READING

1.  What two tests were run on children by researchers at the University of Illinois? Explain all parts of the tests and the results.

2.  What did a study in Sweden reveal?

3.  What kind of fitness seems to be the key? What is the impact on the brain?

QUESTIONS FOR REASONING AND ANALYSIS

4.  Reynolds and the researchers she writes about are all careful with their discussions of test results. Where in her essay do you find qualified statements?

5.  Still, what inference do the studies seem to invite?

6.  What action by parents and schools seems appropriate?

QUESTIONS FOR REFLECTION AND WRITING

7.  Do the results of the tests surprise you? Why or why not?

8.  If you were a parent reading this article, would you be moved to action? If so, what would you do? If not, why not?

9.  Some companies have put gyms in their buildings; others help pay for gym memberships. Are fit employees smarter? More productive? If you were the CEO, would you spend the money for fitness?

## A DAUNTING CHILDREN'S DIVIDE | GEORGE WILL

A syndicated columnist since 1974, George Will is the author of a number of books, including ones about his great love—baseball. He is also a regular participant in television shows of political analysis. The following column appeared August 29, 2010.

PREREADING QUESTIONS What divides—relating to education—might be part of Will's discussion? What are at least three differences in the lives of children affecting their educational achievement that you would select to write about?

Various figures denote vexing social problems. They include 10,000 (the 1 number of new baby boomers eligible for Social Security and Medicare every day), 10.2 percent (what the unemployment rate would be if 1.2 million discouraged workers had not recently stopped looking for jobs), $9.9 trillion (the Government Accountability Office calculation of the gap between the expected revenue and outlays for state and local governments during the next 50 years), $76.4 trillion (the GAO's similar estimate of the federal government's 75-year fiscal shortfall).

Remedies for these problems can at least be imagined. But America's 2 tragic number—tragic because it is difficult to conceive remedial policies—is 70 percent. This is the portion of African American children born to unmarried women. It may explain what puzzles Nathan Glazer.

Writing in the *American Interest*, Glazer, a sociology professor emeritus 3 at Harvard, considers it a "paradox" that the election of Barack Obama "coincided with the almost complete disappearance from American public life of discussion of the black condition and what public policy might do to improve it." This, says Glazer, is the black condition:

Employment prospects for young black men worsened even when the 4 economy was robust. By the early 2000s, more than a third of all young black non-college men were under the supervision of the corrections system. More than 60 percent of black high school dropouts born since the mid-1960s go to prison. Mass incarceration blights the prospects of black women seeking husbands. So does another trend noted by sociologist William Julius Wilson: "In 2003–2004, for every 100 bachelor's degrees conferred on black men, 200 were conferred on black women."

5    Because changes in laws and mores have lowered barriers, the black middle class has been able to leave inner cities, which have become, Glazer says, "concentrations of the poor, the poorly educated, the unemployed and unemployable." High out-of-wedlock birthrates mean a constantly renewed cohort of adolescent males without male parenting, which means disorderly neighborhoods and schools. Glazer thinks it is possible that for some young black men, "acting white"—trying to excel in school—is considered "a betrayal of their group culture." This severely limits opportunities in an increasingly service-based economy where working with people matters more than working with things in manufacturing.

6    Now, from the Educational Testing Service, comes a report about "The Black-White Achievement Gap: When Progress Stopped," written by Paul E. Barton and Richard J. Coley. It examines the "startling" fact that most of the progress in closing the gap in reading and mathematics occurred in the 1970s and '80s. This means "progress generally halted for those born around the mid-1960s, a time when landmark legislative victories heralded an end to racial discrimination."

7    Only 35 percent of black children live with two parents, which partly explains why, while only 24 percent of white eighth-graders watch four or more hours of television on an average day, 59 percent of their black peers do. (Privileged children waste their time on new social media and other very mixed blessings of computers and fancy phones.) Black children also are disproportionately handicapped by this class-based disparity: By age 4, the average child in a professional family hears about 20 million more words than the average child in a working-class family and about 35 million more than the average child in a welfare family—a child often alone with a mother who is a high school dropout.

8    After surveying much research concerning many possible explanations of why progress stopped, particularly in neighborhoods characterized by a "concentration of deprivation," the ETS report says: "It is very hard to imagine progress resuming in reducing the education attainment and achievement gap without turning these family trends around—i.e., increasing marriage rates, and getting fathers back into the business of nurturing children." And: "It is similarly difficult to envision direct policy levers" to effect that.

9    So, two final numbers: Two decades, five factors. Two decades have passed since Barton wrote "America's Smallest School: The Family." He has estimated that about 90 percent of the difference in schools' proficiencies can be explained by five factors: the number of days students are absent from school, the number of hours students spend watching television, the number of pages read for homework, the quantity and quality of reading material in the students' homes—and much the most important, the presence of two

parents in the home. Public policies can have little purchase on these five, and least of all on the fifth.

## QUESTIONS FOR READING

1. What percentage of black children are born to unmarried mothers? What are some of the reasons Will gives for this?
2. What irony puzzles and bothers Glazer?
3. When did the achievement gap between blacks and whites stop shrinking?
4. How many more words do the children of professional parents hear by age 4 than do the children of poor parents?
5. What are Barton's "five factors"?

## QUESTIONS FOR REASONING AND ANALYSIS

6. What kind (genre) of argument is this? State Will's claim to make the genre clear.
7. What is clever about the author's introduction? How do the numbers in paragraph 1 serve his purpose?
8. Examine Barton's "five factors." Based on your own school experience, would you agree that these five are crucial to predicting success or failure in school? How might one of the five be updated to 2010?

## QUESTIONS FOR REFLECTION AND WRITING

9. Look again at all the details of black life that Will provides. Would you agree with him that closing the education gap is a daunting task? Why or why not?
10. Daunting does not mean impossible. If you were education czar, where would you start to seek to close the gap? What specific strategies and programs would you initiate? Why these?

# 10 STEPS TO WORLD-CLASS SCHOOLS | WILLIAM BROCK, RAY MARSHALL, and MARC TUCKER

William Brock was President Reagan's secretary of labor. Ray Marshall was secretary of labor in the Carter administration. Marc Tucker is president of the National Center on Education and the Economy (NCEE). All three are involved in the New Commission on the Skills of the American Workforce, an initiative of the NCEE. They published the following article in the *Washington Post* on May 30, 2009.

PREREADING QUESTIONS What steps to better schools would appear on your list? What might go at the top of your list? Compare your list to that of the three authors.

1     The key to U.S. global stature after World War II was the world's best-educated workforce. But now the United States ranks No. 12, according to the Organization for Economic Cooperation and Development, and today's younger generation is the first to be less educated than the preceding one.

2     No Child Left Behind is about getting our lowest-performing students to minimum standards. That is nowhere near enough. To get us where we need to go, we propose the National World Class Schools Act to replace NCLB. To get its fair share of federal education funds, a state would need to:

3   •  Set standards for licensing teachers that are high enough to recruit from the top third of college graduates—that's what the top-performing countries do—and never waive them during a shortage. If we insisted on high standards for our teachers and didn't waive them, teachers' pay would have to rise, a lot, and the pay for those in the shortest supply—math and science teachers, and teachers willing to work in tough inner-city schools and isolated rural areas—would rise the most.

4   •  Get outstanding students to go into teaching and treat them like professionals, not blue-collar workers in dead-end jobs. That means putting teachers in charge of their schools.

5   •  Reward schools that do a great job. NCLB penalizes schools when they fail but offers no rewards for outstanding work. Provide cash payments of 10 percent of the school budget every year to every school whose students significantly exceed the statistical predictions of performance for students with the same characteristics. Tell principals and faculties that they will get their normal budgets if their students are making adequate progress toward the standard of ready-for-college-without-remediation by graduation, and that they will be handsomely rewarded if their students are making substantially more progress toward that goal than other schools with similar student bodies. The financial reward should come as a big bonus for the school, and the faculty should decide how to spend it. This is better than rewarding individual teachers on the basis of their students' performance, which is hard to measure and will destroy the team spirit essential to a good school.

6   •  Hold faculty accountable for student achievement. Take over every school that, after three years, is unable to get at least 90 percent of all major groups of students on track to leave high school ready to enter college without the need to take any remedial courses; do the same for every district in which more than a quarter of the schools are under review for underperformance for three years or more. Declare such schools and districts bankrupt and void all contracts with their staffs.

- Replace the current accountability tests with high-quality, course-based 7 exams. The way we measure student performance is crucial. Rigor, creativity and innovation in student performance require a high-quality curriculum and exams, and will be impossible to achieve if we continue to use the kind of multiple-choice, computer-scored tests that are common today.

- Collect a variety of information on school and student performance and 8 make it easily accessible to parents, students and teachers. Allow parents to choose freely among the available public schools.

- Provide high-quality training and technical assistance to every school 9 whose students are not on track to succeed. Most struggling schools are in chaos; their morale is in the basement and their faculties don't know how to improve things. States have little capacity to fix this; the federal government needs to help.

- Limit variations in any states' per-pupil expenditures to no more than 5 10 percent by school, except for the differential cost of educating disadvantaged students and those with disabilities to the same standards as students who don't face those obstacles. In this country, students who need the most help have the lowest school budgets—a formula for national failure.

- Make a range of social services available to children from low-income fam- 11 ilies and coordinate those services with those students' school programs. We have the most unequal distribution of income of any industrialized nation. If the problems posed by students' poverty are not dealt with, it may be nearly impossible for schools to educate the students to world-class standards. The state cannot eliminate students' poverty, but it can take steps to alleviate its effects on students' capacity to learn.

- Offer high-quality early-childhood education to, at a minimum, all 12 4-year-olds and all low-income 3-year-olds. Students from low-income families entering kindergarten have less than half the vocabulary of other students. In kindergarten and the early grades, those with the smallest vocabularies cannot follow what is going on and fall further behind. By the end of fourth grade, they are so far behind they can never catch up. By the time they are 16 and can legally drop out of school, they do so because they can no longer stand the humiliation of not being able to follow what is going on in their classes. That is why we lead the industrialized world in the proportion of students who drop out.

Yes, these are radical proposals. But decades of incremental proposals 13 have brought steadily increasing costs and flat performance. Time is running out. It is hard to make a case that the federal government should continue to fund the states to maintain the status quo.

Source: From *The Washington Post,* May 30, 2009. Reprinted by permission of Marc Tucker.

QUESTIONS FOR READING

1. How does today's younger generation compare to their parents in education?
2. What legislation do the authors propose to improve schools?
3. What would the authors do to improve teaching? To evaluate and improve schools?
4. How should students be evaluated? How should they be prepared for school and for learning?
5. How would the proposed legislation seek to make schools more equal throughout a state?

QUESTIONS FOR REASONING AND ANALYSIS

6. How do some of these proposals differ from those established by the Bush initiative of No Child Left Behind? How do the authors argue for their different approaches? Is their argument convincing?
7. What makes their opening paragraph effective? How does it establish both their subject and the kind of argument they will present?
8. What about the essay's tone and style makes the authors' approach effective for this kind of argument?

QUESTIONS FOR REFLECTION AND WRITING

9. Organize your thinking about these proposals by first grouping the 10 under three general headings: teachers, students, and funding. Further subdivide within each of the three categories. Why do you suppose that the authors did not use your "more organized" approach? What do they gain by their strategy?
10. Which two of the 10 proposals do you think are the most revolutionary—different from the Bush initiative and/or different from the ways states and localities have managed public schooling for a long time? Do you think the two are good proposals? Why or why not? Do you think they can be implemented—or will they encounter resistance? Explain.

# 5 MYTHS ABOUT WHO GETS INTO COLLEGE | RICHARD D. KAHLENBERG

A senior fellow at the Century Foundation, Richard Kahlenberg is an expert on K–12 schooling. He is the author of four books on education and the editor of seven more, most recently *Rewarding Strivers: Helping Low-Income Students Succeed in College* (2010). His articles are widely published, and he is a frequent guest on TV talk shows. The following article appeared in the *Washington Post* on May 23, 2010.

PREREADING QUESTIONS In preparation for reading, glance at the five myths the author will examine. Which, if any, myths do you think are accurate? Even if there is just one that you thought was an accurate statement, is that sufficient reason to study Kahlenberg's analysis?

This spring, more than 3 million students will graduate from America's high schools, and more than 2 million of them will head off to college in the fall. At the top colleges, competition has been increasingly fierce, leaving many high school seniors licking their wounds and wondering what they did "wrong." But do selective colleges and universities do a good job of identifying the best and brightest? And is the concern about who gets into the best colleges justified?

These students enjoy one another and their beautiful campus.

**1. Admissions officers have figured out how to reward merit above wealth and connections.** A 2004 Century Foundation study found that at the most selective universities and colleges, 74 percent of students come from the richest quarter of the population, while just 3 percent come from the bottom quarter. Rich kids can't possibly be 25 times as likely to be smart as poor kids, so wealth and connections must still matter.

Leading schools have two main admissions policies that favor wealthy students. The more glaring of these is legacy preferences—an admissions boost for the children of alumni. Legacy preferences increase a student's chances of admission by, on average, 20 percentage points over non-legacies. Schools use such preferences on the theory that they increase donations from alumni, but new research by Chad Coffman questions that premise. Those universities that have abandoned legacy preferences—or never used them—have plenty of alumni donors. Examples include Caltech, Texas A&M and the University of Georgia.

Less obvious is the role of the SAT, which was, when it was introduced in 1926, supposed to help identify talented students from across all schools and backgrounds. Instead, it seems to amplify the advantages enjoyed by the most privileged students. New research by Georgetown University's Anthony Carnevale and Jeff Strohl finds that the most disadvantaged applicants (those who, among other characteristics, are black, attend public schools with high poverty rates, come from low-income families and have parents who are high school dropouts) score, on average, 784 points lower on the SAT than the most advantaged students (those who, among other things, are white, attend private schools and have wealthy, highly educated parents). This gap is equivalent to about two-thirds of the test's total score range. If the SAT were a 100-yard dash, advantaged kids would start off 65 yards ahead before the race even began.

5    **2. Disadvantages based on race are still the biggest obstacle to getting into college.** More than race, it's class: The effects of racial discrimination are increasingly dwarfed by the impact of socioeconomic status. Take that 784-point difference in SAT scores between the most advantaged and the most disadvantaged students. All other things being equal, the researchers found that there was a 56-point difference between black and white students. Most of the rest of the gap was the result of socioeconomic factors. To truly even the playing field, the system would therefore need to provide a lot of affirmative action to economically disadvantaged students who beat the odds and a little bit of affirmative action based on race.

6    Yet colleges and universities today do the opposite: They provide substantial preferences based on race and virtually none based on class. According to researchers William Bowen, Martin Kurzweil and Eugene Tobin, at highly selective institutions, for students within a given SAT range, being a member of an underrepresented minority increases one's chance of admission by 28 percentage points. That is, a white student might have a 30 percent chance of admission, but a black or Latino student with a similar record would have a 58 percent chance of admission. By contrast, Bowen and his colleagues found, students from poor families don't receive any leg up in the process—they fare neither better nor worse than wealthier applicants.

7    **3. Generous financial aid policies are the key to boosting socioeconomic diversity.** In response to the growing scarcity of poor and working-class students on campus, roughly 100 universities and colleges have boosted financial aid in the past several years. But these programs have not been enough to change the socioeconomic profile of these schools' student bodies. At the University of North Carolina at Chapel Hill, for example, a generous financial aid program, the Carolina Covenant, was instituted in 2004. Under its terms, low-income students are not required to take out loans as part of their financial aid packages.

8    According to research by Edward B. Fiske, the program has been successful in accomplishing one important goal: boosting the graduation rate among low-income students. Traditionally, low-income and working-class students drop out at much higher rates than do higher-income students, as financial worries and jobs with long hours distract from their studies. Fiske found that the Carolina Covenant raised the four-year graduation rates of low-income students by almost 10 percent.

9    Yet the proportion of low-income students at UNC-Chapel Hill remained flat between 2003 and 2008, because the university has not given such students (those eligible for federal Pell grants, 90 percent of which go to students from families making less than $40,000 a year) any break in the admissions process. A few other institutions, including Amherst and Harvard, have begun to consider a student's socioeconomic status in their admissions decisions;

these schools provide a promising example. At Harvard, the percentage of students receiving Pell grants has shot up from 9.4 percent in the 2003–2004 school year to 15 percent in the 2008–2009 school year.

**4. Selective colleges are too expensive and aren't worth the investment.** 10 A selective institution with a large endowment may indeed be worth the money. The least selective colleges spend about $12,000 per student, compared with $92,000 per student at the most selective schools. Put another way, at the wealthiest 10 percent of institutions, students pay, on average, just 20 cents in fees for every dollar the school spends on them, while at the poorest 10 percent of institutions, students pay 78 cents for every dollar spent on them.

Furthermore, selective colleges are quite a bit better at retention: If a 11 more selective school and a less selective school enroll two equally qualified students, the more selective school is much more likely to graduate its student. Future earnings are, on average, 45 percent higher for students who graduated from more selective institutions than for those from less selective ones, and the difference in earnings is widest among low-income students. And according to research by Thomas Dye, 54 percent of America's top 4,325 corporate leaders are graduates of just 12 institutions.

**5. With more students going to college, we're closer to the goal of** 12 **equal opportunity.** The good news is that students are going to college at a higher rate than ever before; the bad news is that stratification is increasing at colleges and universities. Much as urban elementary and secondary schools saw white, affluent parents flee to suburban schools in the 1970s and 1980s, less selective colleges are now experiencing white flight. According to Carnevale and Strohl, white student representation declined from 79 percent to 58 percent at less selective and noncompetitive institutions between 1994 and 2006, while black student representation soared from 11 percent to 28 percent. American higher education is in danger of quickly becoming both separate and unequal.

Source: From *The Washington Post*, May 23, 2010. Reprinted by permission of the author.

## QUESTIONS FOR READING

1.  What numbers demonstrate that selective colleges are not rewarding merit above wealth and connections? What two admissions policies favor the rich?
2.  What is the biggest obstacle to getting into college? Why are racial minorities not the most disadvantaged in the college selection process?
3.  Why has increased financial aid not changed the socioeconomic mix at most colleges? Which colleges have begun to consider socioeconomic status in the admissions process?
4.  For what three reasons is the cost of highly selective colleges possibly worth the price?
5.  In spite of the increase in the numbers of students attending college, why is this not a sign of equal opportunity in higher education?

6. What kind of evidence does Kahlenberg provide in support of each of his arguments counter to current views regarding college admissions?

7. What is the author's purpose in writing? To expose myths about changes in college admissions is, ultimately, to write what kind of argument? Write a claim statement that reveals Kahlenberg's purpose in writing.

8. Is the information convincing? Why or why not?

9. Are you surprised by any of the statistics? If so, which ones? If not, why not?

10. To embrace the five myths about college admissions is to see American society going in what direction? Presumably we would agree that this direction is good for our society. So, if these myths don't hold up to the facts, then what should we be doing to correct this problem? What are your suggestions—or the suggestions implied in much of the essay—for making a college education more available to all who wish to attend?

## SO MUCH FOR THE INFORMATION AGE | TED GUP

Chair of the journalism department at Emerson College, Ted Gup is a former staff writer for the *Washington Post* and *Time*. He is the author of two books on the intelligence community, including *Nation of Secrets: The Threat to Democracy and the American Way of Life* (2007). His latest book is *A Secret Life: How One Man's Kindness—and a Trove of Letters—Revealed the Hidden History of the Great Depression* (2010). His article on education was published in the *Chronicle of Higher Education* on April 11, 2008.

PREREADING QUESTIONS Considering just Gup's title, what do you think his topic will be? If you add the context of this chapter, does that alter your expectation?

1    Today's college students have tuned out the world, and it's partly our fault. I teach a seminar called "Secrecy: Forbidden Knowledge." I recently asked my class of 16 freshmen and sophomores, many of whom had graduated in the top 10 percent of their high-school classes and had dazzling SAT scores, how many had heard the word "rendition."

2    Not one hand went up.

3    This is after four years of the word appearing on the front pages of the nation's newspapers, on network and cable news, and online. This is after years of highly publicized lawsuits, Congressional inquiries, and international controversy and condemnation. This is after the release of a Hollywood film of that title, starring Jake Gyllenhaal, Meryl Streep, and Reese Witherspoon.

4    I was dumbstruck. Finally one hand went up, and the student sheepishly asked if rendition had anything to do with a version of a movie or a play.

I nodded charitably, then attempted to define the word in its more public ₅ context. I described specific accounts of U.S. abductions of foreign citizens, of the likely treatment accorded such prisoners when placed in the hands of countries like Syria and Egypt, of the months and years of detention. I spoke of the lack of formal charges, of some prisoners' eventual release and how their subsequent lawsuits against the U.S. government were stymied in the name of national security and secrecy.

The students were visibly disturbed. They expressed astonishment, then ₆ revulsion. They asked how such practices could go on.

I told them to look around the room at one another's faces; they were ₇ seated next to the answer. I suggested that they were, in part, the reason that rendition, waterboarding, Guantánamo detention, warrantless searches and intercepts, and a host of other such practices have not been more roundly discredited. I admit it was harsh.

That instance was no aberration. In recent years I have administered a ₈ dumbed-down quiz on current events and history early in each semester to get a sense of what my students know and don't know. Initially I worried that its simplicity would insult them, but my fears were unfounded. The results have been, well, horrifying.

Nearly half of a recent class could not name a single country that bordered ₉ Israel. In an introductory journalism class, 11 of 18 students could not name what country Kabul was in, although we have been at war there for half a decade. Last fall only one in 21 students could name the U.S. secretary of defense. Given a list of four countries—China, Cuba, India, and Japan—not one of those same 21 students could identify India and Japan as democracies. Their grasp of history was little better. The question of when the Civil War was fought invited an array of responses—half a dozen were off by a decade or more. Some students thought that Islam was the principal religion of South America, that *Roe v. Wade* was about slavery, that 50 justices sit on the U.S. Supreme Court, that the atom bomb was dropped on Hiroshima in 1975. You get the picture, and it isn't pretty.

As a journalist, professor, and citizen, I find it profoundly discouraging to ₁₀ encounter such ignorance of critical issues. But it would be both unfair and inaccurate to hold those young people accountable for the moral and legal morass we now find ourselves in as a nation. They are earnest, readily educable, and, when informed, impassioned.

I make it clear to my students that it is not only their right but their duty to ₁₁ arrive at their own conclusions. They are free to defend rendition, waterboarding, or any other aspect of America's post-9/11 armamentarium. But I challenge their right to tune out the world, and I question any system or society that can produce such students and call them educated. I am concerned for the nation when a cohort of students so talented and bright is oblivious to all such matters. If they are failing us, it is because we have failed them.

Still, it is hard to reconcile the students' lack of knowledge with the notion ₁₂ that they are a part of the celebrated information age, creatures of the Internet who arguably have at their disposal more information than all the preceding generations combined. Despite their BlackBerrys, cellphones, and Wi-Fi, they are, in their own way, as isolated as the remote tribes of New Guinea. They disprove the notion that technology fosters engagement, that connectivity and community are synonymous. I despair to think that this is the generation brought up under the banner of "No Child Left Behind." What I see is the specter of an entire generation left behind and left out.

13   It is not easy to explain how we got into this sad state, or to separate symptoms from causes. Newspaper readership is in steep decline. My students simply do not read newspapers, online or otherwise, and many grew up in households that did not subscribe to a paper. Those who tune in to television "news" are subjected to a barrage of opinions from talking heads like CNN's demagogic Lou Dobbs and MSNBC's Chris Matthews and Fox's Bill O'Reilly and his dizzying "No Spin Zone." In today's journalistic world, opinion trumps fact (the former being cheaper to produce), and rank partisanship and virulent culture wars make the middle ground uninhabitable. Small wonder, then, that my students shrink from it.

14   Then, too, there is the explosion of citizen journalism. An army of average Joes, equipped with cellphones, laptops, and video cameras, has commandeered our news media. The mantra of "We want to hear from you!" is all the rage, from CNN to NPR; but, although invigorating and democratizing, it has failed to supplant the provision of essential facts, generating more heat than light. Many of my students can report on the latest travails of celebrities or the sexual follies of politicos, and can be forgiven for thinking that such matters dominate the news—they do. Even those students whose home pages open onto news sites have tailored them to parochial interests—sports, entertainment, weather—that are a pale substitute for the scope and sweep of a good front page or the PBS *NewsHour with Jim Lehrer* (which many students seem ready to pickle in formaldehyde).

15   Civics is decidedly out of fashion in the high-school classroom, a quaint throwback superseded by courses in technology. As teachers scramble to "teach to the test," civics is increasingly relegated to after-school clubs and geeky graduation prizes. Somehow my students sailed through high-school courses in government and social studies without acquiring the habit of keeping abreast of national and international events. What little they know of such matters they have absorbed through popular culture—song lyrics, parody, and comedy. *The Daily Show with Jon Stewart* is as close as many dare get to actual news.

16   Yes, the post-9/11 world is a scary place, and plenty of diversions can absorb young people's attention and energies, as well as distract them from the anxieties of preparing for a career in an increasingly uncertain economy. But that respite comes at a cost.

17   As a journalist, I have spent my career promoting transparency and accountability. But my experiences in the classroom humble and chasten me. They remind me that challenges to secrecy and opacity are moot if society does not avail itself of information that is readily accessible. Indeed, our very failure to digest the accessible helps to create an environment in which secrecy can run rampant.

It is time to once again make current events an essential part of the 18 curriculum. Families and schools must instill in students the habit of following what is happening in the world. A global economy will have little use for a country whose people are so self-absorbed that they know nothing of their own nation's present or past, much less the world's. There is a fundamental difference between shouldering the rights and responsibilities that come with citizenship—engagement, participation, debate—and merely inhabiting the land.

As a nation, we spend an inordinate amount of time fretting about illegal 19 immigration and painfully little on what it means to be a citizen, beyond the legal status conferred by accident of birth or public processing. We are too busy building a wall around us to notice that we are shutting ourselves in. Intent on exporting democracy—spending blood and billions in pursuit of it abroad—we have shown a decided lack of interest in exercising or promoting democracy at home.

The noted American scholar Robert M. Hutchins said, decades ago: "The 20 object of the educational system, taken as a whole, is not to produce hands for industry or to teach the young how to make a living. It is to produce responsible citizens." He warned that "the death of a democracy is not likely to be an assassination from ambush. It will be a slow extinction from apathy, indifference, and undernourishment." I fear he was right.

I tell the students in my secrecy class that they are required to attend. 21 After all, we count on one another; without student participation, it just doesn't work. The same might be said of democracy. Attendance is mandatory.

---

Source: Originally appeared in *The Chronicle of Higher Education,* April 11, 2008. Reprinted by permission of the author.

## QUESTIONS FOR READING

1.  What does the word *rendition* mean—in its public context?
2.  How knowledgeable were Gup's students?
3.  What may explain the lack of knowledge of history and current events among today's college students?
4.  What can happen in a society when citizens are uninformed?
5.  What does democracy require?

## QUESTIONS FOR REASONING AND ANALYSIS

6.  Gup spends nine paragraphs demonstrating his students' lack of knowledge. That is a long introduction. Why does he do it? What is his purpose?
7.  What is the author's claim? Where does he state it? Put his claim in your own words as a claim for a problem/solution argument.
8.  What solution does Gup propose?
9.  What makes his concluding paragraph effective?

10. Do you agree that today's college students lack knowledge of history and current events? Why or why not?

11. Do you accept Gup's explanation of causes? If you disagree, what do you think are the causes?

12. Do you agree that citizens have a duty to participate in a democracy? Can you participate meaningfully when you don't understand your country's history or know current events? Explain and defend your views.

## LAPTOPS VS. LEARNING | DAVID COLE

A professor at Georgetown University's Law Center, David Cole is also legal affairs correspondent to *The Nation* and the author of several books, including *No Equal Justice: Race and Class in the Criminal Justice System* (1999). The following op-ed piece on his students' use of laptops appeared in the *Washington Post* on April 7, 2007.

PREREADING QUESTIONS Do you take a laptop to class? If so, why? How often do you shift attention from class to e-mail or the Internet?

1   "Could you repeat the question?"

2   In recent years, that has become the most common response to questions I pose to my law students at Georgetown University. It is usually asked while the student glances up from the laptop screen that otherwise occupies his or her field of vision. After I repeat the question, the student's gaze as often as not returns to the computer screen, as if the answer might magically appear there. Who knows, with instant messaging, maybe it will.

3   Some years back, our law school, like many around the country, wired its classrooms with Internet hookups. It's the way of the future, I was told. Now we are a wireless campus, and incoming students are required to have laptops. So my first-year students were a bit surprised when I announced at the first class this year that laptops were banned from my classroom.

I did this for two reasons, I explained. Note-taking on a laptop encourages 4
verbatim transcription. The note-taker tends to go into stenographic mode
and no longer processes information in a way that is conductive to the give
and take of classroom discussion. Because taking notes the old-fashioned way,
by hand, is so much slower, one actually has to listen, think and prioritize the
most important themes.

In addition, laptops create temptation to surf the Web, check e-mail, shop 5
for shoes or instant-message friends. That's not only distracting to the student
who is checking Red Sox statistics but for all those who see him, and many
others, doing something besides being involved in class. Together, the stenographic mode and Web surfing make for a much less engaged classroom, and
that affects all students (not to mention me).

I agreed to permit two volunteers to use laptops to take notes that would 6
be made available to all students. And that first day I allowed everyone to use
the laptops they had with them. I posed a question, and a student volunteered
an answer. I answered her with a follow-up question. As if on cue, as soon as I
started to respond, the student went back to typing—and then asked, "Could
you repeat the question?"

When I have raised with my colleagues the idea of cutting off laptop 7
access, some accuse me of being paternalistic, authoritarian or worse. We
daydreamed and did crosswords when we were students, they argue, so how
can we prohibit our students, who are adults after all, from using their time in
class as they deem fit?

A crossword hidden under a book is one thing. With the aid of Microsoft 8
and Google, we have effectively put at every seat a library of magazines, a
television and the opportunity for real-time side conversations and invited our
students to check out whenever they find their attention wandering.

I feel especially strongly about this issue because I'm addicted to the 9
Internet myself. I checked my e-mail at least a dozen times while writing this
op-ed. I've often resolved, after a rare and liberating weekend away from
e-mail, that I will wait till the end of the day to read e-mail at the office. Yet,
almost as if it is beyond my control, e-mail is the first thing I check when I log
on each morning. As for multitasking, I don't buy it. Attention diverted is
attention diverted.

But this is all theory. How does banning laptops work in practice? My own 10
sense has been that my class is much more engaged than recent past classes.
I'm biased, I know. So I conducted an anonymous survey of my students after
about six weeks—by computer, of course.

The results were striking. About 80 percent reported that they are more 11
engaged in class discussion when they are laptop-free. Seventy percent said
that, on balance, they liked the no-laptop policy. And perhaps most surprising,
95 percent admitted that they use their laptops in class for "purposes other
than taking notes, such as surfing the Web, checking e-mail, instant messaging
and the like." Ninety-eight percent reported seeing fellow students do the
same.

I am sure that the Internet can be a useful pedagogical tool in some set- 12
tings and for some subjects. But for most classes, it is little more than an

attractive nuisance. Technology has outstripped us on this one, and we need to reassess its appropriate and inappropriate role in teaching. The personal computer has revolutionized our lives, in many ways for the better. But it also threatens to take over our lives. At least for some purposes, unplugging may still be the best response.

---

Source: *The Washington Post,* April 7, 2007. Reprinted by permission of the author.

### QUESTIONS FOR READING

1. Why did the author ban laptops from his law classes?
2. What student behavior the first day of class seemed to support Cole's argument?
3. How did some of his colleagues react?
4. What did his student survey reveal?

### QUESTIONS FOR REASONING AND ANALYSIS

5. What is Cole's claim? Where does he state it most emphatically?
6. How does Cole rebut his colleagues' argument in support of laptops in the classroom?
7. What does the author gain in paragraph 9 when he describes himself as "addicted to the Internet"?

### QUESTIONS FOR REFLECTION AND WRITING

8. Cole observes that the results of his survey were "striking." Are you surprised by the students' responses? Would you have agreed with the great majority of students on the questions? Why or why not?
9. Cole asserts that the Internet can be a teaching tool for some classes. In what kinds of courses or for what types of class environments might having a laptop be an aid to learning? Explain and defend your answer.

# CHAPTER 21

# Censorship and Free Speech Debates

Jim Morin, *The Miami Herald*, CartoonArts International, Inc.

READ: What is the situation?

REASON: What is ironic about the signs and speech of one of the figures?

REFLECT/WRITE: Why are protections of speech essential to a democracy?

If we have freedom of speech, why do people keep debating it? Why an entire chapter on the topic? As you explore the specific issues debated in this chapter, keep in mind that the Supreme Court continues to hand down rulings that shape our understanding of First Amendment rights. What is protected speech under the First Amendment is never absolute—it continues to evolve or be reinterpreted, depending on your point of view.

We also need to consider that there is no such thing as absolute freedom in any society and that the First Amendment does not pretend to offer absolute freedoms. For example, you cannot go into a crowded theater and yell "Fire!" when there is no fire. You will be arrested for this behavior that puts others at risk.

And so the debates continue, as we consider what the rules are for exposing someone else's activities on your website or what we think about the building of an Islamic cultural center a few blocks from Ground Zero. Parents place controls on their TVs and computers to restrict their children's access to some shows and sites. What restrictions are appropriate for governments to establish remains the ongoing question.

## PREREADING QUESTIONS

1. What, if any, restrictions should be placed on the publication of obscene, pornographic, or treasonable works? Are there some restrictions that most people can agree to?

2. What, if any, restrictions should be placed on hate speech? Should hate speech be a crime? Are there restrictions that colleges, in particular, should—or should not—establish?

3. What, if any, restrictions should be placed on violent video games?

4. What are some ways to control what is published (in any medium) without always resorting to legal restrictions? Are there feasible alternatives to legal battles?

## GROUND ZERO FOR FREE SPEECH | KATHA POLLITT

Associate editor of *The Nation*, Katha Pollitt contributes to periodicals, has collected her essays in *Reasonable Creatures: Essays on Women and Feminism* (1994), and has books of poetry, *Antarctic Traveller* (1982) and *The Mind-Body Problem: Poems* (2009). Her very successful collection of stories, *Learning to Drive: And Other Life Stories*, was published in 2008. "Ground Zero for Free Speech" appeared in *The Nation* on August 12, 2010.

PREREADING QUESTIONS How does Pollitt's title announce her subject? How does it indicate her position on this issue?

1    Park51, *aka* Cordoba House, won't be a mosque; it will be a $100 million, thirteen-story cultural center with a pool, gym, auditorium and prayer room. It won't be at Ground Zero; it will be two blocks away. (By the way, two mosques

A still-desolate Ground Zero in September 2009, although some construction is under way.

have existed in the neighborhood for years.) It won't be a shadowy storefront where radical clerics recruit young suicide bombers; it will be a showplace of moderate Islam, an Islam for the pluralist West—the very thing wise heads in the United States and Europe agree is essential to integrate Muslim immigrants and prevent them from becoming fundamentalists and even terrorists. "It's a shame we even have to talk about this," says Mayor Michael Bloomberg, a longtime supporter of the project.

Apparently we do, because the same right-wingers who talk about the 2 Constitution as if Sarah Palin had tweeted it herself apparently skipped over the First Amendment, where freedom of speech and worship are guaranteed to all. "America is experiencing an Islamist cultural-political offensive designed to undermine and destroy our civilization," claims Newt Gingrich, who argues that the United States can't let Muslims build a "mosque" "at Ground Zero" because Saudi Arabia doesn't permit the building of churches and synagogues. For a man who warns that Sharia law is coming soon to a courthouse near you, Gingrich seems strangely eager to accept Saudi standards of religious tolerance. Isn't the whole point that ours is an open society and theirs is closed? "This is a desecration," says former Mayor Rudy Giuliani. "Nobody would allow something like that at Pearl Harbor. Let's have some respect for who died there and why they died there. Let's not put this off on some kind of politically correct theory." I'm not aware of any Japanese-Americans trying to build a Shinto shrine at Pearl Harbor, but what if they had? Why would that be so terrible?

(Oh, and "politically correct theory"? Would that be the First Amendment? Giuliani never did have much fondness for pesky old free speech.)

3   And then there's Sarah Palin, America's Tweetheart: "Peace-seeking Muslims, pls understand, Ground Zero mosque is UNNECESSARY provocation; it stabs hearts. Pls reject it in interest of healing." Yes, peace-seeking Muslims, just crawl back into your cave and leave us real Americans alone so we can get over the terrible crime committed by people who are not you! Thirty-three years ago, the language of healing wasn't powerful enough to keep the National Socialists of America from marching in Skokie, Illinois—home to many Holocaust survivors—and kudos to the ACLU for defending the freedom of assembly even of those worst of the worst, a position that was not at all obvious at the time. But we've been thoroughly bathed in psychobabble since then, so it's not surprising that sophisticated opponents like Abraham Foxman, national director of the Anti-Defamation League, have adopted that cloying lingo: "strong passions . . . keen sensitivities . . . counterproductive to the healing process." As Foxman wrote in a statement, "ultimately this is not a question of rights, but a question of what is right. In our judgment, building an Islamic Center in the shadow of the World Trade Center will cause some victims more pain—unnecessarily—and that is not right."

4   Actually, there are 9/11 survivors and families on both sides of the Park51 proposal. Opening the center is "consistent with fundamental American values of freedom and justice for all," said the group September 11 Families for Peaceful Tomorrows. And although a Marist poll found that 53 percent of New York City residents oppose the center, 53 percent of Manhattanites support it—let's hear it for the much-mocked Upper West Side. But even if all the survivors, and every inhabitant of the World Trade Center's home borough, were united against it, that should not carry the day. The Constitution is not a Tylenol pill. It's not about making hurt people feel better—or pandering to the resentments of bigots, either. Nor is it about polls or majority votes. If it were, freedom of speech would not be possible, because as Rosa Luxemburg said, freedom is "always . . . for the one who thinks differently." It would be nice if our elected officials, who swore an oath to defend the Constitution, got the message. Instead, we have mostly silence, with Governor David Paterson offering state land if Park51 agreed to move elsewhere. That man just can't seem to do anything right.

5   What's especially odd about the Park51 flap is that Palin, Gingrich and other right-wing opponents delight in waving the Constitution about and professing to revere its every word. They, after all, are the ones who love religion so much, they think the First Amendment is all about privileging it over secularism. Don't tread on me with your evil humanist jackboot! The argument that religion should not be imposed on public spaces—a public-school classroom, say—has never made sense to them. In their mythology, believers are a persecuted minority because the ACLU won't let biology teachers suggest that Earth might well be only 10,000 years old. It turns out that by religion they mean only Christianity. Indeed, Tennessee Tea Party gubernatorial candidate Ron Ramsey suggests that Islam isn't a religion but a cult—as if the world's 1.5 billion Muslims are sleep-deprived runaways controlled by an evil mastermind.

The attempt by Gingrich and others to portray Park51 as part of a planned  6
Islamic takeover of the United States is shameful and ridiculous. America is a
secular democracy in which at least three-quarters of the population are committed Christians, and hedonism is a way of life. Almost nobody, even among
American Muslims, is interested in the supposed aims of militant Islam—
polygyny, forcing women into burqas, banning pork and alcohol and music,
instituting Sharia law. Fear of Muslim rule is even more preposterous than
what it has so efficiently replaced—fear of communist rule—and one day it will
look just as bizarre.

By then, I hope Park51 will be a modern landmark in the city Mayor  7
Bloomberg proudly called the freest in the world.

---

Source: From *The Nation*, August 30/September 6, 2010. Online August 12, 2010. Reprinted by
permission of the author.

## QUESTIONS FOR READING

1. What point does Pollitt want to make in paragraph 2, with quotations from
   Gingrich and Giuliani? Whom do they represent?
2. What group held a march thirty-three years ago? What do they represent for
   the author?
3. What is *psychobabble*?
4. Why is the Park51 decision not based on a vote? For whom do we have freedom
   of speech?
5. What, according to Pollitt, is the double standard over religious freedom that is
   held by the right wing?

## QUESTIONS FOR REASONING AND ANALYSIS

6. What is significant about the facts Pollitt presents in her opening paragraph?
   What makes this an effective opening?
7. Pollitt finds repeated irony in the position of conservative Republican leaders.
   What is the irony?
8. What type (genre) of argument is this? Is it appropriate to say that Pollitt has
   two goals in writing?
9. How would you describe the author's tone? What elements of style shape that
   tone?

## QUESTIONS FOR REFLECTION AND WRITING

10. The facts in this case are simple; what is the argument about?
11. Has Pollitt written an effective argument for her primary audience? (Where is
    *The Nation* on the political spectrum?)
12. Are you moved by her argument? If yes, why? If no, how would you counter
    her?

## WHY THE FIRST AMENDMENT (AND JOURNALISM) MIGHT BE IN TROUBLE

KEN DAUTRICH and JOHN BARE

Ken Dautrich, chair of the department of public policy at the University of Connecticut, directed the study "The Future of the First Amendment" with colleague David Yalof. They are coauthors of the book *The First Amendment and the Media in the Court of Public Opinion* (2002). John Bare, Dautrich's coauthor for this article, is vice president for strategic planning and evaluation at the Arthur M. Blank Family Foundation in Atlanta. Their article appeared in the Summer 2005 issue of *Nieman Reports,* published by Harvard University.

PREREADING QUESTIONS  Should the government control content on the Internet? Does the First Amendment protect flag burning?

1    Our first-of-its-kind exploration of the future of the First Amendment among American high school students—a highly visible study of 112,000 students and 8,000 teachers in over 300 high schools—suggests a fragile future for key constitutional freedoms while also pointing us to potential remedies. This study, "The Future of the First Amendment," which was released earlier this year, arrived at a timely moment in American history, on the heels of a national election and amid a war the President is using, by his account, to spread democratic freedoms. The results drew remarkable media attention, which tended to focus on one of the more fearful statistics to emerge from the study: Only 51 percent of 9th to 12th graders agree that newspapers should be allowed to publish freely without government approval of stories—in other words, nearly half entertain the idea of newspaper censorship.

2    Beyond that flashpoint finding, the study allows for a more thorough understanding of today's high school students and can point us to potential remedies. The research also suggests ways to improve support for the First Amendment. While many of the findings raise concern, some are not so bad. Some are even encouraging. Most of all, the results should be viewed within the context of the history of the First Amendment, which faced challenges— some would say it was compromised—as soon as it was adopted.

### FIRST AMENDMENT CHALLENGES

3    One of the first acts of the first Congress in 1789 was to append a Bill of Rights to the U.S. Constitution, which, among other things, explicitly denied Congress the ability to tamper with Americans' rights of free expression. Indeed, through the course of our history, Americans and their leaders have proclaimed a commitment to freedom and liberty. Most recently, President Bush, in his second inaugural address, justified the Iraqi and Afghani military operations as a vehicle to spread freedom and liberty throughout the world.

4    Despite a long history of veneration to these values, freedom of expression has met with a number of challenges. Not long after adoption of the First Amendment, President John Adams and the Federalist Congress passed the

Alien and Sedition Acts, severely thwarting the freedom to speak out against government. Abraham Lincoln's suspension of habeas corpus, the internment of Japanese Americans during Franklin Roosevelt's administration after Pearl Harbor, Senator Joseph McCarthy's "red scare," and Attorney General John Ashcroft's aggressive implementation of the USA Patriot Act represent just a few of the more notable breaches to liberty in America.

Like any value in our society, the health and vitality of freedom and liberty 5 are largely dependent upon the public's attention to, appreciation for, and support of them. When Americans are willing to compromise freedom of expression in return for a sense of being more secure, then government officials can more readily take action to curtail freedom. Public fear of Communism allowed McCarthy to tread on people's liberty, just as fear of terrorism allowed Ashcroft to curb freedoms.

The real protection of free expression rights lies not in the words of the 6 First Amendment. Rather, it lies in the people's willingness to appreciate and support those rights. That idea led the Freedom Forum's First Amendment Center to commission an annual survey on public knowledge, appreciation and support for free expression rights since 1997 to gauge the health and well-being of the First Amendment.

If public opinion is a good measure of the First Amendment's well-being, 7 then its annual checkup has been fraught with health problems.

- While more than 9-in-10 agree that "people should be allowed to express unpopular opinions," a paltry 4-in-10 believe that high school students should be able to report on controversial issues in school newspapers without the consent of school officials.

- More than one-third say the press has too much freedom.

- Fewer than 6-in-10 say that musicians should be able to sing songs with lyrics that may be offensive to some.

These annual checkups have shown over time that half of adults think that 8 flag burning as a method of protest should not be tolerated. In general, the surveys have revealed that the public holds low support for, a lack of appreciation for, and dangerously low levels of knowledge of free expression rights. Is it no wonder, then, that the suspension of liberty in this land of freedom has been so readily accomplished by its leaders from time to time?

It was these rather anemic annual checkups that convinced the John S. 9 and James L. Knight Foundation to commission this unique survey of American high school students and to begin a wider discussion about how to strengthen the polity's commitment to the democratic ideal of freedom and liberty.

What follows are some findings from the Knight Foundation survey of high 10 school students that explain, in part, why Americans should be concerned about the First Amendment's future.

- Thirty-six percent of high school students openly admit that they take their First Amendment rights for granted and another 37 percent say they never thought enough about this to have an opinion.

- Seventy-five percent incorrectly believe that it is illegal to burn the flag as a means of political protest, and 49 percent wrongly think that government has the right to restrict indecent material on the Internet.

- A source of the lack of support for free press rights might be due to the fact that only four percent of students trust journalists to tell the truth all of the time.

- Thirty-five percent say the First Amendment goes too far in the rights it guarantees, and 32 percent think the press has too much freedom to do what it wants.

**PROPOSING SOME REMEDIES**

11    This is a bleak picture of what may be in store for the First Amendment as this group matures into adulthood. More importantly, however, a number of findings from the study suggest policies or actions that might better prepare students to value and use their constitutional freedoms. While the suggestions below grow out of findings that are based on correlations, not causation, the logic of the policy ideas holds up against both our experience and our understanding of the data.

12    1. Instruction on the First Amendment matters. Education works! Students who have taken classes that deal with journalism, the role of the media in society, and the First Amendment exhibit higher levels of knowledge and support for free expression rights than those who haven't. The problem, of course, is that the strong trend toward math and science and "teaching to the standardized test" has crowded out instruction that could help students develop good citizenship skills. The less the schools focus on developing strong citizens, the weaker our democracy becomes. The positive lesson to learn from this is that through enhancements to the high school curriculum, students can become better prepared to value and use their freedoms.

13    2. Use leads to greater appreciation. When students are given an opportunity to use their freedoms, they develop a better appreciation for them. The Knight project found that students who are engaged in extracurricular student media (such as school newspaper, Internet sites, etc.) are more aware and much more supportive of free expression rights.

14    3. School leaders need lessons, too. Most high school principals need to be reminded of the value of experiential learning and its implications for the future of the First Amendment. While 80 percent of principals agree that "newspapers should be allowed to publish freely without government approval of a story," only 39 percent say their students should be afforded the same rights for publishing in the school newspaper. Granted, principals have many issues to deal with (like parents and school board members calling and asking how they could have ever allowed a story to be printed in a school paper). But if we are to expect students to mature into responsible democratic citizens, they should be given the freedom to express themselves and act responsibly while in school.

15    4. Place the issues in the context of their daily lives. The project suggests that, as with most people, when issues affecting one's freedom are brought close to home, students are best able to discern the true meaning and value of

freedom. When asked if they agreed or disagreed with this statement—
"Musicians should be allowed to sing songs with lyrics that might be offensive
to others"—70 percent agreed (only 43 percent of principals and 57 percent
of adults agree with this). Music matters to many young people. When this
form of free expression is challenged, most students come to its defense. The
lesson, of course, is that in teaching students about the virtues of free expression, showing how it relates to things important to them will best instill in
students why it is so important to the life of a democracy.

The future of the First Amendment is, at best, tenuous. As the current 16
group of high school students takes on their important role as citizens in our
democracy, their lack of appreciation and support for free expression rights
will provide a ripe atmosphere for government to further intrude on these
freedoms. Many institutions in society should shoulder part of the responsibility to ensure good citizenship skills for our youth. Parents, religious institutions,
the media, as well as leadership from public officials, just to name a few. But
the public schools play an especially important role in socializing youngsters in
how to be responsible citizens, and through the schools the future health and
vitality of the First Amendment might be restored.

Source: From *Nieman Reports,* Summer 2005, pp. 49–50. Reprinted by permission of The Nieman
Foundation for Journalism at Harvard University.

## QUESTIONS FOR READING

1. What is the occasion for the authors' article? What was the purpose of the study?

2. What is the primary source of protection for free expression? For what reason
   do Americans allow free expression to be restricted?

3. What views revealed in the nation's "annual checkup" put First Amendment
   rights at risk, according to the authors? What did the study reveal about high
   school students' views?

4. State the four remedies proposed by the authors in your own words.

## QUESTIONS FOR REASONING AND ANALYSIS

5. What, specifically, is the essay's topic? What is the authors' claim?

6. What assumption about freedom is part of this argument?

7. Analyze the four proposals. Do they seem logical remedies to you? Do some
   seem more likely to produce change than others?

## QUESTIONS FOR REFLECTION AND WRITING

8. What statistic is most surprising to you? Why?

9. Do you share the authors' concerns for the tenuous state of free speech in the
   United States? If you disagree, how would you rebut them?

10. Can democracy survive without First Amendment rights? Be prepared to
    debate this issue.

# CHIPPING AWAY AT FREE SPEECH | ANNE APPLEBAUM

Currently a columnist and editorial board member of the *Washington Post,* Anne Applebaum was a journalist and writer in Poland and London for twenty years before returning to the United States. She is the author of *Gulag: A History* (2003). The following column appeared September 15, 2009.

PREREADING QUESTIONS  Considering Applebaum's title, what do you anticipate her subject to be? And what kinds of issues will she examine?

1    Item One: When it comes out in print soon, look carefully through Yale University Press's book *The Cartoons That Shook the World.* The book is a scholarly account of the controversy that surrounded a Danish newspaper's 2005 publication of 12 cartoons depicting the prophet Muhammad. The author Jytte Klausen argues, among other things, that the controversy was manipulated by Danish imams who showed their followers false, sexually offensive depictions of Muhammad alongside the real images, which she says were not inherently offensive. She consulted with several Muslim scholars, who agreed. Nevertheless, you will not find the cartoons in the finished manuscript.

2    Item Two: Pick up a copy of the September issue of *GQ* magazine. Buried deep inside is an article titled "Vladimir Putin's Dark Rise to Power," by Scott Anderson. The article, based on extensive reporting, argues that Russian security services helped create a series of bomb explosions in Moscow in 2000—explosions that were blamed on Chechen terrorists at the time. But you will not find this article in *GQ*'s Russian edition. As of this writing, you will not find this article on *GQ*'s Web site either; Conde Nast, the media company that owns *GQ,* has ordered its magazines and affiliates around the world to refrain from mentioning or promoting this article in any way.

3    Item Three: If your knowledge of written Chinese characters is up to it, type the word "Tiananmen" into Google.cn (www.google.cn). I do not know Chinese myself but am reliably informed that your search will retrieve little or no useful information on this subject, nor will it tell you much about Taiwan or Tibet or democracy. This is not an accident: In 2006, Google agreed to a modicum of censorship in China, in exchange for being allowed to operate there at all.

4    These three incidents are not identical. Yale Press refused to print the cartoons because the university fears retaliatory violence on its campus. Conde Nast refused to promote an article on the Russian secret service because it fears a loss of Russian advertisers. Google refuses to let its Chinese users search for "Tiananmen" and other taboo subjects because Google wants to compete against Chinese search engines for a share of the huge Chinese market. All three companies exhibit greatly varying degrees of remorse, too, from Conde Nast (none) to the Yale Press (a lot) to Google (ambivalent: Google founder Sergey Brin initially argued that the company would at least bring more information to China, if not complete information).

5    Nevertheless, the three stories lead to one conclusion: In different ways, the Russian government, the Chinese government and unnamed Islamic terrorists

are now capable of placing de facto controls on American companies—something that would have been unthinkable a decade ago. In a world that seems more dangerous and less profitable than it did in the past, either greed or fear proved stronger than these companies' commitment to free speech.

By caving to pressure, they have not made the world a safer place, however, either for themselves or for anyone else. Google's submission to Chinese censorship in 2006 has not prevented the Chinese government from continuing to harass the company, allegedly for distributing pornography. On the contrary, it may have encouraged China to attempt, quite recently, to force companies to place filters on all computers sold in the country. By the same token, Conde Nast's climb-down will only encourage Russian companies—many of which are de facto state-owned—to exert pressure on their Western partners, making it harder for others to publish controversial material about Russia in the future. The fact that Yale's press, one of the most innovative in the country, will not publish the Danish cartoons only makes it harder for others to publish them, too. [Declaration of interest: I am editing an anthology for Yale University Press and have long admired its commitment to opening Soviet archives.] 6

In fact, each time an American company caves to illiberal pressure, the atmosphere is worse for everyone else. Each alteration made in the name of placating an illiberal group or government makes that group or government stronger. What seems a small lapse of integrity now might well loom larger in the future. All of these companies are making it much harder for everyone else to continue speaking and publishing freely around the world. 7

There is no law or edict that can force these companies, or any American company, to abide by the principles of free speech abroad. But at least it is possible to embarrass them at home. Hence this column. 8

---

Source: From *The Washington Post,* September 15, 2009. Reprinted by permission of the author.

## QUESTIONS FOR READING

1. What are the three "items" discussed in the first three paragraphs? What do they have in common?
2. What are two reasons for the decisions, suggested by Applebaum?
3. What, according to the author, are the consequences of the three companies' decisions?

## QUESTIONS FOR REASONING AND ANALYSIS

4. What is Applebaum's claim? Where does she state it?
5. Consider the author's strategy of describing three separate incidents first and then developing her argument based on them; what does she gain from this strategy?
6. Applebaum asserts that each chip away at free speech makes free speech harder for others in the future. Does this seem like a reasonable prediction? Why or why not?

QUESTIONS FOR REFLECTION AND WRITING

7.  Think about each of the three incidents. Which one is the most serious blow to free speech in your view? Why?

8.  Applebaum hopes to embarrass the three companies with her column. What else can be done to pressure companies to take a stand for free speech?

## WHEN THOUGHTS BECOME A CRIME | RICHARD COHEN

Richard Cohen, a graduate of Columbia University, has been a syndicated columnist since 1976. His columns frequently generate controversy, and he has been a finalist for the Pulitzer Prize for Commentary four times. The following column was published October 19, 2010.

PREREADING QUESTIONS What kind of crimes do you expect Cohen to address? What position do you anticipate that he will take?

1     Last April, Christine Quinn, speaker of New York's City Council, honored members of the police department's Hate Crimes Task Force and jokingly said she looked forward to the day she could put them out of business. Since that day, the city seems to have gone on a hate-crime spree, culminating early this month with the torture of three men in the Bronx, purportedly for being gay. Too soon, you might say, to disband the Hate Crimes Task Force. You would be wrong.

2     Almost as bad as hate crimes themselves is the designation. It is a little piece of totalitarian nonsense, a way for prosecutors to punish miscreants for their thoughts or speech, both of which used to be protected by the Constitution (I am an originalist in this regard). It is not the criminal act alone that matters anymore but the belief that might have triggered the act. For this, you can get an extra five years or so in the clink.

3     Take the sad case of Tyler Clementi. The Rutgers University freshman leapt from the George Washington Bridge three days after his roommate and another person allegedly set up a webcam to watch Clementi's intimate encounter with another man and then streamed it to others. Immediately, the cry of "hate crime" was heard throughout the land, and the authorities said they were considering bringing such a charge. (No decision yet.) But Clementi, by all accounts a very sensitive young man, might have reacted to such spying the same way if his partner had been a woman—or, if he were married and with a woman not his wife. Is, somehow, the life of a homosexual more valuable than the life of a heterosexual?

4     The standard rationale for hate-crime laws is that hate crimes, to quote the proclamation Quinn and the police commissioner issued that day, "tear at the very fabric of our free society." To wit, if one gay man is mugged, other gays are intimidated. A whole class of people is affected. Maybe so. But if there is a rape in the park, women will stay away. And there are whole areas of

town—any town—where I wouldn't go in an armored car on account of a fear of crime. Crime affects everyone.

The torture of those three men in the Bronx is amply covered by a plethora 5 of laws—assault, kidnapping, etc. The victims were not more or less victimized by their assailants' hatred of gays. Their torture was not more painful because their torturers hated them. It was the torture itself that mattered. And if the alleged gang members accused of the crimes either were not somehow aware that there are laws forbidding torture or didn't care one way or another, why do we think an additional law regarding hate is going to deter them?

Hate-crime laws combine the touching conservative belief in the unerring 6 efficacy of deterrence (which rises to its absurd and hideous apogee with executions) with the liberal belief that when it comes to particular groups, basic rights may be suspended. Thus we get affirmative action in which certain people are advantaged at the expense of other people based entirely on race or ethnicity. This tender feeling toward minorities must account for why civil liberties groups have remained so appallingly silent about hate-crimes legislation.

The upshot combines Orwell with Kafka. What is the crime? Attempted 7 murder? Or attempted murder on account of hate? Whom does the perpetrator hate, and how much does he hate him or her? On Long Island, some goons felt a solemn obligation to rid the area of Hispanics. Hate, pure and simple. But one of the perpetrators had black and Hispanic friends—and a swastika tattooed on his leg. Was he racist or, as his father maintained, just a dumb kid? Did he really hate Hispanics or just Hispanic immigrants and, anyway, what did it matter? Their victim was dead—the ultimate crime, Should his killers get life for his death—and another five years for what they thought of him?

Prosecutors have vast powers. Most of them are decent, prudent people 8 with a healthy respect for the law. But hate-crime laws arm the overly ambitious among them with permission to seek punishment for unpopular and often dreadful political views—for *thought*. Those three guys in the Bronx were allegedly tortured by homophobic gang members who deserve jail. Their hatred, however, deserves condemnation.

---

## QUESTIONS FOR READING

1. What does Cohen suggest that Clementi might have done if he were heterosexual?

2. What is the justification for hate-crime laws? What is Cohen's response to the rationale?

3. For what reasons do both conservatives and liberals support hate-crime laws?

4. Who are Orwell and Kafka? (If you don't know, check them out online.)

5.  What is Cohen's attitude toward those whose crimes may be fueled by hateful attitudes toward various groups?

6.  Why does Cohen still oppose hate-crime laws? What is his claim?

7.  Is it possible to know for sure what thoughts may have motivated a crime?

8.  Do you agree with Cohen's position? If yes, why? If no, why not?

# ONLINE LESSONS ON UNPROTECTED SEX | ANDREW J. McCLURG

A graduate of the University of Florida, Andrew McClurg is a law professor at Florida International University and author of many law review articles and two legal humor books. He has frequently been recognized as an outstanding teacher. He maintains a website: *lawhaha.com*. His essay appeared August 15, 2005, in the *Washington Post*.

PREREADING QUESTIONS  Have you posted personal information online? If so, why? Should we post personal details that expose the private lives of others?

1    Kiss-and-tell is as old as love itself. Fortunately, most indiscreet paramours limit their blabbing to a few confidants. Not Jessica Cutler. In May 2004, she spilled out the graphic details of her sexual exploits on Capitol Hill on a blog accessible to hundreds of millions of Internet users.

2    Now a federal lawsuit by one of her past lovers has set up a potentially high-stakes battle between privacy and speech rights and could give new meaning to the idea of safe sex in a wired world.

3    Cutler's blog, written under the pseudonym Washingtonienne, was a daily diary of her sex life while working as a staffer for Sen. Mike DeWine (R-Ohio). It recounted, entertainingly and in considerable—sometimes embarrassing—detail, her ongoing relationships with six men, including plaintiff Robert Steinbuch, a lawyer who also worked for DeWine. Although Cutler never used his full name, and usually referred to the plaintiff by his initials, Steinbuch alleges the blog revealed sufficient information, including his first name, physical description and where he worked, to identify him.

4    The Internet gossip site Wonkette published excerpts from Cutler's blog, touching off a media "feeding frenzy" in which Steinbuch was repeatedly identified by his full name. Cutler capitalized on the publicity. She gave print, broadcast and online interviews, posed nude for *Playboy* and reportedly received a $300,000 advance for her just-published book, a veiled fictional account of a Senate staffer's sexual adventures on Capitol Hill.

5    Steinbuch's argument is compelling. By any normative standard, he suffered a genuine wrong. As he asserts in his complaint, "It is one thing to be manipulated and used by a lover, it is another thing to be cruelly exposed to the world."

The law, however, appears to be against him. This is because Steinbuch 6 does not allege that any of the statements about him are untrue. False statements that damage one's reputation can be actionable as defamation. The essence of Steinbuch's claim is: You humiliated me by publicizing these true details about my private life.

His case hinges on a century-old privacy tort claim known as "public dis- 7 closure of private facts." In theory, the tort provides a remedy when one publicizes private, embarrassing, non-newsworthy facts about a person in a manner that reasonable people would find highly offensive. But while Cutler's actions may meet this standard, courts have long been hostile to such lawsuits because of a fear of inhibiting free speech. The Supreme Court has never upheld punishment, based on a privacy theory, for the publication of true information.

In 1989 the court tossed out a lawsuit against a newspaper for publishing 8 a rape victim's name in violation of Florida law. While it stopped short of ruling that a state may never punish true speech, the test it adopted for when that can be done without violating the First Amendment is so stringent Justice Byron White lamented in dissent that the court had "obliterate[d]" the public disclosure tort.

One might think the non-newsworthiness of Steinbuch's sex life would 9 save his privacy claim from a free-speech defense. It could, but newsworthiness has proved to be a broad and elusive legal test in privacy lawsuits. The rape victim's name in the 1989 Florida case, for example, was deemed to be sufficiently related to the public's interest in crime to doom her claim.

Steinbuch's case spotlights the inadequacy of privacy law—developed 10 back when gossip mostly traveled across backyard fences—for responding to the challenges of the Internet age. Today's technology grants any person—no matter how selfish, irresponsible or malicious—the power to invade privacy globally, at almost no cost. All it takes is a computer and Internet access. Some blogging companies offer free services.

And blogs are just the tip of the iceberg. In May an Oregon woman sued 11 Yahoo after her ex-boyfriend posted nude pictures of her on the site and Yahoo failed to remove them. Expect more litigation.

While we wait to see if old law can adapt to new realities, don't forget the 12 C-word when making safe-sex inquiries. No, not condoms or contraceptives. Ask potential partners if they own a computer.

---

Source: From *The Washington Post,* August 15, 2005. Reprinted by permission of the author.

## QUESTIONS FOR READING

1. Who is Jessica Cutler? What did she do?
2. Who is Robert Steinbuch? What was his response to Cutler's disclosures?
3. What laws protect Cutler? What legal precedent is Steinbuch using? What two issues will affect the outcome of his case?

4.  McClurg can be expected to be interested in this situation as a technical legal debate. What else about this modern example of gossip interests the author?

5.  Is the author just reporting on a current legal debate—or does he have a position? What, if any, is his claim?

6.  What is clever about McClurg's opening and closing paragraphs?

7.  The Internet poses interesting questions regarding free speech. If you were the judge, how would you rule on Steinbuch's suit? Why?

8.  Even if the law supports Cutler, does that make her "wired gossip" right? Defend your position.

## VIRTUAL VIOLENCE IS FREE SPEECH | DANIEL GREENBERG

A freelance game design consultant, scriptwriter, and voice-over director, Daniel Greenberg combines a background in programming, writing, acting, and directing to create or consult on the creating of a host of games published in over twenty years of work in this field. He has designed educational games as well as contributing to *Dungeons and Dragons, Star Wars, and Vampire: The Masquerade*, to name just a few in his long list of credits. Greenberg chairs the anticensorship and social issues committee of the Independent Game Developers Association. His argument on censorship was published in the *Washington Post* on October 31, 2010.

PREREADING QUESTIONS Where do we find "virtual" violence? So, what will be Greenberg's subject?

1    On Election Day, everyone in Washington will be focused on the polls. Everyone except the Supreme Court justices. They'll be busy with video games.

2    Tuesday is the day that the court has agreed to hear *Schwarzenegger v. EMA*, a case in which the state of California says it has the power to regulate the sale of violent video games to minors—in essence, to strip First Amendment free speech protection from video games that "lack serious literary, artistic, political, or scientific value for minors."

3    Since I express myself through the creation of video games, including violent ones, I'd like to know how government bureaucrats are supposed to divine the artistic value that a video game has for a 17-year-old. The man who spearheaded California's law, state Sen. Leland Yee, has not explained that. We've had no more clarity from Gov. Arnold Schwarzenegger, who signed the bill into law.

4    Yee argues in his friend-of-the-court brief that since the government can "prohibit the sale of alcohol, tobacco, firearms, driver's licenses and pornography to minors," then "that same reasoning applies in the foundation and enactment" of his law restricting video games.

A violent video game.

As a game developer, I am disheartened and a little perplexed to see my  5
art and passion lumped in with cigarettes and booze.

The U.S. Court of Appeals struck down the law as unconstitutional, just as  6
other U.S. courts have struck down similar anti-video-game measures.
California appealed to the Supreme Court, which surprisingly agreed to
reconsider the lower court's rejection of the law.

So while everyone else is celebrating their constitutional right to vote, the  7
Supreme Court will ask: Does the First Amendment bar a state from restricting
the sale of violent video games to minors?

It seems clear to me that violent video games deserve at least as much  8
constitutional protection as other forms of media that would not be restricted
under this law, such as violent books and violent movies. Books and movies
enable free expression principally for their authors and makers. But video
games do more than enable the free speech rights of video game developers.
Games—even those incorporating violence—enable a whole new medium of
expression for players.

Gameplay is a dialogue between a player and a game. Reading a book or  9
watching a film can also be considered a dialogue, but the ability of the audience
to respond is far more limited. Books and movies rarely alter their course based
on the emotional reaction of the audience. (One exception would be those old
Choose Your Own Adventure-type books, some of which I wrote before I started
working on video games.)

The exploration and self-discovery available through books and movies is 10
magnified in video games by the power of interactivity.

11    A new generation of games features real changes in the story based on the morality of a player's decisions. Mature-rated games such as "BioShock," "Fable 2" and "Fallout 3" go far beyond allowing players to engage in imaginary violent acts; they also give players meaningful consequences for the choices that they make. In "BioShock," the player meets genetically modified people who have been victimized by a mad ideology. The player can help the unfortunates or exploit them for genetic resources. The game's ending changes radically depending on the player's actions. In "Fallout 3," players can be kind to people or mistreat them, and the people will respond in kind. In "Fable 2," the player must make a painful choice to save his family from death or save thousands of innocent people—but not both.

12    In games such as these, gameplay becomes a powerful meditation on the nature of violence and the context in which it occurs. Some of the most thought-provoking game design is currently in Mature-rated games (similar to R-rated movies). This is because, in order to have a truly meaningful moral choice, the player must be allowed to make an immoral choice and live with the consequences.

13    And that's just in single-player mode.

14    The expressive potential of video games jumps exponentially when players take interactivity online. Players can cooperate with or compete against friends, acquaintances or strangers. They can create unique characters, build original worlds and tell their own stories in multiplayer online universes with a few or a few thousand of their friends.

15    Video games, even the violent ones, enable players' free expression, just like musical instruments enable musicians' free expression. No one in the government is qualified to decide which games don't enable free speech, even when that speech comes from a 15-year-old. The courts settled the question of the First Amendment rights of minors long ago. Those rights are so strong that, for example, the Supreme Court ruled that school boards do not have the power to ban books from school libraries, even if students can obtain those books outside of school (*Board of Education v. Pico* in 1982). In that case, the justices said that "the right to receive ideas is a necessary predicate to the recipient's meaningful exercise of his own rights of speech, press, and political freedom," even when the recipient is a minor.

16    The people allowed to limit a minor's free speech rights are his parents or guardians. And maybe his grandparents and aunts and uncles. But not Sen. Yee and Gov. Schwarzenegger.

17    Most developers of video games will admit that we have barely begun to tap their vast potential to enable player creativity and free speech. In this early stage in the history of video games, the range of expression that we provide to players is too limited. We've done a good job of creating imaginative ways to attack our imaginary enemies, but we have not done nearly as thorough a job exploring all the other forms of human (and nonhuman) interaction.

18    Fortunately, many of the best developers are tackling new ways to increase players' in-game actions. I've seen some amazing early work in this field, from

the biggest video game companies right down to one-person indie developers.

For example, the seemingly simple but emotionally complex online game [19] "Darfur Is Dying" lets the player try to survive in a refugee camp without being killed by militias. "Infamous 2" promises a much richer, open-ended world to help or harm, In "Epic Mickey" Mickey Mouse will have the ability to misbehave.

One of my current projects is a game system that lets players shape and [20] reshape the moral and spiritual development of the game world and the people in it by their actions and alliances.

If California's law is upheld, it is likely that far more onerous measures will [21] appear all over the country. Some stores may stop carrying Mature-rated games. Game publishers might be afraid to finance them. Developers would not know how to avoid triggering censorship because even the creators of such laws don't seem to know. The lawmakers won't tell us their criteria, and their lawyers have refused to reveal which existing games would be covered, even when asked in court.

Such censorship is not only dangerous, it's completely unnecessary. More [22] than 80 scholars and researchers from schools such as George Mason University and Harvard Medical School have written an extensive friend-of-the-court brief in opposition to the law, noting that California failed to produce any real evidence showing that video games cause psychological harm to minors. And even if there was harm, the law's supporters have not shown that the statute could alleviate it.

The game development community has worked hard on creating a rating [23] system that clearly discloses games' content. Even our critics, such as the Federal Trade Commission, have praised our efforts. The FTC's own survey shows that 87 percent of parents are satisfied with the rating system.

Parents have good reason to be concerned about their children's media [24] diet and to ask what possible good can come from blowing out the brains of a character in a game. Make-believe violence appears to have many benefits for minors, such as relieving stress, releasing anger and helping children cope with difficult feelings such as powerlessness and fear of real violence. A recent Texas A&M International study shows that violent games could actually reduce violent tendencies and could be used as a therapy tool for teens and young adults.

There is no small irony that the man helping to spearhead the charge [25] against violent video games is Schwarzenegger, the Terminator himself. He, more than anyone, should understand the thrill of a good fake explosion.

Even when video games contain graphic violence, and even when the [26] players are minors whose parents let them play games with violence, picking up that game controller is a form of expression, and it should be free.

Source: From *The Washington Post*, October 31, 2010. Reprinted by permission of the author.

1. What case has the Supreme Court agreed to hear?
2. What was the justification for the California law?
3. What is the nature of gameplay that Greenberg considers significant?
4. Who, according to the author, should be allowed to limit a minor's free speech rights?
5. What are game developers working on now?
6. In the author's view, how might violent games actually benefit teens?

7. Greenberg identifies himself as a game developer. Does his involvement in violent video games help or hinder him in his argument? How does he try to use this to his advantage in paragraph 5?
8. What are the main arguments in defense of violent video games?
9. Greenberg argues that video games provide more creative expression than books, and this means that video games are less damaging to minors than violent books. Is Greenberg convincing in this step of his argument? Why or why not?

10. Are you a gameplayer? If so, how does this affect your response to Greenberg's argument? If you are not a player, how does that impact your thinking on the issue?
11. Evaluate the author's argument as a whole. Are some parts more effective than others? If so, where do you find problems—and how would you counter the author? If you find no problems, how would you defend Greenberg and/or add to his argument?

# CHAPTER 22

# Ethics and the Law—Current and Enduring Debates

Jim Morin, *The Miami Herald*, CartoonArts International Inc.

**READ:** Who are the five figures? What words have they painted over? Who speaks the words to the right of the group?

**REASON:** What Supreme Court decision is the cartoon's subject? What is Morin's view of the court's decision?

**REFLECT/WRITE:** Does the Constitution need to be reinterpreted for current times? Why or why not?

The visuals and articles in this chapter explore and debate several current criminal justice issues: the Supreme Court's handgun decision, the sanctioning of torture, the tolerating of rape and animal cruelty, and immigration laws. In the spring of 2008, the Supreme Court, in a close decision, struck down the District of Columbia's ban on handguns. The decision is seen as affirming the Second Amendment's guarantee to individuals. But, not everyone thinks that this debate is over.

Do we want our nation using torture, even in the interest of national security? Does the state of Arizona have the right to require its police officers to check a person's status in this country just because that person has done something to get police attention? This chapter raises these and other tough questions. Reflect on the following questions as a guide to your study of this chapter.

### PREREADING QUESTIONS

1. What kinds of restrictions—if any—on guns will be consistent with the Supreme Court's 2008 ruling?
2. Under what circumstances—if any—is torture justified?
3. What role does the United States have in fighting against perpetrators' getting away with rape in other countries?
4. What does a toleration for cruelty to animals say about a society?
5. Should the Arizona law be seen as a way to harass legal immigrants?
6. If you wanted to change any of the current laws on these issues to make them reflect your views, how would you go about trying to get the laws changed?

## GUNS FOR SAFETY? DREAM ON, SCALIA | ARTHUR KELLERMAN

Arthur Kellerman is professor and founding chair of the department of Emergency Medicine at Emory University. He has published widely on emergency cardiac care, health care for the poor, and firearms as a public health hazard. Kellerman has served on many boards and committees exploring these issues and has received recognition for his leadership in the fields of emergency care and prevention. His response to the Supreme Court's decision on handguns appeared in the *Washington Post* on June 28, 2008.

PREREADING QUESTIONS Given his title, what position on the ruling do you expect from Arthur Kellerman? Who is Scalia? (If you do not know, look it up.)

1   The Supreme Court has spoken: Thanks to the court's blockbuster 5 to 4 decision Thursday, Washingtonians now have the right to own a gun for self-defense. I leave the law to lawyers, but the public health lesson is crystal clear: The legal ruling that the District's citizens *can* keep loaded handguns in their homes doesn't mean that they *should*.

2   In his majority opinion, Justice Antonin Scalia explicitly endorsed the wisdom of keeping a handgun in the home for self-defense. Such a weapon,

he wrote, "is easier to store in a location that is readily accessible in an emergency; it cannot easily be redirected or wrestled away by an attacker; it is easier to use for those without the upper-body strength to lift and aim a long rifle; it can be pointed at a burglar with one hand while the other hand dials the police." But Scalia ignored a substantial body of public health research that contradicts his assertions. A number of scientific studies, published in the world's most rigorous, peer-reviewed journals, show that the risks of keeping a loaded gun in the home strongly outweigh the potential benefits.

In the real world, Scalia's scenario—an armed assailant breaks into your home, and you shoot or scare away the bad guy with your handy handgun—happens pretty infrequently. Statistically speaking, these rare success stories are dwarfed by tragedies. The reason is simple: A gun kept loaded and readily available for protection may also be reached by a curious child, an angry spouse or a depressed teen.

More than 20 years ago, I conducted a study of firearm-related deaths in homes in Seattle and surrounding King County, Washington. Over the study's seven-year interval, more than half of all fatal shootings in the county took place in the home where the firearm involved was kept. Just nine of those shootings were legally justifiable homicides or acts of self-defense; guns kept in homes were also involved in 12 accidental deaths, 41 criminal homicides and a shocking 333 suicides. A subsequent study conducted in three U.S. cities found that guns kept in the home were 12 times more likely to be involved in the death or injury of a member of the household than in the killing or wounding of a bad guy in self-defense.

Oh, one more thing: Scalia's ludicrous vision of a little old lady clutching a handgun in one hand while dialing 911 with the other (try it sometime) doesn't fit the facts. According to the Justice Department, far more guns are lost each year to burglary or theft than are used to defend people or property. In Atlanta, a city where approximately a third of households contain guns, a study of 197 home-invasion crimes revealed only three instances (1.5 percent) in which the inhabitants resisted with a gun. Intruders got to the homeowner's gun twice as often as the homeowner did.

The court has spoken, but citizens and lawmakers should base future gun-control decisions—both personal and political—on something more substantive than Scalia's glib opinion.

---

Source: From *The Washington Post*, June 28, 2008. Reprinted by permission of the author.

QUESTIONS FOR READING

1. What is Kellerman's subject?
2. Why are loaded guns in the house a risk?
3. Statistically, who is more likely to use a homeowner's gun, the homeowner or the intruder?

4.   What is Kellerman's claim? Where does he state it?

5.   What is the author's response to Scalia's majority opinion defense? What attitude does he express?

6.   How effective are the author's statistics in support of his position?

7.   Have you been aware of the information provided by Kellerman, or are you surprised by the statistics? Does his evidence affect your thinking on this issue in any way? Explain.

8.   Should handguns be restricted? If so, in what ways? If not, why not?

## FIVE MYTHS ABOUT TORTURE AND TRUTH | DARIUS REJALI

A professor of political science at Reed College, Iranian-born Darius Rejali is a recognized expert on the causes and meaning of violence, especially on torture, in our world. His book *Torture and Democracy* (2007) has won acclaim and resulted in frequent interview sessions for Rejali. His latest book is *Spirituality and the Ethics of Torture* (2009). The following essay appeared on December 16, 2007, in the *Washington Post*.

PREREADING QUESTIONS  Can you think of five myths about torture? What do you expect Rejali to cover in this essay?

1    *So the CIA did indeed torture Abu Zubaida, the first al-Qaeda terrorist suspect to have been waterboarded. So says John Kiriakou, the first former CIA employee directly involved in the questioning of "high-value" al-Qaeda detainees to speak out publicly. He minced no words last week in calling the CIA's "enhanced interrogation techniques" what they are.*

2    *But did they work? Torture's defenders, including the wannabe tough guys who write Fox's "24," insist that the rough stuff gets results. "It was like flipping a switch," said Kiriakou about Abu Zubaida's response to being waterboarded. But the al-Qaeda operative's confessions—descriptions of fantastic plots from a man who intelligence analysts were convinced was mentally ill—probably didn't give the CIA any actionable intelligence. Of course, we may never know the whole truth, since the CIA destroyed the videotapes of Abu Zubaida's interrogation. But here are some other myths that are bound to come up as the debate over torture rages on.*

3    **1. Torture worked for the Gestapo.** Actually, no. Even Hitler's notorious secret police got most of their information from public tips, informers and interagency cooperation. That was still more than enough to let the Gestapo decimate anti-Nazi resistance in Austria, Czechoslovakia, Poland, Denmark, Norway, France, Russia and the concentration camps.

Yes, the Gestapo did torture people for intelligence, especially in later  4
years. But this reflected not torture's efficacy but the loss of many seasoned
professionals to World War II, increasingly desperate competition for intelligence among Gestapo units and an influx of less disciplined younger members. (Why do serious, tedious police work when you have a uniform and a
whip?) It's surprising how unsuccessful the Gestapo's brutal efforts were. They
failed to break senior leaders of the French, Danish, Polish and German resistance. I've spent more than a decade collecting all the cases of Gestapo torture "successes" in multiple languages; the number is small and the results
pathetic, especially compared with the devastating effects of public cooperation and informers.

**2. Everyone talks sooner or later under torture.** Truth is, it's surprisingly  5
hard to get anything under torture, true or false. For example, between 1500
and 1750, French prosecutors tried to torture confessions out of 785 individuals. Torture was legal back then, and the records document such practices as
the bone-crushing use of splints, pumping stomachs with water until they
swelled and pouring boiling oil on the feet. But the number of prisoners who
said anything was low, from 3 percent in Paris to 14 percent in Toulouse (an
exceptional high). Most of the time, the torturers were unable to get any statement whatsoever.

And such examples could be multiplied. The Japanese fascists, no strang-  6
ers to torture, said it best in their field manual, which was found in Burma during World War II: They described torture as the clumsiest possible method of
gathering intelligence. Like most sensible torturers, they preferred to use torture for intimidation, not information.

**3. People will say anything under torture.** Well, no, although this is a  7
favorite chestnut of torture's foes. Think about it: Sure, someone would lie
under torture, but wouldn't they also lie if they were being interrogated without coercion?

In fact, the problem of torture does not stem from the prisoner who *has*  8
information; it stems from the prisoner who doesn't. Such a person is also
likely to lie, to say anything, often convincingly. The torture of the informed
may generate no more lies than normal interrogation, but the torture of the
ignorant and innocent overwhelms investigators with misleading information.
In these cases, nothing is indeed preferable to anything. Anything needs to be
verified, and the CIA's own 1963 interrogation manual explains that "a time-
consuming delay results"—hardly useful when every moment matters.

Intelligence gathering is especially vulnerable to this problem. When  9
police officers torture, they know what the crime is, and all they want is the
confession. When intelligence officers torture, they must gather information
about what they don't know.

**4. Most people can tell when someone is lying under torture.** Not so— 10
and we know quite a bit about this. For about 40 years, psychologists have
been testing police officers as well as normal people to see whether they can
spot lies, and the results aren't encouraging. Ordinary folk have an accuracy
rate of about 57 percent, which is pretty poor considering that 50 percent is

the flip of a coin. Likewise, the cops' accuracy rates fall between 45 percent and 65 percent—that is, sometimes less accurate than a coin toss.

11      Why does this matter? Because even if torturers break a person, they have to recognize it, and most of the time they can't. Torturers assume too much and reject what doesn't fit their assumptions. For instance, Sheila Cassidy, a British physician, cracked under electric-shock torture by the Chilean secret service in the 1970s and identified priests who had helped the country's socialist opposition. But her devout interrogators couldn't believe that priests would ever help the socialists, so they tortured her for another week until they finally became convinced. By that time, she was so damaged that she couldn't remember the location of the safe house.

12      In fact, most torturers are nowhere near as well trained for interrogation as police are. Torturers are usually chosen because they've endured hardship and pain, fought with courage, kept secrets, held the right beliefs and earned a reputation as trustworthy and loyal. They often rely on folklore about what lying behavior looks like—shifty eyes, sweaty palms and so on. And, not surprisingly, they make a lot of mistakes.

13      **5. You can train people to resist torture.** Supposedly, this is why we can't know what the CIA's "enhanced interrogation techniques" are: If Washington admits that it waterboards suspected terrorists, al-Qaeda will set up "waterboarding-resistance camps" across the world. Be that as it may, the truth is that no training will help the bad guys.

14      Simply put, nothing predicts the outcome of one's resistance to pain better than one's own personality. Against some personalities, nothing works; against others, practically anything does. Studies of hundreds of detainees who broke under Soviet and Chinese torture, including Army-funded studies of U.S. prisoners of war, conclude that during, before and after torture, each prisoner displayed strengths and weaknesses dependent on his or her own character. The CIA's own "Human Resources Exploitation Manual" from 1983 and its so-called Kubark manual from 1963 agree. In all matters relating to pain, says Kubark, the "individual remains the determinant."

15      The thing that's most clear from torture-victim studies is that you can't train for the ordeal. There is no secret knowledge out there about how to resist torture. Yes, there are manuals, such as the IRA's "Green Book," the anti-Soviet "Manual for Psychiatry for Dissidents" and "Torture and the Interrogation Experience," an Iranian guerrilla manual from the 1970s. But none of these volumes contains specific techniques of resistance, just general encouragement to hang tough. Even al-Qaeda's vaunted terrorist-training manual offers no tips on how to resist torture, and al-Qaeda was no stranger to the brutal methods of the Saudi police.

16      And yet these myths persist. "The larger problem here, I think," one active CIA officer observed in 2005, "is that this kind of stuff just makes people feel better, even if it doesn't work."

Source: From *The Washington Post*, December 16, 2007. Reprinted by permission of the author.

## QUESTIONS FOR READING

1. What context for his discussion does the author provide in the opening two paragraphs?
2. What worked better than torture for the Gestapo? What led to an increase in torture in the Gestapo?
3. What do the data show about getting people to speak by torturing them?
4. Who are the people most likely to lie under torture?
5. How good are we in recognizing when someone is lying under torture?
6. Is it possible to train people to resist torture?

## QUESTIONS FOR REASONING AND ANALYSIS

7. Rejali explains that most of what the Gestapo learned it learned from public tips and informers. He describes this as having "devastating effects." How can we explain why so many cooperated with the Gestapo?
8. Why is the torturing of innocent people likely to do more harm than good?
9. Why are torturers not very good at recognizing when the tortured are lying?
10. Is Rejali reporting on this topic only, or does he have a position? What do you think is his view of torture?

## QUESTIONS FOR REFLECTION AND WRITING

11. Which of the five discussions has surprised you the most? Why?
12. Has the author convinced you that all five myths lack substance? Why or why not?
13. Why do intelligence and military personnel continue to use harsh interrogation strategies even though the evidence suggests that what, if anything, they learn will not be useful? Ponder this question.

## FIRST THEY DID HARM  |  EUGENE ROBINSON

A graduate of the University of Michigan where he was the first black student to be co-editor-in-chief of the student newspaper, Eugene Robinson joined the *Washington Post* in 1980. He has served as city reporter, foreign correspondent, and managing editor in charge of the lifestyle section. He is now an associate editor and twice-weekly columnist. Robinson focuses on the mix of culture and politics, as the following column, published on September 4, 2009, reveals.

PREREADING QUESTIONS  On what common phrase is the title a variation? What, then, might be Robinson's subject?

For the Bush administration, torture was a delicate business. The aim was to injure but not incapacitate—to inflict precisely enough pain and terror to break a subject's will, but no more. To calibrate the proper degree of abuse, the torturer needed an accurate sense of how much agony the subject's mind and body can tolerate.

2    In the administration's program of "enhanced interrogation," this expertise was provided by doctors and psychologists—professionals who are supposed to heal and comfort. A new report by Physicians for Human Rights assembles the evidence and reaches a sickening but inescapable conclusion: "Health professionals played central roles in developing, implementing and providing justification for torture."

3    Dwell on that for a moment, especially if you believe that the Bush administration's decision to submit terrorism suspects to medieval interrogation practices was somehow justifiable—or even if you believe that torture was wrong, but that now we should "look forward" and pretend it never happened. This is how torture warps a society and distorts its values.

4    Much of the information cited by Physicians for Human Rights had previously been unearthed, but some new details were disclosed in the CIA inspector general's report released last week—revealing "a level of ethical misconduct that had not previously come to light," according to the human rights group.

5    From sources that include published reports, an inquiry by the International Committee of the Red Cross and various documents pried out of the government by organizations such as the American Civil Liberties Union, here is some of what we know:

6    The interrogation program—using 11 abusive "enhanced" techniques, including waterboarding—was designed by two PhD psychologists. The techniques, according to a statement released in April by American Psychological Association President James H. Bray, "are tantamount to torture as defined by APA and international law."

7    Said the APA: "The central tenet of psychology's code of ethics is, like that of medicine, to do no harm. It is unthinkable that any psychologist could assert that stress positions, forced nudity, sleep deprivation, exploiting phobias, and waterboarding—along with other forms of torture techniques that the American Psychological Association has condemned and prohibited—cause no lasting damage to a human being's psyche."

8    According to Bray, "There is one ethical response to an order to torture: *Disobey the order.*"

9    We know that medical doctors were asked to sign off on the "enhanced" techniques. We know from detainees themselves, as quoted by the International Committee of the Red Cross, that there was medical monitoring of waterboarding sessions. We know from the CIA inspector general's report that a 2004 letter from a Justice Department official reauthorizing the use of waterboarding specified a maximum of two two-hour sessions per day, with both a doctor and a psychologist present.

10    From the torturer's point of view, this probably looks like compassion—an attempt to ensure that interrogators don't go too far, that they don't cause permanent harm, that they stay within bureaucratic guidelines. But from any other perspective, it's simply and starkly grotesque.

That any medical doctor would help design or review a program of tor-11 ture, let alone be present when an abusive interrogation amounting to torture was being conducted, would be a gross ethical violation.

The American Medical Association's code of ethics "forcefully states med-12 icine's opposition to torture or coercive interrogation and prohibits physician participation in such activities," according to a letter AMA officials sent President Obama in April. AMA guidelines state that "physicians must neither conduct nor directly participate in an interrogation," and that doctors "must not monitor interrogations with the intention of intervening in the process, because this constitutes direct participation."

So how was our government supposed to conduct abusive interrogations 13 without the guidance of psychologists to say whether it was irreparably damaging the subject's mind or physicians to say whether it was irreparably damaging the subject's body? It would have been impossible.

Doctors and psychologists might have been able to prevent this whole 14 shameful episode by refusing to participate. Instead, professionals who were trained in the healing arts used their experience and skill in a way that facilitated harm. They played a vital role in enabling torture.

I like to believe that some psychologists and physicians took a stand and 15 said no. As for those who said yes, the law should hold them accountable— just as conscience, one hopes, is already doing.

## QUESTIONS FOR READING

1. What did the Bush administration do to "perfect" its torture strategies? Who helped in this process?
2. How did this information become available?
3. What is the view of the APA president on the psychologists' participation?
4. What is the position of the AMA on torture and participation in torture?

## QUESTIONS FOR REASONING AND ANALYSIS

5. What is Robinson's claim? Is it appropriate to conclude that he has two major points to make?
6. Robinson's argument is really quite simple: The APA and AMA oppose any participation in torture. Nevertheless, the Bush administration found some psychologists and doctors who helped it with its torture techniques. The participants should be punished by law. What type (genre) of argument is this?
7. What objections does Robinson anticipate? How does he counter these possible objections to his conclusion?

8.   Has Robinson written convincingly? If you disagree with him, over what basic point must you disagree?

9.   Should we accept that "bad things happen" and "move forward"? What is Robinson's response to this approach? What is your response? Why?

## ENDING IMPUNITY FOR RAPE  |  MARIANNE MOLLMANN

Holding a law degree in international human rights from Essex University, Marianne Mollmann is currently the advocacy director for the Women's Rights Division of the international organization Human Rights Watch. Prior to her current position, Mollmann—who is also fluent in Spanish, French, and Danish—worked for Human Rights Watch in Peru. Her article on rape convictions was published in the *Washington Post* on December 27, 2008.

PREREADING QUESTIONS  How big a problem do you think rape—and getting convictions for rape—is in the United States? In other countries?

1      I have a project for Joseph Biden and Hillary Clinton to work on together: ending impunity for rape. Rape-conviction rates are appallingly low across the globe. I don't mean only in countries that many would think of as lacking good justice systems: Conviction rates hover just above 10 percent of complaints filed in the United States and are a measly 6 percent in Britain. Because the vast majority of rape victims don't file complaints, it does not take precise studies or statistics to conclude that most sexual assaults in most parts of the world end without punishment for the perpetrators.

2      Over the years, in the course of my work at Human Rights Watch, I have spoken with dozens of rape victims around the world, read rape-related court files from many countries and scrutinized legislation. Although most people agree that rape is bad, legislation and government action on sexual crimes are not always that clear. Indeed, rape seems to be graded on a scale from "unconscionable" through "bad luck" to "much deserved." Exactly where a particular incident falls on that scale often seems to depend on factors that include family status, sobriety and ethnicity. In all too many cases, laws and judicial systems have determined that forced sex is not really rape.

3      To understand this better, consider this short list of successful defenses:

4      *It's not rape if she is my wife.* Marriage is perhaps the most commonly used cover for rape, so internalized that many women themselves seem to accept it. When I asked a woman in the Dominican Republic in 2004 if her husband ever forced her to have sex, she shrugged and said: "I guess he is a bit violent. He rapes me at times." Unfortunately, this atrocity is often sanctioned by law. Some countries, such as Ethiopia and Indonesia, define rape as something that happens only outside of marriage. In many others, rape is defined more broadly but is interpreted by courts and police as excluding marital rape. The logic can be applied after the fact, too: Several countries, including Brazil and Libya, exonerate a perpetrator of rape if he agrees to marry the victim.

*It's not rape if she is my daughter.* Though unconscionable to many, incest 5 is seen in some countries as either unfortunate or not all that forced. In Mexico, for example, the rape of a teenage girl by her father is defined as voluntary until it is proved otherwise. Under most state criminal codes in Mexico, incest is considered a crime against the family, not against the physical integrity of the victim, and the underage victim is initially considered as much a criminal as the adult perpetrator.

*It's not rape if she was drunk.* Over the years, Human Rights Watch and 6 other organizations have documented how prosecutors and courts are likely to treat testimony by rape victims with more suspicion than testimony regarding other types of crimes. Routinely, women are aggressively questioned about whether the intercourse was really involuntary, whether the victim somehow provoked or deserved the assault, and whether the assault even occurred. The mistrust is particularly pronounced when the victim admits to being anything other than completely sober before or during the attack. The frenzied media coverage in England last year of a controversial proposal to change the burden of proof in rape cases appeared to perpetuate the belief, which seemed to be widely held, that a drunk rape victim "had it coming."

*It's not rape if my culture mandates intercourse.* When the presumed next 7 president of South Africa, Jacob Zuma, stood trial on rape charges in 2006, he bolstered his defense with references to tradition and culture. Zuma testified that his accuser had signaled her arousal by wearing a knee length skirt to his house and sitting with her legs crossed. He said that it is unacceptable in Zulu culture not to proceed to a sexual encounter once a woman is aroused. Zuma was acquitted, but regardless of the outcome, it is troubling that a high-level politician in any country, much less a country with epidemic levels of sexual violence, peddles the notion that women may mean yes even when they say no.

Joe Biden and Hillary Clinton can change this. During his time in the 8 Senate, Biden has championed draft legislation that would make violence against women a foreign relations priority for the United States, through, for example, supporting legislative reform abroad and a victim-centered approach to violence. As a senator, Clinton supported this legislation. As vice president and secretary of state, Biden and Clinton could make central to U.S. foreign policy the fight against perpetrators' getting away with rape and other forms of violence against women. They should start by creating a coordinating office at the State Department to build on this work. Rape is bad no matter what country it takes place in, whatever the age or marital status of the victim. There is no other way to look at it.

Source: From *The Washington Post*, December 27, 2008. Reprinted by permission of the author.

## QUESTIONS FOR READING

1. What is the conviction rate for rape cases in the United States?
2. Explain each of the excuses for rejecting sexual assault on women as actually rape.

3.   What is Mollmann's claim?

4.   Why might Biden and Clinton be successful in changing conviction rates for rape around the world?

5.   How do the courts and prosecutors treat rape victims, making convictions more difficult?

6.   Which of the four excuses is the most intolerable, in your view? Why?

7.   Should married women be forced to have sex with their husbands? Why or why not?

8.   If you are bothered by the treatment of rape victims in the United States, how would you seek to address this problem? If you do not see this as a problem, how would you counter Mollmann?

# CRUSH ANIMAL CRUELTY | KATHLEEN PARKER

A syndicated columnist since 1987, Kathleen Parker is also a regular guest on TV talk shows. In 2011, she briefly co-hosted her own show on CNN with Eliot Spitzer. In 2010, she won a Pulitzer Prize for Commentary. The following column appeared on April 25, 2010.

PREREADING QUESTIONS Do you know what "crush videos" are? If not, can you imagine what they might be—and therefore what Parker's topic is?

1   Some things are too horrific to consider, and yet consider them we must.

2   "Crush videos," for instance.

3   Somehow I missed the 1999 law, recently nullified by the U.S. Supreme Court, that attempted to outlaw crush videos—definition forthcoming pending recovery from horror-induced swoon. Thus, for the past 11 years, I have been blissfully ignorant of a level of depravity I haven't the imagination to invent.

4   No children beyond this point:

5   Crush videos feature small animals (kittens, puppies and others) being slowly crushed or impaled by a woman wearing stiletto heels, ostensibly for the sexual pleasure of those so attracted.

6   And yes, the Supreme Court decided that such videos are protected by free speech. Or, rather, that the law prohibiting such videos was too broad. As written, for example, the law could be construed to prohibit a deer-hunting video, which, though some might find cruel, relates to a legal activity.

7   Though many experts and scholars defend the 8-to-1 ruling as legally correct, the high court's opinion is surely of a kind that prompted Mr. Bumble in *Oliver Twist* to assert: "The law is a [sic] ass—a [sic] idiot."

Obviously, no one ever intended that the free-speech provision of the 8
Constitution protect the rights of deviants to torture animals and then to market videos for the sexual satisfaction of people who, by their tastes, are a probable threat to society.

The case in question stemmed from the 2005 conviction of Robert J. 9
Stevens of Pittsville, Va., who was charged with marketing videos of dog fighting. Stevens, who identifies himself as a journalist and documentary filmmaker (who doesn't these days?), claimed that he was merely trying to provide a historical perspective of dog fighting. Some of the images included pit bulls tearing at the jaw of a domestic pig.

Some things transcend "to each his own," and animal cruelty is one. Dog 10
fighting, in fact, is illegal in all 50 states. But whether the filming of dog fighting is criminal isn't always clear. Animal rights organizations provide videos of cruelty, after all, though the difference should be obvious. One is reporting on cruelty; the other is setting up an event for the sole purpose of profiting from cruelty.

Although the federal government never prosecuted anyone for making 11
crush videos—the market shriveled significantly after Congress passed the 1999 legislation—prosecutors used the law to convict Stevens, who was sentenced to 37 months in prison. Alas, an appellate court ruled that Stevens's conviction violated his free-speech rights, and the Supreme Court upheld the ruling.

The high court noted that dog fighting remains illegal but that there was 12
no compelling reason to create a special category of exemption from First Amendment protections, as is the case with child pornography. The court's reasoning was that child porn necessarily means the abuse of children in the production of such films.

This is logic that escapes the layman, hardened as he is with common 13
sense. Aren't animals necessarily harmed in the creation of crush videos and in the course of filming dogfights? The natural question follows: How can an act be illegal, but the filming and marketing of the illegal act be legal?

In law, it seems, the answer is never simple. These things are not open and 14
shut but are "a matter of grappling," as PETA President Ingrid Newkirk put it to me during an interview of shared despair.

At least one justice, Samuel Alito, applied the common-sense standard in 15
his dissent.

"The videos record the commission of violent criminal acts, and it appears 16
that these crimes are committed for the sole purpose of creating the videos."

Voilà.    17

In effect, the high court has revived the crush-video industry, if only for a 18
short time. A day after the ruling, Reps. Elton Gallegly (R-Calif.) and Jim Moran (D-Va.), co-chairs of the Animal Protection Caucus, introduced a bipartisan bill (H.R. 5092) to narrowly focus the 1999 bill to deal with crush videos.

Even this bill may be imperfect, however. Although it specifically exempts 19
hunting videos, animal rights advocates worry that it leaves a loop-hole. Hypothetically, a crush video could be built around a legitimate hunting scene and thus be protected from prosecution.

20    Grappling, indeed.

21    The challenge to Congress is at once daunting and uncomplicated: There is no argument ever to justify torturing animals and no defense—ever—for selling videos created to profit from that torture. Figure it out. Fix it.

## QUESTIONS FOR READING

1. What are crush videos?
2. What was the Supreme Court ruling on crush videos? What was the basis for the ruling?
3. What was the argument of Alito in his dissent from the decision?
4. What is the law in this country regarding animal cruelty?

## QUESTIONS FOR REASONING AND ANALYSIS

5. What is Parker's claim? What are the basic steps in her argument?
6. What type (genre) of argument is this?
7. What is Parker's reaction to crush videos? How does she reveal this?
8. What does she gain by her reference to *Oliver Twist*? By paragraphs 17 and 20? By her final two sentences?

## QUESTIONS FOR REFLECTION AND WRITING

9. Is Parker's argument convincing?
10. She writes that there are some things that "transcend 'to each his own.'" Child pornography is one such example. Are crush videos another? Are there other items you would add to this list?

## AT THE CLIFF'S EDGE ON IMMIGRATION  |  RUBEN NAVARRETTE JR.

Ruben Navarrette is a syndicated columnist, a regular commentator on NPR, and a weekly commentator for *CNN.com.* A graduate of Harvard University, Navarrette published a memoir of his Harvard days in *A Darker Shade of Crimson: Odyssey of a Harvard Chicano* (1993). The following column appeared July 31, 2010.

**PREREADING QUESTIONS** Why would a writer think we are on "the cliff's edge" regarding immigration? What do you expect Navarrette to address?

1    Parents, you know how it is with kids. One acts up, and so you have to focus your attention on the troublemaker and take your eye off the others. Then, when you're not looking, another one gets out of line.

States are much the same way. The eyes of the nation are fixed on Arizona, 2 the undisputed problem child in our national immigration debate. But there are other states where lawmakers are eager to follow Arizona's lead and blame Washington for not solving a problem that, in truth, their own residents (i.e., employers) helped create.

At least half a dozen of the states thinking about going on this suicide run 3 can perhaps be forgiven their ignorance because the experience of having a sizable population of illegal immigrants is new to them. In Utah, Georgia, Ohio, Maryland, Oklahoma and South Carolina, illegal immigrants are still a rather exotic import.

But then there's Texas, which used to be part of Mexico and where lenient 4 immigration policies toward white settlers from the South and Northeast led to a famous tenant dispute that included a dustup at the Alamo in 1836. In Texas, Latinos are indigenous and as ubiquitous as bluebonnets. In the Lone Star State, where my mother and grandparents and great-grandparents were born and raised and where I spent five years writing about immigration and other issues for the *Dallas Morning News*, legislators should know better than to even flirt with the idea of adopting a divisive and dangerous law like the one in Arizona.

This was true even before U.S. District Judge Susan Bolton, in defense of 5 the Constitution, ripped the guts out of the Arizona law by striking down its most egregious and indefensible parts. Bolton had her pick of seven lawsuits seeking to block the law's implementation, and she based her ruling on the lawsuit filed by the Obama administration. The Justice Department argued that Arizona had exceeded its authority and trampled on powers reserved for the federal government.

Civilian watches the border with Mexico, determined to spot illegals crossing the desert.

6     Bolton agreed. She was particularly bothered by those elements of the law that all but required racial profiling by forcing police officers to arrest people they suspect are in the country illegally, made it a state crime for the undocumented to seek work, required legal immigrants to carry papers proving their status, and allowed police to detain and arrest people who could not prove their legal status. So the judge issued a preliminary injunction against those parts. The rest of the law—which did things such as making it a state crime to transport illegal immigrants—was allowed to go into effect.

7     So much for Gov. Jan Brewer's bravado in telling the federal government that Arizona would "meet you in court." This battle is far from over, and the issue is probably headed to the Supreme Court. So far, it's Common Sense, 1, Arizona, 0.

8     But like the saying goes, common sense isn't always common—even in Texas. State Rep. Leo Berman, a Republican, is drafting an Arizona-style bill for Texas and plans to introduce it next session.

9     Adding fuel to the bonfire, Texas Republicans recently adopted an over-the-top platform at their state convention that, among other things, encouraged the Legislature to create a Class A misdemeanor criminal offense "for an illegal alien to intentionally or knowingly be within the state of Texas," and to "oppose amnesty in any form leading to citizenship." Texas Republicans also want to deny citizenship to the U.S.-born children of illegal immigrants, ban day-labor work centers, limit bilingual education to three years, and deny non-U.S. citizens access to state or federal financial assistance for college.

10     In Texas, Latinos are forecast to make up nearly 80 percent of the population growth over the next 30 years (compared with only 4 percent for whites), and Latinos could outnumber whites by 2015, the *San Antonio Express-News* reported last month. What the Texas GOP drafted was a pact with the devil.

11     All of which leads me to ask my friends in the Lone Star State the same question my mom used to ask me growing up: "If all the other kids jumped off a cliff, would you do the same?"

12     Apparently they would.

---

Source: From *The Washington Post*, July 31, 2010. Reprinted by permission of the author.

QUESTIONS FOR READING

1.   What law on immigration did Arizona pass in the spring of 2010?

2.   How might employers in Arizona have added to the state's immigration problems?

3.   What elements of the Arizona law has Judge Bolton struck down? Where is debate over this law headed?

4.   What details would proposed immigration legislation in Texas include?

## QUESTIONS FOR REASONING AND ANALYSIS

5. Federal law treats illegal immigration as a civil violation. How does the Arizona law differ?

6. What is Navarrette's claim? (Be sure to connect Texas and Arizona.)

7. What details about Latinos in Texas does the author provide? How does this information advance his argument?

8. Navarrette uses a "frame" for his essay. What does he accomplish in his first and then in his last two paragraphs? What does he imply about some of the Texas legislators?

## QUESTIONS FOR REFLECTION AND WRITING

9. Do you agree with the author that Arizona's law is "divisive" and "dangerous"? Why or why not?

10. What is your response to the legal debate? Has a state taken on powers reserved for the federal government? From a legal perspective, is it sufficient to argue that the federal government has failed to address illegal immigration? Explain your position.

11. At the end of 2010, the Congress failed to enact legislation that would have given children brought into this country illegally a chance to attend college or join the military as a way eventually to achieve U.S. citizenship. What is your reaction to this "Dream Act"? Is this one good way to address some elements of the problem? Or, should children, along with their parents, never have a chance to earn amnesty? Defend your views on this issue.

# CHAPTER 23

# America: Embracing the Future— or Divided by Conflict?

U.S. troops responding to Obama's visit in Afghanistan.

The election of President Obama in November 2008 seems, from the perspective of 2011, a long time ago. On the night of his victory, Obama told 100,000 gathered in Chicago's Grant Park that his election demonstrated the possibility of achieving the American Dream. Could his election redirect America's future, disproving the voices of historians and political commentators asserting that we now live in a post-America world? Would he be able to restore our leadership role in the world, find ways to comfortably share power with China and India, end wars and bitterness in the Middle East, and restore market competitiveness around the globe?

Alas, the housing market collapsed and we slid into a major recession while deciding to increase the war effort in Afghanistan. And we watched helplessly as countries in the European Union faced serious financial woes and weather-based calamities added to the world's misery. By 2010, American voters decided it was time to "throw the bums out" of Washington, giving the House of Representatives to the Republicans. (Historian David Kennedy does remind us, in this chapter, that voters have been "throwing the bums out" for a long time; our recent changes in the mid-term elections are nothing new in America's political history.)

What are our internal conflicts all about that would lead to such voting fluctuations? Apparently we not only cannot all agree on the kind of government we want—to say nothing of how we should pay for government services—we also cannot all get along. The rhetoric of bigotry and hate has increased, fueled certainly by too many people spending too much time blogging and tweeting and by some "news" casters fanning the fires of bitterness.

President Obama acknowledges his greeting before addressing troops in Afghanistan.

Some would say that we need to reinvent America—but according to whose vision? Writer after writer in this anthology has stressed the problems we must address, problems with health care and climate change and paying our debts, with improving education and addressing the continuing problems of immigration. Some writers in this chapter see America's current culture war as a zero-sum game: One side must win and stifle the other's vision. Others are more hopeful that we may be able to work together to address our problems. One good detail: Younger Americans are more concerned about the environment and are far more accepting of diversity than older Americans. If young Americans will commit to becoming and staying informed and to participating in elections (older Americans vote in greater numbers than younger Americans in most elections) based on careful consideration of the candidates, there is hope still.

You can begin by seeking out the authors in this text who have impressed you with their knowledge and wisdom and calm approach to examining problems and suggesting solutions. Learn, and reflect on what you learn. Think about the kind of world you want to have for the rest of your life. You might also ask yourself: What else can I do to make a difference?

## THE CULTURE WAR | ARTHUR C. BROOKS

Formerly a professor of business and government policy at Syracuse University, Arthur C. Brooks is currently president of the American Enterprise Institute. He is the author of eight books, including a textbook on social policy and *The Battle: How the Fight Between Free Enterprise and Big Government Will Shape America's Future* (2010). The following article, a riff on his new book, was published in the *Washington Post* on May 23, 2010.

PREREADING QUESTIONS Given what you know about the author, what do you expect to read about? What does the term "culture war" mean to you?

1    America faces a new culture war.

2    This is not the culture war of the 1990s. It is not a fight over guns, gays or abortion. Those old battles have been eclipsed by a new struggle between two competing visions of the country's future. In one, America will continue to be an exceptional nation organized around the principles of free enterprise— limited government, a reliance on entrepreneurship and rewards determined by market forces. In the other, America will move toward European-style statism grounded in expanding bureaucracies, a managed economy and large-scale income redistribution. These visions are not reconcilable. We must choose.

3    It is not at all clear which side will prevail. The forces of big government are entrenched and enjoy the full arsenal of the administration's money and influence. Our leaders in Washington, aided by the unprecedented economic crisis of recent years and the panic it induced, have seized the moment to introduce breathtaking expansions of state power in huge swaths of the economy, from the health-care takeover to the financial regulatory bill that the

Senate approved Thursday [2010]. If these forces continue to prevail, America will cease to be a free enterprise nation.

I call this a culture war because free enterprise has been integral to American culture from the beginning, and it still lies at the core of our history and character. "A wise and frugal government," Thomas Jefferson declared in his first inaugural address in 1801, "which shall restrain men from injuring one another, shall leave them otherwise free to regulate their own pursuits of industry and improvement, and shall not take from the mouth of labor the bread it has earned. This is the sum of good government." He later warned: "To take from one, because it is thought that his own industry and that of his fathers has acquired too much, in order to spare to others, who, or whose fathers, have not exercised equal industry and skill, is to violate arbitrarily the first principle of association, the guarantee to every one of a free exercise of his industry and the fruits acquired by it." In other words, beware government's economic control, and woe betide the redistributors.

Now, as then, entrepreneurship can flourish only in a culture where individuals are willing to innovate and exert leadership; where people enjoy the rewards and face the consequences of their decisions; and where we can gamble the security of the status quo for a chance of future success.

Yet, in his commencement address at Arizona State University on May 13, 2009, President Obama warned against precisely such impulses: "You're taught to chase after all the usual brass rings; you try to be on this "who's who" list or that Top 100 list; you chase after the big money and you figure out how big your corner office is; you worry about whether you have a fancy enough title or a fancy enough car. That's the message that's sent each and every day, or has been in our culture for far too long—that through material possessions, through a ruthless competition pursued only on your own behalf—that's how you will measure success." Such ambition, he cautioned, "may lead you to compromise your values and your principles."

I appreciate the sentiment that money does not buy happiness. But for the president of the United States to actively warn young adults away from economic ambition is remarkable. And he makes clear that he seeks to change our culture.

The irony is that, by wide margins, Americans support free enterprise. A Gallup poll in January [2010] found that 86 percent of Americans have a positive image of "free enterprise," with only 10 percent viewing it negatively. Similarly, in March 2009, the Pew Research Center asked individuals from a broad range of demographic groups: "Generally, do you think people are better off in a free-market economy, even though there may be severe ups and downs from time to time, or don't you think so?" Almost 70 percent of respondents agreed that they are better off in a free-market economy, while only 20 percent disagreed.

In fact, no matter how the issue is posed, not more than 30 percent of Americans say they believe we would fare better without free markets at the core of our system. When it comes to support for free enterprise, we are essentially a 70-30 nation.

10     So here's a puzzle: If we love free enterprise so much, why are the 30 percent who want to change that culture in charge?

11     It's not simply because of the election of Obama. As much as Republicans may dislike hearing it, statism had effectively taken hold in Washington long before that.

12     The George W. Bush administration began the huge Wall Street and Detroit bailouts, and for years before the economic crisis, the GOP talked about free enterprise while simultaneously expanding the government with borrowed money and increasing the percentage of citizens with no income tax liability. The 30 percent coalition did not start governing this country with the advent of Obama, Nancy Pelosi and Harry Reid. It has been in charge for years.

13     But the real tipping point was the financial crisis, which began in 2008. The meltdown presented a golden opportunity for the 30 percent coalition to attack free enterprise openly and remake America in its own image.

14     And it seized that opportunity. While Republicans had no convincing explanation for the crisis, seemed responsible for it and had no obvious plans to fix it, the statists offered a full and compelling narrative. Ordinary Americans were not to blame for the financial collapse, nor was government. The real culprits were Wall Street and the Bush administration, which had gutted the regulatory system that was supposed to keep banks in line.

15     The solution was obvious: Vote for a new order to expand the powers of government to rein in the dangerous excesses of capitalism.

16     It was a convincing story. For a lot of panicky Americans, the prospect of a paternalistic government rescuing the nation from crisis seemed appealing as stock markets and home prices spiraled downward. According to this narrative, government was at fault in just one way: It wasn't big enough. If only there had been more regulators watching the banks more closely, the case went, the economy wouldn't have collapsed.

17     Yet in truth, it was government housing policy that was at the root of the crisis. Moreover, the financial sector—where the crisis began and where it has had the most serious impact—is already one of the most regulated parts of our economy. The chaos happened despite an extensive, intrusive regulatory framework, not because such a framework didn't exist.

18     More government—including a super-empowered Federal Reserve, a consumer protection watchdog and greater state powers to wind down financial firms and police market risks—does not mean we will be safe. On the contrary, such changes would give us a false sense of security, especially when Washington, a primary culprit in the crisis, is creating and implementing the new rules.

19     The statist narrative also held that only massive deficit spending could restore economic growth. "If nothing is done, this recession could linger for years," Obama warned a few days before taking office. "Only government can provide the short-term boost necessary to lift us from a recession this deep and severe. Only government can break the cycle that is crippling our economy."

20     This proposition is as expensive as it is false. Recessions can and do end without the kind of stimulus we experienced, and attempts to shore up the

economy with huge public spending often do little to improve matters and instead chain future generations with debt. In fact, all the evidence so far tells us that the current $787 billion stimulus package has overpromised and under-delivered, especially when it comes to creating jobs.

If we reject the administration's narrative, the 70-30 nation will remain 21 strong. If we accept it, and base our nation's policies on it, we will be well on our way to a European-style social democracy. Punitive taxes and regulations will make it harder to be an entrepreneur, and the rewards of success will be expropriated for the sake of greater income equality.

The new statism in America, made possible by years of drift and acceler- 22 ated by the panic over the economic crisis, threatens to make us permanently poorer. But that is not the greatest danger. The real risk is that in the new cul-ture war, we will forsake the third unalienable right set out in our Declaration of Independence: the pursuit of happiness.

Free enterprise brings happiness; redistribution does not. The reason is 23 that only free enterprise brings earned success.

Earned success involves the ability to create value honestly—not by inher- 24 iting a fortune, not by picking up a welfare check. It doesn't mean making money in and of itself. Earned success is the creation of value in our lives or in the lives of others. Earned success is the stuff of entrepreneurs who seek value through innovation, hard work and passion. Earned success is what parents feel when their children do wonderful things, what social innovators feel when they change lives, what artists feel when they create something of beauty.

Money is not the same as earned success but is rather a symbol, important 25 not for what it can buy but for what it says about how people are contributing and what kind of difference they are making. Money corresponds to happiness only through earned success.

Not surprisingly, unearned money—while it may help alleviate suffering— 26 carries with it no personal satisfaction. Studies of lottery winners, for instance, show that after a brief period of increased happiness, their moods darken as they no longer derive the same enjoyment from the simple pleasures in life, and as the glow of buying things wears off.

The same results emerge with other kinds of unearned income—welfare 27 payments, for example. According to the University of Michigan's 2001 Panel Study of Income Dynamics, going on the welfare rolls increases by 16 percent the likelihood of a person saying that she or he has felt inconsolably sad over the past month. Of course, the misery of welfare recipients probably goes well beyond the check itself. Nonetheless, studies show that recipients are far unhap-pier than equally poor people who do not receive such government benefits.

Benjamin Franklin (a pretty rich man for his time) grasped the truth about 28 money's inability by itself to deliver satisfaction. "Money never made a man happy yet, nor will it," he declared. "The more a man has, the more he wants. Instead of filling a vacuum, it makes one."

If unearned money does not bring happiness, redistributing money by 29 force won't make for a happier America—and the redistributionists' theory of a better society through income equality falls apart.

30  The goal of our system should be to give all Americans the greatest opportunities possible to succeed based on their work and merit. And that's exactly what the free enterprise system does: It makes earned success possible for the most people. This is the liberty that enables the true pursuit of happiness.

31  To win the culture war, those of us in the 70 percent majority must reclaim—and proclaim—the morality of our worldview.

32  Unfortunately, we often fail to do this. Instead, we sound unabashedly materialistic. We talk about growth rates, inflation and investment, while the 30 percent coalition walks off with the claims to happiness and fairness. (According to Obama, for example, we need to restore "fairness" to our tax code by increasing taxes on the wealthy and exempting more people at the bottom from paying anything.)

33  The irony is that it is the 30 percent coalition, not the 70 percent majority, that is fundamentally materialistic. What do they consider the greatest problem of poor people in America? Insufficient income. What would be evidence of a fairer society? Greater income equality. For the leaders of the 30 percent coalition, money does buy happiness—as long as it is spread evenly. That is why redistribution of income is a fundamental goal and why free enterprise, which rewards some people and penalizes others, cannot be trusted.

34  The 70 percent majority, meanwhile, believes that ingenuity and hard work should be rewarded. We admire creative entrepreneurs and disdain rule making bureaucrats. We know that income inequality by itself is not what makes people unhappy, and that only earned success can make them happy.

35  We must do more to show that while we use the language of commerce and business, we believe in human flourishing and contentment. We must articulate moral principles that set forth our fundamental values, and we must be prepared to defend them.

36  This defense is already underway, in a disorganized, grass-roots, American kind of way. Protests against the new statism have flared around the nation for more than a year. And while some have tried to dismiss the "tea party" demonstrations and the town hall protests of last summer as the work of extremists, ignorant backwoodsmen or agents of the health-care industry, these movements reveal much about the culture war that is underway.

37  Just compare the protests in America with those in Europe. Here, we see tea partiers demonstrating against the government's encroachment on the free enterprise system and protesting the fact that the state is spending too much money bailing out too many people. Why are people protesting in Greece? Because they want the government to give them even more. They are angry because their government—in the face of its worst economic and perhaps existential crisis in decades—won't pay the lavish pensions to which they feel entitled. There's no better example of the cultural difference between America and Europe today, yet it is toward European-style social democracy that the 30 percent coalition wants to move us.

38  Fortunately, it is hard to dismiss the voice of the voters in some of our most recent electoral contests. Scott Brown won the late Ted Kennedy's Senate seat from Massachusetts in January by declaring himself not an apparatchik Republican but a moral enthusiast for markets. "What made America great?"

he asked. "Free market, free enterprise, manufacturing, job creation. That's how we're gonna do it, not by enlarging government." His cultural pitch for free enterprise hit just the right chord, even in liberal Massachusetts. It struck at the heart of the 30 percent coalition's agenda for America.

Brown's victory—and Rand Paul's triumph in Kentucky's Republican Senate 39 primary last week, for that matter—are but warning shots in the burgeoning culture war. The most intense battles are still ahead.

To win, the 70 percent majority must come together around core princi- 40 ples: that the purpose of free enterprise is human flourishing, not materialism; that we stand for equality of opportunity, not equality of income; that we seek to stimulate true prosperity rather than simply treat poverty; and that we believe in principle over power.

This final idea is particularly challenging. In Washington, a lot of people 41 think they know how to win. They say what is needed are telegenic candidates, dirty tricks and lots of campaign money. To them, thinking long-term means thinking all the way to 2012. In other words, they talk only of tactics, parties and power.

They are wrong. What matters most to Americans is the commitment to 42 principle, not the exercise of power. The electorate did not repudiate free enterprise in 2008; it simply punished an unprincipled Republican Party.

But political turmoil can lead to renewal, and the challenges of this new 43 culture war can help us mobilize and reassert our principles. The 2008 election was perhaps exactly what America needed. Today there is a very real threat that the 30 percent coalition may transform our great nation forever. I hope this threat will clear our thinking enough to bring forth leaders—regardless of political party—with our principles at heart and the ideas to match. If free enterprise triumphs over the quest for political power, America will be the stronger for it.

---

Source: From *The Washington Post*, May 23, 2010. Reprinted by permission of the author.

### QUESTIONS FOR READING

1. What were elements of the culture war in the 1990s?
2. How does Brooks define today's culture war?
3. What percentage of Americans support free enterprise, according to the author?
4. What does Brooks mean by *statism*? When did it start to dominate over free enterprise?
5. What, according to Brooks, was the real cause of our economic problems from 2008 on?
6. What is Brooks's view of the effect of the economic stimulus package?
7. What are the main characteristics of a European-styled social democracy?
8. What is the source of happiness? What cannot produce personal satisfaction—according to the author?
9. To win the culture war, what do those who favor free enterprise need to do? How do they need to sell their position?

QUESTIONS FOR REASONING AND ANALYSIS

10. What is Brooks's claim? (Is it more helpful to see this as a problem/solution argument rather than a position paper? Explain.)

11. Evaluate elements of Brooks's argument: Is he correct to assert that statism began with the Bush administration? (Reagan expanded the federal government and increased taxes more than any recent president.)

12. Does Brooks provide convincing evidence that unearned money does not provide satisfaction?

13. How have most economists viewed the impact of the stimulus bill?

14. Does Brooks provide evidence that the free enterprise system makes "earned success possible for the most people"? Does he provide any strategies for helping those who are not successful?

QUESTIONS FOR REFLECTION AND WRITING

15. Are you in the 70 percent or the 30 percent—as Brooks divides us? If you are in the 30 percent, how would you respond to Brooks?

16. Are you prepared to accept the concept that 30 percent can actually have political control through a number of elections? If this is hard to explain, then what other explanations might be helpful?

17. Do you agree that it is the 30 percent for statism who are actually more materialistic than those who embrace free enterprise? Does an acceptance of a progressive tax structure equate with materialism? Explain your response.

## FACES WE'VE SEEN BEFORE | COLBERT I. KING

A native Washingtonian, Colbert King has held a number of positions in the government, including special agent for the State Department, and in banking, including at the World Bank. King joined the *Washington Post* editorial board in 1990, began writing a weekly column in 1995, and became deputy editor of the editorial page in 2000. In 2003 he won a Pulitzer Prize for Commentary. The following column appeared March 27, 2010.

PREREADING QUESTIONS  What are the views of the Tea Party? Who was George Wallace? (If you don't know, seek the answers to these questions online.)

1    If angry faces at Tea Party rallies are eerily familiar. They resemble faces of protesters lining the street at the University of Alabama in 1956 as Autherine Lucy, the school's first black student, bravely tried to walk to class.

2    Those same jeering faces could be seen gathered around the Arkansas National Guard troopers who blocked nine black children from entering Little Rock's Central High School in 1957.

3    "They moved closer and closer," recalled Elizabeth Eekford, one of the Little Rock Nine. "Somebody started yelling; 'Lynch her! Lynch her!' I tried to see a friendly face somewhere in the crowd—someone who maybe could help. I looked into the face of an old woman and it seemed a kind face, but when I looked at her again, she spat on me."

Those were the faces I saw at a David Duke rally in Metairie, La., in 1991: 4 sullen with resentment, wallowing in victimhood, then exploding with yells of excitement as the ex-Klansman and Republican gubernatorial candidate spewed vitriolic white-power rhetoric.

People like that old woman in Little Rock, the Alabama mob that hounded 5 Autherine Lucy, the embracers of Duke's demagoguery in Louisiana, never go away.

They were spotted last weekend on Capitol Hill under the Tea Party ban- 6 ner protesting the health-care-reform bill. Some carried signs that read "If Brown [Scott Brown (R-Mass.)] can't stop it, a Browning [high power weapon] can." Some shouted racial and homophobic epithets at members of Congress. Others assumed the role of rabble, responding to the calls of instigating Republican representatives gathered on a Capitol balcony.

Tea Party members, as with their forerunners who showed up at the 7 University of Alabama and Central High School, behave as they do because they have been culturally conditioned to believe they are entitled to do whatever they want, and to whomever they want, because they are the "real Americans," while all who don't think or look like them are not.

And they are consequential. Without folks like them, there would be no 8 Rush Limbaugh, Glenn Beck, Sean Hannity or Pat Buchanan. There would never have been a George Corley Wallace, the Alabama governor dubbed by Pulitzer Prize–winning author Diane McWhorter in a 2008 *Slate* article as "the godfather, avatar of a national uprising against the three G's of government, Godlessness, and gun control."

Hence, an explanation for the familiarity of faces: today's Tea Party adher- 9 ents are George Wallace legacies.

They, like Wallace's followers, smolder with anger. They fear they are being 10 driven from their rightful place in America.

They see the world through the eyes of the anti-civil-rights alumni. 11 "Washington, D.C." now, as then, is regarded as the Great Satan. This is the place that created the civil rights laws that were shoved down their throats. This is the birthplace of their much-feared "Big Government" and the playground of the "elite national news media."

And they are faithful to the old Wallace playbook. 12

McWhorter wrote how Wallace, in a 1963 speech to the political arm of 13 Alabama's Ku Klux Klan, "referred to the recent bombings in Birmingham against prominent black citizens, citing the lack of fatalities as proof that the 'nigras' were throwing the dynamite themselves in order to attract publicity and money."

Fast-forward to today. Note the pro–Tea Party conservative commentary 14 debunking last weekend's racist and homophobic slurs as a work of fiction and exaggeration strictly for political reasons. Noticeable, too, is the influence of George Wallace, Limbaugh, Beck and their followers on outcomes.

The angry '50s and '60s crowds threatened and intimidated; some among 15 them even murdered. That notwithstanding, Americans of goodwill gathered in the White House to witness the signing of landmark civil rights laws.

16    Schoolhouse doors were blocked, and little children were demeaned. Yet the bigots didn't get the last word. Justice rolled down like a mighty river, sweeping them aside.

17    They insulted, abused, lied and vandalized. Still, President Obama fulfilled his promise to sign historic health-care reform into law by the end of his first term.

18    Those angry faces won't go away. But neither can they stand in the way of progress.

19    The mobs of yesteryear were on the wrong side of history. Tea Party supporters and their right-wing fellow travelers are on the wrong side now. It shows up in their faces.

### QUESTIONS FOR READING

1.  To whom are the Tea Party members compared?
2.  What signs and shouted insults could be seen and heard at a Capitol Hill rally opposing health-care reform?
3.  Why, according to King, do Tea Party members behave as they do?
4.  On what side of history are the Tea Partiers, according to the author?

### QUESTIONS FOR REASONING AND ANALYSIS

5.  What is the central comparison established in the essay?
6.  What is King's claim?
7.  What does the author gain by his descriptions in paragraphs 1–5?

### QUESTIONS FOR REFLECTION AND WRITING

8.  Do you agree with King that Tea Party members seem to be motivated by anger—and by a sense that they are being pushed out of their "rightful" place in this society? Why or why not? (Who are Tea Party members? See what you can learn about them online.)
9.  Is the Tea Party on the wrong side of history? If yes, why? If no, how would you counter King?

## AMERICA IS BETTER THAN THIS | BOB HERBERT

Prior to joining the New York Times in 1993, Bob Herbert was a national correspondent for NBC from 1991 to 1993. In 1990 he became a founding panelist on Sunday Edition, a weekly CBS political talk show. His twice-weekly op-ed columns in the New York Times cover politics, urban affairs, and social trends. The following column appeared August 27, 2010.

PREREADING QUESTIONS  Who is Glenn Beck? What did he organize on August 23, 2010? (If you don't know, find the information online.)

America is better than Glenn Beck. For all of his celebrity, Mr. Beck is an 1
ignorant, divisive, pathetic figure. On the anniversary of the great 1963 March
on Washington he will stand in the shadows of giants—Abraham Lincoln and
the Rev. Dr. Martin Luther King Jr. Who do you think is more representative of
this nation?

Consider a brief sampling of their rhetoric. 2

Lincoln: "A house divided against itself cannot stand." 3

King: "Never succumb to the temptation of becoming bitter." 4

Beck: "I think the president is a racist." 5

Washington was on edge on the morning of Aug. 28, 1963. The day was 6
sunny and very warm and Negroes, as we were called in those days, were
coming into town by the tens of thousands. The sale of liquor was banned.
Troops stood by to restore order if matters got out of control. President John
F. Kennedy waited anxiously in the White House to see how the day would
unfold.

It unfolded splendidly. The crowd for the "March on Washington for Jobs 7
and Freedom" grew to some 250,000. Nearly a quarter of the marchers were
white. They gathered at the Lincoln Memorial, where they were enthralled by
the singing of Mahalia Jackson and Joan Baez. The march was all about inclu-
sion and the day seemed to swell with an extraordinary sense of camaraderie
and good feeling.

The climax, of course, was Dr. King's transcendent "I Have a Dream" 8
speech. Jerald Podair, a professor of American studies at Lawrence University
in Wisconsin, has called Aug. 28, 1963, "the most important single day in civil
rights history." This is the historical legacy that Glenn Beck, a small man with a
mean message, has chosen to tread upon with his cynical rally on Saturday at
that very same Lincoln Memorial.

Beck is a provocateur who likes to play with matches in the tinderbox of 9
racial and ethnic confrontation. He seems oblivious to the real danger of his
execrable behavior. He famously described President Obama as a man "who
has a deep-seated hatred for white people or the white culture."

He is an integral part of the vicious effort by the Tea Party and other ele- 10
ments of the right wing to portray Mr. Obama as somehow alien, a strange
figure who is separate and apart from—outside of—ordinary American life. As
the watchdog group Media Matters for America has noted, Beck said of the
president, "He chose to use the name, Barack, for a reason, to identify not
with America—you don't take the name Barack to identify with America. You
take the name Barack to identify, with what? Your heritage? The heritage,
maybe, of your father in Kenya, who is a radical?"

Facts and reality mean nothing to Beck. And there is no road too low for 11
him to slither upon. The Southern Poverty Law Center tells us that in a twist on
the civil rights movement, Beck said on the air that he "wouldn't be surprised
if in our lifetime dogs and fire hoses are released or opened on us. I wouldn't

be surprised if a few of us get a billy club to the head. I wouldn't be surprised if some of us go to jail—just like Martin Luther King did—on trumped-up charges. Tough times are coming."

12    He makes you want to take a shower.

13    In Beck's view, President Obama is driven by a desire to settle "old racial scores" and his ultimate goal is "reparations" for black Americans. Abe Lincoln and Dr. King could only look on aghast at this clown.

14    Beck has been advertising his rally as nonpolitical, but its main speaker is Sarah Palin. She had her own low moment recently as a racial provocateur, publicly voicing her support for Laura Schlessinger, radio's "Dr. Laura," who went out of her way to humiliate a black caller by continuously using the n-word to make a point, even after the caller had made it clear that she was offended.

15    Palin's advice to Schlessinger: "Don't retreat—reload."

16    There is a great deal of hatred and bigotry in this country, but it does not define the country. The daily experience of most Americans is not a bitter experience and for all of our problems we are in a much better place on these matters than we were a half century ago.

17    But I worry about the potential for violence that grows out of unrestrained, hostile bombast. We've seen it so often. A little more than two weeks after the 1963 March on Washington, the 16th Street Baptist Church in Birmingham was bombed by the Ku Klux Klan and four young black girls were killed. And three months after the march, Jack Kennedy was assassinated.

18    My sincere advice to Beck, Palin and their followers is chill, baby, chill.

---

## QUESTIONS FOR READING

1.   How does Herbert characterize the 1963 March on Washington? What is the implied contrast with the Tea Party and Beck's planned march?

2.   How do Beck and the Tea Party seek to characterize President Obama?

3.   What suggests to Herbert that Beck's rally is political, in spite of what he may say?

4.   How does today's bigotry and hate compare to the past, in the author's view?

## QUESTIONS FOR REASONING AND ANALYSIS

5.   What is Herbert's occasion for writing?

6.   What is his claim? What larger point does he want to make?

7.   What is the author's view of Beck? How do the details he provides support his characterization?

8.   Analyze the metaphor in paragraph 9. Is it effective?

9. Many political analysts have accused Beck of ignoring "facts and reality." Do Herbert's examples convince you of the fairness of this charge? Why or why not?

10. Arthur Brooks (see pp. 544–49) has presented the Tea Party and Beck as a group motivated by commitment to a political philosophy. Both Colbert King and Bob Herbert present a very different view of the activists and the commentator. How do the specifics given by King and Herbert compare to those in Brooks's argument? Can you draw any conclusions? Should you seek more information? Why or why not?

11. Is America better than Beck and his "political bombast"? Why or why not?

## THE CURE FOR PUBLIC ANGER | JENNIFER GRANHOLM

Canadian-born Jennifer Granholm was attorney general of Michigan from 1999 to 2003. She then became Michigan's first female governor in 2003 and was reelected to a second and final (due to term limits) term, which ended January 1, 2011. She is a graduate of UC Berkeley and holds a law degree from Harvard University. Her short article for *U.S. News & World Report* appeared in a special November 2010 issue.

PREREADING QUESTIONS  Do you think there's too much anger in Americans today? If so, what would you recommend as a cure?

The November [2010] election will end a tumultuous campaign season 1 that began with many good public servants losing in the primaries because angry voters wanted to "throw the bums out." If this trend continues on Election Day, it would be because the public has simply grown impatient. That's a warning signal for all newly minted politicians flush with victory that they, too, could soon face an angry electorate if they don't produce results quickly or dramatically enough to sate the hunger of an impatient electorate.

The experience of the past few months reminds us that unleashed cyni- 2 cism and anger are infectious, cancerous. Anyone who has recently visited the badlands of the blogs knows that the digital soapbox roils with angry cynicism. Al Gore once eloquently said: "Cynicism is deadly. It bites everything it can reach—like a dog with a foot caught in a trap. And then it devours itself. It drains us of the will to improve; it diminishes our public spirit; it saps our inventiveness; it withers our souls." Cynicism, however, is just an ugly mask that, when lifted, reveals pain.

Fortunately, there is a sure-fire antidote for the negativity and pain that 3 besets our democracy, an antidote that is the purest act of all: service to others. Even the hardest heart softens when a tutored child overcomes the odds to excel. Even the most virulent antigovernment activist feels compassion in delivering meals to disabled and home-bound seniors. Even the hurting unemployed worker will begin to heal when helping to rebuild a crumpled

Volunteers listen to instructions to help complete the house.

neighborhood in the wake of a hurricane. The acts of kindness occurring each day all over America can begin to heal our pain, soothe our rage, and remind us that we are one human family.

4    But even more importantly, America desperately needs the help. Indeed, this new class of political leaders won't be any more successful than the last ones at a "quick fix" since, darn it, they weren't issued magic wands either. Problems such as child poverty, blight, poor education, and homelessness are too big to leave only to the politicians. America's problems and America's pain belong to all of us. So there's a sign on the door of your local Big Brothers Big Sisters or AmeriCorps or Habitat for Humanity. The sign reads: Help Wanted. The pay is lousy, but the rewards are limitless.

5    And perhaps the biggest reward for an angry voter is discovering that service to others can be the most effective painkiller of all.

## QUESTIONS FOR READING

1.    What is the context of the anger that Granholm examines?
2.    Where can one find much of this anger expressed?
3.    What, in the author's view, does cynicism actually hide?
4.    What is the author's suggestion of a cure for anger and pain?

QUESTIONS FOR REASONING AND ANALYSIS

5. What is Granholm's claim?

6. What does the author gain by accepting the anger and acknowledging the pain?

7. Analyze Gore's definition of cynicism, studying it metaphor by metaphor. Is this a good definition?

8. Why does Granholm think her solution of helping others is important for America?

QUESTIONS FOR REFLECTION AND WRITING

9. Has Granholm convinced you that helping others can ease one's pain and anger? Why or why not?

10. Have the authors throughout this chapter provided enough evidence that we need to work together to help solve the country's problems? Why or why not?

11. Have you done any volunteer work? If so, what did you gain from the experience? If not, do you think that now you will seek some volunteer experience?

## THROWING THE BUMS OUT FOR 140 YEARS | DAVID M. KENNEDY

On the faculty of Stanford University since 1967, David Kennedy is now professor emeritus and director of the Bill Lane Center for the American West at Stanford. His PhD from Yale University is in American Studies, and he is the author or editor of ten books. His book *Freedom from Fear* won the Pulitzer Prize for History in 2000. His analysis of the mid-term elections was published in the *New York Times* on November 6, 2010.

PREREADING QUESTIONS  Considering the article's title and what you now know about the author, what do you expect to read about? Who are the "bums"?

So we have had three "wave" elections in a row: control of both chambers  1
of Congress changed hands in 2006, as did the presidency in 2008, and the House flipped back to Republican domination last week [November 2010]. All this apparently incoherent back-and-forth has left the political class reeling and set the commentariat aflutter.

Explanations for our current political volatility abound: toxic partisanship,  2
the ever more fragmented and strident news media, high unemployment, economic upheaval and the clamorous upwelling of inchoate populist angst.

But the political instability of our own time pales when compared with the  3
late 19th century. In the Gilded Age the American ship of state pitched and yawed on a howling sea of electoral turbulence. For decades on end, "divided government" was the norm. In only 12 of the 30 years after 1870 did the same party control the House, the Senate and the White House.

4    The majority party in the House—intended to be the branch of government—most responsive to swings in popular sentiment—shifted six times in the era's 15 Congressional elections. Three of those shifts in power entailed losses of more than 70 seats by the majority party (at a time when there were roughly 100 fewer seats than today's 435). In 1894, Democrats shed more than 100. Today's electoral oscillations, for all their drama, seem modest by comparison.

5    And yet there are features of the Gilded Age that suggest some disturbing parallels with our own time. Generations of American scholars have struggled to find a coherent narrative or to identify heroic leaders in that era's messy and inconclusive political scene. The history books give us a succession of Lilliputian presidents often described as "bearded, bland and boring."

6    These men left but the faintest of tracks in the historical record. Chester A. Arthur? He is best remembered, if at all, for reportedly possessing more than 80 pairs of trousers. Benjamin Harrison? Of him can be said virtually nothing memorable at all. The likes of the monumental figures who strode the national stage in the early years of the Republic—Jefferson, Jackson, Calhoun, Clay, Webster, Lincoln—were nowhere to be found in the years after the Civil War. Nor were there any leaders of the caliber that would emerge in the 20th century—from the two Roosevelts to Ronald Reagan.

7    It is not as if the Gilded Age did not have plenty of urgent and potentially galvanizing issues: healing the wounds of the Civil War; managing enormous nation-building agendas in the conquered South and the dauntingly arid West; navigating the enormous and rushed transition from an agricultural to an industrial economic base, and from countryside to city; quelling the labor unrest that repeatedly erupted into bloodshed; accommodating the millions of immigrants who streamed ashore in the century's closing decades; and defining an international role for an increasingly prosperous and powerful country, just to name a few.

8    Yet the era's political system proved unable to grapple effectively with any of those matters.

9    What's instructive to us now is the similarity between the Gilded Age's combination of extraordinary social and economic dynamism and abject political paralysis. We face a no-less-formidable array of issues, and there is little mystery about their nature. Some have a familiar face: unemployment, sadly, as well as immigration and the quest for an appropriate national security strategy and foreign policy.

10    Others are almost wholly novel: the passage to a post-industrial information age; mounting competition in virtually all the world's marketplaces; worsening educational achievement; giddily levitating health costs; a looming fiscal apocalypse in entitlement programs like Medicare and Medicaid; environmental degradation and climate change; and the search for sustainable energy supplies.

11    In the face of all those challenges, like our Gilded Age forebears, we have a political system that manages to be both volatile and gridlocked—indeed, it

may be gridlocked not least because it is so volatile. And, like their 19th-century forebears, today's politicians have great difficulty gaining traction on any of those challenges. Now as then, it's hard to lead citizens who are so eager to "throw the bums out" at every opportunity.

Yet the Gilded Age was but a chapter in American history, and we are per- 12 mitted to hope that the sorry spectacle of our own time may well come to a similar conclusion. The pent-up demand for some kind of meaningful approach to the great issues that hung so heavily on the land more than a century ago eventually produced the Progressive Era.

Eventually, leaders emerged in both major parties—most conspicuously 13 the Republican Theodore Roosevelt and the Democrat Woodrow Wilson— who breathed vitality into the wheezing political system and effectively initiated the tortuous process of building institutions and writing laws commensurate with the scope and complexity of the society over which they presided.

So perhaps the stasis of the Gilded Age and the stalemate of our recent 14 years reflect not so much the defects of our political structures as the monumental scale of the issues at hand. From that perspective, "wave" elections mark a necessary stage of indecision, shuffling, avoidance and confusion before a fractious democratic people can at last summon the courage to make tough choices, the creativity to find innovative solutions, the will to take consequential action and the old-fashioned moxie to put the ship of state again on an even keel.

---

Source: From *The New York Times*, November 6, 2010. Reprinted by permission of the author.

## QUESTIONS FOR READING

1. What does Kennedy mean by a "wave" election?
2. What does the author mean by "inchoate populist angst"? (Look up any words you do not know.)
3. What are the similarities between the Gilded Age and our own? (Be sure you know the years that have been labeled the Gilded Age.)
4. How does Kennedy characterize our current political system?
5. How did the Gilded Age eventually change?

## QUESTIONS FOR REASONING AND ANALYSIS

6. What is Kennedy's claim? What type of argument is this?
7. Kennedy uses a demanding style, with interesting metaphors and clever word choice. Select several passages and explain their effectiveness.
8. Kennedy suggests that our current problems may not be a flawed political system but a necessary stage of indecision. Why are we indecisive? What must we do to work through the problems, in the author's view?

9. Other writers look closely at current issues and conflicts. Kennedy chooses to put the present in a historical perspective. What do we gain by using a wider lens and a knowledge of history?

10. Many (including E. J. Dionne Jr.) have argued that our political system is dysfunctional. Kennedy is more hopeful. Where do you stand in this debate? Explain your position and your reasons.

## THE DESIGN OF YOUR LIFE | VIRGINIA POSTREL

Virginia Postrel, a graduate of Princeton University with a degree in literature, has been a columnist for *Forbes,* was the editor of *Reason* magazine from 1989 to 2000, is a popular speaker on business and design subjects, and publishes articles in a range of journals on commercial and cultural issues. She is the author of *The Future and Its Enemies* (1999) and *The Substance of Style* (2003). "The Design of Your Life" appeared in 2003 in *Men's Journal.*

PREREADING QUESTIONS In a chapter on America's future, not all articles need to be about politics and cultural battles. What might you expect Postrel to write about?

1   Those old sci-fi movies were wrong. The twenty-first century doesn't look at all the way they said it would. We citizens of the future aren't wearing conformist jumpsuits, living in utilitarian high-rises, or getting our food in the form of dreary-looking pills. On the contrary, we are demanding and creating a stimulating, diverse, and strikingly well-designed world. We like our vacuum cleaners and mobile phones to sparkle, our backpacks and laptops to express our personalities. We expect trees and careful landscaping in our parking lots, peaked roofs and decorative facades on our supermarkets, and auto dealerships as swoopy and stylish as the cars they sell.

2   "Design is everywhere, and everywhere is now designed," says David Brown, a design consultant and the former president of Art Center College of Design in Pasadena, California. And it all happened so fast. It wasn't that long ago that Apple's iMac turned the personal computer from a utilitarian, putty-colored box into curvy eye candy—blueberry, strawberry, tangerine, grape, lime. Translucent jewel tones spread to staplers and surge protectors and microwaves—even American Express cards.

3   Since then everything around us has been getting a much needed facelift. Volkswagen reinvented the Beetle. Karirn Rashid reinvented the ordinary trash can. Oxo reinvented the potato peeler (thus proving that people will happily pay an extra five bucks for a kitchen tool if it looks and feels better). Even toilet brushes have become design objects, with something for every personality. The handle on Phillippe Starck's sleek Excalibur brush looks ready for a duel, while Alessi's Merdolino brush (designed by Stefano Giovannoni) sprouts like a bright green cartoon plant.

When Target introduced a line of housewares developed by architect- 4 designer Michael Graves, few customers had ever heard of Graves. But his playful toaster quickly became the chain's most talked about, and most expensive, model. Target increased the number of Graves offerings to more than five hundred and is still adding more Graves items—and more designers.

"We're seeing design creep into everything," says Chicago industrial 5 designer Mark Dziersk. The 1990s were the decade of distribution. Wal-Mart set the standard for low-cost, hyperefficient retailing, while the Internet made everything available everywhere. You can live in a small town and still buy stylish goods. "I see 2000–2010 as the decade of design," says Dziersk.

This trend doesn't mean that a particular style has triumphed or that we're 6 necessarily living in a period of unprecedented creativity. It doesn't mean everything is now beautiful, or that people agree on basic standards of taste. Instead of a single dominant standard, we see aesthetic fluidity. Diversity and choice, not uniformity and consistency, are our new ideals. The holy grail of modern product designers is mass customization, not mass production. "Mass production offered millions of one thing to everybody," writes Bruce Sterling, the science fiction author and design champion, in *Metropolis*. "Mass customization offers millions of different models to one guy."

Ours is a pluralist age in which different styles can coexist, as long as they 7 please the individuals who choose them. You don't just buy blue jeans anymore; you customize, picking the exact wash and cut you like best. If you don't like the look of the nearest Starbucks, the company gives you choices. "You can go three stores down to a different Starbucks and say,—I like this better. I just feel better here,'" explains a Starbucks executive. And once you're there you don't order just a cup of coffee. You navigate a long menu of customized combinations, including different beans, styles, and flavors.

All this choice required technological and business innovations, but the 8 shift expresses deeper cultural changes, too. The extension of liberal individualism—the primacy of self-definition over hierarchy and inherited, group-determined status—has altered our aesthetic universe. Try as they may, official tastemakers no longer determine the "right way" to look. The issue is no longer what style is used but rather that style is used, consciously and conscientiously, even in areas where function used to stand alone.

Not that other values have gone away. We may crave a barbecue grill that 9 looks like a piece of sculpture, but we still want it to work well. We get pleasure from the bright colors of Nalgene's plastic water bottles, but we also appreciate their indestructibility. We continue to care about cost, comfort, and convenience. It's just that on the margin aesthetics matters more than before.

Designers themselves are finally abandoning the modernist idea of the 10 one best way and embracing the pleasures of personalization. "Good design is not about the perfect thing anymore but about helping a lot of different people build their own personal identities," says David Kelley, the founder of the IDEO design firm (which designed the look and feel of your iPod).

This attitude marks a huge shift. Designers and other cultural opinion 11 leaders used to believe that a single aesthetic standard was right—that style was a manifestation of truth, virtue, even sanity. What if someone didn't like the way Bauhaus architect Walter Gropius had arranged the furniture in the new Harvard dorm he designed? "Then they are a neurotic," Gropius replied.

12    Today's modernists don't talk like that. They emphasize pleasure and personality. "Instead of finding a style and adhering to its tenets, modern design allows you to grapple with your own ideas about how you want to live," says Lara Hedberg, publisher of *Dwell*, the architecture and interiors magazine for "nice modernists." Just because you like austere high-tech lighting and a chrome and glass coffee table doesn't mean you can't have a comfortable upholstered chair.

13    The current design revolution recognizes that sensory experience is as valid a part of our nature as our capacity to speak or to reason. "We are by nature—by deep, biological nature—visual, tactile creatures," says David Brown. The objects we desire don't need any other justification for pleasing our visual, tactile, emotional nature, as long as they make life more enjoyable.

14    Those prophets who forecast a sterile, uniform future got it wrong because they imagined a society shaped by impersonal laws of history and technology, divorced from individuality, pleasure, and imagination. But "form follows emotion" has supplanted "form follows function" as the defining mantra of the day, along with "I'd like a grande mint mocha Frappuccino."

---

Source: From *Men's Journal*, October 2003. Reprinted by permission of the author.

## QUESTIONS FOR READING

1.   What images of the twenty-first century were depicted in sci-fi movies?
2.   Instead of those images, what do we find all around us?
3.   What is meant by "mass customization"?
4.   What motivates the design revolution?

## QUESTIONS FOR REASONING AND ANALYSIS

5.   What is Postrel's claim?
6.   How does she develop and support her claim?
7.   Postrel quotes a number of design specialists; how does this strategy advance her argument?

## QUESTIONS FOR REFLECTION AND WRITING

8.   Has it occurred to you to think about the *Star Trek* uniforms, for example, and the varied dress of today? Do you think that the similarity of dress is still coming in our future, or will our "customized" demands continue? Explain your response.

9. Look around your campus. Do you see a variety of styles—or do most students seem to be dressed much alike? Is it possible to suggest that young people embrace uniformity of dress more than older adults?

10. When Starbucks first moved onto every third corner of many cities, some cultural analysts declared that all those fancy drink choices were elitist—expensive, indulgent, a way for yuppies to show off. Do you think that most people hold this view today—is this a symbol of the culture war, of the separation of red states and blue states? Does it depend somewhat on where people live? What is your view?

## HOW THE FUTURE WILL JUDGE US  |  KWAME ANTHONY APPIAH

The son of a Ghanian lawyer and politician and British novelist, Appiah was educated in both Ghana and England. He holds a PhD in philosophy from Cambridge University, and, since 2002, he has held appointments in both the philosophy department at Princeton University and the university's Center for Human Values. Appiah is the author of many books, including *The Ethics of Identity* (2003) and *The Honor Code: How Moral Revolutions Happen* (2010). He is recognized as one of the world's most significant contemporary thinkers. His essay here was first published on September 26, 2010, in the *Washington Post*.

PREREADING QUESTIONS  Given Appiah's areas of study and interest, what kinds of current problems do you think he will select for future judgment? What have we repudiated from our country's past?

Once, pretty much everywhere, beating your wife and children was 1 regarded as a father's duty, homosexuality was a hanging offense, and water-boarding was approved—in fact, invented—by the Catholic Church. Through the middle of the 19th century, the United States and other nations in the Americas condoned plantation slavery. Many of our grandparents were born in states where women were forbidden to vote. And well into the 20th century, lynch mobs in this country stripped, tortured, hanged and burned human beings at picnics.

Looking back at such horrors, it is easy to ask: What were people 2 thinking?

Yet, the chances are that our own descendants will ask the same question, 3 with the same incomprehension, about some of our practices today.

Is there a way to guess which ones? After all, not every disputed institution 4 or practice is destined to be discredited. And it can be hard to distinguish in real time between movements, such as abolition, that will come to represent moral common sense and those, such as prohibition, that will come to seem quaint or misguided. Recall the book-burners of Boston's old Watch and Ward Society or the organizations for the suppression of vice, with their crusades against claret, contraceptives and sexually candid novels.

Still, a look at the past suggests three signs that a particular practice is 5 destined for future condemnation.

6     First, people have already heard the arguments against the practice. The case against slavery didn't emerge in a blinding moment of moral clarity, for instance; it had been around for centuries.

7     Second, defenders of the custom tend not to offer moral counterarguments but instead invoke tradition, human nature or necessity. (As in, "We've always had slaves, and how could we grow cotton without them?")

8     And third, supporters engage in what one might call strategic ignorance, avoiding truths that might force them to face the evils in which they're complicit. Those who ate the sugar or wore the cotton that the slaves grew simply didn't think about what made those goods possible. That's why abolitionists sought to direct attention toward the conditions of the Middle Passage, through detailed illustrations of slave ships and horrifying stories of the suffering below decks.

9     With these signs in mind, here are four contenders for future moral condemnation.

## OUR PRISON SYSTEM

10     We already know that the massive waste of life in our prisons is morally troubling; those who defend the conditions of incarceration usually do so in non-moral terms (citing costs or the administrative difficulty of reforms); and we're inclined to avert our eyes from the details. Check, check and check.

11     Roughly 1 percent of adults in this country are incarcerated. We have 4 percent of the world's population but 25 percent of its prisoners. No other nation has as large a proportion of its population in prison; even China's rate is less than half of ours. What's more, the majority of our prisoners are non-violent offenders, many of them detained on drug charges. (Whether a country that was truly free would criminalize recreational drug use is a related question worth pondering.)

12     And the full extent of the punishment prisoners face isn't detailed in any judge's sentence. More than 100,000 inmates suffer sexual abuse, including rape, each year; some contract HIV as a result. Our country holds at least 25,000 prisoners in isolation in so-called supermax facilities, under conditions that many psychologists say amount to torture.

## INDUSTRIAL MEAT PRODUCTION

13     The arguments against the cruelty of factory farming have certainly been around a long time; it was Jeremy Bentham, in the 18th century, who observed that, when it comes to the treatment of animals, the key question is not whether animals can reason but whether they can suffer. People who eat factory-farmed bacon or chicken rarely offer a moral justification for what they're doing. Instead, they try not to think about it too much, shying away from stomach-turning stories about what goes on in our industrial abattoirs.

14     Of the more than 90 million cattle in our country, at least 10 million at any time are packed into feedlots, saved from the inevitable diseases of overcrowding only by regular doses of antibiotics, surrounded by piles of their own feces, their nostrils filled with the smell of their own urine. Picture it—and then

imagine your grandchildren seeing that picture. In the European Union, many of the most inhumane conditions we allow are already illegal or—like the sow stalls into which pregnant pigs are often crammed in the United States—will be illegal soon.

## THE INSTITUTIONALIZED AND ISOLATED ELDERLY

Nearly 2 million of America's elderly are warehoused in nursing homes, 15 out of sight and, to some extent, out of mind. Some 10,000 for-profit facilities have arisen across the country in recent decades to hold them. Other elderly Americans may live independently, but often they are isolated and cut off from their families. (The United States is not alone among advanced democracies in this. Consider the heat wave that hit France in 2003: While many families were enjoying their summer vacations, some 14,000 elderly parents and grandparents were left to perish in the stifling temperatures.) Is this what Western modernity amounts to—societies that feel no filial obligations to their inconvenient elders?

Sometimes we can learn from societies much poorer than ours. My English 16 mother spent the last 50 years of her life in Ghana, where I grew up. In her final years, it was her good fortune not only to have the resources to stay at home, but also to live in a country where doing so was customary. She had family next door who visited her every day, and she was cared for by doctors and nurses who were willing to come to her when she was too ill to come to them. In short, she had the advantages of a society in which older people are treated with respect and concern.

Keeping aging parents and their children closer is a challenge, particularly 17 in a society where almost everybody has a job outside the home (if not across the country). Yet the three signs apply here as well: When we see old people who, despite many living relatives, suffer growing isolation, we know something is wrong. We scarcely try to defend the situation; when we can, we put it out of our minds. Self-interest, if nothing else, should make us hope that our descendants will have worked out a better way.

## THE ENVIRONMENT

Of course, most transgenerational obligations run the other way—from 18 parents to children—and of these the most obvious candidate for opprobrium is our wasteful attitude toward the planet's natural resources and ecology. Look at a satellite picture of Russia, and you'll see a vast expanse of parched wasteland where decades earlier was a lush and verdant landscape. That's the Republic of Kalmykia, home to what was recognized in the 1990s as Europe's first man-made desert. Desertification, which is primarily the result of destructive land-management practices, threatens a third of the Earth's surface; tens of thousands of Chinese villages have been overrun by sand drifts in the past few decades.

It's not as though we're unaware of what we're doing to the planet: We 19 know the harm done by deforestation, wetland destruction, pollution, overfishing, greenhouse gas emissions—the whole litany. Our descendants, who will

inherit this devastated Earth, are unlikely to have the luxury of such reckless-
ness. Chances are, they won't be able to avert their eyes, even if they want to.

20      Let's not stop there, though. We will all have our own suspicions about
which practices will someday prompt people to ask, in dismay: What were
they thinking?

21      Even when we don't have a good answer, we'll be better off for anticipating the question.

---

Source: From *The Washington Post,* September 26, 2010. Reprinted by permission of the author.

## QUESTIONS FOR READING

1. On what basis are current practices likely to be repudiated by future Americans? What three signs mark a practice for future condemnation?

2. How do the three signs suggest that our prison system is likely to be condemned?

3. What are the problems with our industrial meat production?

4. What in our work situations contributes to the isolation of the elderly? What happened to many older people in France in 2003?

5. How will the next generation have to react to the environment?

## QUESTIONS FOR REASONING AND ANALYSIS

6. What is Appiah's claim? (You will need a complex statement that combines both a general idea and specific practices.)

7. How do Appiah's four practices illustrate his idea of the three warning signs?

8. What else does the author provide to defend his choice of the specific four practices?

9. Appiah is making some devastating judgments of people past and present. How would you describe his tone? How does his tone help him keep readers from feeling attacked or judged?

## QUESTIONS FOR REFLECTION AND WRITING

10. Has Appiah convinced you that the future will judge the four practices he discusses? Why or why not?

11. Did any of the four practices chosen by the author surprise you? If so, which one(s)? Why?

12. If you had been asked to select four current practices for condemnation, would you have included any of Appiah's? Why or why not? What other(s) would have been on your list? Why?

# Understanding Literature

The same process of reading nonfiction can be used to understand literature—fiction, poetry, and drama. You still need to read what is on the page, looking up unfamiliar words and tracking down references you don't understand. You still need to examine the context, to think about who is writing to whom, under what circumstances, and in what literary format. And, to respond fully to the words, you need to analyze the writer's techniques for developing ideas and expressing attitudes.

Although it seems logical that the reading process should be much the same regardless of the work, not all readers of literature are willing to accept that logic. Some readers want a work of literature to mean whatever they think it means. But what happened to the writer's desire to communicate? If you decide that a Robert Frost poem, for example, should mean whatever you are feeling when you read it, you might as well skip the reading of Frost and just commune with your feelings. Presumably you read Frost to gain some new insight from him, to get beyond just your vision and see something of human experience and emotion from a new vantage point.

Other readers of literature hesitate over the concept of *literary analysis*, or at least over the word *analysis*. These readers complain that analysis will "tear the work apart" and "ruin it." If you are inclined to share this attitude, stop for a minute and think about the last sports event you watched. Perhaps a friend explained: "North Carolina is so good at stalling to use up the clock; Duke will have to foul to get the ball and have a chance to tie the game." The game is being analyzed! And that analysis makes the event more fully experienced by those who understand at least some of the elements of basketball.

The analogy is clear. You, too, can be a fan of literature. You can enjoy reading and discussing your reading once you learn to use your active reading and analytic skills to open up a poem or story, and once you sharpen your knowledge of literary terms and concepts so that you can "speak the language" of literary criticism with the same confidence with which you discuss the merits of a full court press.

## GETTING THE FACTS: ACTIVE READING, SUMMARY, AND PARAPHRASE

Let's begin with the following poem by Paul Dunbar. As you read, make marginal notes, circling a phrase you fancy, putting a question mark next to a difficult line, underscoring words you need to look up. Note, too, your emotional reactions as you read.

## PROMISE | PAUL LAWRENCE DUNBAR

Born of former slave parents, Dunbar (1872–1906) was educated in Dayton, Ohio. After a first booklet of poems, *Oak and Ivy*, was printed in 1893, several friends helped Dunbar get a second collection, *Majors and Minors,* published in 1895. A copy was given to author and editor William Dean Howells, who reviewed the book favorably, increasing sales and Dunbar's reputation. This led to a national publisher issuing *Lyrics of Lowly Life* in 1896, the collection that secured Dunbar's fame.

> I grew a rose within a garden fair,
> And, tending it with more than loving care,
> I thought how, with the glory of its bloom,
> I should the darkness of my life illume;
> 5   And, watching, ever smiled to see the lusty bud
> Drink freely in the summer sun to tinct its blood.
>
> My rose began to open, and its hue
> Was sweet to me as to it sun and dew;
> I watched it taking on its ruddy flame
> 10   Until the day of perfect blooming came,
> Then hasted I with smiles to find it blushing red—
> Too late! Some thoughtless child had plucked my rose and fled!

*[Handwritten marginal notes: "Double start"; "life blooming"; "illuminate life"; "symbol of hope."; "nature"; "someone took his freedom or opportunity his life"]*

"Promise" should not have been especially difficult to read, although you may have paused a moment over "illume" before connecting it to "illuminate," and you may have to check the dictionary for a definition of "tinct." Test your knowledge of content by listing all the facts of the poem. Pay attention to the poem's basic situation. Who is speaking? What is happening, or what thoughts is the speaker sharing? In this poem, the "I" is not further identified, so you will have to refer to him or her as the "speaker." You should not call the speaker "Dunbar," however, because you do not know if Dunbar ever grew a rose.

In "Promise" the speaker is describing an event that has taken place. The speaker grew a rose, tended to it with care, and watched it begin to bloom. Then, when the rose was in full bloom, some child picked the rose and took it away. The situation is fairly simple, isn't it? Too simple, unfortunately, for some readers who decide that the speaker never grew a rose at all. But when anyone writes, "I grew a rose within a garden fair," it is wise to assume that the writer means just that. People do grow roses, most often in gardens, and then the gardens are made "fair" or beautiful by the flowers growing there. Read first for the facts; try not to jump too quickly to broad generalizations.

As with nonfiction, one of the best ways to make certain you have understood a literary work is to write a summary or paraphrase. Since a summary condenses, you are most likely to write a summary of a story, novel, or play, whereas a paraphrase is usually reserved for poems or complex short passages. When you paraphrase a difficult poem, you are likely to end up with more words than in the original because your purpose is to turn cryptic lines into more ordinary sentences. For example, Dunbar's "Then hasted I with smiles" can be paraphrased to read: "Then, full of smiles, I hurried."

When summarizing a literary work, remember to use your own words, draw no conclusions, giving only the facts, but focus your summary on the key events in the story. (Of course the selecting you do to write a summary represents preliminary analysis; you are making some choices about what is important in the work.) Read the following short story by Kate Chopin and then write your own summary. Finally, compare yours to the summary that follows the story.

## THE STORY OF AN HOUR | KATE CHOPIN

Now recognized as an important voice from nineteenth-century America, Kate Chopin (1851–1904) enjoyed popularity for her short stories from 1890 to 1900 and then condemnation and neglect for sixty years. She saw two collections of stories published—*Bayou Folk* in 1984 and *A Night in Acadie* in 1897—before losing popularity and critical acclaim with the publication of her short novel *The Awakening* in 1899, the story of a woman struggling to free herself from years of repression and subservience.

1  Knowing that Mrs. Mallard was afflicted with a heart trouble, great care was taken to break to her as gently as possible the news of her husband's death.

2  It was her sister Josephine who told her, in broken sentences; veiled hints that revealed in half concealing. Her husband's friend Richards was there, too, near her. It was he who had been in the newspaper office when intelligence of the railroad disaster was received, with Brently Mallard's name leading the list of "killed." He had only taken the time to assure himself of its truth by a second telegram, and had hastened to forestall any less careful, less tender friend in bearing the sad message.

3  She did not hear the story as many women have heard the same, with a paralyzed inability to accept its significance. She wept at once, with sudden, wild abandonment, in her sister's arms. When the storm of grief had spent itself she went away to her room alone. She would have no one follow her.

4  There stood, facing the open window, a comfortable, roomy armchair. Into this she sank, pressed down by a physical exhaustion that haunted her body and seemed to reach into her soul.

5  She could see in the open square before her house the tops of trees that were all aquiver with the new spring life. The delicious breath of rain was in the

air. In the street below a peddler was crying his wares. The notes of a distant song which some one was singing reached her faintly, and countless sparrows were twittering in the eaves.

6    There were patches of blue sky showing here and there through the clouds that had met and piled one above the other in the west facing her window.

7    She sat with her head thrown back upon the cushion of the chair, quite motionless, except when a sob came up into her throat and shook her, as a child who has cried itself to sleep continues to sob in its dreams.

8    She was young, with a fair, calm face, whose lines bespoke repression and even a certain strength. But now there was a dull stare in her eyes, whose gaze was fixed away off yonder on one of those patches of blue sky. It was not a glance of reflection, but rather indicated a suspension of intelligent thought.

9    There was something coming to her and she was waiting for it, fearfully. What was it? She did not know; it was too subtle and elusive to name. But she felt it, creeping out of the sky, reaching toward her through the sounds, the scents, the color that filled the air.

10   Now her bosom rose and fell tumultuously. She was beginning to recognize this thing that was approaching to possess her, and she was striving to beat it back with her will—as powerless as her two white slender hands would have been.

11   When she abandoned herself a little whispered word escaped her slightly parted lips. She said it over and over under her breath: "free, free, free!" The vacant stare and the look of terror that had followed it went from her eyes. They stayed keen and bright. Her pulses beat fast, and the coursing blood warmed and relaxed every inch of her body.

12   She did not stop to ask if it were or were not a monstrous joy that held her. A clear and exalted perception enabled her to dismiss the suggestion as trivial.

13   She knew that she would weep again when she saw the kind, tender hands folded in death; the face that had never looked save with love upon her, fixed and gray and dead. But she saw beyond that bitter moment a long procession of years to come that would belong to her absolutely. And she opened and spread her arms out to them in welcome.

14   There would be no one to live for her during those coming years; she would live for herself. There would be no powerful will bending hers in that blind persistence with which men and women believe they have a right to impose a private will upon a fellow-creature. A kind intention or a cruel intention made the act seem no less a crime as she looked upon it in that brief moment of illumination.

15   And yet she had loved him—sometimes. Often she had not. What did it matter! What could love, the unsolved mystery, count for in face of this possession of self-assertion which she suddenly recognized as the strongest impulse of her being!

16   "Free! Body and soul free!" she kept whispering.

17   Josephine was kneeling before the closed door with her lips to the keyhole, imploring for admission. "Louise, open the door! I beg; open the

door—you will make yourself ill. What are you doing, Louise? For heaven's sake open the door."

"Go away. I am not making myself ill." No; she was drinking in a very elixir 18 *freedom* of life through that open window.

Her fancy was running riot along those days ahead of her. Spring days, and 19 summer days, and all sorts of days that would be her own. She breathed a quick prayer that life might be long. It was only yesterday she had thought with a shudder that life might be long.

*grow*  She arose at length and opened the door to her sister's importunities. 20 There was a feverish triumph in her eyes, and she carried herself unwittingly like a goddess of Victory. She clasped her sister's waist, and together they descended the stairs. Richards stood waiting for them at the bottom.

Someone was opening the front door with a latchkey. It was Brently 21 Mallard who entered, a little travel-stained, composedly carrying his grip-sack and umbrella. He had been far from the scene of accident, and did not even know there had been one. He stood amazed at Josephine's piercing cry; at Richards' quick motion to screen him from the view of his wife.

But Richards was too late.                                                      22

When the doctors came they said she had died of heart disease—of joy 23 that kills.

---

## Summary of "The Story of an Hour"

> Mrs. Mallard's sister Josephine and her husband's friend Richards come to tell her that her husband has been listed as killed in a train accident. They try to be gentle because Mrs. Mallard has a heart condition. She cries and then goes to her bedroom alone. She sits in an armchair and gazes out the open window. Her dull stare gives way to some new thought that she cannot push away. She whispers the word "free" and thinks about a future directed by herself. Responding to Josephine's pleas, she leaves the bedroom and sees Richards below—and then Mr. Mallard letting himself in the front door. Mrs. Mallard dies, and the doctors who attend her say she died of heart disease—of "joy that kills."

Note that the summary is written in the present tense. Brevity is achieved by leaving out dialogue and the details of what Mrs. Mallard sees outside her window and the future life she imagines. Observe that the summary is not the same as the original story. The drama and emotion are missing, details that help us to understand the story's ending.

Now for a paraphrase. Read the following sonnet by Shakespeare, looking up unfamiliar words and making notes. Remember to read to the end of a unit of thought, not just to the end of a line. Some sentences continue through several lines; if you pause before you reach punctuation, you will be confused. Write your own paraphrase, not looking ahead in the text, and then compare yours with the one that follows the poem.

# SONNET 116 | WILLIAM SHAKESPEARE

Surely the best-known name in literature, William Shakespeare (1564–1616) is famous as both a dramatist and a poet. Rural Warwickshire and the market town of Stratford-on-Avon, where he grew up, showed him many of the character types who were to enliven his plays, as did the bustling life of a young actor in London. Apparently his sonnets were intended to be circulated only among his friends, but they were published nonetheless in 1609. His thirty-seven plays were first published together in 1623. Shakespeare's 154 sonnets vary, some focusing on separation and world-weariness, others on the endurance of love.

> Let me not to the marriage of true minds
> Admit impediments. Love is not love
> Which alters when it alteration finds,
> Or bends with the remover to remove.
> 5   O, no! it is an ever-fixed mark
> That looks on tempests and is never shaken;
> It is the star to every wand'ring bark,
> Whose worth's unknown, although his height be taken.
> Love's not Time's fool, though rosy lips and cheeks
> 10  Within his bending sickle's compass come;
> Love alters not with his brief hours and weeks,
> But bears it out even to the edge of doom.
>     If this be error and upon me proved,
>     I never writ, nor no man ever loved.

## Paraphrase of "Sonnet 116"

I cannot accept barriers to the union of steadfast spirits. We cannot call love love if it changes because it discovers change or if it disappears during absence. On the contrary, love is a steady guide that, in spite of difficulties, remains unwavering. Love can define the inherent value in all who lack self-knowledge, though superficially they know who they are. Love does not lessen with time, though signs of physical beauty may fade. Love endures, changeless, eternally. If anyone can show me to be wrong in this position, I am no writer and no man can be said to have loved.

We have examined the facts of a literary work, what we can call the internal situation. But, as we noted in Chapter 2, there is also the external situation or context of any piece of writing. For many literary works, the context is not as essential to understanding as it is with nonfiction. You can read "The Story of an Hour," for instance, without knowing much about Kate Chopin, or the circumstances in which she wrote the story, although such information would enrich your reading experience. There is a body of information, however, that is important: the external literary situation. Readers should take note of these details before they begin to read:

- First, don't make the mistake of calling every work a "story." Make clear distinctions among stories, novels, plays, and poems.
- Poems can be further divided into narrative, dramatic, and lyric poems.
- A *narrative poem*, such as Homer's *The Iliad,* tells a story in verse. A *dramatic poem* records the speech of at least one character.
- A poem in which only one figure speaks—but clearly addresses words to someone who is present in a particular situation—is called a *dramatic monologue.*
- *Lyric poems*, Dunbar's "Promise" for example, may place the speaker in a situation or may express a thought or feeling with few, if any, situational details, but lyric poems have in common the convention that we as readers are listening in on someone's thoughts, not listening to words directed to a second, created figure. These distinctions make us aware of how the words of the poem are coming to us. Are we hearing a storyteller or someone speaking? Or, are we overhearing someone's thoughts?

> **REMEMBER:** Active reading includes looking over a work first and predicting what will come next. Do not just start reading words without first understanding what kind of work you are about to read.

Lyric poems can be further divided into many subcategories or types. Most instructors will expect you to be able to recognize some of these types. You should be able to distinguish between a poem in *free verse* (no prevailing metrical pattern) and one in *blank verse* (continuous unrhymed lines of iambic pentameter). (*Note:* A metrical line will contain a particular number—pentameter is five—of one kind of metrical "foot." The iambic foot consists of one unstressed syllable followed by one stressed syllable.) You should also be able to tell if a poem is written in some type of *stanza* form (repeated units with the same number of lines, same metrical pattern, and same rhyme scheme), or if it is a *sonnet* (always fourteen lines of iambic pentameter with one of two complex rhyme schemes labeled either "English" or "Italian"). You want to make it a habit to observe these external elements before you read. To sharpen your observation, complete the following exercise.

## EXERCISE: Observing Literary Types and Using Literary Terms

1. After surveying this appendix, make a list of all the works of literature by primary type: short story, poem, play.

2. For each work on your list, add two more pieces of information: whether the author is American or British, and in what century the work was written. Why should you be aware of the writer's dates and nationality as you read?
3. Further divide the poems into narrative, dramatic, or lyric.
4. List as many of the details of type or form as you can for each poem. For example, if the poem is written in stanzas, describe the stanza form used: the number of lines, the meter, the rhyme scheme. If the poem is a sonnet, determine the rhyme scheme. (*Note:* Rhyme scheme is indicated by using letters, assigning *a* to the first sound and using a new letter for each new sound. Thus, if two consecutive lines rhyme, the scheme is *aa, bb, cc, dd,* and so on.)

# SEEING CONNECTIONS: ANALYSIS

Although we read first for the facts and an initial emotional response, we do not stop there, because as humans we seek meaning. Surely there is more to "The Story of an Hour" than the summary suggests; emotionally we know this to be true. As with nonfiction, one of the best places to start analysis is with a work's organization or structure. Lyric poems will be shaped by many of the same structures found in essays: chronological, spatial, general to particular, particular to general, a list of particulars with an unstated general point, and so forth. In "Promise," Dunbar gives one illustration, recounted chronologically, to make a point that is left unstated. "Sonnet 116" contains a list of characteristics of love underscored in the conclusion by the speaker's conviction that he is right.

## Analysis of Narrative Structure

In stories (and plays and narrative poems) we are given a series of events, in time sequence, involving one or more characters. In some stories, episodes are only loosely connected but are unified around a central character (Mark Twain's *Adventures of Huckleberry Finn,* for example). Most stories present events that are at least to some extent related causally; that is, action A by the main character leads to event B, which requires action C by the main character. This kind of plot structure can be diagrammed, as in Figure 1.

Figure 1 introduces some terms and concepts useful in analyzing and discussing narratives. The story's *exposition* refers to the background details

**FIGURE 1** Plot Structure

needed to get the story started, including the time and place of the story and relationships of the characters. In "The Story of an Hour," a key detail of exposition is the fact that Mrs. Mallard has a heart condition. The *complication* refers to an event: Something happens to produce tension or *conflict*. In Chopin's story, the announcement of Mr. Mallard's death seems to be an immediate complication. But, after her initial tears, we do not see Mrs. Mallard dealing with this complication in the "typical" way. Instead, when she sits in her bedroom, she experiences a *conflict*. She struggles within herself. Why does she struggle? Why not just embrace the new idea that comes to her?

Although some stories present one major complication leading to a *climax* of decision or insight for the main character, many actually repeat the pattern, presenting several complications—each with an attempted resolution that causes yet another complication—until we reach the high point of tension, the *climax*. The action—or inaction—of the climactic moment leads to the story's *resolution* and ending.

These terms are helpful in analysis, even though some stories end abruptly, with little apparent resolution. A stark "resolution" is part of the modern writer's view of reality, that life goes on, with problems often remaining unresolved. A character in an unpleasant marriage continues in that marriage, perhaps ruefully, perhaps a bit wiser but no happier and unable to act to change the situation. What is the climactic moment in "The Story of an Hour"? How is the story resolved? What is significant about the doctors' explanation at the end? Are they correct?

## Analysis of Character

An analysis of plot structure suggests to us that Mrs. Mallard is not in conflict over her husband's death. She is in conflict, initially, over her reaction to that death, but she resolves her conflict, only to have Mr. Mallard open the front door. Note the close connection between complication (event) and conflict (what the characters are feeling). Fiction requires both plot and character, events and players in those events. In serious literature the greater emphasis is usually on character, on what we learn about human life through the interplay of character and incident.

As we shift from plot to character, we can enhance our analysis by considering how writers present character. Writers will usually employ several techniques from the following list:

- Descriptive details. (Mrs. Mallard's heart condition. Josephine and Richards worry about her health.)

- Dramatic scenes. (Instead of telling, they show us. Much of "The Story of an Hour" is dialogue. When Mrs. Mallard is in her bedroom alone, we overhear her internal dialogue.)

- Contrast among characters. (Josephine assumes that Mrs. Mallard continues to be the distraught, bereft widow, whereas she is actually embracing a future on her own. Note the contrast between the gentle, kind control of Mr. Mallard in their marriage and the way the control actually feels in his wife's experience of it.)

- Other elements in the work. (Names can be significant, or characters can become associated with significant objects, or details of setting can become symbolic. Note all of the specific details of events outside Mrs. Mallard's window. What, altogether, do they represent?)

Understanding character can be a challenge because we must infer from a few words, gestures, and actions. Looking at all of a writer's options for presenting character will keep us from overlooking important details.

## Analysis of Elements of Style and Tone

All the elements, discussed in Chapter 2, that shape a writer's style and create tone can be found in literary works as well and need to be considered as part of your analysis. We can begin with Chopin's title. How much can happen in one hour? Well, the person we thought was dead is alive, and the "widow" ends up dead, quite a reversal of fortunes in such a short time. This situation is filled with irony. The doctors' misunderstanding of the cause of Mrs. Mallard's shock at the sight of her husband also adds irony to the story. The doctors express society's conventional thinking: Dear Mrs. Mallard is so happy that her husband is really alive that her heart cannot stand it. But is that really what shocks her into an early death?

Shakespeare's "Sonnet 116" develops the speaker's ideas about love through a series of metaphors. The rose in Dunbar's "Promise" is not a metaphor, though, because it is not part of a comparison. Yet, as we read the poem we sense that it is about something more serious than the nurturing and then stealing of one flower, no matter how beautiful. The poem's title gives us a clue that the rose stands for something more than itself; it is a symbol. Traditionally the red rose is a symbol of love. To tie the poem together, we will have to see how the title, the usual symbolic value of the rose, and specifics of the poem connect.

# DRAWING CONCLUSIONS: INTERPRETATION

We have studied the facts of several works and analyzed their structures and other key elements. To reach some conclusions and shape our thinking into a coherent whole is to offer an interpretation of the work. At this point, readers can be expected to disagree somewhat, but if we have all read carefully and applied our knowledge of literature, differences should, most of the time, be ones of focus and emphasis. Presumably no one is prepared to argue that "Promise" is about pink elephants or "The Story of an Hour" about the Queen of England. Neither work contains any facts to support those conclusions.

What conclusions can we reach about "Promise"? A beautiful flower has been nurtured into bloom by a speaker who expects it to brighten his or her life. The title lets us know that the rose represents great promise. Has a rival stolen the speaker's loved one, represented symbolically by the rose? A thoughtless child would not be an appropriate rival for an adult speaker. In the context of this poem, the rose represents, more generally, something that the speaker cherishes in anticipation of the pleasure it will bring, only to lose that something.

What conclusions have you reached about "The Story of an Hour"? What is the real irony of the story? When Mr. Mallard, very much alive, opens the door to his home, what door does he shut for Mrs. Mallard?

## WRITING ABOUT LITERATURE

When you are assigned a literary essay, you will usually be asked to write either an explication or an analysis. An *explication* presents a reading of a complex poem. It will combine paraphrase and explanation to clarify the poem's meaning. A *literary analysis* can take many forms. You may be asked to analyze one element in a work: character conflict, the use of setting, the tone of a poem. Or you could be asked to contrast two works. Usually an analytic assignment requires you to connect analysis to interpretation, for we analyze the parts to better understand the whole. If you are asked to examine the metaphors in a Shakespeare sonnet, for example, you will want to show how understanding the metaphors contributes to an understanding of the entire poem. In short, literary analysis is much the same as a style analysis of an essay. Thus the guidelines for writing about style discussed in Chapter 2 apply here as well.* Successful analyses are based on accurate reading, reflection on the work's emotional impact, and the use of details from the work to support conclusions.

Literary analyses can also incorporate material beyond the particular work. We can analyze a work in the light of biographical information or from a particular political ideology. Or we can study the social-cultural context of the work, or relate it to a literary tradition. These are only a few of the many approaches to the study of literature, and they depend on the application of knowledge outside the work itself. For undergraduates, topics based on these approaches usually require research. The student research essay at the end of the Appendix is a literary analysis. Alan examines Faulkner's *Intruder in the Dust* as an initiation novel. He connects his analysis to works by Hawthorne and Arthur Miller. What is taken from his research is documented and helps develop and support his own conclusions about the story.

To practice close reading, analysis, and interpretation of literature, read the following works. Use the questions after each work to aid your response.

---

* Remember: The guidelines for referring to authors, titles, and direct quotations—presented in Chapter 1—also apply.

## TO HIS COY MISTRESS | ANDREW MARVELL

One of the last poets of the English Renaissance, Andrew Marvell (1621–1678) graduated from Cambridge University, spent much of his young life as a tutor, and was elected to Parliament in 1659. He continued in public service until his death. Most of his best-loved lyric poems come from his years as a tutor. "To His Coy Mistress" was published in 1681.

Had we but world enough, and time,
This coyness, lady, were no crime.
We would sit down, and think which way
To walk, and pass our long love's day.
5   Thou by the Indian Ganges' side
Shouldst rubies find; I by the tide
Of Humber would complain. I would
Love you ten years before the Flood,
And you should, if you please, refuse
10   Till the conversion of the Jews.
My vegetable° love should grow     *slowly vegetative*
Vaster than empires, and more slow;
An hundred years should go to praise
Thine eyes, and on thy forehead gaze;
15   Two hundred to adore each breast,
But thirty thousand to the rest;
An age at least to every part,
And the last age should show your heart.
For, lady, you deserve this state,
Nor would I love at lower rate.
20     But at my back I always hear
Time's wingèd chariot hurrying near;
And yonder all before us lie
Deserts of vast eternity.
25   Thy beauty shall no more be found,
Nor in thy marble vault shall sound
My echoing song; then worms shall try
That long preserved virginity,
And your quaint honor turn to dust,
30   And into ashes all my lust.
The grave's a fine and private place,
But none, I think, do there embrace.
   Now therefore, while the youthful hue
Sits on thy skin like morning dew,
35   And while thy willing soul transpires
At every pore with instant fires,
Now let us sport us while we may,
And now, like amorous birds of prey,
Rather at once our time devour

Than languish in his slow-chapped power.                                                40
Let us roll all our strength and all
Our sweetness up into one ball,
And tear our pleasures with rough strife
Thorough° the iron gates of life.                        *through*                       45
Thus, though we cannot make our sun
Stand still, yet we will make him run.

---

QUESTIONS FOR READING, REASONING, AND REFLECTION

1. Describe the poem's external form.
2. How are the words coming to us? That is, is this a narrative, dramatic, or lyric poem?
3. Summarize the speaker's argument, using the structures *if, but,* and *therefore.*
4. What figure of speech do we find throughout the first verse paragraph? What is its effect on the speaker's tone?
5. Find examples of irony and understatement in the second verse paragraph.
6. How does the tone shift in the second section?
7. Explain the personification in line 22.
8. Explain the metaphors in lines 30 and 45.
9. What is the paradox of the last two lines? How can it be explained?
10. What is the idea of this poem? What does the writer want us to reflect on?

# THE PASSIONATE SHEPHERD TO HIS LOVE | CHRISTOPHER MARLOWE

Cambridge graduate, Renaissance dramatist second only to Shakespeare, Christopher Marlowe (1564–1593) may be best known for this lyric poem. Not only is it widely anthologized, it has also spawned a number of responses by such significant writers as the seventeenth-century poet John Donne and the twentieth-century humorous poet Ogden Nash. For the Renaissance period the shepherd was a standard figure of the lover.

Come live with me and be my love,
And we will all the pleasures prove
That valleys, groves, hills, and fields,
Woods, or steepy mountain yields.

And we will sit upon the rocks,                                                          5
Seeing the shepherds feed their flocks,
By shallow rivers to whose falls
Melodious birds sing madrigals.

And I will make thee beds of roses
10    And a thousand fragrant posies,
A cap of flowers, and a kirtle
Embroidered all with leaves of myrtle;

A gown made of the finest wool
Which from our pretty lambs we pull;
15    Fair lined slippers for the cold,
With buckles of the purest gold;

A belt of straw and ivy buds,
With coral clasps and amber studs:
And if these pleasures may thee move,
20    Come live with me, and be my love.

The shepherds' swains shall dance and sing
For thy delight each May morning:
If these delights thy mind may move,
Then live with me and be my love.

---

## QUESTIONS FOR READING, REASONING, AND REFLECTION

1. Describe the poem's external structure.
2. What is the speaker's subject? What does he want to accomplish?
3. Summarize his "argument." How does he seek to convince his love?
4. What do the details of his argument have in common—that is, what kind of world or life does the speaker describe? Is there anything missing from the shepherd's world?
5. Would you like to be courted in this way? Would you say yes to the shepherd? If not, why?

## THE NYMPH'S REPLY TO THE SHEPHERD | SIR WALTER RALEIGH

The renowned Elizabethan courtier, Sir Walter Raleigh (1552–1618) led a varied life as both a favorite of Queen Elizabeth and out of favor at court, as a colonizer and writer, and as one of many to be imprisoned in the Tower of London. In the following poem, Raleigh offers a response to Marlowe, using the nymph as the voice of the female lover.

If all the world and love were young,
And truth in every shepherd's tongue,
These pretty pleasures might me move
To live with thee and be thy love.

5    Time drives the flocks from field to fold
When rivers rage and rocks grow cold,

And Philomel becometh dumb;
The rest complains of cares to come.

The flowers do fade, and wanton fields
To wayward winter reckoning yields;                                    10
A honey tongue, a heart of gall,
Is fancy's spring, but sorrow's fall.

Thy gowns, thy shoes, thy beds of roses,
Thy cap, thy kirtle, and thy posies
Soon break, soon wither, soon forgotten,—                              15
In folly ripe, in reason rotten.

Thy belt of straw and ivy buds,
Thy coral clasps and amber studs,
All these in me no means can move
To come to thee and be thy love.                                       20

But could youth last and love still breed,
Had joys no date nor age no need,
Then these delights my mind might move
To live with thee and be thy love.

---

QUESTIONS FOR READING, REASONING, AND REFLECTION

1.  Describe the poem's external structure.
2.  What is the context of the poem, the reason the speaker offers her words?
3.  Analyze the speaker's argument, using *if* and *but* as your basic structure—and then the concluding, qualifying *but.*
4.  What evidence does the speaker provide to support her argument?
5.  Who has the more convincing argument: Marlowe's shepherd or Raleigh's nymph? Why?

## IS MY TEAM PLOUGHING | A. E. HOUSMAN

British poet A. E. Housman (1859–1936) was a classicist, first a professor of Latin at University College, London, and then at the University of Cambridge. He spent the rest of his life at Trinity College, Cambridge. He is best known for his first volume of poetry, *A Shropshire Lad* (1896), a collection of crystal clear and deceptively simple verses that give expression to a world that has been lost—perhaps the innocence of youth.

"Is my team ploughing,
    That I was used to drive

And hear the harness jingle
    When I was man alive?"

5    Ay, the horses trample,
    The harness jingles now:
No change though you lie under
    The land you used to plough.

"Is football playing
10    Along the river shore,
With lads to chase the leather,
    Now I stand up no more?"

Ay, the ball is flying,
    The lads play heart and soul;
15    The goal stands up, the keeper
    Stands up to keep the goal.

"Is my girl happy,
    That I thought hard to leave,
And has she tired of weeping
20    As she lies down at eve?"

Ay, she lies down lightly,
    She lies not down to weep:
Your girl is well contented.
    Be still, my lad, and sleep.

25    "Is my friend hearty,
    Now I am thin and pine,
And has he found to sleep in
    A better bed than mine?"

Yes, lad, I lie easy,
30    I lie as lads would choose;
I cheer a dead man's sweetheart,
    Never ask me whose.

---

## QUESTIONS FOR READING, REASONING, AND REFLECTION

1. Classify the poem according to its external structure.
2. Is this a narrative, dramatic, or lyric poem? How are we to read the words coming to us?
3. What is the relationship between the two speakers? What has happened to the first speaker? What has changed in the life of the second speaker?
4. What ideas are suggested by the poem? What does Housman want us to take from his poem?

## TAXI | AMY LOWELL

Educated at private schools and widely traveled, American Amy Lowell (1874–1925) was both a poet and a critic. Lowell frequently read her poetry and lectured on poetic techniques, defending her verse and that of other modern poets.

> When I go away from you
> The world beats dead
> Like a slackened drum.
> I call out for you against the jutted stars
> And shout into the ridges of the wind.                          5
> Streets coming fast,
> One after the other,
> Wedge you away from me,
> And the lamps of the city prick my eyes
> So that I can no longer see your face.                          10
> Why should I leave you,
> To wound myself upon the sharp edges of the night?

### QUESTIONS FOR READING, REASONING, AND REFLECTION

1. Classify the poem according to its external structure.
2. Is this a narrative, dramatic, or lyric poem?
3. Explain the simile in the opening three lines and the metaphor in the last line of the poem.
4. What is the poem's subject? What seems to be the situation in which we find the speaker?
5. How would you describe the tone of the poem? How do the details and the emotional impact of the metaphors help to create tone?
6. What is the poem's meaning or theme? In other words, what does the poet want us to understand from reading her poem?

## THE ONES WHO WALK AWAY FROM OMELAS | URSULA K. LE GUIN

A graduate of Radcliffe College and Columbia University, Ursula K. Le Guin is the author of more than twenty novels and juvenile books, several volumes of poetry, and numerous stories and essays published in science fiction, scholarly, and popular journals. Her fiction stretches the categories of science fiction or fantasy and challenges a reader's moral understanding. First published in 1973, the following story, according to Le Guin, was inspired by a passage in William James's "The Moral Philosopher and the Moral Life" in which he asserts that we could not tolerate a situation in which the happiness of many people was purchased by the "lonely torment" of one "lost soul."

1    With a clamor of bells that set the swallows soaring, the Festival of Summer came to the city Omelas, bright-towered by the sea. The rigging of the boats in harbor sparkled with flags. In the streets between houses with red roofs and painted walls, between the old moss-grown gardens and under avenues of trees, past great parks and public buildings, processions moved. Some were decorous: old people in long stiff robes of mauve and gray, grave master workmen, quiet, merry women carrying their babies and chatting as they walked. In other streets the music beat faster, a shimmering of gong and tambourine, and the people went dancing, the procession was a dance. Children dodged in and out, their high calls rising like the swallows' crossing flights over the music and the singing. All the processions wound towards the north side of the city, where on the great water-meadow called the Green Fields boys and girls, naked in the bright air, with mudstained feet and ankles and long, lithe arms, exercised their restive horses before the race. The horses wore no gear at all but a halter without bit. Their manes were braided with streamers of silver, gold, and green. They flared their nostrils and pranced and boasted to one another; they were vastly excited, the horse being the only animal who has adopted our ceremonies as his own. Far off to the north and west the mountains stood up half circling Omelas on her bay. The air of morning was so clear that the snow still crowning the Eighteen Peaks burned with white-gold fire across the miles of sunlit air, under the dark blue of the sky. There was just enough wind to make the banners that marked the racecourse snap and flutter now and then. In the silence of the broad green meadows one could hear the music winding through the city streets, farther and nearer and ever approaching, a cheerful faint sweetness of the air that from time to time trembled and gathered together and broke out into the great joyous clanging of the bells.

2    Joyous! How is one to tell about joy? How describe the citizens of Omelas?

3    They were not simple folk, you see, though they were happy. But we do not say the words of cheer much any more. All smiles have become archaic. Given a description such as this one tends to make certain assumptions. Given a description such as this one tends to look next for the King, mounted on a splendid stallion and surrounded by his noble knights, or perhaps in a golden litter borne by great-muscled slaves. But there was no king. They did not use swords, or keep slaves. They were not barbarians. I do not know the rules and laws of their society, but I suspect that they were singularly few. As they did without monarchy and slavery, so they also got on without the stock exchange, the advertisement, the secret police, and the bomb. Yet I repeat that these were not simple folk, not dulcet shepherds, noble savages, bland utopians. They were not less complex than us. The trouble is that we have a bad habit, encouraged by pedants and sophisticates, of considering happiness as something rather stupid. Only pain is intellectual, only evil interesting. This is the treason of the artist: a refusal to admit the banality of evil and the terrible boredom of pain. If you can't lick 'em, join 'em. If it hurts, repeat it. But to praise despair is to condemn delight, to embrace violence is to lose hold of everything else. We have almost lost hold, we can no longer describe a happy

man, nor make any celebration of joy. How can I tell you about the people of Omelas? They were not naïve and happy children—though their children were, in fact, happy. They were mature, intelligent, passionate adults whose lives were not wretched. O miracle! But I wish I could describe it better. I wish I could convince you. Omelas sounds in my words like a city in a fairy tale, long ago and far away, once upon a time. Perhaps it would be best if you imagined it as your own fancy bids, assuming it will rise to the occasion, for certainly I cannot suit you all. For instance, how about technology? I think that there would be no cars or helicopters in and above the streets; this follows from the fact that the people of Omelas are happy people. Happiness is based on a just discrimination of what is necessary, what is neither necessary nor destructive, and what is destructive. In the middle category, however—that of the unnecessary but undestructive, that of comfort, luxury, exuberance, etc.—they could perfectly well have central heating, subway trains, washing machines, and all kinds of marvelous devises not yet invented here, floating light-sources, fuelless power, a cure for the common cold. Or they could have none of that: it doesn't matter. As you like it. I incline to think that people from towns up and down the coast have been coming in to Omelas during the last days before the Festival on very fast trains and double-decked trams, and that the train station of Omelas is actually the handsomest building in town, though plainer than the magnificent Farmers' Market. But even granted trains, I fear that Omelas so far strikes some of you as goody-goody. Smiles, bells, parades, horses, bleh. If so, please add an orgy. If an orgy would help, don't hesitate. Let us not, however, have temples from which issue beautiful nude priests and priestesses already half in ecstasy and ready to copulate with any man or woman, lover or stranger, who desires union with the deep godhead of the blood, although that was my first idea. But really it would be better not to have any temples in Omelas—at least, not manned temples. Religion yes, clergy no. Surely the beautiful nudes can just wander about, offering themselves like divine soufflés to the hunger of the needy and the rapture of the flesh. Let them join the processions. Let tambourines be struck above the copulations, and the glory of desire be proclaimed upon the gongs, and (a not unimportant point) let the offspring of these delightful rituals be beloved and looked after by all. One thing I know there is none of in Omelas is guilt. But what else should there be? I thought that first there were no drugs, but that is puritanical. For those who like it, the faint insistent sweetness of *drooz* may perfume the ways of the city, *drooz* which first brings a great lightness and brilliance to the mind and limbs, and then after some hours a dreamy languor, and wonderful visions at last of the very arcana and inmost secrets of the Universe, as well as exciting the pleasure of sex beyond all belief; and it is not habit-forming. For more modest tastes I think there ought to be beer. What else, what else belongs in the joyous city? The sense of victory, surely, the celebration of courage. But as we did without clergy, let us do without soldiers. The joy built upon successful slaughter is not the right kind of joy; it will not do; it is fearful and it is trivial. A boundless and generous contentment, a magnanimous triumph felt not against some outer enemy but in communion with the finest and fairest in the souls of all men everywhere and the splendor of the world's summer; this is what swells the hearts of the people of Omelas, and the victory they celebrate is that of life. I really don't think many of them need to take *drooz*.

4     Most of the processions have reached the Green Fields by now. A marvelous smell of cooking goes forth from the red and blue tents of the provisioners. The faces of small children are amiably sticky; in the benign grey beard of a man a couple of crumbs of rich pastry are entangled. The youths and girls have mounted their horses and are beginning to group around the starting line of the course. An old woman, small, fat, and laughing, is passing out flowers from a basket, and tall young men wear her flowers in their shining hair. A child of nine or ten sits at the edge of the crowd, alone, playing on a wooden flute. People pause to listen, and they smile, but they do not speak to him, for he never ceases playing and never sees them, his dark eyes wholly rapt in the sweet, thin magic of the tune.

5     He finishes, and slowly lowers his hands holding the wooden flute.

6     As if that little private silence were the signal, all at once a trumpet sounds from the pavilion near the starting line: imperious, melancholy, piercing. The horses rear on their slender legs, and some of them neigh in answer. Soberfaced, the young riders stroke the horses' necks and soothe them, whispering, "Quiet, quiet, there my beauty, my hope." They begin to form in rank along the starting line. The crowds along the racecourse are like a field of grass and flowers in the wind. The Festival of Summer has begun.

7     Do you believe? Do you accept the festival, the city, the joy? No? Then let me describe this one more thing.

8     In a basement under one of the beautiful public buildings of Omelas, or perhaps in the cellar of one of its spacious private homes, there is a room. It has one locked door, and no window. A little light seeps in dustily between cracks in the boards, secondhand from the cobwebbed window somewhere across the cellar. In one corner of the little room a couple of mops, with stiff, clotted, foul-smelling heads, stand near a rusty bucket. The floor is dirt, a little damp to the touch, as cellar dirt usually is. The room is about three paces long and two wide: a mere broom closet or disused tool room. In the room a child is sitting. It could be a boy or a girl. It looks about six, but actually is nearly ten. It is feeble-minded. Perhaps it was born defective, or perhaps it has become imbecile through fear, malnutrition, and neglect. It picks its nose and occasionally fumbles vaguely with its toes or genitals, as it sits hunched in the corner farthest from the bucket and the two mops. It is afraid of the mops. It finds them horrible. It shuts its eyes, but it knows the mops are still standing there; and the door is locked; and nobody will come. The door is always locked; and nobody ever comes, except that sometimes—the child has no understanding of time or interval—sometimes the door rattles terribly and opens, and a person, or several people, are there. One of them may come in and kick the child to make it stand up. The others never come close, but peer in at it with frightened, disgusted eyes. The food bowl and the water jug are hastily filled, the door is locked, the eyes disappear. The people at the

door never say anything, but the child, who has not always lived in the tool room, and can remember sunlight and its mother's voice, sometimes speaks. "I will be good," it says. "Please let me out. I will be good!" They never answer. The child used to scream for help at night, and cry a good deal, but now it only makes a kind of whining, "eh-haa-eh-haa," and it speaks less and less often. It is so thin there are no calves to its legs; its belly protrudes; it lives on a half-bowl of corn meal and grease a day. It is naked. Its buttocks and thighs are a mass of festered sores, as it sits in its own excrement continually.

They all know it is there, all the people of Omelas. Some of them have 9 come to see it, others are content merely to know it is there. They all know that it has to be there. Some of them understand why, and some do not, but they all understand that their happiness, the beauty of their city, the tenderness of their friendships, the health of their children, the wisdom of their scholars, the skill of their makers, even the abundance of their harvest and the kindly weathers of their skies, depend wholly upon this child's abominable misery.

This is usually explained to children when they are between eight and 10 twelve, whenever they seem capable of understanding; and most of those who come to see the child are young people, though often enough an adult comes, or comes back, to see the child. No matter how well the matter has been explained to them, these young spectators are always shocked and sickened at the sight. They feel disgust, which they had thought themselves superior to. They feel anger, outrage, impotence, despite all the explanations. They would like to do something for the child. But there is nothing they can do. If the child were brought up into the sunlight out of that vile place, if it were cleaned and fed and comforted, that would be a good thing, indeed; but if it were done, in that day and hour all the prosperity and beauty and delight of Omelas would wither and be destroyed. Those are the terms. To exchange all the goodness and grace of every life in Omelas for that single, small improvement: to throw away the happiness of thousands for the chance of the happiness of one: that would be to let guilt within the walls indeed.

The terms are strict and absolute; there may not even be a kind word spo- 11 ken to the child.

Often the young people go home in tears, or in a tearless rage, when they 12 have seen the child and faced this terrible paradox. They may brood over it for weeks or years. But as time goes on they begin to realize that even if the child could be released, it would not get much good of its freedom: a little vague pleasure of warmth and food, no doubt, but little more. It is too degraded and imbecile to know any real joy. It has been afraid too long ever to be free of fear. Its habits are too uncouth for it to respond to humane treatment. Indeed, after so long it would probably be wretched without walls about it to protect it, and darkness for its eyes, and its own excrement to sit in. Their tears at the bitter injustice dry when they begin to perceive the terrible justice of reality, and to accept it. Yet it is their tears and anger, the trying of their generosity and the acceptance of their helplessness, which are perhaps the true source of the splendor of their lives. Theirs is no vapid, irresponsible happiness. They know that they, like the child, are not free. They know compassion. It is the existence of the child, and their knowledge of its existence, that makes possible the nobility of their architecture, the poignancy of their music, the profundity of their science. It is because of the child that they are so gentle with children. They know that if the wretched one were not there snivelling in the dark, the other one, the flute-player, could make no joyful music as the young riders line up in their beauty for the race in the sunlight of the first morning of summer.

13    Now do you believe in them? Are they not more credible? But there is one more thing to tell, and this is quite incredible.

14    At times one of the adolescent girls or boys who go to see the child, does not go home to weep or rage, does not, in fact, go home at all. Sometimes also a man or woman much older falls silent for a day or two, and then leaves home. These people go out into the street, and walk down the street alone. They keep walking, and walk straight out of the city of Omelas, through the beautiful gates. They keep walking across the farmlands of Omelas. Each one goes alone, youth or girl, man or woman. Night falls; the traveler must pass down village streets, between the houses with yellow-lit windows, and on out into the darkness of the fields. Each alone, they go west or north, towards the mountains. They go on. They leave Omelas, they walk ahead into the darkness, and they do not come back. The place they go towards is a place even less imaginable to most of us than the city of happiness. I cannot describe it at all. It is possible that it does not exist. But they seem to know where they are going, the ones who walk away from Omelas.

---

Source: Copyright © 1973 by Ursula K. Le Guin; first appeared in *New Dimensions 3,* reprinted by permission of the author and the author's agent, Virginia Kidd.

### QUESTIONS FOR READING, REASONING, AND REFLECTION

1. What is the general impression you get of the city of Omelas from the opening paragraph? To what senses does the author appeal?

2. Describe the people of Omelas. Are they happy? Do they have technology? Guilt? Religion? Soldiers? Drugs?

3. What shocking detail emerges about Omelas? On what does this ideal community thrive?

4. How do the children and teens respond to the locked-up child at first? How do they reconcile themselves to the situation? What do some residents do?

5. Can you understand the reason most residents accept the situation? Can you understand those who walk away? With which group do you most identify? Why?

6. On what does Le Guin want us to reflect? How would you state the story's theme?

# TRIFLES | SUSAN GLASPELL

Born in Iowa, Susan Glaspell (1882?–1948) attended Drake University and then began her writing career as a reporter with the *Des Moines Daily News.* She also started writing and selling short stories; her first collection, *Lifted Masks,* was published in 1912. She completed several novels before moving to Provincetown with her husband, who started the Provincetown Players in 1915. Glaspell wrote seven short plays and four long plays for this group, including *Trifles* (1916). The well-known "Jury of Her Peers" (1917) is a short-story version of the play *Trifles.* Glaspell must have recognized that the plot of *Trifles* was a gem worth working with in more than one literary form.

*Characters*

George Henderson, County Attorney
Henry Peters, Sheriff
Lewis Hale, A Neighboring Farmer
Mrs. Peters
Mrs. Hale

SCENE: *The kitchen in the now abandoned farmhouse of* JOHN WRIGHT, *a gloomy kitchen, and left without having been put in order—unwashed pans under the sink, a loaf of bread outside the bread-box, a dish-towel on the table—other signs of incompleted work. At the rear, the outer door opens and the* SHERIFF *comes in followed by the* COUNTY ATTORNEY *and* HALE. *The* SHERIFF *and* HALE *are men in middle life; the* COUNTY ATTORNEY *is a young man; all are much bundled up and go at once to the stove. They are followed by the two women—the* SHERIFF's *wife first; she is a slight wiry woman, a thin nervous face.* MRS. HALE *is larger and would ordinarily be called more comfortable looking, but she is disturbed now and looks fearfully about as she enters. The women have come in slowly, and stand close together near the door.*

COUNTY ATTORNEY

[*Rubbing his hands.*] This feels good. Come up to the fire, ladies.

MRS. PETERS

[*After taking a step forward.*] I'm not—cold.

SHERIFF

[*Unbuttoning his overcoat and stepping away from the stove as if to mark the beginning of official business.*] Now, Mr. Hale, before we move things about, you explain to Mr. Henderson just what you saw when you came here yesterday morning.

COUNTY ATTORNEY

By the way, has anything been moved? Are things just as you left them yesterday?

SHERIFF

[*Looking about.*] It's just the same. When it dropped below zero last night I thought I'd better send Frank out this morning to make a fire for us—no use getting pneumonia with a big case on, but I told him not to touch anything except the stove—and you know Frank.

COUNTY ATTORNEY

Somebody should have been left here yesterday.

SHERIFF

Oh—yesterday. When I had to send Frank to Morris Center for that man who went crazy—I want you to know I had my hands full yesterday. I knew you could get back from Omaha by today and as long as I went over everything here myself—

COUNTY ATTORNEY

Well, Mr. Hale, tell just what happened when you came here yesterday morning.

HALE

Harry and I had started to town with a load of potatoes. We came along the road from my place and as I got here I said, "I'm going to see if I can't get John Wright to go in with me on a party telephone." I spoke to Wright about it once before and he put me off, saying folks talked too much anyway, and all he asked was peace and quiet—I guess you know about how much he talked himself; but I thought maybe if I went to the house and talked about it before his wife, though I said to Harry that I didn't know as what his wife wanted made much difference to John—

COUNTY ATTORNEY

Let's talk about that later, Mr. Hale. I do want to talk about that, but tell now just what happened when you got to the house.

HALE

I didn't hear or see anything; I knocked at the door, and still it was all quiet inside. I knew they must be up, it was past eight o'clock. So I knocked again, and I thought I heard somebody say, "Come in." I wasn't sure, I'm not sure yet, but I opened the door—this door [*indicating the door by which the two women are still standing*] and there in that rocker—[*pointing to it*] sat Mrs. Wright.
[*They all look at the rocker.*]

COUNTY ATTORNEY

What—was she doing?

HALE

She was rockin' back and forth. She had her apron in her hand and was kind of—pleating it.

COUNTY ATTORNEY

And how did she—look?


HALE

Well, she looked queer.


COUNTY ATTORNEY

How do you mean—queer?


HALE

Well, as if she didn't know what she was going to do next. And kind of done up.


COUNTY ATTORNEY

How did she seem to feel about your coming?


HALE

Why, I don't think she minded—one way or other. She didn't pay much attention. I said, "How do, Mrs. Wright, it's cold, ain't it?" And she said, "Is it?"—and went on kind of pleating at her apron. Well, I was surprised; she didn't ask me to come up to the stove, or to set down, but just sat there, not even looking at me, so I said, "I want to see John." And then she—laughed. I guess you would call it a laugh. I thought of Harry and the team outside, so I said a little sharp: "Can't I see John?" "No," she says, kind o' dull like. "Ain't he home?" says I. "Yes," says she, "he's home." "Then why can't I see him?" I asked her, out of patience. " 'Cause he's dead," says she. "*Dead?*" says I. She just nodded her head, not getting a bit excited, but rockin' back and forth. "Why—where is he?" says I, not knowing what to say. She just pointed upstairs—like that [*himself pointing to the room above*]. I got up, with the idea of going up there. I walked from there to here—then I says, "Why, what did he die of?" "He died of a rope around his neck," says she, and just went on pleatin' at her apron. Well, I went out and called Harry. I thought I might— need help. We went upstairs and there he was lyin'—


COUNTY ATTORNEY

I think I'd rather have you go into that upstairs, where you can point it all out. Just go on now with the rest of the story.


HALE

Well, my first thought was to get that rope off. It looked . . . [*Stops, his face twitches*] . . . but Harry, he went up to him, and he said, "No, he's dead all right, and we'd better not touch anything." So we went back downstairs. She was still sitting that same way. "Has anybody been notified?" said Harry. He said it business-like—and she stopped pleatin' of her apron. "I don't know," she says. "You don't *know*?" says Harry. "No," says she. "Weren't you sleepin' in the bed with him?" says Harry. "Yes," says she, "but I was on the inside."

"Somebody slipped a rope round his neck and strangled him and you didn't wake up?" says Harry. "I didn't wake up," she said after him. We must'a looked as if we didn't see how that could be, for after a minute she said, "I sleep sound." Harry was going to ask her more questions but I said maybe we ought to let her tell her story first to the coroner, or the sheriff, so Harry went fast as he could to Rivers' place, where there's a telephone.

### COUNTY ATTORNEY

And what did Mrs. Wright do when she knew that you had gone for the coroner?

### HALE

She moved from that chair to this one over here [*Pointing to a small chair in the corner*] and just sat there with her hands held together and looking down. I got a feeling that I ought to make some conversation, so I said I had come in to see if John wanted to put in a telephone, and at that she started to laugh, and then she stopped and looked at me—scared. [*The County Attorney, who has had his notebook out, makes a note.*] I dunno, maybe it wasn't scared. I wouldn't like to say it was. Soon Harry got back, and then Dr. Lloyd came, and you, Mr. Peters, and so I guess that's all I know that you don't.

### COUNTY ATTORNEY

[*Looking around.*] I guess we'll go upstairs first—and then out to the barn and around there. [*To the Sheriff.*] You're convinced that there was nothing important here—nothing that would point to any motive.

### SHERIFF

Nothing here but kitchen things.
[*The County Attorney, after again looking around the kitchen, opens the door of a cupboard closet. He gets up on a chair and looks on a shelf. Pulls his hand away, sticky.*]

### COUNTY ATTORNEY

Here's a nice mess.
[*The women draw nearer.*]

### MRS. PETERS

[*To the other woman.*] Oh, her fruit; it did freeze. [*To the Lawyer.*] She worried about that when it turned so cold. She said the fire'd go out and her jars would break.

### SHERIFF

Well, can you beat the woman! Held for murder and worryin' about her preserves.

COUNTY ATTORNEY
I guess before we're through she may have something more serious than preserves to worry about.

HALE
Well, women are used to worrying over trifles.
[*The two women move a little closer together.*]

COUNTY ATTORNEY
[*With the gallantry of a young politician.*] And yet, for all their worries, what would we do without the ladies? [*The women do not unbend. He goes to the sink, takes a dipperful of water from the pail and pouring it into a basin, washes his hands. Starts to wipe them on the roller-towel, turns it for a cleaner place.*] Dirty towels! [*Kicks his foot against the pans under the sink.*] Not much of a housekeeper, would you say, ladies?

MRS. HALE
[*Stiffly.*] There's a great deal of work to be done on a farm.

COUNTY ATTORNEY
To be sure. And yet [*with a little bow to her*] I know there are some Dickson County farmhouses which do not have such roller towels.
[*He gives it a pull to expose its full length again.*]

MRS. HALE
Those towels get dirty awful quick. Men's hands aren't always as clean as they might be.

COUNTY ATTORNEY
Ah, loyal to your sex, I see. But you and Mrs. Wright were neighbors. I suppose you were friends, too.

MRS. HALE
[*Shaking her head.*] I've not seen much of her of late years. I've not been in this house—it's more than a year.

COUNTY ATTORNEY
And why was that? You didn't like her?

MRS. HALE
I liked her all well enough. Farmers' wives have their hands full, Mr. Henderson. And then—

COUNTY ATTORNEY
Yes—?

MRS. HALE
[*Looking about.*] It never seemed a very cheerful place.

COUNTY ATTORNEY
No—it's not cheerful. I shouldn't say she had the homemaking instinct.

MRS. HALE
Well, I don't know as Wright had, either.

COUNTY ATTORNEY
You mean that they didn't get on very well?

MRS. HALE
No, I don't mean anything. But I don't think a place'd be any cheerfuller for John Wright's being in it.

COUNTY ATTORNEY
I'd like to talk more of that a little later. I want to get the lay of things upstairs now.
[*He goes to the left, where three steps lead to a stair door.*]

SHERIFF
I suppose anything Mrs. Peters does'll be all right. She was to take in some clothes for her, you know, and a few little things. We left in such a hurry yesterday.

COUNTY ATTORNEY
Yes, but I would like to see what you take, Mrs. Peters, and keep an eye out for anything that might be of use to us.

MRS. PETERS
Yes, Mr. Henderson.
[*The women listen to the men's steps on the stairs, then look about the kitchen.*]

MRS. HALE
I'd hate to have men coming into my kitchen, snooping around and criticizing.
[*She arranges the pans under the sink which the Lawyer had shoved out of place.*]

MRS. PETERS
Of course it's no more than their duty.

Mrs. Hale

Duty's all right, but I guess that deputy sheriff that came out to make the fire might have got a little of this on. [*Gives the roller towel a pull.*] Wish I'd thought of that sooner. Seems mean to talk about her for not having things slicked up when she had to come away in such a hurry.

Mrs. Peters

[*Who has gone to a small table in the left corner of the room, and lifted one end of a towel that covers a pan.*] She had bread set.
　　[*Stands still.*]

Mrs. Hale

[*Eyes fixed on a loaf of bread beside the breadbox, which is on a low shelf at the other side of the room. Moves slowly toward it.*] She was going to put this in there. [*Picks up loaf, then abruptly drops it. In a manner of returning to familiar things.*] It's a shame about her fruit. I wonder if it's all gone. [*Gets up on the chair and looks.*] I think there's some here that's all right, Mrs. Peters. Yes—here; [*holding it toward the window*] this is cherries, too. [*Looking again.*] I declare I believe that's the only one. [*Gets down, bottle in her hand. Goes to the sink and wipes it off on the outside.*] She'll feel awful bad after all her hard work in the hot weather. I remember the afternoon I put up my cherries last summer.
　　[*She puts the bottle on the big kitchen table, center of the room. With a sigh, is about to sit down in the rocking-chair. Before she is seated realizes what chair it is; with a slow look at it, steps back. The chair which she has touched rocks back and forth.*]

Mrs. Peters

Well, I must get those things from the front room closet. [*She goes to the door at the right, but after looking into the other room, steps back.*] You coming with me, Mrs. Hale? You could help me carry them.
　　[*They go in the other room; reappear, Mrs. Peters carrying a dress and skirt, Mrs. Hale following with a pair of shoes.*]

Mrs. Peters

My, it's cold in there.
　　[*She puts the clothes on the big table, and hurries to the stove.*]

Mrs. Hale

[*Examining the skirt.*] Wright was close. I think maybe that's why she kept so much to herself. She didn't even belong to the Ladies Aid. I suppose she felt she couldn't do her part, and then you don't enjoy things when you feel shabby. She used to wear pretty clothes and be lively, when she was Minnie Foster, one of the town girls singing in the choir. But that—oh, that was thirty years ago. This all you was to take in?

MRS. PETERS

She said she wanted an apron. Funny thing to want, for there isn't much to get you dirty in jail, goodness knows. But I suppose just to make her feel more natural. She said they was in the top drawer in this cupboard. Yes, here. And then her little shawl that always hung behind the door. [*Opens stair door and looks.*] Yes, here it is.

[*Quickly shuts door leading upstairs.*]

MRS. HALE

[*Abruptly moving toward her.*] Mrs. Peters?

MRS. PETERS

Yes, Mrs. Hale?

MRS. HALE

Do you think she did it?

MRS. PETERS

[*In a frightened voice.*] Oh, I don't know.

MRS. HALE

Well, I don't think she did. Asking for an apron and her little shawl. Worrying about her fruit.

MRS. PETERS

[*Starts to speak, glances up, where footsteps are heard in the room above. In a low voice.*] Mr. Peters says it looks bad for her. Mr. Henderson is awful sarcastic in a speech and he'll make fun of her sayin' she didn't wake up.

MRS. HALE

Well, I guess John Wright didn't wake when they was slipping that rope under his neck.

MRS. PETERS

No, it's strange. It must have been done awful crafty and still. They say it was such a—funny way to kill a man, rigging it all up like that.

MRS. HALE

That's just what Mr. Hale said. There was a gun in the house. He says that's what he can't understand.

MRS. PETERS

Mr. Henderson said coming out that what was needed for the case was a motive; something to show anger, or—sudden feeling.

Mrs. Hale

[*Who is standing by the table.*] Well, I don't see any signs of anger around here. [*She puts her hand on the dish towel which lies on the table, stands looking down at table, one half of which is clean, the other half messy.*] It's wiped to here. [*Makes a move as if to finish work, then turns and looks at loaf of bread outside the breadbox. Drops towel. In that voice of coming-back to familiar things.*] Wonder how they are finding things upstairs. I hope she had it a little more red-up up there. You know, it seems kind of sneaking. Locking her up in town and then coming out here and trying to get her own house to turn against her!

Mrs. Peters

But Mrs. Hale, the law is the law.

Mrs. Hale

I s'pose 'tis. [*Unbuttoning her coat.*] Better loosen up your things, Mrs. Peters. You won't feel them when you go out.

[*Mrs. Peters takes off her fur tippet, goes to hang it on hook at back of room, stands looking at the under part of the small corner table.*]

Mrs. Peters

She was piecing a quilt.

[*She brings the large sewing basket and they look at the bright pieces.*]

Mrs. Hale

It's log cabin pattern. Pretty, isn't it? I wonder if she was goin' to quilt it or just knot it? [*Footsteps have been heard coming down the stairs. The Sheriff enters followed by Hale and the County Attorney.*]

Sheriff

They wonder if she was going to quilt it or just knot it!

[*The men laugh, the women look abashed.*]

County Attorney

[*Rubbing his hands over the stove.*] Frank's fire didn't do much up there, did it? Well, let's go out to the barn and get that cleared up.

[*The men go outside.*]

Mrs. Hale

[*Resentfully.*] I don't know as there's anything so strange, our takin' up our time with little things while we're waiting for them to get the evidence. [*She sits down at the big table smoothing out a block with decision.*] I don't see as it's anything to laugh about.

MRS. PETERS

[*Apologetically.*] Of course they've got awful important things on their minds. [*Pulls up a chair and joins Mrs. Hale at the table.*]

MRS. HALE

[*Examining another block.*] Mrs. Peters, look at this one. Here, this is the one she was working on, and look at the sewing! All the rest of it has been so nice and even. And look at this! It's all over the place! Why, it looks as if she didn't know what she was about!

[*After she has said this they look at each other, then start to glance back at the door. After an instant Mrs. Hale has pulled at a knot and ripped the sewing.*]

MRS. PETERS

Oh, what are you doing, Mrs. Hale?

MRS. HALE

[*Mildly.*] Just pulling out a stitch or two that's not sewed very good. [*Threading a needle.*] Bad sewing always made me fidgety.

MRS. PETERS

[*Nervously.*] I don't think we ought to touch things.

MRS. HALE

I'll just finish up this end. [*Suddenly stopping and leaning forward.*] Mrs. Peters?

MRS. PETERS

Yes, Mrs. Hale?

MRS. HALE

What do you suppose she was so nervous about?

MRS. PETERS

Oh—I don't know. I don't know as she was nervous. I sometimes sew awful queer when I'm just tired. [*Mrs. Hale starts to say something, looks at Mrs. Peters, then goes on sewing.*] Well I must get these things wrapped up. They may be through sooner than we think. [*Putting apron and other things together.*] I wonder where I can find a piece of paper, and string.

MRS. HALE

In that cupboard, maybe.

MRS. PETERS

[*Looking in cupboard.*] Why, here's a bird-cage. [*Holds it up.*] Did she have a bird, Mrs. Hale?

Mrs. Hale

Why, I don't know whether she did or not—I've not been here for so long. There was a man around last year selling canaries cheap, but I don't know as she took one; maybe she did. She used to sing real pretty herself.

Mrs. Peters

[*Glancing around.*] Seems funny to think of a bird here. But she must have had one, or why would she have a cage? I wonder what happened to it.

Mrs. Hale

I s'pose maybe the cat got it.

Mrs. Peters

No, she didn't have a cat. She's got that feeling some people have about cats—being afraid of them. My cat got in her room and she was real upset and asked me to take it out.

Mrs. Hale

My sister Bessie was like that. Queer, ain't it?

Mrs. Peters

[*Examining the cage.*] Why, look at this door. It's broke. One hinge is pulled apart.

Mrs. Hale

[*Looking too.*] Looks as if someone must have been rough with it.

Mrs. Peters

Why, yes.
[*She brings the cage forward and puts it on the table.*]

Mrs. Hale

I wish if they're going to find any evidence they'd be about it. I don't like this place.

Mrs. Peters

But I'm awful glad you came with me, Mrs. Hale. It would be lonesome for me sitting here alone.

Mrs. Hale

It would, wouldn't it? [*Dropping her sewing.*] But I tell you what I do wish, Mrs. Peters. I wish I had come over sometimes when *she* was here. I—[*looking around the room*]—wish I had.

MRS. PETERS

But of course you were awful busy, Mrs. Hale—your house and your children.


MRS. HALE

I could've come. I stayed away because it weren't cheerful—and that's why I ought to have come. I—I've never liked this place. Maybe because it's down in a hollow and you don't see the road. I dunno what it is, but it's a lonesome place and always was. I wish I had come over to see Minnie Foster sometimes. I can see now—
[*Shakes her head.*]


MRS. PETERS

Well, you mustn't reproach yourself, Mrs. Hale. Somehow we just don't see how it is with other folks until—something comes up.


MRS. HALE

Not having children makes less work—but it makes a quiet house, and Wright out to work all day, and no company when he did come in. Did you know John Wright, Mrs. Peters?


MRS. PETERS

Not to know him; I've seen him in town. They say he was a good man.


MRS. HALE

Yes—good; he didn't drink, and kept his word as well as most, I guess, and paid his debts. But he was a hard man, Mrs. Peters. Just to pass the time of day with him—[*Shivers.*] Like a raw wind that gets to the bone. [*Pauses, her eye falling on the cage.*] I should think she would'a wanted a bird. But what do you suppose went with it?


MRS. PETERS

I don't know, unless it got sick and died.
[*She reaches over and swings the broken door, swings it again, both women watch it.*]


MRS. HALE

You weren't raised round here, were you? [*Mrs. Peters shakes her head.*] You didn't know—her?


MRS. PETERS

Not till they brought her yesterday.


MRS. HALE

She—come to think of it, she was kind of like a bird herself—real sweet and pretty, but kind of timid and—fluttery. How—she—did—change. [*Silence;*

*then as if struck by a happy thought and relieved to get back to everyday things.*] Tell you what, Mrs. Peters, why don't you take the quilt in with you? It might take up her mind.

MRS. PETERS

Why, I think that's a real nice idea, Mrs. Hale. There couldn't possibly be any objection to it, could there? Now, just what would I take? I wonder if her patches are in here—and her things.
[*They look in the sewing basket.*]

MRS. HALE

Here's some red. I expect this has got sewing things in it. [*Brings out a fancy box.*] What a pretty box. Looks like something somebody would give you. Maybe her scissors are in here. [*Opens box. Suddenly puts her hand to her nose.*] Why—[*Mrs. Peters bends nearer, then turns her face away.*] There's something wrapped up in this piece of silk.

MRS. PETERS

Why, this isn't her scissors.

MRS. HALE

[*Lifting the silk.*] Oh, Mrs. Peters—it's—
[*Mrs. Peters bends closer.*]

MRS. PETERS

It's the bird.

MRS. HALE

[*Jumping up.*] But, Mrs. Peters—look at it! Its neck! Look at its neck! It's all—other side *to*.

MRS. PETERS

Somebody—wrung—its—neck.
[*Their eyes meet. A look of growing comprehension, or horror. Steps are heard outside. Mrs. Hale slips box under quilt pieces, and sinks into her chair. Enter Sheriff and County Attorney. Mrs. Peters rises.*]

COUNTY ATTORNEY

[*As one turning from serious things to little pleasantries.*] Well ladies, have you decided whether she was going to quilt it or knot it?

MRS. PETERS

We think she was going to—knot it.

COUNTY ATTORNEY

Well, that's interesting, I'm sure. [*Seeing the bird-cage.*] Has the bird flown?

MRS. HALE

[*Putting more quilt pieces over the box.*] We think the—cat got it.

COUNTY ATTORNEY

[*Preoccupied.*] Is there a cat?
[*Mrs. Hale glances in a quick covert way at Mrs. Peters.*]

MRS. PETERS

Well, not now. They're superstitious, you know. They leave.

COUNTY ATTORNEY

[*To Sheriff Peters, continuing an interrupted conversation.*] No sign at all of anyone having come from the outside. Their own rope. Now let's go up again and go over it piece by piece. [*They start upstairs.*] It would have to have been someone who knew just the—
[*Mrs. Peters sits down. The two women sit there not looking at one another, but as if peering into something and at the same time holding back. When they talk now it is in the manner of feeling their way over strange ground, as if afraid of what they are saying, but as if they can not help saying it.*]

MRS. HALE

She liked the bird. She was going to bury it in that pretty box.

MRS. PETERS

[*In a whisper.*] When I was a girl—my kitten—there was a boy took a hatchet, and before my eyes—and before I could get there—[*Covers her face an instant.*] If they hadn't held me back I would have—[*Catches herself, looks upstairs where steps are heard, falters weakly*]—hurt him.

MRS. HALE

[*With a slow look around her.*] I wonder how it would seem never to have had any children around. [*Pause.*] No, Wright wouldn't like the bird—a thing that sang. She used to sing. He killed that, too.

MRS. PETERS

[*Moving uneasily.*] We don't know who killed the bird.

MRS. HALE

I knew John Wright.

Mrs. Peters

It was an awful thing was done in this house that night, Mrs. Hale. Killing a man while he slept, slipping a rope around his neck that choked the life out of him.

Mrs. Hale

His neck. Choked the life out of him.
[*Her hand goes out and rests on the bird-cage.*]

Mrs. Peters

We don't know who killed him. We don't *know.*

Mrs. Hale

[*Her own feeling not interrupted.*] If there'd been years and years of nothing, then a bird to sing to you, it would be awful—still, after the bird was still.

Mrs. Peters

[*Something within her speaking.*] I know what stillness is. When we homesteaded in Dakota, and my first baby died—after he was two years old, and me with no other then—

Mrs. Hale

[*Moving.*] How soon do you suppose they'll be through, looking for the evidence?

Mrs. Peters

I know what stillness is. [*Pulling herself back.*] The law has got to punish crime, Mrs. Hale.

Mrs. Hale

[*Not as if answering that.*] I wish you'd seen Minnie Foster when she wore a white dress with blue ribbons and stood up there in the choir and sang. [*A look around the room.*] Oh, I *wish* I'd come over here once in a while! That was a crime! That was a crime! Who's going to punish that?

Mrs. Peters

[*Looking upstairs.*] We mustn't—take on.

Mrs. Hale

I might have known she needed help! I know how things can be—for women. I tell you, it's queer, Mrs. Peters. We live close together and we live far apart. We all go through the same things—it's all just a different kind of the same thing. [*Brushes her eyes, noticing the bottle of fruit, reaches out for it.*] If I was you I wouldn't tell her her fruit was gone. Tell her it *ain't.* Tell her it's all right. Take this in to prove it to her. She—she may never know whether it was broke or not.

MRS. PETERS

[*Takes the bottle, looks about for something to wrap it in; takes petticoat from the clothes brought from the other room, very nervously begins winding this around the bottle. In a false voice.*] My, it's a good thing the men couldn't hear us. Wouldn't they just laugh! Getting all stirred up over a little thing like a—dead canary. As if that could have anything to do with—with—wouldn't they *laugh*!

[*The men are heard coming downstairs.*]

MRS. HALE

[*Under her breath.*] Maybe they would—maybe they wouldn't.

COUNTY ATTORNEY

No, Peters, it's all perfectly clear except a reason for doing it. But you know juries when it comes to women. If there was some definite thing. Something to show—something to make a story about—a thing that would connect up with this strange way of doing it—

[*The women's eyes meet for an instant. Enter Hale from outer door.*]

HALE

Well, I've got the team around. Pretty cold out there.

COUNTY ATTORNEY

I'm going to stay here awhile by myself. [*To the Sheriff.*] You can send Frank out for me, can't you? I want to go over everything. I'm not satisfied that we can't do better.

SHERIFF

Do you want to see what Mrs. Peters is going to take in?

[*The Lawyer goes to the table, picks up the apron, laughs.*]

COUNTY ATTORNEY

Oh, I guess they're not very dangerous things the ladies have picked out. [*Moves a few things about, disturbing the quilt pieces which cover the box. Steps back.*] No, Mrs. Peters doesn't need supervising. For that matter, a sheriff's wife is married to the law. Ever think of it that way, Mrs. Peters?

MRS. PETERS

Not—just that way.

SHERIFF

[*Chuckling.*] Married to the law. [*Moves toward the other room.*] I just want you to come in here a minute, George. We ought to take a look at these windows.

COUNTY ATTORNEY

[*Scoffingly.*] Oh, windows!

SHERIFF

We'll be right out, Mr. Hale.

[*Hale goes outside. The Sheriff follows the County Attorney into the other room. Then Mrs. Hale rises, hands tight together, looking intensely at Mrs. Peters, whose eyes make a slow turn, finally meeting Mrs. Hale's. A moment Mrs. Hale holds her, then her own eyes point the way to where the box is concealed. Suddenly Mrs. Peters throws back quilt pieces and tries to put the box in the bag she is wearing. It is too big. She opens box, starts to take bird out, cannot touch it, goes to pieces, stands there helpless. Sound of a knob turning in the other room. Mrs. Hale snatches the box and puts it in the pocket of her big coat. Enter County Attorney and Sheriff.*]

COUNTY ATTORNEY

[*Facetiously.*] Well, Henry, at least we found out that she was not going to quilt it. She was going to—what is it you call it, ladies?

MRS. HALE

[*Her hand against her pocket.*] We call it—knot it, Mr. Henderson.

---

QUESTIONS FOR READING, REASONING, AND REFLECTION

1. Explain the situation as the play begins.
2. Examine the dialogue of the men. What attitudes about themselves—their work, their abilities, their importance—are revealed? What is their collective opinion of women?
3. When Mrs. Hale and Mrs. Peters discover the dead bird, what do they begin to understand?
4. What other "trifles" in the kitchen provide additional evidence as to what has happened?
5. What trifles can be seen as symbols? What do they reveal about Mrs. Wright's life and character?
6. What is the play about primarily? Is it a murder mystery? Does it speak for feminist values? Is it about not seeing—not really knowing—others? In a few sentences, state what you consider to be the play's dominant theme. Then list the evidence you would use to support your conclusion.
7. Is there any sense in which one could argue that Mrs. Wright had a right to kill her husband? If you were a lawyer, how would you plan her defense? If you were on the jury, what sentence would you recommend?

# SAMPLE STUDENT LITERARY ANALYSIS

Peterson 1

Alan Peterson

American Literature 242

May 5, 2010

Faulkner's Realistic Initiation Theme

    William Faulkner braids a universal theme, the theme of initiation, into the fiber of his novel *Intruder in the Dust.* From ancient times to the present, a prominent focus of literature, of life, has been rites of passage, particularly those of childhood to adulthood. Joseph Campbell defines rites of passage as "distinguished by formal, and usually very severe, exercises of severance." A "candidate" for initiation into adult society, Campbell explains, experiences a shearing away of the "attitudes, attachments and life patterns" of childhood (9). This severe, painful stripping away of the child and installation of the adult is presented somewhat differently in several works by American writers.

    One technique of handling this theme of initiation is used by Nathaniel Hawthorne in his story "My Kinsman, Major Molineaux." The story's main character, Robin, is suddenly awakened to the real world, the adult world, when he sees Major Molineaux "in tar-and-feathery dignity" (Hawthorne 528). A terrified and amazed Robin gapes at his kinsman as the large and colorful crowd laughs at and ridicules the Major; then an acquiescent Robin joins with the crowd in the mirthful shouting (Hawthorne 529). This moment is Robin's epiphany, his sudden realization of reality. Robin goes from unsophisticated rube to resigned cynical adult in one quick scene. Hawthorne does hold out hope that Robin will not let this event ruin his life, indeed that he will perhaps prosper from it.

    A similar, but decidedly less optimistic, example of an epiphanic initiation occurs in Arthur Miller's play *Death of a Salesman.* Miller develops an initiation theme within a flashback. A teenaged Biff, shockingly confronted with Willy's

Peterson 2

infidelity and weakness, has his boyhood dreams, ambitions—his vision—
shattered, leaving his life in ruins, a truth borne out in scenes in which Biff is
an adult during the play (1083–84, 1101). Biff's discovery of the vices and
shortcomings of his father overwhelms him. His realization of adult life is a
revelation made more piercing when put into the context of his naive and overly
hopeful upbringing. A ravaged and defeated Biff has adulthood wantonly thrust
upon him. Unlike Hawthorne's Robin, Biff never recovers.

¶ concludes with emphasis on contrast.

William Faulkner does not follow these examples when dealing with the
initiation of his character Chick in *Intruder in the Dust*. In Robin's and Biff's cases,
each character's passage into adulthood was brought about by realization of
and disillusionment with the failings and weaknesses of a male adult playing an
important role in his life. By contrast, Chick's male role models are vital, moral
men with integrity. Chick's awakening develops as he begins to comprehend the
mechanisms of the adult society in which he would be a member.

Transition to Faulkner's story by contrast with Hawthorne and Miller.

Faulkner uses several techniques for illustrating Chick's growth into a man.
Early in the novel, at the end of the scene in which Chick tries to pay for his dinner,
Lucas warns Chick to "stay out of that creek" (Faulkner 16).[1] The creek is an
effective symbol: it is both a physical creek and a metaphor for the boy's tendency
to slide into gaffes that perhaps a man could avoid. The creek's symbolic meaning
is more evident when, after receiving the molasses, Chick encounters Lucas in
town. Lucas again reminds Chick not to "fall in no more creeks this winter" (24).
At the end of the novel, Lucas meets Chick in Gavin's office and states: "you ain't
fell in no more creeks lately, have you?" (241). Although Lucas phrases this as a
question, the answer is obvious to Lucas, as well as to the reader, that indeed
Chick has not blundered into his naive boyhood quagmire lately. When Lucas asks
his question, Chick's actual falling into a creek does not occur to the reader.

Footnote first paren-thetical reference to inform readers that subsequent citations will exclude the author's name and give only the page number.

---

1. Subsequent references to Faulkner's novel cite page numbers only.

Note transition.

Another image Faulkner employs to show Chick growing into a man is the single-file line. After Chick gets out of the creek, he follows Lucas into the house, the group walking in single file. In the face of Lucas's much stronger adult will, Chick is powerless to get out of the line, to go to Edmonds's house (7). Later in the novel, when Miss Habersham, Aleck Sander, and Chick are walking back from digging up the grave, Chick again finds himself in a single-file line with a strong-willed adult in front. Again he protests, then relents, but

Note interpolation in square brackets.

clearly he feels slighted and wonders to himself "what good that [walking single file] would do" (130). The contrast between these two scenes illustrates Chick's growth, although he is not yet a man.

Good use of brief quotations combined with analysis.

Faulkner gives the reader other hints of Chick's passage into manhood. As the novel progresses, Chick is referred to (and refers to himself) as a "boy" (24), a "child" (25), a "young man" (46), "almost a man" (190), a "man" (194), and one of two "gentlemen" (241). Other clues crop up from time to time. Chick wrestles with himself about getting on his horse and riding away, far away, until Lucas's lynching is "all over finished done" (41). But his growing sense of responsibility and outrage quell his boyish desire to escape, to bury his head in the sand. Chick looks in the mirror at himself with amazement at his deeds (125). Chick's mother serves him coffee for the first time, despite the agreement she has with his father to withhold coffee until his eighteenth birthday (127). Chick's father looks at him with pride and envy (128–29).

Characteristics of Chick's gradual and positive initiation explained. Observe coherence techniques.

Perhaps the most important differences between the epiphanic initiations of Robin and Biff and that experienced by Chick are the facts that Chick's epiphany does not come all at once and it does not devastate him. Chick learns about adulthood—and enters adulthood—piecemeal and with support. His first eye-opening experience occurs as he tries to pay Lucas for dinner and is rebuffed (15–16). Chick learns, after trying again to buy a clear conscience, the impropriety and affront of his actions (24). Lucas teaches

Peterson 4

Chick how he should resolve *his* dilemma by setting him "free" (26–27). Later, Chick feels outrage at the adults crowding into the town, presumably to see a lynching, then disgrace and shame as they eventually flee (196–97, 210). As in most lives, Chick's passage into adulthood is a gradual process; he learns a little bit at a time and has support in his growing. Gavin is there for him, to act as a sounding board, to lay a strong intellectual foundation, to confirm his beliefs. Chick's initiation is consistent with Joseph Campbell's explanation: "all rites of passage are intended to touch not only the candidate, but also every member of his circle" (9). Perhaps Gavin is affected the most, but Chick's mother and father, and Lucas as well, are influenced by the change in Chick.

In *Intruder in the Dust,* William Faulkner has much to say about the role of and the actions of adults in society. He depicts racism, ignorance, resignation, violence, fratricide, citizenship, hope, righteousness, lemming-like aggregation, fear, and a host of other emotions and actions. Chick learns not only right and wrong, but that in order to be a part of society, of his community, he cannot completely forsake those with whom he disagrees or whose ideas he challenges. There is much compromise in growing up; Chick learns to compromise on some issues, but not all. Gavin's appeal to Chick to "just don't stop" (210) directs him to conform enough to be a part of the adult world, but not to lose sight of, indeed instead to embrace, his own values and ideals.

*Student concludes by explaining the values Chick develops in growing up.*

Paging is
continuous.

Works Cited

Place Works Cited
on separate page.

Campbell, Joseph. *The Hero with a Thousand Faces.* Princeton: Princeton UP,

1949. Print.

Faulkner, William. *Intruder in the Dust.* New York: Random, 1948. Print.

Double-space
throughout.

Hawthorne, Nathaniel. "My Kinsman, Major Molineaux." 1832.

*The Complete Short Stories of Nathaniel Hawthorne.* New York: Hanover/

Use hanging
indentation.

Doubleday, 1959. 517–30. Print.

Miller, Arthur. *Death of a Salesman.* 1949. *An Introduction to Literature.* 9th ed.

Eds. Sylvan Barnet, Morton Berman, and William Burto. Boston: Little,

1985. 1025–111. Print.

# SUGGESTIONS FOR DISCUSSION AND WRITING

1. Prepare an explication of either Amy Lowell's "Taxi" or Sir Walter Raleigh's "The Nymph's Reply to the Shepherd." You will need to explain both what the poem says and what it means—or what it accomplishes.

2. Analyze A. E. Housman's attitudes toward life and human relationships in "Is My Team Ploughing."

3. Analyze Mrs. Mallard's conflict, and decision about that conflict, as the basis for your understanding of the dominant theme in "The Story of an Hour."

4. You are Mrs. Wright's attorney (see *Trifles,* p. 589). Write your closing argument in her defense, explaining why only a light sentence is warranted for Mrs. Wright. Select details from the play to support your assertions about Mrs. Wright's character and motivation.

5. Explain what you think are the most important ideas about community in Ursula K. Le Guin's "The Ones Who Walk Away from Omelas."

6. John Donne in "The Bait" and Ogden Nash in "Love Under the Republicans (or Democrats)" also have responses to Marlowe's "The Passionate Shepherd to His Love." Select one of these poems, find a copy, read and analyze it, and then evaluate its argument as a response to Marlowe's shepherd.

# Photo Credits

**Section openers**: © Hans Neleman/Taxi/Getty Images, © Kevin Lamarque/Reuters/Corbis, Columbia Pictures/The Kobal Collection

**Page 2**: Erik Isakson/Getty Images; **8**: © image100/PunchStock; **25**: © Digital Vision/PunchStock; **26**: © PM Images/Getty Images; **48**: © Hans Neleman/Taxi/Getty Images; **54**: © Alex Wong/Getty Images; **70**: Stockbyte/Punchstock Images; **87**: © BananaStock/PunchStock; **92**: SuperStock/Getty Images; **108**: © Ingram Publishing/age fotostock; **114**: © Spencer Platt/Getty Images; **117**: © George Tames/The New York Times; **118**: Courtesy Exxon Mobil Corporation; **119**: Courtesy of Wm. Wrigley Jr. Company; **120**: Courtesy Bridgestone Corporation; **136**: Courtesy of OMEGA; **167**: © Gamble/TopFoto/The Image Works; **184**: (left) AP Photo/Joel Ryan, (right) AP Photo/Lisa Rose; **188**: Tim Pannell/Corbis; **199**: © Mark Peterson/Corbis; **223**: AFP/Getty Images; **241**: Yellow Dog Productions Inc./Getty Images; **244**: Courtesy American Indian College Fund; **256**: © Kevin Lamarque/Reuters/Corbis; **258**: The Bridgeman Art Library/Getty Images; **268**: BananaStock/JupiterImages; **275**: © Comstock Images; **278**: Infotrac screen reprinted courtesy of Gale Group; **286**: © Tetra Images/Getty Images; **313**: © Goodshoot/Punchstock; **331**: BananaStock/JupiterImages; **353**: © Michael Newman/PhotoEdit, Inc.; **361**: Courtesy of Lowe Worldwide Inc.; **362**: Courtesy of BASF; photo by Ed James/represented by Anderson Hopkins, Inc.; **363**: Artist: Richard Borge, www.richardborge.com; Creative Director: Dan Greenwald; Design Studio: White Rhino; Client: AVID. © 2008 Avid Technology, Inc.; **372**: Columbia Pictures/The Kobal Collection; **390**: Franko Lee/AFP/Getty Images; **394**: Nicholas Kamm/AFP/Getty Images; **403**: © INTERFOTO/Alamy; **417**: The Alliance for Climate Protection; **418**: Geostock/Getty Images; **430**: AP Photo/Bill Sikes; **432**: © Images.com/Corbis; **448**: Jesse D. Garrabrant/NBAE via Getty Images; **451**: Image Courtesy of The Advertising Archives; **456**: © Stockbyte/Punchstock; **466**: © Ted Horowitz/Corbis; **487**: Mario Tama/Getty Images; **495**: Photodisc Red/Getty Images; **502**: © Erik Isakson/Tetra Images/Corbis; **507**: © David Brabyn/Corbis; **521**: © Doug Steley A/Alamy; **539**: © Saul Loeb/epa/Corbis; **542**: AP Photo/Pablo Martinez Monsivais; **543**: Jim Watson/AFP/Getty Images; **556**: Photodisc/Superstock

# Index

*Note:* Page numbers followed by an italicized *f* refer to illustrations and figures.

**615**